THE REGULARS

THE REGULARS

EDWARD M. COFFMAN

The Belknap Press of Harvard University Press

Cambridge, Massachusetts, and London, England

2004

THE AMERICAN ARMY

1898–1941

To our grandchildren

Book design by Dean Bornstein

Library of Congress Cataloging-in-Publication Data
Coffman, Edward M.
The regulars : the American Army, 1898–1941 / Edward M. Coffman.
p. cm.
Includes bibliographical references (p.) and index.
ISBN 0-674-01299-2 (alk. paper)
1. United States. Army—History—20th century. 2. United States.
Army—Military life. I. Title.
UA25.C6223 2004
355′.09′04—dc22   2003056908

Preface

D URING the forty-three years from 1898 to 1941, the American Regular Army made the great transformation from a frontier constabulary to a modern army. In this period the Army conquered and controlled a colonial empire, fought the German Army in World War I, and prepared to fight not only the Germans but also the Japanese. To meet these formidable challenges, the regulars had to develop a professionalism of the highest order. A managerial revolution at the turn of the century provided the organizational framework and the educational foundation for this transformation, while the continuous technological revolution demanded adaptation of individuals and organizations to make the best use of the new tools of war.

The Regular Army of this period was a relatively small community within the total American population. These officers and soldiers, their wives, and their children lived in distinctive communities in posts wherever they served, from China and the Philippines to the heartland of the United States. This book is about their lives and their roles in this era of momentous change.

In the fall of 1969 a conversation with Francis Paul Prucha, author of the landmark military social history, *Broadax and Bayonet: The Role of the United States Army in the Development of the Northwest 1815–1860*, crystallized my thinking about a social history of the Regular Army from the War of Independence to World War II. I assumed that I could base the earlier history on published primary and secondary works and then develop many of my sources for the twentieth century through oral history and questionnaires. As I researched the earlier period, however, I came across a good many manuscript collections and unpublished records from the nineteenth century. A conversation with Russell F. Weigley, whose *History of the United States Army* remains the standard, convinced me that would be the proper course. The result was two books: *The Old Army: A Portrait of the American Army in Peacetime, 1784–1898* (1986) and this one.

Unlike *The Old Army*, which did not include wars, this book takes the regulars through the Spanish-American War, other fighting in the Philippines, and World War I. It does not cover the evolution of all branches of the Army but concentrates on the combat arms—the infantry, cavalry, artillery, Air Corps, and Armored Force.

Although I acknowledge elsewhere those who helped make this book possible, I want to express special thanks to a few people here. Charles L. and Adelaide Poore Bolté encouraged me from the start and gave me invaluable aid in my research, and their children, Phil, David, and Damara, have continued to do so. The Orville W. Martins, father and son, and Alice Duncanson Martin also helped me a great deal over the years. Elnora Davis McLendon and her brother, Benjamin O. Davis Jr., and Noel F. Parrish and his widow, Florence Parrish St. John, contributed to my research and have been enthusiastic supporters. Jerry M. Cooper, Brian M. Linn, Allan R. Millett, and Russell F. Weigley read all or part of the manuscript and gave invaluable advice. Timothy K. Nenninger and Larry I. Bland also deserve my special appreciation for their great help in my research. I am also grateful to Paul J. Jacobsmeyer and Michael T. Johnson for help with the index. No author could ask for better editors than Joyce Seltzer, Ann Hawthorne, and Maria Ascher. The Graduate School of the University of Wisconsin–Madison contributed to the financial support of this project, as did the John Simon Guggenheim Foundation. The results are, of course, my responsibility.

I am most grateful to my family. My parents, Howard B. and Mada Wright Coffman, encouraged my interest in history from my early childhood on. My wife, Anne, has given me her devotion and wise counsel, while our children, Anne Wright, Lucia, and Ted, supported me in living the double life that scholars live—one in their world and the other in the world of their subject. I dedicate this book to our grandchildren—Tom, Carl, Mike, Anne Rose, Greg, and any others who may come along later—in the hope that they will appreciate the significance of history.

CONTENTS

Prologue

———◆◆◆———

In 1898 the United States intervened on the side of rebels against Spanish rule in Cuba. Within months American troops were fighting not only on that island but also in Puerto Rico and, across the Pacific, in the Philippines. This nation thus established a colonial empire and became a world power. No other national institution was as much affected by this great transition as the American Regular Army.

Since its creation in 1784, the Army had served as a frontier constabulary. While some artillerymen garrisoned the forts that dotted the coasts, most soldiers policed the Indians and, on occasion, the settlers. In the early years, the continuance of a standing army was endangered by the citizenry's fear of a military threat to civil government coupled with the Minuteman ideal of civilian volunteers springing to arms in an emergency. Besides, a regular force cost more to maintain than a militia system. The Jefferson administration settled the issue by recognizing the necessity of a frontier constabulary. In 1802 Secretary of the Treasury Albert Gallatin grudgingly acknowledged this but voiced a concern that was representative of public opinion throughout that century and which lingered into the next: "The distribution of our little army to distant garrisons where hardly any other inhabitant is to be found is the most eligible arrangement of that perhaps necessary evil that can be contrived."[1]

By the 1880s it was apparent that the days of the Indian-fighting army were coming to an end. Army thinkers considered their future in terms of becoming an urban constabulary to deal with the strikes and riots or, more to their liking, of creating a larger and more modern army capable of defending against a European invader. By 1898 the question of mission was still undecided, but the field artillery and the infantry had new weapons, and both were better trained, since the Army had abandoned many of the frontier posts and moved into larger garrisons.

From 1898 to 1941 the Army reflected the nation's ascendancy as a world power—fighting small wars in the Philippines and Mexico, playing a significant role in World War I, and preparing in its first large peacetime mobilization to take part in World War II. Civil War veterans and Indian fighters led the Army into the new century; those in charge of the Army in 1941 were professionally educated soldiers who had adapted to the great technological advances in machines and weapons as well as the organizational changes that are the requisites of a modern army of a world power.

ONE

The Army Begins a New Era

It was really a very fateful experience, for it destroyed forever our quiet home life, and projected us into the role of world power which has developed into the tragic responsibilities with which we are laden to-day.

—LEWIS S. SORLEY

T HE sinking of the *Maine,* a warship in Havana harbor to protect American citizens, in mid-February 1898 sent a shock wave throughout the United States. Fueled by lurid newspaper accounts of Spanish atrocities in Cuba, the American temper was already almost at the exploding point when the inflammatory news came. War now became a serious possibility.

Although hundreds of thousands were ready to spring to arms, those most immediately affected by the news of the day were the men already in uniform. Scattered about the nation in seventy-eight posts (with the largest garrison under 850), the 28,000 officers and men in the Regular Army might have varied attitudes toward the situation in Cuba, but all knew that if war came they would be the first to go. It would probably be a naval war, with the major Army activity being to bolster the coastal defense. The first congressional action endorsed that belief as, in early March, Congress passed a special appropriation act to build up the coastal defense and to create two regiments of artillery (Sixth and Seventh) to man those forts. This was the first increase in the strength of the regulars since the reorganization of the Army following the Civil War. Indeed, while the nation's population had more than doubled since 1865, to 73 million, the Army had leveled off at around 28,000 since the mid-1870s.[1]

During the post–Civil War years the nation's economy had also grown as it took its place among the world's manufacturing nations.

The population, steadily augmented by waves of immigrants, reflected the increasing industrialization by moving to cities; the percentage of Americans in urban areas doubled between 1860 and 1900. Social tensions, not surprisingly, increased throughout this time of great change and occasionally broke out into widespread civil disorders. During the same period the frontier disappeared, and with it, apparently, the threat of Indian hostilities. Since the Army's basic mission was to serve as a frontier constabulary, these developments raised the question of the Army's future. Although some officers suggested a change to an urban constabulary, the most prevalent view within the Army was that of developing a standing force that would, in peacetime, prepare to defend against the armies of major powers.

In early 1898 an infantry lieutenant, George B. Duncan, published a powerful argument for such a force in the *North American Review,* highlighting the changes wrought in the strategic position of the United States by advances in technology and the vulnerability of its relatively diminutive Army. Armored steamships made the ocean barriers less formidable while improved weapons required the expertise of trained professional soldiers. As it was, the American Army was roughly one-twentieth that of Germany, one-thirteenth the combined armies of Britain and India, less than a third of Spain's, and some 10,000 less than Mexico's regular army.[2]

Such arguments, however, confronted both severe budgetary restraint and the traditional distrust, if not, outright fear, of standing armies and professional soldiers. For most Americans, the major role in national security was best left to the citizenry who had demonstrated their potential as soldiers in all past wars. It was a lesson that Army reformers relearned in the month before the Spanish-American War began when they attempted to obtain congressional authorization of a permanent, as opposed to a temporary emergency, change in Army organization. The proposal was to create a third skeleton battalion in infantry regiments and to authorize the expansion from peacetime strength to full strength of all infantry, cavalry, and artillery units. On the surface, this did not seem like a drastic step, as the existing Army was already at the appropriate cadre strength; but the implication of being able to use this organization to expand quickly from 27,000 to 104,000 by recruiting privates into existing units was very clear not only to antimilitary people but also to supporters of the National Guard. It was also, in part, a ploy on the part of the regulars to make it possible to fight what was evidently going to be a relatively small war without calling on the citizen soldiery. One congressman struck the chords that had resonated throughout all anti–standing Army debates when he pointed out that citizen soldiers were more idealistic and an all-round better sort than Regular Army "hirelings," and, above all, they "do not menace our liberties." The bill was killed for the time being, but starting on April 19 Congress authorized intervention, called for volunteers, and on April 25 declared war. Only after those momentous steps did the legislature approve a modified version of the bill, authorizing an increase in enlisted regulars up to 61,000 and including a 20 percent wartime pay raise for both regulars and volunteers.[3]

In the massive gray stone building next door to the White House, War Department officials were overwhelmed by the rapid move to war. For more than three decades the major consideration in military affairs had been economy, and, as Secretary of War Russell A. Alger later said: "The governmental machinery . . . had become quite fixed in the narrow grooves of peace." When the president called out more than twice as many volunteers as the bureaucrats had expected and added another 75,000 to the original 125,000 a few weeks later, the problems of mobilizing, clothing, feeding, equipping, moving, and then finding places for tens of thousands of recruits were greatly compounded. Typewriters clattered, messages piled up, and men seeking commissions or favors of one kind or the other filled the corridors. One who got more attention than most was Assistant Secretary of the Navy Theodore Roosevelt, who was busy organizing a volunteer regiment of cavalry. On his fourth attempt to pry some horses and wagons from one of the bureau chiefs, Roosevelt reported that the old general finally gave in, sank back in his chair, and sighed: "Oh, dear! I had this bureau running in such great shape and along came a war!"[4]

Before war was declared and the avalanche of volunteers swept aside existing plans, the War Department had already, on April 15, ordered twenty-two of the twenty-five infantry regiments and six of the ten cavalry regiments to concentrate at New Orleans, Mobile, Tampa, and on the Chickamauga battlefield near Chattanooga. For some days before the order, in the headquarters of the Sixth Infantry at Fort Thomas, Kentucky, a soldier sat by the telephone waiting for this message. When it came, it created a great stir there and at other posts as officers and men checked equipment, packed, and got ready for long train rides and, eventually, war.[5]

On the afternoon of April 25 (the day war was declared), at West Point, the fifty-nine first classmen were attending a law lecture when an orderly brought a message to the professor, who told the cadets that they were going to graduate at noon the next day. Guy V. Henry Jr. was elated to graduate early and get the chance to go to war, but he was not pleased that his commission was in the infantry. The son of a distinguished cavalry officer, he had spent his life in the cavalry from his birth in a tent through his youth in assorted frontier posts. By the time he reached West Point, he claimed to have had "far more" field service than most young officers.

Many regular officers used whatever political influence they had to seek higher ranks in the volunteers, but John Bigelow Jr. simply wanted to return to his regiment. He had been on detached service for almost four years as a professor of military science and tactics at the Massachusetts Institute of Technology, where he and his family had certainly enjoyed the delights of Boston after so many years on the frontier. But first he had to persuade his young son, Braxton, who had crawled under his father's bed with his BB gun and was all packed to go, that he could not take him. It is a comment on the long-serving veterans in the black units that when this captain joined his troop, he found First Sergeant William H. Givens, who had been one of his sergeants twenty-one years before when he came to the Tenth Cavalry straight from West Point.[6]

Meantime, at Fort Reno, Oklahoma Territory, Lieutenant Eli A. Helmick was particularly busy as the regimental quartermaster, and hence responsible for much of the preparation. Once the troops were off he seized the opportunity to say goodbye to his family, but six-year-old Gardiner was not at home. When Helmick caught up with the command, half a mile from the post, he saw his son trudging along beside it. He took him in his arms and told him that he could not go but would have to stay home and look after his mother and sister. As the disappointed little boy started back, the soldiers called out: "Goodbye, Gardiner, sorry you can't go along."[7]

Civil War veterans were among those who marched off to war. In 1895 the War Department reported that 271 captains and lieutenants had fought in that war, and many of them remained on active duty—including sixty-three-year-old John W. Summerhayes, who had been a captain in that war. In that turbulent spring of 1898, more than 100,000 Civil War veterans volunteered (most of whom presumably were not accepted). During these weeks the reconciliation of North and South was much celebrated. Congressman Joseph Wheeler, a year younger than Summerhayes, enjoyed considerable fame as a Confederate cavalry major general. President William McKinley offered him and another former Confederate major general, Fitzhugh Lee, major generalcies in the volunteers. Given the melodramatic aura of those days, it is perhaps not surprising that when Wheeler first put on his new blue uniform and stepped out of his tent at Chickamauga, the guidon of the troop trotting past identified it as belonging to Troop A, Third Cavalry, the unit he had left to join the Confederacy in 1861.[8]

Cheering crowds at nearly every station greeted the troop trains as they wound their way south. People waved flags and thrust flowers and small gifts upon the regulars while some girls begged for collar ornaments in return. Southerners were as enthusiastic as northerners in welcoming these men in blue. For white units, like the Tenth Infantry, it was a small matter of having the regimental bands change their music from songs like "Marching through Georgia" to "Dixie" or some nonoffensive tune. Such was not the case, however, with the four black regiments. Sergeant Horace W. Bivens of the Tenth Cavalry, which consisted of black soldiers and white officers recalled that as long as they were in the North, "We received great ovations . . . Thousands of people were thronged at the places where we would stop and we were treated royally." For the black soldiers, however, there was little cheering or even courteous treatment once they reached the South. During the weeks in Florida while they waited to go to Cuba, there were many confrontations as these soldiers from the frontier clashed with civilian bigots.[9]

Some of the officers' families went with them to the southern camps, some stayed where they were, and still others went to live with their parents for the duration. Florence Kuykendall Pickering packed up the three children she had with her (a son was away at school) at Fort Yates and followed her husband's company of the Second Infantry in a Dougherty wagon for the fifty-mile march to Bismarck. From there on the southern-bound troop train, they also enjoyed the cheering crowds.

The First Infantry regiment leaving the Presidio of San Francisco to join the Cuban expedition, 1898. Courtesy of Hester Nolan Donovan.

Seven-year-old Mauree, in particular, was thrilled by the excitement of it all.[10]

An officer or two and a handful of soldiers remained behind as caretakers at each of the virtually abandoned posts. At Fort Sill, Oklahoma Territory, more seemed to be at risk than property for a few tense hours shortly after the garrison left. A rumor spread quickly that Geronimo and the approximately 270 Apaches on the post were planning an uprising. The young lieutenant left in charge telegraphed the column then on the march to send back the cavalry troop. Grace Paulding and her stepdaughter lived close to the guardhouse, so other wives and their children gathered at her house and other nearby quarters, waited, and tried not to think of "the dreadful possibility" of an Indian attack. Around midnight they heard the faint sound of a cavalry bugle: "No sound was ever more beautiful and the relief almost too great."[11]

At Tampa, where those bound for Cuba were assembled for embarkation, the regulars set up their tents and proceeded with their camp routine and drills, sweltering in their heavy blue uniforms. George Kennan, one of the reporters who watched them work out and liked what he saw, wrote: "The soldiers were generally stalwart, sunburnt, resolute-looking men, twenty-five to thirty-five years of age, who seemed to be in perfect physical condition, and who looked as if they had already seen hard service and were ready and anxious for more." In fact they were veterans. The year before the adjutant general had noted that more than a third of the enlisted men had served at least five years, and according to the official records, in April 1898 there were only forty soldiers under the age of twenty-one in the entire Regular Army. Recruits who enlisted for the duration of the war in May, June, and July almost doubled the strength of the Army, but they represented only 11 percent of total enlistments during that period, as McKinley promptly got his 200,000 volunteers. But very few of these men, regulars or volunteers, reached Tampa in time to go to Cuba.[12]

George Duncan arrived in Tampa in late April as a lieutenant in the Fourth Infantry but soon received a staff appointment as a captain of volunteers. For him, the beginnings of the new era in military affairs that he had pleaded for in his article just weeks before must have seemed messier than he had envisioned. He saw those hectic days chiefly as "a nightmare of indecision." Certainly it was a time filled by changes of plans. During this period President McKinley personally took over the conduct of the war from his secretary of war and the commanding general, Nelson A. Miles, neither of whom he trusted. He came to rely increasingly on his new adjutant general, Henry C. Corbin, who in 1866 had picked his single star as a brevet brigadier general out of his shoulder straps to produce the plain insignia of a second lieutenant when he became a regular. A few days before the declaration of war, McKinley had told Corbin: "I deplore the war, but it must be short and quick to the finish." From that desire for haste came many of the problems of the war.[13]

In early June Major General William R. Shafter supervised the loading of his expeditionary force. Although he had been a brevet brigadier general in the Civil War and was a Medal of Honor recipient, he had no experience of commanding a force larger than a regiment. His obesity and his coarse manner irritated Duncan as well as others.

The embarkation, Eli Helmick recalled, was "a classic of confusion and inefficiency." Eventually the 17,000 men and at least some of their supplies got on the twenty-nine leased ships. Before they sailed, Florence Pickering took her children and joined a friend in a rowboat to wave a final goodbye to her husband. The ship "looked like a mountain" to little Mauree, while her father high up on the deck "looked very tiny." As the ship turned, it gave all of them a scare as it seemed about to suck their small boat under its stern.[14]

The Fifth Corps spent only two months in Cuba during which it unsystematically provided a classic example of how not to fight a war. They landed on open beaches, moving from ship to shore in lifeboats. Animals had to swim. When one group started out to sea, an alert regular had a bugler sound calls that prompted the well-trained horses to turn and swim toward the shore, but the untrained mules kept on going. Stores stacked up willy-nilly on the beach while the troops suffered from lack of food, changes of clothing, and medical supplies.

The major action was an assault on Spanish positions on the high ground near Santiago on July 1. Lieutenant Lewis S. Sorley, who took part in the attack with the 16th Infantry, recalled that it was a "company officers' battle." At that level, the officers and men in the half-strength regular regiments that made up 85 percent of the entire command knew very well what to do. An old German sergeant, Necker, in Paulding's company of the Tenth Infantry made that bluntly clear as they pushed to the front past a regiment of volunteers. One of them called out: "Don't go up there; you'll be killed." Necker responded: "What in Hell are we here for?" and kept his men moving toward San Juan Ridge.[15]

After they had swept the Spanish out of their positions on the hills, the troops dug trenches and awaited developments, occasionally exchanging shots with their reluctant enemies. In one of these outbursts on the day after the battle, Sorley was wounded in the left chest and arm. On the third day, the Navy won the decisive victory of the campaign by sinking the Spanish fleet as it attempted to escape from Santiago Harbor. Two weeks later the Spanish surrendered.[16]

This was not, however, the end of the war. Although Cuba had been the focal point of popular hostility toward the Spanish, the War Department's recently created Military Information Division (MID) had also distributed to various commands information about other Spanish possessions—Puerto Rico and the Philippines—even before the war began. The Navy's Asiatic Squadron sank the Spanish fleet in Manila Bay on May 1, less than a week after the declaration of war. With American warships lying at anchor awaiting ground reinforcements, MID officers hastily looked up the Philippines in the *Encylopaedia Britannica* and passed on all they knew to the staff of the commander of the rapidly forming expedition. The first contingent to join Commodore George Dewey set out in late May, but the full force of some 10,000 was not ready for battle around Manila until August. The Spanish were more willing to give up the fight here than in Cuba, and Major General Wesley Merritt, who had served as a Union cavalry major general in the Civil War, handled his troops with more finesse than Shafter. The one battle was an almost bloodless victory at Manila on August 13.

Casualties also were very low in the Puerto Rican campaign, which was carried out by another Civil War major general who had regained his two stars in 1890—Nelson A. Miles. His 18,000 troops saw limited action from the last week in July until the end of the war on August 12. Unlike the Cuban expedition, the forces in both Puerto Rico and the Philippines consisted predominantly of volunteers, who outnumbered regulars by as much as four to one. One of the soldiers who went to Puerto Rico in a volunteer engineer unit was Benjamin D. Foulois. An apprentice plumber in a small Connecticut town, Foulois had never heard of the Regular Army until the war. After a couple of attempts to enlist in the Navy, the eighteen-year-old went to an Army recruiting station in the summer and showed them his older brother's birth certificate (at that time the minimum age for enlistment without parental permission was twenty-one). Within a few weeks of putting on a uniform in a volunteer engineer regiment, he was in Puerto Rico.[17]

Disease became a much more formidable enemy than the Spanish. Those who were wounded like Sorley and Captain Bigelow, who was shot down in the charge up San Juan Hill, were fortunate, since they were taken out of Cuba before tropical fevers flattened the Fifth Corps. Yellow fever infected many of the men, but it was malaria that struck 75 percent of the troops by August 3. Later typhoid took a heavy toll. Since it was widely believed that blacks were less likely than whites to catch tropical diseases, the 24th Infantry was asked to volunteer to work at the yellow fever hospital in mid-July. Of the 456 black soldiers who took up this onerous task (all of those left in the half-strength regiment), only 24 escaped sickness. The obvious conclusion, made by the regimental commander in his report, was "that colored soldiers were not more immune from Cuban fever than white."

Mansfield Robinson, a nine-year veteran, was one of those who left the trenches to nurse the sick. A Kentuckian, he had not planned to stay in the Army, but after being unable to find a job during a visit home at the end of his first enlistment in 1894, he decided to make the Army his career. In Cuba, about a week after he got to the hospital, he came down with yellow fever. A few weeks later he and the other fever victims boarded a makeshift transport whose deck served as his bed. The food was bad, but he did not feel like eating anyway. He had weighed 180 pounds when he left for Cuba in June. By September 2, when he reached Montauk Point at the tip of Long Island, where the War Department had hastily prepared a temporary camp, he weighed 126 pounds.

Despite winning laurels at San Juan Hill, black troops returned to continuing discrimination in what their chaplain referred to as "the land of prejudice and contempt." In Huntsville, Alabama, whites and troopers of the Tenth Cavalry clashed violently, and their troop train was fired on in Mississippi and Texas. These soldiers were probably happy to return to Cuba the next spring.[18]

Most of the officers and men of the Fifth Corps who filled up the tents at Montauk Point looked like scarecrows. Families and friends sent and brought food and other supplies to the volunteers to the point that the regulars felt neglected. But John Jacob Astor and Helen Gould made large contributions to even the balance. Grace Paulding had gone to Martha's Vineyard to wait out the war, which she anxiously followed in the daily newspaper. In August a friend in the War Department wired her that her husband was due in New York the next day. Because of his terrible condition, Will was in a civilian hospital some distance from Montauk Point. When she saw him, she was appalled at the "heartbreaking sight." Yellow fever had wasted him from 165 to 89 pounds. It was touch and go as she nursed him over the next few days until, with the help of friends, she was able to get him to Martha's Vineyard. But he would need a year's sick leave before he was ready to return to duty.[19]

Although 280 were killed in this war, another 2,500 died of disease. Of the latter, 137 died in Puerto Rico and only 63 in the Philippines. At the time, medical officers credited the impressively better record in

Mansfield Robinsin, recently returned from his first of three tours in the Philippines, at Fort Missoula, Montana, 1902. Author's collection.

the Philippines to the fact that the long sea voyage helped hold down typhoid fever, in particular. Most of the deaths from disease, however, were in the camps in the United States. Here some 165,000 of the volunteers and a few regulars spent the war in hastily prepared camps with poor sanitary conditions, where typhoid fever in August and September killed as many as 1,500. While awaiting assignment in May, Guy V. Henry spent three weeks with his father at the camp at Chickamauga. When he returned home to Washington, D.C., he became ill with typhoid. Visits to the hospital and flowers from President and Mrs. McKinley were scant consolation for an ambitious young officer; he missed the war completely. Later, after the War Department had come under heavy attack for the tragic situation at the several camps, the secretary of war pointed out that the Army deaths from disease were less than those in the Civil War, those of the British Army in the continuing Boer War, and even those in several American cities. But however accurate the statistics were, the surgeon general's report in 1899 and Secretary Alger's book in 1900 came a bit late to offset the newspaper headlines of 1898.[20]

When young Henry was well enough to return to service in the fall, he sailed to Puerto Rico to join his father. As he remembered, he and his fellow passengers pondered their future in an "unknown and dreaded world." They realized that disease was rampant, but otherwise "Americans knew little of the tropics in those days." One proof of this ignorance was the congressional authorization to form ten infantry regiments of men who were immune to tropical disease. At least five of these had to be white, but the rest would consist of blacks, who it was generally assumed were naturally immune to tropical disease. In the end, six white and four black regiments of so-called Immunes were organized in June and July. Apparently the dramatic experience of the men of the 24th Infantry with yellow fever had little effect on the formation of these units. Indeed, thirty black noncommissioned officers (NCOs) who had distinguished themselves in Cuba or in their service generally were given commissions in the black regiments. Among them was the veteran Tenth Cavalry Sergeant Givens, who became a second lieutenant in the Tenth Volunteer Infantry. When the volunteers were mustered out, however, many of these men who had given up their stripes to serve as officers had to return as privates to their old companies.

Two of the regiments promptly went to Cuba to help take the place of the invalided Fifth Corps, but the Eighth Volunteer Infantry got only as far as Chickamauga. The first lieutenant of Company G was a particularly enthusiastic officer. The son of a messenger in the Department of Interior in Washington, D.C., Benjamin O. Davis had grown up listening to stories about the Civil War and wanting to be a soldier. The Ninth Cavalry troop stationed at Fort Myer, Virginia, in the early 1890s was a particular inspiration. In high school, from which he graduated in the spring of 1898, he captained the football team but really thrived on the drills of the cadet corps. Offered a first lieutenancy if he would recruit and drill men under the command of a white captain who had no military experience, Davis filled up the ranks in less than three days and began teaching the rudiments of drill. He learned much from the regulars who had taken commissions in the Eighth. A former first sergeant in the Ninth Cavalry, John C. Proctor, who taught him to ride, became a particularly good friend. At Fort Thomas and later at Chickamauga, the eighteen-year-old lieutenant made a very good impression as battalion adjutant. He knew he had found his life's work.[21]

In November 1898, three months after the cessation of hostilities, Secretary of War Alger, General Corbin, and John A. T. Hull, who chaired the House Military Affairs Committee, started to work up a bill to create a Regular Army of 100,000. Despite its seemingly strong backers, the bill failed. A key reason was that the public had begun to make Alger the scapegoat for the many problems of the war; hence his support became a liability. A report by the presidentially appointed Dodge Commission in early February 1899 more or less exonerated him, but too late to help the bill. Then there were assorted other Army reorganization bills proposed, including one by the commanding general, Nelson A. Miles, who was bitter because McKinley had stopped consulting him. Finally, there was fairly strong opposition from the antiimperialists, who understood clearly the purpose of this quadrupling of the Regular Army.

War broke out in the Philippines on February 4, 1899, and if the nation was going to stay in that fight, it needed troops. Accordingly, Congress in early March passed a bill that authorized a Regular Army of 65,000 supplemented by 35,000 volunteers to serve until July 1, 1901, at which time all but 29,000 of the regulars would also be discharged.

That summer and fall the Army organized twenty-five regiments of volunteers, including two black regiments, which would have all-black captains and lieutenants. All officers were to be selected from regulars and volunteers who had distinguished themselves in the Spanish-American War.[22]

Guy Henry had not been able to get into the war, but he knew President McKinley, so he waited outside his door for three days until a friendly usher slipped him in to see the president. When Guy asked him for an appointment in one of these regiments, McKinley wanted to know what rank he desired. "Whatever you think I am capable of having, Mr. President," was Guy's reply. The president told him that he would see what he could do and closed the interview. Later he confided to friends that young Henry was the only applicant who had not asked for at least a colonelcy. So Guy, who got a captaincy, became one of 136 regular officers commissioned in the volunteers. Within two months, however, he was promoted in the 26th Volunteer Infantry and was, at twenty-six, he believed, the youngest major in the Army.[23]

Although the shooting in the war with Spain stopped in mid-August, final ratification of the peace treaty did not occur until March 1899, some six weeks after fighting had broken out in the Philippines. By the fall of 1899 most of the regulars (30,578) were in the new theater of war while occupation forces garrisoned Cuba (10,796), Puerto Rico (2,855), and Hawaii (453), with the remaining 17,317 in the United States. Few of these men had served in the war against Spain. During that turbulent year the War Department had to discharge most of the wartime Army and simultaneously recruit a new one. Within three months after the war had ended, some 100,000 of the volunteers (roughly half) were mustered out, with the 30,000 who had enlisted in the regulars only for the duration soon following them into civilian life. As a result of the insurrection in the Philippines, however, some units were kept in service, with the last regiment of volunteers not being discharged until the end of November 1899. The winding down of the war against Spain, for those who stayed in the Army, meant the end of the 20 percent increase in pay. There was a compensation in comfort, however, in the Army's new light-weight khaki uniform for tropical service. Then, too, the July authorization for the recruitment of competent cooks—one per company or equivalent unit—was probably beginning to have an effect in better meals.[24]

During this transition period the Army's recruiting effort was impressive. It tripled the number of stations to 134 and brought into the ranks more than 62,000 men, 30 percent of those who applied for enlistment. Roughly 10 percent were black, in keeping with the ratio of black to white regiments established after the Civil War. The adjutant general thought that "a better class of men are now entering the ranks than formerly." Enlistment standards had been upgraded in the mid-1890s. Then, in contrast to the large numbers of foreign-born recruits who had populated the Army throughout the century, peaking at two-thirds in the 1850s and declining to little more than a third in the 1880s and 1890s, just 12 percent of the recruits in this period had been born outside the United States. The inspector general noted that most of the new men were either farmers or laborers.[25]

Among those who enlisted at this time was Louis S. Yassel, while Foulois, the apprentice plumber from Connecticut, and Davis, the messenger's son from Washington, D.C., also decided to try the regulars after their stints in volunteer units. Although he was only twenty-one in late 1898, Yassel had already had an eventful life. His parents had brought him to a coal-mining village in northern Pennsylvania from Austria when he was three. He had driven a mule cart at the mine, but after his father's death and his mother's return to Austria, he had gone to Connecticut to work first in a silk mill and then in a machine shop. While still a boy, he began to play the cornet in the local band. He had never seen soldiers before the war, but his landlady's son, who had been slightly wounded in Cuba, convinced him to look into the Army as a career that would further his music.

In the winter, during a ten-day break when his shop was taking inventory, Louis visited his friend at Plattsburg Barracks, New York. The Army made a very good impression on him. Since it was the dead of winter, there was virtually no training, and the soldiers seemed to be merely sitting around, shooting pool, and enjoying themselves. "I thought, gee, those fellows are living a fine life here." The combination of what he saw of Army life, his friend's encouragement, and the fact that there was soon going to be a vacancy as bugler led him to enlist on January 14, 1899, in Company E, 21st Infantry.[26]

When Foulois came home after several months in Puerto Rico, he was heartily sick of the Army. He had made sergeant and handled the responsibility well, but Washington, Connecticut, looked very good upon his return. After a few months he began to remember what he liked about his service—the discipline and the camaraderie. Besides, as the weeks passed, it seemed that his hometown had "shrunk a lot." Since he was still only nineteen, he checked into appointments to the Military Academy but found that he was too late to get one for the coming year. Finally, he got his parents' permission and this time enlisted under his real name on June 17 in the 19th Infantry.[27]

There was more opposition in the Davis family to their son's enlisting in the regulars. In the black middle class in Washington, D.C., enlisted men "were looked down upon." Benjamin O. Davis recalled: "Several boys who had gotten into difficulty with the police had escaped arrest by enlisting in the Army or Navy." When his unit was mustered out in March, he was determined to regain a commission. Besides not being enthusiastic about the Army, his mother wanted him to be a Baptist minister. His father did try to get his nineteen-year-old son an appointment to West Point from President McKinley, but the president let it be known that "for political reasons" it was not feasible for him to appoint "a colored boy" at that time. A half-century later Davis commented: "This matter of color has always presented a problem to me." He knew that he was not inferior. His school work and his months in the Army had given him confidence. When an effort to secure a commission in one of the new black volunteer regiments failed, he began to consider enlisting and then trying for a competitive commission from the ranks. His friend, John Proctor, who was visiting in Washington, encouraged him to enlist with him in the Ninth Cavalry. Although the unit was up to strength, Major Martin B. Hughes, who knew Proctor and had asked him to try to get a recruit with clerical skills, made a special appeal to the War Department to permit the enlistment of his old sergeant and Davis. Despite his family's protests, young Davis and his friend went to the Washington Barracks and were sworn in on June 14.[28]

After serving in the Santiago campaign, the Ninth was scattered in posts in Arizona, Utah, and Texas. Davis and Proctor joined Troop I, which was the entire garrison at Fort Duchesne, Utah. This frontier post, built to separate two Indian tribes, afforded the same duties that soldiers had performed for the past century. Within Davis' first months there, troopers were called out to drive settlers off government land and to bring back some Indians who had gone to Colorado to hunt. While many might have found the routine monotonous at this garrison of less than a hundred men, Davis thought "life there very interesting." The business course that he had taken in high school worked to his advantage. He could write a good hand, take dictation, and type, and, as he recalled, "There was a need for clerks." Soon he was troop clerk and a corporal. He learned about the ways of the Regular Army from the old soldiers, and in turn he taught the illiterates among them how to write their names.[29]

At this time there was only one black line officer in the four segregated regiments. Charles Young, an 1889 graduate of the Military Academy, was a lieutenant in the Ninth Cavalry. Whites filled whatever officer vacancies existed. One of the West Pointers whose class graduated in February 1899, George Van Horn Moseley, joined the Ninth Cavalry after completing the last leg of his journey via stagecoach. Since Fort Grant, Arizona Territory, was regimental headquarters, there were more troops in the garrison, but any amenities of a larger post were offset by the presence of the colonel and his wife. For an ambitious young officer, this situation was very discouraging. Colonel Thomas McGregor had enlisted in the First Dragoon Regiment in 1858 and served in the ranks until he earned a commission during the Civil War. Whatever his prowess in earlier times (he had two brevets for gallantry), he was not inspiring in 1899. Moseley made that point bluntly by remarking that he saw him mounted only twice during the time he spent in the regiment. McGregor's wife, Jennie, was much more formidable. She was an impressive figure at some 300 pounds. Moseley remembered her well: "Equipped with cavalry gauntlets which extended half way up her arms, and armed with a serious looking whip, she drove two fast trotting mules in a buckboard. Cowboys, drunk or sober, put spurs to their ponies . . . when they saw the old lady coming." Circumstances—that the McGregors expected bachelor officers to pay court to their daughter, that Moseley's troop commander was "the worst product I have ever seen from West Point," and exposure to the old Army tradition of payday drunken sprees—combined to encourage the young lieutenant to get out of Fort Grant as soon as possible.

There was a detachment of the regiment at Eagle Pass located in a camp on the site of old Fort Duncan near the Rio Grande. Moseley avidly seized the chance to go there as the commander. He ran into another part of the Old West when he stepped off the train at Eagle Pass to be grabbed by a saloonkeeper who wanted him to break up a melee in his bar. He pulled out his Colt revolver, dispersed the unruly drinkers, and thereby earned free beers for his black troopers whenever they came to town. Moseley enjoyed his independent command and was proud of his soldiers' record during his eight months there.[30]

Although both Davis and Moseley witnessed and participated in many of the experiences that would have been familiar to frontier soldiers of an earlier time, they did not fight Indians. Although it is assumed that the Indian Wars ended with the Pine Ridge campaign in 1890, some officers and men of the Third Infantry did battle with Chippewas in northern Minnesota in October 1898. After its return from Cuba, the Third took up station at Fort Snelling and began to recruit up to strength. In late September the secretary of the interior requested a small detail to go to Leech Lake to support the civilian authorities. The Pillager band of Chippewas were disgruntled over timber-cutting incidents and the requirement to journey to distant courts to make their claims. They were well armed, so when they refused to give up two men for whom there were warrants, the marshals called for the Army. It was a familiar scenario that had played out in hundreds of variations on the frontier. A lieutenant, less than five months out of West Point, and twenty men arrived, but the problem was obviously bigger than they could handle. Then the department commander sent eighty more men, nearly all recruits, under an experienced Indian fighter, Captain Melville C. Wilkinson, a vintage Civil War captain, who had earned a brevet for gallantry in the Nez Percé campaign in 1877. When the troops and assorted civilians arrived by two steamboats at Sugar Point on Leech Lake, they seized the two wanted Indians and were preparing to spend the night when one of the men apparently accidentally fired his weapon. The Indians then opened fire from ambush and pinned them down for almost two days until more troops arrived. Wilkinson and five soldiers died in the battle; ten enlisted men and four civilians were wounded. These killed and wounded almost matched the regiment's combat casualties in the Santiago campaign.[31]

While the vestiges of the old frontier were fading in the United States, regulars were moving into the new frontier in Alaska. Although a small contingent of troops had garrisoned that territory in 1867, after the evacuation of the last two companies in 1877 there had been no military presence until the discovery of gold in the late 1890s. The first troops went there in the fall of 1897 on the humanitarian mission of feeding and caring for destitute miners. They were also supposed to establish law and order. By the summer of 1899 there was still ample work to do to restrain the lawlessness. In late June, Second Lieutenant Oliver L. Spaulding Jr. took ten men into the wide-open boom town of Anvil City to stop claim-jumping, to disarm miners, and to enforce liquor licensing. He also broke up an illegal mob meeting and won the praise of the deputy collector of customs for his efforts.[32]

Meantime, reinforcements were on their way, and they were ordered to build forts. Captain Charles A. Booth and his company of the Seventh Infantry had just about recovered from the Santiago campaign when they had to go to Alaska. After the last lap of ten days by steamboat on the Yukon River, they reached their destination at the mouth of the Tanana River on July 25. The two companies (150 soldiers, including a medical detachment) then fell to the chore of cutting logs and laying out the grounds of what would be Fort Gibbon. The work they did seven days a week was just like that performed by their predecessors during the past century. The snow that fell for three days in mid-September provided ample warning, and on October 10 the soldiers were able to move into their new barracks.[33]

Another reminder of traditional Army duties came in the spring, when the governor of Idaho called for federal troops to put down lawlessness in the Coeur d'Alene region. Thus, for the third time in the 1890s, troops went into those mining camps. The conflict arose over recognition of unionized workers, while the immediate cause was the seizure and blowing up of a nonunion mine plant by a large armed and masked mob. The state government was on the side of management and used the federal troops accordingly to uphold property rights. Eight companies of the 24th Infantry arrived in early May and stayed several weeks while elements of three other regiments reinforced and eventually replaced these black troops. They assisted in the arrest and holding of those suspected of having taken part in the violence—which broadly meant any union member or sympathizer—but met no armed resistance. Before the summer was out, other soldiers of the 24th found themselves on another traditional duty of protecting government land—in these instances, in the Sequoia and Yosemite areas.[34]

Mansfield Robinson probably was not healthy enough to take part in these duties. He had had a difficult time breaking the siege of yellow fever. Finally, his company commander came to his rescue by obtaining a prescription from his own private doctor that did cure him. In June, however, when the 24th was ordered to the Philippines, War Department instructions were to leave behind all men not considered able to stand field service in the tropics. When Robinson was told that he could not go, he made his case "that I had no place to go, that I had gotten sick in the service and that they ought to take care of me. If I got outside, I would be at the mercy of society. If I stayed in and died in the Philippines, at least they would bury me." It was a convincing argument when combined with this private's good record over his ten years in the regiment. By the end of the summer he was in the Philippines in one of the first contingents of black troops to cross the Pacific.[35]

In his annual report for 1899, General Miles recognized the extraordinary hardships that Robinson and other regulars suffered: "Within the last eighteen months several regiments have been required to leave their stations in the extreme North, move to the islands of the West Indies, there engage in a campaign in summer, return to northern stations in the autumn and winter, and move again to tropical islands in the Pacific and engage in campaigns under the most difficult circumstances." In the process, as another general lamented, the "old character" of these units disappeared through the losses in combat and disease as well as discharges of those wartime regulars and the men deemed unable to return to the tropics. The ranks were then filled with "green men . . . awkward, and undrilled."[36]

Louis Yassel fell into the recruit category although he had learned bugle calls and close-order drill at Plattsburg Barracks before the 21st left for the Philippines. Benny Foulois was not a recruit, but he had not been in the regulars before. He soon learned that there was a difference between a volunteer and a regular. Within a month after his enlistment, the 19th left for the Philippines. When the troop train stopped in Lake Tahoe, Nevada, two elderly ladies with a tray of doughnuts came up to Foulois and some of his fellow soldiers and asked the name of their unit. When they heard the 19th, they asked if it was a volunteer or regular unit. The answer—"regulars"—was not what they wanted to hear. As Foulois remembered, "They stared at us a moment as if we had just run off with the town's bank funds, then turned and hurried away."[37]

For most regular veterans, duty in the States was a rather brief interlude in which it was hoped they would recover from disease before returning to the tropics. Eli Helmick, who was not entirely over malaria, had more than the usual reasons for hurrying to his family in October 1898. His wife, whom he had left at Fort Reno, was expecting their third child. He was delighted to be home, but the virtually deserted fort had gone to seed. Since there were no competent doctors nearby, the Helmicks had to depend upon the hospital steward, the wife of the bandmaster, and a soldier's wife to help with the birth. All went well, but five months later he had to rejoin his regiment in Cuba. His wife and the three children stayed at Reno until summer. After spending the warm months with her family in New England, she, the children, the maid, and their bulldog "Taps" journeyed to Cuba in October.[38]

George Duncan returned from Puerto Rico for sick leave and then a staff job in Chicago, but with the discharge of the wartime volunteers he lost his temporary rank and rejoined the Fourth Infantry as a first lieutenant. In mid-January he, his wife, and his sister sailed with the regiment from New York for Manila on the *Grant,* one of the first three transports purchased and fitted out by the Army. As the secretary of war confirmed in October 1899, immediate family members of military personnel could travel on transports, apparently paying only for their meals. It was a memorable two-month trip via the Mediterranean and the Suez Canal, the spicy breezes off the shore of Ceylon, and Singapore.

For Duncan, the most impressive event of the trip was a formal dinner with the officers of the 19th Yorkshire, the Prince of Wales's Own Regiment, during a coaling stop at Gibraltar. It was, indeed, an occasion for an American officer whose military service had begun at frontier posts. The British lavished good food and drink on Duncan and his two fellow officers while the regimental commander graciously toasted them. This friendliness on the part of the British Army was not unique. The adjutant general noted with pleasure in his annual report for 1899 the more elaborate courtesies extended by the garrison at Malta to the officers and men on the *Sheridan,* which sailed a month later than the

Grant. The results of the war against Spain included not only increased amity between Great Britain and the United States but also a more sympathetic understanding among American officers of what it meant to be an imperial Army. In this context, it is not strange that a department commander in the Philippines ordered all American flags on public buildings to be lowered to half-staff out of respect for Queen Victoria when he heard of her death in January 1901 or that the Army and Navy Club in Manila cancelled the regular monthly dance on that occasion.[39]

At Suez, Duncan learned of the outbreak of the insurrection in the Philippines; entering Manila Bay, the troops aboard the *Grant* saw Dewey's warships lobbing shells into the countryside. Since April 1898, when his article on the need for a larger Army because of the changing world had appeared, he had been in two war zones, Cuba and Puerto Rico, and was now entering a third halfway around the world. His experience had certainly illustrated the accuracy of his words: "The world grows smaller and nations formerly but little known to each other now rub elbows in the march of civilization." He thrilled at the sights of the flag flying on Corregidor at the entrance to the bay and of the warships of England and Germany as well as Dewey's fleet. His response probably reflected a view common to a good many Americans: "the tide of white civilization had been moving Westward through the centuries and now our country, young as it was . . . had stepped across the Pacific . . . I could foresee tremendous opportunities in advancing our political creed of government for the betterment of people generally, and at the same time an overwhelming responsibility in showing ourselves worthy of the opportunity given by an all-wise Providence."

At the time, not the least of his worries was what to do with his wife, Mary Kercheval Duncan, and his sister, Nana. Since the outbreak of the Philippine Insurrection in February 1899, the Army had not permitted dependents to go to the Philippines. Duncan recommended that they simply return on the *Grant.* Their decision to stay evoked this comment from him: "I found then that the spirit of adventure is just as strong, if not stronger, in women as it is in men. They remained and were fated to listen to many an engagement around Manila in which they knew that I was engaged."[40]

When the Sixth Infantry left for the Philippines that spring, the wives had to stay but the Army permitted them to retain their quarters. At

Fort Sam Houston, after the regiment departed, the so-called "Philippine widows" anxiously read the news of this war and waited. It had been only a few months since their men had returned from another war. Among them was Adelaide Carleton Poore who gave birth to her third daughter on December 29, 1899. She named her Adelaide but called her "Benny" after her father, Benjamin A. Poore. It would be long months before this family reunited.[41]

Since the Tenth Infantry was in Cuba, Grace Paulding had no problem joining her husband in the fall of 1899. The voyage was uneventful, but Grace sensed that for those who had served on the frontier posts, "it was a strange and eventful occurrence to be going to a post in the tropics and on foreign soil. The old continuity of Army life had been broken and no one could guess what was to take its place, but certainly the change was more tremendous than anyone could have possibly realized. The 'Old Army' was gone." Guy Henry was too caught up in the preparations for combat when he crossed the Pacific to be pensive about what this meant to the "Old Army," but he also clearly recognized that "all of this was new and strange." Eight-year-old Mauree Pickering, who went with her mother and brother to Cuba in the spring of 1899, likewise discovered "so many new and interesting experiences . . . the strangest one was not understanding a word we heard spoken."[42]

Throughout this period from 1897 to 1901, the Army had an increasingly interested observer in a lanky cadet at the Virginia Military Institute (VMI)—George C. Marshall. In the spring of 1898 the VMI cadets unanimously offered their services, but the Army thought it better that they remain in school. Marshall was then a freshman—a "Rat"—and thus had little opportunity to read or think much about what was happening outside VMI. He did, however, catch up on war news that summer, and in August 1899, at home in Uniontown, Pennsylvania, he witnessed the return of the local company from the Philippines. He recalled it as a great emotional experience and considered it "the determining effect on my choice of a profession."[43]

✴

On the eve of the twentieth century, the United States had seized an empire as the spoils of one war and was in the midst of another and greater war. After stumbling through the war against Spain, the new and much larger Army began to show more efficiency in dealing with the myriad logistical problems of the new day in military affairs. General Shafter, who had commanded the Cuban expedition, summed up the reason for this in a letter to General Corbin in August 1900: "We are getting used to war now and have the necessary appliances and means to do with."[44]

There was a new secretary of war, Elihu Root, in August 1899. McKinley, who had come to rely less and less on Alger, was probably not unhappy to see him blamed for the wartime scandals. After the tribulations of the spring and summer of 1898, War Department bureaucrats had not only brought order out of what sometimes seemed to be chaos but had also begun to think of the future. General Corbin, for one, thought the government ought to obtain land for military reservations in newly annexed Hawaii. Already transports such as Henry's were briefly stopping there en route to the Philippines, and its strategic importance seemed obvious. The chief signal officer, meantime, had already purchased an electrical "field carriage" and was planning to test its possibilities not only as an "automobile" but also as a means of providing power for telephones, telegraphy, and lights in the field.[45]

In 1957, in the midst of the Cold War, ninety-year-old Lewis S. Sorley pondered the meaning of the war against Spain: "it was really a very fateful experience, for it destroyed forever our quiet home life, and projected us into the role of world power which has developed into the tragic responsibilities with which we are laden to-day." He had commanded an Indian company in 1892 yet would remain on active duty until 1931. Others would stay with the Army longer: Foulois until 1935, and Henry, Yassel, Davis, and Marshall into the 1940s. Mauree Pickering and Benny Poore would also spend this entire period with the service. Their lives and those of other officers, soldiers, wives, and children reflected the course of the American Army during the first four decades of the twentieth century.[46]

TWO

The Colonial Army

You in civil life are but indirectly, often unappreciably, affected by changes in national policy; but we of the Service are intimately affected by every such change.

—JOHN H. PARKER

———————◆◆◆———————

WHEN the United States emerged as a world power, its Army had to assume large additional responsibilities. For most Americans, the colonial experience remained as superficial as the proud Uncle Sam sticking American flags in the globe in an 1898 cartoon. Both opponents and enthusiasts of this "Roman candle foreign policy" had to depend upon what they read in the newspapers, but for soldiers who planted those flags, it was different.[1]

From 1899 through 1916, the Army fluctuated in strength from some 64,000 in the fall of 1899, to just under 54,000 in 1907, to 107,000 in 1916. Although this force was much larger than the Army America had maintained in the late nineteenth century, it still was relatively small when compared to other armies. Germany and France had forces of more than a half-million in 1899, while Britain's peacetime regulars numbered more than 250,000. Before the mobilization for World War I in 1914, Germany increased its army to 620,000; France fielded 560,000 men; Britain still maintained some 250,000 in its army; and Japan had 230,000 regulars, while the American Army numbered less than 98,000.[2]

At the turn of the century, when "the doors of the wide world had just come ajar" for the United States, almost three-quarters of the American troops were overseas. Until World War I, a fourth or more were in overseas garrisons. The war in the Philippines was the reason for the early disproportionate figure. During that conflict, in December 1900, there were at peak strength 69,420 regulars and volunteers plus about 1,500 native troops serving in the Philippines. In contrast, in 1899 the British kept 74,000 regulars in India and supplemented them with some 145,000 native troops.[3]

✳

Conditions in Cuba had ignited the powder train to America's imperialistic explosion. The brief, successful campaign produced a governmental vacuum that added a collapsed economy and rampant disease to the problems of a war-torn society. In the fall of 1898, American military officials recommended an occupation force of 50,000 that would presumably have an extended stay. By February 1899 the last of the Spanish troops were out, and 45,000 Americans were scattered throughout the island. Under the supervision of the military government, however, restoration proceeded so well that most of the occupation troops were back in the United States by November. A crucial part of the effort had been the massive sanitary campaign carried on in Havana, which was a pest hole. In the last months of 1900, when less than 5,700 troops remained, an Army doctor, Walter Reed, led the team that made the significant discovery that mosquitoes were the cause of yellow fever. Major William C. Gorgas carried through in a campaign to eradicate this dread disease.[4]

Although the American military governor turned over power to the newly elected Cuban president in May 1902, the United States retained a special relationship, under the Platt Amendment, which provided the right of intervention if deemed necessary. Then, too, some 700 men in four coast artillery companies remained in garrison until February 5, 1904. The political situation in Cuba deteriorated two years later to the point that President Theodore Roosevelt sent in the Army of Cuban Pacification of 6,000 (of whom 17 percent were Marines) in October 1906. During their two-and-a-half-year stay, these troops trained and went on lengthy practice marches. When they left in the spring of 1909, the Havana newspaper *La Lucha* referred to them as friends and said of them: "Their discretion has been equaled only by their discipline."[5]

Since there were fewer problems in Puerto Rico than in Cuba, there was no need for a large occupation force. By the end of 1899, fewer than 3,000 American soldiers remained. Two years later there were only a couple of coast artillery companies, and these left in May 1904. The military garrison then consisted of the 600 officers and men of the Puerto Rican regiment. Begun as a battalion in 1899 and increased to two battalions the next year, this force initially had American veterans as officers and as most of the sergeants. The Puerto Ricans soon replaced the latter and gradually took over from the former. These soldiers received the same pay, rations, and allowances of regular enlisted men, and in 1908 the Puerto Rican regiment was incorporated into the Regular Army. One of those who enlisted when the unit expanded in 1900 was Ramón Gómez-Cintrón, who had been working in a store as a sales clerk. He later recalled that it was curiosity that caused him to enlist just before his nineteenth birthday. Although he was not sure what he was getting into, he quickly adapted and advanced through the noncommissioned grades. In World War I he became a temporary captain. After his retirement with thirty years' service, he became a colonel and the acting adjutant general of Puerto Rico during World War II.[6]

Panama became a part of American strategic planning once work began on the canal and its defense became a matter of national security. Initially Army medics had to apply what they had learned in Cuba to free the area of yellow fever and malaria. Colonel Gorgas spent ten years in Panama leading this effort, which resulted in a lower disease rate in the Canal Zone than in any American city or state. After an abortive start by a civilian engineer, a small coterie of Army engineers headed by Colonel George W. Goethals came in 1907 to supervise the building of the canal, which opened to traffic in 1914. Army planners thought that Panama would require a defensive force of more than 6,500 men. In early October 1911, the Army transport *Kilpatrick* brought in the first contingent—854 officers and men of the Tenth Infantry—to take station at Las Cascadas, where some of their quarters had been built by the French during their earlier failed canal-building effort. This regiment was the garrison until reinforcements came in 1914, but it was still another year before the strength neared the projected goal. The men soon became used to marching along jungle trails and to drilling in the tropics. Off duty, there was cheap liquor (homemade rum was twenty-five cents a quart) and a convenient red-light district—a combination that led to altercations with the Panamanian police. For officers, life could be very easy. Stories circulated about those who fended off duties to the point that they would have their first sergeants bring the morning reports to their bedroom for them to sign.[7]

The American interest in the Caribbean area expanded to include Mexico, and two expeditions were dispatched into that country. As revolution racked Mexicans and aroused American fears, 4,100 American troops went into Veracruz for seven months in 1914, and John J. Pershing took another 10,000 into northern Mexico in 1916 and stayed eleven months. The longest-lasting results of these interventions were the hostility of the Mexicans and, for a shorter period, the maintenance of border posts.[8]

Seeking a stronger defense of the northern edge of the Pacific Rim, the Army had settled in Alaska by the turn of the century and bolstered the number of troops from under 500 to more than 1,100. Although these numbers would vary during the next fifteen years, usually a peace-strength regiment of some 1,100 occupied the several small posts in this northernmost region. Year in and year out, as the surgeon general reported, this was the Army's "healthiest region." After helping to establish order and provide relief for unsuccessful prospectors during the Gold Rush period and later for destitute Indians as well as, on occasion, suppressing restive miners, the Army's major concern in Alaska became the building and maintenance of communication lines. Billy Mitchell headed one of the teams that set up the telegraph system. Later he recalled that this was the hardest service of his career, but it helped make him at twenty-four probably the youngest captain in the Army in 1903. Scattered along the telegraph line were three-man outposts to keep it in good repair. An Indiana farm boy turned soldier, Samuel Woodfill came from the Philippines to Fort Egbert and then went out to one of the telegraph maintenance details. Although one winter he and another soldier had to go out in a blizzard when the thermometer read 62 degrees below zero to find and fix a break in the line, he loved Alaska. The magnificent scenery and, most of all, the great hunting kept him there for eight years; as he simply explained, "it sure put the spell on me." Halfway through his long tour, in 1908, the Signal Corps began to install radio stations. Two years later, Benny Poore was ten when her father took his family to Fort William H. Seward. She thought this beautiful post on the Lynn Canal was "heaven for kids." There was no school, but she did have the job of visiting the radio shack daily to see if there was any news.[9]

The most distant and exotic of the outposts in the Pacific was China. When, in 1900, nationalist fanatics, the Boxers, attacked Americans and other foreigners in north China, the United States sent some 500 Marines and more than 5,000 soldiers to join the multinational relief force. The Ninth and 14th Infantry regiments and supporting artillery and cavalry units (some 2,500 in all) and the Marines took part in the march to Peking. Although all suffered from the terrible heat in that August, they quickly overcame Boxer opposition at a cost of 199 casualties among the Army units and 33 Marines. During this campaign Chaplain Leslie R. Groves won the admiration of both officers and men of the 14th Infantry as he helped men along the march and cared for the wounded and the dead. Although the great buildings in Peking impressed him, he was generally repelled by the sights and smells in what he called "this abominable town." He was also disgusted by the wholesale looting and knew that, despite restrictions, some Americans had participated. Before the end of August he was suffering from the cold at night, and it got colder before his regiment and most of the American troops left in the fall.[10]

Although the United States retained the right to station troops in China, only a company of the 15th Infantry remained as legation guard until the fall of 1905, when Marines replaced them. To protect the evacuation route from Peking to the sea when revolution swept over China a few years later, the Army, early in 1912, sent two battalions of the 15th Infantry (1,256 officers and men) to Tientsin, where other powers had also stationed troops. A few months later Pat Hayes volunteered for the 15th. He was looking for excitement and found enough of it guarding the trains, living in a tent, and watching the shelling between opposing Chinese forces. When his battalion was rushed by rail to Peking to protect the foreign settlement, it looked as though there might be a fight, but things settled down, and within a few months his contingent returned to Tientsin. They got along well enough with the French, Germans, Italians, and Japanese troops, but this son of Irish immigrants and some of the other American soldiers had an occasional "rumpus" with the Welsh and Scots. Drill and appearance meant a lot, as the 15th

A blindfolded 15th Infantryman reassembles his rifle before American, British, and Japanese officers, Tientsin, 1916. Courtesy of Adelaide Poore Bolté.

was in competition with the other foreign troops. The result was that, as Walter J. Rouse, first sergeant of Company A during World War I, remembered, "We were really a spit & polish outfit."

By that time, duty had become routine with the 15th's garrisons at Tientsin and halfway to the coast at Tongshan. John M. Palmer had been with the regiment during its brief stint in China in 1900, so the great growth in size of Tientsin and the new houses in the suburbs impressed him when he returned as a captain in 1913. He rented one of these homes, employed seven servants, and recalled: "We probably never lived more comfortably in all of our lives." Benny Poore, who had become a vivacious and attractive sixteen-year-old, loved the six months at Tientsin in 1916 when her father was the regimental executive officer. In addition to riding, which she enjoyed almost every day, she took part in tennis, swimming, and sightseeing. China service was for her and the other Americans, as an officer's wife put it, "an exciting adventure."[11]

Service in China also afforded the Americans the opportunity to observe Japanese soldiers. During the Boxer campaign, a cavalry lieutenant confided to his diary: "The Japs, in my humble opinion, are the best soldiers in China." Chaplain Groves wrote his wife: "Only the Japs can equal Americans and I hope we will never have to find out which is better." The rise of this Asiatic world power, which so prominently flexed its muscle in the defeat of Russia in 1905, put the American position in the Pacific in a different light. In the decade following the Russo-Japanese War, several war scares in the Philippines prompted planners to seek a solution. Army staff officers projected a defensive withdrawal to the Manila Bay area and by August 1908 worked out the core of the plan that would remain dominant into World War II. When Army leaders flatly said they could not defend the proposed major naval base at Subic Bay in Luzon, Navy planners turned to Pearl Harbor in Hawaii as their principal base. This meant that, if Japan struck, the troops in the Philippines would have to wait months for reinforcement. In effect, they were "hostages of fortune," as the Philippines had become, in Theodore Roosevelt's dramatic term, the "Achilles heel" of American Pacific strategy.[12]

When the Navy decided on Pearl Harbor, the Army had to build up its force on Oahu. For most soldiers, Hawaii, aptly called "the Paradise of the Pacific," was merely a pleasant stop on their long journey to the Philippines. Until 1909, 250 or fewer officers and men made up the usual garrison of two coast artillery companies there. In November 1908 Major E. Eveleth Winslow arrived in Honolulu to superintend the construction of forts on Diamond Head and Waikiki beach. While he worked on Forts Ruger and DeRussy, his wife and two small children gloried in life on Waikiki. It was, as Anne Goodwin Winslow wrote her mother, "such a beautiful monotony that you cannot want even the least ripple of change." In mid-January 1909 Colonel Walter S. Schuyler arrived with his Fifth Cavalry Regiment as the first increment of the new garrison. They set up a temporary camp at Leilehua in a large plain of some 18,000 acres surrounded by mountains twenty-five miles northwest of Honolulu. The old Indian fighter commander, whom Mrs. Winslow thought "none too energetic" until she climbed a mountain with him, spent much of his time in Honolulu working with staff officers and others in planning and creating Schofield Barracks. Water supply was a particular concern, and sewage disposal became a real problem. But there was for Schuyler always the social whirl of Honolulu and an occasional visit with the Winslows to take his mind off his troubles.

For younger officers and the soldiers, polo and baseball were the great pastimes. Walter Rouse, a twenty-year-old recruit from Oklahoma who joined the Fifth in 1912, remembered that his days were spent drilling in the morning and playing baseball in the afternoon. He made the Troop F team, and there was a lot of competition with the many other soldier teams in the greatly enlarged garrison. By 1915 there were some 9,500 officers and men, almost 9 percent of the total strength of the Army, in Hawaii. Garrison life had settled into a routine that a just-graduated West Pointer in the 25th Infantry found boring. Carl Spaatz recalled that officers "got up in the morning and marched around a bit with the troops and then went back to the club and drank and gambled the rest of the day." This second lieutenant thought "it was a monotonous life," so "I decided to get out of it and get in the flying game." Duty for lieutenants in that period might not have been very exciting, but it was exciting enough for senior officers, who were haunted by the potential for war with Japan. In 1915 the Army's top planner issued a prophetic warning after a study of the defensive problem that faced Oahu: "perfect coordination between the Army and Navy at this station is absolutely essential to success in holding this key to the Pacific."[13]

Even after the buildup in Hawaii, the Philippines remained the Army's largest overseas station. By the end of 1903, eighteen months after the end of the war, less than a fourth (15,500) of its wartime maximum force remained. Over the next dozen years, the garrison ranged from its nadir at 9,500 (less than 10 percent of the Army's total strength) in 1914 to its highest number of some 12,900 in 1915. The Philippines represented the United States' greatest experiment in colonization, and in those early years the Army was the key to success. President McKinley attempted to set a different course from that followed by imperial European powers when he ordered the commander, Major General Elwell S. Otis, in December 1899 to follow a policy of "benevolent assimilation." Simply establishing control over the population of more than seven million in the 7,000 islands resulted in several different conflicts during the next fifteen years, and combat was not benevolent. Nor was assimilation entirely successful, if indeed it was ever possible, despite the American efforts in creating municipal governments, a civil service, and an educational system. For the common soldier during those early years, the song "Civilize 'em with a Krag," with its emphasis on the service rifle, indicated how he interpreted the mission.

Even while war raged, soldiers and later civilian officials worked with Filipinos to create a different kind of colonial government. Unlike European colonizers, the Americans attempted to educate their new subjects and encouraged them to share in governance. In part, both the American soldiers and civilians were influenced by the Progressive reform movement that swept the United States during this period. Particularly during the Philippine-American War (1899–1902), or the Insurrection, as the Army called it, there was friction between soldiers and civilians regarding policies and power. As the Americans turned over more of both government and policing to the Filipinos, the Army withdrew from governmental functions. By 1914 it was a garrison force with the basic mission of preparing to defend against a foreign invader.[14]

Throughout virtually all of this period Filipino troops, Philippine Scouts, and the Philippine Constabulary, reinforced the American garrison. As hostilities subsided in the islands, their presence enabled a reduction in the American force. In the fall of 1899 Lieutenant Matthew A. Batson received permission to recruit Macabebes, who lived on the northern side of Manila Bay. Within days he had these men, some of whom were veterans of the Spanish colonial army, in action. Their success spawned similar units. In February 1901 Congress recognized the Scouts and laid out their organization. The ranking officers were to be regular officers on temporary assignments while the lieutenants were regular NCOs or former volunteer officers and NCOs. Scout companies supplemented the American troops in the field and, in March 1901, helped capture Emilio Aguinaldo, the leader of the insurrection.[15]

The Constabulary, created in July 1901, was the civil government's police force; yet initially it had Army officers as chiefs and other Americans as officers. From 1902 through 1905 they worked closely with the Scouts to spread and sustain American control. At times Captain Henry T. Allen, who held the temporary rank of brigadier general while serving as chief, had command of as many as 70 percent of the Scout companies (3,500 men) to work with his Constabulary, which peaked at 7,200

Matthew Batson and two of the first Philippine Scouts, Luzon, 1899.
Courtesy of the U.S. Army Military History Institute.

officers and men. Though armed with obsolete black-powder Spring-field rifles, this was still a formidable force. As the guerrilla wars abated, the two organizations went their separate ways. While the Constabulary continued to police the hinterland, the Scouts withdrew into garrisons and polished conventional military skills. In June 1913 they again proved their value when they played a dominant role in the four-day battle against the Moros at Bud Bagsak.[16]

American regulars on duty overseas including Alaska received additional benefits. Congress voted in 1900 to give foreign-service pay increments of 10 percent to officers and 20 percent to enlisted men. The soldiers also received double-time retirement credit (that is, two years' credit for every year toward the thirty-year goal) for their time overseas. There were qualifications. For one, they did not collect extra pay for maintenance and construction tasks. Then, four years later, Congress took away the extra retirement credit from those serving in Puerto Rico and Hawaii. Later those men and their comrades in Panama also lost their foreign-service increment. Finally, in 1912 Congress stopped the additional retirement credit for all overseas service. What this meant in dollars and cents to a private in his first two years of service was $15.60 monthly instead of $13.00. Even the Scouts' pay ($7.80) compared favorably with that of French Foreign Legionnaires, who got roughly $.01 a day, while as late as the 1930s Gurkhas serving with the British Army made the equivalent of about $5.00 dollars a month.[17]

Philippine service presented several variables for Army people. For those who went in the early years and some who went later there were the dangers of combat while others, and indeed all in the last years, followed the routine of garrison duty. Terrain and climate varied through the islands from tropical beaches and dense jungles to mountains. In June 1899, after troops had been there for a year, a captain who sailed with his troop of cavalry commented: "People had little idea of the Philippines . . . it was a voyage into the unknown, where sickness and death prevailed." One officer commented on the effect of three years in the islands: "A number of lieutenants gave every appearance of having already missed more home-bound boats than was to their best interests." After the war the length of the tour in the Philippines became increasingly controversial. Some senior officers noted the extended tours that European nations expected their colonial troops to serve and believed that three years was the least the Army should require. Others thought that physical and mental health suffered after more than two years in the tropics.

Regardless of whether the prescribed tour was three years (as it was in 1900–1902 and in 1912–1915) or two (1902–1912 and after 1915), the concept of rotating regiments created problems not only in personnel turbulence but also in equity for individuals. The requirement that units on orders leave behind soldiers with limited time left in their enlistments had a disruptive effect. In 1903 the Department of Texas commander said that such transfers "so radically changed as almost to emasculate some of the organizations." As for individuals, the promotion system, which as a rule moved the newly promoted officer to another regiment, meant that some would have to stay much longer in the Philippines while others might avoid foreign service. For noncommissioned officers, transfers meant losing one's stripes.

Leonard Wood, who had a large reputation as a colonial proconsul because of his years of administration in both Cuba and in the Philippines, thought that establishing a permanent colonial Army was the answer. As chief of staff, he was able to carry out this policy in 1912 and to designate certain regiments that would remain in the Philippines. Unlike the rest of the Army, these units would be at full strength. Creation of a foreign-service roster would create an equitable situation for officers. Eventually a similar roster was set up for NCOs, who were also permitted to hold their ranks upon transfer—at least for six months. Within five years the demands of the Mexican border troubles and then World War I wrecked Wood's design.[18]

Throughout the first fifteen years the Army was in the Philippines, soldiers were either actively waging war or in a state of alert for possible action. From the night of February 4, 1899, until President Theodore Roosevelt declared it officially ended on July 4, 1902, the Americans fought a war against Filipino nationalists whom they termed insurgents. At first the conflict developed on conventional lines, but in November 1899, after a series of defeats, the Filipino president and commanding general, Emilio Aguinaldo, called for a guerrilla war. The war continued even after Aguinaldo's capture in March 1901 and, indeed, escalated in southern Luzon and Samar. Punitive campaigns in those areas made it possible for President Roosevelt to claim that the war was over.

Within a year an entirely separate war erupted in the southernmost islands of Mindanao and the Sulu archipelago. The dominant group there were Muslims, commonly called Moros, whose fierceness had limited the dominion of the Spanish and of the initial American occupation troops. For the next eleven years, until June 1913, there would be a state of hostility in Moroland that would occasionally explode into fighting. From August 1904 to June 1907 the Americans also had to fight the *pulahanes* in Samar, Leyte, and Cebu. These highlanders maintained a traditional enmity toward lowlanders whom the new American governors were pledged to protect, but they were also inspired by religious beliefs. In Samar alone, it took three infantry regiments and elements from three others as well as several Scout companies to suppress the *pulahanes*. Finally, the Army and increasingly the Scout and Constabulary units in several of the islands had to deal with *ladrones,* or bandits, who in some instances moved about in large bands and terrorized the countryside.[19]

Of these several wars, the Philippine-American War or Philippine Insurrection engaged the most troops and caused the most casualties. The maximum strength of 69,420 (including some 30,400 in the twenty-five volunteer regiments) was reached in December 1900. Eventually the Army garrisoned 502 stations in an effort to establish control. In 1902 the War Department reported 1,004 deaths and another 2,921 wounded among the regular and volunteer forces in the 2,811 recorded combats of that conflict. Another 2,748 American soldiers died of disease during this period.[20]

A quarter-century after the war, a former infantry officer recalled the dominant memories of fighting in the Philippines: "the constant 'alert,' night and day, for attack from ambush by the wily natives along the trails through dense tropical jungle and tall cogon grass . . . numerous treacherous, bridgeless streams to cross, enemy pitfalls, scarcity of food, and the constant dread of cholera, dysentery, and other tropical diseases to say nothing of the 'torments of the damned' heaped upon one by an endless variety of annoying insects." Another veteran later tersely commented on the logistical difficulties: "I often wondered if we convinced Aguinaldo [the nationalist leader] that we could hike without food, clothes, shoes, or rest." Benny Foulois never forgot his first "scout" on Panay during which he waded in waist-deep mud and lived

Jack Norwood's company of the 23rd Infantry making its way through the cogon grass in the Rio Grande Valley of Mindanao, circa 1904. Courtesy of John W. Norwood.

in wet clothes for six days. As Mansfield Robinson recalled, "the filth was awful." Such conditions infected him and many others with "dhobi itch." Scalding water would eliminate the ulcerous sores, but if the feet got wet again the sores came back. Throughout the various campaigns in the Philippines, the basic problems that the Americans faced were succinctly described by two infantry officers on Luzon during the Philippine-American War. When George B. Duncan took over a company of the Fourth Infantry in Cavite Province near Manila in December 1900, he noted that his troops "were only certain of the ground upon which they stood." Michael J. Lenihan, who was in the 25th Infantry in Zambales, added: "Every tree seemed to shoot at us."[21]

Benny Foulois's company saw a good deal of action. In February 1900, shortly after they moved to Cebu, the captain was killed. The next time they had a skirmish with the *insurrectos,* the soldiers caught and threatened to hang a prisoner until he told them where the enemy was. A few days later they drove the enemy out of a village and burned it. Soon the company settled into a routine of "drilling, scouting, guard duty, and target practice." Later they split up, as did many companies,

Benny Foulois (standing), the twenty-one-year-old first sergeant of Company G, 19th Infantry, with a friend by their barracks at Naga, Cebu, 1901. Courtesy of the Special Collections Branch, U.S. Air Force Academy Library.

into four detachments, to take over four towns; but the sweeps continued. In April 1901 Foulois, by then a sergeant, went out on a four-day "hike" into the mountains. After a day's march and a poor night's sleep, thanks to the mosquitoes, his detachment met another unit and converged on a "hot-bed of insurrection," but the village *presidente* had warned the enemy, who had vanished. After a fourteen-mile march that afternoon they encountered a band of *ladrones,* shot four of them, and burned that village. They marched another few miles before camping for the night. The next day, Easter Sunday, they surprised and captured a group of insurgents and then marched the rest of that day and part of the next back to their base at Naga.[22]

Some of the infantry units resorted to horses to increase their mobility. Foulois's company had a mounted detachment, and John H. Parker, a regular first lieutenant serving as a major in the 39th Volunteers, made extensive use of his "cavalry." Since he had only 200 men and was responsible for some 26,000 people in an area about the size of Rhode Island in his subdistrict in southern Luzon, Parker mounted some men on native ponies to patrol his area. He estimated that they rode some 600 miles per month and averaged two enemy contacts a week. Charles D. Herron, who was only a year out of West Point in 1900, had a company on Panay with orders "to get the rifles out of the country and kill off as many" of the enemy as he could. He also put some of his men on horseback to carry out his mission.[23]

During the guerrilla war the level of hostility fluctuated by time and region. The Americans rarely felt certain about the loyalty of the local officials or, indeed, of anyone. This pervasive suspicion fueled the contempt mixed with fear in which most Americans held the Filipinos. Samuel P. Lyon, a lieutenant in the 25th Infantry, thought American policy was a mistake and that the United States should get out of the Philippines: "My but I'm sick of these dark skinned people. They are practically all liars and thieves and most of them murderers."[24]

Guerrilla warfare encouraged atrocities. When Americans found prisoners who had been tortured and killed, they sometimes took out their anger on their captives. Then the Filipinos used torture, murder, and property destruction to coerce their own people. Terror thus served to maintain the secrecy that was necessary for their very existence. Although the Army did not sanction such measures and warned against their use, some Americans used torture to break the shield that kept their enemy invisible. When Duncan sought information, he put a prisoner "on the spot"—made the man stand without moving and without food or water until he talked. Usually the prisoner did so within twenty-four hours. Others were more brutal. Corporal William Eggenberger of the Third Infantry wrote home about how he and his comrades beat a prisoner, gave him the "water cure," and then hung him by his thumbs until he told them where his comrades were. In his journal, Lieutenant Warren Dean described the infamous water cure. A former insurgent officer who had escaped after being sentenced to be hanged by the insurgents did the torturing. He and another man held the victim down, forced a stick into his mouth to keep it open, and then poured water down his throat and nose until he told them what they wanted to know.[25]

Filipino turncoats helped the Americans win this war. Dean pointed out that in the two weeks Major Miranda had been with them, they had been more successful than they had been in the past two years. Duncan's source of help stumbled into the convent where his company was quartered early on the morning of December 29, 1900. Mecario Bautista, bleeding and half naked, had been with the insurgents for two years but had just escaped after being tortured and sentenced to be hanged when he voiced peace sentiments. He knew the enemy and named names, including the servant of one of the officers. He was, as Duncan said, "the initial fulcrum to break down the insurrection in Cavite Province." Both Miranda and Bautista were later murdered. In La Union Province, it was Crispulo Patajo who identified the insurgents and explained to Lieutenant William T. Johnston how they operated. Such breakthroughs, combined with the constant patrolling and the evidence of good intentions in the leniency generally shown to captives as well as in the various American reforms, eventually brought an end to the conflict in most of the Philippines.[26]

The fact that some Americans encouraged the Filipino opposition and condemned Army atrocities galled the soldiers in the field. Antiexpansionists had their greatest influence on the conduct of the war in the months leading up to the presidential election of 1900. The Filipino nationalists stepped up their propaganda and military actions because of the Democrats' opposition to Republican policy in the Philippines. William Jennings Bryan's message was not lost on the soldiers, as Corporal Eggenberger reported: "the niggers are getting more active all over. It is just before election and they want to make a showing they think if bryan gets elected they will get their independence." Even an officer who told his wife that "we are making a big mistake in taking the Philippines" railed in his next letter against the "traitors"—the antiexpanionists whose speeches inflamed Filipino resistance. McKinley's victory elated the American troops as much as it must have disappointed their enemies. Sergeant Foulois wrote home: "Our boys are all crazy over the 'Election.' You can't find a Bryan man in the Co."[27]

In the spring of 1902, when news of courts-martial resulting from the punitive campaign in Samar reached the public, there was another surge in criticism of the Army. Although Brigadier General Jacob H. "Hell-roaring Jake" Smith's instructions "to kill and burn" and to make the interior of Samar "a howling wilderness" were outrageous and, according to the testimony in his court-martial, were not carried out, they certainly reinforced charges that antiexpansionists had made since 1899. A War Department and Senate investigation brought out reports of all trials of Americans and Filipinos accused of atrocities. John Parker, who had helped collect the Filipino cases, thought that they put American actions in context and effectively countered the indictment against the Army. Although antiexpansionists then as in 1900 never gained majority support and the outrage of the spring died out within a few months, the facts of the water cure and other atrocities lingered.

Mary Reaume, who was engaged to an infantry lieutenant in the Philippines, wrote in anguish about what she had read in the Indianapolis newspapers and anxiously pleaded: "I hope you can feel, Hugh, that you have never been unnecessarily cruel, and I know you have not been, you couldn't be." One might well wonder what thoughts these words evoked in Hugh A. Drum's mind. His reality in the 27th Infantry in Panay was far different from that of anyone in the United States. Whether they were bitter or philosophical about it, soldiers certainly became aware of the gulf that separated them from civilian Americans.[28]

For the soldiers in the field, there was little difference between the guerrilla-war stage of the Insurrection and the later conflict against the *pulahanes*. But there were differences in fighting the Moros. Foulois, for one, thought: "The Filipino insurrection was mild compared to the difficulties we had with the Moros." These colorfully dressed Muslim warriors maintained a feudal society throughout much of Mindanao—an island roughly the size of Ireland—and the Sulu archipelago, which stretched toward Borneo. Power rested in the hands of hundreds of *datus,* local chieftains, who ruled their people and slaves from villages that could be formidable fortresses. The one captured by John J. Pershing's troops at Bacolod had stone and bamboo walls twelve feet high and fifteen feet thick. The Moros wielded long knives—krisses, barongs, and campilans (a kind of spear)—and could resort to their small cannon, or *lantacas,* as well as some Remington rifles while their war drums and gongs added to the martial din. At any time, a Moro might work himself into a religious frenzy and then kill as many Christians as he could before he was killed. John Norwood, who served two tours in this part of the Philippines, considered the Moros superior to the Filipinos but described them as a "combination of Moor, Malay, tiger, wildcat, skunk and nitro glycerine."[29]

John J. Pershing (standing beside the Moro in black) and a few of his officers with the sultan of Sulu and his entourage, Jolo, 1911. Courtesy of Ralph A. Curtin.

Initially Foulois was not much impressed by the Moros. He had earned a commission from the ranks through a competitive examination and so was a second lieutenant before he first made their acquaintance in 1901. In late March of the following year he wrote home: "We don't anticipate much trouble from these Moros as they have very few firearms, and are a cowardly lot of savages." After a respite of fourteen months in the States, his regiment, the 17th Infantry, returned to garrison several posts in Moro country. Two companies were at the beautiful port city of Zamboanga, where department headquarters was located. While his duties as post quartermaster and commissary kept him busy, there was still time for tennis. He and his doubles partner, the youthful and very energetic Major General Leonard Wood, defeated all comers. They also saw eye to eye off the court in their opinion of recalcitrant Moros. Wood thought they should be "spanked," while Foulois believed "thrashing" appropriate, since, as he later explained, "They are a race of children . . . and have to be treated accordingly." The lieutenant probably went further than the general would have gone for a solution to the "Moro question": he thought "gradual extermination" was the only answer.

In a campaign against the Lake Lanao Moros, Foulois added three notches on his pistol. One of those represented a Moro who had wielded a kris and a knife in an ambush. After the fight, he was shocked to find that this warrior was a woman. In May 1904 two officers and thirteen men from F Company were killed in another ambush by Datu Ali's men. All of them were known to Foulois, who joined in the sweeps through the Rio Grande Valley to track down the chieftain. This was the hardest campaigning he ever experienced. "We have to march hours through tall jungle grass, from ten to fifteen feet high, and with a trail in which the mud is anywhere from six to eighteen inches deep."[30]

A veteran of three tours in Moroland thought that a Jesuit who had spent forty years there had it right in his book—*What I Know about the Moros*—300 blank pages bound in leather. Many others probably agreed, but Hugh L. Scott would not. As the governor of Sulu from 1903 to 1906, he brought a greater understanding of different cultures than most to his perception of the Moros. Already noted in the Army for his work with American Indians, Scott quickly became aware of the differences between those plainsmen and these warriors of the jungle and the sea. He fought them and was badly wounded in both hands, but he also threatened, cajoled, and, most of all, listened to them. In the process he advanced civilization, as he understood it, and earned the loyalty of the sultan and several of his leaders, who begged him to take them with him to the United States when his term was up. Years later, in 1923, when Colonel Percy P. Bishop visited Jolo and mentioned that he knew Scott, one of the old chiefs followed him to the dock. As Bishop's ship sailed, the old Moro stood waving and yelling: "Tell General Scott, come back."[31]

Scott, Wood, and Pershing were among those older officers who had seen service in the Indian Wars. They could draw parallels between the small outposts, the patrolling and sweeps, the ambushes, and, in general, the characteristics of guerrilla war that they experienced in the American West and the Philippines. Yet there were also significant differences. There was an exotic, alien atmosphere about the tropical jungles that was not to be found in the West. Although in the 1840s frontiersmen encountered vestiges of Spanish government and religion in the territory seized from Mexico, such trappings of what they considered civilization were more widespread in the Philippines. Most of the Indians whom the Army fought were nomads, whereas the Christian Filipinos and the Muslim Moros were settled in villages. Moreover, the Philippine-American War began along conventional lines, with American troops attacking entrenched Filipinos. In order to quell the nationalist guerrillas, the senior military commander in late 1900 turned to the Civil War rather than the Indian Wars for guidance, using General Order No. 100 of 1863 to protect sympathetic Filipinos and to punish hostile elements in the population. Most significantly, there was no wave of settlers pressing against the frontier and involved in the fighting in the islands. Even if the characteristics of the frontier wars and the Philippines had been more similar, the junior officers who commanded the small garrisons, led the patrols, and fought most of the battles were too young to have experienced those earlier campaigns.[32]

Black troops played a prominent role in the fighting in the Philippines. During three and a half weeks in late November and early December 1899, a battalion of the 24th Infantry and a company of native scouts—some 350 in all—made an epic march of 310 miles over the mountainous spine of northern Luzon. They crossed one mountain range on a foot-and-a-half-wide trail. Mansfield Robinson remembered that there were times when they could look down from precipices and see where they had camped the previous night. In the lowlands, they hiked through water and mud and shoulder-high grass that cut their hands and legs. The commander, Captain Joseph B. Batchelor Jr., estimated that they had forded rivers 123 times. They had little food, and hard use wore out their shoes and shredded their clothes. Despite their condition, they fought two battles and brought in an impressive number of weapons and prisoners.[33]

Black troops certainly did their share in the fighting in the Philippines. Brigadier General Henry B. Freeman told Chaplain Groves that the 24th was "the best regiment in the service," while another senior officer hailed the 25th Infantry as the best in the Philippines. Not only the regulars—the two infantry regiments, the Ninth Cavalry, and a squadron of the Tenth—but also two black regiments (48th and 49th) in the volunteers, almost 7,000 in all, helped, as one of them reminded a white heckler, "to take up the white man's burden." It appeared to be a paradox, particularly since many black leaders, including the noted educator Booker T. Washington, questioned the entire colonial venture. And those who went to the Philippines found that white Americans had already firmly established the color line. Indeed, "nigger" was a common epithet applied to the Filipinos. But these were soldiers, and they did their duty and did it well. They were, after all, Americans, and most shared with the white soldiers not only experiences in camp, on the march, and in battle but also similar attitudes toward the people with whom they lived and fought. They called them "gugus." The Filipinos propagandized them and tried to gain their support, but only a dozen or so went over to the enemy. Nevertheless, they did get along with these people better. Richard W. Johnson of the 48th Volunteers remembered feeling at ease among "these people who were generally hospitable and easy to become friendly with."[34]

A southern senator and others thought that the Philippines might be the solution to the "Negro Problem." Senator John T. Morgan wanted the Army to garrison the islands with black troops who would stay on after their discharges. Neither the Army nor the black community liked that idea, but some black soldiers did settle. About 20 of the 106 in Johnson's company decided to stay in 1901, and he looked for a job there nine years later after his fourth enlistment. Since his only job offer was at a leper colony and he had lost most of his savings in poor investments, he went back into the Army. By 1917, having spent some ten years in the Philippines, he was a true "sunshine soldier."[35]

More than eighty blacks, veterans from the regular and volunteer regiments of the Spanish-American War, served as lieutenants and captains in the two volunteer regiments. With the discharge of all the volunteers in mid-1901, however, only one who held a commission in the Regular Army remained an officer. Each of the four regular regiments had a black chaplain; the Ninth Cavalry had the lone black line officer. A West Pointer, the only one of the three black graduates still in the Army, Charles Young had been a major of volunteers during the war and commanded a troop in Samar in 1901 when he was promoted to captain.[36]

The expansion of the officer corps that year brought in three others. One, John R. Lynch, a former congressman and major of volunteers, received a captaincy as a paymaster. The other two were the first blacks to earn appointment from the ranks through competitive examination.

Corporal John E. Green of the 24th was on duty in northern Luzon when he was called to take the examination. Because of the threat of a Filipino ambush, an armed escort accompanied him to a railhead where he could catch the train to Manila. Sergeant Major Benjamin O. Davis, who was still in Utah, had to worry about the attitude of the old soldiers.[37]

Davis had turned down an opportunity to apply for a commission in the volunteers because he wanted to spend the two years in the ranks needed to be eligible for the Regular Army examination. Three of the noncoms at Fort Duchesne, including his good friend John Proctor, took volunteer commissions, and Davis succeeded one of the others as squadron sergeant major. In the fall of 1899 Charles Young arrived on post and not only encouraged his ambition but also tutored him in mathematics. When the old soldiers learned that he was going to try for a commission, they accosted him: "We thought that you had some sense." They knew that no black had been commissioned from the regular ranks before, and they thought it unlikely that this would change. He mollified them by saying that "Old Man" Hughes, the post commander Major Martin B. Hughes, approved.

In February 1901 Davis went to Fort Leavenworth to take the two-week examination. Physical ability and drill-field knowledge and recommendations were evaluated as well as written tests that ranged from grammar and mathematics to the Constitution, international law, and history. Twelve of the twenty-three soldiers who took the exams with him passed, and he ranked third. When he returned to Duchesne, the old soldiers who had doubted that such a thing could ever happen warmly congratulated him.

There was a dilemma, however. His squadron was on orders for the Philippines. Should be go with them or await his commission? On the advice of Major Hughes, he went with them and thus learned that his commission had come through a few days after he landed in Manila in May. Since he received his commission a few weeks before Green, he was the first black to become a regular officer from the ranks. Soon he was leading a detachment on a scout in Samar. At this time disease was more of a threat than the Filipinos, and he came down with dengue fever, which debilitated him for several weeks. In August he transferred, as was the custom with those commissioned from the ranks, to another regiment, the Tenth, on Panay. For a year he commanded the twenty-five or so men who garrisoned the town of Lambunao. He helped himself and them in their occupation duties by learning to speak both Spanish and Visayan.[38]

During this guerrilla war, when the Army occupied more than 500 stations, the responsibilities of junior officers greatly increased. In late 1899, when he wrote his annual report, Inspector General Joseph C. Breckinridge acknowledged this fact: "it should be recognized how largely the burden of field work fell upon the regular company officers; who not only had the duties of their grade to perform, but were assigned by the score to every type of duty, both of the line and staff, and civil duties; while the simply superb organizations were subsequently swamped with untrained recruits."[39]

This was a young officers' war. Slightly more than 62 percent of the combat-branch officers in 1902 (1,818 of 2,900) had been commissioned since the beginning of the war with Spain. A few (276, or 15 percent) had the benefit of a West Point education, while more than half had earned appointments either as regular enlisted men (414; 22.7 percent) or as veterans of the volunteers (616; 33.8 percent). The rest (512, or 28 percent) entered the officer corps directly from civil life. Before he received his commission, Foulois wrote home expressing concern about those inexperienced civilians: "It will be a sorry day for the Army if they are commissioned."[40]

Some of the older officers also complained about the new officers who came in what became known as the "Crime of Ninety-eight." George Duncan and Samuel Lyon complained when they took command of companies that had been badly run by lieutenants. As Lyon explained to his wife: "The Army is full of young officers who . . . have never been properly grounded and probably never will be." Conditions were so bad in Duncan's company that he put the lieutenant under arrest and forced him to resign his commission. Duncan was more concerned, however, about the older officers' inadequacy. "The average field officer of that day was just a larva hatched from the egg of the Civil War, feeding upon the routine of petty administration and its paper work." The long stagnant interwar period of slow promotion combined with a late retirement age of sixty-four fastened this incubus on the troops who fought the wars in the Philippines. In December 1899 all of the artillery, infantry, and cavalry colonels and almost 70 percent of the lieutenant colonels and majors as well as 37 captains were Civil War veterans.

Overage officers accustomed to years of peacetime garrison rounds were likely not be mentally or physically up to warfare in the tropics. When George Van Horn Moseley and his squadron of the Ninth Cavalry landed on a beach in southern Luzon and started marching inland, they were fired upon. The advance guard dismounted, formed a skirmish line, and drove off the enemy, whereupon the squadron commander demanded to know why they had stopped, and started drilling. The old major was deaf and hence had not heard the shooting. In the 21st Infantry in southern Luzon, a captain commanded the regiment for almost a year because all the elderly field grade officers had become ill and been sent home. Given the problem with field officers, it is not surprising that a captain, John J. Pershing, commanded a major expedition against the Lake Lanao Moros.[41]

Second lieutenants of that day might expect to begin their careers with the routine round of drills, guard duty, and patrolling; but small outposts and shortage of officers combined to thrust greater responsibilities upon them. Foulois was probably still stealing glances at the handsome sword and Mauser revolver that the men in his old company gave him upon his commissioning when he started wrestling with the paperwork of a company commander. To complicate matters, Company D, 17th Infantry, was preparing to move to a new station. When he reached Cotabato, on the western shore of Mindanao, he wrote his mother: "I thought that I had my hands full when I was put in command of my Co. . . . Yesterday I was appointed Inspector of Customs and Collector of Internal Revenue, and if I come home gray-headed, you will know what caused it." He could have added that he was also captain of the port, city treasurer, chief of police, and fire chief. At least he had his experience as a former first sergeant to help him understand some of the administrative chores.[42]

Benjamin O. Davis, Benjamin D. Foulois, and George C. Marshall shared the same date of rank—February 2, 1901. On that day the congressional authorization for expanding the Army took effect, and they were 3 of the 1,135 new officers. While Davis and Foulois served in the ranks, Marshall completed his education at VMI. The two veterans accepted their commissions later in 1901, but Marshall did not enter the Army until

February 1902. Assigned to the 30th Infantry in Mindoro, he reported in May to Lieutenant Colonel Charles B. Hall, a Civil War veteran who had lost his arm in that war. In less than two months he saw a cholera epidemic kill hundreds of local civilians, but he and nearly all of the soldiers escaped it. At this, his first post, Marshall observed the effects of bad leadership on morale. His imaginative handling of the task of arranging the Fourth of July entertainment helped restore the spirits that a former tyrannical commander had wrecked. In mid-July 1902 he took command of the detachment of twenty-six men at Mangarin and became the governor of southern Mindoro. For two months, as the sole officer, he carried on the business of that post and led expeditions to search for *ladrones* and to seek out a primitive tribe in the mountains. Two sergeants and the confidence he had gained as a first captain at VMI were his bulwarks in this demanding situation. The soldiers in the 30th were a tough lot—he remembered them as "about the wildest crowd I had ever seen before or since"—but he mastered them. On one hike, just after they had seen a pony badly bitten by a crocodile, he was leading seven of his men single file across a creek when someone shouted, "Crocodile!" The men knocked him down and ran over him. He picked himself up, waded up on the bank, called the sheepish-looking soldiers to attention, and marched them across the water and back again. He halted them, inspected their rifles, and then led them back on the trail. He thus regained command and their respect.[43]

The combination of overage senior officers, newly commissioned officers, and a large proportion of recruits in the Regular Army meant that the regulars did not have the professional edge that one would expect over the volunteer units formed to fight in the Philippines. Robert L. Bullard, a regular captain who wore a colonel's eagles as the commander of the 39th Volunteers, thought that his volunteers had more spirit and adaptability. Other regulars-turned-volunteers shared his belief. The experience and youth of the officers of the volunteers were key factors. While many of the regular officers were appointed from civil life, the volunteer officers were all veterans of the regulars or the wartime volunteers. The field-grade officers were picked from among the best regular company officers. Then a sizable number, an estimated 30 percent or more, of the enlisted men were also veterans.[44]

After war erupted in the Philippines, Theodore Roosevelt wrote a friend that the Army would have to abandon its traditional promotion system if it expected to win. "We have got to push up our best men, wholly without regard for seniority, just as they were pushed up in the Civil War." Roosevelt had in mind his close friend, Leonard Wood, who jumped in regular rank from assistant surgeon to brigadier general; but a few other young men also came to the fore and won spectacular promotions. J. Franklin Bell and John J. Pershing were regular captains promoted to brigadier generals because of their actions in the Philippines, while Frederick Funston, a volunteer colonel who captured Emilio Aguinaldo, the leader of the nationalists, also won a star in the regulars. Such promotions were rarities. Most of the younger regular officers who did such good work as senior officers in the volunteers had to return to their old units with the ranks their years in service had earned them rather than what their merit deserved.[45]

As it had the Indian Wars, the Army generally treated the insurgencies in the Philippines as aberrations. Yet these conflicts were a crucible for the officer corps, and in particular for the sizable group of new officers who entered the Army in the four years after 1898. Foulois thought that the most valuable lessons were in leadership and logistics. Marshall singled out as his most memorable lesson the regaining of control after his men had run over him in the creek. These young officers at the start of their careers had to make the difficult decisions demanded by combat and the onerous responsibilities of isolated command.[46] Leonard Wood, in his annual report as commanding general of the Department of Mindanao in 1905, stated: "The degree of excellence has corresponded to the efficiency of the officers in command of posts and organizations." That is a military truism, but in those trying days in the Philippines, both officers and men who were new to the service learned it the hard and most impressive way. Some failed, of course, but others succeeded, and the full extent of their success bore fruit years later.

For them and the nation, as George Van Horn Moseley pointed out, "The dawn of a new Army was . . . on the horizon." George C. Marshall agreed: "The Army had to virtually be remade . . . It was a long time before this new Army, with all of the new blood that had been taken into it . . . and the exciting things that had happened, were absorbed and boiled down." One effort Marshall made to absorb what had happened in the Philippines was to read the voluminous reports and correspondence that the War Department published. This material gave him a much better understanding not just of events but of the different levels of command. In 1914 he was not surprised to learn that Frederick Funston, who commanded the expedition to Veracruz in 1914, called for copies of these reports as he was creating the occupation government. Four years later, Marshall was a senior staff officer in the American Expeditionary Forces in France. A sizable majority of the senior commanders and staff officers in the AEF were veterans of one or more of the Philippine wars. A few of those veterans, including Marshall and Davis, were still on active duty during World War II. As tragedy unfolded in the Philippines in the early days of 1942, one wonders what Marshall, who in 1903 had served on Corregidor, thought.[47]

THREE

Life and Training in the Philippines

It is impossible . . . to realize how far away the Philippines looked then. "The other side of the world" really meant something in the early 1900s.

—GRACE BUNCE PAULDING

———◆———

THE Philippines loomed large in the experience of Army people during the early years of the twentieth century. When the fighting was at its peak, more than 60 percent of the Regular Army was in the islands. Until 1908, a fifth or more served there, and 10 percent until World War I. Thus most Army people served more than one tour. Benjamin O. Davis, Benjamin D. Foulois, and George C. Marshall served two tours; Benny Poore made three and Mauree Pickering four trips to the islands. The promise of extra pay and double-time toward retirement for years spent in the Philippines brought back soldiers again and again. Richard Johnson spent four tours—one of which was six years—at different posts in the islands. In those days, the Army's purpose was to restore and maintain internal stability throughout the archipelago and to train in preparation for possible invasion by Japan.

In 1971, as she looked back on a lifetime in the Army, Benny Poore Bolté commented: "The greatest advantage is travel and, at the same time, the greatest disadvantage is travel. I mean, it isn't easy." A great journey was the first stage of foreign service. In those days of trains and ships, this was a lengthy initiation. Even for those going to Caribbean stations, Alaska, and Hawaii, the train trip to the port and the ocean voyage might last up to two weeks. Going to the Philippines, the "Big Adventure" as Mauree Pickering called it, took a month or more. And most Army travelers went to the Philippines. The adjutant general reported that by 1910, 188,094 had gone since the first expedition in 1898. Although this is an inflated figure, since those who made more than one trip were counted each time, a lot of people made that journey.[1]

Troop trains had Pullman coaches for officers and their families, sleeper cars for the soldiers, and baggage cars for their equipment and baggage. Since they were on slow freight-train schedules, it took almost a week to cross from the East to West Coast. Soldiers had their canned rations and hard tack and hot coffee while officers and their families shifted for themselves at railroad restaurant stops. When the 23d Infantry journeyed from Plattsburg Barracks in upstate New York to San Francisco in the spring of 1903, each battalion was in a separate train, but they were within minutes of each other on the same track. This meant overlapping at the restaurant stops and occasional practical jokes. Naturally there were card games, and some of the officers put their mandolins and guitars to good use. "It was great fun," Rita Wherry Hines recalled.

This leg of the journey was not as much fun for the Pickerings, who traveled on a regular passenger train. Captain Pickering was already in the Philippines in the spring of 1901 when his wife, ten-year-old Mauree, and her brother and sister set out to join him. The trip was pleasant enough until the train derailed in Nevada. Florence Kuykendall Pickering got her children out of the coach, which had turned over on its side, and then helped care for the casualties. Fortunately, they rescued their luggage before the baggage car burned.

This cross-country journey with its magnificent and varied scenery was awesome for those who simply looked out the windows of the trains. Benjamin O. Davis, who saw the Grand Canyon for the first time en route from Fort Duchesne, Utah, to San Francisco in 1901 remembered: "I really began to appreciate what a large and beautiful country we lived in." Benjamin D. Foulois had his hands full as one of the two NCOs in charge of twenty-nine soldiers in his sleeper car, but he spent much of one night in the Rockies simply drinking in the extraordinary vistas.[2]

San Francisco was the embarkation port, and troops and sometimes officers and their families had to wait in tents for their departure date. When the time came for the 23d Infantry regiment to board ship, it was a lengthy process to load them, a squadron of cavalry and a battalion of engineers, some 1,800 in all, on the *Thomas,* the largest of the transports at almost 4,300 tons and 460 feet long and 50 feet wide. On May 1, 1903, they sailed. John Norwood remembered that a band played and friends on shore united in a mighty cheer with the passengers who crowded the decks as the transport pulled away from the pier. Such events, which had been inconceivable before 1898, were routine by then.[3]

During the Spanish-American War, Secretary of War Russell A. Alger created a Transportation Division with the Army Transport Service as one of its two major branches and proceeded to purchase ships to be refitted as transports. By 1901 the Army owned twenty-five vessels and leased another twenty-nine. Conditions in Cuba and Puerto Rico had improved to the point that regular service was discontinued in the Atlantic that year. In 1902 the waning of the war in the Philippines permitted the sale of several of these ships and the switch from twice-a-month to monthly service across the Pacific. Eventually four ships made the regular monthly crossings of the Pacific while four other transports covered the interisland routes in the Philippines.[4]

When the *Thomas* sailed, it was so crowded that captains and lieutenants and their wives were separated. Rita Hines and her little girl had to share a cabin with another wife, while her husband, Captain John L. Hines, was quartered elsewhere. Meantime, Norwood had to share a cabin with two other first lieutenants while his wife stayed with two other wives. Rank made a difference, as did the demands of the occasion. Under normal conditions, only two would occupy one of those staterooms, and couples would not be separated. Officers and their dependents had to pay $1.00 or $1.50 per day, depending on the ship, for board, which varied in quality on the transports. In 1906 it cost an officer on average $362.40 to carry his family from his Stateside post to his colonial station, and that cost was going up that year with the abolition of half-fare on railroads.[5]

Whatever the living conditions of officers and their families on troop ships, enlisted men had it worse. When a soldier carried his barracks bag, blanket roll, rifle, and equipment below, he sought out a canvas bunk, which would be his cramped home for the four weeks it took to cross the Pacific. On the *Thomas* the soldiers were fortunate: their bunks were in tiers of three, but there were 80 cubic feet of airspace per man and good air circulation. Other ships were more crowded, and a third of the transports had inadequate ventilation or lacked laundry facilities.

Richard Johnson, a black soldier in the 48th Volunteers, remembered his first Pacific crossing with horror. The food was awful, and he and the other soldiers only had one change of clothing and underwear. Since there were no laundry facilities, a soldier had to wash his clothes and hang them on the rail and then watch carefully to keep someone from stealing them. The odors of saltwater, fresh paint, food preparation, lavatories, and hundreds of men combined with poor ventilation to make his trip memorable. Indeed, he came to wonder whether he would survive.[6]

There were duties—exercises, drills, and inspections—but there was also a lot of free time. Storytelling, home-talent shows, various kinds of sports contests, and the inevitable gambling with cards and dice helped pass the hours. Church services (which were held daily on the *Sherman* in early 1899) and regular band concerts added variety to shipboard life. Leslie R. Groves's unit was fortunate: the chaplain set up a lending library and provided stationery as well as religious services to the men of the 14th Infantry during their voyage. And the food was not always bad.[7]

Officers inspected and supervised the soldiers, and they and their families also attended the concerts, church services, the amateur productions as well as the sporting events. They also played cards and told their stories. One of the most detailed accounts of a Pacific crossing is in the lengthy letters that Matthew F. Steele wrote his wife in 1899. From the going rate for Japanese prostitutes in Honolulu—seventy-five cents—through the varied shipboard occurrences to the size of the *Sherman* and its daily progress, Steele kept "Tellie" well informed. He even mentioned the embalmer whom the Quartermaster Department had assigned to the ship. During this time of war in the Philippines, one embalmer was discovered to have a lucrative side business of bootlegging whiskey. More of a student than most of his contemporaries, Steele read three novels (one of them in Spanish), Dean Worcester's book on the Philippines, Arthur Wagner's *System of Security and Information,* and the Army Regulations. He also studied Spanish and brushed up speaking the language with a Spanish priest.

Steele was very interested in the eleven nurses on board, although he carefully explained to his wife that he kept his distance from them. On every transport there were bachelor officers and some young women

The officers' deck on the transport *Buford;* a common scene for more than four decades.
Courtesy of Louise Adams Browne.

traveling alone. They might be nurses or sisters, wives, or teenage daughters of officers. In the close quarters of a transport for a month, not surprisingly, romance blossomed. Steele noted that all the nurses were paired off with officers within a few days. Mauree Pickering remembered her older sister and the other nubile girls with their swains racing for the dark corners after dinner. This could take a dangerous turn, as it did when the 16th Infantry came back from the Philippines in 1907. One of the lieutenants and another officer's wife had a shipboard romance that ended in divorce, then their marriage, and ostracism.[8]

Children livened up these long journeys. When the 23d Infantry crossed on the *Thomas* in 1903, Rita Hines recalled that they "swarmed everywhere." It got so bad that some wag suggested that all of them be loaded on a tender and towed behind the transport. A few years later, on another voyage, the ship captain ordered parents to keep their children shut up in the staterooms for a specified period during the day. Grace Paulding and another mother solved their problem by tethering their four-year-olds to a post while they had their regular morning bridge game. Some wives had maids; others let soldiers babysit the boys.

Almost every Army child of that generation had his or her memories of the adventures of transpacific travel. But the story told by the sons of Captain Louis C. Scherer topped all others. Scherer shipped the boys, ages twelve and nine, unaccompanied via transports and railroad from the Philippines to Massachusetts. Each boy had a bill-of-lading tag with appropriate information, including scheduling and routing details and destinations as well as relatives' addresses for ship stewards and pursers and train conductors. And in their two suitcases were appropriately dated packages of clothing. Not surprisingly, their journey became an Old Army legend.[9]

A fixture on some transports was the bath steward, who maintained the appointment roster for baths for officers and their families. A tall black man whose face resembled that of the Cream of Wheat logo, George was particularly well known, as his service spanned the pre–World War I period into the 1930s. He was known to break up bridge games when he announced that one of the players had not bathed for several days. Benny Poore, who made three round trips across the Pacific and one round trip to Alaska before she was eighteen and then saw George again when she went to China in the 1930s, remembered him fondly. Thus she and all the other Army folk were shocked when he was picked up for smuggling drugs.[10]

Seasickness was common, but smallpox and cholera also occasionally broke out among passengers. The diseases could and did cause death to the sufferers and quarantined others on board. In 1902 Benny Foulois encountered smallpox on the interisland transport and then cholera on the transpacific ship. That same year cholera broke out on the *Sherman* when Mauree Pickering and her family were en route home. Seventeen died, and the passengers spent fifty-two days in quarantine on that unforgettable journey.[11]

Storms took their toll. When Benny Poore was coming home with her family in the summer of 1917, the *Thomas* ran into a typhoon that lasted for several days. The wind roared, and the ship rolled heavily. When it hit a reef, the captain ordered the officers and their families to put on life jackets and meet in the salon. As they nervously stood there, the ship began rocking again, and they were off the reef. It put into Formosa for makeshift repairs and then went on to Japan for a complete overhauling. In 1900 life turned miserable rapidly for Lieutenant Charles D. Rhodes on the chartered *Leelanaw* as it passed the Golden Gate and hit a heavy sea. Rhodes, two veterinarians, and thirty-one troopers were charged with taking 253 horses to the Sixth Cavalry in the China Relief Expedition. These seasick men wrestled with animals that had fallen and torn up their stalls. By the fourth day out, the sea had calmed, and the soldiers had recovered enough to clean and disinfect the ship. Six horses died on that ten-day journey to Honolulu. With brief layovers in Hawaii and Japan, it was another month before Rhodes and his men got their horses to China, losing another two on the way.[12]

After the long voyage that brought most of them to Manila, virtually all were eager to land. In the early years, ships had to anchor offshore while the men, women, and children crowded the officers' deck to see if they could pick out husbands, fathers, or friends among the officers on the launches that approached the ship. In early May 1901, Abner Pickering bounded up the gangway of the *Thomas* to greet Florence, Mauree, and her older brother and sister. Lighters, or *cascos,* came up to take off troops and luggage. A few years later, the construction of a wharf enabled the transports to offload directly to shore in a welter of sound as a band played and assorted vendors hawked their wares.[13]

Not all families were welcomed. The Ninth Cavalry and its commander might well have been relieved to be ordered to the Philippines because the formidable wife of Colonel McGregor did not accompany them. A few months later, while involved in the war in southern Luzon, McGregor got a wire from Jennie: "We arrived on the *Sherman,* what shall we do?" He promptly wired back: "Go back on the *Sherman.*" For several weeks in Manila, she fumed and made life miserable for the general, who refused to let her and her daughters go to her husband. Apparently the colonel resolved this difficult situation by taking retirement leave and joining them.[14]

It was hot in Manila, but Chaplain Groves, who suffered from prickly heat, wrote his wife: "I don't know that it has been worse . . . than a July in Albany. But it was hot all the time." Almost a year later he confided to her: "There is almost a constant and uncontainable desire to go back to my room and get my clothes off." Stella Folsom Steele was of similar mind as she told her husband: "My but I'm cooked alive & shall be so glad when lunch is over & I can shed my clothes."[15]

Manila was exotic to the new arrivals with its assorted sounds, sights, and smells, which Groves said were a mixture of coconut oil and sandalwood with whatever odor emanated from the nearest shop. According to Matthew Steele, "it is a queer looking old city—strange houses & stranger people." Filipinos, Chinese, Japanese, Spaniards, Englishmen, and Americans filled the streets; a good many of the Filipinos lived on the Pasig River. It was hard, Mauree Pickering remembered, "to take in all the new sights," but she carefully noted the different clothing styles. Private William Eggenberger also commented on native dress in a letter to his mother: "they are dirty and it is nothing to see a niger (we call them nigers) woman pretty near naked." Americans had been in the islands less than a year when Eggnebeger arrived, but already their racial standards and the common epithet were in place.[16]

For three years after the Americans seized Manila in August 1898, the city was under military rule. Officers supervised municipal services with understandable emphasis on law and order, the collection of taxes and tariffs, the establishment of an education system, and the imposition of sanitary regulations. In the disruption resulting from the overthrow of the Spanish government, followed a few months later by the outbreak of open warfare with Filipino nationalists, the necessity for military control seemed obvious. There was another dimension, however: these American military governors sought to move away from the traditional colonial practices and to create a model governmental system that they expected to turn over to civilians. With nearly a quarter of a million inhabitants, some—perhaps many—of whom were not particularly friendly, and the spate of troops passing through the city as well as the garrison consisting of those officers and men required to maintain the logistical hub of an Army at war, Manila was booming in those early years. It was no easy task to govern such a city during those tumultuous days.[17]

When Captain William W. Wotherspoon and his family arrived during the early days of the insurrection, they lived for several weeks in a tent camp that was frequently fired on at night. There were two hotels, the Oriente and the Delmonico, as well as the Army and Navy Club, but some found them full or too expensive. The Pickerings stayed in a boardinghouse; the Hineses simply stayed on the transport, which would carry them on to Mindanao in a few days. While in the city,

Grace Paulding remembered that the daily round consisted of shopping in the morning, a siesta in the afternoon, a drive around the Luneta in the late afternoon, then a late dinner.[18]

Some were stationed either in the infantry regiment in garrison or in the headquarters of the Philippines Division. While headquarters was in Fort Santiago, the 1590 Spanish fort, the troops were at Spanish barracks scattered about the city. Most officers found homes for their families in the community. During the war, when larger number of troops were in the area, they lived in tent camps or temporary barracks. In those days, soldiers stood guard for twenty-four hours every third day, and three-fourths of the unit had to remain in their quarters during the rest of the time. By 1907, five years after the war ended, a soldier could expect to have only an hour's daily drill and infrequent guard or fatigue duty. By that time, staff officer duty hours at division headquarters were from 8:00 a.m to 1:00 p.m.[19]

The most vivid and detailed account of an officer's life in Manila at the turn of the century is contained in the almost daily letters of Chaplain Leslie R. Groves to his wife and children. This forty-three-year-old Presbyterian minister had been in the chaplaincy just three years when he arrived in Manila in January 1900. Except for the four months from mid-July to mid-November, when he went to China with his regiment, and a later brief interisland tour, he lived in Manila until mid-July 1901. Since the 14th Infantry had six companies at one of the old Spanish barracks, Cuartel de Meisic, he initially moved into a nearby room with a captain.

Groves was a most energetic chaplain and won the respect of the officers and men of his regiment. He conducted up to twelve services a week at ten different locations—the six company outposts, the guardhouse, the hospital, and the YMCA, as well as Cuartel de Meisic. "This field was ripe for the harvest," he wrote his wife, "but I fear some grain is spoiled already." In addition to these regular services, he counseled individuals and developed a library. Separation was a burden for both him and his wife. Gwen Griffith Groves kept up their home with the help of a hired girl, nurtured their three young sons, and kept an eye on the welfare of the wives of the soldiers who were with her husband. But however much he missed his wife and boys, the chaplain led an active social life. There were more than 200 Army wives and daughters

Leslie R. Groves on his rounds with the 14th Infantry in the Manila area, circa 1900. Courtesy of Richard H. Groves

in Manila when he arrived, and some of them were friends. He called on them as well as on nurses and missionaries. If nothing else offered, he could go to the Luneta for the evening promenade.[20]

The Luneta was the hub of Manila social life. From 5:30 to 7:30 in the evening there were so many carriages that, as one officer said, "it takes sometimes half an hour to drive 100 yards." For young Mauree Pickering, however, the beautiful bayside park, with bands playing and carriages filled with officers and their ladies or gaily dressed Filipino couples, it was a "Fairyland." Rita Hines agreed that "it was a place for romance" but added "and, alas, for many a scandal. It is a curious thing about the Tropics, it certainly does something to one's moral standards." Chaplain Groves also was aware that "some of the girls here are talked about and have been indiscreet."[21]

Army society was exotic to the wife of a University of California professor who came to Manila as a member of the Philippine Commission. Officers and their wives to Edith Moses were "a new and interesting variety of American. They are delightful people. The women are vivacious, talkative, and always in a rush. They find the climate 'awful,' but it certainly puts no visible damper on their gay spirits. They are kind-hearted too, and good-natured."[22]

They were also under a good deal of stress during the periods when war loomed about them. "'These is awful times' for married people who are fond of each other," Stella Folsom Steele wrote her husband in 1901 when he was at Lucban, in southern Luzon, with his command. Two of her friends had just called, and one reported that she had been able to spend only eighteen hours with her husband when she visited him. Stella had spent ten months at Lucban with Matthew, but now they were separated again. Her complaints were minor compared with those of Eugenia Bradford Roberts, who waited in Manila for news of her husband, who was held prisoner by the guerrillas for several weeks, or of those whose husbands were killed. When the volunteer regiments were disbanded, the Steeles returned with them to the States. A few months later, when Matthew received orders to the Philippines, Stella was furious: "I'm so mad I'm crying . . . I just loathe those old islands . . . it would just kill me to go now and take that same old trip." But back across the Pacific they both went for another tour.[23]

⚜

In that era, the Army developed a resort to provide officers, their families, and convalescent soldiers a respite from the tropical heat. The British had pioneered the concept in India with their hill stations in the nineteenth century. To Simla and various other mountain towns, individuals, families, and even the governments went during the hottest months of the year. As early as 1902, a few Americans had made the then-difficult journey 175 miles north of Manila to the mountain village of Baguio. At what became known as Camp John Hay, the Army originally planned to build a post large enough to house a brigade. This never materialized, but by 1913 there were enough quarters to house the headquarters of the Philippine Department during the summer, when the civil government also moved to Baguio, as well as to support troops and convalescents and Army vacationers.

Mauree Pickering was in her early twenties and on her third tour in the Philippines before she visited this lovely spot in 1912. The post, which was in a pine grove at an altitude of 4,500 feet on a mountain ridge with splendid vistas, was already, as Mauree recalled, "fast becoming a popular health resort." The temperature never got over eighty or under forty degrees, so fires were in order in the evening. While there were cottages for higher ranks, lower-ranking officers and their families lived in tents during their temporary stays. Later they shared a dormitory. There were golf, sightseeing, picnics, and—most of all—the delightful climate. After this, going back to the Manila Bay area, was, as one officer said, like "stepping out of a refrigerator and into an oven."[24]

Major Johnson Hagood, who went to Camp John Hay in 1913, was fascinated by the Igorots, the tribe that inhabited that area of Luzon. They worked as servants and were striking figures in their loincloths as caddies on the golf course or as waiters in the dining room. The latter nodded toward convention by wearing white jackets but still refused to wear trousers. These people had been headhunters until very recently, and one did not have to venture very far from Baguio to see warriors with their head-axes and spears along the trail. Of more interest to Hagood were the women, who customarily worked nude in the fields. They did not appreciate the rude stares of Americans, so he felt fortunate on one occasion to be able to take some snapshots of a group of young women "in their innocence." He was so preoccupied with these girls that he did not notice a warrior with a head-ax observing him. As he tried to get away, the Igorot accosted him and asked in good English if he wanted to take his picture also. He explained that he had lived in the States as an officer's servant for several years.[25]

While this parable of colonialism illustrates the feeling of superiority and the interest in the exotic of the colonial as well as the changing of the world of the native, it is only part of the story. Army people brought to the Philippines the mores of turn-of-the-century Americans, including attitudes toward race, morality, and social conventions. In writing of how he felt about being in the Philippines to fight a war, the black soldier Richard Johnson probably spoke for most of the officers and men, black and white: "I was filled with the spirit of venture and also possessed a reasonable share of bigotry." After the war, Army people came on limited tours of duty, and, as one would expect, they lived essentially in their own society. While they noted the exotic Moros and Igorots, they paid less attention to Filipinos generally. As the occasion demanded, they did attend dances, receptions, and other social functions with Filipino government officials or, on the village level, with anyone who cared to come. For the most part, however, these people were part of the background scenery. They were servants, tradesmen, people one saw on the street every day, but they were not part of Army society. In this regard the American experience resembled that of the British Army in India.[26]

Richard Johnson, like many others, was at first suspicious of the Filipinos, yet the native customs amused him. Language posed a problem for most soldiers in getting to know these people better. It did not take long for the men in Johnson's volunteer regiment to become better acquainted with the children who hung around the camp and the women who came into the camp to sell fruits and trinkets. Then there was desire, as Johnson pointed out: "The Americans were inclined to treat the natives as a whole with contempt, but with no other feminine association these soldiers made exceptions with any woman who appealed to their sex instinct." Indeed, some whites feared that the association between the black troops and the Filipinos was too close, and accordingly the War Department kept the black troops out of the regular rotation during Secretary of War William H. Taft's administration.[27]

There were significant differences among the Filipinos. Wealth and education made a difference there as it did everywhere, and there were many diverse tribes, with fear and hatred distancing some more than others. As Edith Moses noted: "There is far more difference between the Igorrote of Benguet and the Tagalog of Manila than between the latter and ourselves." And there was hostility between the Macabebes and the Tagalogs, while Filipinos generally feared, with good reason, the headhunters of northern Luzon and the Moros. In 1900 Lewis S. Sorley learned firsthand about attitudes toward the former when a group came to his garrison at Ilagan. The Spanish and Filipino villagers demanded that he kill them outright, so he had to explain that that was not the American way. In turn, he explained to the headhunters that their practice was no longer acceptable and would be punished if continued. In Moro land Filipinos were realistically concerned about the *juramentados,* or suicide killers.[28]

There were differences among the Americans as well. James Parker, a regular cavalry officer who served as a lieutenant colonel in the 45th Volunteers, was antiexpansion. This perspective was not unusual among regular officers. "I think the Army is all anti-expansion," Chaplain Groves wrote his wife in July 1900. But Parker evidently gave the Filipinos more thought than most. Besides, he liked them. Their "docility, kind-heartedness, and friendliness" appealed to him. He was concerned that he had to fight a revolution that was inspired by the ideals of the American Revolution and embarrassed when he was ordered to explain the Constitution to people who were barred from its protection. He thought that their admiration for Americans made them more humane toward the prisoners they held during the war. Even the Moros, whom Parker did not like, never harmed women, and Steele pointed out that no woman or child was injured by Filipinos or Moros even during hostilities.[29]

Some, perhaps many, Filipinos, in turn, seemed to lack animosity toward the Americans, as Edith Moses discovered when she discussed the war with four Filipina girls while fighting continued in Batangas. Later, in 1914, Captain John Parker was impressed as he hiked alone in Laguna Province, where he had fought during the war, and was received with the "most generous hospitality." As civil government gained power and more Filipinos participated in government, attitudes changed, and this development irritated some veterans. A particular grievance was the handling of the Grafton case by the civil judiciary. While on guard, Private Homer E. Grafton was attacked by two men, whom he killed. A general court-martial acquitted him of murder, but an American judge in the civil court convicted and sentenced him to twelve years' imprisonment. The Supreme Court, which consisted of both American and Filipino judges, upheld the sentence. Even Richard Johnson, who loved the islands and the people and had come to believe that the suppression of the nationalists and the Moros was wrong, knew it was time to go because "there was a marked lessening of that once awesome respect these people had once felt obliged to show toward their 'masters.'"[30]

One could regard this as a mark of the success of American efforts to democratize the Filipinos. But then it could also signify a stereotyping of and contempt for the Americans on the part of the Filipinos. Major William Lassiter, who as an inspector general toured much of the islands in 1909, told of a revealing play that he saw staged in a remote village. The local playwright depicted the Spanish regime in the first act as "very decorous and extremely dignified." The second act, which covered the period of the Philippine-American War before the Americans had gained control, showed a time "of confusion." The last act showed several American soldiers getting drunk at a Filipino bar. Their dialogue consisted "mostly of Got damn!—Got damn!—Got damn!" As Lassiter explained: "it was perfectly easy to catch the general drift of what was going on."[31]

To maintain communications with the garrisons scattered throughout the islands, the Army had to assemble a fleet of ships to transport troops and maintain communications with their stations scattered throughout the islands. In the early days, travel was apt to be uncomfortable, on dirty, overcrowded ships; but on occasion storms or other problems made the journey harrowing. In late 1903 Florence Pickering and thirteen-year-old Mauree boarded a small chartered English ship in Manila to go to Mindanao. The first two days passed pleasantly, but Florence became worried when she heard the captain say that this was the first time that he had been in these waters without a pilot. On the night of the third day, he ran the ship on a reef. No one knew where they were, but since they believed it was Mindanao, they assumed that they were in danger from the Moros. The English and American ship's officers armed themselves and some of the Filipino crew and also gave a rifle to Florence. Then the captain drank himself into a stupor. The next morning a storm enlarged the gash in the hull but did not dislodge it from the reef. In the midst of the storm, the crew gathered on deck. The acting captain, who feared that a mutiny was brewing, asked Florence to talk to them. With her rifle on her arm, she appealed to the Filipinos to obey the acting captain. If they did not, she warned that she and the officers would shoot them. "Now God bless us all," she concluded, and "may He bring us to another and better tomorrow." The men dispersed. On the following day the storm abated, and a passing ship rescued them.[32]

At the end of their hectic trip, Florence and Mauree Pickering were welcomed by Major Pickering at Camp Overton on northern Mindanao. Since the 22d Infantry was living in tents at Camp Marahui (later renamed Keithley) twenty miles away on the shore of Lake Lanao, the major rented a house in nearby Ilagan, where his family stayed for several months. Finally, they began the last leg of their journey in a down-

Florence Pickering, whose strong character carried her through many difficult times in her years as an Army wife. First published in Mauree P. Mahin, *Life in the American Army from Frontier to Distaff Hall;* courtesy of Helen L. Rosson.

pour at four in the morning on January 14, 1904. The three Pickerings and two officers' wives boarded an Army ambulance pulled by four mules and joined the bimonthly supply train to Marahui. A troop of cavalry escorted them and the supplies. It took them sixteen hours to make the fifteen-mile journey over a treacherous, muddy road that soldiers had recently built to a way station where they spent the night in a tent. The last stretch of the road was still bad, little more than a trail, but the weather had cleared, and the scenery was spectacular, with mahogany and mango trees, clumps of bamboo, colorful orchids, and beautiful birds, with the sound of chattering monkeys in the background. When they reached the cleared plateau where two houses constructed with nipa palm leaves for the officer families and tents for the troops made up the camp, they enjoyed the glorious vista of Lake Lanao amidst the mountains as well as the cooler temperatures.[33]

When the Americans established outposts, soldiers set up tents, moved into stone Spanish barracks, church buildings, nipa houses, or built their own nipa quarters while the officers and their families tried to find a good stone or nipa house. When Captain Charles D. Herron

Mrs. John W. Norwood and a servant in front of her quarters at Malabang, Mindanao, circa 1904. She hated the tropics. Courtesy of John W. Norwood.

landed in Leyte with his company of the 18th Infantry, they brought lumber and 100 kegs of nails to build their quarters. In their construction work on quarters and roads, these soldiers followed the example of their predecessors throughout the frontier period. On Samar in 1903, the 14th Infantry replaced the First Infantry Regiment in a seaside tent camp and immediately set about constructing nipa quarters and clearing a parade ground. Meantime the wives and children of several of the officers shared a house in nearby Calbayog, where, as Lewis Sorley pointed out, their privacy in the curtained cubicles approached "absolute zero." But then nipa houses were not conducive to privacy, as John Norwood noted at Malabang: "Frequently, we could hear the conversation in the third house down the line . . . provided the conversation of our next door neighbors was not too animated."[34]

When soldiers were not working, on guard, or chasing enemies, they trained. For infantrymen, this meant close-order drill and marksmanship. A Hoosier farm boy, Sam Woodfill, had no training before he joined the 11th Infantry at the port, so he began to learn the intricacies of close-order drill on Leyte. It was an infuriating process for both the recruit and the drill instructor. Woodfill simply could not get it right. Even carrying a stone in his left hand so he could tell right from left did not help. Sergeant O'Shaughnessey turned red in the face as he bawled at the hapless rookie. On the target range, Woodfill's military career took a turn for the better as he scored eight bull's-eyes and two fours out of his first ten shots—the highest score of the day.

Cavalrymen also trained and had the additional chore of taking care of their horses. Captain George B. Rodney left a record of his troop's routine on Luzon. After reveille at 5:15, the men got their quarters in shape and breakfasted at 6:00. Then they cleaned up the area around their barracks before watering and grooming their horses and saddling up for mounted drill, which lasted until 11:00. They returned to the stables to rub down and water the horses before their own noon meal. In the afternoon there were a summary court-martial and various classes as well as inspections and always another hour's work with the horses from 3:00 to 4:00. Retreat sounded at 5:00, and supper was an hour later.[35]

A few men in each unit were always involved in maintenance chores from administration to cooking. Quince J. Boone of the 28th Infantry wrote in a beautiful hand, which was probably a key reason he was picked as a company clerk. He was also smart, so he moved ahead quickly to more responsible tasks. In January 1902 he explained his duties as post commissary sergeant in a station near Manila to friends back home in Indiana: "First I am in charge of the rations for all troops at the post. Every ten days I issue foods consisting of bacon, coffee, flour, hard bread ('hard tack'), sugar, potatoes, onions, beans, evaporated apples, peaches, prunes, soap, candles, salt, pepper, vinegar, etc." In addition, for two hours each morning he ran the commissary, which sold "almost anything" soldiers wanted. Keeping the records initially drove him to distraction as he had to deal with such figures as $.027375 per pound of potatoes, but he soon adjusted.[36]

Some officers relied on their families to help out. At Puerto Princesa, on Palawan, Elizabeth Clarke Helmick not only kept house and looked after nine-year-old Gardiner and two-year-old Florence but also handled the clerical work for the commissary after her husband became the only officer in the garrison. Fortunately for Major William W. Wotherspoon, during his stint as collector of customs at Iloilo, on Panay, his son, Alexander, hung around the office during business hours. When he overheard a conversation and the translation by the interpreter, Alexander complained to his father: "That man is not telling you what that other man says." He had picked up both Tagalog and Visayan, so, still not yet ten years old, he became the official interpreter.[37]

Some wives and soldiers also became involved in teaching in the schools that the Army established. One of the first acts of the commanding general when the Americans seized Manila in August 1898 was to order a chaplain to open the schools. During the Philippine-American War, his successors recognized the value of education as a pacification measure. Even after the Army turned the schools over to civilian authorities in the fall of 1900, wives and soldiers continued to help run the schools. Elizabeth Helmick opened the school at Puerto Princesa and taught until Corporal Cobb relieved her. He continued to teach even after his discharge and eventually married a Filipina and stayed in the islands.[38]

Soon after Ida Burr Parker brought her two children to join her husband, Major John H. Parker, at Tanauan in the spring of 1900, she organized the schools in his district and supervised the eighteen soldier-teachers in the classrooms. Parker was impressed: "it was plainly evident that every new school established out in an outlying *barrio* meant an effective extension of lawful authority deeper not only into the territory, but also into the hearts of the Filipinos." When they moved to Taal, also in Batangas, she again organized the schools, this time with twenty soldiers and twenty Filipinos as teachers. Even though Batangas was one of the hottest spots of the insurrection, Ida Parker, whom the locals called "Maestra," according to her husband, met "only friendly people."

Not everyone was so enthusiastic about the American schools. There were instances when local police or soldiers had to bring the children to school. Sam Woodfill remembered going from house to house "draggin' the kids out from under the beds and from behind the furniture." In two sizable Batangas cities of a combined population of some 80,000 in August 1900, there was an obvious boycott, as the total number of students enrolled was less than 400. Louis S. Yassel of the 21st Infantry, who was stationed at one of these cities, Lipa, discovered one of the reasons for the low enrollment. He had quickly picked up Spanish, so was conversing with a priest, who acknowledged that he did not like the American approach because he did not want the natives "to know too much . . . if they want to know something they all come to me, but if you educate them, they'll tell me what to do."[39]

Benny Foulois also ran into opposition from local padres when he began teaching school at Naga, Cebu, but with the help of police, who on one occasion brought in eight boys tied together, he persevered. On the first day, November 8, 1900, he had 28 boys in class, most of whom were "attired in a breech cloth and a smile." He told them that they would have to wear more clothes, and they did. Within ten days, there were 126 ranging in age from six to fifteen, all "just crazy to learn English." Not only the boys but some of the older Filipinos were interested, and several offered to pay him to tutor them.[40]

American children were in some of the schools. Twelve-year-old Edith Morgan and her sister and a sergeant's daughter were the only Americans and the only girls in a missionary school near Iloilo. The Filipino boys crowded around them at recess to practice their English and often left small gifts on their desks. Boys did not fare as well. Frederick Munson, who was about Edith's age, frequently got into fights with the Filipinos in his class at Albay, while Bradford Chynoweth, a teenager, sensed racial tension in his class of Filipino and Moro boys. Paul Febiger was only seven, and the teacher at Jolo in 1900 was an Indian who used only Spanish in the classroom. All he remembered learning was "how to sit on the floor all day long."[41]

Seventy years later, Thomas D. Finley, who had lived for several months at Iloilo in 1903 when he was seven, recalled "the enervating heat, the violent thunder storms, the flies and insects in profusion, the strangeness and isolation of living surrounded by natives, the boredom and complete dependence on parents for every activity." Among Benny Poore's first memories were Tacloban, Leyte, and Borongan, Samar, in 1904. Adelaide Carlton Poore arrived with her three daughters before her husband, who was delayed in the States as a witness in a court-martial. One of the old sergeants in his company, Red Wright, lent them money to get by until the paymaster came. They lived in a nipa shack, and Benny never forgot the stark terror when a wildcat burst through the wall one night or the foreboding when, early one morning in pitch dark, Benny and her sister awoke to see the soldiers forming up by torchlight to go after *pulajanes,* religious fanatics who raided in

A quiet interlude in the Philippine War as Sidney Graves walks on the beach with his sister, Dorothy, and Daisy Grimes near the outpost at Candon, Luzon, 1901. Courtesy of Sidney C. Graves.

the area. In those years, war was close to the families. From their post on Lake Lanao, Mauree Pickering and later Grace Paulding watched firefights in the distance. When the *insurrectos* fired into the Luzon village where Captain William S. Graves and his family lived, seven-year-old Sidney cried out: "Mother, they wouldn't hurt a nice woman with two little children, would they?" As a rule, they did not. Some boys, among them Alexander Wotherspoon and Jack Heard, even went into the field with the troops.

Jack was thirteen or fourteen when he went on a patrol with the

Third Cavalry near Vigan, in northern Luzon, for a very specific purpose. He collected stamps and had heard that the Philippine government had issued some. When he asked his father about it, Captain John W. Heard facetiously answered, "Why don't you write General Aguinaldo?" Jack took this seriously and went with the patrol so he could leave his letter on a forked stick by the trail in enemy territory. Eventually he received "a courteous letter" from the general, who explained that he was only fighting for his rights just as the Americans had done against the British. He also enclosed several sets of the much-desired stamps. Another experience was not as pleasant. One night, Jack noticed that a sentinel did not sing out "All's well." When he and others checked, they found his mutilated body.[42]

✳

Zamboanga, Parang, Cotabato, Malabang, Marahui, and Jolo were Moro country. The very names are poetic. And there was beauty. Rita Wherry Hines thought Zamboanga with its "gem-like post beside the sea . . . a little Paradise." And it was—for a child like Ruth Harrison, who was nine in 1905 when she swam off the beach, sailed an outrigger on the canal, rode in the afternoon, and roller skated on the sidewalks. For a young bride, Carolyn Richards Whipple, it was enchanting. More than six decades after leaving, she remarked: "It is the only place I ever was homesick for." There was no fear among the Americans at Zamboanga.[43]

Elsewhere it was different. At Camp Keithley the trees were cleared and a barbed-wire fence erected and the guard doubled. It was a dangerous place when the Pickerings were there, with up to 100 men on guard. Later, in 1908, when the Pauldings lived there, although it was then the largest post in Moro country, with 1,000 troops, one still took precautions. Grace Paulding could not go for a walk except with an armed escort, and at night they pulled beds away from the nipa walls to avoid a possible thrust with a *bolo* (long knife). Three times during that winter, Grace heard the dreaded "call to arms" sounded in the middle of the night, and "nothing can be much more alarming than that."[44]

Rita Hines simply passed through Zamboanga. The destination of the 23d Infantry was Malabang and Parang. Regimental headquarters and a battalion including the Hineses and the Norwoods wound up at

Malabang. Here too sentries were doubled, and after one was wounded there was a "reign of terror." Both Jack Norwood and his wife slept with pistols at hand. Indeed she so disliked her stay at Malabang that he resigned from the Army at the end of this tour. Rita Hines's own fears peaked one morning when she woke up to the sound of voices and found her small daughter showing her dolls to half a dozen Moros on the veranda. When she appeared at the door, they chorused "goodbye Babee" to the child and left.[45]

To ease the "deadly monotony of unoccupied hours," even during periods of hostility, soldiers fished and swam in nearby streams or hunted. "We had to create our own amusement or go without—and we did go without a lot." What Richard Johnson recalled about his months in the 48th Volunteers was true not just for volunteers during the fighting but also for regulars throughout these years before World War I. When there were enough men and the opportunity, there were baseball games. Benny Foulois played on teams as a sergeant and later as a lieutenant. At Malabang the men of the 23d staged a minstrel show for themselves and the officers and their families. There were jokes and "hits" on the officers in the vein of the Gridiron Club or other latter-day roasts.[46]

When the athletic general, Leonard Wood, took command of the Department of Mindanao, he gave a strong impetus to organized sports. Each post had to have a field day every month, and then Wood brought the top athletes to Zamboanga to compete annually in a five-day meet. His successor, Tasker H. Bliss, who had no pretensions to athleticism, cut the number of required field days to twice a year but did maintain the annual departmental event. By 1911, while field days apparently were not as frequent, the department commander, John J. Pershing, attended all but one held at the various posts and was proud that the weeklong meet in Zamboanga, which coincided with the annual Moro Province Fair, had an audience of 20,000 Moros.[47]

As the commanding general of the Philippines Division in 1907, Wood promoted contests not just as sports events but also as a means of military instruction. The best units from each regiment matched skills in such events as digging hasty entrenchments, traversing unfordable bodies of water, and marches. After 1908 such field exercises and athletic competitions combined with an annual carnival staged by

American businessmen in Manila became a major social event. Richard Johnson, who was at Batangas in 1911 in the Hospital Corps, accompanied the entire Eighth Cavalry on its five-day march to Manila to take part in this great event. He was particularly impressed by the Filipinos' enthusiasm for the carnival. As an observer rather than a participant, he had a delightful time frolicking for ten days. Then it was time to go home with the regiment; besides, he had spent most of his money.[48]

In the Philippines as elsewhere, payday meant gambling and drinking. After three or four days a few cleaned out the rest in poker, monte, or craps. Some soldiers bet on the traditional weekly cockfights staged by the Filipinos. In Batangas, Louis Yassel even purchased and fought some cocks that proved to be winners; the Filipinos began to call him "Don Louis." When Sam Woodfill's company finally got paid after four months at Carigara, Leyte, there was a monumental binge of gambling and drinking. Woodfill did not gamble and seldom drank much, but on that occasion he spent twenty-four hours sampling the local drink, Japanese sake, Schlitz beer, and Kentucky rye. His friends found him able to talk but unable to walk. The weeklong hangover convinced him that he should limit his drinking in the future.[49]

There were more serious problems. When Richard Johnson joined Company I, 25th Infantry, in Luzon in late 1901, he expected the regulars unit to be better than his volunteer company. Yet within the previous six months, the men of I Company had been involved in three murders and discipline had virtually disappeared. Later Johnson understood why—a rapid turnover in officers and noncoms and too few of the former, while 85 percent of the men were first-time enlistees. Then they also had a lot of free time with no recreational outlets. When a new captain, an experienced West Pointer, took command, Johnson thought that things would get better, but this officer not only caroused as much as the men but also borrowed money from Johnson and other men. When pressed for payment, he would bluster about insubordination. Eventually, after the 25th returned to the States, he was cashiered and sentenced to Leavenworth for his various crimes, but Company I suffered until then.[50]

In other units there were officers and men who drank too much and got into more or less trouble. While at Malabang, the commander of the 23d had to deal with a drunken lieutenant and with another who was caught stealing funds, but his greatest difficulty was with his senior major, who had stopped eating and merely drank. In the 11th Infantry one of the officers, crazed after drinking native *vino,* started shooting up the area. The post commander three times ordered soldiers to fire before they finally obeyed and shot him down. At Camp Keithley in 1908, soldiers' desire for liquor led to an even greater tragedy. In an effort to make their own, they mixed a lethal brew of methyl alcohol that killed eleven.[51]

Since its earliest days, the Army had had to deal with drunkenness and the disciplinary problems it induced. The statistics of alcoholism (the number of sick-call cases per 1,000) illustrate the ebb and flow of the problem from 1873 to 1915. In 1876 it peaked at 72 but decreased to 27 by 1897 and lower yet during the Spanish-American War into the early years of the twentieth century. With the passage of a bill in 1912 to stop the pay of those men on the sick list because of liquor, drugs, or venereal disease and the increasing outside pressure of the prohibition movement in society generally, it declined to 13 in 1915. The next year, acceding to the prevailing social mood of the time, the surgeon general banned alcohol from all garrisons and camps. Drugs, however, were not considered a serious problem.[52]

While the Army in the Philippines came under that mandate, one had to recognize the fact that, as the commanding general there said in 1903: "The Philippines are about as far away from the capital of the United States as it is possible to get." So things might well be somewhat different. Prohibition was the law in many states, but it had little effect in Batangas in 1911. When the Eighth Cavalry made its five-day march to Manila, a local saloonkeeper followed along with several bull carts loaded with cold beer to sell to the troopers at the end of the day. Since they had spent their money during their ten days in the capital, there was no reason for the portable saloonkeeper to join them on the return march. Not surprisingly, it took one day less.[53]

In the early days of American occupation, the alcoholism rate, despite the availability of the native *vino,* was lower in the Philippines than in the United States. As years passed, however, the admission rates were higher than in the States. In 1915, for example, it was 18 per 1,000 as opposed to the Armywide average of 13.49. Since the statisticians kept tabs by race, it is interesting to note that the black average was 2.46.

Since their incorporation into the Army after the Civil War, blacks had a significantly lower rate than whites. Alcoholism was a greater problem in the American Army than in foreign armies. In 1909 the American admissions rate of sick soldiers was almost twenty-two times that of British troops.[54]

Venereal disease (VD) emerged as the greatest health problem in the Army during this period. After three years of organized effort to control it, in 1912 Secretary of War Henry L. Stimson had to admit: "The high percentage of venereal disease continues to be the reproach of the American Army, and the daily average number of those sick from that cause during the past calendar year was larger than the daily average number of those sick from all other of the more important diseases combined." That year the overall rate of admissions was almost 164 per 1,000 with the rate of 305 for the troops in the Philippines leading the rest of the Army. A year earlier the surgeon general attempted to explain why the rate was so high in the islands. There was such a large number of prostitutes, many diseased and most ignorant of basic sanitary measures; they charged as little as twenty-five cents.[55]

The efforts to bring VD under control included twice-monthly examinations, required records of individual infections and treatments, publication of the rates at each post in the surgeon general's annual report, court-martial if a soldier turned up infected after failing to take advantage of the prophylaxis available at every post, and, after 1912, stoppage of pay for time lost because of what had officially come to be considered "misconduct." There were also detailed lectures about the dangerous consequences of venereal disease by doctors or chaplains. In the year after the imposition of mandatory examinations and pay stoppages, the rate dropped drastically, but Army doctors were fighting a problem that was apparently as great outside the service, as another surgeon general noted in 1914: "From recent investigation it is, indeed, probable that the frequency of venereal disease among our soldiers is less than among adult males in the cities of this country."[56]

Among those who succumbed to temptation was Edgar H. Price. A teenager in San Jose, California, he heard a veteran of Philippine service recount the life he had led in that exotic land. What stuck in young Price's mind was the comment: "Those girls are good looking and good screwing." In 1917 Price enlisted and got the prized assignment to the

15th Cavalry, stationed near Manila. Before he got his first pass, one old soldier warned him to be sure to go to the prophylaxis station (marked by a green light) located near the brothels. "If you get a dose, and your name isn't on the station book," you would have to spend time in the guardhouse as well as lose some pay. Another offered advice about the choice of women: "The Gugu girls are the best screwing, but the Japanese are the cleanest. Only, they're expensive and they're cold. Stay away from Chinese *hoors*" because they had an incurable strain of clap. Forewarned, Price and two companions promptly began looking for prostitutes.[57]

The veteran who first alerted him to the possibilities of the Philippines also told Price about the "squaws" with whom some soldiers lived off post. When Richard Johnson joined the 25th Infantry, he found that many of the men in his company were "shacking." Even the poor excuse for a captain had a *querida* (sweetheart), as these women were also called. This practice served to keep soldiers, to a certain extent, out of trouble and the women off the streets or out of the brothels. When the 15th left the Philippines, Price was appalled by the sad spectacle of these forsaken women, some of them with small blond or red-headed children, saying goodbye. Such scenes were less moving to Johnson, who served several tours. He was impressed by the "competitive scramble" among these women for new "squawmen" when a new regiment moved in.[58]

There were other dangerous diseases rampant in the Philippines. When Eli Helmick took his family and his company of the Tenth Infantry into Puerto Princesa in 1901, he well knew of the danger of disease as well as the necessity for sanitation and the elimination of mosquitoes. Since he had some money for that purpose, he hired local workers to do the necessary cleanup. He also required each family to build a latrine and taught them how to use it. "As the town was small we soon had it clean; constant inspections and reasonable disciplinary action kept it so." And so it went, from Manila, which was described as having the sanitation of a fifteenth-century European city, to the least *barrio* occupied by Americans. A couple of years later, when the Hines family and the 23d Infantry took station at Malabang, Rita took all the prescribed precautions against cholera, and they certainly helped prevent other diseases: "We could eat no raw vegetables or uncooked fruit, and had to boil all the kitchen utensils, china and silver . . . we never ate uncooked food without washing it in boiling water." And the measures worked. Although cholera raged from March 1902 to April 1903 and caused 109,461 deaths in the Philippines, only 305 American soldiers and 81 Philippine Scouts died in the epidemic.[59]

During the period when most of the troops were in the field, it was impossible to practice many of the routine safeguards; thus dysentery made 12.5 times the number of soldiers ineffective in the decade following the Spanish war than in the decade before that war, while the percentage of men who had diarrhea doubled. On the extended hikes that might take up to four months, as Matthew Steele explained, all he and his troopers had to eat was hard bread, bacon, and coffee, and they usually drank unboiled water. Understandably, he suffered from chronic diarrhea. Although Colonel Philip Reade saw little field service on Mindanao, he had a stomach disorder, which he described: "I weigh 182 pounds, one hundred and one pounds of which is stomach paroxysms."

Soon after Private William Eggenberger arrived in March 1899, he developed diarrhea, and the ailment lingered with brief remissions throughout his twenty-five months in the islands. During his first bout, he sought medical attention but was disappointed, as he wrote his family: "them dam doctors made me worse . . . they give you the same pills if you got tooth ache or diarrhea or fever." After almost twenty months in the Philippines, he reported on the devastating effect of disease on his company in the Third Infantry. Of the 106 who had left Fort Snelling, 11 were dead, 7 disabled, and 43 discharged for various disease. Of the 45 left, 3 were in the hospital. Within a few months, he was invalided home.[60]

Despite Eggenberger's bad experience with the medics, Army doctors made a remarkable record improving health within the service during the first years of this century. In 1913 Secretary of War Lindley M. Garrison proudly announced that the Army's health was better than it had been at any time since the Army had begun keeping records almost a century earlier. The development of a vaccine for typhoid fever and the compulsory immunization of all troops were the immediate reasons for the new record in 1912. Typhoid, which had swept through the Stateside camps during the Spanish war and infected perhaps 82 percent of those who were sick at that time virtually ceased to be a health statistic. Although it remained a problem in civilian life, there were only four cases in the entire Army the next year.[61]

The Army, the nation, and the citizens of the new colonies owed much to Walter Reed and the other Army doctors in Cuba, Puerto Rico, and the Philippines who closely studied tropical diseases and those officers who employed military discipline to enforce their solutions not just on the soldiers but also on the civilians in the islands. Eradicating the breeding areas of mosquitoes, using mosquito nets and screens, killing the rats, and even changing sanitary habits—there was an Army regulation mandating the washing of hands after visiting the latrine and before each meal—all helped improve health problems that had seemed inevitable a few years earlier. While there were still cases of malaria, diarrhea, dysentery, and, of course, venereal disease and alcoholism, doctors had proven that it was possible to bring them under control.[62]

Healthier quarters in permanent posts not only helped lower disease rates but also enhanced training and discipline. Even before the end of the Philippine-American War, the commanding general, Adna R. Chaffee, began to think about establishing permanent garrisons for his troops. Of first priority was the building of a large post near Manila. He purchased a three-square-mile site on the Pasig River six miles from Manila and put the chief engineer of the Department of Luzon, Captain William W. Harts, to work designing a brigade-size post. Construction was well under way in 1903, and, through a general order, Fort William McKinley officially came into being in May 1904. Three years later the Army had to lease another 6,000 adjacent acres for training purposes.[63]

There were two strategic purposes for garrisons. One was to control the populace; hence there should be posts scattered throughout the islands. The other, which was considered more crucial, was the threat of war with Japan, which had increased since the Japanese victory over Russia in 1904–05. In 1910 a board of officers recommended building twelve posts: five on Mindanao, one each on Panay and Cebu, and five more on Luzon. Since Manila Bay seemed to be the most crucial strategic area, three of the Luzon posts were in or near Manila. The collapse of large-scale hostilities in Moroland in 1913 and the increasingly obvious ability of the Philippine Scouts and Constabulary to handle local disturbances throughout the islands changed the situation, and all

American troops concentrated in Luzon. In planning, Corregidor was critical. Shaped like a tadpole with the head the highest point (the Americans called it Topside), this island of more than 1,700 acres, thirty-two miles across the bay from Manila, was the cork in the entrance to Manila Bay. In the summer of 1904 Army engineers began to build batteries, and the work continued, at times with the assistance of 2,000 convicts, over the years on additional fortifications, connecting roads, and the buildings of what became Fort Mills.[64]

As early as the fall of 1902, a troop of the Second Cavalry staked out a camp fifty-five miles north of Manila in the Pampanga Valley. With mountains, volcanoes, and jungles in the background, the troopers pitched their tents while their captain and his family took up residence in a nipa shack. The next year, construction began on a regimental-size post. Within six years there were more than 150,000 acres in this reservation, which made it almost eight times larger than the largest Stateside post, Fort Riley, Kansas. In 1911 the post was expanded with new concrete buildings to accommodate an entire artillery regiment. Guy V. Henry Jr., who was there three years later, thought it "ideal from a cavalry-military standpoint. The terrain was excellent and you could maneuver almost anywhere."[65]

Stotsenburg, however, was not healthy. Sergeant Richard Johnson, now in the Medical Corps, dreaded going there, since he knew of its high malarial rate. The year he arrived, 1916, on his fourth journey to the Philippines, Stotsenburg had the highest malaria rate in the Army. Ten years before, the disease had been so rampant that the Army had seriously considered abandoning this post in what some called a "death valley." During Johnson's year there, a sergeant and a crew of a dozen men worked fulltime trying to get control of mosquitoes and their breeding ground, but they could do nothing about the unhealthy wooden quarters that many still occupied.[66]

Caroline Pratt Shunk, a lieutenant colonel's wife, spent eight months at Stotsenburg in 1909–10. For her, as she wrote home, "It is a never-ending battle against heat, damp, typhoons, earthquakes, vermin, and disease." She had malaria within a few weeks of her arrival—about the time she experienced an earthquake—and readily joined in the precautionary measures against cholera. The rainy season brought downpours that made such a noise on the metal roof that one had to scream to be heard. Then there was the continual battle against mold. Shoes and other leather objects turned green overnight, while one had to put clothes under a raincoat in the hope that they would be dry enough to wear the next day. Caroline feared snakes and worried about them. As she started to take a shower one morning, she was petrified to see a huge snake coiled behind the door. She screamed, ran out of the room, and waited for her husband to return from morning drill. When he and his orderly rode up, she blurted out the news. The soldier grabbed an ax, the colonel pulled out his sword, and they quickly dispatched the snake. The houseboy was disgusted: "him very good snake. He eat rats, and sleep up above the Senora's room."[67]

At Stotsenburg, school-age children had their classes in a room that served later in the day as a schoolroom for soldiers and on Sunday as the chapel. Since Fort William McKinley was only six miles from Manila, officers' children were taken into the city to school. Grace Wilson's parents, however, kept her home, where her father, Lieutenant Colonel Richard H. Wilson, taught her literature, Latin, French, and some history. When the trolley line to Manila was finished, her mother took her shopping in the city. Twenty years younger than her husband, Grace Chaffin Wilson knew that her little girl—also named Grace—would probably be interested in matters beyond books. Over his objection, she took her one night to the officers' club and found a secluded spot for her to sit so she could observe a masquerade ball. For young Grace, it was "a great thrill for a nine-year-old . . . Mother said it was good for me and gave me 'something to think about.'" And she never forgot.[68]

Grace and five other girls formed a club called "The Industrious Six." They met regularly after the other girls had come home from school and discussed the Little Colonel series and other novels that they had checked out from the large post library. They also did some sewing. Others pursued more vigorous forms of recreation. Some very small children started playing baseball exuberantly next to George C. Marshall's quarters during the afternoon siesta time. Since he could not sleep for the noise, Marshall went out and pitched for both sides and umpired.[69]

There were parties, of course. St. Aubin Bell celebrated his fifth birthday at Stotsenburg with about twenty children. More spectacular was the party on Christmas Eve 1909, which he and his sister attended. Since his father's cavalry regiment was moving into the post and the other regiment had not yet left, ninety-five children awaited Santa Claus. He came in the form of an appropriately garbed, portly lieutenant who gave out presents contributed by the officers and purchased in Manila by a ladies' committee.[70]

Life could also be fun for adults. In 1910 a captain at Fort William McKinley wrote a friend: "Life at McKinley is delightful with one exception. The social strain is intense." Lieutenant Colonel William Lassiter, who arrived at Stotsenburg in 1915, likewise found it pleasant. "This post is like a big country club. A little work in the morning. Golf, polo, tennis, riding in the hills in the afternoon. The Club at sunset. Dinner in the evenings. A lazy man's paradise." Caroline Shunk added the woman's perspective and provided a more detailed schedule. Her husband got up, breakfasted at 5:00 and went to drill his command at 6:00. She arose at 6:30, had some coffee and fruit, then showered, dressed, and worked with her flowers, read, sewed, or wrote letters until 1:00. Meantime, her husband ducked in at 10:30, changed uniforms, and went to work in his office at 11:00. He returned at 1:00, lunched with Caroline, then they napped through the heat of the afternoon. After another shower and change of uniform for him and more formal dress for her, they walked to the officers' club, met with friends, returned home for dinner, unless they were going to go to a dinner party or, on Tuesday night, for the weekly dance. If they went home for dinner, they would later call on friends or receive calls, listen to the regular evening concert by the regimental band, or play bridge.[71]

Chinese seemed to have monopolized the positions of cook and head servant. Lassiter, being a bachelor, needed only a cook and a Filipino houseboy, while the Shunks had two additional houseboys and two *lavanderas* to do the washing and ironing that was necessary with so many daily changes of clothing. Families with children might not have as many houseboys but would have a nurse. Lassiter recalled that once settled into the comfortable concrete house (which he considered the best quarters he had lived in during his twenty-six years of service), he left the running of the household entirely up to the cook. He would merely tell him how many he expected for dinner.[72]

There were many diversions. Peddlers—Indian, Japanese, Chinese, Filipino—came to the door with their exotic wares. If one were a reader, there was certainly ample time for books. Caroline Shunk belonged to a reading club while Lassiter pored over a philosophic tome and George Marshall studied the published War Department records of the Philippine War and toured the battlefields. Katharine Cochran Kingman, who came to McKinley as a young bride in 1906, was caught up in the social whirl but also had time to ride horseback and even play a role in a home-talent play. Marshall played tennis and began his regimen of riding an hour in the morning while there. He also enjoyed hunting and went out with two younger lieutenants, Henry H. Arnold and Courtney H. Hodges. He bought his first car and enjoyed driving over the good road network around Manila. He did not suffer the embarrassment of Jack Heard, who returned to the Philippines as a cavalry lieutenant. Jack picked up his new car at the dock. Although he had never driven before, he bravely drove it back to McKinley, where he realized that he did not know how to stop. He drove through the back of his garage, where the car rammed to a halt against a tree as the garage collapsed.[73]

For young cavalry and artillery officers, polo became a rage. In the 1890s, cadets at West Point began to play this exciting game. A few years later the War Department encouraged all mounted units to field teams. The requisites—skilled horsemanship, quick thinking, and sheer courage—were powerful appeals, so much so that Ola Bell was oblivious to other entertainment possibilities at Stotsenburg, confiding to his diary: "Polo is our only recreation here." There were two playing fields there and others scattered throughout the islands. Even General Pershing took a turn on the one at Zamboanga. In 1909, with the arrival of an athletic, wealthy businessman as governor general, the sport came into its own. W. Cameron Forbes played, and, indeed, the civil government team frequently beat its military rivals. At his own expense Forbes built the Manila Polo Club, where officers from McKinley practiced and played their games. Frank P. Lahm, an enthusiastic player on the Seventh Cavalry's second team, wrote his father in 1912, during the four-month break necessitated by the rainy season: "I was enjoying it very much and will be glad when it starts again." Like his friend Heard, he bought a car, but he was much more interested in his purchase of an Australian polo pony.[74]

While energetic young and athletic middle-aged officers enjoyed polo, slow promotion and the high retirement age of sixty-four meant that some officers were not physically able to carry out even regular duties. An inspector general in the Philippines Division reported in 1907 that of nine colonels he had observed, only two were fully fit for their duties. The next year, the commanding general of that division wrote that he believed that "a very large percentage of field officers are physically unfit to take the field in time of war." Shortly before he left the office of secretary of war, William H. Taft recommended an elimination system and warned that the current system meant that an officer could expect to spend almost six and half years as a second lieutenant, slightly more than nine years as a first lieutenant, thirteen and a half years as a captain—thus almost twenty-nine years as a company-grade officer. Once a major, an officer's ascent should accelerate, with only a little over five years in that grade and then just under two and half years as a lieutenant colonel. As an indication of the longevity of those nearing the end of their careers, as late as 1909 there were still thirteen Civil War veterans on active duty, including five field-grade officers and one captain.[75]

President Theodore Roosevelt, who was an exceptionally vigorous forty-nine-year-old in 1907, solved the problem by ordering field-grade officers to take fitness tests. The War Department followed through with a general order that required all field grade officers to ride thirty miles a day for three straight days. Coast artillery officers and some staff officers were permitted to walk fifty miles in three days rather than take the riding test. Lieutenants and captains had to start taking annual physicals. A few in both categories did not make the grade, and of course there were complaints, but Teddy Roosevelt would not be swayed. Indeed, to emphasize his point he took the Army General Staff on one of his Rock Creek Park walks, which included scaling cliffs and plunging into the chest-high icy water of Rock Creek. After Roosevelt left office the Navy abandoned its version of the physical test, but the Army kept up the riding requirement until 1917.[76]

As the Army settled into the large posts in the Philippines, there were amenities for the soldiers. Stotsenburg had a garrison of two regiments while McKinley had three regiments. These brigade-size posts were very different from the garrisons that the veterans who had served in the pre–Spanish war Army remembered. In 1914 Stotsenburg had 1,112 enlisted men alone and Fort William McKinley 2,694. In contrast, the largest post in the Army in the mid-1890s had a garrison of only 750 officers and men. At McKinley, Bill Adams, who had seen Philippine service as a Marine, came back in the 29th Infantry and was pleasantly impressed with the quarters and life generally. The spacious, airy two-story barracks were just like the ones he had seen British troops occupy in India. There were excellent showers and laundry service as well as two company bootblacks who came in at night and shined all of one's shoes. He also appreciated the library and entertainment offered by the Young Men's Christian Association (YMCA). One of the black cavalry regiments (the Tenth) shared McKinley at this time with Adams' 29th and another white infantry regiment. The Tenth's Chaplain Anderson reported that the reading rooms were always full and that the various phonograph concerts and stereopticon slide shows were well attended.

Trooper Price appreciated the laundry and the fact that Filipinos performed kitchen police (helped the cooks) and mucked out the stables. A cavalryman still had to groom his own horse and take care of riding gear. Like all new soldiers over there, he hastened to get a tailored uniform, which cost only six dollars and was more comfortable as well as better-looking than the issue uniform. He was also tempted by the tattoo artists and had a dragon portrayed on one arm.

Price liked most of the men in his troop. "The genuinely good guys outnumbered the surly bastards, of which there were a few, and the slick operators." He soon found out that by slipping the NCO in charge of quarters a half-pint of Old Crow one could stay out all night in Manila. He also learned that theft from a comrade was considered one of the most serious crimes in the Army. A rookie he knew was sentenced to three years at hard labor and a dishonorable discharge for stealing a shirt.[77]

Stotsenburg was some four hours by train from Manila and did not have a YMCA. As in the days of the temporary posts, there were hunting, baseball, and the varied activities of the occasional field days. There were also troop gardens to cultivate. Others might satisfy their competitive urge in the traditional contest for the position of commander's orderly in the daily guard mounts. The soldier whose bearing, uniform, and equipment were the best won the prize of not having to stand guard; instead, he ran errands for the commanding officer, an assignment that allowed him to spend much of his day in the shade. For many, a post-payday "hooter"—a spree in dives in nearby *barrios*—was the most they wanted or could expect in recreation.[78]

Occasionally tragedy broke the round of scheduled duties and the search for amusement. The First Cavalry had a particularly dramatic incident during its tour from 1907 to 1910. One day, as the command was settling down at noon after the morning's work, shots rang out. Officers who raced to the scene found a sergeant with rifle in hand, the first sergeant, the top of his head almost blown off, lying on the floor, and a trooper struggling to hold his intestines in. Several others had also been shot. Captain Conrad Babcock ordered: "Drop that rifle." After a moment of hesitation, he did, and the officers seized him. It was clear that he was "as mad as a hatter."[79]

Sergeant Richard Johnson's tour at Stotsenburg with the Ninth Cavalry was less eventful. The medical detachment to which he belonged had only one problem, but it was a serious one: the mess sergeant was more concerned with graft than with feeding the men. It was not uncommon for mess sergeants to be bribed to look the other way when merchants provided short weights and inferior foods. But this particular sergeant was too greedy and made no effort to keep the cooks at their job. The commander fired him and appointed Johnson to take his place. In turn, Johnson fired the chief cook and brought in a replacement who could both cook and obey orders. Then he informed the tradesmen that the scam had ended. The results were good meals and an honest handling of the mess fund, which showed a sizable surplus within a year and half. Johnson got more fun out of the additional duty of recreation NCO. He procured uniforms and equipment for the hospital's baseball team and began to play tennis. Though in his late thirties and never having played before, he soon was able to hold his own with the best players.[80]

Peacetime training was virtually an oxymoron for the Army throughout most of the nineteenth century. The tiny garrisons were barely large enough to carry on the necessary maintenance chores. What training there was took the form of repetitive drill carried on beyond any real utility. With the great increase in larger garrisons in the twentieth century, there were possibilities for training beyond the lowest level of routine. The Philippines offered the greatest opportunity for realistic training.

Recruits who came over irregularly in batches until 1912, when they began to come in units twice a year, had to learn the drill and the basics of soldiering. Infantrymen worked on the manual of arms and close-order drill while field artillery recruits had to learn to take care of their horses as well as to be able to perform crew drill on the guns. For a cavalryman, even if he thought he knew how to handle a horse, there was much to unlearn and to learn. First, fold the saddle blanket properly so no wrinkle will gall the horse. Then mount the Army way and control the horse with precision. A cavalryman needed a strong arm to handle the heavy saber in mounted saber drill and also make the thrust in and out fast or he would break his wrist. Finally, there was no smoking or chewing tobacco on horseback. For all soldiers, recruits or veterans, who carried small arms, there were long hours on the target ranges. Marksmanship was competitive and could bring awards that piqued soldiers' interest as much as any sport.[81]

In March 1906 the War Department mandated an Armywide systematic training program with emphasis on realism. While the traditional training was to be carried on, commands now were expected to conduct rigorous field training to include regular practice marches and tactical problems. Already in 1904 the troops on Luzon had to go out periodically on marches that would last up to two weeks, but there was no specification for tactical problems. While many senior officers carped at the requirement, one of the newest generals, John J. Pershing, enthusiastically put it into effect at his first command, Fort William McKinley. Aside from the value of such training in acquainting officers and men with the situations and conditions of warfare as well as the corollary effect of physically hardening them, Pershing recognized that turning marches into tactical problems was intrinsically more interesting than the regular drill routines. Second Lieutenant Ralph W. Kingman of the 16th Infantry took part in those sham battles in 1907, in which his company practiced both offense and defense. They attacked another company and, on another occasion, set up outposts. Patrolling was the focus of still another problem. There were also a couple of exercises in which his men went into position and had to dig trenches. There were still Saturday inspections and regular parades, but soldiering changed under Pershing during his eighteen months at McKinley.[82]

At Stotsenburg in 1910 there were an occasional practice march and, for officers, a terrain ride in addition to the regular drills but not as much emphasis on practical training as at McKinley. Training at Mc-

Kinley also probably became less strenuous after Pershing left. In 1912, when the colonial Army plan went into effect, training got an impetus. Then six full-strength regiments (Eighth, 13th, 15th, 24th Infantry, Seventh and Eighth Cavalry) were permanently stationed in the Philippines. Three years later the Ninth Cavalry replaced the Seventh and the 27th Infantry relieved the 24th, while in 1916 the 31st Infantry was formed at Fort William McKinley. After the Philippine-American War, companies and troops had been reduced to 65-man units throughout the Army. With the new plan, there would be 150 in the infantry companies and 100 in the cavalry troops. Now officers had the opportunity to work with units whose size corresponded to war strength while soldiers could also get used to the more realistic strengths.[83]

When war came in 1917, it was on the other side of the world. The colonial Army continued to train as its strength diminished with the shipment of two regiments to Siberia in 1918, leaving very few American troops in the Philippines. To maintain garrisons, the Army increased the number of Philippine Scouts and organized them into regiments. One of the regiments that stayed behind was the Ninth Cavalry at Stotsenburg. As a matter of policy, the War Department did not send any regular black units to France.

In July 1917 Captain Benjamin O. Davis arrived at Stotsenburg. Since he had last served in the islands, he had had assorted assignments, including attaché duty in Liberia, teaching at Wilberforce University in Ohio, and troop duty at three posts. He had married and had three children, but his wife had died in early 1916. In addition to this sorrow, he carried the weight of being one of just three black line officers in the entire Army. What happened to his mentor Charles Young in the early months of the war indicated just how difficult life could become when a black man reached field-officer rank. Though a lieutenant colonel with a good record, Young was forced to retire.[84]

Soon after Davis arrived he pinned on the gold leaves of a major and took command of a squadron. He wrote Sarah Overton, who would become his second wife: "I have been given a free hand and I have made good use of it." Occasionally he even drilled the entire regiment as well as training his squadron. His hard work paid off when the department commander came to inspect the regiment and Davis' squadron got the highest rating. In seven months he had turned the worst squadron in the regiment into the best in field training. He was particularly pleased by the support his officers and men had given him. "I have never seen such loyalty to a comdr as I am getting." Officers from other squadrons began to ask his views about training and copied his orders and training schedules. A new regimental commander who came in 1918 told him that he considered him "his mainstay" and that he had "absolute confidence" in his judgment and ability. A lieutenant colonel by then, Davis continued his good work, kept up his professional reading, and took young officers on a tactical ride.[85]

Training, ideally, should progress from the individual through the various-size units until the largest could compete in a maneuver. While the strength of available forces and the large maneuver areas made it more likely that the Philippine garrison could approach this ideal, there was another factor that enhanced the realism—the Japanese threat. Although the Japanese evidently did not seriously consider invading the Philippines in this period, they did carry out espionage efforts, and American officers certainly feared the possibility of an attack. In 1907 young Kingman at Fort McKinley talked with a captain and came away with the impression that "it seems like we might have war with Japan, that would be bad luck for us over here in the Philippines." Shortly after he arrived in the fall of 1909, Major William Lassiter was told by the commanding general that "the situation is such that we are liable to be jumped at any moment." He soon found "everybody gossiping about war with Japan."[86]

In late May 1913 the War Department warned the Philippines Division commander of a Japanese surprise attack. J. Franklin Bell immediately began strengthening the coast artillery garrison at Corregidor. He ordered the 24th Infantry and companies from two other infantry regiments as well as some Scout units and a field artillery battalion to the island and then dispatched a year's supply of food and other stores. Fortunately, it was a false alarm, and most of the reinforcements returned to their original posts. While the 24th was still on Corregidor, Mansfield Robinson, a company cook, retired. The tall, lanky, soft-spoken, forty-six-year-old veteran, on his third tour in the islands, retired and went home to western Kentucky.[87]

A few months after the May 1913 war scare, George C. Marshall arrived and became deeply involved in a maneuver to test the defenses of Manila Bay. Within a few weeks after he moved into McKinley, he was given the job of adjutant to one of the maneuver detachments. Since the commander was an incompetent on the verge of retirement and the chief of staff had gone on leave hunting in Indochina, much of the work of planning and preparing orders for the mobilization, concentration, and supply of this force of almost 4,900 fell on this first lieutenant. This was an additional duty to his regular regimental tasks; hence throughout the fall and into the winter months he spent his evenings and weekends working on the maneuver.

Unlike previous exercises, this began with a surprise announcement and continued night and day without cessation. Marshall and others assumed that it would begin in mid-February, but on the morning of January 22 they were told that it had begun. The chief of staff was present but became ill, so Marshall had to take over. The commanding general, aware of the detachment commander's inadequacy, informed him that he should, in effect, let the lieutenant command Detachment No. 1. The operation began with this force making an amphibious landing at Batangas and fighting (with blanks) its way through the enemy (some 3,200 officers and men) to Manila. Until the maneuver ended on February 4, as Marshall explained to his brother, "I had practically the entire burden of the thing, coupled with the difficulties connected with a first lieutenant's ordering colonels, &c, in the Regular Army."[88]

Another infantry lieutenant, Henry H. Arnold, glimpsed Marshall, in the midst of the maneuver, studying a map and dictating the order that resulted in victory. Impressed by Marshall's success, Arnold realized that it was "a job that any lieutenant colonel or major in the outfit would have given his eyeteeth to have." In truth, because of his experience in an even larger New England maneuver of 1912, Marshall was the best-prepared officer for this task. There were differences, however: this was a more realistic maneuver, and he was the de facto commander. The chief umpire who watched him closely throughout the exercise paid him the highest compliment by writing in his report that his orders showed "a clear grasp of the situation, and attention to every necessary point of tactics, and are so clear and definitive as to be impossible to misconstrue."[89]

Exhausted by the stress of those hectic days, Marshall went into the hospital for two weeks; then he and his wife enjoyed a lengthy leave in Japan, Manchuria, and Korea. A highlight of this trip was a ten-day tour of the battlefields of the Russo-Japanese War in Manchuria. Japanese officers from the military governor down treated him "royally," and he was particularly pleased by a lengthy interview with Japan's greatest cavalry leader of the war. It must have been a letdown to return to the routine of a company officer, but in the spring of 1915 the brigade commander, whom he had tutored in tactics at Fort Leavenworth, made him his aide. Hunter Liggett was portly to the point of obesity, but he had one of the finest minds in the Army. When he became the commander of the Philippine Department, Marshall continued as his aide until his foreign-service tour ended in the summer of 1916.[90]

No matter how well trained the troops were or how brilliant their planners and leaders were, its relatively small size and the great distance from the States dictated that the Army in the Philippines would remain hostage to Japanese ambitions. In 1915 the secretary of war emphasized their predicament when he pointed out that the defense of the Philippines "is a matter of national and not of military policy . . . it must be remembered that, under conditions of modern warfare, unless our navy has undisputed control of the sea, we can not reinforce the peace garrison after a declaration of war or while war is imminent." Although the sword of Damocles hung over them, Army people worked and diverted themselves from day to day. Sentinels walked their posts, called out the hours, and reassuringly added: "All's well." And, for the time being, it was.[91]

FOUR

Enlisted Men in the New Army

They thought I had gone to Hell.

—GILMER M. BELL

———————◆———————

WHEN the Army published a promotional booklet, *The Life of an Enlisted Man in the United States Army,* in 1904, the author, a lieutenant colonel, first addressed the stereotype that recruiters had to overcome: "In many parts of the United States there seems to prevail the idea that to be a soldier of our Regular Army is to be in a position which is below that of the ordinary citizen, and which entails duties or labors degrading to an American . . . and that an enlistment in the Army . . . means that those years of a man's life have been wasted." This was certainly the view held by the middle-class family and friends of Gilmer Bell when he enlisted in 1915. The facts that judges, on occasion, gave miscreants the option of enlisting rather than going to jail and that a well-meaning New Jersey businessmen would suggest that selected inmates at the state penitentiary be enlisted, thereby saving the state money and helping the Army meet its recruiting goals, also indicate the prevailing attitude toward soldiers.[1]

Initially the term of enlistment was three years, but in 1912 this was changed to seven years, with the first four on active service and the last three in reserve. Four years later, Congress changed this to three years' active duty followed by four in the reserve. Rather than criminals, the Army sought unmarried men between the ages of twenty-one and thirty-five "of good antecedents and habits and free from bodily defects and diseases. They must be citizens . . . or have declared their intention to become citizens, and must be able to speak, read, and write the English language." After the turbulence of 1898 and 1899, when the Army in effect had to recruit three different forces, recruiting began to settle into a routine. Yet stability was difficult as Congress periodically raised or lowered strength goals (although the general trend was to higher numbers), while the rise and fall of the economy had the reverse effect on prospective volunteers. Throughout the years between the Spanish-American War and World War I, the Army set up recruiting stations in about 100 cities and sent out details to scour smaller towns as well. Each regiment contributed an officer on a two-year assignment, later supplemented by retired officers recalled to active duty, and an appropriate number of enlisted men to carry out this crucial mission.[2]

Constant complaints about the quality of recruits and the necessity to discharge many for conditions they suffered from at the time of enlistment led to a significant change in the recruiting system in 1905. Rather than have civilian doctors examine and accept or reject applicants at the recruiting station and dispatch the recruit on to his unit, the War Department made enlistment contingent upon the examination of an Army doctor at a recruit depot. Thus, recruiters still rejected a sizable majority on the basis of "lacking either legal, mental, moral, or physical qualifications," but the Army doctor retained the final verdict on those remaining. In 1913 the average weight and height of those accepted was just under 144 pounds and five feet seven inches. During the fiscal year ending June 30, 1914, incidentally, recruiters rejected 76 percent while doctors failed 13 percent of those who reached them. Throughout the period 1900–1916, the annual rejections ranged from 70 percent to 81 percent.[3]

Year in and year out, they came—drawn by the flag at the recruiting station or one of the colorful posters or a newspaper advertisement. In the seventeen years beginning in 1900, 30,000 or more enlisted in nine of those years, with the number falling below 20,000 only twice. In contrast, the Navy, which had a four-year enlistment term throughout this period and a smaller authorized strength, reached above 20,000 recruits in only two years and fell below 10,000 in two other years. Their rejection rate was in the same general area as the Army's.[4]

While many were summarily rejected for illiteracy or alien status, the predominant physical causes were venereal disease and problems with vision, hearing, or the heart. Although VD did not emerge as one of the top four medical reasons for rejection until 1904, from then through 1915 it ranked as first in nine of those twelve years. Despite the requirement for citizenship or at least the declared intention of becoming a citizen and the ability to read, write, and speak English, approximately 12 percent (slightly more than the Navy accepted in those years) of recruits were foreign-born in this period. Usually about half of that number were Germans and Irish, but in 1912 Russians supplanted the Irish, and two years later they took over first place from the Germans.[5]

In 1905 the Army sought to determine the enlistment rate as a proportion of those men in the militia age of eighteen to forty-four in the various regions of the nation. The minuscule actual number of enlistments per 100,000 indicates the relatively small place of the Army in American society. The Western Division was decidedly the most fertile recruiting area (286 per 100,000), followed by the South Central Division (169), with the North Central Division (144) close behind and the virtually identical North Atlantic (115) and South Atlantic Divisions (113) trailing.[6]

✳

On November 2, 1911, William L. Banks, who had turned nineteen about three weeks earlier, walked into the recruiting station at Lexington, Kentucky and signed up. During the fiscal year from July 1, 1911, to June 30, 1912, he was one of 1,827 who applied at this particular station. This small, wiry man was one of the 496 who were accepted. Later, 43 failed the physical examination at the recruit depot; thus approximately 24 percent finally got into the Army. Officially, Banks was designated a "colored" recruit, one of the 2,672 blacks who made up 6.6 percent of all enlistments and reenlistments during that fiscal year.

Banks knew nothing about the Army except what he had heard from an old veteran who lived in the small all-black community where he had grown up. He did know, however, what civilian life had to offer. Although he was bright and energetic and had a high school education, he knew that his job as an orderly at St. Joseph's Hospital in Lexington was probably about as much as he could hope for. Army pay was as good as he was getting at the hospital, while the service also offered travel and the possibility of adventure. He also felt patriotic. His grandparents, who had raised him, were not enthusiastic; they thought he was too young. But his friends thought it was a good idea. He lied about his age in order to be accepted and warned his family that if they reported him he might have to go to jail. The statement of a secretary of war in 1889 still held true: "To the colored man the service offers a career; to the white man too often only a refuge." At a time when race relations were deteriorating in American society, the Army still maintained two segregated infantry and two cavalry regiments and permitted a few to serve in the Signal Corps and Hospital Corps. The Navy, meantime, took steps to curtail recruitment of blacks and downgraded the jobs available to those who were able to enlist.[7]

George S. Schuyler, who enlisted some months after Banks in 1912, was just seventeen. But he was old enough to understand clearly that blacks in his hometown, Syracuse, New York, could aspire to only marginal jobs. The only black people he had ever seen "in any position of authority" were the noncoms in a regular unit that had camped temporarily at Syracuse three years before. Besides, he realized that "in the Army I could see the world I wanted to see and have a chance to advance myself." So he was pleased that his mother willingly signed the papers approving his enlistment as a minor.

The Army looked good to other young black men. Mike Henley in 1915 liked the security it offered; Dorsie W. Willis in 1904 thought the pay was good and that soldiering was a step up from the menial jobs he had in the Indian Territory (Oklahoma). The fact that his girlfriend admired soldiers—her brother-in-law was a sergeant—also nudged him into the recruiting station. Edward Warfield, like Schuyler, had been impressed by some black regulars he had seen, and his family and friends were proud of him when he enlisted in 1905.[8]

Economic necessity, the possibility of advancement, the desire for adventure, and the apparent glamor of military life also attracted whites to the Army. Samuel Woodfill grew up on a farm in southern Indiana. At fourteen, with an education that had not reached the multiplication tables, he had to take on a man's work. His aged father had regaled him with tales of his service in the Mexican and Civil Wars, so Woodfill was ready to go when he was fifteen in 1898, but he had to wait until he reached eighteen. Sidney M. Martin had been operating his own business in western Kentucky before he enlisted in January 1901 at age twenty-five. That winter his timber business had failed when he lost his logs in the Cumberland River; thus the recruiter in Paducah seemed to be the only possibility open to him. His family was surprised when he enlisted, but they considered the move a wise choice.

George E. Maker had a sixth-grade education but had had to start working fulltime when he was fourteen. The sight of a mounted bugler excited him—"that is for me"—so he joined the cavalry in 1911 when he was seventeen. There were a lot of sailors in Massachusetts, and Patrick J. Hayes, who had got through the third reader at school, knew what it was like to work as a cod fisherman and did not like it, so he also signed up in the Army in 1911. The next year Walter J. Rouse, who made relatively good pay in a machine shop, "decided I would like to see some of the world" and joined the Army in Trinidad, Colorado.[9]

Some recruits were ambitious to become officers. One was Clarence R. Huebner, who had grown up on a farm near Fort Riley and thus knew about soldiers. His parents were religious and very antimilitary, so he deferred pursuing his ambition. After a couple of years in high school, he went to a business college and got a job as a secretary-stenographer in a business in Nebraska. There was a nearby cavalry post, and he saw a good deal of the troopers. "I liked what I saw and I was not particularly enamored with being the secretary type so when I got old enough to be my own boss, I enlisted." He was a few weeks past his twenty-first birthday. He spent almost seven years in the ranks before he put on the insignia of a second lieutenant in November 1916.

For another recruit who aspired to a commission, the wait was only three years. Troy H. Middleton, a Mississippi planter's son, had graduated from college, where he had been an athlete, a cadet leader, and class president; but he wanted to be an Army officer. Although his family and friends "took a dim view" of what he was doing, he traveled to Fort Porter, New York, in order to enlist in the company of a friend of the regular officer he had known in college. He was not yet twenty-one when he took the oath in March 1910 and began working toward that commission.[10]

In 1905 the War Department changed the recruiting procedure not only by mandating physical examinations by Army doctors but also by prescribing a stay at one of three recruit depots. Although the newly designated depots—Fort Slocum, New York, Columbus Barracks, Ohio, and Jefferson Barracks, Missouri—had served this function in the late nineteenth century, the Army had abandoned this method of introduction to the service in 1894 and begun to ship new men straight from the recruiting station to their respective units. This policy proved to be, as one officer bluntly put it, "a complete and dismal failure." A recruit could now expect to spend twenty-five days learning to be a soldier at a depot before he went out to his unit.[11]

There were some problems. In 1906 the War Department quickly responded to one criticism by establishing permanent parties, as had been the nineteenth-century custom to operate these depots. This arrangement was much more efficient administratively than assigning random companies to that task. In the same year the Army named eleven posts (seven of which were in the West) as depot posts, which would be closer to many of the recruiting stations than the recruit depots to carry out the initial training. Three years later, the average number of recruits on any day at the original depots was 767 at Columbus Barracks, 748 at Fort Slocum, and 711 at Jefferson Barracks. That year, two of the depot posts, Fort McDowell in California and Fort Logan in Colorado, were upgraded to recruit depots.[12]

"Elopers" constituted a problem that officers more or less accepted. These were men who passed the recruiting-station tests but disappeared either en route or after they reached the depots. Others simply refused to take the oath. In the first year, 5.8 percent of recruits fell into this category. Traditionally there was a high rate of desertion in the first year of enlistment, so the adjutant general concluded that these elopers would probably have deserted anyway. As to those who declined to enlist, the commanding officer at Fort Slocum reported that their reasons were that, despite recruiters' promises, they could not immediately get into special organizations or, generally, the Army was different from what they expected. This officer argued that the Army was well rid of such men, as they probably would have become "an element of discontent" and deserted anyway. The judge advocate general was not as dismissive of these people and against a few preferred charges of embezzlement to the amount of the costs of their transportation and subsistence. He did win some convictions, but the problem did not abate.[13]

Although George Schuyler had grown up in New York and had attended an integrated school, he was apparently not surprised that blacks were segregated at Fort Slocum. On the other hand, William L. Banks, who had spent his entire life in a segregated society, was impressed that white and black recruits slept in the same barracks, ate in the same mess hall, and drilled as well as did kitchen police together. This situation evidently changed within the next few months, for in April 1912 a black leader from Chicago wrote President William H. Taft demanding to know why black soldiers were segregated in the mess halls at Columbus Barracks. The commanding officer responded through channels that this was the only such complaint and that mixing the races "would lead to endless strife and friction." The adjutant general backed him up: "The existence of race prejudice may be deplored, but that it exists in varying intensity is a patent fact everywhere. For the commanding officer of a recruit depot to shut his eyes to this fact and to try and administer his post as if it did not exist, would be to invite serious trouble."

Three years later, a lieutenant on recruiting duty in Charlotte, North Carolina, informed the adjutant general that seven recruits from his area had declined to enlist because they found themselves in integrated quarters at Columbus Barracks. As it happened, the same old cavalry colonel who had responded in 1912 was still in command. He said that this was a temporary situation brought on by overcrowding and pointed out that none of the men specifically mentioned had complained about this when questioned about why they refused to enlist at the time. When Banks returned to reenlist in 1916, there were partitions to segregate the sleeping quarters of the races.[14]

In the spring of 1916 C. C. Lyon, a reporter who also happened to be a friend of the secretary of war, got permission to go through the recruit processing and training at Columbus Barracks without actually enlisting. He published his experiences in four articles in the *Columbus Citizen* which the War Department published a few weeks later as a pamphlet to give to prospective recruits.

Lyon noted that only a few of his new comrades were well dressed when they arrived, and that "several looked like down-and-outers." One of the first steps a recruit went through was to answer questions about his past to determine his occupation. The surgeon general published this information annually, beginning in 1910, so we know that the most common occupations were laborers and farmers, with 40 percent or more coming from those categories for most of the years 1909–1915. Beyond those two jobs, enlistees indicated a wide variety of work experience, with sixty-one occupations listed for 1909 and ninety-five for 1915. Times were changing; in the last couple of years in this period, a few said that they were moving-picture operators and aviators.[15]

The sergeant who met Lyon and his comrades when they arrived at the depot explained: "The first thing you learn in the Army is to keep clean." Those who were in obvious need of a wash had to take a bath at that time. After that, noncoms marched all of them to the baths twice a week, and officers staged surprise weekly inspections at which the men had to take off their shoes and strip to their underwear to demonstrate their cleanliness. Earlier, in 1905, the commander at Columbus Barracks reported that his greatest problem was care of the bathrooms. He attributed this to many recruits' ignorance of modern conveniences. Indeed, he commented, if left on their own, some might blow out the gas lights. After three months he came up with the solution of placing guards armed with clubs in each bathroom to ensure proper treatment of the facilities.

Once Lyon and his group reached their platoon, their sergeant informed them about the two-baths-a-week rule and added that they would also have to wash their hands and faces with soap and hot water before each meal, brush their teeth three times a day, and be clean-shaven with shoes shined and uniform spotless at all times. One of the men confided to Lyon that he doubted if he had brushed his teeth three times in his lifetime. The next morning Sergeant Watt showed that he meant business as he singled out one soldier and ordered him to go back and wash his face and hands again—"this time put a little more enthusiasm and soap into it."[16]

Recruits learned that they were expected to keep not only themselves but also their barracks, mess hall, latrines, and the grounds clean. Schuyler recalled daily inspections at which the officer put on white gloves and rubbed the tops of shelves, under the radiators, and other such places and remonstrated with the sergeant if his gloves showed any dirt. If there was a spot on the floor, a new soldier had to scrape it off with a piece of glass.[17]

There were three categories of recruits at the depot: those who had been there less than fifteen days, the ones with fifteen to thirty days on post, and the reenlistment group. The schedule that ordered the lives of the first two groups started with reveille at 5:30. In the mornings recruits had three drill periods in which they learned to stand at attention, turn in the Army way, march, and salute. The more advanced group drilled more but continued to have readings of the Articles of

War as well as assorted lectures on other introductory material. In the afternoon, physical exercises and games kept them occupied. There were also formations daily as recruits graduated to the other sections, which also meant moving to different barracks. Although the advanced recruits could also expect to work on fatigue details about the post, most of such work fell on the old soldiers in the last section.

Originally recruits moved out to their assigned regiments on the basis of monthly reports of personnel requirements from each unit. This policy proved unsatisfactory, as Brigadier General John J. Pershing pointed out in 1911, because "driblets" of men arriving frequently during the year made recruit training an "endless chain," with both trainers and trainees bored by a process that seemed to have neither a beginning nor an end. Pershing advocated that all recruits be sent out once a year so the units could set up a proper training program. He did not get exactly what he wanted, but the next year the secretary of war changed the system so that recruits joined units twice a year. At the depots, this meant a longer stay of at least thirty-six days. In contrast, the British Army did all of its recruit training—twenty-two weeks of it—at the depots.[18]

When George Schuyler left Fort Slocum to join the 25th Infantry, he had the exciting prospect of a cross-country trip since the first battalion of the 25th was at Fort Lawton, Washington. After the fascinating trip, he joined Company B. One of the first things he and all other new men learned was that the most important soldier in the company was First Sergeant William Blaney, a soft-spoken but brusque man with piercing eyes. If a recruit smiled at his initial encounter with the sergeant, Blaney would quickly put him in his place: "Don't show me your teeth, I'm no dentist." Strict but fair, he ran a good company. Since Schuyler's mother died not long after he arrived, the company did in fact become his home; "It was very much like a family."

Walter Rouse came to believe in the Fifth Cavalry that the first sergeant was "God." In his second enlistment he became first sergeant in the 15th Infantry, so he spoke from experience. "A first sergeant don't have very many problems. If he does, he isn't a good top cutter, because you've got all the authority in the world behind you and you use it." When Schuyler reenlisted in 1915, he joined H Company, where he had a particularly awesome first sergeant, William "Woof" Glass. Every day at the noon meal, Glass announced: "Ah want you people to understan' that Ah'm First Sergeant of H Company." And they could never forget it. He and his company lived by "The Book"—Army Regulations. There was no letup in the rigid discipline. H Company excelled—best-drilled, best marksmen, cleanest equipment, neatest barracks. This stocky, tough veteran demanded perfection. The men feared, respected, and hated Glass. As Schuyler recalled, "Woof was always taking the joy out of life." One soldier fired at him but missed; another attacked him with a knife; but the sergeant always held his own. On another occasion he confronted a soldier who had gone berserk and shot up the barracks. Woof snatched the rifle away and knocked the man unconscious with the butt. As the men gaped, Glass promptly returned to business: "All Right, all right: you people hurry up and get ready for inspection."[19]

Although he now belonged to a unit, the new infantryman still had another two weeks to a month, while the trooper had at least twenty days and maybe as long as two months of special instruction, before he was ready to take part in regular training. Life was complicated for the new artilleryman, who had to learn how to care for and handle horses as well as crew drill on the guns and pistol marksmanship. When he joined the Seventh Infantry, Patrick J. Hayes remembered that "those old tobacco chewing, whiskey drinking corporals put it to you." Even though it was wartime, conditions in the Seventh Cavalry at Fort Bliss were much as they had been before the war when Arthur J. Stanley joined it in the spring of 1918. Recruit training was "rather intense" for new cavalrymen. There was more dismounted drill, but the emphasis was on horsemanship. Stanley had ridden before, but most of the other recruits going through training with him had not. They came to realize that in the cavalry "the horse was a part of you."

Training was more complicated for troopers. In addition to dismounted, close-order drill and familiarization with the rifle, they had to learn how to shoot a pistol and to wield a saber in the appropriate manner. Most of all, they had to learn how to ride. William L. Banks gave one of the most detailed accounts of this training. At Columbus Barracks, he asked for and got the Tenth Cavalry, which was stationed at Fort Ethan Allen, Vermont. There, in F Troop, a sergeant took charge of about six recruits. Banks had ridden before but never used a saddle; however, training began barebacked. First they had to mount and dismount properly. Once that was accomplished and practiced, they had to keep their balance with the help of stirrups on the blanket (held in place by a circingle, a large web belt) on the horse's back as the horses walked around the ring. From a walk, they progressed to a trot, then to a gallop. After the new men mastered these basics, the sergeant issued them saddles and they went through the entire process again until they did it well. Finally, he taught them the rudiments of mounted drill—staying together in fours and the various maneuvers. Then they were perhaps ready for an exciting ride down the steep, sandy bridle path that ended on the bank of the Winooski River. If the trooper lost control, he and his mount wound up in the river.[20]

In the unit, as at the recruit depot, the soldier had to devote time to keeping himself, his clothing and equipment, the barracks, the mess hall, and the kitchen, as well as the grounds, neat. "Fatigue" duty was a given.

In the winter months, soldiers who needed a basic education were supposed to go to school part of the day. Originally designed for illiterates after the Civil War, such a school seemed superfluous after the 1894 requirement that all recruits be literate. Many who were supposed to attend did not want to (at Fort Mason, California, several were reported to have deserted to avoid going), and those like Richard Johnson in the 25th Infantry who wanted to go found that fatigue and guard duties took precedence and interrupted the program. The teachers were other soldiers—George Schuyler taught English and geography for a while at Fort Lawton—and they varied in competence.[21]

When Colonel Reynolds described the soldier's routine in his booklet for prospective recruits, he emphasized that guard duty, though "trying and tedious," was the "most important" of the soldier's duties. For twenty-four hours, beginning with guard mount at 9:00 A.M., the soldier marched or stood guard for two hours and then spent four in the guardhouse. In a small garrison, this duty was more frequent. In 1903 the average interval in the States was seven days between tours, but more than a third had a shorter respite. Guard and the general housekeeping chores left time for little else at the small posts. Since the end of the Indian Wars, the trend had been to larger garrisons, for as Secretary of War Root pointed out in 1902, life in the one or two company posts was "narrowing and dwarfing." Yet even with such an efficient and hard-driving secretary, some such posts remained. In 1905 there were eighteen one-to-three-company posts scattered throughout the States.[22]

Even at the larger posts, when war raged in the Philippines, systematic training was difficult. For one thing, there were fewer troops in the States at the turn of the century than there had been during the Indian Wars. Personnel turbulence resulting from troop movements, the creation of new units, and an increase in recruitment also complicated matters to the point that training, for most, in those years was limited to ordinary drills. Only the relatively stable coast artillery units were able to complete training programs.[23]

A perennial shortage of officers throughout line units (including the coast artillery) also hampered training. With so many on detached service, it was rare to find a captain with his company. In turn, the companies were commanded, as one inspector general reported, "by young, inexperienced officers who are continually changing." In 1911 an inspector general found that only four captains and fourteen lieutenants were present for duty with the twelve companies of the 24th Infantry. Four years earlier there was a shortage of officers in the Sixth Field Artillery but an even greater shortage of men. Early that summer they had to turn 400 of their horses out to pasture, since there were not enough soldiers to care for and train them with the guns.[24]

Ideally, training should progress from the individual through his squad and on to the regiment with simulated combat conditions to provide the proper edge. In 1906 Lieutenant General John C. Bates, during his three-month tenure as chief of staff, issued General Order no. 44, which prescribed a rigorous and realistic training program. He divided the year into periods for garrison training (the winter months) and field training. During the former, soldiers and units would carry on training within the confines of the post, while field training incorporated tactical exercises and included weekly practice marches of twelve miles for the infantry (eighteen for cavalry and artillery) and a monthly march of three days as well as target practice. Finally, each unit would spend twenty-one days marching and living in the field, with night exercises included in this training. Neither garrison and field training seasons nor practice marches were innovations, but the emphasis on marches and realism was. A flood of complaints to the point that the too-frequent marches were an imposition resulted the next year in a reduction of the marches and a relinquishing of more authority for training to company commanders. Tactical drills for the infantry continued along the rigid Civil War lines until the revised *Infantry Drill Regulations* in 1911 authorized more flexibility and realism.[25]

The goal, as enunciated by Bates's successor, J. Franklin Bell, remained to keep "the Army in such condition as to make it available for active service at shortest notice." The experience of the Sixth Field Artillery and of Private Banks in the Tenth Cavalry illustrates what this meant down the chain of command. In the Sixth, batteries went into the field and carried out tactical problems there twice a month, and the long practice marches (258 miles in 1908 and 332 in 1909) involved at least three at night. At Fort Ethan Allen, Vermont, Banks was impressed by the periodic practice alerts, when bugles sounded "Call to Arms" and troopers dropped whatever they were doing, took their weapons, and formed in front of the barracks. Officers timed these drills as they did the other exercise of having the men double-time to the stables, saddle their horses, and lead them into line. In 1913 the Tenth Cavalry marched from Vermont to Winchester, Virginia. If a horse's back was sore, the trooper had to walk until it healed. In camp together with two other cavalry regiments at Winchester, the men of the Tenth learned to go through their drills guided by leaders' hand signals rather than voice or bugle.[26]

Target practice was a significant part of the field training. In the two decades before the Spanish war, the Army had developed an intensive, highly competitive marksmanship program, but, like training generally, it declined during the period 1898–1902. The increased range of small arms and the fact that fewer recruits were familiar with weapons prompted Secretary Root to emphasize its importance in 1903. That year the Army sponsored a national meet and was embarrassed to have National Guard teams score higher. Few soldiers reached that level of competition, but there were monthly pay increases for all who achieved the levels of expert (three dollars), sharpshooter (two dollars), and marksman (one dollar). In 1907 a General Staff study showed that these awards were not commensurate with the Navy awards, which ranged from two to ten dollars according to gun pointers' level of skill and recommended that the extra pay be increased to five, three, and two dollars. According to this recommendation, coast artillery and field artillery gunners should also pick up two or three dollars in additional monthly pay if they qualified as second- or first-class gunners. When Congress enacted these increases, the enthusiasm naturally increased in the ranks.

Private Schuyler well remembered the tension and excitement of going on the range. In the 25th Infantry and probably in most line units, soldiers got in shape, perhaps gave up smoking and drinking, in order to be clear-headed and at the top of their form when they fired for record. There was pride as well as money riding on those scores. Nearly everyone in his company qualified and got the extra cash as well as the appropriate silver badge.

During the late nineteenth century, the rage over marksmanship reached the point that many officers began to complain that it was overemphasized. The same happened after the revival in the first years of the twentieth century. In 1911 one inspector general charged that "the time required to complete the course is out of all proportion to the time left for other instruction . . . As conducted at present target practice . . . is a menace to the general efficiency of the Army." He also recommended abolition of the extra pay. The next year an infantry sergeant wrote to the *Army and Navy Journal* and objected to this effort to take away one of the few incentives available to soldiers, one that had resulted in improved marksmanship. This was too crucial a part of a soldier's life and training to give up.[27]

Another important part of training was physical fitness. Secretary of War William H. Taft was hardly its best example, but he recognized its value in his annual report in 1905. As in the case of marksmanship, this training had developed to a high level in the 1890s—so much so that Nelson A. Miles referred to the Army of those days as a "corps of athletes." Although few posts (only seven out of sixty-six in 1902) had properly equipped gymnasiums, soldiers went through a daily routine of calisthenics, with infantrymen also doing bayonet drills and various exercises with their rifles, while those in the cavalry and field artillery had their workouts with horses. The Army encouraged athletics and even provided expense money for competitors to visit other posts. In 1903 the acting adjutant general of the Army published the names and records of the top track men, such as Corporal Bessmer of the 22d Infantry, who ran the 100-yard dash in ten seconds. Enlisted men in

A baseball game at Fort Warren, Massachusetts, circa 1913.
Courtesy of Charles E. McCombs.

mounted units, such as Walter Rouse, played on polo teams as well as baseball teams.[28]

Regular field days, monthly at some posts, quarterly at others, had men and units competing in a variety of track and field as well as military sports. At these events there might be monetary prizes, and there was always recognition. In the Tenth Cavalry at Fort Ethan Allen, Vermont, the latter included using the saber to pick up rings or to thrust at dummies while at a gallop, wrestling on horseback, and a race to prepare a fire and cook a meal in the open. Banks, who had rapidly developed into a skilled rider, competed with representatives from three cavalry regiments and took top honors in high-jumping in 1913. There was a good gymnasium at Fort Ethan Allen as well as a riding hall, so the troopers got instruction in tumbling and working out on parallel bars and the leather horses. They also had regular mounted training in the riding hall during the winter. Some of the men got permission to come back after duty hours and practice trick riding—vaulting from one galloping horse to another—forming pyramids on horseback. Banks remembered: "It would take hours and hours of training to get the horses to act right."

Sports were very much a part of soldiers' lives. On the long march from Fort Niobrara, Nebraska, to Fort Riley, Kansas, in 1903, on several occasions the baseball players in the 25th Infantry marched twenty miles, pitched camp, and then played a local team. Richard Johnson boasted: "we did not lose a single game." In the athletic competition that followed the maneuvers at Riley, the 25th won the baseball playoff with other regular regiments by beating the Tenth Cavalry four to three. Black athletic teams were apt to hold their own or to beat all comers. Schuyler attributed their impressive record to the fact that in the 25th there was less turnover, and so the teams had honed their skills for years. He recalled that victories over the white units were "extremely relished." At least one officer complained earlier, in 1905, that the Army had gone too far in promoting sports. Major Robert L. Bullard, who was then in charge of athletics at Fort Snelling, believed that many officers and men regarded a field day "as an infernal nuisance and bore." He thought that the Army should play down the sporting aspect and emphasize systematic physical training. The interest in games and competition, however, was much more attractive than any exercise routine.[29]

The logical culmination of the annual progressive training program was a maneuver with regiments or even brigades engaged in sham battles. In the fall of 1902 the Army brought together some 6,000, including some National Guard units, at Fort Riley for what was hailed as the first attempt to carry out tactical field exercises on such a large scale and the first combined regular-militia maneuver. Although maneuvers and the later camps of instruction were not held every fall, they were held most years until the crisis with Mexico in 1914 diverted most of the line units to border stations. In the summer of 1910 an estimated 37,000 regulars and 70,000 Guardsmen got together at several camps of instruction for this valuable training. These maneuvers and camps also afforded regiments the opportunity to make their required annual three-week march. The black soldiers in the 25th Infantry were enthusiastically greeted as they passed through the small Nebraska and Kansas towns en route to Fort Riley for the 1903 maneuver. During the maneuver, Richard Johnson recalled that the marching was strenuous and that he and other enlisted men never knew who won the sham battles. He and the others in the 25th did understand, however, that their incompetent regimental commander was relieved from command and retired because of his poor showing during the tactical problems.[30]

On the border, some individual and small-unit training was possible. After the Tenth Cavalry went to Arizona in late 1913, troopers built a 500-yard range for target practice and carried on mounted drill as well as training in signaling, but their basic mission was to guard a stretch of the border. William Banks was in the squadron stationed at Naco. He and his fellow troopers took turns going on guard, with two hours of riding along the border and four hours of rest. In that mountainous area, one could see for miles and be fully aware of the Mexicans, who occasionally fired across the border. The troopers, however, were not supposed to fire back unless the Mexicans crossed the line.[31]

Some soldiers had to keep up with advances in technology and were crucial in its practical application, as Captain Benny Foulois jotted down in his black notebook when he was commander of the First Aero Squadron: "Entire success of development depends on enlisted men." The coast artillery had ranks of engineer, electrician sergeant, electrician sergeant first class, and master electrician, while by 1904 the Signal Corps had the rank of master signal electrician. Operating the huge guns at the coastal forts required a variety of technical skills on the part of the enlisted men, while the Signal Corps was responsible for telephones, telegraphy, cables, and even installing electric lights on Army posts. This branch also became the home to developing aviation.[32]

The first enlisted man in the embryonic aviation program was Edward Ward. In fact Corporal Ward and Private First Class (PFC) Joseph E. Barrett were assigned shortly before the chief signal officer created the Aeronautical Division on August 1, 1907, to take charge of "all matters pertaining to military ballooning, air machines, and all kindred subjects." Ward, a twenty-five-year-old Kentuckian, had worked on the railroad before he enlisted, and he served a tour in a coastal fort and reached the rank of quartermaster sergeant, which he had given up when he reenlisted in the Signal Corps in 1904. Barrett at twenty-nine already had eight years of service in the Navy. Their initial assignment took them from their station at Fort Wood, on Bedloe's Island in New York Harbor, to Leo Stevens' Balloon Plant on Ninth Avenue in Manhattan. Stevens, a balloonist himself, passed on his skills to the two

Eddie Ward (seated on left) with his balloon detachment, among them Vernon Burge (in dark sweater behind Ward), probably near Norfolk, Virginia, in 1907. Courtesy of the Airmen Memorial Museum and College Park Aviation Museum.

soldiers. The most memorable aspect of this training, as far as Ward was concerned, was the opportunity that he and Barrett had to buy a beer for a nickel and to get a free lunch consisting of hamburger steak, french fries, and trimmings in a nearby saloon, thus saving most of the fifty cents each received for a meal. After a few weeks of this training and fattening up, the two soldiers left for Virginia to assist in an air exhibit at the Jamestown Exposition. There Barrett deserted and joined the Navy, but Ward did not have to go it alone, as eight more Signal Corps PFCs were sent to help him. One of them was Vernon L. Burge, a short, stocky, eighteen-year-old native of Illinois who had enlisted just four months earlier. His company commander at Fort Omaha called him into his office and asked him if he was afraid to go up in a balloon. Burge, who had seen hot-air balloons at carnivals, answered that he would chance it. Over the next couple of years, these men worked with balloons and dirigibles.

Ward did some flying and eventually got his balloonist certificate. When the Wrights brought their plane to Fort Myer to take the Army tests, Ward supervised unpacking the crates. Later he served in the Philippines and helped repair the Wright machine that Lieutenant Frank P. Lahm flew at Fort McKinley. In retirement he recalled: "I was more interested in the mechanical features of the thing than fond of flying. I never took to flying." As for Burge, he served in the ground crew for the Army's first airplane, and in 1912, when the Army shipped a plane to the Philippines, he went out as the NCO in charge of the two-man detail. While there, he became the first enlisted man to become a qualified pilot. During the World War both he and Ward received commissions, but afterward Ward reverted to his enlisted rank while Burge stayed on as a regular captain.[33]

In the spring of 1907 President Theodore Roosevelt recommended to the secretary of war that the Army prepare a paper illustrating that service's attractions as a career for enlisted men. He had seen a paper about the Navy and thought that it would only be fair for the Army also to parade its advantages. Three days later the chief of staff detailed Captain George H. Shelton to this project. Two months later, on July 31, Shelton submitted his seventy-four-legal-size-page report, "The Army as Life Occupation for Enlisted Men," which was published in the secretary of war's annual report for that year. This move was timely, as the Army was in the midst of a personnel crisis. Conditions in the larger society had changed markedly from the waning years of the frontier Army, when soldiers were more isolated from civil life and soldiers' pay went far. Since then, as Shelton pointed out, "Opportunities outside have vastly increased while the inducements to enter the Army have remained the same or relatively lessened." A booming economy with unemployment at less than one percent in 1906 and a steadily rising consumer price index for the past ten years added up to trouble for Army recruitment. Fewer applied for enlistment and reenlistment. Although soldiers had since 1890 had the right to purchase their discharges before the end of their enlistments and many did, others simply deserted, with the annual rate peaking at 7.4 percent in 1906. This was the highest since 1889 but considerably lower than the Navy's rate, which did not dip below 14 percent from 1900 through 1908. Depleted units hampered training and meant more fatigue or maintenance work for the soldiers. One division commander's report corroborated this with a dramatic example of the result of imposing so much labor on a few men. One of his posts was down to just fifty-six men, of whom eleven deserted in one month.[34]

Shelton's report turned out to be about what the Army needed to make it an attractive career possibility for enlisted men rather than an alluring portrayal of what the Army currently offered. Throughout he discussed such matters as pay, rations, quarters, restoration of canteens in the post exchanges, and the status of noncoms and then concluded with a page and half of recommendations to improve the soldier's lot.

Pay was a particularly sore point. When a general queried first sergeants and their unit commanders in his division about causes of desertion in 1907, each group ranked low pay as number one. A private earned $13 a month, which increased to $14 in his third year of enlistment. Sergeants received only $18, with first sergeants an additional $7 monthly. Pay varied widely among specialists and technicians, with master electricians topping the scale at $75. The fact that the American soldier was much better paid than those in foreign countries—almost double British pay, the closest second—was no consolation. More to the point were the higher wages earned by American workers. In 1907 the average worker's yearly wage was $542, a figure that was lowered considerably by the inclusion of farm laborers' annual pay of $319. Even though the latter was the lowest civilian wage listed, it was more than double a private's pay and slightly more than a sergeant's income. There was a marked difference between the situation of whites and blacks. When asked to compare his Army pay with that of his friends, William L. Banks answered that his friends worked either on the farm or in domestic service and made less than Army privates. Gilmer M. Bell, on the other hand, thought that his friends made about six times more than his private's pay.

Knowing about the even lower wages paid to soldiers in European armies probably would have made little difference. Shelton and others who wrote about the pay problem pointed out that compulsory service minimized a private's pay and that the difference between that and a noncom's income was markedly greater in those armies. On the other hand, the discrepancy between the pay of the Navy and the Army was much more likely to come to a soldier's attention. A Navy recruit received $16 monthly, while the lowest-ranking noncom, a third-class petty officer, earned $30. Shelton spent more than three pages comparing Army and Navy pay and allowances, showing that sailors got more money in almost every instance.[35]

When comparing the pay of servicemen with that of civilians, one has to take into consideration the fact that the former received clothing, rations, quarters, and health care. After 1902, when the Army shifted to olive drab and khakis for everyday wear and retained blues only for dress, Shelton and other officers considered the uniform allowance sufficient. Indeed, Reynolds thought that the soldier should be able to accumulate savings from it during his three-year enlistment, but Shelton pointed out that alterations and laundering had to come out of the man's pay. Tailoring was provided gratis to sailors, and Shelton thought that the government should provide that service as well as cleaning to soldiers.[36]

He also recommended that the Army add butter, milk, molasses, or syrup to the ration. As it was, even Reynolds, who was trying to make the Army attractive to prospective recruits, could not make the ration of meat, potatoes, beans, dried fruit, vegetables, coffee, salt, pepper, and vinegar very appealing. The cost of this individual daily ration in 1902 varied from post to post in the United States, from twenty-five cents at two East Coast artillery stations to ten and half cents at Fort Crook, Nebraska. Major General A. W. Greeley commented: "While excellent in quality and doubtless of sufficient nutritive value . . . it furnishes only a meager and monotonous diet." He pointed out that "'white meats,' butter, cheese, eggs, and milk found on every American table, even of the poorest people, are entirely lacking in the Army ration, although they appear on the naval list." In an effort to add variety, half of the posts in the States in 1902 raised gardens. Ten years later, when Banks was at Fort Ethan Allen, he appreciated what the post garden added to the "pretty poor" ration.[37]

As for living quarters, a soldier could expect to find himself in a squad bay with fourteen to twenty iron cots spaced four feet apart and a shelf and pegs on the wall and a locker at the foot of his bed for his clothing, equipment, and personal items. In addition to other squad rooms, the barracks should contain a bathroom, mess room, and recreation or day room. It was very much a sign of the times that in 1900 the Army began to issue toilet paper (one package of 1,000 sheets to every two soldiers per month). Since the new quarters had indoor toilets, it was less costly to issue appropriate tissue than to clear the frequent stoppages caused by other kinds of paper. The Signal Corps also tried to electrify posts during the first decade of the century. As late as 1908, however, some barracks still did not have electric lights. Those who did have electricity had to carefully monitor its usage. Going over the allowance of electric current established in 1906 was serious business, as the post commander at Fort Benjamin Harrison discovered when two papers on the subject went to the assistant secretary of war for decision.[38]

Not all soldiers enjoyed the amenities of the ideal barracks. Although the Army invested a great deal in construction during this period to enlarge and modernize housing, many of the troops lived in old frontier-era posts and coast artillery forts. The commanding general of the Department of the East reported in 1905 that the quarters and barracks at three of his coastal forts (Constitution, Hamilton, and Schuyler) were "dilapidated old rattletraps, uncomfortable, and, I believe, unsanitary in every way." The next year his counterpart in the Department of the Missouri recommended that Fort Washakie be abandoned because of its general dilapidation. Recent reports indicated that "the walls of the quarters are in danger of falling." Meantime, he had just abandoned Fort Niobrara because of "the deplorable condition of the buildings."[39]

In his report, Shelton assumed that soldiers lived in modern barracks and simply ignored those who did not. He did recommend that the Army try to make the recreation rooms more pleasant by providing comfortable furniture and perhaps a rug. After all, as he said, "These are the living rooms of the soldiers." George Schuyler remembered that there were two billiard tables, a piano, assorted tables, and newspapers and magazines in the recreation room of his quarters at Schofield Barracks. Although neither Shelton nor Schuyler mentioned it, many companies maintained libraries in their day rooms. Since the post libraries generally had, as Chaplain Leslie R. Groves noted, "many books that seem to have been given to the library because they were no longer of interest elsewhere," not surprisingly soldiers preferred their own company or troop libraries.[40]

Aside from conducting religious services, Groves and other chaplains were the morale officers of their day. Not all posts had chapels, so they had to hold services in whatever room was available, and they stayed busy. They usually supervised the post school and library, gave lectures on assorted topics, and used stereopticon and lantern slides as well as movies to entertain the troops. Chaplain Edmund P. Easterbrook, who was with the coast artillery in the forts on Puget Sound, bought a movie projector as early as 1908. He also regularly visited the barracks day rooms but did so discreetly: he did not drop in after payday, when there was a good deal of gambling along with the customary card games.[41]

Most chaplains deplored one significant effort the Army made toward the amusement and recreation of soldiers—namely, making beer and wine available on post in the canteen. In contrast, Secretary of War Elihu Root went on record in 1899, ten years after the provision went into effect, in support. As he bluntly put it: "The practical question . . . is not whether soldiers should drink or not drink, but whether they should be permitted to drink beer in the camp, surrounded by the restraining influences of discipline and good association, or whether they should be driven to drink bad whisky in the vile resorts." Statistics showing a decline in alcoholism, desertion, and other disciplinary problems seemed to support the Secretary's position. And most officers and noncoms (83 percent of 1,065 polled in 1899) agreed. A lieutenant in the Seventh Cavalry responded that taking beer out of the canteens would result in "a calamity to the welfare and contentment of the enlisted men and a serious blow to discipline and morality." The post quartermaster sergeant at Fort McPherson was more specific: "The effect of the absolute prohibition of beer at this post would be that men would be strung out between Fort McPherson and Atlanta, Ga., drinking and carousing."[42]

The Women's Christian Temperance Union and other "dries," who paid little or no attention to the secretary of war and the overwhelming majority of officers and noncoms, persuaded Congress to bar spirits from Army post exchanges in early 1901. Two years later Major General Frederick D. Grant, a teetotaler himself, pointed to the rising desertion rate and gave as a key reason the fact that the soldier now sought "pleasure outside of the military reservation at low doggeries or bawdish dives where lewd women and degraded men assemble to help fleece and ruin him." In addition to the usual forms of debauchery, there were also at least two reports of soldiers beginning to use drugs. Nevertheless, Congress flatly rejected the War Department's appeal in 1903 to reconsider the ban. A couple of years later the chief of staff suppressed the complaints of department and division commanders by ordering them not to give their opinions on the issue. When Shelton discussed the life of soldiers in 1907, he recommended the restoration of beer, but already the issue was dying down. For one reason, the statistics did not show as drastic an increase in alcoholism and disciplinary problems as the Army polemicists suggested. After 1907, desertion and alcoholism generally declined. In regard to the latter, the surgeon general commented in 1916 that the decline was in keeping with the "general public sentiment and decreased use of stimulants of this character among all classes in all walks of life in this country." By that time, the issue over beer in post canteens was dead.[43]

Shelton did not consider it necessary to comment on military justice in his treatise, nor did Reynolds comment directly in his booklet for prospective recruits. Those who did read the latter, however, should have noted carefully what he said under the heading "Discipline." He warned that the Army was strict about what seemed "little things" to civilians. While this policy might appear to be harsh, the soldier's rights were protected, and he need not fear the military code as long as he did "his duty in the right spirit." Once in the Army, a man soon learned a good deal more about military justice. First, as Reynolds warned, there were many seemingly trivial matters that could result in a court-martial, and one's chances of being tried were high. From 1908 through 1911, for example, an average of 58.25 percent of enlisted men were court-martialed in lowest summary courts, while another 6 percent during three of those years (1909–1911) had to appear before general courts-martial. The Navy had a better court-martial record from 1909 through 1911, with an average of only 2.5 percent of the enlisted force appearing before general courts-martial and 27 percent before lower courts.

A general court-martial with five to thirteen officers on the panel could pass judgment on officers as well as enlisted men for serious crimes, while lower courts (regimental and garrison, which were replaced in 1913 by special courts) could award punishments to enlisted men of up to three months' confinement and forfeiture of pay and demotion, with the summary court (one officer) permitted to sentence a soldier to confinement and forfeiture of pay and allowances up to a month. The overwhelming majority of men tried appeared before summary courts. The conviction rate was very high. From 1912 through 1916 it was more than 92 percent in the superior court and 97 percent in the summary court.[44]

In 1912 the judge advocate general listed eighty-eight offenses for which men could be tried. While theft, forgery, assault, being drunk and disorderly, and assorted other crimes would also have brought a civilian into court, fifty-five of these offenses were military matters. A soldier, for example, could find himself in serious trouble for being absent from his workplace, losing equipment, disobedience, or sitting down while on guard. After 1908 selling one's uniform could net a man a year's confinement at hard labor and a dishonorable discharge. Although desertion was a serious crime, courts exercised wide latitude in sentencing; some were let off with fines, while others received prison terms and dishonorable discharges.[45]

Sidney M. Martin, who served in the 26th Infantry from 1901 to 1904, complained that military justice assumed the guilt of the accused. The peculiarities of the military system made it appear so and did result in a high level of convictions. So many of the military crimes hinged on the records or on the word of a superior officer or noncom. If a man was absent or missing a part of his uniform or fell asleep while on guard, his guilt was obvious. The court simply referred to the written report in which the absence, missing item, or sleeping was recorded and had it confirmed by an officer or noncom. In cases of disobedience, drunkenness, or negligence, the key witness was probably the officer or noncom who had made the initial complaint. In some cases soldiers, as Patrick Hayes (15th Infantry) pointed out, "took care of their own." Men in barracks might not report a thief but instead administer vigilante justice with a beating and force him to desert. They might also deem fighting, although it could be construed as an offense under Article of War 62, the best way to settle an argument; hence no one would turn up in court.[46]

Soldiers evidently usually dealt with homosexuals themselves instead of preferring charges. As Gilmer Bell remembered, "Homos were run over the hill," and Patrick Hayes reported that a "degenerate" in his company also deserted. Matters of this nature were not as publicly aired then as they would be later. George Schuyler was the only memoirist to refer to homosexual activity. When authorities closed the red-light district in Honolulu in 1915, he noticed an increase in such activity at Schofield Barracks to the point that officers ordered lights kept on all night in the barracks. He did not mention whether any legal action was taken against practicing homosexuals. Sodomy was a crime, as was, from 1902 through 1911, "disgraceful conduct, indecent, infamous, and unnatural practices." In the next year the judge advocate general lumped "Sodomy and other unnatural practices" together in his report. From 1901 through 1910 there were only 64 convictions for sodomy. From 1911 through 1917, convictions increased greatly, to 304. Even if one added the 155 convictions in the earlier years for "Disgraceful conduct etc." to the sodomy convictions, there was still a substantial increase in the last seven years. The judge advocate general did not attempt to explain this phenomenon.[47]

The huge number of summary court trials irked judge advocates, who thought that unit commanders should settle many of these cases by using their discretionary powers. The fact that so many captains were absent on detached service and that relatively inexperienced lieutenants commanded in their stead was a likely reason for referring to court what a commander should have settled in his orderly room. During this period the various company commanders did begin to exert more authority in this area. Thus the number of these trials decreased from more than 42,000 in 1910 to less than 38,000 six years later while the Army increased in strength by roughly a third.[48]

Although the Army had its own prisons at Fort Leavenworth and Alcatraz for several years in the late nineteenth century, it had given them up in 1895. The results were that prisoners overflowed post guardhouses, where serious and petty criminals were housed together, and that garrisons had to provide guards. The Army regained control of the prison at Leavenworth in 1906 and the next year the one at Alcatraz and thereafter had places to put offenders with a year or more sentence to serve.

In 1911 Enoch H. Crowder, an outstanding bureaucrat, became judge advocate general and began to campaign for various reforms. One was to segregate prisoners convicted of military offenses from those who were serving time for crimes that would have brought them within prison gates in civilian life. In 1912 he succeeded in getting the latter sent to state penitentiaries. The next year he persuaded the secretary of war to authorize the formation of disciplinary companies within the military prisons. Prison officials selected prisoners on the basis of good behavior for these units, which would engage in military training rather than hard labor. They wore uniforms rather than convict garb and were known by their names instead of merely by numbers. If they performed well in these units, they became eligible to return to active duty. This reform proved to be more successful than Crowder expected. As an indication of this change of focus from punishment to rehabilitation, in 1915 he persuaded Congress to redesignate the military prisons as disciplinary barracks.[49]

Sexual harassment (a term not common then) of subordinates was the subject of one of the most controversial legal cases between the Spanish-American War and World War I. Two officers, one civilian government employee, nine NCOs, and four privates alleged that a major, a commander of a coast artillery post, had either fondled them, exposed himself, or made lewd and suggestive remarks to them. Repercussions of this case reached the highest levels of government. Major Benjamin M. Koehler, a forty-two-year-old West Pointer, had an excellent record, including combat in both the Spanish war and the Philippine War. In the summer of 1913 a captain serving under Koehler heard rumors of his commander's relationships with enlisted men but did nothing about this until at a Halloween party Koehler grabbed his testicles. He then requested an investigation by the inspector general, which turned up other victims. In December 1913 the major was arrested. Secretary of State William Jennings Bryan and a senator wrote on his behalf, and another senator accompanied by a congressman came to Secretary of War Lindley M. Garrison's office. At least one ex-soldier wrote that a few years earlier Koehler had made lascivious advances to him and several of his comrades and had maltreated them when they refused and that he hoped that Koehler got his just deserts.

Eleven officers sat on the general court-martial that went into session on the last day of February in 1914 at Koehler's post, Fort Terry, on Plum Island, off the tip of Long Island Sound. Charged with "conduct unbecoming an officer and a gentleman" and "conduct to the prejudice of good order and military discipline," Koehler hired a civilian lawyer to join with a coast artillery colonel in representing him. For four weeks, alleged victims gave explicit testimony and attempted to counter the defense's efforts to discredit their veracity and character. The defense also argued that this was a conspiracy against the major. In addition, a number of officers and enlisted men appeared as character witnesses. Finally, Koehler categorically denied every charge. Although the court did find in his favor as far as one lieutenant, two sergeants, and two privates were concerned, it believed him guilty of the allegations made by eleven others and sentenced him to dismissal. After General Crowder reviewed the case, Woodrow Wilson signed the dismissal order in June 1914. Koehler became one of eight officers dismissed of the thirty-two tried by general courts-martial that year.[50]

✳

Soldiers could hope for a commission, but except in wartime the chances for such promotion were slim. After each year's Military Academy graduates were commissioned, any vacancies in the officer corps went to enlisted men and then to civilians who had passed appropriate examinations. Since 1892 any unmarried soldier under the age of thirty and with two years of service could apply for a commission. He then competed with others in his area at a regional examination in the spring. Those who scored the highest would vie in an Armywide examination that fall. In addition to good moral character and an aptitude for the military, the examining board tested candidates on mathematics, grammar, history, constitutional and international law, and Army and drill regulations, with the greatest weight being given to knowledge of math and regulations.

In March 1907 the chief of staff, J. Franklin Bell, asked for an answer to the question "Does the present method of promoting men from the ranks benefit the Army?" One respondent argued that the current system was not a benefit, since it "feeds the list of second lieutenants from an acknowledged inferior source while not rewarding tried and faithful service." He believed that only noncoms with fifteen years of service should be eligible. This would not only be an appropriate reward for those men but also provide a host of capable and experienced company-grade officers who presumably would retire before advancing to field grade. Lieutenant Colonel T. W. Jones rebutted this argument by indicating that such a proposal would glut the junior officer ranks with overage former noncoms who would probably be frustrated by their faint hope of advancement. Such a group certainly would not make for a "happy garrison." Besides, he and others in his staff division believed that having a long term of enlisted service was a detriment for an officer. Rather than making such a drastic change in the current system, he recommended extending the two-year rule to three and having candidates attend a prep school in that last year prior to taking the examinations. As with so many staff exercises, in the end nothing changed.[51]

While those staff officers contemplated the future of soldiers who hoped to become officers, Private Vernon G. Olsmith, a twenty-two-year-old former Oklahoma newspaperman, was working hard toward that goal. An older friend had persuaded him to enlist with him for that purpose. Olsmith was not sanguine about his chances, since he had only an eighth-grade education, while his friend was a college graduate. In the end, however, he took all the hurdles in stride and earned his commission in 1909, while his friend was commissioned a year earlier. Just 22 of the 273 officers commissioned that year were from the ranks. The largest number, 160, were appointed from civil life. Four of these civilian appointees were Naval Academy graduates. During the next few years, several other Annapolis men received Army commissions. At that time the officer corps consisted of almost equal numbers of West Pointers and civilian appointees, while former regular enlisted men accounted for slightly less than 13 percent. In the next seven years, 1910 through 1916, only 110 of the 1,615 officers commissioned came from the Army, with West Point graduates making up 63 percent and civilians almost 30 percent of that group. The Navy offered significantly less opportunity for promotion from the ranks. From 1910 to 1916, just 16 sailors were commissioned. In 1901 the expansion of the Army brought in the largest number of regular soldiers, 215 (including Benjamin O. Davis and Benjamin D. Foulois).[52]

In 1911 controversy swirled about the process when an old cavalry colonel's bigotry apparently quashed one soldier's effort to attain a commission. Anti-Semitism, which permeated American society of that time, was well represented in the Army. That same year, Captain Leroy Eltinge, an instructor at the School of the Line at Leavenworth, published a paper on the "Psychology of War" in which he said that Jews did not know the meaning of patriotism. He added that their traditional background as traders and their contempt for physical labor made them unsuited for military service. Since the Army did not record a soldier's religion, no one knew how many Jews were in the service. In 1916 the Young Men's Hebrew Association polled unit commanders and tenuously based its estimate that Jews made up some 6 percent of the Army's strength on an interpolation of the responses received from 47 percent of those queried. During this period the Army did not have a rabbi among its chaplains but did grant furloughs to Jews for special holidays.[53]

Frank Bloom, the son of a tailor at Fort Myer, wanted to be an officer. The Episcopal chaplain checked out possibilities for an appointment to West Point for him but to no avail. When he graduated from high school in 1909, he enlisted in the field artillery battalion at Fort Myer. A year later he applied to take the examination. Although his battery commander endorsed him, the battalion commander, who declared privately that he was against recommending him, refused to go on record. The post commander, Colonel Joseph Garrard, a West Pointer of thirty-seven years' service, however, flatly declared: "I would not desire him in my command as an officer and a social and personal associate . . . From an experience of many years, I have found . . . few communities where Jews are received as desirable social associates." Not surprisingly, Bloom failed the examination that he took the next month. He made low grades on the grammar and geography parts and very low grades on the regulations and military record and aptitude. In the last category, Garrard's opinion must have been a factor. Private Bloom and his father, who suspected that Garrard had a baleful influence on the decision, set about to get a copy of his comments, and his mother forwarded it to a prominent Washington lawyer and Jewish leader with a plea to obtain justice for her son.

On May 3, 1911, attorney Simon Wolf wrote President William H. Taft a three-page typescript letter about the case. Taft immediately forwarded Wolf's letter to the secretary of war with a request that he verify the details. He added that it was difficult for him to read Garrard's comments "with patience and without condemnatory words that had better not be written . . . The statements made . . . are not true with reference to the standing that Jews have in this country; and I resent, as Commander in Chief of the Army and the Navy, that any officer of either should permit himself in an official document to give evidence of such unfounded and narrow race prejudice." Secretary of War Jacob M. Dickinson responded the next day that he agreed wholeheartedly but that Bloom had failed the exam. Nevertheless, "to show that the Department has no sympathy whatever" with anti-Semitism, he would permit him to take the final examination that fall. But Taft did not let the matter rest and asked the secretary to discipline Garrard. A strong letter of reprimand accordingly was sent. The *Army and Navy Journal* complained that Garrard's remarks were confidential and that Taft had been too harsh. It supported its position on this case by quoting El-tinge's anti-Semitic comments.[54]

Bloom's grades markedly improved in the fall examination, and he scored high enough to obtain a commission. In October 1911 he became a second lieutenant of field artillery before he was twenty-one years old. His early days in the officer corps were not easy. Youthful indiscretions accounted for some of the trouble, but one ill-timed drinking spree and running up debts were serious matters. Unfortunately for him, his first regimental commander was the same officer who, as his battalion com-mander at Fort Myer, had refused to recommend him for a commission. Within a year and half, Colonel Lucien G. Berry had court-martialed him once and dropped charges against him for another incident only after the inspector general persuaded him that he had no case. Bloom was no fool, so he applied for a transfer, and his lot improved in a different regiment. His promotions came through on schedule, and he even became a temporary lieutenant colonel during World War I. Along with many other officers, however, he left the Army after the war, ac-cepting an honorable discharge in 1921.

The man who attempted to be his nemesis fared better than one might expect. One of President Taft's last acts in office on March 4, 1913, was to withdraw the reprimand that he had urged the War Depart-ment to give Colonel Garrard. His reason was "the excellent record of this officer both before and after the occurrence." Thirteen months later, Garrard retired.[55]

✴

During the two decades between the Spanish-American War and World War I, racism was on the rise in American society. In this charged atmo-sphere, the position of blacks in the Army was threatened. In 1901, when the Army expanded from twenty-five to thirty infantry regiments and from ten to fifteen cavalry regiments, none were added to the two regiments of blacks in each branch. Efforts by black leaders to add blacks to the new artillery units failed, and the percentage of black regulars thus decreased.

In fact from 1906 to 1916, proposals to eliminate blacks from the Army were presented in Congress annually. None of these bills actually came to a vote, and the War Department officially showed no interest in eliminating the 24th and 25th Infantry and the Ninth and Tenth Cavalry regiments. Nevertheless, the Army bent to the pressure of prevailing social mores. In November 1916, for example, when the War Department prepared to bring out another edition of C. C. Lyon's pamphlet about a recruit's experience at Columbus Barracks, the adjutant general ordered one revision—the cropping of two blacks from comparison photographs of ten recruits on the day of enlistment and after a dozen days of training.

In 1903 Captain Charles Young, the ranking black officer among the three who held commissions in the line, appealed to an audience at Stanford University: "All the Negro asks is a white man's chance; will you give it?" The fact that no other blacks were commissioned in the combat branches after Davis and Green in 1901 until World War I was one answer to his question. Another was inherent in a comment made by the adjutant general in 1910: "our colored soldiers . . . are treated in every way precisely the same as our white soldiers." While this was true in regard to pay, rations, training, and general duties, it indicated blindness to the true dimensions of the race problem.

Despite excellent records in combat during the Spanish war and the fighting in the Philippines, despite the fact that their desertion rate year in and year out was much lower than in white units, despite any soldierly achievement, blacks were considered inferior by most whites, and this basic assumption established and maintained their position in or out of the Army. This meant, as an officer reported on conditions in El Paso, Texas, in 1900, "A negro soldier in uniform is frequently subjected to insult though behaving with perfect propriety for no other reason than his color." Coupled with this bigotry on the part of many was fear. The stationing of black units became increasingly difficult, since white communities usually protested when news of the imminent move of black troops into nearby forts became known.[56]

When the Army abandoned Fort Niobrara, Nebraska, in 1906, three

TOP ROW SHOWS 10 RECRUITS THE DAY THEY ENLISTED.
BOTTOM ROW SHOWS SAME 10 MEN, IN THE SAME RELATIVE POSITIONS, AFTER 12 DAYS UNDER THE DRILL
SERGEANTS.

Although a few blacks remained in the Army throughout the peacetime years, the official attitude was changing, as indicated by the editorial comment on this illustration in the Army publication *Experience of a Recruit in the United States Army*, originally published in 1916. Courtesy of the National Archives.

companies of the garrison moved to Fort Brown, in Brownsville, Texas, on the Rio Grande River. Since part of the all-black 25th was already at Fort Bliss in El Paso, another Texas post was a logical location for Companies B, C, and D. When Senator Charles A. Culbertson appealed the decision, Secretary of War Taft refused to reconsider but explained his reasoning at length. He pointed out that prejudice has brought about objections "no matter where colored troops are sent." Yet they "are quite as well disciplined and behaved as the average of other troops." Indeed, they might cause less trouble, since they were less prone to drunkenness, the most frequent cause of trouble, than white soldiers. He added a hopeful note: "It has sometimes happened that communities which objected to the coming of colored soldiers have, on account of their good conduct, entirely changed their view." Such was not the case with Brownsville.[57]

Despite protests from the governor and other Texans, the War Department also planned to send the 25th to the Texas militia maneuver camp in July. When he heard of this, the commanding officer of the 25th, Colonel Ralph W. Hoyt, registered his second protest about the assignment to Brown and added a strong complaint about being sent to the maneuver camp. He also forwarded letters from several of the officers and the chaplain. In the fall of 1903, before Hoyt came to the regiment, at a joint maneuver at Fort Riley, Texas militiamen had threatened and abused the soldiers of the 25th to the point that open warfare almost broke out. These officers recalled those events and predicted trouble if the orders were carried out. The only black officer in the regiment, Chaplain Theophilus Steward, went further as he flatly asserted: "Texas, I fear means a *quasi* battleground for the 25th Infantry."[58]

The Army relented as far as the maneuver was concerned but did not give up the transfer to Fort Brown. Foreboding aside, orders were orders, so Major Charles W. Penrose and some 170 officers and men of his battalion arrived in Brownsville in late July. From the moment they got off the train, the animosity of the community was obvious. Aside from the segregated bars and overt hostility, several incidents brought the situation to an explosive point. Within a couple of weeks, a customs inspector pistol whipped "in the manner of the South" (as a later investigating officer described it) a soldier who he said had jostled his wife on the sidewalk. Another customs inspector pushed a soldier into the Rio Grande because he did not move promptly. Then, as they began their third week, a local matron claimed that a soldier had attempted to attack her.

About ten minutes after midnight on August 13, 1906, the night after the last incident, shots rang out. A mob of perhaps nine to fifteen men roamed the streets near the fort and killed a bartender and wounded a policeman. The sergeant of the guard, who assumed the garrison was under attack, ordered the bugler to sound "Call to Arms." Within a few minutes all was quiet, and roll calls revealed no absences. NCOs swore that they had found no rifles missing when they unlocked the racks to arm their men at the sound of the alarm.

By the time an inspector general from Southwestern Division headquarters arrived four days later, even Major Penrose had come around to believing that some of his men were involved, although, after hearing additional testimony, he reversed himself again. Major Augustus P. Blocksom interviewed the officers and assorted civilians but apparently did not talk with any of the soldiers. He and the later investigating officers started from the premise that the mob consisted of soldiers. For them the only question was which of the soldiers were involved. At any rate, both soldiers and civilians got what they wanted when, within a month after their arrival, the Army moved the battalion to Fort Reno, Oklahoma. But the troubles of the soldiers were just beginning, as Blocksom recommended that all be discharged if none came forward to confess or named those who took part in the raid.

Before the Army pursued the investigation, the local grand jury discovered over a three-week period that no one could identify any specific person; hence there were no indictments. In late September, another inspector general looked into the case. This time he talked with many of the soldiers but to no avail. By this time President Theodore Roosevelt was irate. He ordered Brigadier General Ernest A. Garlington, the inspector general, to go out to Reno and make it clear that if no one came forward all enlisted men would be discharged "without honor" and barred from enlistment in any of the services and from any federal employment. Garlington interviewed every one of the soldiers and came away convinced that there was a "conspiracy of silence." Later he admitted that he would not believe a black under oath anyway.

In early November the Army carried out the threat and discharged all 167 men present that August night. More than half had more than five years of service, and ten had served fifteen or more years. War Department Special Order no. 266 thus wiped out what Major Penrose, who had served in three white regiments before coming to the 25th, called "the best drilled and best disciplined battalion that I have ever seen in the Army."

Aside from the black community, there were cries of outrage from the white press—the *Evening Post,* the *Sun,* and the *World* in New York and the Springfield, Massachusetts, *Republican* excoriated the Army for taking such action without a trial. In his annual report, Secretary Taft used all of his lawyerly skill to argue that a "discharge without honor" was not a punishment, but this did not mollify critics. In early 1907

Major Penrose and the officer of the guard the night of the raid, Captain Edgar A. Macklin, were court-martialed but acquitted of charges of negligence. Later Senator Joseph B. Foraker, a Civil War veteran from Ohio, took up the case and went over the details in a lengthy Senate hearing. Although the majority supported the Army's decision, Foraker led the minority, which pointed out the confused and inconsistent testimony of the civilians and the injustice of the group punishment.

One of Roosevelt's last acts in office was to authorize a court of inquiry, which eventually reported in March 1910. These officers simply confirmed the Army's position but did name fourteen men who could reenlist. All but one did within three months and were given back pay from the date of their discharge to the time of their reenlistment. More than sixty years later, in 1972, the Army, prodded by Congressman Augustus F. Hawkins, upgraded the discharges of the remaining 153 to honorable. There were two survivors: Edward Warfield, who was one of those permitted to reenlist; and Dorsie Willis, who had spent fifty-nine years shining shoes in a Minneapolis barbershop. The latter lived to collect a $25,000 payment from the government the next year. When asked, he summed up the case: "None of us said anything 'cause we didn't have anything to say."

No one will ever know who did the shooting that night in Brownsville. To be sure, no one was ever tried for it. Even such a staunch champion of the Army as the *Army and Navy Journal* was offended by the way this case was handled. After the announcement of the dismissal, an editorial writer nevertheless still put the Army first: "The fate of a few score of soldiers is of less concern to us than the fair fame of the Army and its reputation for doing exact justice." Later, after applauding Senator Foraker's efforts on behalf of the soldiers, however, the *Journal* editorialized: "The great mistake was in treating the men of the 25th Infantry as a lot of 'plantation niggers,' instead of as soldiers."[59]

What made this case such an appalling example of racism and mistreatment of blacks was the very different way in which the Army handled two somewhat similar cases involving white troops. In August 1904, when friction developed between regulars and civilians during a maneuver camp at Athens, Ohio, about 100 soldiers marched into town and shot and killed one man and wounded three others. In this instance, 3 admitted taking part and named others. Yet, in stark contrast to his handling of the Brownsville case, Secretary Taft was prompt to offer legal defense for the soldiers who were charged.

The other case was more similar, as older officers in the Army recalled and the *New York Evening Post* explained. In 1891 a mob from Fort Walla Walla went into town, broke into the jail, and lynched a gambler accused of shooting a soldier. When no one confessed or offered to name anyone, the general who headed the board of inquiry advocated discharging all the men in the garrison. The acting judge advocate general overruled him. Meantime, the commanding officer was court-martialed and found guilty of negligence. Shortly after the Brownsville decision was announced in November 1906, the *Army and Navy Journal* reprinted the *Evening Post* article, comparing the Walla Walla case with the Brownsville affair. Later, when the Department of Texas was drawing up charges against Penrose and Macklin, a staff officer called upon the judge advocate general for the reports of the Walla Walla court of inquiry and of that commander's trial.[60]

Despite such injustice, it is a comment on the situation of their race in American society of the time that blacks continued to find the Army attractive. In 1910 a comparison of the desertion rates showed that the black rate (1.35 percent) was roughly a third of the white rate, and this figure was not unusual in the years before World War I. Although communities still protested the stationing of black troops in their vicinity, there were no major incidents as there had been at Brownsville, but there was a riot in Honolulu inn January 1916. The Army handled this episode very differently. The 25th Infantry at Schofield Barracks entertained the Ninth Cavalry during their stopover en route to the Philippines with a dinner at the National Guard Armory. Afterward, when many of the soldiers drifted over to Iwilei, the red-light district, trouble began when some of the white prostitutes refused to entertain the blacks. The soldiers began to beat up the women and wreck the houses. George Schuyler did not want to go, because he feared there would be trouble, but an old friend in the Ninth persuaded him. By the time they reached Iwilei, the riot was in progress. Remembering Brownsville, Schuyler and his friend got out as quickly as they could, before white troops arrived to restore order. There were many arrests, but no punishments were meted out, and there were no national repercussions. Afterward Schuyler reasoned that the investigators were sympathetic to the soldiers because they considered the cause of the riot a misunder-standing. The recalcitrant prostitutes had infuriated the black soldiers with their refusals and received little sympathy because their occupation was beyond the pale as far as society was concerned. Then, too, no one was killed, and, after all, Hawaii was a long way from the States.[61]

❋

"Married men in the Army are unquestionably a burden," George Shelton commented in "The Army as a Life Occupation for Enlisted Men," but if the Army expected to keep good men for a career it would have to accept marriage and provide proper quarters for their families. Of course, this was the case only for noncoms. As far as he was concerned, privates should not marry. That same year, 1907, a first sergeant spelled out a harsher view in a letter to the *Army and Navy Journal:* marriage should be limited to a few senior-staff noncoms; men in line units should not marry. Indeed, he advocated trial by court-martial and sum-mary discharge if they did.[62]

What both Shelton and the letter writer feared did happen on occa-sion. Privates did marry and lived where they could. At Fort Robinson in the summer of 1904 a difficult situation resulted in murder. The post commander had barred women whom he considered troublemakers from the fort. Lulu Bell, the wife of Sergeant William Bell, a veteran of twenty-three years' service, had to move to the nearby town of Craw-ford, but she continued to come back on post to attend assorted enter-tainments. At a ball on the night of July 25, she and her husband quar-reled, and she pulled out a pistol and killed him. Chaplain William T. Anderson reported that another soldier had just missed a similar fate not long before. He concluded in an understatement: "The presence of these women in the garrison has a demoralizing effect."[63]

Throughout most of the nineteenth century, the Army officially pro-vided for some enlisted men's wives by giving rations, quarters, and fuel to four laundresses assigned to each company. Soap Suds Row, as their area was called, was an accepted neighborhood on posts. In 1878 Congress abolished laundresses and their provisions, but Soap Suds Rows continued to exist. Soldiers still married, and there was laundry to be done and work available as officers' servants to eke out livings. Over the years, the shacks on Soap Suds Row deteriorated until, at

Fort Leavenworth in 1897, the inspector general vigorously complained: "These pest holes have been a menace to the health of this garrison for years, and it is time now that they should be destroyed." Two years later, the recommendation was renewed. At Fort Sill, a similar situation was met promptly with the department commander's approval of simply burning down the offensive buildings. By 1905, at least at some coastal forts in the Carolinas and Florida, the government authorized the construction of new quarters for noncoms.[64]

At coastal forts, most enlisted families lived in casements—rooms within the fortress walls. In 1904 a doctor pointed out the need for more heat, ventilation, and sunlight in those at Fort Monroe. Yet, to a child growing up there, the casements were warm in the winter, cool in the summer—"a good place to live." Roy F. Sulzberger, who was born in 1894 was one of twelve children of a Hospital Corps private at Fort Monroe. For the first three or four grades, he and the other kids went to school on post and had a sergeant as their teacher. Later they would go to the nearby town of Phoebus. When he got older, he could fish out the window of the casement. There were also swimming and the various childhood games with the officers' children as well as those from the other enlisted families. Since there were so many Sulzbergers, if there was any mischief, word went out to see if a Sulzberger boy had done it. In one instance at least, they had. Roy and his brother tried out their BB guns by taking shots at cables. Punishment was swift and sure; their father threw the guns in the moat.[65]

George L. Stackhouse did not have as fond memories of his childhood. His mother, Maggie, who died when he was eight, was a full-blooded Cherokee which, as he pointed out, "was frowned on in those days." So they did not live on post. When he reached age ten in 1915, however, his father, a first sergeant in the 13th Infantry, let him come to live with him during the summer. He took part in formations, went on the practice marches with the soldiers, and was generally accepted.[66]

Education was a problem for parents. As a rule, there were not very many children at even the largest posts; hence it was difficult to maintain a school. Schools in nearby towns offered the solution. Statistics from the Department of Texas in 1904 give an idea of the dimensions of this situation. There were only ninety-six children in six posts, ranging from twenty-four each at Fort Sam Houston and Fort Sill to one at Fort Logan H. Roots. Five others had no children present. Forty-four of those ninety-six children went off post to school. By 1910 there were no post schools, so all the children had to go to civilian schools.[67]

The one outstanding exception was the garrison at West Point, where there were a lot of children—293 (including 230 from enlisted families) in 1907. Although it was not a particularly large post, the soldiers there were permanently stationed. Many were artisans, mechanics, and laborers who maintained the post. Some of them had been born on post, and a few could count three generations in the service of the Academy. The school building was inadequate for the 130 children in the first eight grades; the 45 teenagers went to high school in Highland Falls. Nor were the four soldier teachers considered adequate. Finally, in 1908, after several annual appeals, Congress authorized hiring civilian teachers.

Robert Johnson was one of some twenty black children on post. His parents, Robert and Armead Johnson, kept him busy. His father, a bugler in the cavalry troop who did not make corporal until Bob was eleven, was strict. He taught his only child "to never lie . . . if you're wrong, take the consequences." He also taught him to ride when he was five and had him cleaning out stables and doing other chores as he got older. At the same time, his parents did not neglect Bob's artistic potential; they saw to it that he took violin lessons from a sergeant in the band.

In addition to school during the week, there were Sunday school and, of course, ample opportunity to play. The officers' and enlisted men's children enjoyed together various games, fighting, fishing, and wandering along Flirtation Walk, with skating and sledding in the winter. As the boys matured, cadets helped instruct them in the finer points of baseball and football. It was a life brimming with activity.[68]

The experiences and observations of three children at Fort Warren, a fort on a fifty-five-acre island in Boston Harbor, from 1910 to 1916 provide a glimpse of the life of an NCO family in this era. Orville K. and Katie Gonder McCombs brought their children there in January 1910. As an engineer in the coast artillery, he was a senior noncom and was responsible for running the power plant for the post. Orphaned at an early age, he was working in a logging camp in upstate New York by the time he was thirteen. Five years later, in 1891, he enlisted in the

Army. While stationed at Fort Thomas, in northern Kentucky, he met Katie, a farm girl from Ohio. Several years later, in 1901, they married. Their first child, born in 1902, was Charles, followed a year later by Ruth, then in 1905 by Martha. Before he married, O. K. went into the coast artillery and studied hard to educate himself in the technical skills necessary for his specialty. As an engineer with his length of service, he was among the highest-paid noncoms, with $85 a month when he was at Fort Warren.

While McCombs and his family were assigned to one of the best NCO quarters, a freestanding brick house in the interior courtyard, most of the NCOs had to live in the casements. Lillian Auring Perry, the wife of Fred Perry, McCombs' assistant at the power plant, recalled: "I mopped every hallway in those casements" as they were often "ranked out" by a higher-ranking NCO and had to move about. She was used to this, as she had grown up in the Army on the frontier and had come to Warren with her father, a commissary sergeant, in 1904. Even so, it shocked her when the post commander made a surprise inspection of family quarters before eight o'clock one Sunday morning. But she took it philosophically: "Some of them needed checking."

Although there were only some 200 officers and men in the garrison, there were a dozen or more children. They played hide-and-seek, run, sheep, run, and other such games but also took advantage of the possibilities offered by their surroundings. The vacant casements and storerooms in the walls of the fort were fascinating to explore or to use as locations for playing house or school. In the winter, there was sledding; in the summer, swimming. Charlie loved to watch the passing ships and enjoyed sports. Since he was a boy, his parents let him hang around the barracks with the soldiers, and he was the batboy for the baseball team.

When not in school, the children would go to the commissary to pick up groceries in the morning and then stop by the company to pick up freshly baked bread. One day the baker commented to Ruth: "You children just don't know how well you have it . . . If you were on the outside this bread would cost six cents a loaf." But they were on the inside and felt very secure. It was a pleasant life. For the NCO wives there were a sewing club and a whist club. Croquet was a rage after duty hours when the husbands joined them. For everyone, there were ball games, band concerts, parades, the firing of the guns and

O. K. McCombs and his family next to their quarters at Fort Warren, Massachusetts, circa 1910. Mrs. Kate McCombs is standing on the right and her sister on the left. In front, Martha (left) and Ruth are enjoying their parasols while Charles has his baseball and glove. Courtesy of Charles E. McCombs.

mines, and, after 1912, weekly movies. When they practiced exploding the mines, soldiers collected the dead fish and delivered part of the "catch" to the families. Before the twelve-inch guns were fired, a soldier would go around and warn each family to take pictures off the wall and raise the windows and stop their ears. No matter what was going on, however, at four o'clock the McCombs children had to come home, wash up, and get dressed for dinner.

School was a problem. Although she had never taught, their mother had attended a normal school and did tutor them before they came to Warren. There, a corporal tried to teach Charles, Ruth, and two other children, but he was ineffective, so their parents started sending them to school at Hull. A boat went the rounds of the harbor forts each morning, Monday through Friday, and picked up children for school. After school they had to leave promptly to catch the outgoing boat; hence they missed some activities. The boat journey could be very rough in the winter. Worse yet, on occasion the children missed the boat. During one cold winter afternoon, a group of officers and their wives from another post noticed them and took care of them until the next boat came.

The Army was home, and its ways were all that the children who grew up in it knew. When Ruth spent the night with a school friend at Hull, she noticed that there were no sentries. "I . . . couldn't sleep because I was just petrified, being used to the post and all that protection I had there." On the Army boats, officers and their families always got on first and sat on separate sides of the cabin. The enlisted wives and their children would sit quietly and listen as the others talked. Then, when they arrived at the wharf, the officers' families would get off first. As Ruth remembered, "Nobody was resentful. That's just the way things were."[69]

✳

When Shelton surveyed the career opportunities in the Army, he recognized the significance of able noncoms and sought to reward them not only with pay raises but with "privileges, allowances, and dignity." For the highest ranking noncoms, he recommended the creation of the rank of warrant officer. The Navy already had the grade, as did the British Army. He believed that this rank should go to men who were then first sergeants, sergeants major, staff noncommissioned officers, chief musicians, master electricians, and engineers. O. K. McCombs would have benefited from that promotion, as would Louis S. Yassel.

Since he had enlisted as a bugler in 1898, Yassel had come a long way. While in the Philippines he transferred to the regimental band as a cornet player. Unlike some of the bandsmen, he practiced a great deal—five or six hours a day. He became so proficient that when the 21st Infantry returned to the States to garrison Fort Snelling, he played in the local symphony orchestra. At one of those concerts, he met a small-town Minnesota girl, whom he married. By 1911 he was the band-master at Fort Monroe and off duty led the Chamberlain Hotel orchestra.

Although Congress responded to Shelton's recommendations about pay the next year, in 1908, it ignored his appeal to create this new rank. A few years later the Army eliminated some of the specialist grades, including engineer, and made the men who held those ranks master sergeants. When that happened, O. K.'s daughter thought that it was a blow to his pride to be addressed as sergeant instead of engineer.[70]

When an article in the November 1912 issue of the *American Magazine* heartily lambasted the Army with stereotypes of enlisted men as idle, profane, and vice-ridden, an old soldier's wife at Fort Des Moines was so infuriated that she wrote a letter to President Taft. Mrs. E. J. Erazmus complained that "the public at large is all too ready to believe all the bad they hear of our Army." and such articles encouraged prejudice against soldiers. "It is an outrage! and my American blood boils with the injustice of it." The article provoked a different reaction from Brigadier General Robert K. Evans, the commander of the Department of the Gulf. While he thought it "intemperate" to assert that soldiers merely "acquired habits of confirmed idleness and viciousness" during their enlistments, he did admit that idleness was a "prominent feature of barrack life." Since he believed that military training took only two hours a day for nine months each year, he advocated a program of vocational education, including twenty-two specific courses from military-related courses to stenography. Evans' superior, Major General Thomas H. Barry, forwarded this letter to the War Department but added his own view: "If the troops properly attend to their legitimate duties there will not be the necessary time to carry out this proposed scheme."[71]

What officers and soldiers knew and presumably what few if any of those who held antimilitary views realized was that there was already in place a rather substantial educational system in the Army. For those who desired instruction in basic grammar, mathematics, and other such subjects, post schools had offered them for years. Attendance was voluntary, and so few soldiers took advantage of this opportunity that several commanders recommended their abolition. Since the Army needed skilled technicians and artisans, there were also specialist schools, which offered a wide variety of courses. Among programs available in the Hospital Corps were x-ray and laboratory techniques as well as pharmacology, while the Signal Corps and coast artillery trained men in various electrical fields. Then there were the cooks' and bakers' schools, as well as courses for saddlers, mechanics, and carpenters. The plate was full for anyone who wanted to partake of it.[72]

Besides, as many officers thought—but none articulated as well as one of the youngest officers on the General Staff, Captain Douglas MacArthur—the Army should not cater to a diminution of its primary mission. In his staff paper of November 15, 1913, MacArthur argued: "In order to make a fighting machine efficient it is necessary to devote practically all the time and ability of those involved to the fulfillment of its purpose . . . The military man needs no excuse for his existence other than his value as a national protection. Too long already has the idea been prevalent in [the] civilian mind that little or nothing is done in the Army, that loafing is the rule. Too long have soldiers been employed on . . . non-military work. Such tendencies should be discouraged not nurtured and occasion taken to create respect for the purely military attributes."[73]

Despite MacArthur's and other officers' misgivings, it was likely that the Army would establish a compulsory education program after the Navy did so in late 1913. The National Defense Act of 1916, which authorized an expansion of the Army's strength from 97,013—in five annual increments—to 217,750, also mandated an educational program to enable enlistees "to return to civil life better equipped for industrial, commercial, and general business occupations." Within a year, war made this act virtually a dead letter. Although the few months were hardly enough to determine the effectiveness of such a program in enhancing recruitment, the chief of staff in his annual report that year did comment that the spirit of voluntarism was low. This, despite the enthusiasm of tens of thousands in the Preparedness movement for defense against a possible invader as war raged in Europe.[74]

Neither the Preparedness parades and associated hoopla nor vocational training had much to do with those who were committed to the Army. William Banks, for one, had taken his discharge in the fall of 1914 and returned to central Kentucky to try to make a living. He soon found that, for a farm laborer, the hours were longer and the pay less than in the Army. In April 1916 he reenlisted and was sent to the cavalry detachment at West Point, where he found a home. Sam Woodfill had made that commitment years before. While war raged in Europe, he was a sergeant in the Ninth Infantry on the Mexican border. The possibility of taking classes apparently never crossed his mind. He still enjoyed spending his spare time hunting, while chasing rattlesnakes was a newly acquired diversion. In April 1917, when he heard of the declaration of war, he confided to a friend: "I've been practicing shooting all my life, and now it looks as though I'll have plenty of chance to try out my marksmanship on the sort of targets that we soldiers are supposed to be ready for." World War I proved to be a severe test for him, the other regulars, and their nation.[75]

FIVE

The Managerial Revolution

We had started just knocking on the door to become a more modern
Army when World War I came along.

—WILLIAM H. SIMPSON

———————•◆•———————

W ITHIN four months after he took office as secretary of war in
1899, Elihu Root articulated his plan for a very different Army
from the constabulary that had patrolled the frontier and guarded the
coasts for more than a century. It would be based on two fundamental
principles: "the real object of having an Army is to provide for war"
and "the regular establishment . . . will probably never be by itself the
whole machine with which any war will be fought." With a large force
then at war in the Philippines and a public outraged by the inefficiency
of the mobilization in 1898, Root seized the moment not just to make
piecemeal reforms but to lay the groundwork for an organization to
meet the demands of the new century. This brilliant New York corporation lawyer sought to improve the existing system, as he put it, "in
the direction of simplicity and effectiveness." Specifically, he called for
organized study and planning toward the solution of problems, keeping
up with technological developments, emphasis on merit in the officer
corps, enhancement and better coordination of the Army's educational
and training programs, and a more coherent relationship between the
Regular Army and the citizen soldiery.[1]

During the four and half years that he served in the War Department,
Root fought for the legislation necessary to bring about his reforms.
His greatest battle was for a general staff. In this, his opponents were
traditionalists whose power rested in the very institutions he hoped to
change. The heads of the several bureaus that supplied, armed, fed,
paid, and kept the records of the Army had run their own agencies
more or less independently since early in the nineteenth century. There

142

was a commanding general, but he had authority only over the line—the combat units. There was no centralized planning or coordinating agency, and the secretary of war was the only coordinating official. In times of peace, this system worked well enough to maintain a small Army. In an emergency, when a large force had to be mobilized, the system virtually collapsed. A general staff, in theory, would centralize both planning and coordination and avoid such a debacle as the mobilization in 1898.

Root attempted to sway Congress by using a modern business analogy to point out the irrationality of the existing system in the War Department: "What would become of a railroad, or a steel corporation, or any great business concern if it should divide its business in that way?" This very argument perhaps fueled the fire of the opposition, which included not just the bureau chiefs but also many legislators who were uneasy with the transition from a rural, seemingly simpler, country to the turbulent, urban nation at the turn of the century. But in President Theodore Roosevelt Root had a powerful ally, so he got his General Staff in 1903. He would also create the Army War College and begin a revolution in Army education. Then he was able to persuade Congress to make the first major change in the federal government's relationship with the state militias since George Washington's administration.

It would take time for such basic reforms to evolve into what Root and his advisers had hoped they would become. As other Progressives would later discover, simply getting legislation enacted did not solve the problem. The newly established system needed men educated to develop the planned design. An initial difficulty, for example, was to have a properly functioning general staff when there were no trained general staff officers. The Army was still struggling with these organizations when the Military Academy class of 1909 entered the Army. For second lieutenants, the Army War College or service on the general staff would have seemed so distant as to be hardly worth a moment's thought. But the institutions were in place, and these young officers would be affected by them from the day they received their commissions. In time, sooner than they would have dreamed, they would play their roles in this managerial revolution.[2]

The great changes that the Army had recently undergone were not as evident to the 101 newly commissioned graduates as the ongoing

Jacob L. Devers, energetic and enthusiastic, soon to graduate and begin his career in the field artillery in 1909. Courtesy of Special Collections and Archives, U.S. Military Academy.

Gothic building project that was reshaping West Point's architecture. Except for the few who had grown up in the Army, they were entering the only Army they knew. With more than 4,000 officers and 72,000 troops occupying an empire, it was far different from the nineteenth-century peacetime establishment. Just as significant in their future was Root's vision, which would govern the professional careers of these new second lieutenants.[3]

Jacob L. Devers, George S. Patton Jr., and William H. Simpson were three members of that 1909 class who made the Army their career. And theirs were particularly successful careers. While hardly representative of the more than 1,500 graduates of West Point between the Spanish-American War and World War I, many of their experiences as they gained appointment to the Military Academy, survived its rigors, and then carried on through eight years of service before World War I, would have a familiar ring to their contemporaries.

The large number of congressional and senatorial appointments guaranteed broad geographical representation among the cadets. Devers, a jeweler's son, came from Pennsylvania, while Patton and

William H. Simpson, steady and dependable, ready for whatever the infantry had to offer in 1909. Courtesy of Special Collections and Archives, U.S. Military Academy.

Simpson were, respectively, from California and Texas. Simpson's father was a rancher; Patton's father, who was the wealthiest of the group, had married a fortune and then managed the estate and a land company. The memory of the Civil War was strongly reinforced for two of these boys. Patton was named for a grandfather who died as a Confederate colonel. The war was kept alive in his family through books and conversation, and he even had the privilege of getting to know the famous Confederate raider John Singleton Mosby. Simpson's father was a Confederate veteran who told him: "It'll seem kind of funny seeing you wearing a blue uniform. I still don't like it too doggone much, but it's all right."[4]

Given the desire to go to West Point, the problem was to get an appointment. Patton's father used his influence with political figures in California to gain a senatorial appointment for his son. More was involved in Simpson's and Devers' struggles to clear this hurdle. Simpson had been impressed by the West Point cadets he had seen at the St. Louis Fair in 1904. When his congressman announced that he would appoint someone from his county, Simp worried, since he was

George S. Patton Jr., shortly before graduation in 1909, already dreaming of battlefield glory in the cavalry. Courtesy of Special Collections and Archives, U.S. Military Academy.

only sixteen and had not finished high school and there was another candidate. The congressman decided the issue after several interviews and chose Simpson.

The football accomplishments of Charles Daly inspired Devers to go to West Point. Since his family were Democrats and his congressman was a Republican, he considered abandoning his ambition. Several factors, however, outweighed the political difference. Devers never missed Sunday school, and the congressman was the superintendent of the Sunday school. Then, his father and the congressman were both Masons, and the brother of the congressman was a friend who lived across the street. Finally, the congressman had not had much luck in appointing boys who could complete the course at the Academy. So Jakie got the appointment.[5]

Many of the cadets in this period had attended college before entering West Point. Patton, for one, had completed a year at the Virginia Military Institute. Four others in the class of 1909 had graduated from college. Simpson's first roommates had both attended Kansas State University for two years. At not yet a month over seventeen when he entered, he was the next-to-youngest in the class, and Devers was only a few months older. Jakie did finish high school with a good mathematics program, but Simp left school to take a cram course in the village of Highland Falls, just outside West Point's south gate, to help him pass the entrance examination.[6]

In mid-June 1905 the class of 1909 began its education. Simp later admitted: "I didn't have the faintest idea what West Point would be like . . . except I knew it was a military school." As the librarian, a graduate who had become a prominent astronomer and had served as president of the University of California, bluntly put it: "The Academy is a technical school for war." In addition to various military subjects, each cadet was required to take a range of courses that included mathematics, engineering, law, chemistry, English, French, Spanish, and history. There were no electives, and virtually all the instructors were graduates. Simpson had troubles with his studies throughout all four years. The traditional West Point system, which accentuated reciting and being graded in every class every day with no emphasis on teaching, was almost too much for him. He recalled that if one got an incorrect answer, the instructor seldom explained the proper solution. Only Second Lieutenant Joseph W. Stilwell made an effort in his Spanish classes, as Simp remembered, "to help us out . . . We all liked him." Despite his difficulties in the classroom, Simp, whom his classmates also called "Cheerful Charlie," enjoyed West Point, excelled in the military subjects, and became a cadet captain his last year.[7]

Sports had attracted Jakie Devers to West Point, and he attempted to take full advantage of athletic opportunities while he was there. He captained the basketball team, played shortstop on the baseball team, went out for lacrosse and for the class football team. As in his high school days, he showed a lot of energy in everything and, as he put it, "I was willing to do anything." He worried about classes but worked hard and consistently improved his academic standing. His favorite instructor, who also coached the basketball team, was Stilwell, who had already begun to hone his acerbic trait. "He was sarcastic. He could squeeze the last ounce of water out of you, and say the meanest damn things, and," Devers added, "I liked it."[8]

Although his impeccable military manner gave no hint, Georgic Patton had the hardest time of these three at West Point. After a year at VMI, he had entered the Academy in 1904 only to fail mathematics at the end of his first year. Thus he joined the class of 1909 at the end of their grueling plebe summer. On their first night in barracks, Patton strolled into Simpson's room. Neither Simp nor his roommates had seen him before, so they wondered who this man was who looked like an upper classman in his well-tailored uniform. He promptly informed them that he was going to be the cadet adjutant. Shortly before his return, he had bought a notebook and had made the first entry: "Do your damdest always." And his efforts did win him the position of adjutant. Throughout his years at West Point and, indeed, his entire life, he struggled with the effects of dyslexia, which was never diagnosed. Aside from the problems it caused with his academic work, dyslexia also induced periods of doubt when he belittled his abilities.

He worked hard at everything he did. Athletics rated high in the cadet's universe, so Georgie went out for football all four years. Simpson really got to know him when both were on the scrub team. He well remembered practice, when "the first team would just pound the hell out of us." In games, the first team played sixty minutes. No one left a game unless he was hurt. The scrubs huddled under blankets on the sideline waiting for a chance to play. When someone was injured and the coach turned to the bench, Georgie would throw his blanket off and jump up. He was carrying out another dictum in his notebook: "Do everything possible to attract attention." But the coach never called on him. The first team broke both of his arms in scrimmage, and he kept coming back, but he never played in a game. He did earn a coveted letter, however, by breaking the school record in the 220-yard hurdles. Simpson liked him, but generally Patton was not popular. His classmates caricatured his overweening ambition in two spoofs in their yearbook. Even the commandant of cadets warned him about being too military. He knew that he was unpopular, but he was conscientiously working to fulfill his destiny.[9]

Since the Spanish-American War cadets had received considerably more practical training rather than merely close-order drill. The class of 1909 ran various tactical problems, went on a lengthy practice march, and were introduced to artillery. Shortly before classes began in their last year, they went to a coast artillery post for a week's additional training with the heavy guns. A few years earlier, in 1902, the Academy had begun to send the first classmen on a tour of a Civil War battlefield. A month before their graduation, the men of 1909 spent two days touring Gettysburg. Being able to combine their knowledge of the battle with the actual terrain could teach those willing to make the necessary leap in imagination much—not just about this battle but also about the eternal verities of men at war. As Patton mused, after an additional solitary stroll over the field that Pickett's men had made immortal, it makes "one understand what men will do in battle."[10]

The staff and faculty served as role models for the cadets. Theodore Roosevelt understood this when he announced: "What I want *is* a soldier, and I am getting one!" So he brought Major Hugh L. Scott back from his post as governor of the Sulu archipelago to be superintendent in August 1906. The commandant, Robert L. Howze, through most of the time the class of 1909 was at the Academy was a Medal of Honor recipient from the Indian Wars, and younger graduates such as Charles D. Herron, Charles P. Summerall, and Guy V. Henry were also combat veterans. The background of all these officers, including their class standing as cadets, was common knowledge to cadets. Not surprisingly, Patton tried to impress Henry, who was the senior instructor of cavalry. In turn, Captain Henry certainly impressed him: "I have never met a more charming man. While off duty he is very friendly. On duty he is strictness its self. You ought to see him ride . . . it is wonderful."[11]

Although Congress had expanded the authorized number of cadets to 533 in 1900, there were only some 400 in the six cadet companies at the Academy in 1909. Attrition took its toll. That year's graduating class of 103 had originally numbered 160. This was one of the largest classes in West Point's history and was significantly larger than nineteenth-century classes. During those years, the largest class, John J. Pershing's class of 1886, graduated only 77 members. When it came time for the class of 1909 to choose a branch, Simpson did not have to make a decision. His class ranking was so low that infantry was the only choice available. Patton had difficulty deciding between the infantry and the cavalry. On the one hand, he mused in October 1908, "There seems to be a nicer class of people in the cavalry." And the drills were more pleasant. On the other, he thought that a cavalryman might have to wait thirteen years for promotion to first lieutenant, while an infantryman could expect this advance in at most seven years. Finally, he went to see a neutral observer, the well-liked artillery instructor Captain Charles P. Summerall, who advised him that the cavalry would be better because "there was more to do and therefore a man was likely to be happier." Besides, Summerall added, promotions in peacetime did not mean that much. When war comes, the powers that be disregard rank and look for someone who could win. So Patton opted for the cavalry.

Devers wanted the field artillery but feared that his class ranking would be too low to get that choice. He had worked hard, and he would graduate near the top third of the class. He had tried to impress Summerall, but he thought it might take more, so he contacted his congressman. His earnest desire must have made a good impression, as he did get that branch—one of only nine in his class to do so. Thirty-seven got the infantry, and twenty each the cavalry and the coast artillery. Traditionally, the top men in the class were able to choose the engineers, and the first fifteen in this class did so.[12]

Whatever their choice, all were undoubtedly pleased that Congress, just the year before, had raised the Army base pay for the first time since 1870. Because of the general deflationary trend in the last years of the nineteenth century, this had not been a hardship, but with an upturn in the new century, officers and soldiers felt the pinch. With the new pay in effect, the 101 second lieutenants could expect to get $1,700 annually as base pay. Although they had saved up to buy their uniforms upon graduation, the array of full-dress blues and regular service uniforms might force them to borrow from their families. When and if they went to a tropical assignment, they also had to buy whites, including a mess jacket.[13]

After the graduation ceremony, the class went to New York City, where they celebrated by attending a show at the Casino followed by a dinner together at the Hotel Astor. Then they went their separate ways for a three-month leave before joining their first units. Since there was a shortage of officers, they could hope for a welcome. A key reason for the shortage was the practice of detaching officers from units for various other assignments. In 1909, 27 percent of the line officers were on detached service. In the newly established coast artillery corps, the rapid expansion in strength forced the War Department to set a special examination in January 1910 to commission more civilians.

In 1909 the officer corps included a few more commissioned from civil life (43.67 percent) than West Point graduates (43.36 percent). Another 13 percent were appointed from the ranks. Almost 49 percent of those civilian appointees were former volunteer officers commissioned during the Spanish and Philippine wars. And the Civil War still had its representatives. The class of 1909 had received their diplomas from Jacob M. Dickinson, a Confederate veteran who was the secretary of war, and they would find thirteen Union veterans on active duty. Since the retirement age was sixty-four, unless there was another war with a concomitant expansion, the new second lieutenants could expect a slow progression through the ranks. The year before, an official estimate was that they would spend six and a half years as second lieutenants, just over nine as first lieutenants, thirteen years and four months as captains, five and a half years as majors, and almost two and a half years as lieutenant colonels before reaching the rank of colonel. While thirty-seven years might seem like an eternity to a brand-new officer, it was certainly a good deal better than the estimate in the 1830s of fifty-eight years of service to a colonelcy.[14]

The coast artillery corps offered the fastest lane for promotions. Devers and Patton received their first promotion in the spring of 1916, while Simpson became a first lieutenant on July 1 of that year. Meantime, their coast artillery classmates were promoted two years after graduation. There were other advantages of that branch. If one had a mechanical or mathematical bent, the variety of heavy weapons and the technical (including electrical) paraphernalia that went with them as well as the recently developed fire-control system offered much to engage the mind. Thus a later graduate, Henry S. Aurand, in the class of 1915, who liked mathematics and admired his instructor in ordnance and gunnery, opted for coast artillery even though he could have gone into the engineers. For some, the location of many of the posts near major cities may have influenced their choice.

Artillery had undergone a revolution in the past quarter-century. As Secretary of War Luke E. Wright noted in 1908, the seacoast defense branch "had been more radically affected by this development" than any other part of the Army. Until the 1880s the emphasis had been on fortifications, but new technology had brought the weapons to the fore. In 1886 the Endicott Board (named for the then secretary of war) had explained the need for great change, and over the years the huge eight-, ten-, and twelve-inch guns with newly developed disappearing carriages had supplanted those of earlier days. While the class of 1909 was still at the Academy, another high-level board reaffirmed the commitment to a strong coastal force with fourteen-inch guns. The great forts would now also have searchlights and the new triangulation aiming system. Mortars and mines completed the armament of this force, which made up one-fourth of the Army in 1909.[15]

In addition to increases in strength, drastic organizational changes accompanied the technological developments. During the previous century, the artillery consisted of regiments, with the so-called heavy batteries stationed in the coastal forts, while the light batteries operated in the field. Officers rotated between the different kinds of service. The Reorganization Act of 1901 authorized a chief of artillery to supervise branch activities but eliminated the regiments. Officers still rotated service in the field batteries, of which there were 30, and the 126 coast batteries. Meantime, technology made advances in field artillery. The adoption of a new three-inch gun with a hydrospring recoil system and panoramic sights in 1902, followed by the experiments of provisional regiments at Fort Riley with the demonstrated value of artillery in the Russo-Japanese War, led to the basic doctrinal change to indirect fire and the massing of this fire.[16]

The increasing sophistication of weaponry and technique in both kinds of artillery made it more difficult for officers to move from one to the other. In 1907 Congress separated and increased both elements to 6 regiments (of six batteries each) of field artillery and 170 batteries of coast artillery. At this point, officers had to choose. First Lieutenant Beverly F. Browne, who had served in one of the field batteries, asked his former commander, Major Peyton C. March, for advice on this crucial decision. March replied that he preferred the branch "that went to *meet the* enemy rather than the one that . . . *waited for* the enemy." Besides, Browne loved horses, and the field artillery was a mounted service, so his decision was easy. The School of Application for Cavalry and Field Artillery (later the Mounted Service School) at Fort Riley attempted to give instruction in the new indirect-fire techniques, but officers needed more than this school could offer, so the Army created the School of Fire at Fort Sill in 1911.[17]

Beverly F. Browne (in shako) and friends on the traditional New Year's calling rounds at Fort Riley, Kansas, 1903. Courtesy of Louise Adams Browne.

Although the field artillery had less than a third (5,456 officers and men) of the personnel of the coast artillery, it quickly developed a special spirit and pride. In the spring of 1908 three graduates of the West Point Class of 1904 who had opted for the field shared bachelor quarters at Stotsenburg. To celebrate the fact that both battalions of their regiment (the Fifth) were soon going to be united, William Bryden, Robert M. Danford, and Edmund L. Gruber got together with some other officers one night and started working out a regimental song. Gruber composed the lilting melody while all contributed to the words of the famed "Caisson Song."[18]

In their first years in the Army, Devers, Patton, and Simpson learned in the hard school of experience how to be officers. Assigned to the

Fourth Field Artillery at Fort D. A. Russell, in Wyoming, Jake Devers began to find out more about mules, soldiers, and himself than he would have previously thought possible. In a pack-mule outfit, first of all, he had to learn how to load a mule. It was intimidating, as he recalled: "I used to dread that . . . because I wasn't sure I could do this." Under the instruction of an experienced soldier, he had to maneuver a side of beef or bale of hay onto the back of the mule and then tie it on securely. Although he was an athlete, he did not have the upper-body strength to easily heave that much weight. Again and again, he worked at it with determination, and he noticed that the soldier always gave a little help at just the right moment. Over time, he gained not only the physical strength but also the confidence that he needed.

He was fortunate in having an outstanding battery commander, First Lieutenant Lesley J. McNair, with whom he worked to prepare C Battery for a grueling mission. Their battalion of mountain pack artillery was brought up to full strength, supplied with three pack trains of fifty mules each, and sent on a 1,000-mile march from Cheyenne, south to Denver, on through Colorado Springs to Canyon City, then back and forth over the Rockies as they returned to Wyoming. They carried some rations but had to pick up additional supplies at various railheads. One of Devers' jobs was to take a pack train to pick up those supplies. There were not enough mules to maintain the 250-pound load limit, so he had to overload some mules one day and then change the loads the next. An additional chore was to clean up the camp areas after the main column moved on. He also learned how to tend to minor medical problems such as blisters, as the soldiers were also wearing new issue shoes. It was a grueling two or three months.

After three years in this regiment, he had an interim assignment as a mathematics instructor at West Point for three and half years before going to Hawaii to join the Ninth Field Artillery. There he had to brush up on the military law he had learned at the Academy and apply it in his work as judge advocate on a general court. When one of the batteries neared mutiny because of a commander who was too rigid and did not know how to handle men, the battalion commander turned the problem over to Devers. After some sleepless nights, he came up with the solution. First, replace the noncoms and bring in new ones to whom he explained that he did not want to court-martial and send men to the guardhouse except for the most serious offenses. It was their responsibility to keep the men in line. And this delegation of authority worked.[19]

Patton's first assignment was with a troop of the 15th Cavalry at Fort Sheridan. Not surprisingly, his avid efforts to make good as a troop officer impressed his commander, who wrote in his first efficiency report: "He is the most enthusiastic soldier of my acquaintance and misses no chance to improve." Captain Francis C. Marshall either ignored or perhaps did not know about a lapse of judgment. When Patton found a horse untethered in the stable, he cursed and humiliated a trooper. On reflection, he recognized his mistake and called together the man and the other soldiers who had witnessed the scene and apologized.[20]

Although Sheridan had its amenities, in particular Chicago, where George put to use his new civilian dress clothes in going to the theater, opera, and various social functions, Washington, D.C. was obviously more desirable. Patton's transfer to the squadron of the 15th Cavalry at Fort Myer paid off as he soon met and became friendly with Secretary of War Henry L. Stimson and the chief of staff, Major General Leonard Wood, in whose office he served briefly as an action officer. While this was heady experience for a second lieutenant, going to the Olympics in 1912 as the first Army officer to represent the United States in the pentathlon was still more exciting. Given that he had little time to prepare and faced seasoned opposition, he did well in the marksmanship, fencing, swimming, running, and steeplechase events and placed fifth in the overall competition. He also used a couple of weeks in Europe to study swordsmanship under the master at the French Cavalry School at Saumur.[21]

In the summer of 1913 Patton got his orders to report to the Mounted Service School at Fort Riley. Before that he was permitted, at his own expense, to go to Saumur again for a five-week course with the master swordsman. While in France, he drove his automobile through Normandy, where he spent several days at St.-Lô. He had purchased his first car while at Sheridan and would later, at Riley, attempt to take one apart and put it together again. His acquaintance with automobiles, however, did not cause him to question the future of cavalry. Certainly, the Army was not rapidly taking advantage of the military possibilities of the gasoline engine. In one of his last recommendations as commanding general in 1903, Nelson A. Miles, who had been a major general in the Civil War, called for taking horses away from five cavalry regiments and mounting the men on motorcycles, automobiles, and bicycles. While careful not to intrude on the cavalry's prerogatives, the Army cautiously began to employ motorized vehicles. As late as 1915 the quartermaster general listed every automobile and truck in the Army together with make, date of purchase, mileage, and cost of operation. The twenty-five motorcycles were not described in detail, but anyone interested could check into the data on the thirty-five automobiles and the eighty-five trucks then in the Army's inventory. The next year trucks showed their value in a dramatic fashion by carrying supplies to the Punitive Expedition undertaken by the United States in northern Mexico.[22]

Patton went to the Mounted Service School as a student, but he also taught swordsmanship. He wondered about the support that he would get from the senior instructor of equitation, Captain Guy V. Henry Jr., who had been his instructor at West Point. There was no need to worry, as Henry proved to be an enthusiastic backer. Teaching classes and taking the rugged course proved to be, as Patton wrote his father, "more work than I have ever done in the Army." During his two years there, he also wrote the drill regulations for the cavalry sword that he had designed as well as an instruction pamphlet and a tract on racing in the Army.[23]

He plunged full-force into a renaissance of equestrian activities, and by the time he left he had accumulated a stable of eleven personal mounts. The Mounted Service School had offered equitation courses for only ten years, but now they dominated the course. Officer students rode virtually all the time and then spent their time away from school playing polo, hunting, racing, or enjoying recreational riding. They studied the care and management of horses, including shoeing, but the only hint of war in the course was a few hours devoted to explosives and demolitions. Their yearbook, the *Rasp,* carried individual pictures of horses as well as students, while most of the photographs were of men on horseback. There were details of results of races (in which Lieutenant Patton's name turned up), polo matches, and horse shows. In the 1912 *Rasp,* one could also read essays about the riding schools of France, Germany, Britain, Italy, Austria-Hungary, and Russia.[24]

Guy V. Henry Jr., where he always wanted to be, on horseback as the senior instructor of equitation at the Mounted Service School, Fort Riley, Kansas, 1912. Reproduced from *The Rasp* (1912).

Guy V. Henry played a major role in teaching the cavalrymen how to ride. He brought to the Army the techniques of horsemanship that he learned during his year at Saumur in 1906–07. He returned to be the senior instructor at Riley and to attempt to undo what he considered the harm done by the "western cowboy and circus" approach to the art that his predecessor had taught. From Riley, he carried his message to West Point and then back for another tour at the Mounted Service School. There was a philosophical difference between Henry and his predecessor, who also held the senior instructor position during Henry's West Point tour. Though also a graduate of Saumur, Captain Walter C. Short was an older officer who feared that emphasis on horse shows, polo, and hunting would detract from the instruction. As he bluntly put it to a friend, "I do not care to see . . . this school become a play ground." When it became apparent that to Chief of Staff Leonard Wood sports were considered necessities, he requested and got a transfer to regimental duties.

Henry returned and soon requested government funds for maintenance of a pack of fox hounds: "There is nothing that will teach bold, courageous, and strong riding better than following the hounds." In addition to his teaching and riding to the hounds, he published assorted works on equitation, starred in horse shows in New York and London, and captained the Army's equestrian team, which won a bronze for the United States in the 1912 Olympics. His assistant instructors included such dedicated horsemen as Adna R. Chaffee Jr., Ben Lear, and the field artilleryman Edmund L. Gruber. Their efforts raised horsemanship to an art in the Army, and Patton was a most willing disciple.[25]

In General Wood, Henry and the cavalry had "an ardent supporter." In his annual report for 1913 Wood lauded the improvement in horsemanship over recent years and chided those who thought of cavalry as merely mounted infantry. Two years earlier he had queried surviving Civil War cavalry leaders as to the advisability of dropping the revolver because he did not consider it as effective as a saber in a mounted charge. After all, European mounted troopers did not use revolvers. In the same report he pointed out that "European armies, living always in the shadow of war, are devoting every energy to building up good cavalry." Henry could attest to that. He would never forget the glorious month he spent with the French 31st Dragoons in 1907. At the end of each day's maneuvers, when the mounted regiments assembled, "it was an inspiring sight to see them charge across the terrain like the waves of the sea."[26]

There was no such romance in Simpson's infantry. Although he showed no resentment of the cavalry, branch rivalry did exist. Wade H. Haislip, who graduated from the Military Academy into the infantry three years later, summed up the attitude of some infantrymen: "The cavalry always thought they were the corps d'élite, but they weren't worth a damn . . . they dashed around on horses, galloping all over hell . . . the artillery . . . would have to handle mathematics . . . but the real business was the infantry."

In Stateside garrisons, life in the infantry was, in Simpson's term, "simple." He found Company E, Sixth Infantry, in a beautiful little battalion post, Fort Lincoln, near Bismarck, North Dakota. Each of the four companies had some sixty to sixty-five men, and there were fewer than twenty officers in all. His company commander, a bachelor, shared his quarters with the new officer, and they went about the routine of drills, which ended before noon. Simp did have to attend garrison school in the afternoon, and because of his football experience at West Point, he coached the battalion football team. It was a "very quiet—pleasant" sort of life.[27]

Since he was in the infantry, Simpson could expect to go on foreign service while still a second lieutenant. With its sizable garrisons, the Philippines was the most likely assignment. Some of his classmates went directly there after graduation leave, while all but four of the thirty-seven in the class who were commissioned in the infantry served in one of the overseas outposts before World War I. Patton was able to use influence to get out of going to the Philippines, but most of his cavalry classmates had a tour of foreign service while all the engineers at least went to Panama for a brief tour. In contrast, 70 percent of their coast artillery classmates and more than half of the field artillerymen remained in Stateside garrisons.[28]

Simp was on a transport with the rest of his regiment within four months of reporting to Fort Lincoln. Although he took part in a maneuver on Luzon and later spent several months mapping in the mountains near Camp Stotsenburg, most of his time was spent on Mindanao. Camp Keithley was the base, but he reckoned that he was in the field on patrols and company sweeps for at least half of his time there. For a while he even commanded a Philippine Scout company, and on at least one occasion he went into the field with a Constabulary detachment. At night, for two or three hours, the Moros made their presence known by banging their brass cymbals. They were a threat not to be taken lightly. One of his West Point roommates, Hugh McGee, was wounded fighting them. Simpson learned to lead small detachments and to live in the jungle, but it was still a shock to have a seemingly endless python crawl over him at night.[29]

Another classmate, Robert L. Eichelberger, served in the States until the fall of 1911, but he saw a great deal of field service as well as rattlesnakes in the spring and summer of that year when his regiment, the Tenth Infantry, joined other units in the Maneuver Division near San Antonio, Texas. Trouble in Mexico occasioned this effort to make a show of strength by pulling together this division of some 12,000 officers and men. Another 10,000 collected in smaller units at Galveston and at stations along the border. The division was a makeshift affair, but the troops involved did get a lot of experience maneuvering, going on long marches, and living in tents for months on end. Eichelberger recalled: "It was a rugged life." For him, the highlight of the monotonous evenings in camp came when he "listened big eyed" to the stories of the veterans of the fighting in the Philippines. This large troop concentration also afforded him his first glimpses of two young officers with the reputation of comers: Douglas MacArthur, a dashing, aloof, newly promoted captain; and First Lieutenant George C. Marshall, who had become known as a "high brow." There were experiments with field telephones, wireless transmitters, and even two airplanes. Eichelberger was particularly impressed by how hardened the troops became, but the chief of staff, Leonard Wood, saw the event from a larger perspective. He concluded that the problems of the troop concentration, which lasted some five months, "demonstrated conclusively our helplessness to meet with trained troops any sudden emergency."[30]

When the Maneuver Division dispersed, the Tenth Infantry went to Panama. There, as well as in the Philippines, the Army perceived Japan as the potential enemy, and the regulars trained for that possibility. For the next four years, except for one brief home leave, Eichelberger served in the Canal Zone. Although some officers succumbed to the lure of indolence, he worked hard at learning his trade. He learned more about handling men, whether getting them out of street fights in the red-light district or forcing them to go beyond what they thought was the limit of their endurance on long marches through the jungle. Those hikes and a mapping assignment taught him that seemingly impenetrable jungles could be traversed.[31]

In this period the infantry's basic weapons remained the rifle and pistol. There were machine guns in the regiments, but, as Simp Simpson remembered, there were only two in his regiment, and they did not work. One of the outstanding officers of that day, Hunter Liggett, who took part in the arguments over the efficacy of machine-gun units, thought that the generally held belief that there should be only two to six guns per regiment was absurd. If the Army could get a reliable gun, it would need many more than that.[32]

Although the Army had purchased a hundred Gatling guns shortly after the Civil War, the questions of appropriate doctrine and organization for these weapons were still unsettled fifty years later. The problem of securing a reliable gun was crucial, but the process of developing such a weapon to its full potential mired down in bureaucratic complications. As different models of machine guns emerged after the turn of the century, some officers began to consider the possibilities of the weapon. Within weeks after he became chief of staff, in 1906, J. Franklin Bell emphasized the importance of such a gun in a twenty-two-page memo that recommended the formation of a platoon consisting of two machine guns in each of the infantry and cavalry regiments. Meantime Captain John H. Parker, the most famed machine-gun expert in the Army, had demonstrated what machine guns could do with an experimental squad in the Fort Riley maneuver of 1903. He had published a book about his exploits with the Gatling guns in Cuba and kept badgering superiors, including President Theodore Roosevelt, with recommendations to create a machine-gun corps with himself as a brigadier general at its head. His manner and self-promotion infuriated Bell. "He's a pestiferous, immodest ass," Bell wrote to the assistant secretary of war, "but has much ability notwithstanding and his disagreeable qualities must simply be tolerated for the sake of his usefulness." Bell did let Parker work with another experimental unit—Company A, 20th Infantry—in 1908. Again, under his tutelage the men and the guns did well, but his organizational theory of a separate branch went against the obvious need for close support in both the infantry and cavalry.[33]

In 1911 the Army gave some recognition to the weapon in the new *Infantry Drill Regulations (IDR)*. "Machine guns must be considered as weapons of emergency." And the authors assumed that their use would be infrequent. After all, neither the Russians nor Japanese had used this weapon much in their recent war. The same year the new *IDR* came out, the platoons began to receive the light, air-cooled Benet-Mercie machine gun and to try to cope with its persistent problems of weak parts, jamming, and lack of stability while firing. Such deficiencies made it virtually impossible to develop tactical doctrine for the use of these guns. Platoon leaders were given little guidance, and they had to cope also with the problems of what Parker called "an orphan outfit." Company or troop commanders did not send their best men to this unit. A tough officer like Patton might be able to whip them into shape, as he did when he took over the 15th Cavalry's machine-gun platoon for a couple of months in 1910, but others might well find such a unit impossible to train properly. Even if the guns worked, soldiers could not fire them much. In 1907 the annual allowance was 1,000 rounds, which could be used up in less than five minutes.

Meantime the European powers were making more progress bringing machine guns into their armies, but none approached the numbers that World War I would demand. By late 1916 there was a machine-gun company with four guns in each infantry regiment, but, as C. D. Herron, who commanded the company in the Tenth Infantry in 1916, complained: "The problem was to keep the guns firing. If you had all four guns going at one time, it was a great triumph." By this time, many American officers' interest was jaded. Before the United States intervened in World War I, interest remained minimal. Joe Stilwell, who was back at West Point for another tour as an instructor, tried to excite some interest in this weapon, which had demonstrated how effective it was on the Western Front. But only sixteen officers and cadets showed up at the exhibition he staged.[34]

During this period the airplane became an integral part of the Army. As late as 1911, however, when the Maneuver Division concentrated near San Antonio, few soldiers had even seen one. Young Eichelberger was awed by the sight of two airplanes—the first he had ever seen and all the Army had at the time. Except for the sound of their engines, one might mistake them for large kites. He volunteered for pilot training only to have his request pigeonholed by the regimental adjutant. George C. Marshall, who was assigned to the Signal Corps company, the organizational home of the aviation contingent, was not as impressed by the airplanes. One crashed and killed the pilot, while the other ran into a horse and buggy. After the fatal crash, the commanding general of the Maneuver Division banned all flying, and what was left of the air unit moved to College Park, Maryland.[35]

Although the Army had used balloons in the Civil War and in Cuba, and had invested in Professor Samuel P. Langley's unsuccessful attempts to build an airplane, the real beginning of Army aviation came in 1907, when the chief signal officer created the Aeronautical Division with Captain Charles DeForest Chandler as its head. Balloons were the major concern initially, but in December Brigadier General James Allen published specifications for a "heavier-than-air flying machine" and asked for bids. Among other things, it should be able to average a speed of forty miles per hour and stay in the air for at least one hour with a pilot and passenger. For practical field service, it should have the capability of being transported in an Army wagon. In 1905 the War Department had turned down the Wright brothers' offer to build a plane. Three years later, however, the secretary of war in his annual report pointed out that "many military men" believed that when fully developed, "mechanical flight . . . will profoundly affect modern warfare."[36]

Benny Foulois was one of those believers. Just back from the Philippines, he had become interested in the potential of air warfare as a student at the Infantry and Cavalry School. The next year, 1907, while attending the Signal Corps School, he went into detail in his thesis, "The Tactical and Strategical Value of Dirigible Balloon and Aerodynamical Flying Machines." The reconnaissance and artillery-spotting possibilities seemed obvious to him, as did the likelihood that there would be great battles between aerial fleets. He even had the audacity to predict that an air force would replace horse cavalry.[37]

In 1908 Foulois and two West Pointers, Frank P. Lahm and Thomas E. Selfridge, were the cutting edge of Army aviation. At first they mastered the dirigible that had just been purchased. Lahm, a lanky cavalryman, outranked the others and had considerable experience in ballooning as well as having observed aerial activities in Europe. Selfridge, a field artilleryman, had the advantage of having worked on some aeronautical experiments with Alexander Graham Bell. Benny, however, was an enthusiastic learner. From July 1908 to October 1909, he made fifty-five flights in free balloons and dirigibles. In August 1908 Orville Wright brought his plane to Fort Myer. Although the turnouts to see the airplane were sizable, they were not as large as the crowds at the regular weekend cavalry exhibitions. Foulois was one of those thrilled to see for the first time a heavier-than-air flight. A few days later, he had to leave to take the dirigible to Missouri. On September 9 Wright chose his friend Lahm to be his first passenger on a six-minute hop and proceeded over the next week to break nine world records. Unfortunately when Selfridge flew with Wright on September 17, a defective propeller caused the plane to dive into the ground. Selfridge was killed, and Orville was severely injured.[38]

After he recuperated, Wright brought a new plane to Fort Myer in June 1909. Benny donned coveralls and helped assemble this machine. July 27 started out windy and rainy but cleared in the afternoon. Lahm took the seat next to Wright, and they catapulted into the air at 6:35. For the first ten minutes, the eight-inch string with a small weight that Orville had attached to the horizontal bar between the skids to indicate balance wobbled a good deal, and both fliers became airsick, but the rest of the flight was smooth and, as Lahm wrote his father, "decidedly enjoyable and instructive." Their time of one hour, twelve minutes, and forty seconds set a world's record, and President William H. Taft greeted them when they landed.[39]

Foulois laid out the round-trip ten-mile course from Fort Myer to Shooter's Hill (now the site of the Masonic Memorial) in Alexandria, Virginia, for the speed test. Three days later, another windy, rainy day that cleared in the afternoon, Benny joined Orville for the test flight. At 6:46 the plane shot into the air. It was Benny's first flight, and, as the plane bobbed up and down at times, he felt "as if someone on the ground had a string attached to us and would pull it occasionally as they would a kite." Throughout the flight, he had to guide Wright over the course and to keep time with his two stopwatches. When they landed, they knew that they had set three world records: speed—42.5 miles per hour; distance—ten miles; altitude—400 feet.[40]

The Army now had a plane that met its specifications, and the chief signal officer designated Lahm and Foulois to take pilot training. Lahm had already located a better landing field at College Park for their base. But the acting chief signal officer, who was also president of the Aeronautical Board, Major George O. Squier, sent Foulois to observe aviation activities in France and Germany. This decision enraged both officers. Lahm, who was already acquainted with European flying circles, thought that Squier had done this because he knew that "I do not think much of him." Foulois, who wanted very much to be one of the first two rated military pilots, thought that he was being punished for his criticism of balloons. Thus, the first officer to solo—on October 26—under Wilbur Wright's tutelage was Second Lieutenant Frederic E. Humphreys, a West Point trained engineer who had been assigned to the Aeronautical Board in June. Lahm followed him a few minutes later.[41]

Benny got back a few days before the others soloed, and he was able to get in some instruction before Lahm cracked up the plane in early November. Then the cavalryman and Humphreys had to return to their units while Foulois took the repaired plane and eight soldiers to Fort Sam Houston, where they hoped the weather would be more conducive to flying. On March 2 he took the plane up for his first solo—seven and half minutes. He reached an altitude of 150 feet and awed spectators as he soared around the parade ground. After he landed, someone asked: "Was it difficult breathing up there?" He followed up with three more flights that day, but a broken fuel line brought him down hard and ended flying for a few days. During that month he made ten other flights and suffered through more rough landings and another crash. But with the help of a "lively correspondence" with the Wrights, he taught himself to fly. When later asked how he lived through those early flying days, he responded that "anyone who lived through the fighting in the Philippines could live through anything."[42]

It was an exciting year for Foulois. In August 1910 he even put wheels on the machine and duly noted in his monthly report: "One of the unpleasant features in landing on wheels is the difficulty experienced in stopping the machine." When he was not flying he was working to get the plane back in the air. He soon exhausted the $150 maintenance stipend and dipped into his own funds for double that amount (a

The Army Air arm: one pilot—Benjamin D. Foulois (second from right)—a civilian mechanic, and five soldiers, including Vernon Burge (second from left) at Fort Sam Houston, Texas, 1910–11. Courtesy of the National Archives.

month and half of his pay) for parts. Secretary of War Dickinson pressed Congress for more funds, emphasizing "that all European first-class powers are devoting a great deal of attention to the subject of military aeronautics . . . while the United States is practically at a standstill." Indeed, Benny, his small detail of soldiers, and their airplane were, as the secretary indicated in his annual report, the entire United States military aviation force except for one licensed balloonist, a small dirigible, and three captive balloons.[43]

In the fall of 1910 the *Army and Navy Journal* laid the blame for the inadequacy of the aviation program on congressional parsimony. Admittedly, "Predictions that battleships would be wrecked, forts and cities destroyed by a rain of explosives, were exaggerated enough to turn away, rather than stimulate Congressional interest." Nevertheless "the time has come when in our Army and Navy there should be developed a body of young men trained in the manipulation of airships of all kinds." In March 1911 Congress came through with $125,000, five times larger than any previous appropriation. This sum was paltry, however, in a period when England, France, and Germany were annually spending more than a million dollars on military aviation.[44]

It was a start, nevertheless, and the Army purchased additional aircraft and assigned more officers to flight training. Among the latter were two West Pointers, Second Lieutenants Thomas D. Milling and Henry H. Arnold. Milling was the first man from the class of 1909 to go into aviation, to be followed by five others before the United States intervened in World War I. Meantime Frank Lahm introduced aviation in the Philippines. After completing the Mounted Service School course in 1911, Lahm had returned to the Seventh Cavalry at Fort William McKinley. The Army shipped a plane and instructed him to set up a flying school in 1912. By the fall of the next year he thought aviation was on firm enough footing for him to return to troop duties. He had been in a couple of crashes and confided to his father: "I have done my share . . . In case of war, if they need me, I will go back to it." When war began in Europe in the summer of 1914, there were 18 officers and 104 enlisted men on aviation duty in the American Army, and there had been 15 planes in inventory at the end of the previous year.[45]

While it was a struggle simply to keep planes flyable and stay alive in the process, these pioneers began experiments that would expand the potential of military aircraft. Foulois was particularly interested in radio, and on a flight along the Mexican border he succeeded in contacting signal corps stations. Milling piloted the plane while Captain Chandler fired on ground targets with a machine gun. Lieutenants Paul W. Beck and Myron S. Crissy designed a sight and dropped thirty-six-pound bombs from 1,500 feet and almost hit the target. In the Philippines, Lahm took time from training students to try taking off and landing with pontoons in place of wheels on Manila Bay. After the demonstration of successful takeoffs and landings on the deck of a ship in 1910 and 1911, the Navy also began to move into the air. In 1913 Lieutenant John H. Towers made the first scouting flight during a fleet exercise.[46]

With the increase in activities, the death rate rose. By the end of 1913, eleven officers and one noncommissioned officer had been killed in accidents, seven of them that year. Congress recognized the dangers of this profession by authorizing giving lieutenants the rank and pay of one higher grade plus hazardous-duty pay as pilots. That same act of July 18, 1914, specified that only unmarried lieutenants under the age of thirty were eligible for pilot training. This constraint worried the chief signal officer, who had the responsibility for the newly created Aviation Section, in that it severely limited the selection pool. He also had to consider that virtually all these officers came from the line; hence under the strict provisions of the so-called Manchu Law they could serve only four years before they had to return to their original branch.[47]

By 1916 the flight school, which had been moved from College Park to North Island, near San Diego, was flourishing, and Foulois commanded the First Aero Squadron of Curtiss planes, which were not armed but at least did not look like kites. Meantime one of the senior Signal Corps captains, Billy Mitchell, became temporary head of the Aviation Section and began to take private flying lessons. Among those who earned a pilot's rating at North Island that year was Carl Spaatz. A few months later, while stationed at Fort Sam Houston, he started dating Ruth Harrison. When they began to be serious, her cavalryman father complained: "he's in that fly by night thing . . . It will never amount to anything. He'll never amount to anything." Regardless of the colonel's misgivings, Ruth married her airman shortly before he sailed for France in the summer of 1917.[48]

✸

Some senior officers had always fretted about the marriage of young officers. In 1915 the General Staff even considered barring the marriage of second lieutenants on the basis that it interfered with their work and was "too expensive a luxury." A dozen years earlier, one of the most powerful officers in the Army, Major General Henry C. Corbin, had led the fight to keep junior officers single. Others joined in with the argument that married lieutenants lost interest in their profession when caught up in domestic life or that they and their wives received special privileges. Throughout the debate, nature took its course, and lieutenants continued to marry.[49]

George Patton married less than a year after his graduation in a society wedding complete with the crossed sabers of groomsmen and the traditional cutting of the cake with his sword. Guests must have been impressed and perhaps moved when the orchestra played "The Star-

Spangled Banner" after his bride cut the cake. The transition to Army wife was particularly jarring for Beatrice Ayer Patton. After a honeymoon in England, she and George began their Army life together in a small set of quarters at Fort Sheridan, Illinois. They had known each other since childhood, and their families were friends. Both had had the privileged youth of the rich, but the Ayers were much wealthier than the Pattons. When her father failed in his effort to persuade George to give up the Army, he endowed his daughter with a sizable monthly allowance. Aside from the quarters, Beatrice was not enthusiastic about some of the other officers and their wives. She was shocked when she started to drop in on the neighbors to see the husband bolt out of the door followed closely by his wife waving a rolling pin above her head. It was a relief to return to the family mansion and summer home in Massachusetts when her husband went on a maneuver in Wisconsin.

Quarters were better at Fort Myer, and Washington was more interesting to the Pattons than Chicago, while a maid and chauffeur added to the graciousness of their life. Servants and a car were luxuries that perhaps only 10 percent of American families could afford. Beatrice, however, did not become entirely reconciled to the world of the Army until they moved to Fort Riley. There she experienced a "waking up"—a recognition of the possibilities of discovering and appreciating what the Flint Hills of Kansas—and by inference any locale—had to offer. Far different from the Boston area that she knew so well, in this landscape she came to understand that what had been alien and barren to her had been a prehistoric seabed. Then, too, she found in a captain's wife a friend who made her feel at home in the Army.[50]

Another bride of this era, Carolyn Richards, the daughter of a Seattle banker, adjusted to the Army more readily than Beatrice. Married to Sherburne Whipple in 1908, she appreciated the camaraderie and the regimental spirit and enjoyed their Philippines tour, but she did not find Madison Barracks as pleasant. Their quarters were a hundred years old and poorly insulated, so winters were grueling. There was bowling, and, one winter when Lake Ontario froze over, she and her husband even skated across to Canada. But it was cold—very cold. Milk left out in the kitchen froze overnight, and one had to crack the frozen eggs with a hammer. The nadir came when she tripped over a frozen diaper and broke her toe. Fort Sill was a good deal warmer, but they stayed there only three months before Sherburne was ordered to the Mexican border. At that point Carolyn took the children and went to stay with her sister in Rhode Island and then with her father in Spokane until she could join her husband at Fort Leavenworth.[51]

Even so, the military life offered security and more than a touch of glamor to young married couples. Louise Adams grew up in the artillery and, not surprisingly, married an artillery officer—Beverly F. Browne—in 1907. Looking back, she reflected on the advantages of living on posts where the Army kept the quarters in repair, mowed their lawns, and provided stabling for their horses. Prices were lower at the commissary and post exchange, and medical and dental care was free. Besides, there was a colorful aspect, a charm, that one did not find in civilian life. Louise never forgot the morning ritual of the simultaneous arrival in front of Officers' Row of mounted orderlies, with their bugles hanging by red cords from their shoulders, leading their officers' horses, each duty day. The uniformed officers came out, wearing their swords, gauntlets, and spurs, exchanged salutes, mounted, and then clattered off to their work.[52]

For couples, both young and old, there was much social activity. In addition to the obligatory calls and frequent dances, which they called hops, there were dinner parties. At a regimental post where there were a sizable number of officers, older officers and their wives, in particular, might find the social whirl almost overwhelming. When Captain Eli Helmick and his family joined the Tenth Infantry at Fort Benjamin Harrison in January 1911, their social card was filled. After their first three weeks, Elizabeth Clarke Helmick told her mother about the bridge games and the constant dinner parties: "Last week we dined out five out of the seven evenings, and regretted one dinner invitation because we had invited guests ourselves; we have eaten just four dinners at home since we came to the post . . . now I shall have to get busy and give a series of dinner parties."[53]

Army children from the pre–World War I era had fond memories of growing up in the Army. The posts were "full of interest and things to do" for Tom Finley, while Marjorie Hinds recalled that "children on an Army post really had fun." Benny Poore dramatically made the point: "I felt that an evil fate had banished me to limbo if I couldn't be on a post." And Brad Chynoweth flatly declared: "I used to wish that I would never grow up." Family life was ordered by the father's assignments, so moves to different stations were a way of life. Finley lived in six states as well as the Philippines before he went to West Point in 1912. Benny Poore lived in only three states and the District of Columbia between 1900 and 1917, but she had seen much of the Philippines as well as Alaska and China. Before she married in 1913, Mauree Pickering had experienced a particularly busy dozen years, residing in seven states as well as Cuba and the Philippines. No matter how much of the country or, indeed the world, they saw, there was a constant that Tom Finley pointed out: "the Army was a *Home* which you took with you."[54]

The little ones played hopscotch, hide-and-seek, run, sheep, run, jacks, jumprope, and marbles, and the girls had their dolls. When the boys were older, they began to play football and baseball and, as did the girls, tennis. Riding was a pleasant pastime for many. Girls were apt to be tomboys. The commanding officer of Fort Crook brought a jarring conclusion to that phase for Mauree Pickering, who was on the verge of teenage when he saw her in a tree and ordered her to stop tree climbing. There were dancing classes and children's dances or hops to introduce them to the social graces. The location of the post and the number of children governed the types of recreation. Coast artillery forts, as one would expect, offered opportunities for fishing, swimming, and digging clams.

At some posts there might be only two or three children, as the Poore girls found at Fort Missoula, while at West Point there might be as many as a hundred. NCOs' children lived in a different part of the post. With some exceptions, officers' and NCOs' children rarely played together. As they got older, however, the boys played together on teams. Where there are boys there is, inevitably, some fighting. Bernard Byrne fought every day with another officer's boy. A sergeant's son bloodied Brad Chynoweth's nose, but the only repercussion was that his father started giving him boxing lessons. Jack Hines's black eye resulted from his taking umbrage when he forcefully resented a playmate's insulting northerners after they had seen *Birth of a Nation*. And at Fort Riley, a group of white officers' sons rigged up a tripcord with cans of water that doused the black chaplain's feet as he came down the sidewalk.[55]

With the encouragement of their fathers, some of the boys took to the outdoors. Mark Clark's father introduced him to fishing and duck hunting when he was in his early teens, while Matt Ridgway's parents turned him loose in the prairies and woods near Fort Snelling before he was ten. Swimming in mudholes and chasing snakes were exciting, but the real adventure began when he got a Daisy air rifle; then, he thought "I was a big game hunter." By the time Matt was a teenager he had a .22 rifle and a 12-gauge shotgun. At seventeen, he led the smaller boys at Fort Andrews on fishing or clam-digging expeditions or took them out for some target shooting.[56]

There were chores. Matt had to clean the lampshades, trim the wicks, and then fill the kerosene lamps each morning at Fort Snelling. As a teenager at Fort Robinson, Nebraska, Tom Hay herded the officers' cattle out on the plains in the morning and brought them back in the evening. Jenny Bigelow mended her stockings, picked up the morning mail, and helped with housework, while the Poore girls made their own clothes and served as maids when company came to dinner.[57]

Education was a hit-or-miss affair for most children. Most posts did not have schools, but some had classes taught by soldiers or, in the case of Riley and Leavenworth, private schools operated by women. If schools were nearby, the old frontier ambulance, the Dougherty wagon, drawn by horses or mules took children to and from school. At some coastal forts, kids could look forward to daily boat rides to the towns where there were schools. Benny and Priscilla Poore had to walk a mile and half each way across the prairie at Fort Missoula to a one-room school where the teacher tried to instruct eight classes. The three months she went to this school together with the five years she later spent at the Holton School completed Benny's formal education. Grace Wilson started first grade with a class of Eskimo children in Alaska. A year or so later at Fort Slocum, in New York, she went to a post school taught by a corporal who was unable to maintain order. Whatever the quality of the schools, frequent moves presented a major problem, as was impressed on Tom Finley when he went to four high schools in one year.[58]

Some families sent their children to boarding schools; others tried to teach them at home. Benny and Pris Poore's mother used the Calvert system, while the Finleys cut letters from newspaper headlines to teach Tom and his brother how to read. The Bigelows hired governesses;

Hester Nolan's parents brought a University of Chicago student out to Fort Meade to tutor her. Richard Wilson was the most dedicated of the home-school teachers, taking Grace through the basics of botany, mathematics, and three foreign languages as well as Latin over the years. Nor was reading neglected. Colonel Wilson required Grace to read the Bible and Shakespeare. Matt Ridgway's father encouraged him to read the novels of Victor Hugo and James Fenimore Cooper, and Matt was able to slip in some of the adventure stories of G. A. Henty and the Buffalo Bill dime thrillers. Both Tom Finley and Mark Clark also read the Henty books as well as the Mark Twain and Horatio Alger novels. Both also looked ahead to being soldiers as Tom read Paul B. Malone's novels about cadet life at West Point, while Mark, or Wayne, as he was called, pored over military history books. In Hester Nolan's home, there were nightly readings aloud of the works of Dickens, Dumas, Hugo, or Kipling.[59]

Soldiers were an integral part of these children's world. Strikers (enlisted men who worked part time as servants) shined their fathers' shoes and leather and brass uniform items and, on occasion, were paid to perform other chores. When Sidney Graves was old enough, his father took him to the company barber to cut his hair. Mess sergeants could usually be relied upon to give a piece of pie to the company commander's son. Children often attended the colorful ceremonies—guard mounts and parades. Indeed, soldiers were interesting to the children. In turn, the men were kind to them. Some fathers warned their children to stay away from them, but it was difficult to do in the confines of a post. Despite his father's concern, Red Reeder was delighted to be the company baseball team's mascot. Older boys played on teams with or against enlisted men and sometimes were coached by them. Brad Chynoweth hunted and fished with soldier friends, while Paul Febiger ignored his father's warning with the result that he learned how to curse and smoke. Others learned how to be soldiers. Red Reeder went on hikes with his father's company and even fired with them on the small-arms range and went out on the mine planters. Mark Clark's father took his teenage son along on summer training, billeting him in a pup tent with the bugler. He also fired on the range and, all in all, learned "what it was all about."

These children grew up expecting men in uniform to be helpful.

Benny Poore was around four and Priscilla almost four years older when the rope broke on their swing in front of their quarters at Fort Leavenworth. Seeing an officer passing, Pris asked if he would fix the swing, which he did. Their mother was shocked when she glanced out the window and saw Brigadier General J. Franklin Bell repairing the swing. As soon as he was gone, she called in the girls and warned them never to bother such a high-ranking officer. That night, Benny paused as she said her prayers and asked if God outranked a brigadier general. Captain Poore responded: "Not J. Franklin Bell."[60]

Jenny Bigelow provided the most intimate glimpse into childhood on an Army post in this period. For five months, from the fall of 1902 to early March 1903, during which she turned thirteen at Fort Robinson, Nebraska, she kept a diary. She was young enough to play hide-and-seek and baseball with the boys and get into a snowball fight yet old enough to play tennis with an officer's wife and to start playing golf. Mature enough, also, to go to tea and dinner at a neighbor's, to shop at nearby Crawford, and to take dancing and music lessons. She had gone to school in Massachusetts and Maryland and had governesses, so she did well in the classes taught each afternoon for two and half hours by the wife of William T. Anderson, the black chaplain of the Tenth Cavalry, at her home. Mrs. Anderson made history, arithmetic, and grammar interesting for a small class consisting of Jenny and the sons of Captain William H. Hay. Jenny liked her and never forgot her soft voice. She also took an occasional French lesson from her father and a few guitar lessons from Mrs. Anderson. Watching the soldiers at drill or in their ceremonies or sports was endlessly fascinating to Jenny. She had learned how to ride a cavalry horse in Cuba. The first time she was boosted up in the saddle of one, she recalled: "I felt like I was going to hit the sky." At Robinson, in the mornings, even when it was snowing hard, she would frequently go out with a lieutenant at the head of the troop for the various mounted exercises and even took part in one sham battle. She left Fort Robinson in the spring of 1903, but her pleasant memories of Fort Robinson never dimmed.[61]

The friendships formed in their youth continued throughout their lives for many of these children. Some of the boys became officers, and their sisters tended to marry the lieutenants, who were the most eligible bachelors they knew. All three of the Poore daughters married officers,

Jenny Bigelow at her studies in Holquin, Cuba, 1902, not long before she started keeping her diary. Courtesy of Jane Bigelow Stevenson.

with eighteen-year-old Katherine leading off by eloping at Fort Missoula. Mauree Pickering's older sister married a captain who had courted her for four years. This was a big event for Mauree, who at sixteen was permitted to wear her first long evening dress and attend her first hop with an officer. Five years later, she was with her parents at Fort D. A. Russell, a large brigade post in Wyoming, which had nine other marriageable girls on Officers' Row and a good many available lieutenants. Mauree remembered it as "heaven," with "dances, teas, skating parties in the winter, and picnics in the summer" as well as amateur theatricals. She soon fixed her attention on Frank C. Mahin. And their romance lasted through the difficulties imposed by a transfer and a mobilization on the Mexican border. In September 1913, when she turned twenty-three, they married in Washington, D.C., and, after a three-day honeymoon in New York City and a sea voyage to New Orleans, took up residence in a hotel room in Texas City.[62]

For many of the boys, West Point and a career in the Army seemed logical. When Eli Helmick was unable to get an appointment to the Military Academy for his son, Gardiner took the proffered appointment to Annapolis but received an Army commission shortly after graduation. Major Charles C. Clark put it bluntly to Wayne: "I will support you at the college of your choice . . . provided it's West Point." So when the Clarks had to go to China in 1913, they left their son at a prep school with the promise of an appointment. As far as Mark Wayne Clark was concerned, there "was always no question" as to his future profession. Other West Pointers did not pressure their sons in this matter. The fathers of Brad Chynoweth and Tom Finley talked up possibilities in engineering, but both boys chose the Military Academy. Matt Ridgway's father encouraged him to check out opportunities in industry and construction. He even sent Matt to New York City, where he could spend some time with an uncle involved in building the subway system. But a short visit to West Point had already made up the boy's mind. Army life was what these youngsters knew best, and most of them loved it. It was not surprising that so many would be in the next generation of officers and their wives.[63]

✳

When the graduates of 1909 started their first assignments, they had to go to garrison school—the first step in one of Secretary Root's most innovative reforms. A well-organized educational system was a necessity to prepare officers to manage the continuing managerial revolution. Although there had been specialized schools at several posts and, beginning in 1891, an officers' lyceum at every post, there was no coordinated progressive education system in the nineteenth-century Army. Besides, the lyceums, with their emphasis on discussion and papers, might, as Matthew F. Steele found, be merely "a constipation of ideas in a flux of words." With the outbreak of the war with Spain, the schools closed, and continued personnel turbulence hampered an effective reopening after the turn of the century. Root considered the lyceum approach "unsatisfactory and futile" anyway, so he assigned his closest adviser, Lieutenant Colonel William H. Carter, to work up a proper education program. The garrison school, which all lieutenants and captains with less than ten years of service had to attend for two hours on ninety days between the first of November and the end of April, was, in Root's words, "the foundation of the whole system."

In the fall of 1902, Carter, who had become a brigadier general and acting adjutant general, issued General Order no. 102, which spelled out in detail the subjects, the appropriate texts, and the amount of time to be spent on each subject. Except for a few deviations, which were detailed for different branches, this order established a uniform system throughout the Army for a two-year program that included a basic knowledge of administrative and drill regulations, weapons, tactics, law, field engineering, and care of horses. All students would have to take examinations, and the results were noted in each officer's permanent record. Over the years until World War I, there were only minor changes in the program. Success was rewarded. If an officer scored 95 or above in a subject, he would receive an exemption in that subject on his next promotion exam if he took the latter within five years. A grade of 90 to 94 would exempt him over a three-year period.[64]

The next step in the Root-Carter educational system was the General Service and Staff College. Although the specialized branch schools re-opened their doors and others (including the Signal and Field Engineering Schools at Leavenworth) were established in the early days of the century, this school was supposed to be at a higher level. From 1881 until 1898 there had been an Infantry and Cavalry School at Fort Leavenworth. Initially created to bring undereducated lieutenants up to the general level of their colleagues, and, as a result, customarily referred to as a "kindergarten," the school advanced beyond that in the 1890s. Under the leadership of such imaginative instructors as Arthur L. Wagner and Eben Swift, the course evolved into a more sophisticated study of tactics.[65]

In its first two years, 1902–1904, the General Service and Staff College was a throwback to the remedial program. Instead of carefully selecting promising officers, the Army sent more than ninety recently commissioned officers, of whom only fourteen were college graduates, in order to provide them with a basic education. Although they read

Wagner's books, there was apparently more emphasis on memorization than on understanding. Energetic and ambitious officers such as Ewing E. Booth worked hard and profited from the course, but the large number of failures in the midyear examinations attracted public attention. Eventually some 20 percent did not complete the course.[66]

During this inaugural year, the commandant was not present. Brigadier General J. Franklin Bell still served in the Philippines and took an extended leave in Europe before reaching his new duty station. A vigorous man, with a brilliant combat record in the Philippine Insurrection, Bell had earned a Medal of Honor and a direct promotion from captain to brigadier general. When he arrived in 1903 he galvanized the school. Matthew F. Steele, who was a member of the faculty, described Bell to his wife: "he is so active and his life is so given up to work . . . yet, he is the best, the kindest, the biggest hearted man in the Army today." Bell was often out among the students, talking with them, watching them work both in the classroom and in the field. He played sports with them and began the practice of calling them by their first names, a break with the customary last-name formality.[67]

In addition to inspiring the students, Bell combined his own observations with the advice of Wagner to change the system by upgrading the quality of the instruction and increasing the amount of practical work. He also added to the competitive stress by creating a second-year course. In 1904 the first-year course was renamed the Infantry and Cavalry School (changed to School of the Line in 1907), while the newly created second-year course became the Staff College. Only half of the first-year students could expect to be accepted for the latter. In the future, selection of students would be based on an officer's aptitude, potential, and merit as displayed in garrison school rather than on lack of background. General orders prescribed that there be one student from each infantry and cavalry regiment stationed in the United States, while two could come from the engineers, three or so from the artillery, and slots would also be available for National Guard officers.[68]

The core of the first-year course was tactics. Aside from Wagner's work, the translated textbooks and the approach were German. Far from being theoretical, the emphasis was on application—problems that called upon the student to grasp the essential principles involved and to produce the appropriate course of action. Although Swift returned, at Bell's express request, the tactical instructor whom graduates from 1907 to 1912 remembered best was a chunky infantry major, John F. Morrison, a West Pointer who had distinguished himself in combat in Cuba and was later an observer with the Japanese during the Russo-Japanese War. Morrison was always "simple and clear," as Eli Helmick of the class of 1910 remembered. George Marshall (class of 1907) liked him because "he appealed to our common sense," while his classmate, Fay W. Brabson, summed up this master teacher's appeal: "Maj. Morrison talks very interestingly of tactics as they are applied up to date and not school book blarney."[69]

Two other instructors who left their marks were Matthew F. Steele and Arthur L. Conger. They attempted to reinforce students' developing skill in tactics with historical background. Steele, an excellent lecturer, eventually published his lectures in 1909 as the Army's first text in American military history, *American Campaigns*, which was used at the Military Academy until 1959. Conger, a Harvard graduate turned infantry officer and School of the Line (1906) and Staff College (1907) graduate, brought the graduate seminar approach to the Staff College and attempted to stretch students' minds as they explored historical examples.[70]

Situated on a bluff overlooking a great bend in the Missouri River, Fort Leavenworth was a beautiful post and one bustling with a lot of construction in progress during the first decade of the century. It was also very hot during the summer; Steele thought it hotter than the Philippines. Students were so busy, however, that they had little time for the scenery and could not afford to let the heat or the construction activity distract them. Helmick summed up the School of the Line course "as a race from start to finish." In addition to the goal of making a high enough grade to get into the Staff College, students were spurred on by their desire to do well for the sake of regimental and branch pride. This resulted in competition so fierce, as George Marshall pointed out, that "95 percent wasn't sufficient at all. It had to be 99, or at least a fraction, if not perfect." And grades were scored to the third decimal point.[71]

Although the first-year course evolved throughout this period, the subjects and relative weight given them in 1910 indicate what the students had to master. Half of the credits (500) were in Military Art, which included tactics, military history, and other subjects related to the conduct of war, with 275 points given to military engineering, 125 to law, and 100 to Spanish. Understandably, the students had to do a good deal of memorization, particularly in the last two subjects, but the stress on practical application also placed them in moot courts in law and forced them to display their conversational skills on a gramophone record. The heavy demands of the school work, as Helmick recalled, "precluded all home or social life." There were some dinners and a few dances, but the student wives had to carry on social life in assorted interest clubs and in various card games.[72]

Beginning in 1907, lieutenants could no longer enter the School of the Line. This policy change resulted from the difficulties of such junior graduates when they returned to their units, as many older officers who had not attended any postgraduate schools ridiculed the graduates. The last class before this change went into effect had fifteen first lieutenants, thirteen second lieutenants, and only ten captains. One of the most junior officers in this class of 1907 was George C. Marshall. A classmate, Captain Charles. D. Herron, remembered him as "tall, raw-boned, homely," with "an appealing simplicity of manner and speech." Another classmate, Fay W. Brabson, was impressed most by his "quickly comprehending genius." Although Marshall had consistently done well in garrison school, he had not been told to prepare, so was shocked to find that cavalry officers had been coached and even sent problems by their predecessors. In contrast, he had never seen a tactical problem before. Determined not just to succeed but to excel, he worked relentlessly. "It was the hardest work I ever did." Even though he had also to prepare and take his promotion examinations in the midst of the course, which meant forgoing any break at Christmas, he wound up as the first man in the class.[73]

Brabson's diary provides insight into the rigorous routine of that school year. Like Marshall, he was an infantry second lieutenant who also had to struggle with the promotion examination. Even before classes started, as the incoming students began to find out what was in store from the Staff College students, Brabson noted: "More and more strenuous. People go around with long faces." On the fourth day of classes, "This certainly is a strenuous day beginning with four hours hard mathematical work on an exam this morning and two hours map problems that afternoon." He soon found out that there was a lot of practical work. One of the early terrain exercises involved "three and half hours galloping to three places, dismounting and writing. It is a devil of a job to sit in the middle of a road after you have just galloped wildly to the place and think calmly, and draw a sketch." Later, when they got into the engineering phase of their course, he and his classmates discovered that practical work meant hard physical labor as they dug trenches, dragged trees about to construct a barricade, built rafts and a bridge in the tiny lake near the housing area.

Since he was ambitious, Brabson studied long and hard. On February 17 he wrote: "Study all day. If possible I want to make the Staff class—that is all I think about and I am leaving no effort untried on my part." On other days he recorded thirteen, fourteen, and even fifteen hours of studying, which he would get in by arising as early as 3:00 A.M. On the night before graduation, he learned that his best was not good enough, so he left the post a few hours after the final ceremony.[74]

Marshall, Herron, and the others who stayed on for the Staff College found it more pleasant and interesting than the pressure-driven first year. After a fumbling beginning in 1904, when the several departments merely assigned additional and, often, overlapping work to the first Staff College students, the course had become more coherent. The emphasis was on developing both command and staff skills in handling large bodies of troops in campaign. Although there were neither examinations nor grades, students continued to work hard as they attempted to master the managerial, tactical, and logistical problems. For the students in 1907–08, there was more exposure to Morrison and Steele, while Conger inaugurated his seminar approach by having them concentrate on the Civil War Peninsular Campaign in Virginia.

Although they continued to pore over their German textbooks and maps, the availability of a wealth of original sources on the Civil War in the voluminous *Official Records of the Union and Confederate Armies in the War of Rebellion* made the Civil War a logical subject for Conger's seminar. Students alternated in the different positions of commanders and chiefs of staff of divisions, corps, and armies as they refought the battles of less than a half-century earlier. In these war games, instructors expected them to demonstrate not only a firm grasp of the relevant facts but also a talent for imaginative, incisive analysis. For the twenty-four members of Marshall's class, the culmination of the course came in July 1908, when, led by Morrison and Steele, they went on an extensive staff ride over the battlefields of Virginia, Maryland, and Gettysburg. For thirteen days, they rode over the historic countryside and became familiar with the hills, valleys, and rivers that they had long studied on maps. In the Shenandoah Valley, Marshall set up the tactical problems for the daily alternating commanders and staff officers to solve with appropriate orders. At Gettysburg, they camped near Spangler's Spring and had their photo taken on Little Round Top. Marshall also gave the summing-up lecture on that battlefield. He had carefully prepared in eleven legal-sized typescript pages an excellent analysis that put Lee's ill-fated campaign in its larger political-military context.

Following this tour, the group, which had been together for two strenuous and stimulating years, broke up. This intimate association developed friendships and a strong esprit that would serve them and the Army well in later years. Herron probably spoke for all of his classmates when he said that the school experience "enormously enlarged your horizon . . . I had no conception of the big picture until I went to Leavenworth. Then everything was expanded, and it made the rest of it much more interesting." They had learned a systematic way of dealing with problems and a common technical vocabulary. The most valuable asset Leavenworth taught was tersely summed up by Marshall, whom Morrison picked to stay on as an instructor: "I learnt how to learn."[75]

The War College was supposed to be the apex of the Army's education system, but it developed more slowly than did the Leavenworth schools. Tasker H. Bliss, the first president, held that students should work at staff plans rather than receive academic instruction. From 1902 to 1907 the handful of staff, faculty, and students (the first class came in 1904) were quartered in a row house on Lafayette Square, across from the White House. In June 1907 they moved into a large new building at Washington Barracks. From this point until World War I, the college evolved under such leaders as W. W. Wotherspoon and Hunter Liggett. The classes, which consisted mostly of Army line officers, were more rigorously selected over the years. Through the class of 1917, there were 256 graduates, including a few Marine and naval officers. After the first year or so, there was more emphasis on academics, which consisted of twenty or more lectures but mostly of practical work on map problems, war games, and a heavy dose of military history. This was in addition to their mandatory work on plans in what came to be known as the War College Division of the War Department General Staff.[76]

Captain Eli A. Helmick went from the School of the Line straight into the War College in 1909. He and the other students, like all officers in Washington, wore civilian clothes on and off duty. The social life was more demanding than that at Leavenworth, as calling cards had to be left with so many officials, from the president on down, and actual calls had to be exchanged among the many officers in the city. He thought that the academic course resembled the one he had just finished, but, as in the Staff College, there were neither grades nor the competitive atmosphere. And, as at Leavenworth, he appreciated the opportunity to develop professional relationships with fellow students. In order to help older officers who had not been to the Leavenworth schools to prepare for the War College, the Army offered a two-month (later increased to three months) course of instruction at Leavenworth in 1908 and again from 1911 to 1916. This "Get Rich Quick" course concentrated on tactics and ensured that these students would have a solid background in German tactical doctrine.[77]

Lieutenant Colonel Robert L. Bullard was skeptical of the education program. A West Pointer who had achieved an outstanding record in the Philippines, Bullard was an intellectual who believed that there was more art than science to war. He realized, however, that the "Get Rich Quick" course not only sharpened his map reading and tactical skills but also forced him to relearn how to study. At the War College, however, having to come up with the proper school solution to the assorted problems reinforced his doubts about education. What finally convinced him of the value of the course was the six-week staff ride at the conclusion of the school year in May and June 1912. With a support train of wagons and a detachment of cavalry, the students and faculty rode more than 600 miles over the battlefields of northern Virginia, Maryland, and Gettysburg. The year before, an eighty-year-old Confederate cavalry brigade commander, T. T. Munford, joined the column for part of the way and brought personal insight to their study. Being on the actual ground, working out the problems faced by the Civil War leaders, stimulated Bullard. It brought home to him the difficulty a general had in making subordinates understand and properly execute orders. For him and most of the others, the staff ride was the best part of the course. They profited not only from the practical learning in the field but also from the physically hardening exercise after those long months in the classroom.[78]

☀

After World War II, throughout which he served as secretary of war, Henry L. Stimson reminisced about his two years in the same post in the Taft administration. He remembered that the Army of 1911–1913 was "slowly awakening," and he was proud of the efforts he made to animate that service. As a law partner and protégé of Elihu Root, Stimson was fully aware of his older friend's great achievements in the War Department, but he found when he moved into the secretary's office in the State, War, and Navy Building next to the White House that much remained to be done. As George Van Horn Moseley, who graduated from the War College in 1911, pointed out: "the battle was still on between the younger men, led by a few older officers—Wood, Bell, Morrison, Liggett—for a new Army and the older men who were holding fast to old ideas of organization and training, or . . . the almost total lack of both."[79]

To be sure, there were a chief of staff and a General Staff and an impressive educational system, but these reforms were less than ten years old, while older officers who had spent most of their careers in the nineteenth century still dominated the Army. Such generals as Jesse M. Lee, who had served in the ranks and as a captain in the Civil War, disdained those who "burned the midnight oil" in their military studies. When called upon to command a large force in the Manassas Maneuvers in 1904, he led, according to his aide, as a Civil War general might have, "by getting into a terrible rage, waving his hands, while emitting volumes of the choicest profanity." Yet Lee encouraged his aide, Moseley, to go to Leavenworth because he thought it would help the young officer's career. Below Lee in rank were others who were caught up in the minutiae of routine in a small unit. "Too often," a Leavenworth graduate commented, "they are busy going over and accounting for the number of cans of baking powder, or the number of nails of a particular size asked for on the current requisition." Then, some remained of the same mold as the infantry officer in the 1890s who responded to the question of what his duties were: "Mostly social." Not surprisingly, officers of this kind viewed the educated, and usually younger, officers with hostility.[80]

There were relatively few graduates (less than 10 percent of the officer corps in 1916 had attended the War College or the Staff College), and, as the inspector general reported, the educational system was not coordinated to advance them forward through the various stages into the General Staff before World War I. Less than half of the 202 officers selected for the General Staff in that era had any military postgraduate education. That is not to say that graduates necessarily had a good grasp of general staff work. One could expect them to know about the duties of commanders and staff officers of tactical units and to be able to write staff papers, but even the War College did not prepare students to serve on the General Staff. During Helmick's year at the War College, he noted that there was "not much strictly General Staff work taught or performed" by his class. He attributed this to the fact that "the functions of the General Staff were not yet thoroughly understood."[81]

One way to shake the cobwebs out of the Army was to bring regimental commanders up to standard. When Helmick left the War College, he went on a detail to the Inspector General's Department. As a new major, one of his most stressful assignments was to inspect and critique colonels. He and other inspectors general turned in reports that resulted in the relief or retirement of men who were inadequate to hold command. In 1911 another junior major, William Lassiter, was sent out under specific orders from the inspector general to look into the competence of field artillery regimental commanders. Two years earlier he had inspected the Third Field Artillery at Fort Sam Houston and had found Colonel Lotus Niles seriously wanting. Niles, a West Pointer who had graduated from the Artillery School in 1880, made no effort to command his regiment throughout the inspection, which included a tactical problem. Instead, he "treated the whole business as more or less of a joke." Although a general observed this irresponsibility, neither he nor anyone else acted on Lassiter's report. Colonel Niles was still in command of the Third when Lassiter came out to inspect the field artillery regiments in the Maneuver Division. Even Major General William H.

Carter, the division commander who had helped Root lay the foundations of the reforms, was loath to deal with the "jolly, companionable" Niles. This time, Lassiter was determined that Niles would demonstrate how he would command his regiment in a tactical exercise. When the colonel finally and very reluctantly issued an order, it was "so hopelessly wrong that the safety officers had to prevent the guns from being fired." After an "embarrassed silence," Niles admitted to Lassiter that he simply did not know what to do, and the exercise was called off. When Carter showed no inclination to take any action, Lassiter went to Niles and told him that he would prefer court-martial charges for neglect of duty against him. Rather than face that, the old man retired.[82]

One of Niles's battalion commanders, by now Major Charles P. Summerall, saw an even worse colonel when he took his battalion to Fort Myer. The old cavalry colonel in command of the post had forbidden any duty after noon. It seemed to Summerall that this officer's "idea was to have the troops do as little as possible and let the officers run wild." When the diligent battalion commander started holding terrain exercises for his officers in the afternoons, the colonel accused him of overworking them and refused to support him when he tried to discipline an insubordinate lieutenant. His superior, the department commander, however, supported Summerall, who succeeded in turning a poor battalion into an excellent one. The old colonel was forcibly retired.[83]

Army reformers from Secretary Stimson on down found it more difficult to overcome the opposition of recalcitrant bureau chiefs in the War Department. In a real sense these bureaucrats who controlled logistics had run the Army throughout most of its existence. They recognized a threat in the General Staff's coordinating function and did not want to surrender any of their prerogatives to a group of young officers who were on temporary detail as General Staff officers.

A bureaucracy's effectiveness stems in great part from how well it handles information. Root understood that when he specified that the General Staff should make "intelligent command possible by procuring and arranging information and working out plans." The Adjutant General's Office (AGO) served as the clearinghouse for correspondence and included the Military Information Division (created in 1886). During the Spanish-American War, President McKinley turned to the adjutant general, General Corbin, rather than the commanding general to help him run the war. Root recognized the obvious conflict between the powerful AGO and his newly created General Staff. He tried to deal with it by moving the chief of staff next door into the office previously occupied by the adjutant general, by transferring the Military Information Division to the General Staff, and by changing the title of the adjutant general to the military secretary. Yet, whatever the name, the office continued to control the correspondence, and hence the information.

Some eight months after the General Staff came into existence, a brilliant bureaucrat took over as military secretary. Fred C. Ainsworth, a New Englander in his early fifties, had entered the Army as a doctor in 1874. His true talent as an administrator had come to the fore in the Records and Pensions Office before the turn of the century, when he had devised a card-index system that facilitated access to the personnel records of the Civil War. This accomplishment gained him great prestige, as well as a host of friends in the Congress, who were besieged by veterans seeking pensions. He carefully nurtured his reputation by never signing a negative response. If one was necessary, he passed it on to someone else for signature. Not surprisingly, he became known as the man who could get things done. After he had been in his new office for four years, long enough to get its name changed back to the Adjutant General's Office, he evoked awe in President Roosevelt's military aide: "Ainsworth attends to his duties so perfectly that it is a relief for anyone to approach his office."[84]

No one said that about the chief of staff in those days. The first three, all distinguished Civil War veterans, had passed through the office in less than three years. Then, in 1906, J. Franklin Bell assumed the office, which he would hold for four years. Much younger than his predecessors and more dynamic, Bell was the first chief of staff to make his mark. He was able to get significant Army legislation enacted and attempted to coordinate Army affairs. Yet Secretary of War William H. Taft and his two successors were more tolerant of the bureau chief's power than Root, so Ainsworth still remained the man to see in the War Department.

Johnson Hagood, who served as the legislative liaison officer for Bell and later for Leonard Wood, pinpointed a problem in the operation of the General Staff shortly after he became chief of staff in 1910. He suggested that the general randomly pick up a hundred General Staff papers to see how many dealt with matters of consequence. As Captain Hagood expected, Wood found none. One seven-page paper, which bore the approving signatures of the former chief of staff and the acting secretary of war, was a recommendation that no toilet paper be issued. Although George Van Horn Moseley wisely did not take it up with the chief of staff, he was appalled that the General Staff was concerned with such matters as the kind of saber that should be issued to the cavalry and the color of the stripe on uniform trousers. Such matters could have come straight out of the in-boxes of bureaus in the nineteenth century.[85]

The paperwork was generally mind-boggling. When Jesse Lee commanded the Department of Texas in 1905, he complained that the various bureaus had distributed 983 different forms supposedly to help units conduct business. Aside from the multitude of forms, correspondence could become very complicated, as Lieutenant Henry W. Fleet discovered. Assigned to a mapping survey, Fleet requested a bicycle and cyclometer on June 6, 1905. This simple request ultimately received fourteen endorsements as it passed through bureaucratic channels to the chief signal officer and quartermaster general to determine whose responsibility it was to issue such items. It was in the military secretary's office three times and once in the chief of staff's office before a "no" got back to Fleet a month later.[86]

A General Staff was supposed to plan, and there was a planning division isolated from the rest of the staff with the War College. It also had to be conversant with ongoing Army affairs and gather the information necessary to plan on a general policy basis and to coordinate Army activities. In the course of carrying out those functions, however, it became involved in minutiae and duplicated some of the work done by the bureaus. While it was unlikely that he would be able to clear out all of the trivial paperwork, Leonard Wood wanted to establish the supremacy of the General Staff. In Henry L. Stimson, who took over the office of secretary of war in May 1911, thirteen months after Wood became chief of staff, the charismatic former Army doctor had a worthy ally. The most formidable enemy was clearly the military secretary, Fred C. Ainsworth, who paradoxically had been an old friend of Wood's. The crisis came to head when a General Staff committee recommended the abolition of the muster roll—a personnel record of long standing.

Ainsworth spelled out his opposition at great length and concluded with the gratuitous slap at the General Staff and by implication at the chief of staff and secretary of war: "it is most inadvisable ever to intrust to incompetent amateurs" business "that can only be managed prudently, safely, and efficiently by those whom long service has made experts." Wood showed the offensive document to Stimson, who then threatened Ainsworth with court-martial. To the relief of some and surprise of most, Ainsworth retired rather than press the issue.[87]

Neither Stimson nor Wood appeared concerned about the hostility this dispute engendered on Capitol Hill. Some legislators were already furious because of their efforts to abolish obsolete forts that were expensive to maintain and served no strategic purpose. At this time only ten had garrisons of more than 1,000. But it had not been tactful to include Fort D. A. Russell, Wyoming, the second-largest post (with a complement of 2,416 officers and men) in the Army and the pride of the chairman of the Senate Military Affairs Committee on that list. Over the next few years, Congress reacted by cutting the strength of the General Staff by one-third, to thirty officers, by strengthening the limited-term provision for details away from their units for junior officers, and by attempting to limit its function narrowly to planning, as well as by specifically barring Wood from continuing in office. Although President Taft succeeded in blocking the blow against Wood and a later secretary of war, Newton D. Baker, chose to interpret the limitation language to the benefit of the General Staff, the agency that Root called "the directing brain" was weakened. Stimson did succeed, however, in persuading Congress to combine the Subsistence, Pay, and Quartermaster Departments into just one bureau—the Quartermaster Corps.[88]

Stimson considered his greatest achievement the organization of the Army on a tactical basis. When he entered office, the various regiments, battalions, and lesser units of the Army, scattered in too many posts, were organized in administrative departments. As Captain John M. Palmer, who made a special study of this problem while at the Staff College in 1910, indicated, this lack of organizations as divisions, corps, or armies, meant that the Army "was entirely unsuited to peacetime training or to operations in war." Stimson appointed Palmer, Moseley, Lassiter, and Major Richmond P. Davis to a General Staff committee to come up with a solution.

After working for several months, amid pressure from those who saw this as an opportunity to gain special advantage for their branch and from others who tried to impose their favorite foreign military system, the committee, under the careful monitoring of Secretary Stimson, came up with a comprehensive organization. Palmer drafted most of the *Report on the Organization of the Land Forces of the United States*—a lengthy document that not only spelled out details of organization but also set general policy goals. Foremost among them was that the peacetime Regular Army should be organized and brought up to appropriate strength to fight while the National Guard should be organized into large tactical units and, in case of war, there should be provisions for additional citizen soldiery.

Stimson could, and did, order the organization by executive decree. He also collected the generals who would have to shift from being administrators to commanders for a conference in January 1913. Despite this effort by General Staff officers and the secretary to explain the necessity for the change and what they hoped to accomplish, and despite the generals' protestations of loyalty, the meeting was not a success. Lassiter, who attended all the sessions, came to realize that "they didn't know anything about training or leading a Brigade or a Division . . . and it was too late for them to learn." It was clear to him and to the other younger Army progressives that "that generation would have to pass away before much could be done."[89]

Times had changed, and too many of the older officers had not adapted. In the late 1880s and early 1890s, Secretary of War Redfield Proctor and Commanding General John M. Schofield had introduced professional reforms such as regular efficiency reports and examinations for promotion, while the end of the Indian Wars made possible larger garrisons and even an occasional field maneuver. Then, too, various branches organized professional societies and began to publish journals while the Infantry and Cavalry School began to push the limits of professionalism. With the advent of the twentieth century and the Root reforms, the level required of a military professional rose considerably. It was no longer enough to keep a post in good order with proper supply accounts and the garrison appropriately drilled and disciplined. To be professional in this period, as always, required a mastery of the knowledge and skills in one's field, and there had been a notable expansion in the requisite knowledge and skills.

In his great report of 1899, in which Secretary Root laid out his vision for the Army, he used the term "machine" to describe that Army. A machine requires men equipped not only to plan its construction and purpose but also to operate it at full capacity. Rather than depend upon the personal bent of individuals to study and, hopefully, rise to the occasion in war, he wanted a systematic approach to developing leadership. This "safe leadership" meant that officers would follow well-understood methods in staff and command. While they might not have seen a unit larger than a regiment, they would have worked out problems with divisions and armies. While only a relative few had attended the Leavenworth schools or the War College, the Leavenworth influence, at least, was much broader than that of its graduates. Beginning in 1907, officers could request copies of instructional material from Leavenworth, and by 1915 there were 4,000 on this mailing list. Among those who profited from the mailing list was Brigadier General John J. Pershing. More readily available than the assorted lectures, problems, maps, and textbooks was the *Field Service Regulations,* a book small enough to fit into a uniform pocket. As issued by the War Department in 1905 and in the 1910 and 1914 revisions, this work distilled the Leavenworth knowledge as to the logistical and tactical operation of a field Army. Thus current administrative and tactical doctrine was laid out clearly.[90]

National Guardsmen had access to this book, the Leavenworth material, and regular officers. Root had called for a better relationship between the militia and the regulars in 1899, and the Dick Act of four years later was an integral part of his reforms. Upon the request of governors, the federal government provided arms and equipment, while the states had to conform to federal standards as to drill periods and camps of instruction and take part in maneuvers with the Army. In the summer of 1910 almost 47,000 Guardsmen and more than 25,000 regulars trained together at ten different camps of instruction across the country. Army inspectors and instructors also went out to work with Guard units throughout the year. This learning experience worked both ways. Leavenworth trained young officers such as George Marshall who spent a good deal of time with the Pennsylvania units and a year with the Massachusetts militia, passing on their professional knowledge to Guardsmen. In turn, the regulars got to know the strengths and weaknesses of these citizen soldiers. Marshall learned even more when he was called upon to play a key role in planning and helping run a maneuver of 15,000 Guardsmen from six states and 2,300 regulars in Connecticut in 1912. Unlike regulars in the past, he and the other officers who worked with the Guard would not have to wait for a war to become acquainted with citizen soldiers, while the maneuvers offered the chance to deal with troop concentrations the size of which the nation had seen only during wartime.[91]

Marshall fondly recalled his association with the Massachusetts Guard officers: "They treated me splendidly." But then he and the other officers of his age had a lot in common with the civilian middle class. There were many similarities in their socioeconomic background and probably in most of their views. Progressivism, the reform urge that swept through the nation in this period, had many aspects that appealed to officers. Those who governed in the Philippines demonstrated the influence of Progressivism in their efforts to provide justice and to alleviate what they perceived as the ills of society. The reform of military organizations that Root instituted also had its civilian counterparts as Progressives created bureaucracies to bring about and maintain their economic, political, and social reforms.[92]

Some Army reformers also followed the Progressive lead in publicizing their cause. One of the outstanding features of Progressivism was the spate of muckrakers who exposed political and social ills and injustice. John M. Palmer while serving as an instructor at West Point became one when he published a story about businessmen manipulating a street railway system in one of the leading muckraking journals, *McClure's*. He became acquainted with such famed muckrakers as Lincoln Steffens, Ida M. Tarbell, and Ray Stannard Baker and even considered leaving the Army to be a staff writer on *McClure's*.

Other officers dealt with matters directly related to the Army. Captain Merch B. Stewart published two articles in *Harper's Weekly* in an effort to explain the attraction of the military and to improve the larger society's attitude toward soldiers. On the one hand, many civilians seemed to view the Army with ignorance and suspicion, while others regarded it as a waste of money. In 1912 Secretary Stimson, General Wood, and five other officers aired the Army's problems in articles in the *Independent* in an attempt to gain increased understanding and support. Later, during World War I before the American intervention, when there was a public debate about military preparations, Wood was joined by prominent civilians in advocating military training as a means of improving society as well as contributing to national defense. In 1916 Major Douglas MacArthur became chief of the recently created Bureau of Information in the War Department. He made a good impression and succeeded in getting the Army's message across. The journalists on that beat praised his efforts to "shape the public mind" on military affairs.[93]

Although he wore civilian clothes while on duty in the War Department, MacArthur was not readily mistaken for a civilian. He had the bearing and manner as well as the experiences that set soldiers apart. Whatever their affinities with their civilian friends, officers who took their profession seriously thought long and hard about the demands of war. Many of them had seen combat; yet war was not a topic often broached in polite society. As a class, officers had also seen more of the world than their acquaintances in the civilian middle class. Duty had taken them to several regions in the nation as well as to the Caribbean and Pacific islands. Some had served in China, others had visited there and Japan. Pershing, Marshall, and others, including Lewis Sorley, took extended leaves and leisurely toured Europe, where, in Sorley's words, they "absorbed culture." Although those three took time from their holidays to observe some military activities, a few others, Lassiter, Moseley, and Palmer among them, were sent to Europe specifically to attend the grand maneuvers in Germany and France, while Patton and Henry were among those who attended foreign military schools. Ten, including John F. Morrison and Pershing, had the great professional opportunity of observing the Russo-Japanese War.[94]

Even though Guardsmen shared many of the interests of their regular mentors, they differed in loyalties as well as experiences. States' rights and the militia tradition separated them from the nationalist-oriented regulars. This problem came to a head during the Wilson administration when the War Department sought to supplant the Guard as the first line of citizen soldiery with federal volunteers over whom states would have no control. Formidable opposition in Congress maintained the traditional primacy of the Guard as the nation's citizen soldiery.[95]

While many civilians probably never saw a regular during this period, others did see them putting on exhibitions at military tournaments in various cities. In 1909 there was so much demand that the War Department attempted to set limits. Since there were obvious public-relations opportunities involved, sizable contingents did go to seven cities in 1909 and 1910. The largest, which included two infantry regiments, two cavalry squadrons, a battery of field artillery, four bands, and assorted support troops, demonstrated their skills before an estimated million people over ten days in Chicago in July 1910. The next year, because of troubles in Mexico and a concentration of troops in the border area, the Army stopped these public events.[96]

Less pleasant circumstances also brought the Army out of its posts and into the public arena. While there were fewer labor disturbances leading to calls for troops in the new century, there was a notable incident in 1914 when one cavalry regiment and large elements from two others went into the Colorado coal-mining area. For nine months these troops were able to maintain order. Also fewer soldiers were involved in several Indian outbreaks. As a rule, a small show of force or, in 1916, the calming appearance on the scene of the chief of staff, Hugh L. Scott, who knew sign language and was celebrated as a friend of the Indians, was enough to settle problems. There was one skirmish, however, on October 28, 1908, when seventy-eight officers and troopers of the Fifth Cavalry attacked a band of Navajos who had been, according to the commanding general of the Department of Colorado, "causing no end of trouble" in the Four Corners area of Utah, Colorado, Arizona, and New Mexico. Two Indians were killed, and another was wounded in the fight.[97]

The Army's capability of bringing organized relief quickly into an area led to calls during forest fires, tornadoes, and floods. The San Francisco earthquake in April 1906 made the greatest demands of this sort on the service. Awakened by the shock, Brigadier General Frederick Funston, the acting commander of the Division of the Pacific, promptly ordered troops out to fight fires and keep order and make supplies available. For two and half months, the Army directed the relief effort. Food

(4.8 million rations), medical aid, tents, blankets, as well as the support of 6,000 officers and men helped bring the city back to life.[98]

In the last years before the United States entered World War I, as differences between the Army and the Guard became more manifest, the Army made a strong effort to influence public opinion as well as to develop another source for citizen soldiery through training camps. Leonard Wood began this program with two camps for college students in 1913. With regulars as instructors and cadre, some 245 students from ninety colleges and universities paid their own way for six weeks of training. As Wood confided to a friend, he knew this was too short a period in which to turn out trained soldiers, but "we do believe a great deal can be done in the implanting of a sound military policy." The next year there were more camps, and in 1915 business and professional leaders were invited. In 1916 some 16,100 attended sixteen camps for a month's training and six two-week courses. (One of the instructors that year was newly promoted Captain George C. Marshall.) Out of these trainees came influential advocates of a stronger military based on universal military training.[99]

✳

In the early morning of March 9, 1916, Pancho Villa led some 500 men in an attack on Columbus, New Mexico. Since there were some troops of the 13th Cavalry there, this turned into a small battle that precipitated the greatest crisis in Mexican-American relations since the revolution had begun five years earlier. While civil war raged south of the border, reverberations caused several large American troop concentrations. In 1911 the Army organized the Maneuver Division and held it in readiness at Fort Sam Houston for four months. Two years later the War Department formed a division at Galveston and Texas City. When the Navy intervened in Vera Cruz, Funston took 4,000 officers and men from this division and together with more than 3,000 Marines occupied that port for seven months. At that time another 20,000 patrolled the border. Lieutenant Colonel Lassiter, who took a battalion of the Fourth Field Artillery to Vera Cruz, had great misgivings about the expedition. He feared that "the rest of our lives were apt to be spent in Mexico . . . once we invaded . . . we will not turn back but would have to go

Frederick Funston (seated third from left) and his staff, including two of the rising stars in the Army: Douglas MacArthur (seated on extreme left) and Hugh A. Drum (seated on extreme right), Vera Cruz, 1914. Courtesy of Carroll Drum Johnson.

on and organize and rule the country." While this did not turn out to be the case for those in the Vera Cruz expedition, months turned into years for a good many American regulars who patrolled the little towns and the dusty trails along the border.[100]

Where the Army went, families followed. Couples made do with whatever housing they could find. At one border station, a cavalry captain and his family lived in a boxcar. Though in her fourth decade as an Army wife, Florence Kuykendall Pickering was not very comfortable living in what she called "a dinky little 'dobe'" in Douglas, Arizona. Bea Patton did not bring the children when she visited George, who was with an Eighth Cavalry detachment at Sierra Blanca, Texas. She enjoyed her brief stay in what must have seemed to her a very wild western village.[101]

After so many threats and alarms, Villa's attack on Columbus made it look as if war had come. As it happened, the War Department was in transition; a new secretary of war, Newton D. Baker, had just taken office on the day of the raid. When the Wilson administration decided to dispatch an expedition in pursuit, the venerable chief of staff, Hugh Scott, recommended John J. Pershing, who was in command at Fort Bliss, as the commander. Scott also checked on the plan for war with Mexico. He was dismayed when he saw the five or six mimeographed books that made up the largely theoretical and essentially irrelevant plan. Scott asked his assistant, Major General Tasker H. Bliss, to prepare a usable plan. Standing at his shipping-clerk's desk in his office, Bliss dictated a two-page plan for moving troops to the border and then for an all-out invasion. For the time being, however, the president decided to limit the latter to what became known as the Punitive Expedition.[102]

Pershing dispatched two columns in a great enveloping movement into the mountains of Chihuahua. He lived up to his reputation as a tough, hard-driving commander as he pushed his troops to the limits of their capacity. He was a cavalryman, and most of his troops were cavalry (Seventh, Tenth, 11th, and 13th regiments), but there were two infantry regiments (Sixth and 16th) and two field artillery batteries from the Sixth Field Artillery), as well as assorted support troops in the 10,000-man expedition. Logistics could not keep up, so both men and horses went hungry. On one occasion Simp Simpson, who was in the Sixth Infantry, stopped at a Mexican farmhouse to see if there was any food. For a quarter, he got six tortillas, one of which he ate immediately. He saved the others to eat at hourly intervals until they were gone. Fifty-five years later, he well remembered: "They tasted mighty good." At that he was more fortunate than the cavalry captain, whose food supply for three meals was three crackers. It was hard duty, and, as Simp pointed out, "there wasn't a great deal of difference in what we were doing then . . . [from] what they did in the Civil War."[103]

There were two marked differences from Civil War days, and Benny Foulois was much involved in making both happen. One was the First Aero Squadron, and the other was the truck convoys. Benny commanded this first American aviation unit, which had only eight unarmed training planes, Curtiss Jennies; but he hoped that they would serve to reconnoiter for the columns and to deliver messages speedily. On the first day, however, he lost two of the planes, and within a month four more had gone down. The mountains were simply too much for their low-powered engines and limited climbing capacity. "Not only were they inadequate," Benny later recalled; "they were downright dangerous to fly." Nevertheless, he and his pilots were able to contribute some useful information gleaned from their reconnaissance missions and to get some messages through. When he tried to carry a message to the American consul in the city of Chihuahua, Benny had to endure some worrisome moments. Upon landing, local police arrested him and kept him in jail until the consul secured his release.[104]

Pershing was probably more impressed with the 10 trucks that belonged to the First Aero Squadron than with the planes. As he was organizing the expedition, they were the only available trucks. As others began to arrive, he turned them over to Benny and his mechanics to assemble. The War Department did respond to his urgent call and in four and half months purchased 613 trucks—more than seven times the total number (85) the Army had had in its inventory the year before. By the end of 1916 he had nineteen trains or convoys of trucks making the circuit from bases in the United States to his command and back.[105]

A month into the chase, lead elements had reached Parral, some 360 miles south of Columbus. When these troopers were fired on by the forces of Villa's archenemy, President Venustiano Carranza, it was clear that the American soldiers had few—if any—friends in Mexico. Pershing organized a base camp at Colonia Dublán, 245 miles closer to the border than Parral and, over time, brought his command back to this camp and another close to it where the expedition stayed until early February 1917, less than eleven months after it had first crossed the border.[106]

Pershing did not catch Villa, but his aide gained some fervently hoped-for notoriety by killing General Julio Cardenas, the head of Villa's bodyguard. Patton had been appalled when he learned that his regiment had not been chosen to go into Mexico. He went to see Pershing and begged him to take him as an aide. When the general asked why he should choose this one second lieutenant over others, Patton answered: "Because I want to go more than anyone else." The fact that Pershing did take him must have assuaged his disappointment over the order for all cavalry units to leave their sabers behind when they went into Mexico. When he participated in a gun battle in which one of

Villa's generals was killed, he got the writeups in the *New York Times* and other newspapers that he so much craved.[107]

While Pershing kept his troops busy in Mexico, there was a massive buildup on the border. By the end of August, 48,000 regulars (67 percent of the strength of the Army in the States) and more than 111,000 Guardsmen were in camps scattered along the border. Although the president had called out the Arizona, New Mexico, and Texas Guard in May, he waited until summer to call out the rest of the National Guard. By that time Congress had finally, on June 3, enacted the National Defense Act of 1916. This was a compromise in that the Guard retained its traditional position as the nation's first line behind the regulars, but in return, Guardsmen took two oaths—one to the state and one to the federal government, which meant that, once called up, they had to go even abroad if necessary. In this comprehensive act, Congress provided for increases, over a five-year period, in both the Army and the Guard, as well as for a reserve force to include a training program in the Reserve Officers Training Corps. Finally, it gave the federal government power to regulate industry and transportation in a national emergency.[108]

While most of the regular officers stayed with their units during this crisis, some did serve with the Guard regiments. Moseley, for one, became a colonel and chief of staff of Pennsylvania's division. Although he did not exchange his rank temporarily for a Guard commission, Dwight D. Eisenhower went to the Seventh Illinois Infantry as an inspector instructor during their stay in Texas. He had been out of the Military Academy just over a year when he and most of his classmates were promoted to first lieutenant, with the same date of rank—July 1, 1916—as Simpson and Eichelberger of the class of 1909. Eisenhower was told that his job would be "to help straighten out administrative snarls and to supervise training." In effect, the Guard colonel virtually let him run the regiment. It was, as he realized, "one of the most valuable years of preparation in my early career."[109]

As Mexican-American relations calmed down, the War Department ordered Pershing out of Mexico in February 1917 and sent the National Guard home. When Secretary Baker reviewed the experience, he emphasized the importance of demonstrating the national determination to defend its border and the value of the training received by both regulars and Guardsmen in their field service as well as that of the several supply services in the Army. A particularly crucial aspect of the logistics in this callup was the health of the troops. In stark contrast to the serious health problems in the last great mobilization in 1898, the force on the border had an excellent record. It was hard service for regulars as well as Guardsmen, but for the latter it provided an opportunity for continuous service as soldiers over several months, in contrast to their usual nights in the armory and a week or so of field training annually.[110]

By the time Pershing got his troops back across the border, President Wilson had broken relations with Germany. For two and a half years, huge armies had waged war in Europe with no prospect of an end. The United States had declared neutrality but also assumed that American ships could operate freely on the seas. This worked to the advantage of the British, since they controlled the sea-lanes. The German submarines challenged that control and American neutrality. During the first months of 1917, the European war that had seemed so distant loomed increasingly near to Americans.

On the day after the Germans invaded Belgium in August 1914, Captain Hugh A. Drum, one of the Leavenworth men, wrote a prescient letter to his wife: "It is terrible to think of the affairs of Europe. The loss of life will be immense . . . Germany will have a hard time unless she can win in the first few months. If the war lasts for a long period Germany must lose." The day before, another Leavenworth man, Lieutenant Colonel Joseph T. Dickman, who had leaned heavily on German regulations when he prepared the first edition of the *Field Service Regulations,* made his more detailed predictions in a Burlington, Vermont, newspaper. Although Dickman assumed that the Germans planned a quick decisive blow in France and a holding action against Russia, he questioned its success. "There will be fierce fighting in the air, underground in sieges, and beneath the waters of the ocean. The cheapness of human life is likely to be illustrated on an enormous scale." He was also very much aware of the economic aspects of the war, yet, as a good cavalryman, he thought his arm would play a role and would decide the issue of whether the lance or the sword was the better cavalry weapon.[111]

Dickman studiously followed the course of the war, but he did not dream that American troops might fight in France until relations began to deteriorate in the winter of 1916–17. Generally, the war was a matter of academic interest to officers, who knew how poorly prepared the nation was for such a struggle; besides, the Wilson administration seemed dedicated to peace. One of the most thoughtful officers in the Army, Colonel Robert L. Bullard, was somewhat surprised when Congress did declare war on April 6, 1917. There were still real questions as to how much of a role the Army would play in the war when Congress made that great decision. Whether this was the right thing to do and what this meant for the Army, the 5,791 Regular Army officers did not know. But all could agree with Simpson: "We had started just knocking on the door to become a more modern Army when World War I came along." And all could hope that the managerial revolution had prepared them for the roles they would have to play.[112]

SIX

The War to End All Wars

By comparison with our previous wars, we made a
magnificent showing.

—HUNTER LIGGETT

———◆———

A N AURA of disbelief surrounded the American intervention in
World War I. Less than two decades after the momentous events
of 1898, which propelled the United States to world-power status, this
nation intervened decisively in the first great European war since the
Napoleonic era. When war broke out in 1914, who would have thought
that possible? And who could have dreamed of the tremendous American effort and its impact on the American people—particularly those
in the Army? Would they measure up to the great demands thrust upon
them?

After the assassination of the heir to the Austro-Hungarian throne
in Bosnia in late June 1914, the alliance system pitted England, France,
and Russia against Germany and Austria-Hungary. On the Western
Front, which stretched from Switzerland across northern France and
through Belgium to the English Channel, the war soon settled into a
stalemate despite great offensives that cost tens of thousands of casualties. In the East there was greater movement of the lines, but still neither side had struck a decisive blow into the early months of 1917.
Italy joined in the fight against the Austro-Hungarians in 1915, and the
British fought the Germans in Africa and the Turks, who had allied
with the Germans in the Middle East. As the war progressed, German
submarines roamed the Atlantic and challenged British control of the
sea.

The official position of the United States was neutrality, but as long
as the British dominated the sea-lanes, America sold munitions and
other supplies to Britain and France. President Woodrow Wilson

indicated his concern for neutrality in 1915 when he came across a brief news item to the effect that the General Staff was making plans in case of war with Germany. He was furious and ordered the acting secretary of war to relieve every officer of the General Staff if this report was true. When Henry Breckinridge took this message to the assistant chief of staff, Major General Tasker H. Bliss explained that this was what general staffs were supposed to do. Breckinridge accepted this explanation but advised that such planning be camouflaged in the future. No more was heard from the White House.[1]

When war began, the belligerents understandably showed little interest in the Americans. Aside from their naiveté about military matters, dependence on the anachronistic volunteer system, and apparent incompetence of commanders, the Americans had a very small Regular Army. At just under 98,000 in 1914, it was about 16 percent of the peacetime strength of the German army (620,000), less than 18 percent of the French army (560,000), just over 38 percent of the British army (254,500), and not quite 70 percent of the Swiss army (140,000). In 1912 the American military attaché at St. Petersburg had reported that neither the Russians nor any other European officers commented on American military affairs, as there was a "universal belief that our Army is not worthy of serious consideration."[2]

By late 1916 the Allies were glad to get American supplies and munitions, but still neither they nor the Germans thought of the American Army as a factor. Even if it were possible to raise, supply, and train a large enough force to make a difference, where would the commanders and staff officers come from? Even if all those problems were solved, this army would still have to cross the Atlantic. The Germans obviously thought it was a safe gamble in the winter of 1916–17 to risk going to war with the United States by opting for unlimited submarine warfare in the Atlantic. In the tense weeks before the nation went to war in early April 1918, the General Staff did draw up plans for a 4-million man Army based on the assumption that Congress would enact compulsory service. A few days before Congress declared war, however, staff planners estimated it would take almost two years to get 500,000 men to France. Even after war came, a prominent senator who flatly stated that Congress would not allow the Army to send troops to Europe probably expressed a commonly held belief.[3]

Nor did the British or French expect much from the American Army after the United States entered the war. Their political-military missions that came to the States that spring talked only of a division as a token force. Marshal Joseph Joffre, the former commander of the French army, was the one dissenter, declaring flatly that what the Allies needed was men. Only 19 General Staff officers (considerably fewer than had been in the original staff in 1903) were available to talk with the various officers on these missions. The demands of the war eventually led to the expansion of this body to almost 1,100 officers. In the spring of 1917, however, such a number would have been beyond belief to those few who were struggling with the avalanche of work brought on by the war.[4]

One early shock that Major John M. Palmer recalled was that talks with the Allies made it clear that the division organization worked out only the year before was unsuited to the war in France. Within a few days Palmer and his colleagues came up with a square division built around four regiments of infantry. With some 20,000 officers and men, this was double the size of the European divisions, and later reorganizations increased it by 8,000. In this way, planners hoped to make the divisions more self-sufficient and to be able to get by with fewer commanders and staff officers.[5]

By the end of May, Congress enacted the draft, which made possible the large force that Army planners envisaged and the commander of the American Expeditionary Forces (AEF) had been selected and set sail for France. Only four months before, at his headquarters in Mexico, Major General John J. Pershing had discussed the likelihood of war with Major John H. Parker. Parker apparently surprised Pershing when he predicted that within six months the United States would be in the war and Pershing would be either chief of staff or commander of an expedition to France. The tough cavalryman certainly had the most recent experience in such a command with the Punitive Expedition. The other likely candidates were Frederick Funston and Leonard Wood. Funston's sudden death in February and Wood's physical condition and open political opposition to President Wilson made Parker's prediction come true. On May 10 Pershing arrived at the War Department to begin organizing the expedition.[6]

Later, in 1919, the Government Printing Office published a thin volume, *The War with Germany: A Statistical Summary*, which concisely sums up the statistics of the mobilization. This was the work of Colonel Leonard P. Ayres and his officers in the Statistics Branch, one of the quickly organized wartime sections of the General Staff. Two pie charts show the great expansion in manpower from the 200,000 (including 67,000 in the National Guard) in the service when war was declared and the 4 million (13 percent regulars, 10 percent Guardsmen, and 77 percent draftees) in uniform at war's end. In the summer of 1917 the Army contracted for thirty-two temporary camps with a capacity of 1.5 million to house, or at least tent, this great influx, and construction was far enough along to bring in the first draft that fall.

Originally the Army intended to segregate the regulars, the National Guard, and the National Army (the draftees). Thus the first numbered divisions through 20 were regulars, those from 26 through 42 were Guardsmen, and 76 through 93 were allotted to draftees. Wartime volunteers soon came to outnumber peacetime veterans in the regular and Guard units, so that by 1918 there was little difference in the experience level in any of these divisions. In August of that year the Army chief of staff ordered the elimination of those distinctions.

Eventually some 200,000 officers were required in the 4-million man wartime Army. Since there were only 5,791 regular officers at the outbreak of the war, a gigantic effort was launched to create new officers. National Guard and reserve officers were a readily available source, as were qualified regular NCOs. To obtain others, the Army accelerated the course at West Point and established Officer Training Camps (OTCs), which put likely recruits through a three-month course. When the Army reached its peak, only 3 percent of the officers were regulars, 6 percent Guardsmen, 8 percent commissioned from the ranks, with the OTCs furnishing 48 percent. The rest were specialists, including doctors, who were given direct commissions.[7]

Among those who came into the officer corps from civilian life were Charles L. Bolté and Lucian K. Truscott Jr. Both turned twenty-two in 1917, but they had different backgrounds. When war came, Bolté, who was from Chicago, had recently graduated from the Armour Institute of Technology. He had attended four training sessions during the Preparedness period when the Army set up camps to provide military training to civilians. Although his mother was not enthusiastic about his interest in the military, he was pleased to get his reserve commission in November 1916. Truscott had graduated from a normal school and worked as a teacher in Oklahoma. A wartime OTC served as his introduction to the military. He considered the military education he got there "sparse and elementary." For one thing, the instructors "seemed to know little more than the candidates." Charlie Bolté, who was an instructor, would agree. At Fort Benjamin Harrison, Indiana, he had to stay up at night to learn what he had to teach the next day. "It was . . . the blind leading the blind." He received a regular second lieutenant's commission that fall. Lucian, who completed his training course in mid-August and got a reserve commission then, was also given a regular appointment in October 1917.[8]

When his stint as an instructor ended, Bolté went into an infantry division and was soon on his way to France. After OTC, Lucian went in the opposite direction, to Camp Harry J. Jones, near Douglas, Arizona. There the 17th Cavalry, like other regular regiments at that time, had only a few of its regular officers and noncoms as cadre for the wartime influx of officers and recruits. They were enough, however, to make cavalrymen of the neophytes. There were classes and practical instruction on subjects ranging from the Regulations to loading a pack mule and dealing with paperwork. Most of all there were hours on horseback as all learned to ride the Army way. Overseeing this training was the regimental commander, Lieutenant Colonel James J. Hornbrook. A tough West Pointer, Hornbrook seemed to be everywhere. "Sunny Jim," as Lucian recalled, was quick to correct any young officer's error. He was almost apoplectic if he heard a lieutenant address troopers as "boys." The colonel would scream in his high-pitched voice: "they're men, goddamit! They're men! Every one of them! They're men! Men! MEN!" And they had to be if they stayed in his regiment.[9]

In a short-sighted attempt to add more officers, the War Department speeded up the graduation of cadets at the Military Academy. During the nineteen months of the war, five classes graduated 938 cadets (14.3 percent of all graduates since 1802). Guy V. Henry Jr., the commandant of cadets when war came, tried to keep up cadets' morale amidst the turmoil and increased practical training. By the fall of 1918, when Henry was promoted to brigadier general and left to take command of a newly organized division, there were only three classes left. On October 3 the order came to graduate two of those classes the next month. Orville W. Martin, who with his classmates had been at the Academy just sixteen months, remembered: "we tried to catch up a lot of the loose ends in courses" in those four weeks. To complicate matters, the flu epidemic hit West Point during October. The graduation speaker for both classes on November 1 promised that they would be in France within four months, and some of the officers predicted that they would soon be majors.[10]

Many more regular noncoms received commissions than those cadets in the five classes from West Point. Sergeant Sam Woodfill and Corporal George Schuyler were among those who made the transition to officers in 1917. Woodfill was in his late thirties and had been in the Army since before the turn of the century, while Schuyler, at twenty-two, was in his second enlistment. Woodfill, who considered himself and many others he met in the training program "typical old-time non-coms," was anxious to get at the Germans. He received the gold bars of a second lieutenant upon graduation and soon found himself in command of a rifle company at the training camp at Gettysburg. During Christmas leave he married, and within months he was a first lieutenant on the way to France.[11]

Schuyler was at Schofield Barracks when war began. Within weeks, he and some eighty other NCOs in the 25th Infantry were picked to attend the segregated black officer-training course at Fort Des Moines. When his party passed through Oakland, they ran into Lieutenant Colonel Charles Young, the ranking black officer in the Army. Young was in the Bay area for medical observation and examination that might lead to his retirement. What disconcerted him as well as Schuyler and his friends was that Young thought that he was in fine health and that the real reason was his report on the failures of a white colonel during the Punitive Expedition. Both Young and those noncoms would have been more disgusted if they had known the truth. A Mississippian, a lieutenant in the Tenth Cavalry, complained of having to serve under Young because he was black. His senator took this to the White House, and President Wilson suggested the young officer's transfer. Additional white officers' complaints, however, seemed to the secretary of war to indicate another solution—namely, Young's retirement. Such action also put to rest any concern that he might become a general officer.

The course at Fort Des Moines started on July 1, 1917, with 1,250 candidates, 250 of whom were from the four regular black regiments. Schuyler enjoyed the first month, but he and others began to be suspicious when they realized that they were not getting the same training as the white candidates and that their course was a month longer. Nevertheless, he was delighted to get a first lieutenant's commission. He prided himself on being a good drill master, and he put that skill to use at Camp Dix and Camp Meade until the end of the war.[12]

The wartime expansion brought almost overwhelming pressure on the regular officer corps. Promotion, which was very slow and deliberate in peacetime, advanced by leaps and bounds to keep up with the rapidly expanding force. While most rose to the challenges of increased responsibility, some did not. The priority given to seniority, an effort to maintain parity among the branches, and the necessity of finding officers for new branches led to problems. The handful of generals in the peacetime Army and those at the top of the colonels' list were in their late fifties and sixties, and many were physically unfit for the rigors of war. After he visited the French and British armies, Pershing was adamant about eliminating division commanders who were over age and not in good shape. When many of these generals came to France on observation tours in the winter of 1917–18, he looked them over and recommended that seventeen (more than half) be relieved. With the exception of the one National Guardsman, these were long-serving regulars of excellent records, three of whom (J. Franklin Bell, Leonard Wood, and Hugh Scott) had been chiefs of staff.[13]

Pershing's chief of staff, James G. Harbord, noted in his diary after the visit of the first contingent of these officers: "the glimpse of physical inefficiency which would be fatal to our arms lingered in its effects." One of those generals, Hunter Liggett, was sixty and overweight, but, to the ultimate good fortune of the AEF, Pershing changed his mind in his case. Liggett later cited another problem that derailed the careers of other senior regulars: "We had . . . once excellent officers of higher ranks, who had gone to seed in the doldrums of peace and could not shake themselves loose from the cut-and-dried methods of the old Army." The secretary of war supported Pershing in his decisions and relegated those senior officers to posts distant from the battlefield.[14]

The War Department's attempt to promote fairly among the branches led to a problem in the field artillery. When war began there were only 275 field artillery officers who had one year or more of service. This was scarcely enough to officer one brigade, and by war's end there were sixty-one brigades. In the early days of the war, when the first thirty-three brigades were created, only 8 of their commanders were field artillerymen. Understandably this led to failures in the development of these units, as many of the commanders did not have the necessary background to understand what they were supposed to do. The solution was to bring in younger but more experienced field artillery officers, some of whom had been only captains in the prewar Army, to take command. Because of this exigency, 19 of the 37 regular captains who made the great leap to stars during the war were field artillerymen. Not surprisingly, Colonel William Lassiter wound up as a major general and amassed an outstanding record during the war as a brigade commander, as chief of artillery for a corps and later a field army.[15]

The early experience of the First Division, which was the first to reach France, illustrates some of the difficulties that wartime units had to overcome. This division, which was organized in May to follow Pershing to France as soon as possible, consisted of regular units filled with recruits. George C. Marshall, who became the first operations officer of the division, never forgot those hectic early weeks. He was a captain serving as a general's aide when he got the coveted assignment. Indicative of the Army's state of preparation, the division staff met for the first time on board the transport. At that time, Marshall and the others were amazed to learn that infantry regiments were greatly enlarged and contained strange organizations armed with new weapons.

Colonel George B. Duncan, who within a year was a major general in command of a division, commanded one of the four infantry regiments. Not only were many of his troops mere recruits, but he had had to leave behind the best NCOs, as they were slated for commissions. Nor was he happy that only seventeen of his officers had a year or more service. This division, as Marshall said, "was supposed to be the pick of the Regular Army and yet it looked like the rawest of territorial units." When a battalion of the 16th Infantry paraded in Paris soon after their arrival, one of the company commanders lamented that his men did not even know the manual of arms. Even after the division had been in France for six months, the division commander complained of the lack of competent officers: "I have much difficulty in getting officers who know anything . . . many even of our regular officers can never be worth anything in this war, unadaptable and immovable."[16]

The most celebrated new branch of the Army was the Air Service, which separated from the Signal Corps during the war. In 1917 there was speculation that this would be the focus of the nation's military effort. Since the Army arm had only some 1,200 officers and men and fewer than a hundred obsolescent aircraft in April 1917, this was fantasy. Nevertheless, ultimately there would be 190,000 in the Air Service, and American combat squadrons would see a considerable amount of action in the last six months of the war. Shortly before the nation went to war, the chief signal officer brought his most experienced air commander, Captain Benny Foulois, to Washington to help in the rapidly developing—at least on paper—aviation program. Thus when Pershing wanted Foulois to go to France with him, the Signal Corps general would not release him. During these early months of 1917, Major Billy Mitchell, who had worked on aviation matters in the Chief of Signal Corps office, had gone to Europe as an observer. When the Pershing party arrived in Paris, Mitchell met them at the railroad station and soon took over as the AEF aviation officer.

Although they were born in the same month and had roughly the same amount of military service, Foulois and Mitchell had very different backgrounds and military experiences. The former grew up in a working-class family and worked as a plumber before he enlisted in the Army, while Mitchell, whose father had been a U.S. senator, was from a wealthy family. Like Foulois, he had enlisted as a private, but he became a volunteer officer within a month; hence Foulois had considerably more enlisted service, while Mitchell ranked him as an officer. By the time of World War I, Foulois was an aviation pioneer. Meantime, Mitchell learned to fly at his own expense in 1916. The more they came in contact, the more they disliked each other.

When Foulois, who had received his star in August, reached France in November 1917, Mitchell was still a lieutenant colonel and infuriated at Foulois and his staff whom he considered "carpetbaggers." In turn, Foulois came to consider Mitchell a troublemaker who knew much less than he thought he did about aviation matters. Finally, Pershing resolved this difficult situation by placing in command, over both, Mason M. Patrick, who had been his classmate at West Point. Mitchell's eventual command of the forward combat elements in October 1918 brought him a star while his flamboyance won him fame.[17]

The Tank Corps was another new branch created during the war. The first man assigned to work with tanks in the American Army was Captain George S. Patton Jr. He had gone to France with Pershing as the commander of the headquarters company. In September 1917 he heard that there might soon be a new organization in the AEF. Although he had engaged in a debate over the merits of the cavalry saber only a few months before, George leaped at the chance to volunteer for work with the more modern—and more formidable—tanks. On October 3 he submitted his application with the explanation: "I believe that I have quick judgment and that I am willing to take chances. Also I have always believed in getting close to the enemy." When the assignment came through he started a crash course in learning all he could about tanks, since his first job was to set up a tank school.

As in the case of the Air Service, Pershing wisely placed an older officer, Samuel D. Rockenbach, in command of the Tank Corps, but Patton was on the cutting edge. He wrote his wife: "It is so apparently a thing of destiny." By the next spring he was a lieutenant colonel and the commander of the first American light tank battalion. In late August he gained command of a tank brigade. The real war still lay ahead.[18]

✳

During the fall and winter of 1917–18 the AEF slowly grew in strength, but it was not until the British made shipping available that large numbers of Americans reached France. During that winter, after the withdrawal of Russia from the war and the collapse of their Passchendaele offensive with huge losses, the British realized that they needed reinforcement from across the Atlantic. By the spring of 1918 a new and dynamic chief of staff, Peyton C. March, and a greatly enlarged General Staff were able to supply the necessary men. The rub was that the British wanted these men as replacements for their units. In this respect, Pershing was adamant for an independent AEF and withstood repeated efforts by British political and military leaders to wear him down. As Douglas MacArthur commented, Pershing's greatest asset was his "strength and firmness of character."[19]

During those early months when the First Division was the only major American force, Pershing and his staff paid particularly close attention to their activities. It did not help matters that the commander, William L. Sibert, was an engineer officer. Fortunately, he had as his operations officer Major Marshall, who, as one of the company commanders recalled, was a "go-getter . . . If you needed him, he was right there." When Pershing came down to their training area to view a combat exercise, he was infuriated when neither the division commander nor the chief of staff was able to give a proper critique. Marshall, who had set up the maneuver, was stunned when Pershing "just gave everybody hell." Although he assumed that he was sacrificing his career, Marshall went up to explain matters. Even after Pershing made it clear he did not want to listen, Marshall continued to talk. The general's response was that "we have our troubles." The young major countered: "Yes, I know you do, General . . . But ours are immediate and every day and have to be solved before night." Rather than ruining his career, he gained Pershing's respect.[20]

On May 28, 1918, the AEF staged its first assault, at Cantigny. One reinforced regiment of the First Division quickly drove the Germans out, but the difficult part came later as that regiment (the 28th) and later the 16th had to fend off counterattacks. Though wounded a couple of months earlier, Clarence R. Huebner was back in time for the attack. When his major was killed, he took over the battalion throughout the bitter defensive battle. A few weeks later, in mid-July, he led the battalion in the counteroffensive at Soissons. After keeping his men going forward despite the terrible losses they were suffering, he was wounded on the second day. Every officer in that battalion had become a casualty. The Army awarded him two Distinguished Service Crosses (DSCs) for his actions in those two battles and, later, the Distinguished Service Medal (DSM) for his outstanding service as a company, battalion, and regimental commander.[21]

Throughout that summer, American units were in battle. In August Pershing organized a field army—the First Army—which began preparing for the first large-scale American offensive at St.-Mihiel. On September 12 this new army received its baptism of fire, as did Patton and thousands of other officers and men, in a relatively easy victory. Even before the St.-Mihiel operation began, the First Army staff was at work on plans for a much larger effort between the Meuse River and Argonne Forest to threaten the Germans' main supply artery along the Western Front. The First Army chief of staff, Hugh A. Drum, gave the most difficult chore in this planning to his new assistant, George Marshall, who was now a colonel. The problem, which Marshall said was "the hardest nut I had to crack in France," was to move some 400,000 American and French troops, many of whom were about to attack to the north at St.-Mihiel, more than thirty miles west to their jump-off positions on the Meuse-Argonne front. Later he received the DSM for his "untiring, painstaking, and energetic efforts" throughout the war.[22]

Leavenworth really paid high dividends during the war, as so many graduates put their training to good use in key staff positions in the AEF. In early October John M. Palmer visited the front with Drum, who MacArthur said ran the First Army, as Drum conferred with three corps chiefs of staff. He was impressed: "It seemed just like a Staff College conference . . . The technique and the talk were just the same." At war's end, nine of the ten Army and corps chiefs of staff and twenty-two of the thirty division chiefs of staff, with Charles D. Herron among the latter, were graduates. At Pershing's headquarters, four of his top staff officers—including George Van Horn Moseley, who was responsible for coordinating AEF supplies—belonged to that exclusive group. On Armistice Day Drum penned a quick note to his wife: "All the hard hours of study at Leavenworth . . . have borne fruit."[23]

On the first day of the Meuse-Argonne attack, Patton led his tankers from the front and also rallied infantrymen in his area to sustain the advance. A severe wound, however, ended his war before the day was out. He was promoted to colonel while in the hospital and would later receive a DSC for his heroism as well as a DSM for his "high military attainments, zeal, and marked adaptability in a form of warfare comparatively new to the American Army." None of these rewards assuaged his disappointment for missing so much of the war. Afterward he wrote Pershing: "War is the only place where a man really lives."[24]

More than a million Americans took part in the Meuse-Argonne offensive during the almost seven weeks it lasted. More than 26,000 were killed, and almost 97,000 were wounded. In addition to Patton, Charlie Bolté was wounded. During the last five weeks of this great battle, Bill Simpson was the operations officer of the 33d Division. He had missed earlier campaigns because of his detail as a student to the AEF's abbreviated version of Leavenworth—the Army General Staff College at Langres. There he was impressed by the experienced Allied officers on the faculty and recalled that "we just began learning all kinds of things." He learned enough to earn a DSM as the operations officer and chief of staff of the division.

Others who helped make that great battle a victory included John Parker, Troy Middleton, and Sam Woodfill. The Army's machine-gun pioneer had an outstanding record as a regimental commander, earning four DSCs for battlefield gallantry and a DSM for his work with machine guns. But whatever he did was not enough to win him a star; he finished the war and his career as a colonel. Troy Middleton, who was twenty-three years younger than Parker, led a battalion in the Fourth Division on the first day of the campaign but wound up a colonel and regimental commander. At twenty-nine, he was said to be the youngest colonel in the AEF. Woodfill surpassed both of them. On October 12 near Cunel he went ahead of his company and with his rifle, pistol, and pick killed the crews of three machine-gun nests. He received the Medal of Honor and Pershing's accolade as "the outstanding soldier of the AEF."[25]

While so many of the regulars were winning laurels in France, others spent the war in the States. Particularly for younger officers like Matt Ridgway, whose West Point class graduated a couple of months early in 1917, this was a major disappointment. He served on the border and then as an instructor at the Military Academy. To him it seemed that "the soldier who had had no share in this last great victory . . . would be ruined." His classmate, J. Lawton Collins, and two promising members of the class of 1915, Omar N. Bradley and Dwight D. Eisenhower, were others who were unable to get into combat. As the commander of Camp Colt, a training camp for tankers, Eisenhower earned a DSM and had the largest experience of these young officers, but it was certainly not the same as being in France. Jake Devers was older and did achieve the rank of colonel but did not cross the Atlantic until the war was over. When the war began he was in Hawaii, but he got only as far as Fort Sill, where he spent ten months as a "trouble shooter." As he explained, he "did everything there."[26]

Two of the older officers who missed combat were Lewis Sorley and Eli Helmick. Sorley was also in Hawaii when war came. Promoted to colonel, he commanded a regiment in the Eighth Division and got as far as the port of embarkation when the Armistice was signed. His division commander, Helmick, spent most of the war as an inspector general. Like Sorley, he was impressed by the "marvelous spirit" of the temporary soldiers. He did get across the Atlantic with the division advance party, but the war was over. A few days after the Armistice he had the great pleasure of pinning the silver oak leaves of a lieutenant colonel on his son, Gardiner, who commanded a field artillery training camp.[27]

War for the families of regulars, as for those of the civilians temporarily turned soldier, was a time of farewells and anxiety. The fact that many of them had sent their husbands or fathers off to battle in Cuba, the Philippines, or Mexico did not ease the ordeal. The experiences of Beatrice Ayer Patton, Adelaide "Benny" Poore, and Mauree Pickering Mahin give a sense of what happened to the distaff part of the Old Army during the turbulent days of 1917 and 1918.

Beatrice said her goodbyes to George in New York when he sailed with Pershing in late May 1917. Both had hopes of her joining him in France within months. While two-year-old Ruth Ellen might not be up to the trip, they assumed that Beatrice would bring "Little Bee," who was six, along to an apartment in Paris. A ban on AEF wives made George think of London as a possibility, but it soon was apparent that that option was out of the question. Beatrice wrote a relative in mid-August: "This is a hard time on all of us." She and the girls stayed with her family in Massachusetts during the long two years of Patton's absence.[28]

Both Benny Poore and Mauree Mahin traveled a lot during the war. Benny, at seventeen, was in the Philippines when war was declared. Her father's promotion to brigadier general brought him and his family home. A storm buffeted the ship about and damaged it severely, so that they had to stop over in Japan for a few days. Then, as Benny recalled, "we really did have rapid changes"; she and her mother accompanied General Poore to Camp Pike, Arkansas, for three months and on to El Paso, Texas, for another three months. While there Benny came down with scarlet fever, so her parents left her at Fort Bliss when they went to Camp Greene, North Carolina. Poore's new brigade left for the embarkation port just three weeks later, shortly after Benny caught up with them in Charlotte. She and her mother stayed there for almost a year. Benny wanted to contribute to the war effort so applied to a couple of nurses' training programs. When she was not accepted, she took a course in medical technology and began work at Camp Greene as a laboratory technician. In the spring of 1919 the Poores went to stay with a relative in Massachusetts until the general returned in June.[29]

The Mahins were also in the Philippines when the United States entered the war. Married less than four years before, they had come out to the Philippines in the spring of 1915. Within a few weeks of their arrival, Mauree gave birth to twins, Anna and Margaret. Three months later they had to move to another post where a typhoon and a cholera epidemic complicated their lives. In 1917, when Margaret's glands became swollen, a cooler climate seemed a possible cure. Frank took Mauree and the twins to China. On the way back they stopped in Japan, where they learned that he had orders to go to the States. Since the transport was crowded, Mauree and the girls had to share a cabin with a woman while Frank was down the passageway with three other men. The glandular problem continued, and the ship's doctor mistakenly diagnosed the girls' prickly heat as a skin infection, so he quarantined them. Mauree never forgot trying to keep her two-year-old twins entertained in that hot cabin for ten days.

Back in the States, they went by rail to Salt Lake City, where Frank joined his new unit at Fort Douglas; Mauree took the girls on to Georgia, where her father was the commander of Fort Oglethorpe. In late 1917 her mother, whose thirty-eight years of marriage had carried her through all sorts of adventures, from an Indian agency to the Philippines, died just a few months before her husband retired. When Frank went overseas, Mauree took the girls to join her father at Fort Crook, Nebraska. When Colonel Pickering returned to active duty, at Fort McPherson, Georgia, Mauree waited: "those were long dark days, and our news was so scant." In October she was relieved to get a cable from Frank, now a major, with the news that he was only "slightly wounded." Actually he had been severely gassed, but she did not know that, and all she could think of was that he was no longer in combat.[30]

✳

Whatever hopes blacks had that their participation in the war effort might alleviate racial attitudes were soon dashed. A riot in Houston

Mauree and Frank Mahin enjoy their twin daughters, Los Banos, Luzon, 1915. As a daughter and a wife, Mauree witnessed all of the Army's great transitional era from 1898 to 1941. Courtesy of Helen L. Rosson.

confirmed whites' worst fears about black soldiers and helped convince the War Department to cut the originally planned sixteen infantry regiments of black draftees to four. In July 1917 the third battalion of the 24th Infantry was moved to the outskirts of Houston. There were only seven officers, and soon a new white battalion commander, as well as a substantial number of new NCOs; the twenty-five best noncoms had recently departed for the officer-training course. Under the stress of general abuse from Houston whites and police brutality, the unit cracked. On the night of August 23, after police pistol-whipped 2 soldiers, 100 or more of their comrades, intent on revenge, armed themselves and threatened to shoot the battalion commander before they marched into the city. During a two-hour rampage, 16 whites lost their lives and others were wounded, while 4 of the mutineers died. The Army immediately disarmed the battalion and transferred it to New

Mexico. Unlike the Brownsville affair, there was enough evidence to try 118 soldiers. After three trials, 110 of the 118 tried were convicted and 19 were hanged. The black community was outraged when the 13 men sentenced to death in the first court-martial were hanged without recourse to appeal. After the other trials, President Wilson commuted the sentences of 10 of the remaining 16 condemned to death.[31]

The racial climate restricted the wartime role of the 400,000 blacks in the Army. The War Department kept the four regular regiments out of France and used most of the 368,000 draftees as labor troops. Four black infantry regiments (three National Guard and one draftee) won distinction when they served as combat troops with the French throughout the war. The only full-strength black division, the 92d, which had black soldiers and company-grade officers, with whites holding all of the senior positions, had problems in the Argonne Forest when two battalions disintegrated. In large part this division's failure was a self-fulfilling prophecy for white officers; nevertheless, for half a century, the problems of the 92d were remembered by the white community, which, not surprisingly, overlooked the achievements of the other black units.[32]

There had been racial clashes, including a huge riot in East St. Louis, before the Houston riot in 1917. In the months after the Armistice, race problems multiplied. Lynchings were more numerous in 1919 than they had been in more than ten years. During that summer some twenty-five race riots erupted, including major ones in Washington, D.C., Chicago, and Omaha. During the past decade there had been a large migration of blacks out of the South into northern cities. Meantime, the frustration of hopes for better conditions festered in the black community, while racism increased among the whites.[33]

In his quarters at Fort Stotsenburg on Luzon, Lieutenant Colonel Benjamin O. Davis was despondent as he read about deteriorating race relations. He had been successful, and his white subordinates evidently respected him. One captain, the grandson of a Confederate general, openly admired him. It was discouraging that the commissioned white noncoms who had joined the regiment were obviously less capable than the black noncoms. And news from home was all bad. He hid his feelings from those about him, but he poured them out to his fiancé: "the future looks dark . . . I am afraid that before long there will be more open organized persecution." A few days later he wrote: "It is hard to tell where this color prejudice will drive us."[34]

✳

When the war ended on the Western Front, some Americans were fighting Bolsheviks in northern Russia while others were poised precariously among White Russians, partisans, and Japanese in Siberia. In August and September 1918 some 5,000 were deployed to northern Russia and another 9,000 to Vladivostok. The former operated under the overall command of the British and actively fought, while Major General William S. Graves held firm to his orders of neutrality until President Wilson changed them in early 1919. By the end of August 1919 all the smaller contingent were out of Russia, but the Siberian expedition stayed until the spring of 1920.[35]

When the president ordered Graves to protect the Trans-Siberian Railroad, he committed American troops to guard the logistical link for the White Russians. Soon American outposts along the railroad came under attack from partisans. On April 1, 1920, Graves and his command sailed for home, but his operations officer, Robert L. Eichelberger, stayed on for a few days—long enough to see the Japanese shoot up Vladivostok. During his nineteen months in Siberia, his observations of the Japanese troops left him with two dominant impressions. The first was that they were hostile to Americans, and the second was that they were outstanding soldiers—brave, well trained, and superbly disciplined.[36]

Within a week after the Armistice, American troops began to march toward Germany. Ultimately, in February 1919, there were more than 262,000 on occupation duty in the Rhineland enclave, which consisted of the area within a thirty-kilometer radius of Coblenz. Meantime, at AEF general headquarters, staff officers, including George Marshall, worked on contingency plans for a movement beyond the boundaries of the Rhineland zone in case Germany did not sign the peace treaty. As months passed it became increasingly clear that there would be no trouble, and what was known as the Third Army began sending men home in great numbers. After the peace conference at Versailles came to an end, this command, reduced to a third of peak strength, became the American Forces in Germany (AFG). In July Major General Henry

T. Allen, a courtly Kentuckian who was one of the best-known cavalry-man in the Army, took command of the AFG. The exodus continued until by November there were only 15,000 troops left. By the spring of 1922 there were 5,500, in comparison with the 85,000 French and 15,000 British in their occupation zones. By the end of the year there were just 1,200, and they left in January 1923.[37]

Major J. Lawton Collins, who graduated from West Point in April 1917 and, to his disappointment, spent most of the war in the New York City area, joined the occupation force in mid-1919. At first he commanded a battalion; later, after a reduction in rank, he served as assistant to the operations officer, Jonathan M. Wainwright. Collins thought this was "probably the best job for a captain over there" and had "a wonderful experience." There was hard training, but there were also games for the soldiers and horse shows and polo for the officers. Finally, there was a lot of spit and polish. As Lieutenant General Robert L. Bullard noted, the AFG "became . . . the most highly polished and burnished soldiers that the government of the United States ever had."[38]

Soldiers and officers wanted to serve in the AFG. After all, as the chief surgeon pointed out, a private's pay was more "than some of the highest salaried German Government officials." Many were billeted in homes, a practice that, whatever the inconvenience, provided the Germans with some extra income and the men with more comfort than barracks. The Army withdrew its ban on fraternization in September 1919, so open mixing with the German women began. This develop-ment embittered many Germans—young men because of the competi-tion, and middle-class people generally because of the lack of American respect for their social-class system. It also led to a good many marriages, some illegitimate children, and a high rate of venereal disease. During 1920, cases of venereal disease accounted for one-third of all hospital admissions for disease.[39]

In 1920, when the mean strength of the occupation force was 15,219, there were some 2,000 American civilians in the Coblenz bridgehead. Families as well as assorted welfare workers and Rhineland High Commission employees enjoyed life on the Rhine as much as the men in uniform. General Allen brought over his wife, while his son and son-in-law also served in the AFG, which some began to call "Allen's Family in Germany." Joe Collins' two sisters shared his billet, while the daughter of Chief Chaplain Edmund P. Easterbrook, Gladys, came over to work as a secretary for the Rhineland Commission, followed in 1920 by his wife and two sons.[40]

A wounded veteran and newly commissioned regular first lieutenant, Edwin T. Wheatley proposed by cable to his hometown sweetheart, Elizabeth Lewis. Betty crossed the Atlantic and met and married him in Antwerp on May 4, 1921. After a brief honeymoon in Paris, they went to the Coblenz bridgehead, where she was in a bridge-club meeting within hours. In addition to parties, there was much travel. Edwin had already visited the battlefields and London before Betty arrived, and they were soon back in Paris, where she was impressed by "the long haired men and the short haired women" they saw in the Latin Quarter. Then there were the boat trips up and down the Rhine and more extensive journeys into Germany, including one to see the Passion Play at Oberammergau. And there was much shopping—so much so that when the last transport sailed, it could not carry all the officers' household goods.[41]

Joe Collins also did a great deal of traveling, taking his sisters to France, Switzerland, Austria, and Italy; but he began to devote most of his off-duty time to Gladys Easterbrook. After a lengthy courtship, they married in July 1921, just before he had to return to the States. Gladys' twelve-year-old brother, Ernest, also enjoyed his time in the Rhineland. There were enough American children to have their own school, but what he enjoyed most were the travel and the Scouting activities. A Navy veteran, Henry Thomson, who had wound up his walking tour of Europe and taken a job with the Army, organized Rhineland Boy Scout Troop no. 1, which consisted of some twenty Army boys. Sixty years later, Ernie was still in touch with this energetic leader of their hikes and campouts.[42]

In early 1923 the American occupation came to an end. Wheatley was the officer who raised the national flag on the last day, January 24, at the famed German fortress at Ehrenbreitstein. French troops moved in, and the AFG ceased to exist. Edwin probably spoke for many when he looked back on his service in the Rhineland as "the happiest days I ever spent."[43]

Throughout the war and into the postwar era, a considerable number of troops had remained on the Mexican border. In early May 1918, when the AEF was just beginning to make its weight felt on the Western Front, nine cavalry regiments, seven and a half infantry regiments, and assorted other units consisting of 31,500 men kept up the border guard. There were innumerable firings across the boundary and some Mexican raids, which the Americans countered. In addition, there was at least one incident with Indians; in January 1918 a troop of the Tenth Cavalry engaged in a brief battle with ten Yaquis that left one Indian dead.[44]

The most significant action took place in June 1919, when Pancho Villa's Army engaged Carranza forces in Juárez. On this occasion, civilians as well as soldiers in El Paso came under artillery as well as small-arms fire. On the night of June 16, the local American commander sent troops into Juárez with orders to drive Villa out. The 24th Infantry crossed the bridge between the two cities, while the Seventh and two squadrons of the Fifth Cavalry crossed on fords downriver with the intention of catching Villa's force in a double envelopment.

Shortly after nine on the morning of June 17, the Seventh caught up with some of the Villistas and launched a mounted charge. One of the troopers, Arthur J. Stanley, was exhilarated as he yelled and pulled out his pistol only to be somewhat disillusioned. As he recalled, "it wasn't a Jeb Stuart style charge" because their horses had such difficult footing in the irrigated field. Nevertheless, they captured some of the enemy and dispersed the others, who, as the official report stated, "scattered like quail." In fact the four batteries of artillery that had pounded Villa's main force probably did the most damage in this battle, which destroyed Villa's Army. By late afternoon on the seventeenth, the American forces were back across the Rio Grande.[45]

This proved to be the last major action along the border, although patrols continued their grueling routines for more than a decade. There were also air units on duty after the war. Captain Arthur R. Brooks recalled how exhausting it was to fly missions during the summer heat. Officers were not supposed to fly aircraft in their underwear, but Ray Brooks found that wearing just his underwear was more comfortable in the torrid weather. The occasional incidents along the border ended in 1930 with a skirmish between some Tenth Cavalry and Mexican rebels near Naco, Arizona.[46]

✢

While American troops went about their duties in Germany, Siberia, and the various stations in the Pacific as well as along the Mexican border, others in the States had to deal with a rash of race riots and labor disorders and carried out routine garrison duties. At the same time, the overwhelming majority of the wartime Army simply wanted to go home. And they did. Within a year of the Armistice, more than 3.4 million men were demobilized. While many of the wartime units ceased to exist, others continued at skeletal strength. A colonel at Camp Custer reported in August 1919 that his regiment had only 375 men, about a sixth of its authorized strength. At Camp Grant, Major Omar N. Bradley had difficulty mustering as many as two or three squads for drill out of his eviscerated battalion.[47]

In the spring of 1919 the Army launched a recruiting campaign to fill its ranks. Recruiters made a strenuous effort at demobilization centers to persuade those who were about to be discharged to reenlist. One-year enlistments were held out as an inducement, although three-year enlistments were also available. Congress also withdrew the bar on illiterates, and in the fall of 1919 the War Department launched a campaign featuring a new educational program. Secretary of War Newton D. Baker had high hopes for the vocational education plan. On the one hand, it should make the service more appealing; as he pointed out, "the peace-time Army . . . will be . . . an educational institution." On the other, it should provide technical training that would enhance the soldier's value to the Army while giving him a skill that should be useful when he returned to civilian life. Besides, each man would also take a course in American institutions and history. A soldier student could expect to spend fifteen hours a week in classes taught by other soldiers, officers, or, in some instances, civilians. Except for the illiterates, who were required to take courses in order to learn how to read and write English, the program was voluntary.

The Army got its recruits—almost 70,000 in the first four months of the recruiting campaign to June 30, 1919, and another 151,000 in the next fiscal year, with approximately half volunteering only for one year. This short term proved to be ineffective. Then the educational program was not as successful as Secretary Baker hoped. In February 1921, Major General William G. Haan of the General Staff explained to the chairman of the House Military Affairs Committee what had happened: "during the past two years while the Army has been passing through the throes of reorganization, it has been impracticable to make very much headway along these lines."[48]

During those first two years after the war, officers were also caught up in the personnel turbulence that severely strained the morale of the Army. Most of the wartime officers, some 178,000, took their discharges in the first year after the Armistice and went home. This left the older prewar regulars, both officers and NCOs who had become temporary officers, and those emergency-period officers who wanted to make the Army a career. As was the case after the Civil War when a large wartime Army collapsed into a relatively small peacetime establishment, most officers who held higher wartime rank suffered demotions to their regular ranks. This development was particularly onerous to those who had served as officers in the AEF divisions. Although many had distinguished records, when they returned to the States, most of their units were promptly demobilized, and the leaders lost their rank. What galled them was that Stateside officers retained their temporary rank because their units or staff positions remained intact. Frank L. Winn, a wartime major general who had to put on the eagles of a colonel in 1919, struck a common chord when he complained privately: "I am demoted while others hold on who are my juniors in the Regular Army, who have neither right nor reasonable claim to being considered my superiors." Prewar regular NCOs who had received temporary commissions were also caught up in the demobilization. A few obtained regular commissions, but Sam Woodfill did not qualify, so he stayed on as a sergeant. George Schuyler was pleased to get a temporary civil service job as a clerk.[49]

Younger officers also considered their options. During the war they had worked with temporary officers with good connections in civilian life who were impressed by them. Some lawyers-turned-wartime-officers were so impressed by Joe Collins when he took part in courts-martial that they encouraged him to make the law a career. Before he got his orders to the Army of Occupation, Collins applied for Columbia Law School. After all, as he recalled, "I didn't think there would be any more wars, and not having served in action I felt there wasn't much of a future for me in the Army." When his acceptance came, he was already overseas, and one of his friends warned him that the law was not as promising as he had been led to expect, so he gave up his place at Columbia. Another young West Pointer, Dwight Eisenhower, also briefly considered an offer from an Indiana businessman who had served under him at Camp Colt, but also decided to stay.

Simp Simpson retained his temporary lieutenant colonelcy into 1920 but knew that he faced demotion to his regular rank of captain; thus he took seriously an offer to manage a bus company in Illinois. The $18,000 annual salary—almost six times that of a captain—was very tempting. He visited and checked out the company and even wrote out his resignation but left it on his desk until he reached the conclusion that he would stay in the service. When he got an offer the next year to manage a factory, he did not hesitate to turn down the offer: "I said to hell with it." Many did resign—2,103 in 1919 alone—and the rates for the next couple of years were significantly above normal.

As in the case of enlisted men, the Army tried to recruit temporary officers into the regular service. In 1920 alone more than 15,000 applied for the vacancies in the officer corps, and some 5,200 received regular commissions. Ray Brooks and George Hinman were wartime officers who accepted captaincies. Ray, a six-victory ace, enjoyed the hunting near Kelly Field and, most of all, the flying. But as reductions in the Army in 1922 led to a demotion when he thought that he should have been promoted, he resigned. As a Massachusetts Institute of Technology graduate, he had no difficulty finding a good job. For Hinman, who was on duty in the Adjutant General's Department, it became increasingly clear that if he remained he would stay in his rank for about sixteen years. This gloomy prospect, combined with a depressing inspection trip of several posts, swayed him to accept a good offer in journalism.[50]

Adversely affected as well, the Military Academy was in difficulty during the first months after the war. When the Armistice came, there were only two classes there—one had arrived in June 1918 and the other just a few days before. All were told that they would graduate in June 1919. The most recent arrivals were not even issued cadet gray uniforms but wore enlisted men's olive drab. Some of these men resigned before the end of November because, as one explained, "I did not at any time intend following the Army career as a life profession but entered the Academy in view of the war emergency." Meantime the last class to graduate, those who had entered in June 1917, were still on graduation leave when they received orders to report back to West Point in early

December. Although as second lieutenants they had more freedom than cadets, they lived in the barracks and resumed their studies. A few, including Alfred C. Wedemeyer, wanted to stay and complete the entire academic course, but they graduated a second time in June and went as a class on a tour of the recent battlefields.[51]

The Academy needed rehabilitation, and the time was ripe to overhaul the outdated and narrow approach to the education and training of the cadets. Secretary Baker and General March agreed that thirty-nine-year-old Douglas MacArthur was equal to this great task. March told him: "Douglas, things are in great confusion at West Point . . . Mr. Baker and I . . . want you to go up there and revitalize and revamp the Academy." Despite the young brigadier's protests that he was a field soldier, not an educator, and that some of his teachers were still professors there, he took over the superintendent's office in mid-June 1919.

With his crush cap and riding crop and the aura of being one of the top combat commanders in the AEF, MacArthur's very presence must have been irritating to the oligarchy of permanent professors who composed the Academic Board and were adamant about returning the Academy to its prewar state. Nevertheless, he was able to get through a broader social science program and to introduce courses in modern technology. He brought in civilian educators as consultants and succeeded in cracking the academic isolation in which the Academy had existed for decades. He attacked the hazing problem and gave cadet officers more responsibility. Then he liberalized discipline and systematized the honor code. It was a herculean task. After the first few months, he thought of resignation. Whatever his success at West Point, he faced reduction to major with the end of the wartime ranks. He had decided to accept a lucrative offer as vice-president of a New York bank when, in January 1920, word came that he had received an appointment as a regular brigadier general. So he continued in his mission.[52]

Jake Devers, who lost command of his regiment and his colonelcy when he returned from Europe in the summer of 1919, was assigned as a captain to take over the artillery detachment ("an awful detachment it was") at the Academy. His first audience with the superintendent indicated MacArthur's leadership style. Devers entered his office and saluted. MacArthur told him to sit down and offered a cigarette and lit it for him. Then he began pacing back and forth and "thinking aloud . . . talking about problems there." He stopped, asked a few questions, then picked up a large report on his desk, handed it to Devers, and said: "I give you ten days to clean this up." Devers saw that it was an inspector general's report that was filled with the numerous deficiencies of his detachment. MacArthur told him that, in the future, if Jake wanted to see him about anything, the door was open; just "walk right in." He got the response he wanted, as Devers remembered: "I went down and I cleaned it up . . . I swept everything under the rug and in the closets, but I did the best I could in ten days."[53]

Others, both cadets and officers, found MacArthur "aloof and reclusive," as Omar Bradley, who was on the faculty, said. One of the cadets, Maxwell D. Taylor, recalled that MacArthur did not make an effort to impress his personality on them unless they were athletes. He loved sports and regularly attended practices of the football, baseball, and basketball teams. On one occasion he even grabbed a bat, loosened his blouse, and tried to teach a cadet player how to hit a curve ball. His strong belief in sports as a good preparation for military leadership led to his inauguration of an intramural program in which all cadets had to participate.

When MacArthur left the Academy in the summer of 1922, he could take pride in having brought about the rehabilitation and reform that Baker and March had desired. Although his successor tightened restrictions on cadets, the foundation that MacArthur built remained intact. In 1960 he pointed out: "West Point is still running on the lines laid out at that time."[54]

✯

In that uncertain postwar period, amidst such turmoil, trying to forge long-range military policy was difficult. Nevertheless, it had to be done, for, as Secretary of War Newton D. Baker pointed out, "we must live in the world as it is while we struggle to make it what it should be." Baker and his chief of staff, General Peyton C. March, offered a plan for a standing Army of 500,000 within a couple of months after the end of the war. Such a large force, quadruple the size of the Army in April 1917, found few supporters and many enemies. There was a bloc that favored the National Guard, with its leader, Bennett Clark, calling for Congress to "smash the Regular Army." Another group wanted a policy built around a citizen Army with officers trained in camps similar to those held during the Preparedness period and universal military training. Their spokesman attacked the large Army proposed by Baker and March as "uneconomic, undemocratic and un-American." While both groups had their advocates in Congress, most legislators probably had little interest in either the Guard or the reserve but rather simply agreed with Senator Hiram Johnson of California, who said: "I can not quite fathom why at this particular time, when we are facing an era of universal peace, we should have an Army many times larger than we have had in our history before." Besides, as King Swope, the first World War I veteran elected to Congress, said: "Everybody had a bellyful of the damn Army."[55]

Even within the Army there was opposition to the Baker-March plan, which later incorporated a brief universal training program. Major General William G. Haan, who headed the War Plans Division, had to go along with it but privately let it be known that he did not like it. One of his wartime brigade commanders wrote him in November 1919 that "nobody favors the War Department reorganization bill." While many officers grumbled about the Baker-March bill, one who had given a great deal of thought to military policy over the years, Colonel John McAuley Palmer, openly opposed it. As adviser to the Senate Military Affairs Committee, he pushed hard for a program that newly promoted General of the Armies John J. Pershing endorsed in his testimony before the combined Senate and House committees in the fall of 1919. To be sure, the Palmer plan included a Regular Army of 275,000 to 300,000, but it also provided for a substantial National Guard and an organized reserve based on universal military training. In sum, this plan, as its author explained, made the citizen army "the foundation of national defense."[56]

The debate over military policy covered a host of other topics. Bureau chiefs urged that wartime General Staff power over them be reduced, and there were spokesmen for the Air Service, Tank Corps, Chemical Warfare Service, and other wartime branches, while nurses and chaplains wanted a more respected place in the hierarchy. A controversy over military justice simmered in the background as legislators mulled over amending the Articles of War. Thousands of pages of testimony before congressional committees went into the record as dozens of witnesses, most of whom were officers, pleaded for their particular cause.[57]

The place of aviation in the postwar Army was a vociferously debated issue. Some 190,000 men had been in the Air Service at its peak during the war, and no one argued that it should return to its prewar status as a part of the Signal Corps. Indeed, air officers and their civilian supporters pressed for a separate service equal to the Army and Navy, and bills to create a separate department of aviation were before both the House and Senate. Meantime the Air Service captivated public attention with long-distance flights, air races, and flying circuses. In one month in the spring of 1919, three of the latter put on shows in forty-five states.

The director of the Air Service, Charles T. Menoher, was not a flyer but rather a former division commander who had been at West Point with Pershing. As one would expect, he followed a conservative line; however, his assistant, Billy Mitchell, who retained his wartime temporary star because of this appointment, advocated an independent air organization in his testimony before Congress. Major Benny Foulois, who had lost his star in the demobilization, followed Mitchell before the House Committee on Military Affairs on October 7, 1919. Benny testified, at much greater length and more forcefully, for independence and also vehemently attacked the General Staff. That body, he flatly declared, "through lack of vision, lack of practical knowledge, or deliberate intention to subordinate the Air Service needs to the needs of the other combat arms . . . has utterly failed to appreciate the full military value of this new military weapon." The fact that the War Department plan recommended that officers be detailed to the air branch also galled Foulois as another indication that the Army meant to subordinate air interests to those of the other combat branches, whose officers were permanently assigned. He was furious that the official line was that the air arm was important yet the War Department plan "castrated it."[58]

Although the War Department favored maintaining the Tank Corps as a separate branch, it was neither as large nor as popular as the Air Service, and there were no ardent supporters within Congress. Within the Army, many, including General Pershing, believed that the tankers should be a part of the infantry. George Patton and Dwight Eisenhower vehemently disagreed, but Congress did not ask their views. After the war, what was left of the Tank Corps concentrated at Camp Meade, Maryland. It was there that Patton and Eisenhower met and, in the latter's words, "got along famously."

Patton still commanded what was left of the 304th Brigade, and Eisenhower had a battalion, but much of their time was spent with the tactical and technical tank schools and in experimenting with the light and heavy tanks. During one such test, when a heavy tank was pulling three light tanks through a ravine, a cable snapped and came within a few inches of killing both men. They worked Leavenworth problems, discussed tactics together, and agreed that the tank had a greater future as an offensive weapon than merely as a slow-moving support for infantry. Both published articles in service journals about tanks. Although Eisenhower's position was more conservative than Patton's, it still was so different from the standard infantry policy that Ike was berated and threatened with a court-martial by the chief of infantry.

While they might, as Ike recalled, have "the enthusiasm of zealots" for tanks, life at Meade was not all work. Their families got to know each other well as they shared the vicissitudes of living in abandoned barracks. Ike tried his hand at gardening and tried to get around Prohibition by concocting some bathtub gin, while George made some beer. Their tastes also differed in sports, with George enjoying polo and Ike coaching the post football team.

Their interlude came to an end after a year, in the fall of 1920, when both reverted from their temporary ranks of colonel and lieutenant colonel to major and Patton returned to the cavalry. For the younger man, the two years immediately after the war were much more profitable professionally than they had been for virtually all his contemporaries. In addition to his work with Patton, Ike had accompanied the truck convoy that the Army dispatched on an epic two-month journey from Washington, D.C., to San Francisco in the late summer of 1919. This exercise taught him all anyone would want to know about trucks, while he also learned a great deal about the nation that he crossed at a rate of six miles an hour.

Finally, Patton did him a great professional favor by inviting him and Mamie to dinner with Brigadier General and Mrs. Fox Conner.

This introduction to Pershing's wartime plans and operations officer served Eisenhower very well indeed.[59]

When the National Defense Act became law in June 1920, there were mixed reactions. For the first time, Congress did not detail the strength of each unit, granting the Army flexibility in such matters. The authorization to organize the Army generally along tactical rather than administrative lines was also obviously beneficial. A single promotion list would, it was hoped, still the traditional branch arguments over which had the advantage in promotion, and the new classification system should rid the officer corps of deadwood. At last the Army would also have warrant officers. Bureau chiefs were happy to be placed under the assistant secretary of war rather than the chief of staff. Infantry, cavalry, and field artillery officers, meantime, could rejoice that they at last had representation in the War Department through the newly created branch chiefs. Congress also saw fit to make the Air Service, Chemical Warfare Service, and Finance Department permanent branches but abolished the Tank Corps and the Motor Transport Corps. The nurses got a clarification of their authority and relative rank from second lieutenant to major, while the chaplains got a chief who would be a colonel.

The fact that Congress authorized a strength of almost 300,000 officers and men had to please virtually all the pre-1917 officers, who remembered when the Army had been less than half that number. In turn, National Guardsmen were delighted to get a clearly stated place in the military system and the position of chief of the Militia Bureau. Although their principle of basic dependence was accepted, Palmer and UMT supporters were disappointed that there was no provision for UMT, yet they could take solace in the framework for a citizen army and in the civilian training camps. The revised Articles of War did not meet the approval of those who sought a basic change in military justice from emphasis on command authority to individual rights; nevertheless a defense counsel and a board of review were steps in that direction.[60]

Four years later a regular major turned historian, William A. Ganoe, judged this legislation "by all odds the greatest provision for prolonging peace and the efficient control of war ever enacted by the Congress." It is safe to assume that no one said that about the reorganization acts following earlier wars. The only one that some active-duty officers could remember was the one after the Spanish-American War, and that was not as comprehensive. Besides it had become law in the middle of the war in the Philippines. In contrast, in 1920 the Army faced no such immediate demands. Indeed, none seemed likely in the future. This prospect certainly made the authorized-strength figure vulnerable.[61]

In World War I, the Army forged by the demands of colonial wars and the Root reforms met its first great test. Its officers directed the great mobilization and successfully led a force of more than a million into combat on the Western Front. Lieutenant General Hunter Liggett, who performed brilliantly as an AEF corps commander and, in the last weeks of the war, as commander of the First Army, justifiably took pride in the Army's accomplishment in this war as compared with earlier conflicts. It was "magnificent." As the 1920s began, younger officers who had gone through the crucible of this war could reasonably hope that the new National Defense Act provided for a modern force capable of dealing with any national emergencies that they might have to face in the future. Most Americans, however, were no longer interested in military matters. They probably shared the view of an older woman in Columbus, Ohio, who was shocked to see a neighborhood boy still in uniform in 1923. Clovis E. Byers had gone to West Point in 1918, graduated in 1920, and come home for a wedding where he wore his uniform. The woman addressed him: "Clovis, what have you done? Why is the Army still holding you . . . Can't you get out?"[62]

"Normalcy" had returned.

SEVEN

The Army in Limbo

It was our schools that saved the Army.
—J. LAWTON COLLINS

———◆◆◆———

D URING the Roaring 1920s and the Depression-ridden 1930s, public desire to cut government expenditures and traditional antimilitary attitudes combined with the dominant isolationist mood to reduce the Army to the point that it was negligible as a world power. Tight budgets year in and year out meant under-strength units, slow promotion, and restrictions on virtually any activity beyond maintenance of the status quo. At least from 1921 to 1939 the Army was more at peace than ever before in its history. There were no conflicts: no fighting Indians as before 1898 nor, as later, fighting Filipinos, Moros, and Mexicans. These years were marked by increasing professionalism in the form of emphasis on the advanced schools and the opportunities they provided officers to prepare for future possibilities. At the Army War College captains worked on strategic plans and even thought in terms of generals in command of large wartime units. Meantime, innovative officers advanced new infantry and field artillery techniques as those in the cavalry began to think about tanks rather than horses while airmen aspired to winning a future war with great fleets of bombers that were coming into production in the late 1930s.

In 1922 Secretary of War John W. Weeks bluntly declared: "Economy has literally become of primary consideration in every departmental undertaking." Even the prestige of General Pershing could not stem the tide. George Marshall, who was his aide, recalled that "his views didn't count at all," so "the cuts and cuts and cuts came." By the mid-1920s the transportation budget was so tight that the chief of staff of the Army and his aide could not afford to travel in a Pullman compartment when they took the train to inspect posts. The combat arms suffered from severe cuts in ammunition allowances for training. The Depression increased the privations. Even paperwork suffered; during the early 1930s the operations officer of the Eighth Infantry had to beg waste newsprint from Charleston, South Carolina, newspapers to use for mimeographing training schedules. At Fort Sheridan, Illinois, soldiers could have only one small light bulb in an entire squad bay in the barracks, and an officer checked each night to make sure that there were no unauthorized lights. The unkindest cut of all was reported in the 25th Infantry, where the daily ration of toilet paper was limited to three sheets for each soldier.[1]

The force authorized by the National Defense Act of 1920 to provide for immediate military needs as well as to train and serve as the foundation for a large citizen force in an emergency was 18,000 officers and 280,000 men; but Congress never appropriated funds for that host. For twelve of the twenty years from 1920 through 1939, the total force numbered less than 138,000 officers and men, and 28 percent of these troops were stationed outside the continental United States. Most were in small nineteenth-century posts because of lack of money to construct proper housing. Line units were pitifully under strength. A rifle company might have only seven or eight men available for training. Such a shortage created more of a problem in a mounted unit, when eight or ten men had to tend to 100 horses. In 1931 only twenty-seven of the seventy-four posts, bases, and hospitals had more than 1,000 in their garrisons, with Fort Sam Houston the largest with 5,434 officers and men. As Marshall pointed out in 1934, the entire combat force available in the States could be comfortably seated in the stadium at Chicago's Soldiers Field. It was painful for Army leaders to compare their strength with that of other nations. In 1932 the chief of staff, Douglas MacArthur, reported that the Army was seventeenth in size, smaller than those of Belgium and Portugal. Six years later, despite an increase of some 50,000, his successor, Malin Craig, said that the Army's relative strength had dropped to eighteenth among the armies of the world.[2]

The experience of World War I, which clearly demonstrated the need for a larger Army, and the National Defense Act of 1920 laid the foundation for a citizen army that, as MacArthur noted, would be the "ultimate reliance for the Nation's defense." Congressional parsimony hampered the development of this program, as did the difficulty faced by older officers in adjusting to this new mission of instructing the civilian components. In 1923 George Marshall, who had worked with National Guard units before the war, acknowledged this difficulty when he lectured the students at the Army War College about the duties and responsibilities of this new challenge. At that time there were 160,000 Guardsmen, 77,000 reserve officers, 104,000 cadets in Reserve Officer Training Corps (ROTC) programs, and 25,000 volunteers who had just finished that year's summer training in the Citizens' Military Training Camps. The postwar version of the Plattsburg camps, the CMTC offered a month's training each summer for three, later four, years, after which a young man could apply for a reserve commission. In 1926 the chief of staff reported that 49 percent of the Army had been involved in supporting these civilian components. Over the 1920s and 1930s, an estimated 370,000 participated in the CMTC program (only 6 percent lasted through the four years, and even fewer received commissions), while almost 299,000 Guardsmen, some 104,000 reserve officers, and another 3,200 enlisted reservists were available for active service when war was on the horizon in the late 1930s.[3]

Who were the regular officers of this period? A survey based on samples from the 1925, 1933, and 1940 *Official Army Registers* provides general characteristics. The largest group (33.4 percent) came from the Midwest, followed by southerners (29.2 percent). A sizable share (28.5 percent) had spent time in the enlisted ranks before becoming officers. Most of those veterans entered the officer corps when the Army expanded following the Spanish war and the world war. Over 37 percent of the officers were West Pointers, yet 71.1 percent of the generals were graduates. General MacArthur believed that since "the whole Army had been developed spiritually in the image of West Point," at least 50 percent of the officers should be graduates. In 1935 he was delighted when Congress authorized a 42 percent increase in strength to 1,960 in the corps of cadets at West Point.[4]

There were black and Jewish officers during this period, but the *Official Army Register* did not indicate either race or religion. With the retirement of John E. Green in 1929, Benjamin O. Davis was the only black line officer until his son, Benjamin O. Davis Jr., graduated from West Point in 1936. Four years later the father, son, and three chaplains remained the only black officers. The experiences of the Davis family illustrate the quality of life they were able to develop in this segregated era.[5]

Throughout this period the Army discriminated against the elder Davis by keeping him away from regular troops in assignments at black colleges and with black civilian components. He went about his duties conscientiously and tried to make the best of his lot. While in the Philippines, his children had stayed with his parents in Washington, D.C. Upon his return with his new wife, Sadie Overton, who had journeyed across the Pacific to marry him, they took the children to Tuskegee. For faculty and students at the institute, Tuskegee was like "a little island" in a world of segregation. The Davises sent their teenaged daughter to Atlanta to high school but kept eight-year-old Ben and four-year-old Elnora with them. "Punctuality, neatness, and obedience were the rules" in the Davis home.[6]

Racism did intrude in one stark incident, when Ku Klux Klansmen bearing torches staged a night march in the campus area. To avoid trouble, the black residents turned off all lights and attempted to ignore them—except for Lieutenant Colonel Davis, who put on his dress whites, turned on the lights, and sat on the porch with his wife and three children. There was no confrontation, but he made his point, as his son later wrote, "that we need never demand that people like us, but by our actions we must always demand that they respect us."[7]

For several summers Davis and his wife and, on occasion, each daughter went to Europe, where they enjoyed a freedom beyond that possible in the United States. During those years, young Ben excelled in high school, went to college, and thought about becoming a mathematics teacher. His father never urged him to make the Army a career, but when the opportunity to go to West Point came, both were enthusiastic.

Within days of his arrival at the Academy, Ben realized that he was not welcome. Although official amenities were observed, he was silenced by the cadet corps and, with few exceptions, shunned by the other cadets throughout the four years. After three years, a tactical officer recommended him to be a cadet officer, but the commandant, Simon Bolivar Buckner Jr. (son of a Confederate general), refused to promote him. Davis bore the burden of social ostracism with dignity and did not tell his parents of this shameful treatment. Despite the tribute that was paid him in the yearbook—"The courage, tenacity, and intelligence with which he conquered a problem incomparably more difficult than Plebe year won for him the sincere admiration of his classmates"—he found that he was as unwelcome in the Army as he was at West Point. Before he graduated in 1936 (the first black graduate since Charles Young in 1889), the Army rejected his effort to become a pilot, so he went into the infantry. At Fort Benning he served in the 24th Infantry and as a student in the basic officers' course, but he and his wife were ignored by classmates as well as by other white officers. Years later, he explained how he managed to cope with this. He held to the belief "that you are a hell of a lot better morally and you are far superior as individuals than those stupid characters who don't realize that they ought to associate properly with other human beings."[8]

Another form of racism, anti-Semitism, also pervaded American society. There are clues as to what effect this had in the Army in the records of the National Jewish Welfare Board (NJWB). Perhaps it was not as much as one might expect. In 1936, when asked to investigate a rumor that Nazi propaganda was being circulated in the Army, one of the field representatives reported: "While, of course, occasional instances of anti-Semitism have been brought to my attention, I do not believe that it is widespread in the service, and certainly is less evident than in civil life." It is impossible to determine the number of Jews who held commissions, but the NJWB files and fragmentary information do provide some information about this minority. Although some rabbis held reserve commissions, apparently there were no rabbis in the Army throughout this period. Representatives of the NJWB did attempt to stay in touch and provide religious support for soldiers of their faith. When a rabbi visited West Point in 1923, a cadet told him that the eight Jews in the corps did not want to form a group, as doing so might arouse comment. Since chapel was compulsory, they attended Protestant services, but four did go to a high-holy-days service offered by a reserve chaplain. Fourteen years later another reservist who began holding regular services at the Military Academy found both Protestant and Catholic chaplains supportive, yet Jews still had to attend compulsory chapel. When he began his work, there were twenty Jews in the cadet corps. Two years later, there were twenty-five. Rabbi B. A.

A very happy day. Benjamin O. Davis congratulates his son at his graduation from West Point, 1936. Courtesy of Elnora Davis McLendon.

Tintner was pleased by his general reception at West Point and the enthusiasm of the cadets.[9]

Maurice Rose, who would earn the accolade "the top armored commander in the Army" from his corps commander in World War II, did not attend West Point. After wartime service as an infantry lieutenant, he received a regular commission in 1920. As a captain, ten years later, he transferred to the cavalry. "Tall, handsome, always dressed immaculately," Rose was "very much liked" by his classmates at the Command

and General Staff School in the mid-1930s. Elwood R. "Pete" Quesada, a young Air Corps captain, who saw much of him there, found him very congenial. The Roses invited Pete, who was a bachelor, for dinner, and occasionally the two officers attended movies and visited museums in Kansas City. They also exchanged ideas about the value of close air support. Whether or not Quesada and the other students knew that Rose was a Jew, they obviously appreciated him.[10]

When *Fortune,* a leading business magazine, ran two in-depth articles on the Army in its September 1935 issue, the anonymous authors seemed somewhat bemused about officers whose characteristics they perceived as "a queer mixture of the clergy, the college professor, and the small boy playing Indian . . . The Sam Browne belts, the brief, unqualified commands, the perpetual acknowledgment of salutes, the blind worship of rank, are manifestations of the primitive that lies hidden in almost every one of us." They were awed by the only general they discussed at length—MacArthur—whom they called "the Army's mainspring." "Brilliant," with a gift of metaphor and dramatic sense worthy of an Elizabethan actor, he was "the hero" to them.[11]

A colonel at thirty-seven and a general the next year, MacArthur had put on four stars and become chief of staff when he was fifty. Others had similar rapid promotions during World War I, but MacArthur outstripped them during the postwar period. For most officers, promotions were very rare in the 1920s and early 1930s. Indeed, as the secretary of war pointed out in 1935, "Officers were growing old in junior grade" during those years. The problem was that in expectation of the large force authorized by the National Defense Act of 1920 the War Department commissioned 5,229 officers that year. This group of approximately the same age and grade constituted what became known as the "hump." By 1932 almost 4,200 officers (more than a third of the entire officer corps) were between the ages of thirty-seven and forty-three, with 1,885 captains and 234 lieutenants in their forties. This sizable bloc, combined with promotion by seniority and the mandatory retirement age of sixty-four, created a logjam in advancement.[12]

Although promotion was not as glacial as it had been a century earlier, when a new lieutenant could expect to spend fifty-eight years in the service before putting on the eagles of a colonel, still, according to MacArthur, an officer in the early 1930s could expect to take at least thirty-six years to reach that exalted rank. In 1933 the mean age of lieutenants was thirty-two, that of captains forty-three, that of majors forty-five and a half, that of lieutenant colonels fifty-two and a third, and that of colonels just over fifty-nine.[13]

Even those commissioned ahead of the "hump" were frozen in rank for years. Devers, Patton, and Simpson spent fourteen years as majors, while younger West Pointers such as Dwight Eisenhower and Omar Bradley of the class of 1915 were demoted after serving as majors for more than two years and had to spend some two years as captains before regaining their gold leaves, which they then wore for twelve years. Mark Clark, Joe Collins, and Matt Ridgway, who graduated the month war was declared in 1917, spent more than thirteen years as captains. Two non–West Pointers, Charlie Bolté and Lucian Truscott, who received regular commissions ahead of the "hump," served as captains for fifteen years.

Though commissioned before the "hump," the West Point class that graduated in November 1918, then returned as lieutenants to complete a second year at the Academy, was still outranked by many of the World War I veterans who came into the regular officer corps in 1920. Although they were promoted to first lieutenants not long after their graduation, they had to give up their silver bars for several months to a year in the early 1920s and then return to the higher rank where they remained for what must have seemed an eon. As Al Wedemeyer explained later, "I parked in the lieutenant grade for 17 years, all of my class did." A classmate, Anthony C. McAuliffe, became bored with the round of lieutenant's duties in the field artillery. "I thought," he recalled, "that if I had to give another gunners examination, I would go crazy." He considered transferring to the infantry for variety. Jake Devers advised him against it because he was known in his branch and his future might depend on that. During this period, some of these aging lieutenants began to refer to their rank insignia as the "Bars Sinister." Yet most of them stayed on. Years later, McAuliffe admitted that he had thought about resigning, but "I had an idea that we might get into another war and I had the ambition to command troops in combat."

Understandably an officer's position relative to the "hump" made a difference in commitment. Eisenhower's class of 1915 held higher ranks throughout this period of stagnation, and only twelve (7 percent) resigned. By the time the West Point class of 1923 received their diplomas, the impact of the "hump" and tight budgets was clear, and seventy-one (24 percent) ultimately resigned. Of course, specific reasons for resigning varied. Fritz Breidster, who held a commission in the closing days of the war before entering West Point, was the most outstanding man in the class of 1923. He was not only class president and first captain but also an all-American football player who captained the team through an unbeaten season. As a football star he was a marked man, and senior officers wanted him to play or coach for their teams. These assignments were frustrating, as they took him out of the normal routine of his branch, the Signal Corps. Then, in the mid-1920s, it did look as though the last war was the war to end all wars and he might retire as a major. As he put it, "I became somewhat disenchanted" and resigned to go to work for the American Cable Company.[14]

Ten years after Breidster left the Army, Congress finally gave some relief to officers. The 1935 legislation mandated promotion to first lieutenant in three years and to captain seven years later; it also increased the number of field-grade officers to help break the logjam. The secretary of war declared the effect "electrical": almost half of all officers under the rank of colonel received promotion, and others gained from two to eight years on their next promotion. At last those long-serving lieutenants from the class of 1919 became captains, as did others who graduated from West Point or entered the officer corps through the class of 1925. The act meant gold leaves for Charlie Bolté and Lucian Truscott.[15]

When *Fortune* turned its attention to the Army, its writers highlighted details of Army pay. In 1935, in the midst of the Depression, Army pay, particularly that of officers, no doubt looked very good to most Americans. The businessmen who read *Fortune* were probably not as impressed. With second lieutenants making only $1,500 to $2,000, colonels $3,500 to $4,000, and generals $6,000 to $8,000, they were hardly laying the foundations for fortunes. Congress had set those pay levels in 1922 for the first time for the regulars since 1908. During the two decades from 1908 to 1928, Army pay increased only 11 percent while other federal government branches enjoyed salary raises of 25 percent to 175 percent and the Consumer Price Index (CPI) rose almost 87 percent. The effect, as explained by an Army wife, was that "it took some tall figuring to keep up with the Joneses."

The Depression markedly changed the situation. Between 1928 and 1935 the CPI dropped 20 percent, and Army pay along with other federal salaries suffered cuts of 15 percent plus one unpaid month as part of the New Deal economy program. A detailed War Department study, however, showed that in 1933 officers, depending on their grades, paid from over 8 percent to more than 17 percent less for such essentials as food, quarters, clothing, medical expenses, and servants than they had five years earlier. The officers who responded to a questionnaire about their finances that year, however, were not happy with their situations. Some expressed concern about having enough to educate their children; others worried about their insurance premiums, while several reported that they had to dip into savings to get by. A couple complained that duty with the Civilian Conservation Corps (CCC) cost them out of pocket up to a dollar a day. One lieutenant commented that he was doing his best to live within his salary "even to the point of miserliness." A recently promoted captain pointed out: "Every day in every way it's becoming more difficult to keep the chin up." In 1935 salaries were restored to their precut levels, but officers were not reimbursed for the lost month's wages plus the 15 percent difference over those two years. Nevertheless, an officer's wife later pointed out that they were more fortunate than many civilians, and some were able to send money to their needy families.[16]

Two New Deal measures to bolster the economy had a direct impact on the Army. One was the provision of Public Works Administration funds to Army housing. During the first year after Franklin D. Roosevelt entered office, the PWA made more than $61 million available for officer quarters and barracks, and there was more to come to replace the multitude of shabby temporary buildings. The second measure was the creation of the Civilian Conservation Corps, which provided room, board, and medical care as well as wages to young men who worked to enhance the environment. Initially, in the spring of 1933, the Labor Department was supposed to select the men; then the Army would immunize, clothe, organize, and transport them to points where either the Interior or Agriculture Department would put them to work. Within a few days, it was obvious that the Army would have to take over the program although a civilian director remained in nominal control. By June 30, 250,000 men (more than double the number of regulars) were in 200-man companies scattered across the nation in 1,350 CCC camps.

The chief of staff, General MacArthur, was reluctant for the Army to take on the responsibility for such a huge task, since he realized that it would virtually monopolize the Army. As he noted later, in 1933, it did bring training to a "standstill, and has almost destroyed the readiness of units for immediate and effective employment on emergency duty." Despite the fact that the Army assigned 3,109 officers (a fourth of the officer corps) and more than 5,000 soldiers to the CCC, it still had to call on the Navy and Marine Corps (532) and the reserves (1,774) for additional officers to supervise the camps.[17]

With such a great mobilization—larger than that of the Spanish-American War—and construction of camps in terrain ranging from forests to swamps, it was a hectic summer. George Marshall, however, thrived on it. From the routine of commanding a battalion post, he quickly adjusted to supervising the CCC scattered over Florida, Georgia, and South Carolina. Although he left in the fall of 1933 for another assignment, his promotion to brigadier general in the fall of 1936 gave him a brigade with additional responsibility for the CCC in Oregon and southern Washington. "I found," he wrote a friend, "the CCC the most instructive service I have ever had and the most interesting."[18]

Whatever its effect on routine training, the CCC provided for those regulars involved the experience of a large mobilization. MacArthur recognized that in his annual report and pointed out that the Army had done a much better job in the spring of 1933 than it had done during the early months of 1917. There were problems. For one, CCC men got $30.00 a month, while privates were paid only $17.85; hence there was natural resentment. Then, the CCC was a civilian organization; thus officers did not have the Articles of War and regulations to back up their authority. They were also forbidden to drill the men or give them any military instruction. During that first summer, Marshall was concerned about the resulting lack of discipline. His regimental operations officer remembered that there were some New Jersey and New York men who were "anti-everything," and there was certainly little to lift the morale of urbanites in a South Carolina swamp.[19]

Charles T. "Buck" Lanham had a particularly difficult situation with a company that was on the verge of mutiny. Agitators, who he believed were Communists, stirred up trouble in the camps in his area. At one, the CCC people beat up the few regulars and reservists in the cadre and left them tied up in the woods. Lanham called a meeting and never forgot the sound of muttering as the 200 or so men gathered around him. After the leaders made their demands, he got up on a stump (with two lieutenants armed with 45s behind him) and spoke to the entire company. In a few minutes he managed to make the ringleaders look ridiculous. Later, he discharged them from the company.[20]

After that first summer, although men continued to pour into the CCC, the Army withdrew most of its officers as it called up reservists to take over this mission. In 1934 there were fewer than 500 regular officers and more than 5,000 reservists on CCC duty. A year later there were 359 regulars and 9,284 reservists, and those numbers continued to decline. By 1940 more than 3.3 million men had been enrolled, and some 200,000 were currently in camps. By that time civilians had replaced the officers in the camps.[21]

George W. Weber was a reserve second lieutenant who took a job as a civilian "subaltern" to do administrative work at a camp in northern Michigan during the summer and fall of 1940. He had just completed a year's tour at Fort Brady as a Thomason Act officer. In the mid-1930s, to alleviate the shortage of officers, Congress authorized calling up annually 1,000 reservists for a year's active duty. From this group, 50 could win regular commissions through competitive examination. When Weber received his reserve commission in 1939, a lieutenant's pay of $125 plus $18 in ration allowance looked very good compared with the $75-a-month jobs that his classmates at the University of Wisconsin sought in civilian life. He and the other Thomason Act lieutenants who went to Fort Brady were pleasantly surprised at how well they were received and treated by the regulars. The program worked to the advantage of these young men, who were given good jobs in hard times, and to the Army, which needed the officers. Jack Hines, who commanded a troop in the Third Cavalry at Fort Myer, liked the two Thomason Act officers under his command and was disappointed that they did not get regular commissions. Then and later, he thought that "they didn't let enough of them in." Melvin Zais, a University of New Hampshire graduate who spent a year with the 13th Infantry, was one of those. Army life appealed to him. As he said, "I really caught on fire." He studied hard for the competitive examination but was rejected for physical reasons. Two years later, during the mobilization in 1940, he returned to active duty and stayed until he became a four-star general.[22]

In late 1934, a professor recommended adoption of a book on the New Deal for the Military Academy's course in economics. Lieutenant Colonel Herman Beukema argued that the course should cover that important topic and that Schuyler Wallace's *New Deal in Action* was a balanced account. The superintendent, however, turned down the proposal because the New Deal "is a live political issue, and as such, is not suitable for study or discussion in this institution." Furthermore, it "is sponsored by the President, who is Commander-in-Chief of the Army, and whose policies are therefore not properly debatable in this institution."[23]

While this incident was probably not known beyond West Point, another involving one of the most senior officers in the Army reverberated through Congress and the White House. Major General Johnson Hagood, commander of the VIII Corps Area, was outspoken but, from his years in the War Department before the war, should have known the pitfalls of the political arena. Called to testify about government spending before a subcommittee of the House Appropriations Committee in December 1935, Hagood, who assumed the session was secret, harshly criticized New Deal policies for inept handling of labor and funds, thus fueling anti–New Deal attacks. The chief of staff publicly admonished his former close friend for making "remarks so deliberately designed to hold up Government agencies and policies to ridicule and contempt" and relieved him of command. During the period when Hagood awaited orders, President Franklin D. Roosevelt met with him and offered a similar command if he would apologize. Although the general initially refused, he did accept later and made a token appearance at his new command before retiring in the spring of 1936.[24]

Officers were supposed to stay out of politics, and most of them did—even to the point of not voting. Charlie Bolté, who did not vote throughout his active-duty career, recalled being imbued with the concept: "it was none of our business." And wives followed suit. Benny Bolté never voted, and one of the first admonitions Walter M. Johnson gave his bride, Virginia, was not to have "anything to do with politics or politicians." George Marshall, Jake Devers, Ralph Huebner, the Benjamin O. Davises, Matt Ridgway, Al Wedemeyer, Joe Collins, Tony McAuliffe, and Buck Lanham were others who did not vote in this period. Even if they had wanted to vote, it was difficult to establish residency, and some states did not have absentee ballots. Generally, however, they did not even discuss politics much.[25]

John W. Leonard, five years out of West Point, did vote in the presidential election of 1920. The Democratic party leader who had procured his appointment to the Military Academy sent him an absentee ballot, and he voted for that party's candidate, James M. Cox, but it was his only vote until he retired. Wayne Clark voted after he bought a house and established residence in Indianapolis while on duty with the National Guard in the late 1920s and early 1930s. And Clovis Byers, his wife, and Bonner Fellers were regular voters via absentee ballot, while Jack Hines, as a young lieutenant, voted for Franklin D. Roosevelt in 1932 and 1936; but these were exceptions.[26]

In the early nineteenth century, young officers had regularly taken long leaves and spent weeks in Washington mixing with Army and political leaders, including the president. But that practice had faded after the Civil War, and even those officers stationed in Washington were hardly noticeable in the 1920s and 1930s. For one reason, since the early 1920s these officers did not wear their uniforms. Even Douglas MacArthur wore a white civilian suit to his office, although he did don his uniform on the day he observed the eviction of the Bonus Army in the summer of 1932. His appearance on that occasion and his statements about the Bonus marchers confirmed some civilians' fear of a man on horseback. Although Roosevelt was one of those skeptics, he still gave the chief of staff an extra year in office.[27]

While the faint specter of military influence in politics remained just that on the national level, there was an Army bloc that did make its weight count in a local election in the Big Bend country of Texas in 1923. As two factions of Democrats battled evenly in the sheriff's race, one of the leaders who had two daughters married to officers of the First Cavalry regiment stationed at Camp Marfa had the innovative idea of trying to get the votes of the other wives. Although it was then against state law for "convicted felons, insane persons, and members of the Regular Army" to vote, nothing was said about officers' wives. So he and his wife, who were well liked on the post, came out and recruited the wives and took them into town to vote. Those votes decided the race.

Lucian Truscott was shocked when his wife mentioned that she had voted that morning. His forebodings were soon realized when the losing faction complained. The regimental commander gathered the officers and roundly criticized them for letting their wives vote. Inspectors and judge advocates general as well as assorted civilian authorities came in to check on the matter. Eventually, a ruling that they were not legal residents because their husbands could not establish residency led to their votes' being thrown out. As Truscott remembered: "we all set about mending public relations with as much charm as we possessed." And hard feelings dissipated, except perhaps among the disfranchised wives.[28]

When *Fortune* surveyed "Who's in the Army Now?" the writers paid little attention to the women of the Army. There were only mentions of MacArthur's former wife, the honorary commissions given to a couple of movie stars, and a photo of a horse-drawn coach with men and women in hunting costumes. The caption indicated that this was taken during a pageant at Fort Myer and added that "the Army favors the ladies." Depending upon an officer's wife's personality and her particular mood when she read that, it evoked a chuckle or perhaps a snarl. For these women, Army life was not all costumes and pageants. Mauree Mahin, Beatrice Patton, and others who were born into the Army or married into it before World War I already knew that, and the brides who came into garrisons during and after the war soon realized it.[29]

Despite their families' misgivings and warnings, girls who knew little or nothing about the Army met and married officers. In the mid-1930s, Virginia Weisel's mother and grandmother told her that soldiers drank too much and were rootless and that she would never be happy in that life, but it did not take much persuading on the part of a young West Pointer to convince her otherwise. After their elopement, she began to find that it was a different world. An older Army wife explained the round of formal fifteen-minute calls, exactly which and how many calling cards to leave, and that she, not her husband, had to carry packages and push the baby carriage when that became necessary. She learned the bugle calls, how to help her husband take off his boots, and how she could depend on the first sergeant. In fact she spent her first night on the post on Sergeant Meador's cot. The sergeant told her husband when they returned from their honeymoon that he was the officer of the day, and thus would not have the time or opportunity to obtain temporary accommodations for his wife. Sergeant Meador's solution was to take a twenty-four-hour pass and offer the new Mrs. Walter M. Johnson the cot in his separate little house for the night.[30]

Two others who discovered this new world were Maurine Doran and Thelma Fadner. Maurine, or Renie, the daughter of a Ball Brothers Glass Company official in Muncie, Indiana, had finished her musical studies at Northwestern University and was working at the War Department when she met Mark Clark on a blind date. She married the tall, handsome officer in Washington Cathedral in the spring of 1924. Her parents gave them a new Buick as a wedding present. As she began to adjust to Army life, she felt "that I was living in a goldfish bowl." All the officers and their wives knew what each's salary was and what work they did, and secrets were hard to keep. At the same time, the fact that a "post is like a big family," Renie came to realize, had its compensations in the helpfulness of friends and neighbors.[31]

The Depression was making life hard for most civilians when Thelma Fadner, a carpenter's daughter, journeyed to West Point to marry Robert J. Watson in 1930. They had met while in their teens in the First Baptist Church in Fond du Lac, Wisconsin. She enjoyed the festivities of June Week, and the day after he graduated they married in the Cadet Chapel. Bob's mother and the sexton were the only attendees. After several days of sightseeing in New York City, they went to Minneapolis, where he began his first assignment at Fort Snelling. By early October, when Bob received his first pay, Thelma was aware that "money goes fast here as everywhere." She wrote her mother that she had finished the ironing and was fixing goulash for dinner with leftover hamburger meat. Those were common enough experiences, but Thelma's references to a regimental review and an upcoming big party must have struck her family as somewhat exotic.[32]

Marrying an officer was not as great a step for girls who had grown up in the Army. One recalled the assumption that "if an Army girl didn't marry an Army officer, she probably would become an old maid." Another wrote: "My sister and I had always feared we might fall in love with a civilian and we wondered how we'd ever adjust to that way of life." Brigadier General and Mrs. Benjamin A. Poore, according to their daughter, "didn't expect anything else." Benny Poore and Grace Wilson, who had become known as "Boo," were captivating young women in the early postwar years. Benny liked sports and riding above all, while Boo was musically inclined. Their attractiveness and charm brought beaus to their doorsteps, and to no one's surprise they married officers. Boo was fourteen when she met fifteen-year-old Leslie R. "Dick" Groves on New Year's Day 1912. They liked each other, but like other Army children, they soon moved to other posts. However, they kept in touch. After he graduated from West Point, he pressed his suit although she was engaged to another man. Finally Boo returned the other man's ring and accepted Dick's proposal.[33]

Benny enjoyed the amenities of Fort Sam Houston and San Antonio and dated, among others, a Marine officer and became engaged to an older Air Service officer. She had broken up with the latter by the spring of 1922, when she was named the Duchess of the Army for the local Festival of San Jacinto. During a rehearsal she met the handsome "Duke," Captain Charles L. Bolté. He proved to be an ardent swain, although she wondered about the pattern of their courtship, in which she would see much of him in the early days of each month and then see him hardly at all toward the end of the month. By then Charlie had simply run out of money; nevertheless his suit was successful: they were married in April 1923.[34]

Quarters varied greatly during this period. The newlywed Boltés moved into an apartment on K Street in Washington, D.C., since Charlie was the deputy chief of staff's aide. Throughout these years, many officers in Washington had to live off post, where, as one wife pointed out, their commutation allowance sometimes did not cover the expense. Later, when General John L. Hines became the chief of staff, Benny and Charlie moved into quarters at Fort Myer. Their next assignment took them to a "little wooden shack" at Fort Benning. The beaverboard covering the walls did not provide much insulation. Nor were the fireplace and two pot-bellied stoves much help. During the winter Benny stuffed absorbent cotton in the assorted cracks to little avail. At the other extreme, in the summer the heat hovered around 100 degrees in the bedroom, which had no cross-ventilation. Later in the 1930s, at the Army War College, they lived in an old arsenal that had been converted into apartments. Despite all their efforts, they could not get the temperature above 56 degrees during the cold nights. When they finally moved into adequate quarters, Charlie got orders to another assignment after only two months.[35]

Their experiences were not unique. Katharine Hollister Smith recalled that during heavy rains the roofs leaked so badly in the makeshift quarters at Benning that one had to use an umbrella to do housework. One newlywed couple at Benning had to live in four attached tents with vines growing up through the floor. In 1919, when Beatrice Patton moved into a wartime temporary barracks at Camp Meade, she used the only paint available, so the rooms were blue and yellow; as a gesture toward beautification, she planted ivy in the urinals. Since the Pattons were wealthy, however, they were sometimes able to rent lavish quarters off post over the next twenty years.[36]

The Groves often lived among civilians because of Dick's engineer assignments. Their first home, however, consisted of two rooms in the basement of the bachelor officers' quarters during his first assignment after their marriage at the Presidio in San Francisco. There were no cooking facilities, so they had to eat at the officers' mess or go into the city for their meals. When they finally got a house equipped with an old gas stove, Boo waited too long to light it one night, and the gas exploded and burned her face. In 1936 the Watsons, who now had a son, moved to the Presidio, and Thelma was excited by their first temporary home there, as it overlooked the Bay and the new Golden Gate bridge, and she appreciated the flowers that surrounded their more permanent quarters.[37]

Many wives had fulltime help, a combination cook and maid, who could babysit when necessary. But Thelma seldom had this luxury. After she was settled at the Presidio, she wrote her sister: "it is no mean job just to keep the house clean, meals ready, dishes washed, laundry done, kid clean." After several years of this routine, she complained: "I have got so I simply loathe housework . . . particularly getting meals is a boring chore." There was help in an emergency such as the time she discovered on Thanksgiving morning that the turkey was too big for her oven. Bob took it over to his company, where the mess sergeant cooked it together with the twenty others he was preparing for the company's dinner.[38]

Thelma also sometimes had part-time help from a soldier. Most wives welcomed this help, but Dick Groves disapproved of soldiers doing domestic work; hence Grace had to get by with a maid. Enlisted men could pick up some extra money (five to fifteen dollars per month) after duty hours by volunteering to take care of an officer's horse, shine his boots and Sam Browne belt, and keep his insignia polished. They also performed various other chores such as doing heavy housework, bringing in wood for the fires, taking care of the yard, and even babysitting.[39]

Travel, most wives would agree, was one of the greatest advantages of Army life. On the other hand, the constant moves and consequent rootlessness were significant disadvantages. Although, as Benny Bolté remembered, the Army began to pay for moves after World War I, there still remained some cost as well as inconvenience. As it happened, the emergency budget government decree of an unpaid month in 1932 occurred just as the Boltés were preparing to go to China. They could not stay in their quarters at Leavenworth, since a new class was coming in, so they decided to spend the two months until sailing time with his parents in San Diego. While Charlie and six-year-old David drove to California, Benny took Phil (four) and Damara (nine months) via a lengthy (five nights and six days) train trip. They had hoped to stay with his parents but wound up exhausting their savings to rent a house. By the time they boarded the transport, they were flat broke.[40]

Whatever the trials of the moves, once settled in the new home, as one wife pointed out, "each post seemed the same and life went on as always." In addition to the mandatory formal calls, there was an extraordinary array of social activities. Another wife remembered: "You could be as busy as you wanted to be." A separate career was not, however, an option. Nevertheless, a few wives did have work on occasion. Aina Wodehouse Olsmith worked as the riding instructor at a girls' camp in Michigan during parts of four summers. Since her husband was stationed at various schools during those years, he was able to accompany her and was also compensated for his efforts as stable manager and assistant instructor. They had a private cabin and were also reimbursed for their travel costs from his post to the camp. During the summer of 1925, Rachel Forbush Wood and Jared also worked at a girls' camp. At Camp Tahoma in New Hampshire, he was the riding instructor and she was in charge of entertainment. Three summers later they got a free round trip to Europe as the hostess and deck sport leader on a Holland-American ship that catered to students. From 1924, when they returned from an assignment in China, to 1931, Rachel also ran a small Chinese import business, which "added zest and shekels to our life."[41]

The social whirl took up whatever spare time most officers and their wives had. There were frequently dances, or hops, and occasionally costume balls. Thelma went as a hula dancer while Bob Watson dressed up as a gypsy for a ball at the Presidio; the Pattons went to one at Fort Benning as Rhett Butler and Scarlett O'Hara. Dinner parties, buffet suppers, and, a postwar innovation, cocktail parties were other forms of entertainment. There were also a wide variety of interest groups—bridge clubs, book clubs, music groups, theatrical societies—while those with children could help out with the Boy and Girl Scouts or perhaps join the local parent-teachers' association. At Fort Benning in 1925, the Infantry School Woman's Club met weekly. The printed program for the Monday afternoon meeting of March 16 shows three speakers: a major talked about Oriental rugs, another man (presumably a butcher) gave pointers on how to buy meat, and one of the wives discussed the family budget. The program also included recipes for angel drop cakes and two kinds of cookies. At Benning in the late 1920s, with the multi-talented Forrest Harding as the sparkplug, the drama group was very active, even staging some three-act plays. Katharine Smith, who had roles in several of those productions, however, had some doubts about this activity. "On the whole I think amateur theatricals cause more quarrels, hard feelings and flirtations than they are worth." At Leavenworth in the mid-1930s, Grace Groves belonged to thirteen clubs.[42]

There was ample opportunity for the adults to play golf, tennis, bowl, or go swimming. Riding was particularly popular. In addition to recreational riding, hunt clubs were important parts of the social life at Leavenworth and Benning. For those wives who did not know how

The Infantry School Hunt, Fort Benning, Georgia, 1930. Similar photos in the media did not help the Army's image during the Depression. Courtesy of Rachel Forbush Wood.

to ride, classes were available. George Marshall was a great believer in riding for exercise and encouraged it when he was assistant commandant of the Infantry School at Fort Benning. Among those who rode with him there was Benny Bolté, who had ridden since childhood. Those who were not skilled horsewomen could get into trouble. Tere Versace found that out when her horse ran away with her and galloped across a golf course. Her husband heard from his superiors about that and gave her a scolding.[43]

The showcase for Army horsemanship was Fort Myer, across the Potomac from Washington. When Patton returned to the cavalry in the fall of 1920, he took command of a squadron of the Third Cavalry at this post. He saw the possibility of livening up the winter months with weekly exhibitions in the riding hall. During his tenure as regimental commander in the late 1920s, Guy V. Henry took special interest in these exhibitions. Each troop would work hard to develop an acrobatic, trick-riding act, which might draw as many as 1,800 spectators. Troop E, when John L. Hines Jr. commanded in the late 1930s, had a Mongolian ride as its specialty. With troopers costumed as Mongolians and their mounts decorated accordingly, Jack silently directed them through an intricate, wild riding exhibition. Another troop might do a jumping exercise or perform as cossacks. Backing up these two-and-a-half-hour shows each Friday was the excellent Third Cavalry band. In 1926 the adjutant general asked Louis S. Yassel if he could ride a horse. Yassel responded: "Never in my life" but said he was willing to learn, so he took over this mounted band. The exhibition season culminated in the Society Circus, a special show that included Cub Scouts as well as Washington debutantes. In 1933 the theme was technology, but the action, not surprisingly, turned out to be elaborate displays of horsemanship. This proved to be a good fundraiser for the post athletic fund and assorted Army charities.

The Pattons enjoyed their first tour at Myer, but George did not want to return as regimental commander in 1938. He thought that his regiment at Fort Clark, Texas, offered more opportunity for "real soldiering." But the chief of cavalry prevailed. Despite his disgruntlement, Patton, as one would expect, attended to his duties. When he checked out Jack Hines's Mongolian ride, he told Jack to take the tassels off the bridles and not have his men ride so fast. And when the regiment went into field training, he made certain that the live-firing exercise was more realistic. During this period the Pattons' marriage was strained, and Beatrice took solace in riding.[44]

Marital stress in the Army as well as in civilian life came from causes ranging from infidelity through neglect to illness. No one will ever know how many flirtations begun during the continuous social whirl turned into serious affairs, but the marital strain between George and Beatrice Patton did become known later. During their tour in Hawaii in the mid-1930s, at least two women made advances, which George repelled. The third, however, he evidently welcomed. Jean Gordon, the twenty-one-year-old daughter of Beatrice's half-sister, came out to visit her good friend, Ruth Ellen, the Pattons' younger daughter. Apparently they consummated the affair on a trip to another island. The resulting tension in the Patton household was long-lasting, yet Beatrice did not leave George. As she explained to Ruth Ellen, "Your father needs me . . . I am all that he really has, and I love him and he loves me."[45]

Drinking was probably no more of a problem among the officers and their wives than among their peers in civilian life. Prohibition was in force throughout much of this period, yet people who wanted to drink did so in and out of the Army. When the Truman Smiths reported for duty at Fort Benning they understood that the assistant commandant was a teetotaler and would enforce Prohibition. Nevertheless, the officers in Truman's section gave them a five-gallon jug of Georgia corn whiskey as a welcoming gift. At Fort Myer, officers depended on bootleggers who would deliver pure alcohol to the door, which when mixed with an equal amount of water would make gin. Since this was cheaper than corn liquor, it became the drink of choice. Even after the national law was repealed, Kansas remained dry; those at Leavenworth who wanted even beer had to go to Missouri.

Decorum as well as the law had to be observed. Those who could not hold their liquor or who became objectionable could be in trouble. Eleanor Bishop Powell remembered that one colonel regularly sent home from dances two officers' wives who overindulged. Others would call in the husbands and admonish them about their wives' behavior. For an officer, overdrinking could lead to dismissal. As a rule, Al Wedemeyer did not touch liquor, but a couple of years after he graduated from West Point, he did get drunk one night and roused an old colonel with his boisterousness. Faced with a court-martial, he thought about resigning but stayed in and accepted the fine and the six-month restriction to the post. Wayne Clark barely escaped a similar fate when he took the family car and drove to Missouri for some beer one Saturday afternoon. When the military police stopped him, he was in his golfing togs and did not have his military identification with him. After some anxious moments, when he feared that the MP would search the car and find the beer, he persuaded the soldier to go with him to his quarters, where the maid identified him.[46]

When she wrote her memoirs, Maurine Clark remarked: "Life on an Army post in peacetime gives the Army wife far more opportunity, and probably more obligation, to help her husband in his career than most wives find in civilian life." On posts, officers and their families lived close together and were in constant association with their peers and superiors. They were thus exposed to close scrutiny by people whose judgments influenced promotions and assignments throughout their active service.

A good wife and mother, a charming hostess and guest, and a woman who clearly understood the place of the Army in her husband's life was a definite asset. Since Grace Groves had grown up in the Army, she probably already knew when she married what to expect as an Army wife. Dick, however, did tell her early in their marriage that while she could not help him in his career she could hurt him. Certainly, any misstep on the part of a wife or children could lead to the husband's being called to task. What all hoped for was praise such as the George Slineys received when they paid a parting call on the commandant at Leavenworth. As he walked them to the door, the general said: "I always knew that I could count on you, Sliney." Then he turned to Eleanor and added: "And you too."[47]

Children were also very much a part of this life. Bugle calls divided their days just as they did everyone else's. Indeed, one boy did not even learn how to tell time until he was almost eleven. Since he knew the meaning of the calls, there was no need. Edward C. Smith also remembered: "And we had damn good buglers." Children watched parades, and if they were outdoors, they stood at attention during the daily ceremony of retreat. If an older boy was interested and his parents were willing, virtually all military activities were open to him. While in high school, John A. Heintges had the newspaper concession at Fort McKinley, Maine. Aside from affording him the opportunity to get to know the soldiers, this gave him a place at the table on payday to collect from his patrons. His father, a company commander, permitted him to go on range, where he learned to fire a rifle, pistol, and machine gun, and took him on regimental hikes and maneuvers. He played basketball and bowled with the soldiers, snacked at the mess hall, and even attended sex lectures designed to keep the men out of trouble. In fact, he "just became part of them."[48]

Children's misadventures could get their fathers into trouble. When Bill and Ann Clark climbed on the World War I monument at Fort Lewis, the commanding general called their father, Wayne, to task and did not think barring the children from the post movies for a week was sufficient punishment. Colonel Marshall was more lenient with David Bolté. At Fort Benning, he came to dine with the Boltés and, as they chatted on the porch, he became very uncomfortable in the wicker chair. When he got up and examined the seat, he found tacks stuck in the wicker mesh. Fortunately for David, who was four, the colonel liked children.[49]

Although youngsters who had to go to adjacent towns to school could not take part in extracurricular activities because the Army truck or, in some cases, mule-drawn wagon picked them up right after classes, there was certainly enough to occupy them when they returned home. The small children played hide-and-seek, kick the can, hopscotch, and jumped rope, while, as boys will, some formed gangs and fought with dirt clods or whatever came to hand. The location of the post extended the possibilities of recreation. At a northern post such as Fort Brady, Michigan, there were winter sports. At Fort Huachuca, in Arizona, Margaret Forsythe Camp remembered Indians teaching her how to track deer and other animals, while Bill Leonard and his friends at Fort Strong, Massachusetts, watched the seagoing traffic and the seals, ducks, and fish that turned up in the tidal flats or wielded wooden swords and played Count of Monte Cristo or Robin Hood in the casements.[50]

Children of officers and NCOs went to school together, albeit on segregated vehicles on some posts, and in smaller garrisons were more likely to play together because of the paucity of children and proximity of their quarters. On the larger posts, the distance between the officer and NCO housing areas precluded much mingling. Some parents discouraged it, and Hariette Marshall got a good scolding when she went over to play in the NCO area. The best friends, however, of Bill Leonard and Harry N. Rising Jr. were the sons of NCOs. At West Point the fathers even got together to lead and support their sons in the Boy Scout troop. As they got older, they still might compete on teams in various sports, but with the emergence of a social life revolving around the officers' club for the officers' children, there was a distancing. For most, this was simply a fact of life. Even as a teenager, however, Frank Hoskins was ashamed of what he had come to realize was discrimination.[51]

Children off to school in an Army truck at Jefferson Barracks, Missouri, 1932. Courtesy of Edwin Todd Wheatley Jr.

Throughout the Army, horses and riding instruction were almost universally available. The Patton children exercised their father's horses, and Guy V. Henry's daughter, Mary Henry Howze, not surprisingly responded when asked what she did for recreation: "mostly equestrian pursuits." In cavalry and field artillery garrisons, the world revolved around horses. At Leavenworth, West Point, and other posts garrisoned by black troopers, these men taught the children, usually on Saturday mornings. Alice Beukema Miller never forgot the good advice of the "black, kindly, and competent" instructor at West Point: "Ride your horse—don't let it ride you." At Fort Hoyle, Fielding Greaves and the other children got the same training as recruits. The stables were a magnet for him, just as they were for Ted Milton and Karl Scherer, while Adrian St. John pitched in and worked with the soldiers there. He also traveled with them in the vans when they took the polo ponies to away matches. Bob Matte even went on maneuvers and to the firing ranges with his father's troop. Bruce Palmer Jr., who had lived off post for seven years, was sixteen when he arrived at Fort Riley in 1929, so he marveled at the recreational opportunities. Most of all, there were the horses, and, as he recalled: "I literally fell in love with the U.S. CAVALRY!"[52]

Living off post was not unusual among Army brats; some went to boarding schools while their fathers scattered over the nation on assignments with the National Guard, Reserve Officer Training Corps, or on staff duty in large cities. Usually they adapted and made friends with the children they got to know at school. Life at Grand Rapids, Michigan, however, was miserable for Jo Jones; the girls in the high school were a tight clique that would not accept her. Rather than overt antimilitary attitudes, there was, as Bruce Palmer mentioned, "a manifestation of not wanting to acknowledge that the military even existed." There was also sheer ignorance. When Dorothy Devine's schoolmates at New Haven saw her father in uniform, they asked if he was a policeman. Alice Beukema did experience some malicious barbs at boarding school, however; some of the girls who knew that her father taught at West Point taunted her with snide questions: "Does your father only teach killing?" and "Do you sleep in barracks?"[53]

In a real sense their world was different. As Jacqueline Thompson Campbell pointed out, "it was like a small elite club. We had a rich man's life on a small income." For Ted Milton, who loved horses, Fort Riley "was obviously the best place in the world . . . we had everything, and we knew it." To be sure, there were the constant moves, but most Army brats liked to move, and some pitied the civilian youngsters who stayed in one place. A "work hard and play hard atmosphere" permeated garrisons, and fathers had time for their children. The secure sense of belonging was strong. Theodore Conway spoke for many, perhaps most, of his contemporaries who grew up in the Army of the 1920s and 1930s when he said: "I liked its stability and order . . . The Army was a big family, steady, reliable, friendly."[54]

✳

Most West Pointers in this period went to a unit right after graduation leave. When he reported at Fort Howard, Maryland, in 1924, Charles

T. Lanham had a severe shock. Resplendent in his new uniform with sword and gloves, he marched into the regimental commander's office, saluted, and was greeted by the colonel: "Look, I know what you have heard about me." Stunned, Buck remained silent. The colonel added: "You have heard I'm crazy." Lanham then responded: "No, sir. I haven't heard anything like that. I just reported to the post, sir." The colonel ignored that: "Don't tell me. I know you've heard I'm crazy. Everybody on this post has heard I'm crazy. You are going to sit down in that chair, Mr. Lanham, and you're going to read these two documents before you get out of here." He then took two papers from his desk and handed them over. They were statements from two doctors to the effect that he was sane. After he had served for a while at Fort Howard, Buck realized that the doctors "had made one hell of a mistake." When he went to his company he received a second but less severe shock. His company commander told him: "As of tomorrow morning, you will take over all duties in the company . . . report to the First Sergeant and be instructed." Buck did not know what those duties were, but he soon found out and became immersed in paperwork.[55]

Lanham's initiation was probably unique, but all new officers shared other routine experiences in their first assignment. There were also inspections and drills in the morning, with afternoons devoted to schools, boards, athletics, and fatigue. Marksmanship and range firing were significant parts of the training in the combat arms. In mounted units, which included the infantry machine-gun companies with their mules to pull the machine-gun carts, taking care of the animals was a priority. For the soldiers, there were also the fatigue details to cut the grass and tend to other matters of post maintenance. Younger officers attended the schools, but they might also take part in courts-martial or other boards, while some became much involved in athletics. Aside from polo, which dominated the lives of so many officers, there were unit football, basketball, and baseball teams with both officers and men on the squads. Al Wedemeyer played baseball, Max Taylor, basketball; Red Reeder played both baseball and football, while Dwight Eisenhower and James A. Van Fleet coached football teams. Athletics were a significant part of garrison life and an escape from the monotonous routines.[56]

Charles T. Lanham at West Point, a few months before his encounter with the colonel at Fort Howard, 1924. Courtesy of Special Collections and Archives, U.S. Military Academy.

Other escapes from the routine included an exotic recruiting detail and the sesquicentennial of the Declaration of Independence in Philadelphia. In 1921 Wayne Clark toured the eastern part of the country with ten picked soldiers on the Chautauqua circuit. He made a short speech and led the men in precision drills; then one soldier sang and another played the ukulele in the hope of drumming up recruits. Simpson commanded the various units at the sesquicentennial as his battalion of the 12th Infantry from Fort Washington and representatives of other branches put on historical skits. Tom Finley, who had transferred from the engineers to the infantry, commanded the machinegun company and staged a World War I type battle. Finley, who spent a year under Simpson's command, admired him "as much as anybody I've every served with" for his low-key approach and understanding of the officers and men in his battalion.[57]

After two or three years, lieutenants should have mastered the duties of a company, battery, or troop officer. The better ones gained that understanding of men that made officers like Simpson stand out. James M. Gavin was one of those. During his three years with the 25th Infantry in Arizona border stations, he trained with the soldiers, boxed and raced with them in track events, and came to appreciate the NCOs. He never forgot a demonstration of the basic military principle of taking responsibility. After a long day's march in the desert, when the parched and exhausted men were ready to collapse on their bunks, Gavin overheard the captain tell the first sergeant to clean out the areas between the barracks. When the sergeant passed the order on, a dumbfounded NCO asked who had given such an order. The first sergeant snapped: "God-damn it, I said so, and I want it done right now."[58]

Professionalism was well established in the officer corps. Officers understood that they were professionals even though many would probably have been hard pressed to come up with a definition of the term. They expected to make a career of the Army, and they performed the round of duties for which they were paid. There was enough in the events of routine garrison duty to keep many of them occupied. Too much, according to Forrest Harding who was one of the intellectual lights of the Army. While editor of the *Infantry Journal,* he explained in an editorial that there was too much "piddling," as manifested "in eyewash, undue emphasis on competitive athletics, excessive supervision by command and staff, useless paper work, unnecessary reports, requirements that all officers attend all drills, multitudinous administrative checks, daily officers' calls indefinitely prolonged, and a hundred other time-consuming non-essentials that have nothing to do with training for war." Of course, some officers thrived on this, but others, like Harding, deplored those who were caught up in such time-wasting matters. A bright young officer like Buck Lanham simply thought that the Army was "full of stuffed shirts with a very inferior grade of stuffing."[59]

Major John H. Burns, a Columbia University graduate who had been commissioned during the war and stayed on, was one of those who looked beyond the daily routine, as he indicated in an article he wrote for the *Infantry Journal* in 1937: "we are in a great era of change. With lightning rapidity our social and industrial structure is being reshaped by the roaring machines of a mechanical age . . . The infantry regiment is being radically changed to fit the age . . . cavalry is taking to wheels and tractors; already the idea of great motorized and mechanized masses is being toyed with; aircraft have shouldered their way into the battle group. All is fluid . . . Never did we need thinking officers more; never could less trust be placed in custom or tradition. We are on the threshold of a new era of war." Looked at this way, despite the under-strength units, the slow promotion, and the depressingly low budgets, there were some exciting aspects of this interwar period. Although these were certainly not limited to the combat branches mentioned by Major Burns, still the infantry, cavalry, Air Corps, plus the field artillery would be the major elements in any future war.[60]

While still in France after the war, General Pershing attempted to lay the foundation for fighting a future war by establishing boards to evaluate the lessons offered by experience of the several branches in the American Expeditionary Forces. For two months in early 1919, a Superior Board headed by the portly Joseph T. Dickman, who had commanded a corps during the war, went over the reports of these boards and came up with recommendations about organization and tactical doctrine. Controversy developed over the size of the infantry division, which the Dickman board envisaged as being roughly the strength of the wartime division. Upon the advice of Fox Conner, who had headed his operations staff during the war, Pershing disapproved and argued for a more flexible division with less manpower. Arguments over the size and shape of the division continued for the next twenty years until a much smaller and triangular (three infantry regiments rather than four) division was adopted in 1939.[61]

By 1923, however, the General Service School offered a revision of the basic doctrinal guide—the *Field Service Regulations*—based on the lessons learned from the war. The old edition was based on what Ralph Huebner called the "rifle-pistol" Army, in which the soldier simply had to know how to shoot, march, and live in the field. The world war changed that, and the new Regulations acknowledged that infantrymen now had to learn other skills as well: how to employ machine guns, mortars, gas, tanks, and even artillery, since a howitzer company was part of the new infantry regiment. The new Regulations also emphasized a key point made by the Dickman board that "the infantry remains the predominant and basic arm."[62]

Fort Benning was the heart and brain of the infantry. There the Infantry Board tested new weapons and tactical theories and the Infantry School instructed lieutenants and captains in what they needed to know to lead a company. Here students learned doctrine—what to do and how to do it. In logistics, elaborate paperwork to cover every eventuality in Army supply was the standard. In history, the faculty concentrated on the principles of war and tried to get them across in dull lectures and even duller publications. Weapons instructors supervised familiarization with the basic infantry weapons with which virtually all the students were already well acquainted. Finally, tactical instruction concentrated on problems in which students were given more background information and more time for decision than one would find in combat. They were then expected to come up with the school solution after going through detailed checklists.

In the fall of 1927, nine years after the establishment of the Infantry School at Benning, Lieutenant Colonel George Marshall took charge of academics. A month before, he had suffered the loss of his wife of twenty-five years, so he welcomed such an important assignment that might distract him from his grief. He went to Benning determined to "get down to the essentials, make clear the real difficulties, and expunge the bunk . . . we must concentrate on registering in men's minds certain vital considerations, instead of a mass of less important details." The colonel was out and about, listening to lectures, observing tactical problems. Buck Lanham, who came as a student and stayed as an instructor, recalled: "you never knew when to expect him behind you." In one of his tactics classes, Buck disagreed with the school solution and laid out a different one, which the instructor proceeded to lambaste as unorthodox. Marshall, who was sitting in the back of the room, briefly demolished the approved solution and then praised Lanham's as "original" and workable.[63]

Simplicity was one of his major goals. He ordered the directive for Army supply to be cut from 120 pages to 12 and the demonstration of the process from three days to a half-day. He brought in the cantankerous but brilliant Joseph W. Stilwell to head the Tactics Section and to carry on the search for common sense and originality in that crucial field. He made Omar Bradley, whose personality was the opposite of Vinegar Joe's, head of the Weapons Section. His choice for the section that dealt with history and publications was his old friend Forrest

Harding, who soon brought in Lanham as well as other talented lecturers and writers to liven up that subject. Soon students were applauding the exciting lectures, which were good enough for Buck and others to take out on the Chautauqua circuit, while Harding ensured that the publications would be readable. As Buck remembered, "there was an electric current that coursed through that place for people who had anything to offer." For Joe Collins, who had joined the faculty shortly before Marshall arrived, it was "probably the most stimulating period . . . of my entire service."[64]

During his five years at Benning, Marshall gathered and maintained an outstanding faculty. He set up a book-discussion group that met at his home and included Collins, Charlie Bolté, and a few others. And on three occasions he was able to dissuade the commandant from relieving the ever-difficult Stilwell. At a time when infantry units were under strength and neither prepared nor equipped for war, Marshall prepared a generation of officers for whatever the future might bring. Omar Bradley later testified that he learned the "rudiments of effective command" from serving under him. Most of all, Marshall emphasized the practical over the theoretical. And he noted and never forgot those who met his high standards. He wrote on Bolté's efficiency report that he was qualified to command a division in time of war, and a few others probably received similar accolades. They would become known as "Marshall's Men."[65]

The 1923 *Field Service Regulations* emphasized the importance of artillery support for infantry by devoting more coverage to it than to any other topic. The AEF's experience pointed up the need for developing more effective means of providing this support. Under Jake Devers in the late 1920s, the Gunnery Department of the Field Artillery School improved gunnery methods, but, as Joe Collins, who was a student at Fort Sill in 1926–27 noted, the artillerists still had not solved the problem of effective support. In 1929 Lieutenant Colonel Lesley J. McNair began his tour as assistant commandant. Just as Marshall galvanized the Infantry School, McNair encouraged new ideas at the Field Artillery School. A younger officer recalled that the Minnesotan, who had been a brigadier general in 1918, "could get an awful lot out of people" and that he was "extremely thorough and very, very capable." In Major

Carlos Brewer, who succeeded Devers, and the outstanding group of instructors in the Gunnery Department, McNair had men equal to the task.[66]

At the Gunnery Department's Saturday practice firings, Brewer experimented with putting observers closer on the ground and in the air to the front-line infantry and letting them direct the fire. While this was an improvement over the older method of establishing observation posts some distance from the troops, Brewer also developed a firing chart, which enabled batteries to deliver accurate fire even if they did not have maps. Then he and his instructors developed a control center at battalion rather than the traditional battery level. Such a group, by using telephones or radios, could stay in contact with the forward observer and the batteries and carry out the necessary adjusting, plotting, and computing of firing data and direct the fire. In the spring of 1932 Brewer and his instructors tried out this organization, which came to be known as a fire direction center. Major Orlando Ward, the forward observer that Saturday morning, was jubilant at their success in massing so much fire accurately: "It was just like squirting a hose."[67]

Ward succeeded Brewer later in 1932 and continued with his instructors to develop new tools to speed up calculations and to refine the techniques of fire control. The capability of rapidly concentrating the accurate fire of several batteries and, eventually, the massing of fire of battalions, later known as time on target, was a tremendous achievement that would have a devastating effect on the battlefield. McNair recognized the possibilities, but more senior field artillery officers were adamantly opposed, deploring what they saw as a lessening of battery commanders' authority. Nevertheless, progressive officers continued to refine the system until it was generally accepted more than a decade after Brewer and his officers began their experiments.[68]

Throughout the 1920s and 1930s the field artillery, like the infantry, sought to develop better weapons and appropriate organizations, but the artillerists were much more concerned with mobility. In the immediate aftermath of the war, three different boards agreed that motorization was a priority; however, budget cuts severely limited such efforts. Indeed, as late as 1934 the Army had to rely almost entirely on vehicles left over from 1918. In Hawaii the division artillery was motorized, but, as Tony McAuliffe noted in the early 1920s, "We had great difficulty keeping them in operation." When his West Point classmate, Orville W. "Doc" Martin, came out to the same regiment ten years later, he found the same tractors "rather unpredictable." In late 1934, Doc, who returned to the States to take command of a battery of the Sixth Field Artillery at Fort Hoyle, Maryland, had to deal with an unusual problem. His battery had just been issued horses to pull their 75s, after spending some years working with trucks as part of an experiment. Since these soldiers had no training with horses and did not know how to handle the huge Belgians and Clydesdales, accidents were frequent. Day in and day out, Doc was in roadside ditches trying to untangle men, horses, and guns. Fortunately, no one was killed, and in time he had a "smooth running battery." Although his battery relied on horses for transportation, Martin participated in a pioneering aviation event. If not the first, one of the earliest uses of an autogyro (which was somewhat similar to the latter-day helicopter) to help observe fire took place at Fort Hoyle in July 1935. Doc was the observer who went aloft on that occasion. With more funds available in the late 1930s, motorization increased apace, yet there were still horses pulling guns in the American Army into the early 1940s.[69]

John K. Herr loved the cavalry—the tradition, the glamor, the bond between horse and man—everything! As an old man his thoughts lingered on bygone days when he was astride a horse and he "felt like a great king." There was something special about men on horseback. Mounted troops continued to patrol the Mexican border, and at their posts cavalrymen went through the age-old routines of caring for their horses and putting them through their paces. In the Advanced Equitation Class at the Cavalry School, officers worked with four horses each and rode to their hearts' content. James H. Polk, who was there in the late 1930s, remembered it as "the most gorgeous year I have ever spent in my life."[70]

Whenever cavalry officers gathered and swapped stories, the names of Selah R. H. "Tommy" Tompkins and Arthur H. "Jingles" Wilson came up. Tommy, who had to be the last officer on active duty to wear muttonchop whiskers, spent most of his career in the Seventh Cavalry, which he joined in the mid-1880s. He was not much for new things.

When an airplane landed on the field where his beloved Seventh was exercising, he rode up and confronted the pilot: "Why the hell did you drop from the sky onto this cavalry area? You frightened our God damned horses worse than any damned Indians. Get the hell out of here." In this instance he was mollified when the pilot produced a bottle of whiskey. For the sake of sentiment, the Army returned him to command the Seventh briefly before his retirement in 1927. After his final review, he refused to leave in the proffered staff car; instead he rode his horse to the post gate.[71]

In contrast, Jingles Wilson was a very quiet man. One could not help but notice the huge scar around his neck, which he received in a fight with the Moros in the Philippines when he earned the Medal of Honor. What impressed cavalrymen, however, as much if not more, was his ability as a polo player. Jingles along with Lucian Truscott, Terry Allen, and Charlie Gerhardt were among the better-known players. They were tough and aggressive, and, as Lucian told his son, every good player just as every good combat commander "has to have some sonofabitch in him."[72]

Many cavalry officers lived the traditional life of horsemen and ignored the possibilities of mechanization. After all, the slow, unreliable world war–vintage tanks were all the Army had into the early 1930s, and, in some respects, as George Patton and a friend spelled out in an article in *Army Ordnance,* they were no match for horses because of problems with supply, control, and terrain. Besides, the National Defense Act of 1920 had assigned the tanks to the infantry; however, Patton, who had returned to the cavalry, continued to believe that there should be some mechanized cavalry. Infantrymen naturally thought of tanks as support for advancing foot soldiers, but the few cavalrymen who turned their minds to the subject saw possibilities of faster, longer-range, thrusting cavalry missions.[73]

A visit by Secretary of War Dwight Davis to England in 1927, where he was impressed by the British Experimental Mechanised Force, led to greater involvement by cavalry officers. When he returned to Washington, he ordered the formation of a similar force. As it happened, a cavalry officer, Frank Parker, who was the assistant chief of staff for organization and training, projected a role for such a force as a major striking arm. Although the small force that formed and went through

Geoffrey Galwey (left) and Lucian Truscott (third from left) on the First Cavalry's polo team at Camp Marfa, Texas, circa 1923. The troopers holding the horses are in their blue fatigue uniforms. Courtesy of Geoffrey B. Galwey.

a variety of tests for a couple of months in 1928 was hobbled by the obsolete tanks, Parker and the General Staff's Mechanization Board looked to newer, better, and many more tanks in this arm of the future. Meantime the chief of infantry opposed any such expansion of the role of tanks, which would remove them from his control.[74]

The chief of staff, a famed artilleryman and corps commander during the world war, Charles P. Summerall, went ahead and ordered the formation of another combined-arms mechanized force and named a cavalry colonel, Daniel Van Voorhis, as its commander. Although Van Voorhis knew virtually nothing about tanks, he looked upon his assignment as a means of developing a better "horse" for waging cavalry warfare. During this period a junior officer on the Mechanization Board of 1928, Adna R. Chaffee Jr., began to come to the fore as an advocate. A handsome, likable man, Chaffee had grown up on cavalry posts, graduated from both the American and French Cavalry Schools, and competed against the best horsemen in the world in horse shows. When he saw an experimental tank go forty-two miles an hour, however, he decided that the future lay in that direction. Through his service in key positions on the War Department General Staff and in the mechanized force, he did more for the advancement of this new arm than any other officer in the American Army. And his old cavalry friends, as a West Point classmate noted: "never failed to accuse him . . . of betraying them."[75]

Not long after he became chief of staff, Douglas MacArthur called in the chief of cavalry and gave him a blunt message. He gestured toward the parked cars on the street outside his office and said: "Henry, there is your cavalry of the future." There was no more distinguished horseman in the Army than Guy V. Henry Jr., but throughout his remaining years as chief of cavalry and later as commander of a mechanized brigade and as commandant of the Cavalry School, he encouraged mechanization. In his sixties, while at the school he took the course in motor mechanics, and when he retired in 1939, he rode off post in a scout car. Nevertheless, he continued to ride extensively and participate in horse shows.[76]

Although he supported mechanization, MacArthur disbanded the mechanized force that Van Voorhis commanded and encouraged both infantry and cavalry to move forward in that area. Budget constraints precluded a large investment in tanks that might soon be obsolete; hence a few experimental pilot models were preferable. Besides, he wanted to encourage the cavalry to develop its own mechanized organization, and he gave Van Voorhis command of the regiment to do so. To get around the National Defense Act's limitation of tanks to the infantry, the term "combat car" was adopted. These thinly armored tanks were lightly armed with only one .50 caliber and two .30 caliber machine guns, but they could reach a speed of forty-five miles per hour.[77]

Van Voorhis had already relocated the old mechanized force at the relatively undeveloped Camp Knox, in north-central Kentucky. In December 1932 he led a truck column to Marfa, in southwest Texas, to pick up his new troops. Although the officers of the First Cavalry did not show much interest, since they were going to other horse units, the troopers did. On the fourteen-day return journey, according to the executive officer, Robert W. Grow, they were pleased with the comforts of riding such a long distance "fast and smooth" in trucks that did not need grooming.[78]

While the mechanized cavalry troops at Knox experimented with new vehicles and tactics, Grow, who had served as master of the hunt at the Cavalry School and still enjoyed horseback riding, was convinced that if the cavalry did not mechanize it would disappear as a branch. Henry's successor as chief of cavalry, Leon Kromer, was also of that belief. By 1938 there were two regiments in a cavalry mechanized brigade at Fort Knox. Chaffee, who succeeded Van Voorhis in command of that brigade, believed that a separate arm was a better organizational solution. Malin Craig, who became chief of staff in 1935, also reached that conclusion. He was another cavalryman who had grown up on cavalry posts, but as chief of staff he feared that infighting between the chiefs of infantry and cavalry would hamper appropriate development of mechanization.[79]

John K. Herr, who became chief of cavalry in 1938, seemed to confirm that view when he made it clear that whatever mechanization the Army did would not be at the expense of a single horseman. Meantime he encouraged experiments with "porteeing," in which trucks carried horses over long distances in an effort to counter mechanization. In the fall of 1938 he suggested to the chief of staff that the cavalry arm should be greatly increased until it was at least 15 percent of the active forces. At that time it accounted for less than 6 percent—some 10,000 officers and men in fourteen regiments. He warned: "We must not be misled . . . that the untried machine can displace the proved and tried horse. I have an abiding faith in the glorious role that cavalry will play in any future war." He also began to look into ways to restore the saber, which had been abandoned in 1934. Younger officers had a firmer grasp of how warfare had changed. Lucian Truscott later commented on mechanization: "Most thoughtful officers in the branch . . . supported the trend." When Bruce Palmer Jr. and his friend Creighton Abrams, who graduated from West Point in 1936, talked about the prospects of the horse cavalry, they agreed: "We all realized that it was an anachronism . . . it had no battlefield future."[80]

By the late 1930s, even the Cavalry School began to pay more attention to mechanization. It was still theoretical, as there were no tanks

The old gives way to the new as officers and men of the First Cavalry bid farewell to their horses, Fort D. A. Russell (formerly Camp Marfa), Texas. Although the photo is dated 1932, the regiment was mechanized early in 1933. Cropped version of original. Courtesy of the Patton Museum of Cavalry and Armor, Fort Knox, Kentucky.

at Fort Riley, although the students did visit the mechanized brigade at Fort Knox. James Polk remembered Patton emphasizing armor attacks in his instruction. "We were beginning to get caught up in this kind of thinking . . . We were willing to accept change." One of the older cavalryman who liked the trend toward mechanization was Jack Heard. He had already learned to fly in the Air Service and had also served in the Motor Transport Corps before he went to Fort Knox; hence his comment "I loved the clank and roar of the tanks" is not surprising. When the time for choice came, these officers as well as many others recognized, as Jack Hines said, "that the horses had no place in the new war" and opted for tanks.[81]

✷

The Air Service, renamed the Air Corps in 1926, was a field of service in an entirely different dimension from that of the other branches. Pilots received flight pay, 50 percent more than ground officers, and the air officers abandoned the high, stiff-collar uniform in the mid-1920s, a couple of years before the rest of the Army. Unlike the other branches, where newly minted officers immediately plunged into the garrison routine, the air arm imposed the high hurdle of flight school on these neophytes. In addition to West Point graduates, there were flying cadets competing for the silver wings. More than half did not make the grade at Brooks, Randolph, and Kelly Fields—all at San Antonio—which were the training bases throughout most of these years.[82]

Jim Gavin was one of those attracted by the glamor of flying, so after West Point he went to flight school. Looking back on it, he admitted: "I really didn't have my heart in it. I couldn't even drive an automobile." He learned to make turns and to land but fell behind the class and was eliminated. This left him with the impression that the school was trying to wash out the students. Another West Pointer, Jacob E. Smart, who graduated in 1931, two years after Gavin, had an entirely different experience. He had been intrigued by airplanes since childhood. He was also impressed by the Air Corps officers he knew at the Academy. Almost a third of his class of 1931 went into flight training. Although only half successfully completed the year's training, Smart did not think there was any prejudice against West Pointers. Later he served two years as a flight instructor.[83]

In the early 1920s students learned to fly on Curtiss Jennies, which were not much improved from the pre–world war models. Even in the late 1930s they still flew a biplane that Paul Tibbets, who took his training in 1937, said was "nothing but a fuselage and a pair of wings held together by what looked like baling wire." Regardless of the aptitude of the pilot, these craft were not very reliable, so one of the most important parts of training, as Jake Smart pointed out, was to develop the judgment necessary to avoid and cope with difficulties. Among other things, the student had always to keep an eye out for a suitable landing place, as instructors would frequently surprise them by ordering them to bring the craft down. A little bit of knowledge could be dangerous and lead to taking chances, stunting, and perhaps killing oneself. Smart's instructor took him out and flew under high-tension wires and below a bridge. Then he told him: "Now that you have done that you need never to do it again . . . Don't be a show-off."[84]

Flying cadets were paid $75 monthly and followed the same routine as officer students: flying in the morning and ground classes in the afternoon. The cadets, who wore light-blue uniforms, also had additional military training such as close-order drill and went through a hazing period as "dodos." Applicants for the program had to have two years of college and be in good physical condition. During the early 1920s, only a third were accepted. Noel F. Parrish met the requirements and also had served eleven months in the cavalry, which made the military training and hazing easier. But he had an instructor who seemed determined to wash him out. After they watched a student crash and die, this officer told him: "You fly just like him." Fortunately, his next instructor was more sympathetic if no less demanding. When Noel did well on the midcourse check flight and won his praise, it remained "one of life's most reassuring moments."[85]

While the West Pointers already had regular commissions, Parrish and the other flying cadets who completed their training received reserve commissions. By 1932, however, when Parrish graduated, they were awarded a year's service. Flying in the 13th Squadron of the Third Attack Group at Fort Crockett, near Galveston, Texas, naturally dominated pilots' lives, although they were required to go horseback riding one afternoon each week. In the mornings they went aloft in their Curtiss A-3s, flying in formation. As an attack unit, they were expected to fly low, and they did their gyrations at seventy-five feet. Parrish recalled that it was "fascinating, amazing activity. Chickens flying, cattle running, people running out of houses, day after day . . . at such low altitude if you had the slightest collision you'd never have time to jump." Noel lost three good friends at Crockett that year.[86]

Virtually all the reservists who completed their active duty returned to civil life and sought hard-to-find jobs in that Depression year. After a couple of months of unsuccessful job-hunting, however, Noel went to Chanute Field, Illinois, and enlisted as a pilot. By the mid-1930s there were only some eighty of these specialists. They received the base pay of their enlisted rank plus 50 percent flight pay. Generally, they

flew "the odd, flunky jobs . . . that officer pilots considered drudgery."
He flew tests for the Gunnery School, dropped parachutists for the
Riggers School, and carried passengers hither and yon.

Promoted to private first class, which meant a raise in base and flight
pay to $45 a month, he went to the First Provisional Air Transport
Squadron (which consisted of four enlisted pilots and three planes) at
Patterson Field, Ohio. There he tested some of the new airplanes and
flew various transport missions. In order to raise the pay of the handful
of enlisted pilots, the Air Corps gave them the additional specialist ranking of air mechanics, which almost doubled it. Thus, when the opportunity came, after almost two years in the ranks, to apply for a regular
commission, Parrish hesitated, as he enjoyed the relatively carefree life
and the recent increase in pay. Besides, he would lose his date of rank
in the reserves. The master sergeant who ran the squadron convinced
him to go ahead. He applied, received one of the thirty-five appointments, and returned to the 13th Squadron in 1935.[87]

There were some familiar faces, but the Third Attack Group now
flew Curtiss P-36s. The rapidly changing models made flying difficult
for pilots who had learned to fly in the 1920s or earlier. Some younger
pilots, like Noel, sympathized with those veterans "who had been able
to wrestle successfully with . . . slow biplanes but were never at home
in the fast and unforgiving new monoplanes with the distracting radios,
numerous instruments and retractable landing gears." Gone were the
days when one could determine wind direction by leisurely swooping
down low enough to see which direction grazing horses or cattle faced.[88]

Benny Foulois, who had been a major general and chief of the Air
Corps for some six months, spoke at Noel Parrish's graduation from
flight school in the summer of 1932. At fifty-two, he seemed very old
and "a little burned out" to the young fledglings. After all, he had been
flying since before Noel and most of his other classmates were born.
Over the years he had also battled for the air arm. Aside from his efforts
within the Army, in the past dozen years he had testified seventy-five
times in its behalf before various congressional committees. His stand
for an independent air arm was well known.[89]

Yet, despite Foulois's position as the top air officer, his status as a
pioneer, and his wholehearted devotion to the cause, he was eclipsed
by Billy Mitchell. From his farm in Virginia, Billy still turned out arti-

cles and gave speeches that not only made him appear the spokesman for air power to the general public but were an inspiration to ambitious young air officers. Air advocates had continued their fight after their failed attempt to create an air arm coequal with the Army and Navy in the postwar congressional debate about reorganization of the Army. Record distance and endurance flights, races, and exhibitions kept them before the public eye while fifteen different high-level boards addressed their problems in the sixteen years after the war.[90]

Mitchell was involved in the two most dramatic incidents. In the summer of 1921 he supervised the bombing tests in which planes sank a German battleship. Then, in the fall of 1925, he turned his court-martial into an appeal for air power. His polemical attack, in which he blamed accidents on the "incompetency, criminal negligence and almost treasonable administration of the national defense by the War and Navy Departments," understandably brought about the charge that he had acted against "good order and military discipline" and that his "conduct [was] of a nature to bring discredit upon the military service." The spectacle of the handsome and flamboyant Mitchell in the new Air Service uniform of shirt, tie, and blouse arguing the case for air power in front of a court-martial board of generals in their old-fashioned stiff, high collars might well symbolize the futuristic claims he made. But as one of his most ardent admirers, H. H. Arnold, pointed out, "the thing for which Mitchell was really being tried he was guilty of, and except for Billy, everybody knew it, and knew what it meant." He responded to the conviction and the sentence of five years' suspension from active duty by resigning early in 1926.[91]

The issue between the Army leadership and the aviators was clear-cut. The Army believed that the Air Service was a supporting arm for the ground force, and the airmen thought that they would never be used to their full potential under Army control. Mitchell took the lead in arguing that the air weapon would change warfare by striking "the enemy nation's vital centers, paralyzing them and making it impossible for the population to carry on in war." Similar ideas were abroad in Europe, with Giulio Douhet and Basil H. Liddell Hart making the argument. Carried to the extreme, one could reach the conclusion that airpower alone could win wars, hence armies and navies were obsolete. Generals and admirals were not about to make that leap of faith.[92]

Nevertheless, within the limitations of its budget the War Department did well by its airmen. Even Mitchell recognized that in early 1921 when he wrote a friend in the midst of working out the annual budget: "we will come off much better than any other department of the Army." And so they did throughout this period. By the early 1930s the Air Corps was getting 20 percent of all Army funds. In 1940 the secretary of war reported that over the sixteen years from 1925 through 1940, the air arm received almost 60 percent of Army funds that were allocated for modernization.[93]

Two investigative boards also helped the airmen. The Morrow Board, which was appointed in response to the Mitchell crisis in the mid-1920s, influenced the passage of the Air Corps Act of 1926, which changed the name of Air Service to Air Corps and, more significantly, authorized an assistant secretary of war for air, gave the airmen representation on the General Staff, and called for a five-year expansion program. It was, as Foulois noted, "a tremendous shot in the arm." Although later budgets did not provide for the full expansion program, there were more planes, more officers, and more men—the latter taken from the other branches of the Army. In order to provide those soldiers, the War Department had to deactivate five infantry battalions and a field artillery regiment.[94]

The Baker Board in 1934 resulted from the difficulties encountered by the Air Corps when Benny Foulois answered the Post Office's call to deliver the mail. The combination of pilots who were not trained for this kind of flying, ill-equipped planes, and one of the worst winters in years contributed to fatal accidents and bad publicity. This board recommended and the Army implemented in early 1935 the formation of a General Headquarters Air Force, which took the air-combat units distributed about the nation under ground-force commanders and concentrated them under an air commander.[95]

When Mitchell left the service, Major Henry H. Arnold attempted to pick up his torch, and it almost cost him his career. In early 1926 Arnold and another officer in the chief of air service's office ignored regulations and began lobbying for favorable legislation. Exposed by an inspector general's investigation, Arnold was threatened with a court-martial, but a contrite letter and an immediate reassignment to Fort Riley saved him.[96]

A West Pointer who had learned to fly in 1911, Arnold had been a colonel during the war, which he spent in Washington. Called Hap because of a habitual grin, the nickname belied his dynamic, forceful personality. One who knew him well summed up his most significant characteristic: "He had the ability to get things done." During this period his closest associate and friend—they were almost like brothers—was Carl "Tooey" Spaatz. Also an Academy graduate and a prewar military aviator, Tooey had shot down two planes during the war. The two first teamed up in 1919 at Rockwell Field, California, where Hap, the commander, soon learned that Tooey, his executive officer, was "one who can do any job given him." Reliable, taciturn, wise, Tooey and his wife were also known for their jolly parties, where he would entertain with a guitar or start up a poker game.[97]

Ira Eaker met these two at Rockwell when he became the adjutant. He had come into the Army during the war, earned a commission and wings, and was thinking about resigning when he first met Arnold and Spaatz. Their examples and continuous good assignments kept him in the service. Diligent and articulate, he made himself "indispensable" to anyone for whom he worked. During the 1930s he and Arnold would coauthor two books about military aviation.[98]

Arnold was too senior to go to the air arm's branch school established after the war, but Spaatz and Eaker graduated from this citadel of air doctrine. Located at Langley, Virginia, until 1931, when it moved to Maxwell Field, Alabama, the Air Corps Tactical School (ACTS) evolved from emphasizing fighter aircraft to small classes when Tooey went in the mid-1920s to preaching the gospel of strategic bombardment to much larger classes when Ira attended in 1935–36.[99]

Although Billy Mitchell talked and wrote incessantly about the future prospects of bombers, the large, cumbersome, slow planes, which a bombardment group commander in 1927 called "bird cages," were obviously not capable of any such missions. That officer recalled trying to compensate for the lack of a bombsight by aiming with a makeshift web of strings. Nevertheless, in the late 1920s and early 1930s a coterie of ACTS instructors put together a rationale for a war strategy that envisaged a dominant role for bombardment. In one of his lectures to Eaker's class, Harold L. George explained that their strategic objective was "independent of either land or naval forces which can, in itself, accomplish the purpose of war." During their stint as instructors, Robert Olds, Donald Wilson, Robert M. Webster, and Kenneth Walker were among those who also contributed to this concept, which took the shape of high-altitude precision daylight bombardment against specific choke points in the enemy nation's economy. It was predicated upon the invincibility of a bomber attack force, which as Walker stated, "is most difficult, if not impossible, to stop."[100]

As bomber technology began to overtake fighter development, the Maxwell theorists thought it appropriate to abandon classes on fighters. Not only did they think that they did not need a Navy or Army, but fighter escorts also began to seem unnecessary. In the summer of 1935, when Eaker went to the school, the experimental model of the Boeing B-17 flew. This great plane could fly up to 256 miles an hour and reach an altitude of more than 30,000 feet with a five-ton bomb load. With a range of 2,480 miles, it could certainly be considered a strategic weapon. The first of the thirteen ordered by the War Department arrived at Langley in early 1937.[101]

One of the most junior officers in Ira's class was Elwood R. "Pete" Quesada, who had flown with Eaker and Spaatz on the historic endurance flight in 1929, when refueling in air kept them flying more than six days. Well known for his skill as a pilot, Pete also loved horseback riding, hence was one of the few students who welcomed the school's requirement to ride in the mornings. Later he remembered the mania for strategic bombardment and the absence of even much lip service "to the use of tactical airpower." He also recalled the talk among the students about "ourselves and the Goddamn Army." Otto P. Weyland, who attended the school two years after Quesada and Eaker, thought that fliers generally were "scornful of the 'ground pounders,'" whom they considered provincial because of their lack of appreciation for airpower.[102]

Midway through Eaker's and Quesada's school year at Maxwell, Benny Foulois, who flew in the first Army plane with Orville Wright, retired as chief of the Air Corps. Beset by congressional hostility, he was to a large extent, as the chief of staff, Douglas MacArthur, said, "a casualty of political warfare." But Benny had never liked desk jobs, and the administrative side of his duties as chief of the Air Corps had suffered. He much preferred flying and still logged far more hours than

The Question Mark crew: (left to right) Roy Hooe, Pete Quesada, Harry Halverson, Ira Eaker, and Carl Spaatz—all happy to be on the ground after their historic endurance flight of almost seven days in January 1929. Courtesy of the National Archives.

other senior Air Corps officers. On Christmas Day 1935 he took up a Douglas O-38, an open-cockpit biplane, for his last active-duty solo flight. He flew south with no destination in mind. As he daydreamed about his early flying experiences, he found himself over Kill Devil Hill, on the Outer Banks of North Carolina, where the Wright brothers had made the first flights thirty-two years before. When he returned to Bolling Field and landed, he knew that "it was all over," and he was overcome with sadness.[103]

✳

When asked to compare service in the Army before and after World War I, Omar Bradley responded that "the greatest difference . . . was the school system." Pershing was so impressed with the performance of the Leavenworth graduates that he emphasized education in the postwar

Army. The increase in students at what came to be known as the Command and General Staff School was dramatic, with 3,677 graduates in the 1920s and 1930s, compared with 432 in the twelve prewar classes.[104]

Leavenworth could be considered the keystone of the Army's education system. Although all officers could expect to be thoroughly indoctrinated at their branch schools in what they needed to know to be good company officers, only a few went on to Command and General Staff School, and perhaps half of those were selected for the Army War College. In 1936 one estimate was that only 75 of 1,000 eligible infantry officers could go to the CGSS. As Wayne Clark recalled, it was "a great feather in your cap" to be picked to go to Leavenworth. Several of the more promising officers spent much of these two decades either attending or teaching in the schools. In an extreme case, from 1921 to 1941 Joe Collins was a student or instructor during all but three years. Bill Simpson, who graduated from the Infantry School, Command and General Staff School, and Army War College and taught at the latter, explained why schools were crucial. They "made up in a great way for our lack of men." Since the Army did not have enough troops to do much maneuvering, the schools helped officers to "visualize the command of the large units." World War II demonstrated the effectiveness of this method. Of the thirty-four generals who commanded corps, twenty-five spent ten or more years at schools during the interwar decades.[105]

When Leavenworth reopened after the war, it had a two-year program similar to that of the prewar years. In order to turn out more graduates, it shifted to a one-year course in 1923, reverting to a two-year course from 1930 to 1936 and reinstituting the single year for the last four years of the decade. Whatever the length of the course, the purpose remained the same: to prepare officers to hold command and staff positions in divisions and corps, with heavy emphasis on solving tactical problems. For eight hours a day, five days a week, students went to class to learn as much as could be taught in lectures, conferences, and practical problems about the tactics and combined arms operations of divisions, corps, and even armies. At times they would ride horseback into the field to work on problems. There was one extensive individual research paper as well as a committee research effort. The papers in the fall of 1930 ranged from a specific tactical problem such as why one

Union brigade's attack first succeeded but then failed at Spotsylvania, to larger issues such as "Consolidation of Railroads in the United States." Each set of quarters had a study, and students were expected to put in at least two hours every night in preparation.[106]

This schedule, which was much more demanding than routine garrison duty, combined with the belief that one's class standing could make or break a career, meant that there was a lot of pressure on the students. Charlie Bolté recalled officers who were so worried about their standing that they would not look at the grades on their problems when they were returned. He resented being graded like "a student in grammar school."

Rumors of suicides abounded, although there were only two during this entire period. Tom Finley, who graduated in 1932, the year after Bolté, did not think the course was difficult but it was certainly competitive. He had enough free time to meet, court, and marry during the first four months of the course.[107]

After he graduated first in his class in 1926, Dwight Eisenhower wrote a commentary that was published anonymously. He warned prospective students against overestimating the difficulty of the school and reminded them that everyone graduated. Rather than rote memory, the problems required "common sense and clear judgment." Besides, the weekends were free; yet at the cocktail or dinner parties, Lucian Truscott remembered, such topics as "wide envelopment" would inevitably come up.[108]

Air Corps officers generally were not enthusiastic about Leavenworth. Ennis C. Whitehead summed up this attitude in a letter to a friend in 1937: "this school is as valuable to us as a course in advanced English literature would be. Nice to have but of little practical value." The study of past wars and ground-unit tactics left most of them cold. Tooey Spaatz simply treated it as a vacation. There were only two or three days of aviation material in the course during the late 1930s. Although Pete Quesada considered it "old fashioned," he did appreciate the opportunity to work with and become acquainted with ground officers. He and a cavalryman, Maurice Rose, became good friends and talked about the possibilities of air support for ground troops. Earlier, in the late 1920s, the commandant who had been on the Mitchell court-martial board disliked Hap Arnold so much that when he heard he was coming as a student, he wrote him that he would be "crucified"; yet Hap was not crucified and there was some consideration of the aviators' interest. In 1934 St. Clair Streett even submitted as his research paper an argument for strategic bombardment, with books by Mitchell, Douhet, and Liddell Hart among his sources.[109]

While one might expect complaints about the approved solution to this or that problem, some ground officers also criticized the instruction at Leavenworth. Charlie Bolté thought that some of the requirements were "pretty far fetched" and that one learned more about "actually doing things" at Benning. After several months at the school, Buck Lanham was more vociferous than the airmen. In a letter to Forrest Harding, he prophesied that in the next war "there is going to be one hell of a rude awakening . . . We are merely refining and super refining outmoded and antiquated procedure that has no more relation to 1939 than does the kerosene lamp. By God it is pitiful."[110]

Help was on the way. George Marshall had been concerned about Leavenworth since his days at Fort Benning. The concentration of elaborate staff procedures and overly detailed orders had convinced him that the course was "wholly out of date." As the Army's deputy chief of staff in 1939, he appointed Lesley McNair commandant with a mandate to modernize the school. The focus should be on training officers to command and staff a citizen soldier force under conditions of open warfare. He also urged McNair to visit the Air Corps Tactical School before he went to Leavenworth and to pay particular attention to the Air Corps.[111]

A few months before he corresponded with McNair, Marshall gave a speech before the West Virginia American Legion Convention in which he discussed the complexities of mobilization. When he came to the problem of procurement of supplies, he mentioned that most of the officers involved in this were graduates of the Army Industrial College. Established in 1924, this school was the most recent addition to the educational system. At first the program, which was intended to be on the same level as the Command and General Staff School, was rather informal and lasted only five months. Hap Arnold, who was in the second class, found that he was almost as much a teacher as a student because of his wartime service in Air Service logistics. In 1926 the course was expanded to ten months and theoretically became the peer of the Army War College.[112]

The focus of the course, according to Dwight Eisenhower, who attended in the early 1930s, was to develop "logical thought in the problems involved in industrial mobilization." Not surprisingly, most of the students were from the supply branches. Quartered in a World War I temporary building in downtown Washington, the school was a stepchild as far as budget and prestige were concerned. One general referred to it as the "booby prize" for those who were not selected for the Army War College.[113]

When Joe Collins learned of his assignment to the Army Industrial College as a student, he was taken aback, as he had never heard of it. The personnel people had forgotten that he was coming back from the Philippines that year and had not reserved a slot at the War College for him. Because they expected to send him to the War College the next year, they placed him in the Industrial College so that he would not have to make another move within a year. Later he considered it a lucky break that "broadened my managerial horizon" as well as teaching him much about industrial mobilization. Besides, he appreciated the lectures of various business leaders and the visits to various plants and arsenals. Between 1924 and late 1941 there were about 1,000 graduates, including reservists as well as a few Navy and Marine officers. During this period more than 200 officers also attended the two-year graduate program at the Harvard Business School. If war came, the Army would certainly be much better prepared to cope with the problems of supply procurement than it had been in the turbulent days of the world war.[114]

The Army War College was at the peak of the education system, the gateway to high command and staff positions. Thus, as Dwight Eisenhower remarked, "To graduate from the War College had long been the ambition of almost every officer." The war had convinced the Army's leaders of the value of the school system, so they quickly reinstituted it in 1919. At the War College, which was briefly called the General Staff College, classes were much larger, and graduation from Leavenworth was a requisite for virtually all students. Prewar classes had numbered in the twenties, but the first postwar class included 85, with 1,790 graduating in the twenty-one classes through 1940. While the courses varied over these years, the two major themes remained "Preparation of War" and "Conduct of War." Joe Collins, who graduated in 1938, summed up the content of the nine-month course: "political and economic aspects as well as the military considerations involved in wartime mobilization of manpower and industry; the correlation and evaluation of political and military intelligence; the command relations between Army and Navy forces; possible interallied command relations; as well as strategic war plans."[115]

Rather than a highly competitive program, the War College was ungraded and generally more leisurely. There was time for softball, tennis, golf, handball, and, of course, riding. Students organized in small committees to consider an issue for two weeks or so, come up with a solution that was submitted to the class and faculty for discussion and critique, then reorganize into different committees to deal with other problems. Joe Collins was involved in the issue of tactical air support. The issues that Charlie Bolté worked on included "Tactical Instruction at General and Special Service Schools in Aviation," "Chemical War Service," "Signal Communications" (the committee concluded that the War Department dissemination of doctrine was faulty), and a "Survey of Japan" (its military could dominate the northwest Pacific and eastern Asia). The discussions could become very heated, as Brad Chynoweth discovered when he argued for less censorship in wartime.[116]

There was an individual study requirement on a topic of interest to the War Department. George Patton labored long and hard to produce a fifty-six-page paper on "The Probable Characteristics of the Next War and the Organization, Tactics, and Equipment Necessary to Meet Them." He thought a small, well-trained professional force preferable to a hastily organized large citizen army in winning a quick victory and won commendation for his effort. Chynoweth, who was also in the class of 1932, remembered him as "the outstanding worker"—one who "went all-out."[117]

There were also map problems, war games, lectures, and field trips. When an Air Corps officer in Patton's class started to develop a war game involving an airborne envelopment, however, he ran into stiff opposition. The commandant stopped the game, called the class together, and made it clear "that there would be no more of such nonsense!" In 1935 the new commandant restored the historical rides to studying Civil War battles, but using Greyhound buses instead of horses to tour the battlefields.[118]

War planning was a particularly significant part of the course. Since war with Japan was considered virtually inevitable, students year in and year out tried to figure out the best way to defend against Japanese attacks on the Philippines, Hawaii, and Panama. Beginning in the mid-1930s, classes predicated their plans on coalition warfare and the possibility of two fronts as Hitler's Germany emerged as a potential enemy. In 1935, for the first time, one group of student planners began to refer to World War II. The classes that studied this problem made realistic appraisals of the Japanese and German military potential. Their speculations about the course of war were eerie presentiments of much of what later happened. As the crisis neared, the focus of planning changed to mobilization and then, in 1940, back to allied warfare on two fronts.[119]

Joe Collins looked back on his years as a student and instructor as "one of the finest periods of his life." His friend Charlie Bolté, who served with him on the War College faculty, thought the most crucial lesson he learned there was not to be frightened by the large numbers involved in corps, armies, and army groups. Simp Simpson, a 1928 graduate who later spent four years on the faculty, summed up what the school meant to him as well as to Bolté, Collins, Jakie Devers (1933), Ike Eichelberger (1930), and others who got so much out of the college. If war came, he thought: "I'm about as ready as you could be" for high command.[120]

A few officers received more exotic educations, traveling abroad to learn languages or attend foreign schools. In turn, there were officers from other nations in the service schools below the level of the Industrial and War Colleges and on brief tours with troops. In 1931, thirty-two foreign officers were in this country, with nineteen from Latin America (thirteen of whom were Cubans) and the others from China, Japan, Siam, Germany, and Sweden. Nine served with units, two attended the Command and General Staff School, and the others went to various branch schools. In turn, the Army sent forty-two officers abroad, of whom twenty-one were language students, with fifteen studying Chinese and Japanese. Ten went to French military schools, three to German, three to Italian and Polish schools, while four attended Oxford. The Americans usually numbered in the thirties each year, with language students making up perhaps two-thirds. Generally fewer foreign officers came to the United States: there were thirty-two in 1931 but only eighteen three years later.[121]

In 1936, following his completion of the two-year course at Leavenworth, Al Wedemeyer was ordered to spend another two years at the German War College. The tall captain was dissatisfied with Leavenworth. He considered the course too theoretical and many of the instructors "mediocre." Neither was the case in Berlin. German officers, he considered, were "much better trained, much more dedicated" than their American counterparts. He formed close friendships with several of his classmates, including Claus von Stauffenberg, who tried to kill Hitler in 1944. Upon his return to the States, although several General Staff officers questioned him about his experience, only one—George C. Marshall, then head of War Plans—asked significant questions in a meeting that took up much of a day. Wedemeyer told Marshall how the Germans were developing armor and air, emphasizing mobility and maneuver in what would later be known as Blitzkrieg. The Germans had also strongly impressed upon him the importance of the economy in warfare.[122]

The Germans, who had been impressed by the American industrial effort in World War I, sent an artillery captain over to attend the Army Industrial College in 1930. But there was a misunderstanding; the Americans did not want to open up this senior school to foreigners. Walter Warlimont made the best of the situation by visiting various Army installations and several manufacturing firms that would be involved in any mobilization. His visit to Fort Benning, where he was the houseguest of George Marshall, was particularly memorable. When he returned to Washington, the War Department not only permitted him to talk with officers involved in industrial mobilization planning but gave him copies of pertinent manuals. In turn, he gave a few lectures at the Industrial College on the German experience in that area during the recent war. Years later, after his service as a general and key staff officer during World War II, he commented that the German industrial mobilization that was beginning at that time was influenced "by, and partly even adapted to, the regulations and experience of the U.S. Army."[123]

✴

When Tony McAuliffe looked back on the 1920s and 1930s, he mused: "The Army seemed to have a feeling that they had been forgotten." Noel Parrish wrote that most officers "plodded grimly along, stubbornly reminding themselves . . . that the things that they were doing were necessary." If the civilians who stereotyped officers had looked closely, they would have been very surprised at their versatility. Omar Bradley spent part of a summer as a construction worker on the Bear Mountain Bridge across the Hudson. Red Reeder worked out with the New York Giants and made the team but, like Matt Ridgway, who turned down an administrative position with the Giants after a few weeks' trial on the job, gave up his baseball ambitions. While on ROTC duty at the University of Florida, James A. Van Fleet coached the football team to national prominence. At the other end of the spectrum, during his tour as an instructor with the New York National Guard, Geoff Galwey studied art with the well-known painters George Luks and Robert Henri. Hap Arnold supplemented his income by writing boys' books and by collaborating with Ira Eaker on adult books about the Air Corps. And Buck Lanham published poetry in *Harper's* magazine. Despite their varied interests, however, those who stayed in the Army must have shared the feeling that Lanham articulated: "This is my trade . . . I'm a professional soldier." For him, resigning "would be like waiting half of your life for a railroad train at the station and when the damn thing comes along . . . you're not there to get on it."[124]

In an article published in *Scribner's Magazine* in 1935, Marine Major John W. Thomason Jr. rebutted critics of the services and pointed out: "The professional soldiers and sailors of this country are a singularly self-contained and inoffensive group, connected in no way with any one region or caste, but constituting in fact a cross section of the whole population. The Army, as the buffalo and the Indian, subsists remotely on reservations." Throughout the Army's history, this had always been the case in peacetime. Although the reforms of the early years of the century and the tremendous effort in World War I changed the Army, it remained close-knit and relatively unknown and isolated from the rest of American society. It was still small enough that officers knew virtually all others in their branch. An officer found that this situation worked to his advantage when he was considered for a key staff position in 1938. He learned later that he had got it because his superior had come across a bad efficiency report in his file and explained his reasoning: "If that son of a bitch said that about you, you must be all right."[125]

The acquisition of an empire in the Spanish-American War made the United States a world power, and the American effort in World War I had confirmed that status, yet in the 1920s and 1930s the Army was grossly under strength as the military arm of a world power. Budgetary restrictions prevented it from developing its potential. A high level of professionalism, however, meant that many officers grasped the possibilities of the future and prepared for it as best they could. During these decades, the most vital element in the Army was the school system. As Joe Collins bluntly put it, "it was our schools that saved the Army."[126]

EIGHT

Soldiering in the 1920s and 1930s

The career of a soldier is crammed with life and activity.

—THE UNITED STATES ARMY AS A CAREER

———◆———

T HE recruiting booklet that the Army published in 1929 contained facts and figures about the branches, pay, work, and recreation, with emphasis on the opportunities that awaited the new soldier. During the 1920s and 1930s, budget limitations and the lack of hostilities caused the Army to focus on garrison duties with correspondingly relatively little field service. Enlisted men of this period found perhaps more outside life and activity than they desired, and some took advantage of the opportunities offered.

Since the Army was largely left to itself throughout most of these two decades, post commanders sought to attain order, precision, neatness, and the superficial brilliance laboriously achieved with spit and polish. One old soldier regularly and vigorously applied salt, vinegar, scrubbing powder, jeweler's rouge, and finished off with a Blitz cloth to obtain the necessary luster on his brass. Application of a lotion creme and two kinds of polish might be necessary to bring the required gleam on shoes. Then he began work on his canvas leggings and web belt. Riflemen had to polish the stocks of their Springfield '03s, while troopers and gunners had to go over their horse equipage as well as their uniforms and weapons. There was a saying that you were not ready until you could see the reflection of your rifle stock in your shoes and your shoes reflected in your stock.

A soldier took great pride in his uniform, his equipment, and, most of all, his unit. He quickly learned that his company was better than the others and that his regiment was best of all. In 1921 the Army authorized regimental insignia designed to commemorate each unit's actions in

A showcase Army exercise as the corps commander, Frank Parker, inspects Company B, Sixth Infantry, Jefferson Barracks, Missouri, 1931. Courtesy of Edwin Todd Wheatley Jr.

past wars. Every soldier wore this crest on his campaign hat and lapels of his uniform coat to remind him of the proud tradition, while constant competition in inspections, on the firing ranges, and in athletics constantly fueled the pride in his company, troop, or battery.[1]

Old posts and new ones reflected this pride and mandatory neatness. All had a manicured look. The streets were clean and the grassy areas, lawns, and parade grounds carefully trimmed; the uniform houses and barracks appeared primed for inspection. In the 1920s a general at one post deplored the oil stains left on the streets by cars parked in front of officers' quarters; those gentlemen had to get out and scour the pavement.[2]

Bugles marked the routine, and band music was frequently heard as the musicians gave concerts or paraded with the troops in reviews and guard mounts. Those formations provided the pageantry that has been associated with soldiery since time immemorial. Rank on rank of men, their brass and weapons highly burnished, went through the traditional movements with guidons flashing up and down on command. At mounted posts, horses added to the spectacle as troopers and gunners put their animals through their precisely regulated paces. Stirring martial airs mingled with the ring of commands, of hands slapping rifles in unison, or of the jingle-jangle of the horses' accouterments.

There was a glamor about the Army—seductive enough to attract some enlistments. It helped bring John Dulin and Basil Rauch into the recruiting station, while simply seeing a newspaper photo of a cavalry trooper jumping his horse was enough for Louis Wilson. But they were sixteen-year-old boys. It was usually more difficult to get men to commit themselves. Secretary of War John W. Weeks succinctly gave the reason in 1921: "The American people are traditionally opposed to the maintenance of a large standing Army." Besides, civilian jobs generally paid more; hence, as long as there was prosperity, recruiting was an uphill effort.[3]

There was no recruiting from September 1918, when conscription became the only source and Congress barred enlistments in the early postwar months as the Army demobilized. When Congress lifted the ban on recruitment in late February 1919, the War Department hurriedly opened up 513 recruiting stations. By mid-1920 there were an additional 69 in operation. Since only some 50,000 of the pre-war regulars remained after the war and a large peacetime strength was assumed, Army leaders were anxious to build up their ranks. Inducements included keeping their wartime rank for those who reenlisted, choice of branch, and, in some instances, choice of station for recruits, and the option of signing up for only one year instead of three if they desired. Roughly half of those who enlisted in the first sixteen months after recruiting was resumed chose the shorter term.[4]

Both physical and mental standards were lowered. Illiterates, foreigners who had not yet learned English, and men whose intelligence tests showed they were at the eight-year-old level were now accepted. The hope was that the new education and vocational training program that the Army launched in the fall of 1919 would solve their problems as well as make the service generally more attractive.

A recruiting poster with an illustration of an officer instructing a soldier at the blackboard while another soldier sat reading at a desk exhorted readers:

> THE U.S. Army WANTS REAL MEN
> Join the University in Khaki & fit
> yourself for higher rank in Civil Life
> or a commission in the Army.
> You Earn While You Learn.

And it worked. Thousands enlisted to take one or more of the 115 courses offered as they went to class fifteen hours a week. This approach, which helped both the men and the Army, was particularly pleasing to the Progressive spirit of Woodrow Wilson's secretary of war. Newton D. Baker clearly understood how this might enhance the image of the Army, for, as he pointed out in his annual report in 1920, "It removes from a peace-time Army the reproach of wasted time."[5]

Many post surgeons were not pleased with the results of the recruiting effort. One complained of the "morons," another about those who enlisted for the educational and vocational training and hence considered the "duties of a soldier" secondary, while several expressed concern about the youth of the enlistees now that eighteen was the new age standard. A doctor at Camp Grant, Illinois, flatly declared: "Never in the history of the Army has its ranks been filled with such poor physical specimens and such young lads so susceptible to disease." The surgeon general weighed in with the comment that during the first ten months of recruiting only 50 percent were rejected, in comparison with a rejection rate of 83 percent from 1909 to 1915.[6]

Help was on the way for those who despaired of the new recruits and the training program, but not in a way that those doctors would have desired. Although the National Defense Act of 1920 authorized 280,000 enlisted men, Congress appropriated funds for only 175,000. During the calendar year 1921, the enlisted strength was reduced almost 43 percent, followed the next year by another 14 percent; only 113,124 remained in the ranks at the end of 1922. The General Recruiting Service ceased operating for most of 1921, and the vaunted educational and vocational training program was abolished.[7]

From 1923 to 1935 Congress, concerned about holding down expenses, did not permit the Army to have more than 118,750 men, so recruiting ebbed or flowed depending on the difficulty in obtaining that many men. With the advent of the Depression and the dramatic increase in unemployment, the Army raised its physical and mental standards and was able to be still more selective as lines formed at the recruiting stations. Finally, in its appropriations for fiscal year 1936, Congress authorized an increase in strength to 165,000. The rearming of Germany and the increasing threat of Japan in the Pacific had made an impression on the legislators. By mid-1939 there were 167,712 in the ranks.[8]

There was a reduction of the number of blacks in the Army during the 1920s and 1930s. In this era of financial stringency, when personnel had to be reduced, the prevalent racism made black units the obvious choice for cuts. When recruiting resumed after the war, reenlistments filled the quotas for the four segregated regiments during the first months. William L. Banks, who had been in the cavalry detachment at West Point since 1916, was one of those who reenlisted, because he knew that he could find nothing better outside. When recruiting opened up in 1920, Tommie J. Baugh enlisted because he was tired of working as a porter in a barbershop and "the treatment I had to take to hold a job." The $21 monthly private's pay represented an increase to Gussie A. Buckner, who had earned only $4 a week in his part-time work as a delivery boy and janitor in 1925 when he enlisted.

In 1924 there were only 4,186 blacks, less than 4 percent of the Army's enlisted strength, in service. A third of these were stationed at border posts in Arizona. Ten years later there were only 2.5 percent (2,974) on the rolls. Low as these figures are, they were appreciably larger than the Navy's total of 441 blacks, almost all messmen, who represented about 0.5 percent of the strength in 1932. The tendency of former soldiers to reenlist made it very difficult for blacks to get into the Army in those days. Robert P. Johnson, who had grown up at West Point, where his father had been in the cavalry detachment before the war, was one of the fortunate ones. He was able to get into the Ninth Cavalry band at Fort Riley in 1934. Another was Felix L. Goodwin, a college student whose father's long illness had virtually bankrupted the family. He had seen the men in both cavalry regiments while serving in the Civilian Conservation Corps at Leavenworth and Riley, and the life they led looked much better than the prospect of working as a domestic.[9]

Throughout this period the Army used many blacks for housekeeping tasks rather than for regular duty. In the early 1920s the 24th Infantry left the Mexican border for Fort Benning, where its primary duties were, as Ben Davis remembered, "maintaining equipment and grounds, janitorial service for officers' quarters, cleaning stables." In 1931 the Tenth Cavalry took up similar tasks at Leavenworth. Meantime the cavalry detachment at West Point, which was reflagged as the second squadron of the Tenth that year, continued its major chore of taking care of the horses but was available for leaf raking and snow removal as well as cutting ice from the reservoir as needed.[10]

In March 1930 Banks was a corporal when the detachment celebrated its twenty-third year at West Point with an address by its commander, a polo game (in which Banks played), and a ball. A program with a historical sketch and photos and records of the various sports teams also commemorated the occasion. Among the 208 enlisted men was one of the original detachment. The first sergeant, M. T. Dean, had been a major in the 92d Division during World War I. It was a proud unit, and its athletic teams were winners. The polo team, which existed for ten years, from the mid-1920s into the 1930s (perhaps the only black team in the nation), invariably defeated the cadet C squad. Banks, who was a good horseman, competed in horse shows and played polo as well.[11]

During the academic year, when cadets took horsemanship, much of the troopers' routine was devoted to caring for the horses. Each man had to look after four. In the summer the unit would demonstrate cavalry tactics to cadets and help train reservists and National Guardsmen. What irked Banks was the extra duty involved in tending to officers' polo ponies and show horses, which might keep him at work until almost midnight. For a time, when he was helping train horses for the pentathlon in the Olympics, he also had to work on Sundays. One summer an officer took him to help instruct at a girls' camp. There was not much time left for his wife, whom he had married in 1917, and their six children. In the late 1930s, after some twenty-five years in the Army, he made sergeant. It was a hard life, but, as his friend Bob Johnson, who had grown up at West Point, pointed out, "The Army was a sure living with no lay offs."

Racism was a given. Banks and his fellow soldiers understood the injustice but doubted that anything could be done about it. In the early 1920s, when Marcus Garvey started preaching black nationalism and

William L. Banks (left) and other members of the Cavalry Detachment polo team, West Point, circa 1930. Courtesy of Special Collections and Archives, U.S. Military Academy.

called for an exodus to Africa, where he would lead in driving out the white rulers and establishing a black empire, Banks and his comrades were critical. "We didn't think he had a chance." One soldier in the detachment was, like Garvey, a West Indian. On one occasion, when the commanding officer got after this man in the riding hall, the trooper exploded: "I'm a white man just like you are." The officer burst out laughing, and, Banks added, "Naturally we did too." There was a poignance in this situation, but the officer, Jingles Wilson, did not punish the soldier and was remembered by Banks as his favorite officer.[12]

Generally, blacks, like the white soldiers of this day, had little interest in politics. Many had the impression that they could not vote. A 24th Infantry veteran, Mike Henley, went farther to claim: "if they caught you talking about it, they said they'd put you in the stockade." He was one of the few who voted regularly.[13]

Sports was the great morale builder. As Tommie Baugh, who served in the 24th from 1920 to 1940, put it: "Sports was the one thing that

Tommie J. Baugh winning the mile at Fort Benning, Georgia, probably in the 1920s. Courtesy of Tommie J. Baugh.

kept the morale up in my Regiment." He believed that their morale "was the highest in the entire Army." Baugh, a Tennessean who enlisted at seventeen, was a major contributor. In 1929 he won a medal at the Camp Perry national rifle matches, received a letter of commendation from the chief of infantry, and had the regiment honor him and another soldier medalist with a band concert. A few months later, his promotion to corporal after ten years of service was a more material award. An all-around athlete, Baugh played quarterback on the football team, second base on the baseball team, guard on the basketball team, ran the mile and 880, and threw the javelin on the track team. He also starred on the tennis team and was a chief lifeguard at the regimental swimming pool. Most of these contests were intramural within the black regiment, but the baseball team did play against white units. It was not surprising with all of those activities that some black civilians in nearby Columbus, Georgia, would come out to watch the games or don white tennis togs for a set with Baugh or one of the other soldiers. In 1936 Baugh made sergeant and, soon afterward, completed courses in a variety of infantry subjects, including combat intelligence, scouting and patrolling, antiaircraft and antitank defense, and advanced weapons training. Once the black soldiers put their training to use in maneuvers with the white 29th Infantry and captured a group of the white soldiers.[14]

Religion was more of a morale booster for blacks than for whites. Few white soldiers were interested; hence the chaplain was not as influential with them as he was among the blacks. For many who served in this period, the chaplain was probably the only black officer they saw. As Baugh remarked, "You almost had to attend church because the Chaplain was always on you." He considered Alexander W. Thomas, a Methodist who entered the service in 1917, "outstanding" and "a personal friend." At West Point, where the black troopers did not have a black chaplain, Banks and others who were religiously inclined went to churches off post.[15]

Tennis in Georgia, polo in New York, and fox hunting in Kansas as well as the multitude of football, baseball, basketball games and track events—all were outlets and pride builders in this segregated era. Yet the dwindling number of blacks between the mid-1920s and mid-1930s was a very real symbol of their peripheral status in this era.[16]

The Army did not keep statistics on another minority, Jews, who were integrated, unlike the blacks, Philippine Scouts, and Puerto Ricans. Jewish Welfare Board representatives who visited military installations attempted to ascertain the number of Jews. Their status reports survive from 1927. These include figures for each of the many Army posts, naval stations, veterans' hospitals, and disciplinary barracks. The representatives reported a total of 1,273 (1 percent of the enlisted strength) in the Army, with the largest number, 206, among the estimated 12,000 soldiers at Schofield Barracks in Hawaii and the second-largest, 160 (out of 5,299), at Fort Benning. In the late 1930s there were four or five Jews in Company B, 66th Infantry, at Fort Meade, Maryland, Alphonso S. Zawadski remembered that "there was very, very little prejudice" in that "melting pot" of men of Polish, German, and Italian descent.[17]

In the Seventh Infantry regiment, one Jewish soldier is remembered because he earned the admiration of James M. Gavin, his company commander. When Gavin joined the company in 1939, Max Roth, a Polish Jew, had been in the outfit sixteen years. Over their months together, Roth impressed Gavin, whose new captain's bars he helped pin on, because of the humane, warm relationship he maintained with the men. Years later Gavin summed up his regard for this NCO: "He was one of the best First Sergeants, if not the best of all those I knew before and during the war."[18]

The United States Army as a Career, the 1929 recruiting booklet, did not refer to Jews specifically but did make it clear that a soldier's religion was "never interfered with in any manner." It did, however, include a section on "colored men" that detailed the segregated units in which they could enlist. Recruiters focused on those who made up more than 90 percent of the Army. It was this group to which the foreword referred: "The enlisted force . . . is made up of young men from all parts of the country and from all walks of life . . . typical of the American people." While it was true that recruits came from all parts of the country, some sections provided more than others. Each year the Army reported how many came from each of the eight corps areas. During the 1920s the Second, which consisted of New York, New Jersey, and Delaware, furnished the most, while the Eighth (California, Nevada, Utah, Montana, Idaho, Wyoming, Washington, and Oregon) led in the next decade.[19]

The reasons why men and boys walked into recruiting stations varied, as they had traditionally, with many having more than one motive for this drastic step. Some, Jack Bradley, Theodore L. Dobol, and John L. Key among them, thought they would like the Army; and a few, such as Theodore J. Conway, James H. Short, and Robert L. Scott, saw enlistment as the first step toward an appointment to West Point. Others wanted to get away from the farm, small town, or wherever they lived and see the world. Arthur W. Piehl, who came from Wisconsin, was tired of milking cows and the cold weather; besides, he didn't like the politics of the LaFollettes. James C. Hicks, Eugene G. Hogan, and Andrew Pemper were teenage orphans, while Francis T. Dockery did not get along with his father. Louis M. DiCarlo, a sixteen-year-old from New York City, had run away and was in Newport News, Virginia, when he had to choose between the Army or jail for vagrancy.

Although it would be possible to find soldiers from all walks of life, it was stretching the truth to say that the social makeup of the peacetime Army was "typical of the American people." At any given time, most men enlisted because the Army offered a job. Thus, during the Depression years a larger number of middle-class men joined because of the dismal job market. Even in the 1920s there were gaps in prosperity. During the first five months of 1920, an officer found that one in four of the 236 recruits he asked had enlisted because they were out of work. In 1927 John Randall could not find a job and owed eleven weeks' board when he enlisted. Three years later, twenty-six-year-old Heman W. Peirce was "on the bum," far from his Massachusetts home. A man he met at the Salvation Army shelter in New Orleans, where he was staying, suggested that he enlist in the Army, and he did so the next day. Before that, he had thought the Army had been disbanded after the war. John J. Hoodock succinctly summed up his reason for enlisting in 1928: "No work & hungry."[20]

In some instances, enlistment disturbed family and friends. They thought that Leland R. Goodwin "was nuts" and that Otto E. Bauman was going to become a bum. Although Gene E. Harris' brother talked him into enlisting in 1938, his friends thought he was going into "some sort of prison." Michael C. Varhol's father warned him that only the "scum of the earth" were in the Army and that he would have to live on beans and hardtack. Gaylord J. Parrish, minister of a small church in Uvalde, Texas, was even more forceful when his son, Noel, sought his permission to enlist in 1930. Parrish warned: "To be jeered at and cursed and kicked and beaten into helpless submission to the lowest, most vile, and most humiliating experience that can be thought up by the most perverted drill-sergeants . . . will be most *galling* to you. To keep one's self clear of it is like a drop of water trying to keep itself clear in a sea of ink."[21]

A college graduate at eighteen, Noel had spent another year earning a teaching certificate, only to be turned down for a school job because he was too young. Then, in the early months of the Depression, he lost the job he had taken with the Texas Oil Company. He went to San Francisco to look for work but found none. As he walked the streets, the only friendly person he came across was a recruiting sergeant who slapped him on the back and said: "son we need you in the Army." One day he followed the sergeant into his office and enlisted. When asked what branch and station he desired, Noel responded: what was "the toughest outfit"? Told that it was the cavalry and that assignment to Monterey was a possibility, he opted for both and got them. In his World War I surplus uniform with the high-collar blouse, he had a

Noel Parrish wields the mop as the cooks have fun with the kitchen police in F Troop, 11th Cavalry, at the Presidio of Monterey, circa 1931. Courtesy of Noel F. Parrish.

very different, more optimistic attitude when he walked the San Francisco streets as a soldier.[22]

Recruits' stories differ, but most contain a catalytic moment of desperation that caused them to raise their hands and take the oath of enlistment. James M. Gavin was an orphan—adopted and raised in a poor coalminer's family in Mt. Carmel, Pennsylvania. He worked hard in a variety of jobs from early childhood to add to the meager family budget. He loved school and reading Horatio Alger's books about poor boys whose diligence brought them success, and military history fascinated him. He learned about West Point, but it seemed unlikely that he could ever reach such a goal. When he completed the eighth grade, his parents made him quit school and go to work fulltime. Two years later he was doing relatively well as manager of a filling station, but he was frustrated. "I realized . . . that I was standing still . . . just earning money, and not earning much, and not getting any education, and it was stupid as I saw it." On the night he turned seventeen, March 22, 1924, after a row with his family, he slipped away and caught a train to New York City. After several days of checking with employment agencies, it was clear that they had little to offer to further his ambition. Then he walked into a recruiting station at the Battery. At last the possibility of education came up as the sergeant explained that the coast artillery had schools at Fort Monroe. When Jim expressed interest, the NCO asked him if he had venereal disease; Gavin was sure that he did not, but he did admit to being underage. The resourceful sergeant took him to a nearby office, where a lawyer signed permission slips as guardian for him and several other prospective recruits. Before he sailed for Panama to join a coast artillery battery, he wrote his step-parents to let them know he was all right, but he did not tell them that he was in the Army until he reached the Canal Zone.[23]

Wherever the recruit went in the Army, the barracks became his home. While there were various kinds of barracks—large, small, old, new—there was a sameness about them whether it was a small squad bay for eight men that Parrish found at the Presidio of Monterey or the more open tropical quarters that Gavin had in Panama. James W. Twitty, who joined the 29th Infantry in 1931, left a detailed description of his home in one of the larger and newer brick barracks at Fort Benning: "There were small, individual rooms for senior noncommissioned officers. Corporals and privates lived in immense open squad rooms, capable of housing a hundred or more soldiers. Standing in the middle of the highly waxed floor you saw, nearest you, a row of olive drab footlockers parallel to the longer axis of the room. Next, beyond and behind each footlocker, was a steel bunk, alternating head and foot with its neighbors, made up with sheets, O.D. [olive drab] blankets and pillows. Finally, behind the bunks and against the wall, were rows of green wall lockers . . . There were no drapes, no air conditioning, no pictures or other decorations on the walls." At all posts, there was great emphasis on cleanliness, and soldiers took pride in their barracks. As one recalled, "you damn well had better take pride in it, or else."[24]

Despite the lack of privacy, individuals had their own space. In a real sense, their bed and lockers were theirs. Theodore R. Milton saw what this meant soon after he joined the Third Cavalry. A drunken trooper came in and sat on another man's bunk. The soldier asked him twice to get off, and when the drunk did not move, he jerked him up by the collar and hit him hard in the face. The drunk reeled across the room, fell, hit his head on a footlocker, and was out cold. None of the other soldiers said a word. Noel Parrish was more impressed by the mental space that was permitted. It seemed to him that as long as you did your duty, your share of the work, and obeyed to the letter the regulations, no one cared what you thought. If you did what you were supposed to do, "your mind, your soul . . . were your own."[25]

Each unit had its own mess hall where the men gathered three times a day for family-style meals. Jim Twitty described what they could expect: "each found a place setting of a heavy white china plate, placed upside down . . . a white china mug, and a knife, fork, and spoon. The dining room orderlies, detailed daily from the company . . . served food on china platters and the liquids in metallic pitchers . . . The food was plain and plentiful"—but heavy on starch. According to Rufus W. House, a typical day's meals were: Breakfast: eggs to order, bacon, grits, fried potatoes; assorted jams, buttered toast, and coffee; Dinner: roast beef and gravy, mashed potatoes, boiled lima beans, sliced tomatoes, sliced pineapple, hot rolls, ice tea; Supper: beef stew, candied yams, stewed cabbage, peach cobbler, hot biscuits, and coffee. On such a diet, Parrish's weight increased from 120 to 163 in his first six months in the Army.[26]

Francis J. Walski (extreme right), by this time a mess sergeant, in his mess hall at Fort Belvoir, Virginia, 1934. Courtesy of Francis J. Walski.

NCOs usually made sure that manners were observed and that no one took more than his share. Francis L. Walski learned this his second day in the Army, when he scooped up four eggs to go with fried potatoes, ham, and toast. When another soldier arrived and complained that there were no eggs left, a cook waving a cleaver came running out of the kitchen yelling that he would kill "that son of a bitch . . . that pig that ate up all the eggs." Fortunately for Walski, no one told the cook who the culprit was.[27]

The quality of the food depended on the amount of money the Army provided as a ration allowance for each soldier and, more importantly, on the ability of the mess sergeant. In 1927 that allowance was 41 cents per day, which even the *New York Times* thought should be raised. After all, sailors received 52 cents and Marines 49 cents. The president resolved that problem by ordering that all services should have the same allowance of 50 cents. During the 1930s this would continue to increase until it reached, according to a former mess sergeant, $1.08. A good mess sergeant made sure that he had cooks who used this money to the best advantage. A bad one, such as Francis T. Dockery ran into in a coast artillery company, might steal or waste some of the money and provide skimpy and poor meals. Yet most veterans remember how good and plentiful their meals were. William A. Howell thought his meals in a field artillery battery were the "best I have ever had before or since."[28]

At one point early in his Army career, Charles Willeford's first sergeant assigned him to be a cook. Although the work was hard—one worked from 4:00 a.m. to 7:00 p.m.—there were two days off for each workday. When Willeford told the mess sergeant that he had no experience, the NCO responded that he could read recipes as well as anybody; besides, he could learn from the first cook. Charlie's first day began inauspiciously: he found the first cook dead drunk, passed out on the floor in the kitchen. He had at least prepared the bread, but Willeford had to build the fire in the stove and start making the omelets. He followed the recipe but did not realize that the bacon was supposed to be fried before it went into the omelets. The cook revived briefly, but the coffee laced with gin that a friend gave him caused him to pass out again before he could be of any help. Meantime Willeford stirred the grits, which he forgot to salt. The result of his efforts naturally brought complaints from the soldiers, one of whom called the mess sergeant at his home. The sergeant rushed in, accepted Charlie's explanation, but told him that he should have called when he found the cook passed out.

On his next tour in the kitchen, Willeford had to make twenty-four chocolate pies. His misreading of the recipe resulted in what one soldier called "fudge-on-a-crust." This was too much for the mess sergeant, who fired him. His day and a half of this duty convinced him that "cooking for 120 men is not as simple as one thinks." And it gave him more respect for cooks even though many of them were "rummies."[29]

✳

Purpose, training, organization, and, in particular, mission differentiated the military from other institutions. The Army's reason for existence was to fight if the necessity arose. Although organizational systems changed, the living together and the coordination of their efforts toward the common goal were constant for soldiers. Over the years there were also changes in uniform, drill, weapons, and equipment, but training was always necessary to gain the proper efficiency. In the early years of the century, except for the frenzied days of the war, recruits were initiated into military life at large depots before they joined their units for the finishing touches on their training. The War Department, however, abolished these depots in January 1922 and turned all training over to units.[30]

Jim Twitty, who had already served as a noncom in three different National Guard units before he enlisted at twenty in 1931, recognized that the objective of recruit training was "to transform a civilian (who knew absolutely nothing—according to the instructors) into a person who walked, talked and looked like a soldier" and was prepared for the more advanced training he would receive in his permanent unit. At Fort Benning, where Twitty took his training, the program isolated the new men in a small tent camp where two corporals taught them the proper wearing of the uniform, drill, the manual of arms, proper rolling of a field pack, courtesies and customs of the service, and the necessity of knowing one's serial number and the General Orders. Throughout, these veteran noncoms who went about their business quietly and effectively maintained the strictest discipline. If one of the new soldiers even twitched as a fly landed on his face, he was likely to find himself running a half-mile holding his 8.69-pound Springfield rifle above his head.

At the end of two weeks the 29th Infantry regiment, which was the only infantry unit in the States with full-strength companies, formally inducted them into its ranks. At the large post athletic stadium, there was a regimental ceremony with speeches and band music before the recruits were taken into their respective companies and then marched to their new homes in the large brick barracks. Jim never forgot the colorful spectacle of the national colors, the blue guidons, and the white-gloved troops with rifles fixed with gleaming bayonets as they paraded out of the stadium.[31]

Others received a much less formal introduction to the Army. Alphonso S. Zawadski, the son of a Polish immigrant coal miner, enlisted at eighteen in 1936 and was sent to a tank company in the 66th Infantry at Fort Meade. Since Company B was on the range at the time, Zawadski, still in civilian clothes, took weapons and marksmanship training along with the other soldiers. He learned how to disassemble

James W. Twitty, a keen observer and enthuslastic soldier, in the 18th Infantry at Fort Hamilton, New York, circa 1933. Courtesy of James W. Twitty.

and assemble the .30- and .50-caliber machine guns and fired a 37mm cannon with a subcaliber device. Since he qualified as an expert, he received an extra five dollars each month. Back at the barracks, a corporal took him and some other recruits out and taught them the rudiments of drill. Ten days elapsed before he got his first uniform—blue denim fatigues with a floppy-brimmed hat. Properly uniformed at last, he and the others spent several days tearing down the old post theater. A half-century later, Al ruefully commented: "I suppose they considered that part of the training also." Two years earlier, another Pennsylvanian who joined the same company, Michael C. Varhol, had a different experience. A small sergeant who had been in the German army ran the training with an iron fist. For six weeks he delighted in picking on tall recruits, whom he kicked, struck, and ridiculed. He imbued his charges mainly with a fear of all NCOs and officers.[32]

The 11th Field Artillery was at full strength, so training was more systematized, as in the 29th Infantry, except that it was longer. John J. Hannon recalled that in 1933 training lasted for eight weeks and that none of the recruits could even speak to the other soldiers during that period. Eugene G. Hogan joined the same regiment two years later but had to wait at Fort McPherson, Georgia, before he made the trip to Schofield Barracks, Hawaii. In those first days he learned close-order drill and a valuable lesson in Army ways. Thinking that he could get out of a work detail by not answering when his name was called or by not volunteering, he silently watched his entire group assigned to this or that job. When just the sergeant and he were left, the noncom asked him what he could do. Hogan answered, "Nothing." The sergeant said, "Let me teach you." He took Gene to the kitchen, a converted wooden barracks building, gave him a toothbrush, a G.I. (general issue) brush, a bar of brown soap, and a pail and put him to work cleaning the floor. Two days later he finished with his hands scrubbed raw. When the sergeant checked, he noted that Gene had not used the toothbrush to clean the cracks between the boards, so the newcomer had to spent another two days redoing the floor. Throughout the rest of his years in the Army, Hogan always answered loud and clear when his name was called.[33]

Those who joined the Air Corps also found the noncoms on recruit details tough. Close-order drill and lectures on military courtesy made up the two weeks or more that recruits spent in training. At Chanute Field in 1939, Edward R. Halvorsen also received familiarization training with the .45-caliber revolver. At smaller fields, where a recruit might be the only new man, a corporal would simply tell him what he needed to know.[34]

When Charlie Willeford wrote a memoir about his life in the Army during the 1930s, he devoted one clause to his six weeks of basic training at March Field but some twenty pages to the ninety days of training he received when he joined the 11th Cavalry after his enlistment in the Air Corps. He chose the cavalry because he "didn't feel like a soldier" in the air arm. In the Air Corps he learned nothing about weapons, and the drill he had learned at March Field was different from what they did at Monterey. Corporal Royale taught Willeford and his fellow trainees all they needed to know about horses and the Army. In the morning they learned to ride and how to care for the horse. During the afternoon there were map reading, tactics, close-order drill, and weapons training. Royale was a stern taskmaster. When one recruit moved his head as he shifted his rifle to right shoulder arms, the corporal knocked him unconscious. If a man held his reins the wrong way, he would knock him off the horse.

Horses made the cavalry the toughest branch. First, one had to overcome fear of them but still be ever on the alert as one might bite or kick. Noel Parrish, who went through his training at the Presidio of Monterey in 1930, nine years before Willeford, found that out when he was leading a horse and unwisely gave him too much rope. The horse gave him a left rear hoof to the stomach that left him with "temporary indigestion" and "a blue horseshoe mark" for several weeks.

Learning to ride the Army way and caring for the horses was hard work. After six weeks Willeford noticed that he had blood in his urine. When he mentioned it to Royale, the corporal told him that it was to be expected after all that riding and to look forward to lower back pain also, but that after six months or so "every internal organ will shake down nicely and you'll no longer be bothered." Noel was so stiff and sore in the mornings that at times he did not know if he could get up. He kept at it, however, and he did begin to feel better; he was certainly tougher.[35]

Those who went into the combat arms became well acquainted with range firing over the years. The competition for ratings was intense. The extra pay, which had not changed since before the war, mattered. If a soldier did not get in the proper position and adjust his strap properly, he would get a badly bruised shoulder or perhaps a fractured jaw from the recoil of the Springfield '03. Aside from the money, one risked being a social outcast if he "boloed"—failed to qualify as marksman. While not as intense as the firing for official record, working in the butts, where men had to pull down targets, mark them after each shot, and then push them back up for the next shot was hard labor that one soldier compared to wielding a sledge hammer.[36]

There were also the marches and field exercises in the summer. While Jim Twitty was in the 29th, the regiment marched from Benning to Panama City, Florida. In order to avoid this 461-mile trek, two soldiers disappeared only to report when the unit returned. Their punishment was to cover the same distance with full field packs and rifles on the road around the infantry barracks. They had to eat out of their mess kits and sleep each night in a pup tent in the middle of the parade field. The whole regiment turned out to watch the band lead them over their last mile.[37]

Both Mike Varhol and Al Zawadski had to learn to drive tanks in the 66th Infantry. The Renault, a World War I vintage light tank, was, in Al's opinion, "not worth a damn," as it frequently broke down. This was particularly embarrassing when several broke down during a presidential inaugural parade. Because the budget did not allow for much fuel, the tankers rarely got to operate the Renaults, but they still had to simonize them every Friday for the Saturday morning inspection. Mike did not know how to drive a car so was somewhat nervous when a sergeant introduced him to the Renault. The sergeant's instructions were succinct and uninformative: "Drive the damn tank, it's just like a truck except for the steering levers." Although Mike managed to get the tank moving, he could not find the brake and so ran into a building.[38]

Artillerymen, of course, had to learn the intricacies of working the big guns, while those in the field artillery also had to learn how to handle horse teams or tractors. At Fort Scott, California, George S. Pappas was in a gun crew for a 12-inch mortar that fired a 2,000-pound projectile. His job in the intricate procedure was to swab out the chamber with a sponge after firing. In Battery C, 11th Field Artillery, Gene Hogan became so efficient as a loader that he competed on a special award-winning gun crew. It was hard work and could be dangerous, but the money and the pride that went with an expert gunner rating made it worthwhile.[39]

With the increasing level of technology, many soldiers had to take courses to operate equipment that in many instances had not even existed at the turn of the century. This was the case in the Air Corps; hence, during this period men in the Air Corps held the highest percentage of specialist ratings of those in any branch. These ratings meant extra money. The lowest rating added $3 to the private's monthly $21 stipend, while a rating of specialist first class raised his pay to $51. First-class air mechanics drew $84—the pay of a technical sergeant—and those who earned second-class ratings earned $72. During the Depression years, such pay compared well with similar jobs in civilian life.

Elmer Howell and August Linkey were two who were attracted by the obvious opportunity offered by learning the mechanic's trade.

Alfred Saxon even gave up his sergeant's rank in order to take advantage of the Air Corps program. Getting into schools, however, was not easy. When Steve Davis completed basic training at Randolph Field during the winter of 1939—40, he found that the quota for the mechanic's school at Chanute was one per squadron every six months. Ed Halvorson was more fortunate; he was accepted in radio school right after basic.[40]

Going through basic training at Chanute by no means guaranteed a good shot at one of its specialist schools, as Bernard S. Kolp learned. When he completed his initial training, he and several others were sent to the base heating plant, where they shoveled coal eight hours a day. As the weeks passed, his hope of getting into radio school diminished. Then he heard that a key sergeant at the school was short of funds. Since Kolp had just won big in a crap game, he let it be known that he was willing to pay $100 to get into the school. A couple of days later, a friend of the sergeant's asked him if he was serious about that. Kolp gave him the money, and his name appeared on the list the next month.[41]

For those soldiers interested in competing for appointments to West Point, there were, beginning in the late 1920s, preparatory schools in several of the corps areas and overseas departments. A hopeful candidate could enlist for one year, and if he was able to get into one of these schools and win an appointment, he would enter the Military Academy before the year was up. Robert L. Scott in 1928 and, three years later, William P. Yarborough were among those who reached West Point in this manner. All the prep schools emphasized the same subjects, and, as James H. Short, who attended the one at Fort Scott, said, they "worked the hell out of you."[42]

When he enlisted, Jim Gavin, conscious of his lack of education, hoped that he might eventually get into the coast artillery noncom school at Fort Monroe. Within six months at his first station in Panama, he became battery clerk and made corporal because of his mastery of the semaphore code. The first sergeant, an Indian inevitably called "Chief," told him he ought to try for appointment. He was accepted at the prep school and under the tutelage of a Chemical Corps officer he acquired enough background in English, history, and mathematics as well as exam-taking skill to gain an appointment less than fifteen months after he had enlisted.[43]

James M. Gavin, shortly before his graduation from West Point in 1929, on his way to a brilliant career. Courtesy of Special Collections and Archives, U.S. Military Academy.

Soldiers could also compete for reserve commissions. One of the duties of Jim Twitty, who had become a sergeant in the 18th Infantry at Fort Hamilton, New York, was to instruct reserve officers. With the encouragement of the regimental sergeant major, he took the appropriate correspondence course and received his gold bars as a reserve second lieutenant but continued his regular duties as an NCO until called up in his reserve rank shortly before World War II.[44]

Some soldiers did not find the Army congenial. Many of them deserted; others purchased discharges before their enlistments were up. In the 1920s desertion had become a serious problem. For the first time since the early 1880s, for three years in a row—1924 through 1926—the desertion rate was higher than 7 percent. Only once, in 1906, had it reached such a level between the Spanish-American War and World War I. Concerned Army leaders thought that better recruiting, improved housing, and other such measures would solve the problem. There was not much they could do about a probable basic cause—the booming economy. With the coming of the Depression, desertion,

which had been declining since the mid-1920s, sank to an unprecedented level in peacetime. For five years in the 1930s, fewer than 2
percent deserted and gave up the security of the service for the uncer-
tainty of civilian life.[45]

Why did men take this drastic step, which could result, if they were
caught, in six months' confinement and a resulting extension of six
months on their required enlistment? Some could not adjust to Army
life, especially if it meant having to master and care for horses. During
these years the cavalry and field artillery usually had a higher desertion
rate than the other branches. Others got into trouble of some sort.
Norbert L. Craine, who was first sergeant of Company H, 29th Infantry, reported that one of the two deserters from his unit had stolen
money and the other had married without permission. In the 24th Infantry, Tommie J. Baugh thought that the rare deserter feared having
to face "his buddies" if he had done something "to bring discredit to
his unit." Veterans of those years also speculated that homesickness and
boredom were other reasons their comrades deserted.[46]

In the late 1930s two men deserted from Company B, 66th Infantry.
Al Zawadski remembered them as "happy-go-lucky" fellows who perhaps
thought they had had enough of Army life and it was time to move on.
Some seven or eight months after one had left, Al was working in the
orderly room when the phone rang. It was one of the deserters, calling
long distance. He asked how everyone was and then said, "I missed you
guys" and even added, "give my love to the first sergeant." He went on
to tell where he was and what he was doing. Al reported this to Herman
M. "Peso" Brown, the first sergeant, who was not amused; but since deserters could not be pursued, there was nothing he could do.[47]

From 1890 to 1940, soldiers after one year of honorable service could
purchase a discharge. In the 1920s and 1930s the initial fee was $120,
but it decreased as the soldier's length of service increased. Chiefs of the
technical branches complained that many men who had completed their
specialized schools took advantage of this in order to get better-paying
jobs in the civilian economy. While the onset of the Depression caused
a decline in such cases, by the mid-1930s they were again on the increase.
A study in 1938 indicated that more than 30,000 men had left the Army
this way since 1934, including more than 19 percent of the graduates
from the Signal Corps and Quartermaster Schools and 16 percent of

those who finished the Air Corps schools. Among those who bought out were Raymond L. Hammond and Basil G. Rauch. Hammond made his decision in December 1939 soon after completing the ten-month course in the Signal Corps radio repair and operations. A trooper since early 1936 in the Seventh Cavalry, where he served in the communications section, he won a place in the school by placing first in a branch-wide competitive examination. Rather than the possibility of a better job on the outside, his desire to get married prompted his decision.

Although Rauch had been attracted in part by the apparent glamor of the Army, he was quickly disillusioned. In September 1926, Rauch, who had just turned eighteen, was in his thirteenth month of service at Fort Myer as a bugler in a field artillery battery. He disliked "the boredom, the brainless talk [in barracks] . . . the pointlessness of it all." Somewhat interested in trying for a West Point appointment, he had attended a few preparatory classes but had found them "excessively dull." His mother sent him the money, so he was able to leave to begin a new life.[48]

Since soldiers' pay was so low throughout this period, it is remarkable that many were able to amass enough money to purchase discharges. Theodore J. Conway, who knew the Army in the 1920s and 1930s as the son of a regular, a soldier, and an officer, recalled that most soldiers were "in chronic debt." They got through the last week or two before payday by obtaining credit or by borrowing (they called it "Jawbone"). A soldier could draw coupon books for the post exchange and the movie theater, which meant additional deductions from his next pay. Some still had to borrow at exorbitant rates. One soldier recalled that a moneylender he knew expected $1.50 at the end of the month for each dollar he loaned.[49]

During World War I, as millions entered the Army, Congress, as it had done during the Civil War, raised the pay. Indeed, the private's 100 percent raise from $15 to $30 in 1917 was much more generous than the 45 percent Civil War raise. As in the case of the earlier war, after the civilians who had made up the large wartime Army were discharged, Congress reduced the pay of privates. This 1922 legislation, which cut a private's monthly pay to $21, more than doubled the wartime pay of the top enlisted grade and gave significant increases to sergeants. The reasoning was to protect those who were committed to a career.

When the economy boomed in the 1920s, even the sergeants' pay did not keep up with increasing prices. During the Depression, however, when the cost of living declined, the meager Army pay stretched further. In 1933 President Roosevelt made a 15 percent pay cut in all government employees' (including the Army) wages. Soldiers also lost reenlistment bonuses, longevity raises, and the extra marksmanship pay. A private then received only $18.75, which seemed even less when he worked with CCC men, who were paid $30 monthly. Nor did it help soldiers' morale that the lowest-ranking Navy seamen received automatic increases from $21 to $36 at the end of three months of service. As Willeford noted, "Although no soldier in his right mind would have traded places with a swabby, this inequity was resented."[50]

Payday, the last workday of the month, was a holiday. The company commander picked up the pay, brought it to the company area, and stacked the new bills and shiny coins on a table, where he sat next to the first sergeant. The men lined up by rank in alphabetical order. When his name was called, each soldier approached the table, saluted, and gave his name, rank, and serial number. The captain returned the salute; then the sergeant read the amount due, after the various deductions; the officer counted out the exact amount; the soldier saluted again and briskly made way for the next man.[51]

The experience of William R. Dunn, who enlisted at seventeen in 1934, was common. After deductions of $5 for post-exchange coupons, $2 for theater tickets, $3 for laundry, and 25 cents for the Soldiers Home, he had less than $8 "to blow on girls, cigarettes (Bull Durham or Golden Grain), toilet articles, etc." The specific expenses differed, but in many cases, as Jim Twitty, recalled: "the net monthly pay might be zero or close to it."[52]

Some of the soldiers had made more in civilian life—one claimed to have made $200 a month with the National Cash Register Company—but they were aware that jobs of any kind were hard to find during the Depression. Al Zawadski and others thought Army pay, particularly since they did not have to pay for food, clothing, or shelter, was equal to or better than what they earned in civilian jobs. Al was among those, including Mike Varhol and Jim Gavin, who managed to send money home every month.[53]

On payday at Fort Benning in the early 1930s, Jim Twitty recalled that "some soldiers, eternal optimists, were attracted to the many gambling games, usually poker and craps, that bloomed each month. Others donned civilian clothes and went to town, especially to Phenix City, Alabama, in search of sex, usually professional. Others headed for a favorite bar." Gambling was close at hand. Indeed it flourished in the barracks area, with the top-ranking NCOs often running the games or getting their cut of the profits. Zawadski's and Varhol's top sergeant, "Peso" Brown, earned his nickname from his success in gambling in the Philippines and was rumored to have purchased a country club and golf course with his profits after he left the Army. At Clark Field, in Willeford's squadron, the dayroom orderly, who Willeford believed was a former Franciscan monk, ran the games in the dayroom. "Padre" let Willeford start up a blackjack game after specifying his cut but eventually took the game away from him.

One of the more successful gamblers was Jay Smith, a Sixth Infantry bandsman, at Jefferson Barracks. Every payday his wife and children would wait anxiously through the day into the night and perhaps until the next morning to see if he had won or lost. Once, in the early 1920s, when he had not returned by noon the following day, Georgia Campster Smith took her two little boys into town and checked the various speakeasies but did not find him. When they returned home late in the afternoon, there he was, lying on the floor amid wads of bills. He had taken his winnings from the post into the town, and his luck had held until he won some $5,000.[54]

Drinking on payday was traditional. As Noel Parrish pointed out, that was about the only time men could afford it. Even though Prohibition was the law throughout most of this period, soldiers still got their beer, wine, hard liquor, or whatever substitutes bootleggers came up with. Jay Smith, who lived off post, turned his house into a speakeasy that featured his homemade beer. Although his son thought it smelled like "old wet Army shoes" and tasted like "a soggy blanket," it sold well at ten cents a pint. As long as soldiers were ready for duty the next day and did not drink on duty, the authorities apparently condoned the payday excess. Al Zawadski remembered that the men in his company tried to look after those who drank too much and rescue them before they got into trouble. That is not to say that Parrish and the other men in his squad bay appreciated the two drunks who vomited in the barracks after they overdosed on cheap red wine. In that case, "cleanups and retribution" were prompt.

Jay Smith began to drink every day, as did others to the point of alcoholism. The barber in Zawadski's company even sank to the depths of going through men's lockers in the hope of finding aftershave lotion to drink. Al never forgot trying to take care of him when he was overcome by delirium tremens. Even the first sergeant felt sorry for him and did not mete out the usual harsh penalties for stealing. Looking the other way, however, could lead to tragedy. At least that was what one soldier thought when the condition of an alcoholic mess sergeant was ignored and the NCO committed suicide.[55]

Army records indicate some efforts to contain or suppress drinking excesses. An officer or soldier could wind up standing trial before a general court-martial for a variety of charges involving drunkenness; yet in the period 1926–1932 the average annual number of convictions for all of these throughout the entire Army was only eighty-nine. Since alcoholism was considered a disease, medical statistics on admissions are probably more accurate. The rate for blacks was consistently lower than that for white soldiers. Generally, the overall rates in the 1920s were less than the prewar figures, and, even with the repeal of Prohibition, the rate steadily declined in the 1930s to about half of that at the beginning of the decade. Drug usage was minimal throughout these decades. In 1931, for example, there were only twenty-one reported cases in the entire Army.[56]

Everyone expected soldiers to chase women. Civilians who had a low opinion of peacetime regulars certainly did not want their womenfolk to have anything to do with them. In turn, the soldier was not apt to meet nice girls at the bars and other dives where so many went to spend their few dollars. If a soldier wanted sex, prostitutes were the most likely prospect. At Jefferson Barracks in the 1920s, on payday, one could see them in their bright dresses and tennis shoes walking to the post with blankets under their arms, prepared to ply their trade in the woods.[57]

There were homosexuals in the Army, but since sodomy and assault with intent to commit sodomy were crimes under military law, those who indulged risked imprisonment and dishonorable discharge. Those who did not wind up standing before general courts-martial might suffer ridicule or worse from the other soldiers. In one Air Corps unit the NCOs beat up a man and forced him to accept a less-than-honorable discharge rather than be court-martialed. At times an officer or NCO forced himself on men under his authority, a situation that obviously affected the morale and discipline of their units. In a couple of instances, a company commander and sergeant who had been accused of such behavior committed suicide. Others who were caught were court-martialed.[58]

While homosexuality was a topic of contemptuous banter in the barracks of the 11th Cavalry, Noel Parrish noticed only one incident, and it resulted in tragedy. A trooper drank too much one night and made a pass at another soldier. When he sobered up the next day, he was so horrified by what he had done that he shot himself in the head. Off post, Noel thought that homosexuals sought out men in uniform. He politely fended off a subtle advance made by a member of the church he attended. Other soldiers were willing—for a price. Then there were some who would beat up and rob the civilian involved. In the Third Cavalry at Fort Myer, a few would go into Washington and routinely beat up gays at Lafayette Park, across from the White House. The barracks culture condoned such activities. While the level of tolerance for homosexuals varied among individuals as well as units, generally, as one veteran pointed out, life was "hell" for them in the Army of that era.[59]

✵

In 1925 the surgeon general called venereal disease (VD) "the most important sanitary problem of the Army." Only respiratory problems caused more hospital admissions. Annually, the Medical Department prepared elaborately detailed statistics and charts to show the rates and effects of the disease in lost duty time.[60]

To control VD the Army pursued a major prevention effort. Movies, slide shows, and lectures warned soldiers of the dangers of the various sexual diseases. While the official line urged sexual morality and made it clear that continence was "not prejudicial to health" and "the only sure method of avoiding venereal disease," the Army made condoms available and provided prophylactic stations near the brothels. Failure to take advantage of the latter resulted in a court-martial if the man became infected. The prospect of three to six months in confinement with loss of pay (or at least a substantial part of it) and the addition of those months to the original enlistment was a formidable threat. It probably had the negative effect of causing some men to try to hide their infection. Nevertheless, making VD a crime and delegating the responsibility of enforcement to unit commanders were apparently the most effective preventive measures.[61]

Humiliation as well as fear was a part of the prevention campaign. Subjecting men to regular and more or less public inspections of their genitals—"Peter parades"—could easily lead to ridicule. Infected soldiers were probably more embarrassed by being forced in some units' latrines to use only the commode designated as the "VD stool." Charles Willeford, who picked up crabs from a prostitute just before he left the Philippines, suffered the consequences after he got off the transport. In front of a formation of the 600 casuals on Angel Island, he was called out and told to drop his trousers and shorts while a medic sprayed his genitals with a Flit gun. Then he had to bend over and receive additional squirts in the rear while the audience roared with laughter.[62]

Whatever the methods used, the VD rate dropped almost steadily throughout the 1920s and 1930s. In 1923, for the first time in history, there were fewer than 60 cases per 1,000 men; sixteen years later, there were only 29.6. Blacks usually had higher rates than whites in the States, but, year in and year out, the whites' rates in foreign stations topped the list. During the first year of the mobilization in 1940, the rate went up as it customarily did during wartime. Yet the surgeon general could still look with pride on the graph that traced VD rates since 1819 and clearly illustrated the great decline in the interwar decades.[63]

The Army health record generally had improved dramatically since the turn of the century. Advances in medical science, which made possible realistic preventive measures, as well as the development of vaccines reduced the combined rate for venereal disease, typhoid, smallpox, dysentery, diarrhea, dengue, and tuberculosis by 88 percent between 1903 and 1929. Over those years, however, there was relatively little change in such diseases as mumps, measles, and meningitis, and, year in and year out, respiratory illnesses still hospitalized large numbers of soldiers. In 1926 and 1928, flu epidemics again swept through the barracks. Then, during the 1920s and 1930s, increased participation in sports led to more injuries. Curiously enough, baseball led football and boxing in sending men to the hospital.[64]

Although the suicide rate was lower than it had been from the early 1890s to World War I, it was a leading cause of death throughout this period. From 1922 through 1931 it led all other causes. During the ten years from 1926 through 1935, 69 officers and 418 white, 9 black, 6 Puerto Rican, and one Filipino soldiers killed themselves. The surgeon general was disturbed that the Army suicide rate was higher than that of civilian males in the same age group. In the 1930s, increased use of automobiles began to raise the number of those killed in accidents. Although deaths in such accidents were just half of those who committed suicide in 1927, four years later the situation was reversed, and more men continued to die on the roads than by suicide throughout the 1930s.[65]

The Medical Department's published annual reports provide figures and charts that trace the number of incidents over a period of years, but they do not go into the basic question of why men killed themselves. To be sure, perhaps no one knew; but veterans thought they did. Some thought that being exposed as homosexuals and liable for severe punishment was the cause of suicides in their units. Bill Dunn heard that his company commander shot himself because he was having money problems. Another soldier believed a comrade killed himself because of gambling debts. Alberto Garcia remembered a sergeant at Fort Benning who killed his wife and then himself, while two others recalled that family problems were the probable cause.[66]

Several soldiers who served in Panama in the 1930s remarked on the high incidence of suicide in posts in the Canal Zone. Robert L. Bergeron thought that Fort Davis was just a depressing place, while M. J. Thompson surmised that being on alert so much in the 33d Infantry at Fort Clayton might have been a factor. He also wondered about the effect of smoking "goof" (marijuana). Whatever the cause, facts and rumors about suicides reverberated in the units and about the posts long after they had occurred.[67]

✻

At Jefferson Barracks in 1934 Private William F. Alden reported to his company commander and requested permission to marry. The captain blurted out: "You know you're a damn fool. Any man who asks a woman to share the life of the military is a damn fool." Although he proceeded with a detailed list of problems that a wife could expect, the captain ended by giving his approval.[68]

Although the Army traditionally discouraged marriage of enlisted men below the rank of sergeant and, in 1932, issued a regulation that barred the reenlistment of married soldiers below the top three grades of sergeant, it left the decision up to the local commander. Many of these officers were as lenient as Alden's captain. In 1937 the War Department reported that one-fifth of all soldiers below the rank of staff sergeant were married and three-fourths of that number did not have quarters on post. At Fort Sam Houston the next year a count showed that this group had 829 children on and off post. The situation was considered so serious in 1939 that the Army chief of staff ordered that any married soldier other than the top three grades and buck sergeants with eight years of service would be discharged immediately. In the next year 3,382 were, but the mobilization brought an end to this policy; only 2 men were discharged for this reason in fiscal year 1941.[69]

While married senior NCOs could live on post, privates usually had to live off post. As long as they reported for reveille and did their duties, no one said anything other than the occasional razzing from other soldiers. Often commanders would help out those who were not qualified for quarters. At Jefferson Barracks, Jay Smith qualified for housing only briefly when he was a sergeant, but he and others were permitted to fix up abandoned buildings and live in them. There the Smiths and the other families had to prepare for white-glove inspections by an officer every Saturday just like soldiers in the barracks. But the Army did provide furniture and bedding as well as issue woolen underwear that the wives could alter for their children. A small food allowance and the opportunity to buy freshly baked bread for two cents a loaf, hams for not much more than a dollar, and other foodstuffs at the commissary also helped him make ends meet. Georgia Campster Smith took in sewing and worked as a server at officers' parties to bring in additional money.[70]

Evelyn Hruby was a contract nurse working for the Civilian Conservation Corps when she met Private Joe Hruby at Fort Meade, South Dakota. Even with her nurse's income, they had a difficult time. She remembered "never having enough for the smallest luxury—such as an occasional baby sitter" for the two boys. In contrast, during the first years of her marriage in the 1930s, Caroline Rouse said that they "lived quite comfortably." Walter was a sergeant stationed at Fitzsimmons

Hospital, so Caroline and he were able to set up housekeeping in Denver, which was her hometown. It was eight years before she had to move to an Army post.

Ruby Mundell Barry and Florence Ricketts Jackson also enjoyed a long stay at their first station, which was Fort Benjamin Harrison. They had quarters on post and enjoyed the dances, bridge parties, and church, but housekeeping and raising children took up most of their time. Florence's folks lived a few miles away in Indianapolis, so she was able to see them often. As she looked back it seemed to her that "it was like one big family—people in the Army looked after their own." The Christmas parties for the children and the great feasts that the families attended at the mess halls on Thanksgiving and Christmas were memorable occasions. Each company would have its own mimeographed or printed menu, which included the names of all the officers and men. Jay Smith's older son, Bill, had fond memories of these big events at Jefferson Barracks and recalled, with nostalgia, a comment that the commanding officer had printed on one of these menus: "When you think of an Army post you must remember that we are really a small town."[71]

Life for the children in enlisted families had changed little since before World War I. They still lived in different neighborhoods from the officers' children, so they tended to see little of each other outside of school. All, however, were surrounded by soldiers. John Lillie loved sports and was able to learn from soldier teachers, who would also lend the youngsters sports equipment. Marnie Bradley remembered the soldiers as "babysitters . . . It was like having 200 uncles." Cooks in the mess hall even sometimes provided ice cream.

Army children's principal contact with civilians was at school, where the Army trucks took them every day. In the St. Louis schools, Bill Smith impressed his teachers, who encouraged him. Elsewhere some encountered hostility. Jess Cloud thought that the teachers at Hampton, Virginia, seemed to dislike them. Barbara Jane Barry came to realize that many civilians considered her and other Army kids "low class." Her mother, Ruth Mundell Barry, thought that the school board in the small town near Fort Benjamin Harrison resented having so many Army children in the school and were unaware that the Army paid tuition for them. In Riverside, California, where Bob Brockway attended school, the principal lectured the Army children on the point that they "were inferiors and must behave with particular deference to civilians."[72]

✳

Americans traditionally had little interest in and less respect for soldiers in peacetime. Many civilians may have lived through the 1920s and 1930s without ever seeing one, while a few may not even have known of their existence. Yet, year in and year out, their numbers waxing and waning with the rise and fall of the economy, thousands of young men entered the Army. Some got out as soon as they could. Barracks life, with its lack of privacy, the strict discipline, the boredom, and—for those in the mounted branches—the hard labor involved in caring for horses, was more than some could stand.

Others found comfort in the camaraderie, the order and stability of the disciplined life, and the security. Then there was the pride in the company and the regiment. Men would fight, as did soldiers in the Sixth Infantry with men of the Second Infantry who insulted their regimental crest during a maneuver in 1934. All took pride in the campaign hat, which "was worn square on the head, canted slightly forward, carefully blocked and with a brim ironed board-stiff and straight." The color of the hat cord indicated the soldier's branch, and the badge on the crown showed his regiment or unit. As Jim Twitty emphasized, "The campaign hat . . . was a symbol of professionalism, a mark of distinction, a personal treasure." For all these reasons, tangible and intangible, there were those like Bill Dunn who "just liked being a soldier."[73]

NINE

The Army in Pacific Outposts, 1919–1940

There appear to be more prospects for interesting events here than elsewhere.

—GEORGE C. MARSHALL

A LTHOUGH the United States and its Army enjoyed the most peaceful period in history during the years between the two world wars, the troops who garrisoned posts in China, the Philippines, Panama, and Hawaii lived under the threat of a possible war with Japan. They trained in units at or near full strength and were aware that they would be the front line if war came. During the mid-1920s, when George Marshall was in the 15th Infantry, they were in the midst of a Chinese civil war with the Japanese as an increasingly ominous presence. By the late 1930s Japan was fighting in China, and the conflict that American military leaders had pondered since the early years of the century was obviously drawing closer.

In 1925 Eli A. Helmick, now a major general and the inspector general of the Army, toured the American bases in Panama, Hawaii, China, and the Philippines. He had never been to China, and this was his first return to the Philippines since he had left in 1903. There were now paved highways, modern public buildings, and good streets in major cities. As for the Army, the majority of the regular troops were Philippine Scouts. During World War I they had been organized into regiments that, after the war, were integrated into the Regular Army. Most of the officers, however, continued to be Americans. Helmick was impressed by the Scouts. They were "good soldiers . . . well disciplined." Although he was pleased with the one battalion of American infantry

Looking better than in 1925, the 31st Infantry paraded at Fort Santiago, Manila, 1936.
Courtesy of Edwin Todd Wheatley Jr.

from the 15th that he saw at McKinley, he was dismayed by the state of the one complete American infantry regiment—the 31st—and thought that the commander should be relieved. On Corregidor, at the mouth of Manila Bay, he found further reason for concern. The island's defenses were inadequate for the eventuality of an extended siege, and the Scout contingent of coast artillery outnumbered the Americans by two to one. A mutiny in two Scout units the year before, together with growing anti-Americanism and the Philippine independence movement, caused him to ponder the wisdom of having a sizable majority of Philippine troops at the forefront of defense.

From the Philippines Helmick went to Tientsin to see two battalions of the 15th Infantry, which lived up to its reputation as a showcase regiment; he was duly impressed: "any American could be proud to claim [it] as representative of the authority of his country." Yet there were fewer than 1,000 of these men to show the American flag in the turbulence of northern China. The vulnerability to a possible Japanese attack of troops defending American interests in both China and the Philippines was obvious.[1]

During the 1920s and 1930s an average of 27 percent of the Army was on foreign service, which included Alaska and Puerto Rico. In 1934 the War Department had shortened the overseas tour from three to two years, but that still seemed to some like "an eternity." A few, fewer than 400 in most of those years, were in Alaska, while some 1,100 (Puerto Rican enlisted men with American officers) were in Puerto Rico throughout the first decade, only to decline to fewer than 1,000 in the 1930s. The token force in China rarely had more than 1,000 on duty, with fewer than 800 during its last six years in Tientsin. Since both the Army and the Navy assumed that if war came the Japanese would be the most likely enemy, the bulk of the Americans overseas were on the island of Oahu in Hawaii, on Luzon in the Philippines, and in the Panama Canal Zone. Before World War I the largest concentration had been in the Philippines.[2]

More than 14,000 soldiers were stationed on Oahu during most of this period, with a buildup in the late 1930s to 25,000 by 1940. In most of these years troops in the Philippines numbered fewer than 12,000, with Scouts accounting for some 57 percent of this total, while the garrison in the Canal Zone consisted of fewer than 10,000 until it began to increase in the late 1930s. Secretary of War Dwight F. Davis stated in 1925 that a sufficient defense of Oahu required 20,357 soldiers and that the Canal Zone needed 14,437, but neither had that number on hand until the late 1930s. By then the Army had evacuated the 15th Infantry from China and had begun to send reinforcements to the other outposts. Time seemed to be running out.[3]

Between the world wars, regulars and their families could expect to serve at least one tour in the Philippines, Panama, or Hawaii, and a select few in China. The lives they led in those distant places were far different from those led by their civilian contemporaries in the United States.

China was the most exotic and exciting of the foreign stations. After spending five years as General Pershing's aide, George C. Marshall had the pick of assignments in 1924. Not surprisingly, he chose China, since it was considered the prize assignment by both officers and soldiers. Benny Poore Bolté, who had loved her year there in 1916, was also enthusiastic about returning to Tientsin in 1932. Rachel Forbush, who was assigned there by the American Library Service, summed up the attitude for those fortunate few who got the opportunity: "China is the *place!*"[4]

As one of the foreign contingents with the mission of protecting the lives of their nationals and the communication lines from Peking to the coast, the 15th Infantry was a showcase unit. All wore specially tailored uniforms, and coolies even ran out onto the drill field to dust off the soldiers' shoes. Because of the desirability of the station, in the last years soldiers had to be in their second enlistment to qualify, and, once there, many wanted to stay. By 1930, most were in their late thirties. Frank Bozoski, who finally got there in 1936 after nine years in the Army, was impressed by the 15th. It was "a damn good outfit, every soldier knew what he was doing, no one had to give a command other than when we were drilling." Discipline was a hallmark, as Jack Campbell pointed out: when an officer spoke, "you stood straight as a pole. When they said jump you jumped." After he had been there a couple of years, Marshall wrote a friend: "This particular regiment has the most remarkably efficient personnel I have ever seen gathered in one group."[5]

China held another attraction for ambitious officers. With warlord armies occasionally clashing, there was the possibility of action. Marshall, his wife, and her mother arrived in the midst of a civil war. If they had landed five days later, they would not have been able to reach Tientsin by train, as troops had taken over the rail line. During his first two and half months, he commanded the regiment while Chinese troops swarmed in the environs of Tientsin. A division surrounded the company outpost at Tongshan, halfway between Tientsin and the port of Chinwangtao. Marshall's morning horseback ride was both exercise and an opportunity to check the small outposts that were supposed to keep these forces from coming into the city. He estimated that 100,000 Chinese troops passed through the vicinity in those days. The Americans were able to disarm some of them and generally kept them out of critical areas. The language training that the commanding general of the American forces in China had ordered in February 1924 really paid off, as officers and some of the soldiers were able to communicate with these people. Grateful citizens of Tientsin gave a marble monument to their American protectors, while Marshall received a commendation for his skillful handling of the regiment. As he wrote a friend, that reward "is worth my three years in China."[6]

During this crisis Marshall was impressed by the younger officers, who "are pulling on the leash . . . to get the detail for the International Train or for patrols going in the apparent direction of trouble," who did yeoman service protecting the city. One of them was Major Matthew B. Ridgway, who took two men with him to divert a force of 12,000 that was headed in their direction. Fortunately the Chinese forces began to veer away from the city, but Ridgway followed them on horseback for several miles to make sure. Another was Captain William B. Tuttle, who took nine men out to guard a bridge into the American defense sector and turned away a contingent of some 5,000 Chinese.[7]

The day of the white man's influence, however, was waning. In January 1926 Major General William D. Connor, the commander of the American Forces in China, wrote a lengthy plea to the American ambassador that the troops be taken out. "During the recent war we escaped conflict by as narrow a margin as I consider possible." When the 15th had first been sent there, the assumption had been that its potential enemy would consist of mobs, but now they faced "organized armies." The State Department did not act on his recommendation. Instead, the United States reinforced the Marines. Over the next two years the Marines, which had originally had about half as many men as the Army garrison, increased tenfold, to almost 5,000, while the size of the 15th was maintained. During this period the British, French, and Japanese also increased their forces, although the Italians still had fewer troops than the Americans. By June 1928 the British had more than 2,600, the French some 2,500, and the Japanese had more than 6,000.[8]

When General Helmick came for his whirlwind four-day visit in the fall of 1925, he observed three regimental reviews, assorted small-unit drills, and exercises, including athletics. A few weeks later General Connor made a more extensive inspection as he observed field training and tactical problems and was more impressed by those exercises than by close-order drill. His successor, Brigadier General Joseph C. Castner, had a different impression. He thought many of the old soldiers were obese and that the field training was unsatisfactory, so he instituted long marches. Even after he left, the regiment emphasized speed marching. When Lieutenant Alfred C. Wedemeyer arrived in 1930, the troops regularly marched five miles after breakfast. He recalled the nauseating stench of human and animal waste in the countryside and soldiers' frequent departures from the column to vomit. By the mid-1930s, when the executive officer wanted to take the troops out for a field exercise, there was a lengthy discussion as to whether or not it was medically safe. During the summer, however, the regiment went, a battalion at a time, to the seashore near Chinwangtao for several weeks of range firing and some field training.[9]

In China, as elsewhere throughout the Army, there was a strong emphasis on athletics. In addition to intramural contests between the companies, regimental teams competed against the Marines in Peking as well as the other foreign contingents; Wedemeyer even took the baseball team to Japan to play the Kyoto University nine. The British and Americans held annual joint field days, and Wedemeyer learned how to play cricket. In the mid-1930s the regimental commander temporarily halted all competition with the Marines, as they had started winning virtually all the contests.[10]

During the 1930s the Japanese threat to Americans and other foreigners in China increased. In 1931 the Japanese took over Manchuria. The next year their attempt to seize Shanghai caused the Americans to send the 31st Infantry there for five months to reinforce the Marine regiment in defense of the foreign concessions. It became clear to American observers that they could not maintain such a meager military presence in China. At this time Captains Charles L. Bolté and David D. Barrett emphasized in the school for company officers that if there were an incident with the Japanese the 15th could not expect the State Department to support them. The American military was already stretched too thin.[11]

In July 1937, when the Japanese seized Peking and Tientsin and opened up a full-scale campaign against the Chinese, Lieutenant Stephen O. Fuqua Jr. was en route to his assignment with the 15th. His wife accompanied him on the first part of the trip, but because of the volatile international situation, the Army would not let her go on to Tientsin. When he arrived in August, he was impressed that "the Japanese were all around." Every morning when the American troops fell out for reveille, Japanese bombers would fly very low and very slowly over their formation. The Americans joked that they "were taking a head count." At the same time, there was a tendency to underestimate the Japanese, to think of them as "paper tigers." In December they bombed the American gunboat *Panay* in the Yangtze River. Rather than risk an incident against the vulnerable and inadequate Army garrison, the War Department ordered the 15th home; it sailed on March 4, 1938.[12]

Memories were all that remained of China service for those who served and their families. Benny Bolté had enjoyed her months there in 1916 and looked forward to going back. In 1932, after a five-week transpacific journey via Manila, she and her family stood on the deck of the transport *Republic* off Chinwangtao. As a lighter pulled alongside, she saw coffins of six adults and two children who had died of disease being shipped back to the States. With three children under six, she began to wonder "why did I think this was such a good idea to go to China."

After they settled, she began to appreciate again what China offered. "Life was fascinating there—each small expedition from the house an adventure in sights, sounds, and smells." However, one had always to be on the alert about food and water. Fresh vegetables were out, and one had to take great care in cleansing food generally. The regimental quartermaster delivered drinking water every day. Then there were the constant rounds of shots to prevent disease. Benny recalled that "the kids were like pin cushions."[13]

With the abundance of servants and an exchange rate that greatly increased the buying power of the dollar (at least before the United States went off the gold standard), the social whirl was intense. Even the rather staid George Marshall thought the dances, parties, amateur theatricals, and sundry other activities "very attractive." With foreign units nearby, some parties were cosmopolitan. During the summer weeks at Chinwangtao, the women and children enjoyed the beach, and Benny, who loved to ride, rode the Mongolian ponies and taught many of the children to ride.[14]

Shopping was one of the greatest attractions. When the *Infantry Journal* published an article on what one should expect on this assignment, there was great emphasis on what one should buy—rugs, solid silverware, linens, and furs—and what one could expect to pay: the rugs might be around $2 a square foot, while a tablecloth might be as little as $40. Rachel Forbush, who went to China in 1921, was enthralled: "Shopping is truly thrilling." As she explained, "It is simply unbelievable—how much you can get for how little." Peking was even more exciting than Tientsin, as Rachel wrote her parents: "The crowded stores and bazaars, so jam-full of beautiful things, are like the Arabian

Charles L. Bolté (seated on left) and Benny Bolté (fourth from left) at a dinner party given by the Japanese officers for their American, French, British, and Italian colleagues in Tientsin, circa 1935. Courtesy of Adelaide Poore Bolté.

nights. The streets, with their conglomerate push of Peking carts, rickshas, glassed-in Chinese carriages with shouting servants running fore and aft, basket-laden donkeys, with now and then an automobile or a gorgeous funeral or wedding procession, or a camel train—are like a huge fascinating stage setting."[15]

While Peking and the Great Wall, which was near the summer camp, were sightseeing meccas for the Americans, some officers went much farther afield. When conditions permitted, they were encouraged to travel and were annually allowed a month's detached service for this purpose. Some like Matt Ridgway went hunting; others went sightseeing. During his three years in China, Charlie Bolté took one trip to Port Arthur and Darien in Manchuria to go over the Russo-Japanese battlefields and then, with three others, took a trip down the Yangtze from Hangchow to Chungking.[16]

In 1933 Lilian Stewart Burt wrote her mother that there were 105

American children in Tientsin. Most of them were in Army families. China was an adventure for them. The smallest, who were under the constant care of amahs, learned Chinese before they did English. Joe and Winifred Smith Stilwell made certain that all their children learned Chinese and something about the art and culture, but most children did not receive formal instruction. They parroted what they heard, and some of that was not acceptable in polite society. Francis Clune, who learned some choice oaths from ricksha men, was picked up by a Sikh policeman because his language was shocking people on the street.

The American children played with children of several nationalities. Phil Bolté's best friend was a Dutch boy who lived across the street. Bill Clune belonged to a French Boy Scout troop, while the Stilwell girls went by ricksha to play with their friends. Dave Bolté was fascinated by the troops and would walk or ride his bicycle to the compound to watch the parades and various formations. There were movies at the compound and in the city. The Clune boys had to learn their address in Mandarin before they could go to the latter. The Bolté boys were among those who attended Sunday school regularly in the compound. Afterward their parents would take them to their father's company mess hall, where they enjoyed cherry pie. During the summer the families spent six to eight weeks at the beach. In the early years there they lived in tents; later they had bungalows but still ate at a central mess hall.

In the fall, many went to the Tientsin American School. Norma Tuttle was close enough to walk, but a mule-drawn ambulance picked up others, who sat on the two facing benches while a military policeman stood on the step at the back. In Phil Bolté's class about half of the students were Chinese. Dave, who was older, had only two Chinese children in his class. Norma remembered children of businessmen and diplomats in her class. Instruction was in English; Chinese was not taught, but French was offered. Dave's third-grade class had some difficulty in that the teacher was a Russian who could speak Chinese but no English, so a Chinese girl in the class had to translate.

There was a darker side in addition to the many vaccination shots and restrictions on food and water. Generally servants spoiled the American children, but the Boltés' number-one boy threatened to beat the boys with their father's Sam Browne belt. Other matters were more serious. Once the Japanese guards tried to evict the women and children from the train when they were on their way to the beach, and Dave recalled seeing them physically throw off a Russian woman. He also remembered seeing a corpse wash up on the shore and passing one on the street in Tientsin as well as the coffins by the roadside. Norma Tuttle had a more shocking experience. She and her parents were on a train to Peking when Chinese soldiers came into their car and seized a Chinese man who was sitting across from them. Her parents pushed her head down so she could not see, but she later found out that the soldiers had beheaded him by the side of the train.[17]

Soldiers who were lucky enough to get assigned to China had to go through an indoctrination. Frank Bozoski, an old soldier who had served in Hawaii and Panama, was impressed that during the two-week layover in the Philippines any soldier who got into trouble was not permitted to continue on to China. When his group of replacements arrived at Chinwangtao in 1936, a sergeant took charge and warned them against drinking too much of the cheap, strong beer on the train ride to Tientsin. The four men who ignored him and got drunk had to go back on the next ship.

Regardless of their previous service, new arrivals had to undergo a period of training to demonstrate their soldierly skills and to learn what was expected of them as well as where not to go in the city. The message to Bozoski and his group was clear: they were "ambassadors" and "had better act as such or you don't stay." After completing this ten-day course and receiving their new tailored uniforms, they were permitted to leave the compound when they were not on duty but had to be back by taps. After six months, if they behaved themselves they could get passes to stay out overnight. As he became better acquainted with the men of the 15th and life in China, Frank was struck by the quality of the soldiers and the friendliness of the Chinese. He thought that they were easier to get along with than people back in the States.[18]

During the first years in Tientsin, the men of the 15th had been scattered about the city, but in 1917 they moved into the block-square American Compound, which all soon learned to call Mei-Kuo Ying-P'an. They were housed in three-story brick-and-stucco buildings arranged on three parallel courtyards. Poorly constructed and not particularly well suited for barracks—the builders had assumed they might be converted into apartments—the buildings had bad lighting and only one central bathroom. These problems were not solved until just before the regiment left.[19]

Whatever the inconveniences of the living quarters, the availability of cheap servants made a great difference. Much of the work the soldiers did in the States was done by coolies, who polished brass, shined shoes, cleaned uniforms, made beds, cleaned the barracks, and handled kitchen-police chores. In 1920 James McCarthy reported that all this labor cost only a dollar a month. The Christmas dinner menu of E Company in 1935 included not only a group photo of the seventy officers and men but also one of their seventeen coolies.[20]

Some of the NCOs who were married and lived off post also enjoyed having servants. Jack Bradley Jr. was a sergeant when he joined the medical detachment at Tientsin in 1928. He and his wife initially had a houseboy, cook, and gardener; after Margaret was born, they added an amah to the household. A good many other soldiers maintained households off post with local women. Charlie Bolté estimated that as many as 80 percent of the men in Service Company in the mid-1930s lived this way at one time or another. Nevertheless, he believed that in an emergency, they could get to the compound within fifteen minutes. About that time, the regimental executive officer directed company commanders to inspect those places, but Bill Carraway, who commanded E Company, ignored the order, and nothing happened.[21]

Alcoholism and venereal disease (VD) were major problems in the 15th Infantry. The causes, as George Marshall pointed out in 1925, were "cheap liquor and cheaper women." In the 1930s a bottle of Scotch could be had for seventy-five cents, and, as Frank Bozoski recalled, beer was seven cents a quart and a woman only three cents more.[22]

Although they were perhaps not aware of the enormity of the problem when they went to China, Rachel Forbush and two hostesses arrived in Tientsin in the spring of 1921 with the mission of setting up a Service Club and establishing a recreation program. They found the Young Men's Christian Association effort virtually moribund. Rachel tried to build up the library and helped her friends as they organized entertainment. "We dance and play cards or checkers or sing or just talk with them . . . I have danced two hours straight every night since I came." In those early years after the war, many of the soldiers were very young. One confided that before they opened up the Service Club one could go to the movies in the compound or go for a walk, but after a week or so the attraction of "booze" and "the wrong sort of women" became overpowering.[23]

When a soldier walked out of the main gate, bars "seemed to stretch into infinity," and women were always available. During the eleven years from 1928 through 1938, the surgeon general's annual report showed that the troops in China led the Army in alcoholism for nine years and tied with those in the Philippines one year. Their highest rate in this period occurred in 1928, when they reported 43.8 cases per 1,000, more than five times the overall Army average. Yet alcoholism apparently did not bother the authorities as much as venereal disease.[24]

In 1920 the VD rate in the 15th hit 421.73 per 1,000, more than double the rate for white troops in the Philippines and six and half times the Stateside rate. The vigorous effort by George Marshall and other regimental commanders to develop athletic and recreational programs cut the rate more than half by the late 1920s. An Army regulation that placed responsibility for the rate on the unit commanders in 1923 helped galvanize those officers.[25]

During the 1930s two regimental commanders went beyond the increased emphasis on athletics and genital inspections in their efforts to solve the problem. One attempted to impose punishment on an entire company if one man came down with a venereal disease, but complaints brought in an inspector general, who put a stop to that. The War Department also assigned a specialist in VD control, Dr. Francis J. Clune, to the garrison. A combination of all these efforts greatly reduced the rate, to 56 per 1,000 in 1933. For seven of the last nine years that the regiment was in Tientsin, its rate was less than 100 per 1,000 and below that of the Philippines six of those years and tied with it one other year. Another possible cause for this decrease could have been higher standards demanded of those who volunteered for China service.[26]

Transports to China and the Philippines made the Pacific crossing only four times a year. Since regiments were permanently stationed in those overseas garrisons, the passengers consisted chiefly of newly assigned officers and soldiers, most of them raw recruits who had not received any training prior to the voyage. There were also some wives and children on the long journey. In early January 1937, several members of the West Point class of 1936 posed joyfully with their recent

Ready to sail on the first leg of their trip to the Philippines (left to right): John and Betty Heintges, Nancy and William T. Ryder, Marian and William T. Haneke, Eleanor and Edwin Sutherland, Norma and William P. Yarborough, on the transport St. Mihiel, in New York Harbor, January 1937. Courtesy of Norma Tuttle Yarborough.

brides on the deck of the U.S. Army transport *St. Mihiel* just before it sailed from New York. One of the brides was Norma Tuttle, who was returning to the Far East—with William P. Yarborough. He and his good friend William T. Ryder were delighted at the prospect of going to the Philippines. Theirs was the first class in a decade or so that had the choice of foreign service upon graduation.

The two Bills had certainly followed different paths to the Military Academy. Yarborough was an Army brat who had always wanted to go to West Point, and he had enlisted in the Army to attain that goal. Growing up, Ryder had had no interest in the Academy or in the Army. He really wanted to follow his older brother out to Hollywood and become a Busby Berkeley chorus boy. His widowed mother, however, had different plans, and she was able to obtain an appointment for him. Bill made a pact with her: he would go for a year and then decide whether he wanted to stay. He liked the institution and his classmates, so he stayed. During his years there, whenever the opportunity arose, he acted, sang, or danced and became a well-beloved character. Bill Yarborough also belonged to the Dialectic Society, the cadets' theatrical organization, but he had a variety of other interests, including swimming and working on *The Pointer,* the cadet magazine, where he became the managing editor. Neither, however, made a big impression on the supervising tactical officers, and they remained cadet privates through the entire four years.

Since the next transport was not leaving until January, the Army assigned the two Bills and their classmates on orders for the Philippines to Fort Jay, on Governors Island in New York harbor, when they came off leave in early September. Ryder and Yarborough lived at the Algonquin Hotel and took the subway each work day to the pier, where they caught the ferry to Governors Island. In their uniforms, complete with polished boots, Sam Browne belts, and swords, they cut fine figures amidst the blasé commuters. Bill Ryder said that he thought the New Yorkers were amused and perhaps "wondered what hotel door we had vacated." Bill Yarborough remembered that there was no evidence of hostility.

Before the ship sailed, each got married. Yarborough recalled: "I felt that unless I married Norma before I went to the Philippines . . . when I got back she would be gone." It was a six-week journey with stops in San Francisco and Hawaii. As was frequently the case for junior officers, they were quartered separately from their brides on shipboard. Bill Yarborough remembered: "We were pretty ingenious and things seemed to work out all right." He was impressed with the quality of the meals, which compared favorably with those he had on pleasure cruises in later years. The officers and their ladies always dressed formally for dinner. As they made the long passage from Hawaii to their destination, he remembered, we felt a "sense of adventure . . . as the flying fish began to come across the ship, and ultimately you saw in the distance the low, blue Philippine Islands stretched out there, mysterious as hell."[27]

A joyous crowd awaited them at the dock in Manila. The quarterly arrival of a transport was an occasion as officers and their wives greeted newcomers and said farewell to old friends about to depart. Representatives from the regiments welcomed the newly assigned officers and wives and promptly took them out for a drink or two. Then the sponsors escorted the men to tailors to be measured for white dress uniforms, mess jackets, and khakis. If assigned to nearby Fort McKinley, the hosts would take them to their quarters, where food was in the refrigerator and servants were on hand. Bill Yarborough and his friends appreciated the week they were given to get their uniforms and generally to get settled before they had to assume their duties.[28]

The Philippine Scouts to which these young West Pointers were assigned in the 1920s and 1930s were very different from the small units established around the turn of the century. After World War I, two infantry and one each field artillery, cavalry, engineer, and medical regiments were organized as part of the Regular Army, and Scout officers were given regular commissions. Most of the Scouts were at two posts. Four of these regiments, the 45th and 57th Infantry, the 12th Medical and 14th Engineer, were quartered at Fort William McKinley except for two companies of the 45th, which were stationed at Pettit Barracks at Zamboanga. The mounted troops, the 24th Field Artillery and 26th Cavalry, were at Fort Stotsenburg.[29]

Despite the organization of the larger units, their assumption of regular status, and the performance of garrison duties in which they at times excelled the American units, the Scouts, who had initially been paid half the American pay scale, had now received about a third of what their American counterparts received. In July 1924, 602 privates of the 57th Infantry and the medical regiment refused to obey orders. Within days more than half returned to duty, and the mutiny ended without violence. The Army court-martialed 218, who received prison terms of five years or more, and there were no repercussions.[30]

Officers who served later in the Scouts emphasized their loyalty, and all were enthusiastic about their professionalism. John E. Olson, who went out to the 57th after graduation from West Point in 1939, thought that the Filipinos considered service in the Scouts "a coveted honor." Since those who enlisted stayed in, a private first class of less than two enlistments was unusual. At any given time, there were relatively few openings, and competition was stiff. Jim Gavin, who was with the 57th from 1936 to 1938, remembered that recruits had to obtain recommendations from their high school superintendents. Douglas V. Johnson, who was in the 24th Field Artillery, said that the first sergeants actually made the selection and that the recruit was likely to be a relative of a noncom. When the new man reported for duty, his family came with him, and his father charged him to consider the commanding officer his new father.

The iron discipline, high state of training, and long service of these professionals meant that there were few problems with drunkenness, VD, and absence without leave. Courts-martial were so rare that Olson did not recall having to serve on one in two and half years. Language was the one problem that bothered the officers, since many of the soldiers did not understand English. Beginning in 1930, American officers at Stotsenburg had to take lessons in Tagalog, and more Scouts learned English over the years, but communication remained a problem. The practical solution was to give orders through the NCOs. Looking back on his service in the Scouts, Bill Yarborough compared these soldiers to the famed Gurkhas who served the British so well.[31]

A significant reason for the stability and high morale of the Scouts was that many were married and lived with their families in nearby *barrios*. In 1937 at Fort William McKinley, 227 men from the 57th lived in their *barrio,* which had a population of 1,203. Originally built out of whatever was available in 1918, the *barrio* underwent a complete renovation, with new houses and roads, in the early 1930s. Although a lieutenant was technically in charge, two Scout sergeants and a council of other residents governed the community. Beginning in 1932, the *barrio* staged an annual fiesta to which the officers were invited. From Saturday afternoon through Sunday, there were games, dances, a band concert, two plays in Tagalog, and a high mass. In the program of the 1937 fiesta, the brief history of the *barrio* emphasized the "promotion of Christian fellowship" in the community.[32]

At Pettit Barracks in the early 1930s the commanding officer had the huts torn down and put the Scouts to work with government-furnished supplies to build wooden houses. To ensure that they and the quarters were well maintained, he sent his officers to inspect them regularly. Charlie Ivins remembered the "senora of the establishment . . . standing in her doorway all starched up in her best dress" with her children equally well dressed sitting on the porch as they waited for the inspecting officer. Ivins thought that the well-kept new houses were good not only for the general appearance of the post but also for the morale of the Scouts and their families.

There was an unusual situation at this post, in that one of the Scout companies consisted of Moros, who wore khaki headbands instead of campaign hats like other Scouts. Considering the traditional enmity between the two groups, this practice had explosive possibilities, but there were no problems. Charlie Ivins, who served with the Moro company for eighteen months in 1933 and 1934, remembered that "they behaved like angels" because of First Sergeant Damao, "a man of immense dignity" who was not only the ranking soldier but also the *datu* and imam of these men.

A problem did arrive, however, when one of the Scout sergeants was hit by a pitched ball during a baseball game with a local team and died. Whatever benefits his wife and family might receive were in doubt because he had not been legally married in a Christian service. Not surprisingly, a check disclosed that none of the Moros in the *barrio* had been married by a Christian priest. In order to ensure payment of benefits and pensions, the colonel ordered that all must go through a Christian ceremony. Those who refused would have to move out of the *barrio*. On the appointed day all the Moros reported, led by the ranking sergeant with his wife and three sons, all of whom were also sergeants, and were married by an Army chaplain.[33]

Duty hours were in the morning from six or seven until noon unless a special inspection or competitive tests were in the offing. In addition to his company duties, Ivins was also post quartermaster and engineer as well as signal, finance, and ordnance officer. Whatever the duties of the morning, well-trained servants eased the passage of the rest of the day for officers. As Charlie recounted, he would come to his quarters, drop his clothes to the floor to be washed by the *lavendera*, shower, lunch, and then enjoy a siesta—short or long—depending on whether or not he played golf. If the latter, he again changed clothes and showered before dressing in his white formal uniform for cocktails and dinner.

Golf at the Zamboanga Golf and Country Club was an unusual experience—like playing through a zoo. Cows, water buffalo, dogs, pigs, goats, and chickens might wander onto the fairways. There were crocodiles in the pond that served as the water hazard, and monkeys usually harassed players at the fourth tee. Once he killed a cobra near the fifth hole.[34]

Every year the Philippine Division on Luzon would go on a maneuver to practice its role in the Orange Plan, which was drawn up by the War Department to defend against a Japanese attack. In Doug Johnson's first year in the 24th Field Artillery at Stotsenburg, the regimental exercise was to combat a landing in Batangas below Manila. The second year they went north to fight an imaginary attack in Lingayen Gulf. He was one of a group of officers who reconnoitered in Batangas before the main body arrived. Thirty years earlier, Batangas had been one of the hotbeds of the Philippine War. When the artillery officers got out of their cars near a group of Filipinos working in rice paddies, the natives fled. They sent a Scout to explain that they meant no harm, but an old man explained that during the insurrection the Americans had said the same thing but then had killed people. On the next maneuver in the Lingayen Gulf, conditions were unusually hot and dusty, and men and animals collapsed. Some of the officers, including the doctors, suggested to the regimental commander that he abandon the march in such beastly weather. The old colonel bluntly told them that soldiers had to learn to endure such hardships, for they might have to fight in similar weather.[35]

When Bill Ryder took a mule train to Bataan for a maneuver in the late 1930s, he had a problem: much of the movement was at night, and he had to send small parties of six or seven to each company with supplies. As a rule, Bill carried out his mission successfully, but one night he got lost in the jungle. When he radioed the service company commander, the captain told him: "Ryder, I know you think you know where you are, but I know I know where you are. By God, you stay where you are until I find you. You stay lost until I get there." Bill was probably not as amused by that situation as the older lieutenant, Jim Gavin, who was in charge of the regimental trucks. It was one of the few lighter moments for Gavin, as he was acutely aware that, in case of war, "prospects on Bataan were grim at best" with what was available to defend it. During their service together, Gavin formed friendships with Ryder and Yarborough. They and the other officers in the regiment knew that tall, slim Jim Gavin was, as Bill Ryder put it, "a real comer."[36]

With the great reduction in strength of American troops, those who remained were limited to the Manila area, Corregidor, and, after the early 1920s, to Clark Field, near Fort Stotsenburg. In December 1922 the last black soldiers, the Ninth Cavalry, left Stotsenburg and the Philippines. Richard Johnson, who had come to the islands in the 48th Volunteers in 1900 and returned for three more tours, wound up his last tour as a medic attached to the Ninth in the fall of 1921. He had spent more than half of his service in the islands, and before he left, this last time, he took leave and went on a nostalgic tour of the posts where he had served. Yet he did not want to stay. As a family man, he wanted to live in the States after his retirement. At the end of 1922 he retired as a technical sergeant. Although he regretted not being able to retire as a master sergeant, he looked back philosophically on his service. "I fared pretty well in the army and departed with a greater heritage than I might have attained in any other occupational pursuit."[37]

Through the memories of two younger men who served in the islands during the last years of that period, one can catch glimpses of soldier life. Charles Willeford, who later became a professional writer and left the most accessible account, served at Clark throughout most of his tour but did spend a few months at Nichols Field, which was located near Manila. During the last months of peace, David G. Brenzel served in the 59th Coast Artillery on Corregidor.

Bored with driving a truck at March Field, Charles Willeford, who had enlisted at sixteen, volunteered in 1936 for duty in the Philippines. After he arrived at his destination, the Third Pursuit Squadron at Clark Field, it hit him: "Here I was in the middle of nowhere, and here I would remain for two years. A wave of nostalgia overwhelmed me." He was also dissatisfied with the Air Corps and became more so at Clark Field. Civilians could do what he and the other enlisted men did, and there was not much to do. Not surprisingly, since he had driven a truck at March, he drove a truck at Clark. As the fire-truck driver, he was on duty one day and off the next. On the days he was on duty, he merely drove the truck from the garage to the firehouse and then back again a few hours later. Military prisoners cleaned and polished the truck. And there were no fires.

It seemed a waste of time. Aside from the mechanics, who put in four-hour days looking after the planes, the squadron had little or nothing to do. When Charlie transferred to a fuel truck, he had more to do. On duty five days a week, he had to refuel the planes when they

Charles Willeford, who enjoyed life in the Philippines but wanted tougher soldiering so joined the cavalry, Manila, July 1937. Courtesy of Betsy Willeford.

landed. He was also placed in the rotation for guard duty. At least this assignment made time pass more quickly, and it gave him the opportunity to steal gas and sell it to those soldiers who had cars. A corporal with almost twenty years of service helped him to understand how the Army worked. "Everything is always done as it was done before." But this did not ease the ache that he felt because, as far as he was concerned, he was "a flunky in coveralls" rather than a soldier.[38]

Leisure was the up side of his life. For three dollars a month, Filipino houseboys made beds, shined shoes, cleaned the barracks, and did the kitchen-police chores—those routine duties that took up so much of soldiers' time in the States. Willeford was able to read three or four books a week from the Fort Stotsenburg library. He wanted to be a poet and tried to find inspiration in what he saw about him. In an effort to learn more about the art of poetry, he also pored over the back issues of the *Saturday Review of Literature* that an officer's wife had left in the squadron dayroom. For more general information and intelligent conversation, he depended upon Corporal Elmer T. Canavin, who had completed three years at the University of Pennsylvania.[39]

As a street-wise seventeen-year-old who already had a year in the Army, Willeford was ready to take advantage of the debauchery that he found about him in the Philippines. Sex, in particular, was a great attraction. Whores charged a dollar in the four two-story brothels in nearby Angeles. Army medics regularly checked the women and provided a prophylactic station nearby for soldiers to be treated. If a man turned up with venereal disease and had not checked in at the pro station, he could be court-martialed. By the 1930s, punitive measures for VD brought the rate down, but still the men in the Philippines usually vied for the unwelcome distinction of having the highest rate in the Army.[40]

Thirty miles across the bay from Manila was Fort Mills, the island fortress of Corregidor. There were four much smaller islands in or near the entrance to the bay, but Corregidor was the keystone of Army defensive strategy. Since World War I, the Washington Naval Treaty, which restricted work on fortifications in the Pacific, and budgetary constraints had held down further construction except that of Malinta tunnel. Strategy changed over the years, but the concept of Corregidor as the Army's last bastion if the Japanese invaded the Philippines remained.

Most of tadpole-shaped Corregidor's 1,735 acres were in the highest part of the island, Topside, where the Army had built the batteries and quarters for most of the garrison. In the last years of the peace the garrison consisted of four coast artillery regiments, two of them Scout units. Virtually all the soldiers lived in one huge multistoried barracks building. Because of its elevation and sea breezes, Topside was cooler and more comfortable than Manila.[41]

In November 1940 David G. Brenzel arrived on "the Rock." A twenty-four-year-old native of Wisconsin who had been working in southern California, he had enlisted a few weeks earlier and opted for the Philippines because it cut a year off the regular enlistment. Since he had operated a machine that made paper bags, the recruiter identified him as a skilled machinist in his records. The first sergeant of Battery C, 59th Coast Artillery, noticed this designation and assigned him to a special detail that carried extra pay as a specialist—gun mechanic for the battery's two 12-inch disappearing guns.

Other soldiers lived in the barracks and took part in training activities ranging from some infantry tactics on Friday morning to the routine crew drill. They stood guard and had to participate in the retreat parades that each regiment held one day a week. Brenzel avoided all of this when he became part of the permanent battery guard detail. Two gun mechanics, two powerhouse operators (which he later became), and a corporal stayed with the guns. They did not have reveille or lights out. They could get food at any time but had to walk roughly a mile to their mess hall in Topside barracks. Each man worked only a couple of hours a day; hence, other than staying at Battery Wheeler, the rest of his time was free. It was clear to Brenzel that he "had the best job in the outfit. Nobody else could do it and nobody was sure exactly what it was."

Dave aspired to be a writer, so he read a lot and did some writing. Sitting around in his usual uniform of a pair of shorts, he also listened to classical music on the radio and chased the scorpions, lizards, and an occasional snake. There was a large theater near the barracks if he wanted to walk over to see a movie. Then, he could have a real treat by visiting the post exchange and ogling the officers' wives. As he wrote home, "I thought the women in Hollywood and Los Angeles were scantily clad but they looked like nuns compared to some of the few white women on this post." In the spring he got leave to go to Manila, where he soaked up color for his writing by staying with a family in a bamboo shack and learning some Tagalog. For Brenzel, Philippine service meant that "everyday is Sunday in the Army."[42]

Most officers' wives probably shared that view. Phyllis Corbusier Pierson, a lieutenant's wife at Stotsenburg in the mid-1920s, considered life in the Philippines "very free & easy—no cares nor worries." Another young officer's wife who was at Stotsenburg in the same period, Eleanor Fletcher Buckley, remembered: "It was play time for me." Servants relieved them of housekeeping chores, and there were ample opportunities for recreation—riding, golf, tennis, bridge, parties, weekly dances, and occasional home talent shows. On nights when nothing was planned, the officers in their starched white uniforms and the ladies in long dresses sat on the porch and awaited callers or went calling themselves. As Grace Short Weaver recognized after a few weeks on Corregidor in 1939, "There is a lot to do, doing nothing, so that the days fly."[43]

It was not quite as easy as that. Virginia Weisel Johnson never became accustomed to the heat, which brought on an irritating heat rash as well as swollen feet. And she could not stand insects, which were so much a part of daily life. Besides, she was homesick for Montana. Then, servants could be a problem, as Grace Weaver noted when after only a few weeks she had to get rid of one houseboy and his replacement was "terrible." Eleanor Buckley noted some problems. The cook was offended when she asked him to do something in the garden. Then, she had to break up a fight when the cook found the laundress carving a block of soap on his cutting board and he grabbed a knife and began chasing her around the house. He could rise to the occasion, however, as when Eleanor asked him to fix a cake as well as the meal when she and her husband invited the priest to dinner. He proudly iced on top of the cake "Hurrah for Jesus."[44]

Michael, Eleanor's husband, was a field artillery officer; hence riding was a major part of his life. Indeed, everybody rode—except Eleanor. She was game, but her attempt to join a group of other wives on a ride did not turn out well. While they waited, she with one foot in the stirrup, the horse took off. It was bad enough until he came to a ditch; then it got worse, as he made the jump but she did not. She had the courage to try again and then rode regularly.[45]

Despite the formal wear in the evening, by the late 1930s wives had begun to dress more comfortably during the tropical days. Dave Brenzel and his fellow soldiers had certainly noticed the casual apparel of the officers' wives on Corregidor. One of the women he might have glimpsed in the post exchange was Grace Weaver. When she arrived on the Rock, she heeded the advice of the other women and had two shirts and shorts made for her daily wear. A few days after she began wearing these clothes, she wrote home: "I love them though I felt funny wearing them at first." Times and customs change. According to standards of later years, a snapshot of her taken at the time shows her modestly dressed.[46]

With Grace and her husband were their twin sons, who turned five the year they arrived on Corregidor. Despite the similarity of life on Army posts everywhere, even small children could see that there were some differences between Stateside posts such as Carlisle Barracks, which the Weavers had just left, and the Rock. Harriette Marshall, who was there from 1929 to 1932, was six and her brother a year and half older when they moved to Corregidor. Together they roamed the island, riding the trolley from one end to the other and exploring jungle paths. They could go to the movies, swim either in the pool or at the Bottomside beach, or they could stay home and play with their pet monkey. "We had so much freedom."[47]

Children who lived in Manila had less freedom than those on the Rock. Nevertheless, Nina Garfinkel was "most unhappy" to have to go back to the States for her senior year in high school. In the early 1920s Mary and Patricia Henry lived in Military Plaza—the tiny enclave of senior officers in Manila. There were not many children in the compound, and parents did not let them roam freely about the city. A mule-drawn ambulance took them in the morning to the American School; in the afternoons Patricia could play games, while Mary, who was six years older and who became a teenager during their stay, might play tennis on the court next to their house. Then there was riding. As one would expect from a daughter of Guy V. Henry, Patricia commented: "If I had a horse to ride . . . life for me was happy."[48]

Paul and Robert Matte were teenagers when their father was assigned to Fort Stotsenburg in the late 1930s. Officers' wives taught their classes in the high school on post. Since there were only four students, the boys received a lot of personal attention. There were also the usual riding, tennis, and golf available in their free time. Robert played polo and even went to the firing range and on maneuvers with his father's unit. The social round that was so prevalent made its mark on these older children, and Robert thought they matured quickly "aping the social activities of their parents." The formality of the evenings carried over to the older teenagers; the boys had to put on coats and ties if they left their quarters at night. Peter rode in a drag hunt (simulated fox hunt), went on maneuvers, and even climbed Mount Pinatubo. The life at Stotsenburg, however, seemed to him to offer too much opportunity for juvenile delinquency. As he looked back on life in the islands, he recognized its romantic appeal but thought it was like a "B-movie about the tropics."[49]

While families enjoyed their more or less carefree lives in the Philippines, officers and soldiers also appreciated that they had a mission. In the late 1930s, the increasingly obvious Japanese threat and the fact that they were in full-strength units put a greater edge on training than one would encounter in bases in the United States.

The Panama Canal was much farther from Japan than the Philippines, but its significance to American seapower in case of war and to maritime trade in peace made it a very desirable target for any enemy of the Untied States. In the early 1920s there were nine posts and one airfield in the Canal Zone. During that decade after World War I, the garrison at Camp Gaillard, one of the largest in the zone, lived in relics left over from the period of the canal's construction. An officer who lived there from 1923 to 1926 simply called it "a hell hole."[50]

Conditions improved in the 1930s. When a fighter pilot, Jacob E. Smart, arrived at Albrook Field in 1933, the quarters at this recently opened base near the Pacific end of the canal were new. Although air units had been assigned to the Canal Zone as well as Hawaii and the Philippines as early as 1915, they were increased after the war, with coastal defense as their major mission.[51]

Jake welcomed the assignment. After all, one of the reasons he had decided upon the Army as a career was that it offered opportunity for travel. A southerner, he had been attracted to the military by the examples of Civil War and Spanish-American War Army veterans and a Navy veteran in the family. While at West Point, a few flights and the

Jacob Smart in his flying togs at Kelly Field, Texas, circa 1932, a few months before he went to Panama. Courtesy of Jacob E. Smart.

good impression that Air Corps instructors made enhanced an early fascination with barnstorming airplanes and caused him to opt for the Air Corps. Besides, as he later wrote, "I wanted to become a part of an expanding enterprise where horizons seemed unlimited." Upon graduation in 1931, he went to Randolph and Kelly Fields for pilot training, where a year later he was one of about half of the entering class who completed the basic and advanced courses. After his graduation, he stayed on at Kelly for some six months before going to the Canal Zone.[52]

While the work day at Albrook was in the morning, as at the other posts, that was not the case for pilots, who were required to make flights at night as well as familiarization flights in afternoons and weekends. The latter were crucial because of the hazardous conditions fliers encountered as they flew in rainy weather as well as over mountainous jungle terrain and the ocean without radio beacons and inadequate radios. It behooved them to know the terrain features and the auxiliary landing fields, which were merely pastures with a windsock on a pole to mark them. For safety reasons, they flew in pairs when exploring remote regions. In the 78th Pursuit Squadron, Jake spent "many interesting and enjoyable hours" in his P-12 biplane as he learned the features of the rivers, the coastline, and the nearby islands. A multitude of orchids in the flooded jungle near the shore of San Miguel Gulf enchanted him, as did the colorful costumes of the Indians in the San Blas Island villages he passed over.

Regular operational readiness tests demonstrated the capabilities of individual pilots rather than the unit's readiness for combat. All knew that more men, aircraft, munitions, and spare parts were needed before they could sustain themselves in extended action. But, as Smart pointed out, "We were content to try to maintain individual proficiency believing that our leaders would recognize a threat should it appear, and do so in time to take required measures."[53]

While flying was central to a pilot's life, as an Army officer he also had to handle assorted administrative duties ranging from supervising supply, engineering, communication, and food-service activities of his unit to staff jobs and attending schools. Jake added to his record completion of a course at the bakers and cooks school. Then there were the professional lectures, where he learned about mach speed, high-octane fuel, and multispectral photography and heard about marijuana for the first time. He also appreciated the department commander's contribution to professional development. Major General Preston Brown required young officers to come to his quarters, where he would talk about the crucial importance of maintaining integrity and other responsibilities of officers, the traditional bond of trust between the military and the citizenry, and the necessity for a high order of behavior, particularly in a foreign country. He used examples from his own experience to give them pointers on how to judge men and other such matters.[54]

Maneuvers with the ground forces and, on occasion, the Navy were highlights of training. They pointed up differences between the services. As far as some ground officers were concerned, the fliers were a "harebrained and undisciplined group," while the pilots considered the Army generally "hidebound." The simple matter of camping demonstrated this attitudinal conflict. Army commanders tended to make sure that tents were neatly in line without regard to cover, while the Air Corps would disperse the planes and tents in the woods if possible. This practice provoked comments among the ground officers about the fliers' being "sloppy and unmilitary" and confirmed the other branch's view that the Army did not recognize the possibility of aerial observation. Paradoxically, Army officers did not appreciate the limitations of the airplanes. Infantry officers expected air-dropped messages to hit squarely on the panel they had laid out, with no knowledge and little interest in the difficulties of judging wind and altitude. Their antiaircraft counterparts wanted the fliers to maintain straight-line courses at the same altitude. Aside from the assumption that enemy air would be so accommodating, again wind and the lack of adequate altitude gauges made doing this difficult.[55]

In joint maneuvers, the Navy was the aggressor, and the Air Corps's mission was to locate and attack the fleet before it neared the coast. During one maneuver, Smart discovered the fleet and simulated strafing runs on a carrier before the Navy got its planes into action. Once they were airborne, they assumed that he would try to escape to his base, and hence lead them not only there but to the canal as well. Jake led them away from both. Before the official start of another maneuver, a shrewd admiral attempted to get a jump on the Army by hiding his command closer to the Canal Zone in a lagoon near the Costa Rica–Panama border. A formation of bombers on a routine navigation training flight during which they had picked up some fresh fruit happened to fly right over the fleet and bombarded the ships with quantities of fruit. Sailors had to clean up the mess while their commander had to make other attack plans.

Despite the differences, there was much socializing between the officers in different branches and their Navy counterparts. The fliers took them on airborne sightseeing trips, while the Navy took some of them to sea. Jake went on a five-day cruise and also made two dives on a submarine. They also partied, played games, fished, hunted, and sailed together. As Jake recalled, there was "a lot of good-natured raillery." After joint maneuvers, the Army and Navy officers would get together over cocktails and make their exaggerated claims "in high good humor." Smart thought that in both Army and joint maneuvers, resources were too limited to have "realistic operations." Young officers did not think that there was a serious threat, so they did not worry about the situation in the early 1930s.[56]

Holland L. Robb, who arrived in the Canal Zone about a year before Smart in the summer of 1932 and left a few weeks before Jake's tour terminated in 1935, led a less adventurous life, but he, his wife, and two daughters enjoyed life there as much. He was older and a major in command of an engineer battalion at Corazal. There was the usual peacetime routine broken by mapping details and field maneuvers. Later he would remember this as his most pleasant tour. The social activities were particularly memorable. Although her two years at Leavenworth held first place in her memory, Marian Sanford Robb enjoyed the tropical tour. She had no complaint about quarters and liked the climate. She and Holland were acutely aware that they were much better off, even after the mandated pay cut, than friends and relatives who were then coping with the Depression in the States.[57]

Fielding L. Greaves, at Fort Randolph on the Atlantic side, thought of his post as a "paradise" for a boy his age—nine to eleven. He fished and lobstered, and he and a friend, armed with a .22 rifle and a slingshot, went on half-day expeditions into the jungle. Adrian St. John was older when he arrived in 1934. It seemed to him that there were so many posts and troops that the "Canal Zone was almost like one big Army post." Howard Clark, who was there from 1928 to 1931, remembered the competition that resulted from this plethora of units stationed so closely together; but the major fascination for him was the daily stream of ships passing through the canal, with the added excitement of visiting not only the American but also the British Royal Navy ships. It was an exciting life for a child.[58]

For soldiers the garrison routine remained much the same wherever they were, but tropical posts were different from those in the States. Some appreciated the exotic aspects more than others. Indeed, some hated it. Lawrence B. Curtis, a North Carolina farm boy who upped his age a year to eighteen to enlist in 1936 and sailed for Panama to begin his service, was one of those who enjoyed what the Canal Zone had to offer. His first impressions were favorable as the 14th Infantry band met the transport full of recruits at the port. After a brief truck ride they arrived at Fort Davis, near the Gatun Locks. Although the 14th and other infantry regiments went through regular training, each had to furnish a company each month for the particular assignment of patrolling the canal. Curtis liked what he saw of Fort Davis, with its palm tree–lined streets, red-tile roofs on the modern buildings, the parade ground in the quadrangle, and everywhere the trimmed but lush greenery. The next morning he and his fellow recruits marched to the post theater for an orientation as members of this famous infantry regiment. The regimental commander's appearance and remarks were appropriate, but the surgeon, who followed him, struck a chord as he explained the possibilities of service as a medical technician. Lawrence responded to his call for volunteers. Aside from other attractions, he assumed that he would be able to report for duty at the hospital immediately.

Sergeant O'Shea quickly disabused him, informing the recruits that all would belong to him for thirteen weeks of recruit training. It was tough enough to make "any 17 year old youth forget that he was ever born free." Looking back, he added that it was this recruit training "which kept me in the service 34 years still hoping that I would get Sgt. O'Shea in my command." Afterward the new men immediately served thirty days on kitchen-police duty with the San Blas Indian workers. When the new soldier finally joined his unit, he would not have to pull KP again while in Panama.

When Lawrence finally got to the hospital, he found a mentor in Captain William C. Knott, the doctor who handled sick call and was in charge of the pharmacy. Knott encouraged him to become a pharmacist and taught him the basics. Curtis remained at work there through the rest of his two-year tour and eventually became head pharmacist with the rank of private first class and fourth-class specialist, which paid $45 a month—more than twice the private's pay of $21.

During his twenty months in the pharmacy, Lawrence routinely dispensed APC (aspirin, phenacetin, and caffeine) capsules for headaches and colds and Epsom salts for aches and pains and other undiagnosed ailments. Maneuvers took a heavier toll, as malaria, dhobi itch, and ringworm as well as the assorted cuts and bruises associated with field service required treatment. Ringworm spread over the body caused the men to scream in agony. Salicylic acid solutions and ointments would help if the sufferer could keep his skin dry. Iodine was also used but caused more pain, with blisters and the peeling of the skin. Robert Bergeron, who was in the 14th at this time, had never been sick before he arrived in Panama, where he had various skin diseases as well as two bouts of malaria during his tour. Understandably for him, "that place was very depressing."[59]

Although a new colonel abolished the free afternoons and put the troops to work hacking away at the jungle to create space for ranges, golf courses, and other recreation areas, Lawrence still did not find Panama depressing. There was so much to do. He fished on the Chagre River, swam and sailed in Gatun Lake, hunted deer in the jungle, and visited the San Blas Islands as well as Costa Rica and Colombia. He enjoyed the spectacle of the ships moving through the canal and read up on the history of the area. Jim Gavin, who had been at Fort Sherman more than a decade before, found the library a seemingly "unending source of interesting books." Dodge's *Great Captains* evoked ambitious dreams of becoming a great commander.

Sports, a great diversion throughout the service, were particularly emphasized in the zone, where so many units were in such close proximity. On game day, not only the regimental band but large numbers of the men would accompany their team on the train to make the contest more festive. Payday activities were another diversion. James C. Hicks, who was at Fort Clayton in the late 1930s, thought the Panamanians were easier to get along with than Americans. Bars and prostitutes flourished in Colón, where soldiers and sailors from three Army posts and an airfield as well as one naval station converged on paydays. Bar girls were very friendly as long as the soldier continued to pay for another "blue moon" (a watered-down drink that resembled whiskey) every half-hour or so. Sex was also readily available for a price, as indicated by the VD rate, which kept the statistics for the troops in Panama usually third behind China and the Philippines during these two decades. There was also some smoking of marijuana.

The day after always brought a reckoning as sergeants pushed the hungover troops through close-order drill or forced marches and brought them back into the spit and polish. Barracks were spic and span, and one would have to search long and hard to find a scrap of paper on the now-immaculate grounds. The tailored uniforms were laundered and pressed. Appearance meant a lot in those days. After a career in the Army, Curtis recalled that he never again "had the feeling of pride of appearance and military dress" that he did in those years in the 14th Infantry.[60]

Throughout the 1920s and 1930s, military planners considered Hawaii the keystone of the American defense in the Pacific. The buildup had begun on Oahu after the Navy designated Pearl Harbor as its major base before World War I. In addition to the huge post at Schofield Barracks, the Army eventually garrisoned two airfields, three coast artillery forts, and maintained a supply base and a departmental headquarters. More Army personnel served on Oahu in this period than in any other foreign station. And most considered it good duty.

Lucian K. Truscott, a lieutenant in the 17th Cavalry when he came to Hawaii with his regiment in the spring of 1919, never forgot his arrival. "There is one thrill that can come only once in a lifetime . . . the first view of Diamond Head against the blue Hawaiian sky, the entry of the ship into Honolulu harbor . . . the gaiety and excitement of ship and shore as the ship is edged into her berth . . . bands playing . . . friends on shore greeting arrivals on shipboard . . . flowers and leis." As the newcomers journeyed to Schofield Barracks, the lushness of pineapple and sugarcane fields, the varied colors of flowers and the velvet green of the grass, and the vistas of the two craggy mountain ranges that limned the great plain where the huge post was located continued to excite the senses. It was a great change from the Arizona desert outpost the men of the 17th had left a few weeks before.[61]

Their quarters were also an improvement over their camp on the Mexican border. A large quadrangle of four recently constructed three-story concrete barracks housed the troops, while the officers were able to move into nearby houses. They replaced a Hawaiian National Guard regiment and for a year would be the only combat troops on the base. Meantime, builders labored on additional regimental quadrangles, which were not completed before other units began to arrive; hence some of those troops had to live in temporary quarters. Gardens provided fresh fruit and vegetables to supplement the ration, and a small Japanese village supplied gardeners and other workers as well as cooks and servants for the officers' families.[62]

The first year in Hawaii was a busy one for the 17th. Like all other cavalry units, they had to care for their horses and meet training schedules; but they also had to maintain the entire post. In the fall and winter of 1920, three infantry regiments, a field artillery brigade, and an engineer battalion arrived to occupy the empty barracks. Enough units were then available to organize the Hawaiian Division on February 28, 1921. A fourth infantry regiment completed the square division the next year.[63]

One of the lieutenants, William W. Ford, who joined the 11th Field Artillery was impressed by the difference between Schofield Barracks and Stateside posts. "Hawaii was a giant leap forward in almost every respect." The climate, the new quarters, and the over-strength units, which did not have the personnel turbulence of the thinly manned batteries he had known before, made his life not only more pleasant but also more interesting. There was one problem, however. The War Department had shipped tons of war surplus—uniforms, weapons, ammunition, gas masks, and nonperishable food—to Schofield. Stacked in towering piles that filled warehouses and even some open fields, this proved to be an invitation for countless hours of fatigue duty as soldiers opened boxes, inspected the contents, cataloged, and then resealed them. This task took up so much time that one field artillery regiment had five of its six batteries working fulltime on these stores.[64]

The department commander at that time was a famed AEF corps commander, Charles P. Summerall. When he came to Hawaii in August 1921, he began to impress on all the troops that they "were in the front line and must be ready for an attack by Japan at any time." He put his operations officer, Major Lesley J. McNair, who had been a brigadier general during the war, to work on a defense plan. Although he found his Navy counterpart uncooperative at times, he was able to enlist the support of a young naval officer, Chester W. Nimitz, to help McNair. The resulting plan of 1924 assumed that 94,000 troops were needed to repel a Japanese invasion. In addition to the tremendous sixfold increase in the number of troops then on hand, the plan called for more airplanes and coast artillery guns as well as assorted other supplies. The planners also assumed that the Army would use poison gas if an attack came. What Summerall did not assume was the loyalty of the Japanese on Oahu; he believed that he would have to impose martial law in case of war.

Brigadier General Billy Mitchell came through on an informal visit and wrote up an elaborate scenario of a surprise Japanese attack at dawn by planes launched from submarines. His unsurprising conclusion was that the Hawaiian garrison needed more airplanes. This move infuriated Summerall, who pointed out that Mitchell was unable to fly the DeHavilland plane that he had lent him, much less make a practicable defense plan.[65]

Summerall stepped up the field training of the Pineapple Army, as it was called. By the time he left, in 1924, he was satisfied that they were the best-trained troops he had ever seen. The large reservation afforded ample space for maneuvers. There was an excellent rifle range for the infantrymen, while the field artillery units had ample ammunition and firing space. Lieutenant Orville W. Martin, who joined the 11th Field Artillery in 1931, also thought they had "the best soldiers." He had reason to respect those men. His unit, Battery B, won the Knox Trophy, awarded annually to the best artillery battery in the Army, while he was executive officer.[66]

Major George S. Patton Jr., who served on the staff of the Hawaiian Division from 1925 to 1928, like other officers of that era appreciated the opportunity to work with full-strength units. Initially the personnel and intelligence officer, Patton craved the job of operations officer. After a year he got it and, as was his wont, threw himself vigorously into his work. He tried to eke out more effective training time despite the heavy demands of fatigue duty, and tackled the problems of maintaining proper military bearing and saluting habits among both officers and men. In his enthusiasm, he harshly criticized a brigadier general for his handling of his troops in a maneuver, a board's report on defense against aircraft, and a battalion for its ineptness in carrying out a defensive problem. His superiors were disturbed by the resulting hurt feelings among the officers involved and made Patton pay for his lapses in judgment. The division chief of staff gave him a disappointing "average" on his efficiency report, while the commander relieved him from his job as operations officer and returned him to the post of intelligence officer.

During his last months in Hawaii, Patton did get to command the invading force in a shore-defense exercise. As one would expect, he read up on amphibious operations and, in particular, studied the amount of support the landing force would need to succeed. Meantime, as the intelligence officer, he was suspicious of the Japanese. The fact that officers from Japanese warships visiting Honolulu called on their countrymen who farmed near the coast enhanced his concern.[67]

Seven years later, in 1935, Patton, by this time a lieutenant colonel, returned to Hawaii. Nearing fifty, he had spent twenty-six years in the Army and was beginning to think he would never command a host of men in great battles. Again he had a staff assignment, but this time he was intelligence officer of the Hawaiian Department with headquarters at Fort Shafter, only three miles from Honolulu. Despite his experience after submitting harsh critiques in his earlier tour, he started off in a similar manner. Within weeks of his arrival, he turned in a five-page single-space-typed report on the June maneuvers. Commanders were not flexible enough and were too set in lessons they had learned during the war in France. Both troops and commanders seemed more concerned with their comfort than with the purpose of the exercise. They loaded down trucks with nonessential items, illuminated their camps, and neglected basic security. Troop movements generally ignored the possibility of enemy fire, and, rather than personal reconnaissance, commanders relied on telephones. Fortunately for Patton, his superiors on this tour appreciated his efforts. The department chief of staff praised him in his efficiency report—"ambitious, progressive, original, professionally studious"—and concluded that he was "an officer of very high general value to the service."

Patton continued his study of amphibious operations and concentrated at length on the British disaster at Gallipoli in 1915. He gave much thought to the Japanese threat and, shortly before he left Hawaii, presented his conclusions in a paper that laid out the possibility of a surprise attack by a large invasion force supported by carrier-based aircraft. He assumed that many local Japanese were enemy agents and, to thwart their espionage and sabotage activities, planned for mass arrests.[68]

During the two years of Patton's last tour in Hawaii, the War Department added almost 4,000 officers and men to the garrison of 14,800. By 1938 another 3,000 were added to the force. One of the most prominent was Colonel Edwin Forrest Harding, who took command of the 27th Infantry regiment. He had just completed four very successful years as editor of the *Infantry Journal* and was anxious to get back to troops. The outgoing commander told him it was a "grand regiment," but Harding wanted to make it even better. His approach would have pleased his West Point classmate, Patton. As Harding explained to a friend, "I try to maintain a balanced program, with emphasis on the really important part of our business, which is field training. I try to keep away from the . . . cut and dried stuff embalmed in outmoded regulations. There is plenty of room these days for experimenting with ideas."

As his first year in command came to an end, Forrest and the regiment were winding up a maneuver. Unlike the officers Patton had criticized, he did not stay in comfortable quarters, aloof from the men, but was a leader who led and led vigorously. Rather than truck his troops back to their barracks, he led them in a twenty-seven-mile night march. It was a tribute to his efforts to get these men in top physical condition that only 4 of the 848 officers and men fell out. And they had very good excuses.

Forrest had a well-honed sense of the dramatic and built on the regiment's Siberian service, in which it had gained its nickname— the Wolfhounds. In Siberia the regiment had had a real wolfhound as its mascot, so Harding purchased one to parade with the regiment. Within six months of his arrival, he equipped the sixty-piece band with a Russian type uniform featuring Cossack hats, black cartridge cross-belts, and black leggings. It made a colorful appearance, and the men of the regiment believed it to be the best band on the post. Harding made the regiment not only tough but also proud.[69]

For officers and their families, and to a more limited extent for soldiers, life in Hawaii at times resembled that of a resort. The beautiful landscape, the pleasant climate, the beaches, the emphasis on recreation, and, as Verone Gruenther Davidson remembered, the "relaxed and peaceful" pace made the tour delightful. When she and her family arrived there in 1938, they "entered into a very happy way of life." Maida

Davis Turtle, whose husband commanded a coast artillery regiment at Fort Kamehameha from 1927 to 1931, simply declared that it "was as near heaven as I ever expect to get."[70]

The great sport for the officers was polo. During the 1930s there were polo games on Wednesday and Saturday afternoons from May to November. Although there were no cavalry units and the field artillery units were motorized, the horsemanship, team play, and sheer courage of the game attracted players from all branches, including the Air Corps. According to Lucian Truscott, the impetus for postwar polo came from Lieutenant Colonel Beverly F. Browne, a wartime brigadier general, who came to Schofield as commander of the 11th Field Artillery in 1921. An excellent player, Browne brought a great enthusiasm for the game, procured better mounts, and taught a new concept of team play that would eventually result in the Army team's being able to compete at the same level as the excellent civilian teams on the island. The year after Browne's departure, the all-Army team with George Patton, as always playing his hardest, won the island championship over the top civilian teams. Younger officers envied Patton because he had his own private polo ponies and such fluency in profanity.[71]

As it was throughout the Army, riding, jumping, and showing horses were popular in Hawaii. Ruth Ellen, the Pattons' younger daughter, put horses first among her memories of the two Hawaiian tours. Annually, there was a horse show in which enlisted men, officers, wives, and children competed separately for prizes. At Schofield Barracks, a riding club was organized in 1925 that offered classes in riding. In addition to horses, there was a wide variety of other means of amusement available. There were one or more hard-surface tennis courts in each regimental quadrangle, and the golf course had clubhouses for enlisted men as well as for officers. Lucian Truscott was among those who played bridge, and Leslie R. Groves won the tennis championship, while Tony McAuliffe enjoyed golf. Not long after his arrival, Forrest Harding started a dramatic club. Many officers had cars and took their families on weekend drives through the mountains and along the lovely coast.[72]

As in all garrisons, there was an almost exhausting social life. After his first eight months at Schofield Barracks, Forrest wrote a friend that the evenings were taken up "with official, semi-official, and unofficial social activities." He thought that the social demands there were greater than those in the 15th Infantry in China. Officers and their wives dressed formally to await callers nearly every evening or went calling themselves. There were dances at the officers' club, welcoming and farewell parties, dinner parties, and parties just for the sake of having a party. Not surprisingly, life there was expensive.[73]

The beaches, however, were not expensive, and all took advantage of them. In the early 1920s Beverly and Louise Browne rented a cottage for weekends. On a lieutenant's pay, Wallace and Alice Ford could not afford that, but they took their small daughter and spent a week at an Army beach where they stayed in a tent. During their two years, 1938–1940, Gar and Verone Davidson tried to get to the beach on Wednesday and Saturday afternoons and also spend all day Sundays on the Army beach at Haleiwa. Gar taught his small sons to swim and dive in the surf. Their Christmas card that year was a picture of the four of them in swimsuits on the beach.[74]

Some became interested in the people as well as the marvelous scenery. Beatrice Ayer Patton studied Polynesian culture and published a historical novel about Hawaii. She and Ruth Ellen learned to hula. Ruth Ellen also became interested in archaeology. In addition to the social round in the Army, the Pattons made friends with the well-to-do polo set throughout the islands. For Aina Wodehouse Olsmith, it was not a matter of making new friends. She had grown up on Maui. When she and her husband, Vernon, came back to Hawaii in 1937, her uncle lived in Honolulu, her brother and his family on Hawaii, while she still had childhood friends on Maui.[75]

※

While most of the military people lived on post, a few lived in the community. Some had to live off post, at least for a while, and others were stationed in the coast artillery posts, departmental headquarters, and Luke Field, which were in or near Honolulu. Unlike Schofield Barracks, where children could go to school from the first through the twelfth grades, those at the other installations had to go to school with civilians. Frank Hoskins and his brother, whose father was stationed at Fort DeRussy, went to grade school in Honolulu. They made friends with some Japanese boys and were often in each other's homes, but his sister, who was in the eighth grade, was so unhappy that her parents transferred her to a private school. Pat Tansey and his two brothers totaled half of the *haoles* (whites) in their high school of some 1,200 students yet "got along pretty well." When one small boy parroted soldiers and referred to Hawaiians as "gooks," his parents gave him a good scolding.[76]

For most military people, Hawaii was an interlude of two or three years. The Pattons had two tours, but that was unusual. Bob Brockway, however, spent an extraordinary eight years on Oahu as his father, a master sergeant in the Air Corps, served at Wheeler, Luke, and Hickam (which replaced Luke) Fields from 1934 to 1942. Eleven when he arrived, Bob was fascinated by the reviews, bands, and bugle calls at Schofield Barracks. He could ride his bike over and watch the ceremonies in the field artillery area or take in a movie at the Third Engineer Quadrangle. A year later, his father transferred to a bombardment squadron at Luke Field, and the family had to rent a home in Honolulu. Bob got back from the public school he attended around 2:30 just as his father returned from the airfield. Often they would spend the rest of the afternoon lounging and swimming at Waikiki Beach. Rather than other Army brats, his friends in Honolulu were local boys or the sons of Navy noncoms; yet the Army had a real attraction for him. Life in the Pineapple Army seemed to him easygoing and very congenial. During those years, his ambition was to become a corporal in the coast artillery.[77]

On the sunny morning of April 27, 1938, the Army transport *Republic* began running along the coast of Oahu. By 6:00, Thelma Fadner Watson and five-year-old Jimmy were on deck peering at the mountains in the distance. Bob joined them at 6:40 as the ship pulled closer to the island. As the ship docked some two and half hours later, several airplanes flew over, native boys dived for coins, and the Watsons could see old friends awaiting them in the crowd. "It was tremendously exciting"—Thelma described the scene to her parents—"the band playing . . . Hawaiian songs and people waving and laughing." When the gangplank went down, their friends and their new regimental commander came aboard and put leis around her, Bob's, and Jimmy's necks. She had fifteen and "smelled like a perfume counter."

Thelma (fifth from left) and Jim Watson (second from left) picnicking on the officers' beach with the Scanlans, soon after their arrival on Oahu, May 1938. Courtesy of James S. Watson.

Once ashore, their friends took them to Schofield Barracks and later on an even more scenic drive. Thelma was enthralled by the beauty and fragrance of the roadside flowers and awed by the tremendous view from Kolekole Pass. When Bob returned to Honolulu to pick up their car, friends took her and Jimmy to the officers' beach, which had a bath house and a branch post exchange that sold soft drinks and hot dogs. "The sand is clean & white and the waves roll in gently enough so that it is safe for children. Jimmy had a great time." In addition to all that Oahu offered, Thelma was impressed by how cordial everyone was—much more so than at their last station at the Presidio in San Francisco. She assured her parents: "We think we are going to be very happy here." And they were.[78]

For soldiers, arrival in Honolulu was not the gala event that officers and families enjoyed. They were, nevertheless, glad to get there. Many had lived in crowded troop holes for weeks, with only brief breaks in Panama and San Francisco as they made the journey from New York. When they streamed down the gangplank carrying bag and baggage, rather than meet friends waiting to load them down with leis, they formed in ranks on dockside as officers looked them over. There they learned a very significant fact about Hawaii. Athletes were highly prized. Captain Jim Vardi, who liked boxers, spotted Steve Kaydash as a likely light heavyweight and picked him for his battery in the Eighth Field Artillery. Others looked for men to fill vacant positions on their football or other teams. In some instances, Stateside friends had alerted officers to an outstanding athlete who had reenlisted. A company or battery commander might offer an additional stripe or two to such a man. The rest of the soldiers standing in formation could not hope for such preference as they waited to have their destinations determined by officers who went among them and chose men for specialist units such as the military police, signal corps, and quartermaster corps. The rest were distributed among the line units.[79]

Frank Bozoski, who was an eighteen-year-old recruit, never forgot his reception when he finally reached his unit in August 1927. The first sergeant greeted the new men with this advice: "I welcome you to A Company, 19th Infantry, if you make a good soldier I will back you all the way even to hell, but remember this I don't like a liar and I don't like a squealer, just soldier and you will have an easy life here." Eugene Hogan, who arrived a few years later, got a similar message in the 11th Field Artillery. "If you tried to get the job done, you weren't criticized—if you were lax you had problems."[80]

Despite the top-kick's assurance of ease, Frank and his fellow recruits soon found that their basic training "was good and hard," with emphasis on marksmanship. After this initial training, the regular training period would be in the mornings as it was throughout the Army. There was a difference, however, in the Hawaiian Division. For one thing, it was nearly full strength and afforded opportunities for training that were unavailable to most units. Then, there were many field problems, which added realism as the division practiced its defensive role. George C. Hodgen, who served in China, Panama, Alaska, and the Philippines as well as Hawaii, remembered, in particular, the "superb training" in the latter. Another soldier who served in the same period, John J. Hoodock, regarded duty with the 27th Infantry at Schofield Barracks as "better soldiering"; everyone "knew what they were doing."[81]

Emil E. Matula, who joined Company D, 35th Infantry, in 1940, found that platoon sergeants conducted calisthenics, close-order drill, and weapons instruction. Since this was a weapons company, they worked with .30- and .50-caliber machine guns, mortars, and 37mm antitank guns as well as studying compasses and range-finding methods. There was also a good deal of firing practice. In field exercises, he was impressed with the effort made to teach men not only their job but that of a superior; thus privates were expected to take over squads, squad leaders to move up to sections, and so on.[82]

The level of training was high, but there was more enthusiasm about sports. As Frank B. Scahill, a first sergeant in the 13th Field Artillery in the late 1930s, said, "Athletics was # 1." He understood that he would be judged accordingly. "If you had a lot of athletes, you were sitting on top of the world. The more athletes you had the better first sergeant you were." Schofield Barracks was known as the biggest "jock strap" post in the Army, and the other Hawaiian posts attempted to be competitive. Not surprisingly, the Hawaiian garrisons usually led the Army in sports injuries throughout the 1930s.[83]

While companies and batteries competed in basketball, boxing, touch football, cross-country, track, softball, bowling, and baseball, regiments took the better players for their teams. *The Bark*, the 27th Infantry's yearbook for 1939, illustrates the significance of sports by the emphasis on the records and photos of the regimental and champion company teams. A few years earlier, the program for the 1932 Hawaiian Division horse show indicated the amount of competition at the regimental level. In 1931, ten baseball teams played 135 games, and ten football teams played 45 games. During the winter of 1931–32, ten basketball teams played 90 games. In the same period there were four so-called smokers, with a total of 250 boxing matches; a fifth "smoker" in April put the best Army boxers into the ring with sailors. The Army won that one. That spring there were five track and field meets. It is a comment on the level of competition that the successful coach of the Army football team at West Point for five years in the 1930s, Gar Davidson, was the assistant coach of the Third Engineer team his first year at Schofield Barracks.[84]

Boxing was probably the most popular sport, with as many as 10,000, including many civilians, filling the arena for crucial bouts. Summerall encouraged this in the early 1920s and ordered that men who boxed

Camp Lewis Champions — 1926–27.

Kirke. McElfish. Branton.

Lt. Taylor. — Scahill. — Rice. — Black — Lt. McFarland (Coach).

During his days as an athlete before he went to Hawaii, Frank Scahill (second from left) with his battery team, which included Maxwell D. Taylor (left), Camp Lewis, Washington, 1927. It was customary for officers to play on the same unit teams. Courtesy of Frank Scahill.

against Navy boxers be excused from all training. The caliber of the boxers was high throughout this era, and some went professional after they left the Army. Frank Bozoski was a boxer, as were Gene Hogan and Steve "Killer" Kaydash. The name, however, was not entirely accurate: Kaydash, who did not like to train, had to take out his opponent in the first three rounds or he was exhausted.[85]

"For those who participated in sports, Hawaii was a heaven." At least, that is the way it appeared to Francis T. Dockery, who was not an athlete and spent fourteen years between 1923 and 1940 in the coast artillery at Fort Shafter. There was, he added, a "push on participation," and those who did not participate were expected to attend the contests. Gene Hogan did not need a push. In addition to boxing, he played baseball and was a back on the regimental football team. Nor did Sergeant Scahill need any encouragement, but he knew that his battery commander expected him to turn out the men who were not playing to attend the games. John Hannon understood that if he did not go to the 11th Field Artillery games he would have to spend that time doing the onerous work of cleaning off the tracks of the big tractors that pulled the guns.[86]

Unit pride fueled the intensity of the rivalry. One game between two of the regiments caused the officers' wives' tempers to rise to the point that they did not speak to their counterparts in the other regiment for weeks. Violence disrupted a couple of football games in the late 1930s. In one, a lineman on the 35th Infantry team slurred the 27th Infantry by implying that their regiment had lost their colors through cowardice. Fists flew on the field, and the spectators spilled out of the bleachers and joined the melee until the bands played the national anthem. This tactic abruptly ended the fight: all the soldiers came to attention. The 27th was later involved in a similar riot when Gar Davidson coached his Third Engineer team to a narrow victory. Again the 27th's band started playing the "Star Spangled Banner," but this time one rabid Wolfhound continued to go after one of the engineers. Forrest Harding grabbed his arm and ordered him to stand at attention, whereupon the soldier took a swing at him. Forrest ducked and left an opening for the engineer to knock down the miscreant.[87]

Although the Army emphasized sports, it also afforded many other recreational opportunities. Like soldiers throughout the Army, the men in the Pineapple Army could go to the company dayroom, with its pool tables, radio, phonograph, and magazines, or the post movie theaters. Bob Kenney was one of many who paid a dime to see *Gone with the Wind* at Schofield Barracks. When Prohibition came to end, they could get a beer for a dime at beer gardens in each of the infantry regimental quadrangles as well as at a large one for the other troops. Bridge and chess were amusements that some soldiers such as Dick White enjoyed. Many, like Gene Hogan, were among the crowd of 11,000 in the Boxing Bowl to hear the famous Polish pianist Ignace Paderewski play in 1939.[88]

William A. Bowling, who served two tours in the Eighth Field Artillery (1923–1926 and 1930–1932), liked Hawaii because there was "always something to do," and he listed swimming as one of the possibilities. Over the years the Army had obtained beaches near Schofield Barracks for the use of the officers and soldiers. When John Hannon was in the 11th Field Artillery in the mid-1930s he and friends could get three-to-five-day passes, draw rations and a tent, and catch a ride to one of those beaches in a

A battalion championship volleyball match between Companies A and C, 19th Infantry, during the regiment's rest month on the beach, Hawaii, April 1928. Courtesy of Frank Bozoski.

battery truck. Once there, they would bury their keg of beer in the sand, put up the tent, and enjoy themselves. Gene Hogan much preferred one of these Army beaches to Waikiki, where it was obvious that the guests at the Royal Hawaiian Hotel did not want to mingle with soldiers.[89]

During his two years in Hawaii, Hogan went to Honolulu only twice. John Hannon and Frank Bozoski usually visited the city once a month. Honolulu was expensive. In contrast, Bozoski had gone to town once a week in Panama and every day when he was in the 15th in Tientsin. Other men at Schofield Barracks went more often, and those stationed at Forts Ruger and DeRussy merely had to walk a short distance. Some "shacked up" with local women; others frequented the bars and brothels in the Hotel and River Street area. There were a dozen brothels—the Modern Rooms, Senate and Bronx Rooms among them—that were approved and inspected by the Army where white prostitutes were available for three dollars. Soldiers were discouraged from going to other brothels, such as the Honolulu Rooms, where local women offered sex for two dollars. Whether because of the brothel inspections, the availability of prophylactics and the threat of punishment if one became infected, or the vigorous sports and recreation programs, the Hawaiian Department throughout most of the 1920s and 1930s had the lowest VD rate in the Army. In 1936, as an example, the admission rate was approximately three-fifths that of the troops in the States, a fifth of that in the Philippines, and a third of that in Panama. Nor was alcoholism as much of a problem as it was throughout the rest of the Army. That same year, the troops in Hawaii had a rate slightly less than that of the Stateside troops, about four-fifths of the men in Panama, and only about half of the admissions reported in the Philippines. Indeed, the Hawaiian garrison had the lowest alcoholism rate in eight of the ten years from 1927 through 1936.[90]

Payday nights and weekends in Honolulu were apt to be exciting, and they could turn ugly as soldiers mixed with sailors and islanders. As one would expect, race was a factor. Gene Hogan and his friends in the 11th Field Artillery, as they rode in the back of trucks to gun emplacements, baited workers in the pineapple plantations by calling them "gooks" or some other racial slur. The workers hurled pineapples at them, which was the purpose of the exercise, as the soldiers wanted the pineapples. Some soldiers did dislike the islanders; others thought that the locals did not like them; and still others got along well. Don Livesay, who had served in Panama, thought Hawaiians less friendly than Panamanians. James C. Hicks preferred Hawaii to Panama but thought that generally soldiers got along better with civilians in both places than in adjacent towns in the United States.[91]

In the early 1920s, gangs of locals beat up and robbed soldiers, and there was always tension when soldiers and islanders vied for the attention of the same women. Fueled by too many beers or shots of stronger stuff at the Black Cat or some other bar, soldiers and sailors were more belligerent, and there were often young islanders ready to take them on. Fights and even riots were the result. Military police made a valiant effort to keep order. They cooperated with Honolulu police, who taught them judo while the MPs instructed them in riot tactics. Soldiers, of course, wanted to stay out of the hands of any policeman, but if the choice had to be made, most preferred the MPs. Racial prejudice might be involved, but the local police also had a reputation for humiliating and treating soldiers harshly.[92]

If a man committed a serious crime and was convicted by a court-martial, he faced time in the much-dreaded stockade at Schofield Barracks, a concrete building with cells facing an inner courtyard. Only men with sentences of more than six months and those scheduled for transport to the disciplinary barracks at Leavenworth or to a federal prison came to this place. Hard labor, which ranged from sledgehammer work in a rock quarry to "the heaviest and most disagreeable work" around the post, was the lot of these prisoners. Rehabilitation was not a matter of concern. Although he admitted that a few prisoners might return to their units and make good soldiers, Lucian Truscott concluded that most were hardened criminals "lost to the service."[93]

In early 1951, copies of *From Here to Eternity* arrived at bookstores throughout the nation. This epic novel about soldiers at Schofield Barracks before World War II was not only a critical success but also a best-seller. A few years later Hollywood made the movie that won eight Oscars, including the one for best picture, and reached a large audience who had not read the book. Thus hundreds of thousands of Americans were introduced to the world of the peacetime Army in Hawaii. The author, James Jones, served at Hickam and Wheeler Fields as well as Schofield Barracks from January 1940 into 1942. Although he spent several months with air units, he relied more heavily on his experiences and observations as a soldier in the 27th Infantry for his novel. In F Company he knew or heard about a company commander who was the regimental boxing coach, the sergeant who had an affair with the company commander's wife, and the soldier who was a good boxer but who refused to fight after he had injured a man in the ring and suffered the wrath of the boxing coach. Years later, all appeared in his novel, which dramatically captured a slice of life of the Army in Hawaii.[94]

★

In the 1920s and 1930s China, the Philippines, Panama, and Hawaii were virtually inaccessible to most Americans; thus the military people who served in those places realized that they had enjoyed a rare and exotic experience. By the time the end of an enlistment or, for the career people, reassignment came, however, most were ready to leave their temporary homes and return to the States. Yet leavetaking is always poignant. Gene Hogan perhaps articulated the thoughts of many when he described his mood on his departure from Hawaii: "In due time all the guns have been fired, all the guard mounts stood, all the details completed and . . . it is time to return to the starting point. You think of all the friends . . . you are leaving behind and up until the time the ship sails your mind is filled with doubts . . . You get aboard and the ship sails and you think the rest of your life, what would it have been like if I had stayed."[95]

For individuals, foreign service was one of the most memorable experiences of their lives. For the nation, the service of those officers and men was crucial as they maintained the Pacific outposts throughout a period in which Japan was looming large as a threat to American interests. More than just showing the flag, they familiarized themselves with terrain where they might fight in a future war, and the higher level of their training prepared them better for that eventuality.

TEN

Mobilizing for War

Small as it was, the Regular Army personnel has been the invaluable
leaven of the present forces without which developments to date would
have been impossible.

—GEORGE C. MARSHALL

———— ❖ ————

THE summer of 1939 was glorious for four newly graduated West
Pointers. James L. Collins Jr., Charles H. Bowman, Harry W. O.
Kinnard Jr., and George W. R. Zethren had spent their last months at
the Academy planning to spend most of their ninety-day graduation
leave in Europe. They enjoyed Paris and bicycling through the French
countryside. After a brief stay in Switzerland, they took the train to
Munich and then to the Bavarian Alps. While en route to Garmisch,
a German corporal joined them in their compartment. They talked
about military matters and shared their lunch. The corporal confided
that the Germans were going to invade Poland in September.

For the next few days, as Jimmy Collins recalled, "all sorts of wild
schemes" flashed through their minds. If war was imminent, would it
not be a grand adventure to overstay their leave and "be caught by the
war." They could report to the military attaché in Berlin and begin
their careers with a flourish. The more they pondered this possibility,
however, the significance of missing the reporting date for their first
assignment became increasingly clear, so they wisely returned to the
States in August. The German invasion of Poland that initiated World
War II began on September 1, some two weeks before Chuck and
George reported for flight training and Jimmy and Harry joined their
field artillery and infantry regiments.[1]

War in Europe brought about a massive military mobilization in the
United States. During the first two years of the war, the Army made
strategic plans but concentrated primarily on increasing its strength and

housing, arming, equipping, and training the hundreds of thousands of new soldiers. Some were draftees, others were Guardsmen. Relations were often strained among the regulars, the selectees, and the Guardsmen. The race issue also added to the stress. Throughout these hectic days of filling manpower needs, combat branches struggled to develop the technological innovations that the belligerents were already using.

At the helm was George C. Marshall. On September 1, 1939, he raised his right hand and took the oath of office as chief of staff of the Army. As befitted a peaceful nation, he wore a civilian suit, as did the adjutant general who swore him in. Indeed, for more than two years, until December 7, 1941, Marshall and the other officers on duty in the War Department rarely wore uniforms. Four years before, Marshall had despaired of his future as the grinding pace of promotion by seniority in a budget-strapped Army stymied the advancement of many able officers. But in the fall of 1936 he finally received his first star, and the chief of staff, Malin Craig, told him that he would try to get him to Washington as soon as possible. After twenty happy months as a brigade commander at Vancouver Barracks, Washington, Marshall got the call in the summer of 1938. Although General Craig had some trouble scraping together enough money to bring the Marshall family across the country via train, by mid-July he was in his office as chief of the War Plans Division. Three months later, this junior brigadier general was deputy chief of staff. Whether or not he would attain the top office was a matter of conjecture, since he was outranked by all twenty-one major generals and eleven of the brigadier generals. Yet only four of those men had the requisite four years prior to mandatory retirement left to serve. In April President Franklin D. Roosevelt privately told Marshall that he was his choice, and when Craig went on terminal leave in July, he became acting chief of staff. On September 1 he dropped the "acting" from his title and was promoted to the regular rank of major general and the temporary four-star rank of general.[2]

The next two years were a time of momentous change for the Army as war raged in Europe and the Japanese desire for empire tortured China and threatened peace in the Pacific. General Marshall would later say that the years 1940 and 1941 were the hardest during his term as chief of staff. In November 1940, in a radio address, he pointed out that in the summer of 1939 there had been only about 170,000 inadequately armed and

George C. Marshall being sworn in as chief of staff by Adjutant General Emory S. Adams with Secretary of War Harry H. Woodring as witness, Washington, D.C., September 1, 1939. Courtesy of the George C. Marshall Library, Lexington, Virginia.

equipped men in the 3 half-organized divisions, 56 air squadrons, and 2 small mechanized regiments that constituted the U.S. Army. Fifteen months later, there were more than 500,000 men in 18 infantry divisions, 2 armored and one cavalry divisions, and 109 air squadrons. With the recent passage of the Conscription Act on September 14 and the congressional authorization of the callup of the National Guard and Organized Reserves on August 17, the assured growth of the Army would make these figures seem small. By the end of November 1941 there were 1,644,210 officers and men in 29 infantry, 5 armored, and 2 cavalry divisions and almost 200 air squadrons. The years, such as 1923, when Americans spent six times as much annually on soda and confections as they did on their Army were over. Military expenditures zoomed from just under $500 million in fiscal year 1939 to almost $3.7 billion two years later.[3]

In the midst of this turmoil, in October 1940, Marshall wrote his friend Charles D. Herron: "We are doing a great many things, and involvements are numerous and exceedingly complicated." The chief of staff spent long hours at his desk directing the course of this great mobilization. During his first year in office, a feud between Harry H. Woodring and Louis A. Johnson, the secretary and assistant secretary of war, made his task more difficult. With the appointment in July 1940 of the venerable Henry L. Stimson, who had served Taft as secretary of war and Hoover as secretary of state, the War Department had the civilian leadership it deserved. Marshall still made many appearances before Congress as representatives of a largely isolationist constituency made him explain and argue for every cent of military appropriations. Then he tried to get out in the field to see how the troops in the booming newly built camps were progressing. Organizing new units, training the men to fill those camps, and finding officers to lead the units deserved the highest priority. He broke the logjam of seniority for promotion and tried to bring the best men forward as fast as possible. He also had the burden of relieving old friends who were unable to handle the responsibilities of higher rank. The logistics necessary to arm, equip, uniform, and house this massive force were complicated by the demands to send arms to the British as well as to deal with the possibilities of war.[4]

From his desk in the utilitarian Munitions Building, George Marshall eventually exerted his influence throughout the Army. To keep fit, he rode horseback in the morning before reaching his office at seven-thirty, and he tried to leave before five o'clock. While there, he was totally focused on his work—meeting with key subordinates, attending necessary committee meetings, and making the myriad required decisions. A small group of officers in the Secretariat of the General Staff, including Omar Bradley, J. Lawton Collins, and Maxwell D. Taylor in the mobilization period, carefully screened the papers that came to the chief of staff for decision. Each digested daily five to ten papers on a variety of issues, wrote up briefs, and prepared to answer any questions and give their own opinions before they went to the general's office at ten every morning. For the sake of efficiency, anyone who came to see him entered without knocking and took a seat. They were to begin speaking when he looked up from his desk. His reputation for being brusque and a sharp interrogator as well as a man who did not suffer verbosity, inarticulateness, or, for that matter, anyone who appeared foolish was intimidating and could cause the most seasoned officers to quake.

Even Omar Bradley, who knew the general well from their days at Fort Benning, admitted that he "was never entirely comfortable in his presence." He was impressed by how quickly Marshall absorbed information, how he could detect a flaw in an argument and demand from the nervous officer why he had missed it. He would cross-examine the presenter and demand his opinion. Once he reprimanded Bradley and the two other officers in the Secretariat for not disputing recommendations. He told them that he expected them to counter those solutions. "Unless I hear all the arguments against something I am not sure whether I've made the right decision or not."[5]

Plans had first priority. Basically, they had to answer the questions whom and where would we fight? What would be the necessary manpower and logistical support needed for victory? The formation of the Joint Board early in the century brought together the uniformed heads of the Army and Navy and key assistants to consider such matters. Their plans, however, envisioned wars against a single power, designated by a color, in one theater. Since planners considered Japan the most likely enemy, the Orange Plan was the one most carefully detailed and kept current. Between 1924 and 1938 there had been more than half a dozen revisions to this plan. With Japan's attack on China and the increasingly aggressive actions of Nazi Germany in 1937, the possibility of a war against one nation in one theater decreased. Late in 1937, General Craig flatly declared current plans "unsound" and "inappropriate" to the international situation.[6]

The Munich crisis in the fall of 1938, when Europe was on the brink of war, galvanized a new approach to planning as the Joint Board called upon its own Joint Planning Committee for a strategic plan based on the premise that the United States would have to fight against Germany and Italy in the Atlantic as well as Japan in the Pacific. Faced with this problem, the planners recommended that the nation deal with the Atlantic threat first. They also considered the possibility of having allies. In June 1939 the Joint Board asked for plans to deal with specific situations. With the advent of the war, work progressed on these so-called Rainbow Plans. In May 1940, as France collapsed under German blows, staff officers began concentrating on Rainbow No. 5. Its premise was that the United States would fight with British and French allies against the Germans, Italians, and Japanese. The strategy proposed was to defeat the European enemies, then to pursue victory against the Japanese. Staff talks with the British early in 1941 agreed with these general premises, and the Joint Board approved the strategy in May 1941. The strategic framework was in place, but myriad specific plans were necessary to put it into effect.[7]

That spring, General Marshall gave the War Plans Division the assignment to work out a comprehensive plan, to encompass manpower and production requirements, to carry out the grand military design. There was a Protective Mobilization Plan with a complementary Industrial Mobilization Plan on hand, but events had rendered them obsolete. They assumed that the military objective was continental defense and proposed logistical solutions that had already been ignored in the almost two years of the mobilization. Al Wedemeyer, who joined the General Staff in April, was the logical choice to work out a new, more comprehensive plan. General Marshall had trouble remembering names, but he knew who "that long-legged major" was. Wedemeyer's professional reading over the years and his training at the German War College gave him a larger view of strategy than virtually all his fellow officers. He understood that strategy included "all of the so-called instruments of policy—political, economic, psychological . . . as well as military," and he had the intellectual capacity to comprehend those aspects and keep them balanced in his consideration.[8]

For several weeks before he was given this assignment, Wedemeyer had been at work on production requirements. This new task enlarged the scope of his work considerably. Over the next three months he compiled and digested "mountains of data" and conferred with the relevant staff sections, as well as meeting daily with Marshall. On one occasion the chief of staff told him: "don't you ever fail to give me benefit of your thinking and experience." As he tried to gauge how many men and how much material would be needed to carry out the objectives of Rainbow No. 5, he came up with figures for manpower and supply that "flabbergasted" Army logisticians. One told him that he thought it would take the nation more than a hundred years to produce such a magnitude of material.[9]

In the end, he produced a fourteen-page document that provided "data and estimates" of the men, supplies, munitions, and transport required to win a two-front war. He assumed that 10 percent of the nation's population (132 million) would be in uniform. Of that number, almost 8.8 million would be in the Army. He estimated that more than 6.7 million would man 215 divisions (including 61 armored and 61 mechanized) and support troops, while another 2 million men would serve in air units. He then based the logistical requirements on those figures. Although he grossly overestimated the number of divisions, he came close to the total manpower that was actually needed. Later, Wedemeyer concluded that the so-called Victory Plan was the "contingency plan" that provided "a basis for coordinating" the myriad activities involved in mobilization and rearmament.[10]

When the secretary of war forwarded the printed copy of the Victory Plan to the president in late September, he included a copy of the air war plan—AWPD-1. This was the work of four officers in the recently created Air War Plans Division: Lieutenant Colonels Harold L. George and Kenneth N. Walker and Majors Haywood S. Hansell Jr. and Laurence S. Kuter. Given the task of developing an air plan to carry out Rainbow No. 5, with nine days to complete it on August 3, these men worked as a team during those hot, muggy days in the Munitions Building. Hansell had recently returned from an observation tour in England, where the Royal Air Force planners had given him target data. Hansell and the others were imbued with an unshakable belief in strategic bombardment.

While they provided estimates for hemispheric defense and a secondary war in the Pacific, the planners concentrated on the defeat of Germany. They concluded that the vital links that must be attacked were electric power, transportation, and oil. To do this they came up with 154 specific targets and estimated that it would take 4,000 planes six months to carry out this destruction. They believed that such a force could be ready in a year, which fit in with the assumption that the Army would be ready to invade Europe in two years. When the planners made their presentation to Marshall and other members of the General Staff, some critics pointed out that their projections called for a disproportionate amount of men and material. But Marshall assured them with his comment: "I think that the plan has merit."[11]

✻

In late October 1940, when Marshall wrote an old friend about the immensity of his task, he added: "McNair has taken a tremendous load off my shoulders." During that summer he had activated the General Headquarters (GHQ) and named Major General Lesley J. McNair as its chief of staff with responsibility for creating the divisions of the great new Army and supervising their training. He had known this field artillery officer since they had crossed the Atlantic together as roommates in June 1917. McNair, a 1904 graduate of the Military Academy, was then in charge of training in the First Division. By the time World War I ended he was a brigadier general and one of the senior officers in the training section of the American Expeditionary Forces (AEF). Unlike some other promising officers Marshall had known, McNair never lost his drive or his ability to get things done and done well. In addition to his work at the Field Artillery School, he had played a significant role in the development of the new division organization and, in 1939 and 1940, as commandant of the Command and General Staff School, he had carried out Marshall's plans to revitalize that institution.[12]

To help McNair, the chief of staff summoned a newly promoted lieutenant colonel, Mark W. Clark, to Washington. Marshall had had ample opportunity to observe Clark while he commanded a brigade in the Third Division. Since the division commander and the chief of staff were nearing retirement, they let their chief of operations and training virtually run the division. A brilliant, dynamic, ambitious man, Clark made good use of this opportunity in handling one of the two divisions in the States that had the strength to carry out large unit exercises, which he planned and then critiqued. After Marshall became chief of staff, Clark planned and supervised an amphibious maneuver that brought the division from Fort Lewis, Washington, to an invasion site near Monterey, California. McNair, who closely followed Clark's activities in this maneuver, was also very impressed.

When Clark arrived at the Army War College, where General Headquarters was located, he found that there were only fifteen officers on the staff and that McNair was away observing a maneuver in upstate New York. He flew to join him, and for three days they went around the maneuver area looking over the National Guard as well as the regular units. At the beginning of their relationship, he learned that McNair "always wanted to see at first hand how things were working out." When they returned, McNair had seen enough of his new assistant to entrust Clark with the job of operations and training.

Their first major task was to plan the organization and training of the new divisions. As Marshall later recalled, Clark was the one who deserved most of the credit for creating those divisions. Since McNair was deaf, he usually sent the younger officer to confer with the chief of staff; thus the lieutenant colonel and the four-star general worked out the details as they sat in the latter's office. The plan was to select the senior commanders and staff officers, then gather a cadre of non-commissioned officers, send all through a training program, and then collect them at the post where the division would be organized. After a few weeks, enough time for the leaders and their cadres to become accustomed to working together, the troops for the division would arrive and begin a fifty-two-week training program.

Clark pored over the lists of colonels and generals, selected the three generals in each of the infantry divisions, and took his choices to McNair and then the chief of staff for approval. McNair, who was given another star in June 1941, moved his able assistant up to the position of his deputy, and in August 1941 Clark was jumped over hundreds of seniors to be a brigadier general. Having been a major just thirteen months before, Clark was "shocked" and realized that "it made a lot of people mad." Some senior generals were angry for another reason: they did not want to be told how to train their troops. Before he got his star, Clark had to face Lieutenant General Ben Lear, the commander of Second Army, who came to his office and demanded to know why he should be told how to train troops by a field-grade officer. After Clark explained that they had worked out this program, which they thought was the best for a difficult war, Lear accepted the decision. On the other hand, another and more famous lieutenant general, Hugh Drum, the commander of the First Army, refused to go along with this program; as a result no new divisions were created in his area. Despite the mutterings of those officers he had leaped over for promotion, and the senior generals who resented the centralized control, Clark obviously satisfied the two most important people—McNair and Marshall.

As the divisions took shape, Clark and McNair spent much of their time flying from camp to camp to monitor progress. Clark estimated that they flew together 80,000 miles in one year. Throughout this period, his admiration for his superior officer grew. "I found McNair one of the most brilliant, selfless and devoted soldiers I ever knew." In turn, General McNair's respect for Clark increased. One night, after the war they had prepared for had begun, as they walked home from their offices at the War College, Clark remarked that soon the War Department would create a headquarters that would go to Europe. He assumed that McNair would be the commander, and he hoped that he would take him along with him. McNair responded: "You're more apt to have high command than I am. I am too old, and you're in the right age bracket."[13]

✤

During this hectic mobilization period, as hundreds of thousands of men streamed into the ranks of the Army and enormous sums of money poured into construction, equipment, and armaments, life in the Stateside Army began to look like a "squirrel cage" to Forrest Harding in Hawaii. "Time is the dominant factor in all our military preparations," as George Marshall wrote. What this meant to the regulars was spelled out by Dwight Eisenhower in a letter to a friend in the fall of 1941: "Things are moving so rapidly these days that I get almost dizzy trying to keep up." He had just been promoted to brigadier general. Only the year before he had estimated that he would not make colonel until about 1950.[14]

Aviation took the center of the stage even before Europe went to war, while events forced the mechanization issue to a head in the cavalry. Aside from the great expansion in strength, there were significant developments in the field artillery and infantry. During the mobilization, large field maneuvers tested commanders, troops, and new concepts. Old soldiers had to adjust to the flood of civilians who filled the ranks while blacks still struggled with the constraints of a segregated society. Throughout these turbulent years, families moved about from posts to newly established camps in an effort to keep up with their men in uniform.

Shortly after Marshall took over his job as chief of the War Plans Division in July 1938, he received an invitation from the commanding general of the Air Corps GHQ, Major General Frank M. Andrews, to visit Langley Field. When Marshall accepted, Andrews flew to Washington to pick him up and flew him back. Within a few days, he extended the invitation to tour air bases and aircraft plants across the nation. For nine days the two generals flew to the West Coast, with frequent stops as Andrews not only introduced Marshall to senior Air Corps officers but also showed him the awesome B-17s on the assembly line at the Boeing plant in Seattle, as well as the Douglas and Northrup factories.

A West Pointer who had served more than a decade in the cavalry before he earned his wings, Andrews, who had been a friend of the late Billy Mitchell and had served as Foulois's executive officer, had a warm personality with a touch of charisma. Respected by both air and ground officers, he made a most favorable impression on Marshall, who clearly understood what Andrews was trying to get across. "I learned a great deal on this trip, a very great deal." He grasped the vision of the air officers and came to understand their problem of dealing with a hostile General Staff. He also recognized that part of the problem was caused by some Air Corps officers' going directly to Congress and playing politics against the rest of the Army.[15]

In the fall of 1938, air power gained its most significant convert— Franklin D. Roosevelt. Galvanized by the Munich pact, in which the British and French leaders acceded to Hitler's demands, and by the intelligence he later received about the overwhelming advantage the Germans had over the French and British in aircraft, the president called a meeting on November 14 to lay out his program for dealing with what he perceived as a threat to American security. Among the civilian and military leaders present on that Monday afternoon in the White House were Marshall, who had recently been designated deputy chief of staff, and Henry H. Arnold, who had become chief of the Air Corps in late September.

Roosevelt said that he wanted a 20,000-aircraft program but assumed that Congress would provide only half of this number. Since the Air Corps had only some 1,700 planes (less than half of them combat ready), this was a stunning announcement. Arnold was naturally overjoyed, but Marshall was not. When FDR asked him what he thought, he answered bluntly: "I am sorry, Mr. President, but I don't agree with that at all." What concerned him was that there was confusion about the purpose of this great armada: Was it to serve under American command to defend the hemisphere, or was it to be sent to the British and French to use against Germany? Besides, nothing was said about matching crews and armaments with planes or, for that matter, severe shortages in men and material throughout the rest of the Army.[16]

Only a few weeks before, Arnold had been in a fight within the War Department to preserve future production of B-17s. Now, with the president's strong endorsement of air power, he began to worry about the gap between the time it took to produce airplanes and that required to train crews. As he checked on production capabilities, he also began to look into the possibility of contracting civilian flight schools to train the huge number of pilots. Not surprisingly, he called on his most trusted subordinates, Carl Spaatz and Ira Eaker, to help him as his work expanded.[17]

Although Marshall had disagreed with FDR, Arnold knew that air power had a friend in the man who was going to be the next chief of staff. If he needed any proof, he got it the next summer. Despite the opposition of the secretary and assistant secretary of war and the then chief of staff, Marshall demanded that Frank Andrews be appointed chief of the Organization and Training Division. Andrews, who had lost his temporary two stars when he left the command of Air Corps GHQ, not only would be the first airman to hold such a crucial position in the General Staff but also would have to be promoted to brigadier general. In a heated session, Marshall told his civilian superiors: "You just must do it. If you are going to make me chief of staff, you've just got to do it." So Brigadier General Andrews took up those important duties in August 1939.[18]

As the momentum increased through 1939, 1940, and into 1941, Arnold's power and his organization grew apace. The figures are impressive: the force of 1,700 planes and 19,600 officers and men in January 1939 increased to 10,100 planes and 292,000 officers and men in November 1941. While the president probably did not even know the names of other Army branch chiefs, he met with Arnold on several occasions. In turn, Marshall raised him to the position of deputy chief of staff and included him in the highest-level conferences. On June 20, 1941, the Air Corps became the Army Air Force, with Hap Arnold as its commander. Arnold understood and appreciated Marshall's role in the evolution of the air arm. Pete Quesada, whom Arnold brought to Washington, summed up their relationship: "Marshall had endless confidence in Arnold and Arnold had endless devotion to Marshall."[19]

With the collapse of France in 1940, Roosevelt emphasized supplying war material to Britain through "Cash and Carry" and later Lend-Lease programs. Pete Quesada stayed very busy as Arnold's liaison with the various allied air attachés who made requests for material. Through 1941, the Americans shipped some 2,400 planes to Britain. American officers also crossed the Atlantic to observe the war firsthand and consult with their British counterparts. Tooey Spaatz was one of the earliest observers, going to England via Italy and France in May 1940. Arnold and Quesada went in April 1941. In addition to talking with RAF leaders, Hap conferred with Prime Minister Winston Churchill and met King George VI. All experienced air raids and could see clearly that the British were in a desperate situation. As Arnold recalled, "They needed help, needed it badly, and were frank to admit it."[20]

While in England, they visited the RAF's Eagle Squadron, which was manned by American volunteers. On the other side of the world, the Air Force was involved in the American Volunteer Group (AVG) in China. Claire Chennault, who had led the losing case for pursuit aviation at the Air Corps Tactical School, had retired and gone to China to command this unit. With the backing of the White House, agents recruited active-duty flyers in all the services. Jake Smart, at Randolph Field, Texas, was amazed at the success the AVG had in recruiting pilots, while Ira Eaker, who commanded a pursuit group on the West Coast, was dismayed with his orders to pack up all of his unit's P-40s and ship them to Chennault. Although the Flying Tigers did not get into combat until December, they and the Eagles excited as much attention in America as the Escadrille Lafayette had in World War I.[21]

As well as increasing production of aircraft and firming up relations with the RAF, Arnold pressed for more pilots and ground crews. In 1939 the Air Corps hoped to turn out 1,200 new pilots. The objective was raised to 7,000 the next year, and by the fall of 1941 staff planners were discussing the possibility of training 50,000 annually. At that time the actual rate of training technicians had risen to 100,000.[22]

At the beginning of the mobilization, both Noel Parrish and Jake Smart were first lieutenants in the Air Training Command at Randolph

Field. Noel was an instructor, while Jake was on the commanding general's staff. Already in 1939, the signs of coming war were so obvious that Jake, who now had a family, took out additional life insurance. He followed the war news closely and attended intelligence briefings, including some by RAF officers on tactics and techniques; but he was frustrated by his "limited opportunity and ability to do something about matters that really counted."[23]

When Arnold opened up pilot training in civilian contract schools, Parrish was picked to be deputy commander of the program at Glenview, near Chicago. Since the commander at Glenview refused to have anything to do with the contract program that trained black pilots in the Chicago area, Noel visited and talked with the head of the instructors, Charles A. "Chief" Anderson, the first black to hold a commercial pilot's license, and Willa B. Brown, who ran the school. He was "really impressed by them" and wanted to help them.[24]

His interest in the black program was virtually unique in the Air Corps. Although blacks wanted the opportunity to earn wings, the Air Corps was adamant in opposition until political pressure forced the door slightly open with the contract programs at Chicago and Tuskegee, Alabama. In 1941, opportunity was expanded by developing a military base at Tuskegee, home of the famous black college. Originally Glenview had been a possible site, and when it did not work out, Parrish investigated the possibility of Joliet but met with determined resistance. Once the Tuskegee decision was made, Noel, by then a captain, was given the job of setting up the training program.

He had mixed feelings about this assignment. Such a special detail might well mean a dead end to his career, yet it offered an unusual opportunity to deal with a complex mix of politics and racism. Besides Noel was genuinely interested in "the struggle toward decent recognition and advancement" of the blacks. He prepared for his task by talking with experts in anthropology and psychology at the University of Chicago.[25]

There was one obvious candidate for flight training and leadership— Ben Davis. He had been interested in flying for years and had applied for pilot training while at West Point. The Air Corps had rejected him then because of the all-white policy. Since graduation, he had served in the 24th Infantry and attended the company officers' course at the Infantry School. He had spent a couple of years as an ROTC instructor at Tuskegee, and was his father's aide at Fort Riley when the War Department ordered him to take flight training. Over the years, he had been promoted on schedule, and thus had put on the two silver bars of a captain in the fall of 1940.

In July 1941 Davis and twelve aviation cadets began their training under the supervision of white instructors. Later classes had blacks led by Chief Anderson as teachers. Standards were rigorous, and eight of that first class washed out. Ben loved flying, but, perhaps because of the high stakes for himself, his race, and his nation, he was so disciplined and so cautious in his flying during training that there was some concern that he might fail. But he worked hard to meet the requirement, earning his wings and the right to command the first black squadron. The success of Davis and his classmates established the benchmark for black military pilots. In turn, the strength of character and professionalism of Ben Davis set the tone of the Tuskegee program and served as a model for those who followed.

When he looked back on those early days at Tuskegee, Davis praised Noel Parrish for his fairness and recognized that "his goodwill was of major importance." As director of training, it would have been easy for him to go along with the hostility of the Air Force toward the program and simply certify that blacks were not able to make the grade as military pilots. Instead, as a later Tuskegee graduate, Charles W. Dryden wrote, he was "a friendly, enthusiastic supporter . . . sensitive to the needs, aspirations, and obstacles faced by all of us."

The initial unit Davis commanded, and in which those who earned their wings served, was the 99th Pursuit (later Fighter) Squadron. The ground crews went to Chanute Field, Illinois, for their training, which, unlike Tuskegee, was not segregated. Though organized in the spring of 1941, the 99th did not reach its full strength of pilots and ground crews until July of the next year. The first increment of pilots, Ben and his classmates, pinned on their wings in March 1942. Despite all the obstacles, they had firmly established the foundation for blacks in the Air Force.[26]

※

In November 1941 Lucian Truscott took command of the Fifth Cavalry Regiment at Fort Bliss, Texas. It felt good to be back in the saddle at the head of a column of troopers. The pageantry of the mounted reviews was, if anything, more thrilling than he remembered. A First Cavalry Division review was unforgettable as thousands of horsemen "with sunlight gleaming on polished sabers, red-and-white guidons fluttering as they dip in salute, standards rustling as the bugles sound 'Flourishes,' the columns pass, wheel to the left, and wheel again, and sweep past the reviewing stand at the trot as the band plays. Around once more, this time at the gallop amid swirling clouds of dust."[27]

Truscott savored the experience even more deeply because he had been away from the cavalry for more than seven years and he realized that the future of mounted units was limited, if it existed at all. He had taken the two-year course at Leavenworth and then stayed on as an instructor for four years. When his tour neared completion, he requested service in the mechanized arm and reported to the 13th Armored Regiment at Fort Knox in the summer of 1940. In contrast to the steady rhythm of life at the few remaining cavalry posts, he found Knox a "beehive of seething activity," with rigorous training programs and lots of construction in progress. Officers who shared his belief in the future of what had just become the Armored Force were assigned in such numbers that they had to live in tents because no other quarters were available.

He and the other newly arrived officers promptly took a course in driving and care of all types of vehicles in the command before they joined their various regiments. At first Truscott was a battalion executive; then he served as the plans and operations officer of the 13th. Training from the lowest unit of the section to the division went apace, with drills and field problems day and night—"constantly," as Truscott recalled.[28]

After a decade of intraservice bickering, a War Department directive (July 10, 1940) had brought the Armored Force into existence. The shocking spectacle of German panzers spearheading victories in Poland in September 1939 and more immediately in France during May and June 1940 served as dramatic background and, to a certain extent, as a catalytic agent in creating this new branch. The infantry as well as the cavalry had tanks, and during the crucial months from the fall of 1939 into the late spring of 1940, neither branch chief would sacrifice any of his organizations for more mechanization. The chief of cavalry,

Johnny Herr, proffered the "portee" system of transporting men and horses to the scene of action and the combined use of horse and mechanized cavalry, but field tests demonstrated that these concepts were unworkable. Adna Chaffee, the commander of the cavalry's mechanized brigade, and many of the other cavalry officers, including some of Herr's own staff, continued to urge him to recognize that the cavalry must mechanize in order to carry out its traditional mission in modern war. Herr countered that the mobilization would bring in men and money enough to maintain the horse regiments as well as build up the mechanized units.

The issue came to a head in the Third Army maneuver in May as German tanks smashed through the Allied front in western Europe. During the second phase of this exercise, the Seventh Cavalry Brigade (Mechanized) from Fort Knox united with the recently formed infantry counterpart—the Provisional Tank Brigade—from Fort Benning and made an impressive showing in comparison with the First Cavalry Division. On the last day of the maneuver, May 25, the commanders of the two brigades, Chaffee and Brigadier General Bruce Magruder, and a few other officers met with Brigadier General Frank Andrews in the basement of the high school in Alexandria, Louisiana. The time had come to bypass branch intransigence and create an armored force independent of the infantry, cavalry, and field artillery branches. Significantly, neither Herr nor the chief of infantry, Major General George A. Lynch, both of whom were in the maneuver area, were invited. Chaffee and the others made a strong case for an armored force, and Andrews took this message back to Marshall, who was most receptive. Within six weeks the Armored Force was authorized.[29]

Colonel George S. Patton Jr., one of the umpires of the maneuver and the commander of the Third Cavalry Regiment, was present at that conference, but his contribution is unknown. Since he had returned to the cavalry in 1920, he had been a horseman. During the 1930s he had served two tours in the Third, the showcase regiment at Fort Myer that he had commanded since December 1938. Before the maneuver, he had broken rules by passing on information about the role of the cavalry to the commander of the First Cavalry Division. After the relatively poor showing of the horse cavalry, he remained supportive with suggestions to enhance their effectiveness. At the same time he kept his options open with his old friend Chaffee, who responded to his letter in June with the good news that he was on his list as a possible brigade commander in one of the soon-to-be-created armored divisions.

In mid-July at Fort Knox, the First Armored Division, which was organized around the mechanized cavalry brigade, came into being under the command of Magruder. Simultaneously at Fort Benning, the Second Armored Division, with the Provisional Tank Brigade as its cadre, was organized under a cavalryman who had commanded one of the mechanized regiments, Brigadier General Charles L. Scott. It was Scott who selected Patton as one of his brigade commanders.

Soon after he arrived at Benning, Patton wrote General Pershing, with whom he had remained close over the years: "The whole thing is most interesting as most of the tactics have yet to be worked out and there is a great chance for ingenuity and leadership." Within a few weeks two developments arose that shaped Patton's future. One was that Scott went to Knox to take acting command of the First Armored Corps, since Chaffee's cancer was debilitating him. This meant that Patton took over the Second Armored Division. About the same time, he turned down the chief of cavalry's offer of command of the First Cavalry Division. The examples of the German panzer successes, reinforced by his own observation of the mechanized versus horse units' confrontation in the Third Army maneuver, clearly indicated the course of modern war. Besides, as he wrote his wife, promotion would be faster with the tanks.

At this time the Second Armored Division, which was scattered in tents in outlying regions of the Benning reservation, was ill equipped, under strength, and suffering from a morale problem. Mobilization would eventually bring in equipment and men. Indeed, as the War Department learned later, the appeal of the Armored Force was surpassed only by that of the Air Force among volunteers. The new commander applied his particular brand of leadership to improve morale and mold an effective fighting force. He established high training standards in physical conditioning, skill in weapons and in handling vehicles, together with dress and conduct rules—all enforced with strict discipline. He moved constantly about the division area, checking on all aspects of the training. One soldier turned to see the general by his side on the rifle range. When Patton asked him what he was doing, the man answered: "Just trying to hit the target." The general blurted out in his high-pitched voice: "You are like hell! You are trying to kill some German son of a bitch before he can kill you."[30]

From his reading in military history, Patton fully understood the importance of symbolic gestures. In May 1941, a few weeks after he pinned on a second star, he and his wife moved from the large stucco house at the main post to a spacious log cabin, which he partially paid for, near his troops at Sand Hill, at Fort Benning. Before that, he designed a new uniform that he hoped would be adopted for tankers. Raymond S. McLain, a National Guard general from Oklahoma, who was among a group of Guard and reserve generals visiting Benning, described it as a pea-green double-breasted form-fitting jacket with brass buttons and green riding breeches. Instead of a cap or hat, he wore a golden football helmet. When Patton asked him what he thought of it, McLain replied: "I don't quite understand it."

Whether it was understood or not, all could agree that it was different and demonstrated the wearer's flair. Patton wore it as he went about his routine, and, not surprisingly, soldiers began to refer to him as the "Green Hornet," after a comic-book hero. Journalists also noticed him and what he was doing with the Second Armored. *Life* and the *Saturday Evening Post* ran stories about him and his division. The July 7, 1941, issue of *Life* featured him in full color (but not in his Green Hornet outfit), in a tank turret, on the cover, and the accompanying article served the purpose he desired. As he wrote the editor: "The important thing in any organization is the creation of soul which is based on pride, and no member of the division reading your magazine could fail to be filled with pride."[31]

One of the young infantry captains who had been in the Provisional Tank Brigade mentioned other aspects of Patton's leadership. When his tank drivers did as the general ordered and hit ditches at full speed, with the resultant cuts and bruises as well as some broken suspension springs, Patton took full responsibility. Later, in a large maneuver, Richard Steinbach took the initiative of ordering a company to reinforce a flank unit. Patton singled him out for praise: "that is what makes the American Army great. Trained men can take action without orders from above, because they know what they are doing." At the end of that maneuver, during which the Second Armored captured the enemy corps headquarters, the maneuver director harshly condemned Patton for doing what the director thought could not be done in combat. Following that session, Patton called a meeting of all the division officers. He told them of the criticism and then commented: "if anything was wrong, and I don't believe there was, it was my fault. You performed perfectly." Steinbach commented: "He was our 'Georgie,' and we loved the S.O.B."[32]

While at Benning, Patton became acquainted with Brigadier General Omar N. Bradley, who took over as commandant of the Infantry School in March 1941. Earlier, Patton renewed correspondence with his old friend Ike Eisenhower. Not long after he became a brigade commander, he asked Ike if he wanted to come to the Second Armored. Eisenhower was delighted but specified that he wanted to command a regiment. Patton told him that he would prefer to have him as his chief of staff but understood his desire for command. He added: "no matter how we get together, we will go PLACES." Better opportunities kept Eisenhower from joining Patton at that time.[33]

A year after the creation of the Armored Force, it became clear that Chaffee's illness would not permit him to carry on. He retired and died within a few weeks. The next senior officer and logical successor was General Scott, commander of the First Armored Corps, but General Marshall selected a field artillery officer who had not been involved in any of the infantry and cavalry infighting in the 1930s—Jacob L. Devers—to become commander on August 1, 1941. A major general and commander of the Ninth Division at Fort Bragg since October 1940, Devers had done a good job training those troops and giving the division a proper foundation. He had known Chaffee when both served on the War Department General Staff and had worked closely with Van Voorhis as his chief of staff when he commanded the Panama Canal Department. More significantly, during his service as commander of the Washington Provisional Brigade he had gained the confidence of Marshall. Devers became known as a "blowtorch"—a man who got things done, effectively and efficiently.

Patton was surprised at the appointment. Although their dates of rank as colonels were the same, Devers had pinned on his first star five months before Patton and his second seven months before him. But he had no experience with tanks. In early August Patton wrote his wife:

"I was very much impressed with Devers, he has developed a lot and is a very fine leader." Devers lived up to that high regard. He streamlined the headquarters, increased staff efficiency, and stepped up training in small-unit tactics and tank-artillery coordination. He also pressed for improvement of self-propelled guns and better tanks. He was often in the field with his troops, coming into his office at seven in order to get through the paperwork early. He also diplomatically handled racial problems as he depended on the advice of a local black woman, Margaret Collier, who was recreation director for black troops at Fort Knox.

The most delicate problem he had to solve was Patton's going around his back to communicate suggestions to the secretary of war. He solved this, characteristically, by confronting Patton. He went to Benning and, while at dinner with the Pattons, he broached the topic. He was blunt: "I'm a boss and I got to do something about those crazy things that you're doing." This cleared the air, and both men went about their respective duties with Patton understanding where he stood.[34]

In the late summer of 1941, with dynamic leaders, Devers and Patton, and the Victory Plan's projections of sixty-one armored divisions, the Armored Force seemed to have a boundless future. Two factors, however, limited its expansion. First was the demands on tank production that Lend-Lease made. The other was the belief of General McNair, a veteran artilleryman, that antitank units should be pushed as vigorously as tank units, if not more so. The creation of an antitank organization would draw both men and materiel from the Armored Force. While Lend-Lease was beyond their purview, these generals could assume that the General Headquarters maneuvers in the fall would help decide the effectiveness and future expansion of the Armored Force.

During ten days in late September in Louisiana and for another ten days in November in the Carolinas, the Armored Corps joined with a large array of all arms within the Army to test commanders, staffs, and men, as well as organizational concepts and tactics. As could be predicted, Patton led with dash and won some victories. In one instance he was said to have personally paid for gasoline to keep his tanks moving. Nevertheless, the armored units generally did not do as well as their advocates hoped. At the same time, McNair was pleased to see that antitank units were effective, and even Johnny Herr could point to some success of combined horse and mechanized units in Louisiana.

While the efforts of the recently organized antitank groups were not as successful as McNair had hoped, he went ahead and developed a Tank Destroyer Force. Whether or not the combined horse-mechanized concept succeeded in a few minor actions, Herr's hope for a future for horse cavalry was doomed.

There was no question that a future remained for armored units; yet improvements had to be made. Devers thought that the commanders and staff needed more training, but that could be said of virtually every large unit in these maneuvers. Patton made the key point, however, in a talk he gave his division in the interval between these great exercises: "We still fail to use every weapon every time." The problem was inherent in the organization, which made it virtually impossible to coordinate combined arms actions and led to the infantry, tank, and artillery units' fighting their own unsupported battles. While Chaffee and his planners tried to follow the model of German panzer units, they neglected the crucial point of the battle group organization, which led to combined arms being involved and working together whenever they went into battle. Finally, in March 1942, a new division organization, which featured two combat command headquarters to provide specifically for combined arms action, went into effect. But, as was the case with many other of the Victory Plan's organizations, there would never be sixty-one divisions as Wedemeyer projected.[35]

✷

The GHQ maneuvers, in which almost half of the entire Army participated, were the culmination of a progressive training program from the individual through the various units to Army level. These huge exercises tested not only soldiers but commanders, equipment, and organizational and tactical doctrines. By the time they ended in the fall of 1941, the United States, for the first time in its history, had "a field-tested, almost combat-ready Army before the declaration of war." Two years before, in a speech before the National Guard Association, Marshall had emphasized that "the only way to learn how to do things properly is to get out on the ground and do them." He explained that large-scale maneuvers would serve as "our Combat College for troop leading." During the intervening time, McNair had developed and put into effect a standard training program that had reached large-unit maneuver level, but the maneuvers in the fall of 1941 concentrated the largest number of troops ever brought together in the continental United States. There was an obvious difference between the National Guard and regular divisions. The former were larger (22,000) and still organized around four infantry regiments, while the regulars were in the smaller (15,000) triangular organization with three infantry regiments. The two armies that clashed over 30,000 square miles in Louisiana contained 472,000 men, while 295,000 were in the army and corps that maneuvered against each other in more than 9,000 square miles of the Carolinas two months later.[36]

McNair gave Wayne Clark the job of drawing up the basic directive for the Louisiana maneuver, with the admonition to keep it "as simple as possible." Clark took a Standard Oil road map and drew two large goose eggs to represent the two armies, added a line to separate them, and then wrote up a mission for each that would bring them into contact. That was it. The maneuver thus would be free; that is, the commanders could do what they wanted within the geographic boundaries. Conditions would be as close to combat as possible to include the handling of logistics. Moving hundreds of thousands of troops and their equipment and supplies to the designated area and keeping them supplied throughout the maneuver were as crucial as the conduct of the simulated battles.

The commanders of the three armies—Ben Lear of the Second, who faced Walter Krueger of the Third, and Hugh Drum of the First, who maneuvered against a corps—were lieutenant generals who had entered the Army in 1898. Lear and Krueger had started as enlisted men, while Drum had received a direct commission. Drum had worn a star in 1918, when he earned a reputation as a brilliant staff officer in the AEF. He and the solid, hard-working Krueger were infantrymen; the cavalryman Lear was known as a martinet. An incident in the summer of 1941 drew national attention to this characteristic. Lear was playing golf in civilian clothes when a convoy of trucks filled with soldiers from one of the Guard divisions passed by and the men whistled and shouted at the girls on the golf course. When Lear remonstrated with them, they hooted at what appeared to be merely an irate elderly duffer. When the general got back to his office, he ordered those soldiers to take a fifteen-mile hike. Aside from not helping Regular Army and National Guard relations, the resulting publicity pinned the nickname "Yoohoo" on Lear.[37]

The planners and leaders of the Louisiana maneuvers, September 1941 (left to right): Mark W. Clark, Harry J. Malony, Dwight D. Eisenhower, Ben Lear, Walter Krueger, and Lesley J. McNair. The careers of the two opposing commanders, Lear and Krueger, spanned the Spanish-American War and both world wars. Courtesy of the Dwight D. Eisenhower Library, Abilene, Kansas.

The Louisiana maneuver began on a rainy Monday and ended two weeks later with a brief respite between its two phases. While the senior commanders and staffs maneuvered the two great armies, the soldiers and officers attempted to carry out those plans. If they had failed to learn how to live in the field before, they certainly had the opportunity to do so in the heavily wooded areas and swampy river bottoms of Louisiana. Richard Steinbach, a regimental supply officer in Patton's division, recalled that "the terrain was tough, and you had to fight it" as well as the enemy. For those on the ground, there were occasional confusion and mistakes. There were also some casualties, of whom Steinbach was one. On a drizzly night he was in a column on the march when a vehicle got stuck in a ravine. While he was trying to help, the driver got the half-track in gear, shot forward, and threw him into the small stream, where a tank ran over his arm. Fortunately, the muddy bottom kept him from losing the arm.[38]

Joe Collins, chief of staff of the Seventh Corps in Louisiana, appreciated the experience gained from conducting the difficult operations of withdrawals and river crossings and in handling the tactical deployment of combined arms including armor and air units, as well as the necessary complex logistical arrangements. This is what Marshall and McNair expected commanders and staffs to gain from the maneuvers, which were tests of those officers' abilities.[39]

Krueger's Third Army emerged as the victor in Louisiana, while Drum made an even more impressive showing in the Carolinas maneuver. Despite his success, Drum was evidently not in McNair's or Marshall's plans for the future. McNair critiqued his performance as being too much like World War I in his overly detailed orders and in his tactics. They much preferred the Third Army's style, which was more responsive and flexible than Drum's approach.[40]

The man who was credited with the Third Army success was Dwight D. Eisenhower, Krueger's chief of staff. It had been a busy ten months for him since he left his battalion command to be chief of staff of the Third Division in November 1940. Three months later he moved up to the Ninth Corps as chief of staff and soon wore the eagles of a colonel. In July 1941 he became chief of staff of the Third Army, which was preparing for the upcoming maneuvers. He confessed to a friend: "Since none of us has ever functioned on an Army staff in such large maneuvers, we are having some difficulty in deciding just how many individuals are needed in each section." That was only one of the myriad problems that required decisions and kept him at work from six in the morning to eleven every night by late August. In addition to planning for the GHQ maneuvers, Ike dealt with command post exercises for senior commanders and their staffs and preliminary lower-level maneuvers. He quickly became known as the man to see in the Third Army, and, as he wrote an old friend: "Everyone comes in here to discuss his troubles, and I'm often astonished how much better they seem to work after they have had a chance to recite their woes." What he did not say was that this was a good way to keep his finger on the pulse of such a large force. The culmination of his work was the Third Army's sweep of both phases of the maneuver. On September 29, the day after the maneuver ended, he received his reward—promotion to brigadier general.[41]

During the last phase of the maneuver, he took time to write a long letter to Leonard T. Gerow, who was then chief of the General Staff's War Plans Division. He emphasized that one of the most troublesome problems was getting rid of unfit officers. Successful senior commanders, he believed, must have not only a high level of professionalism but also "drive," "an inexhaustible supply of determination," and, finally, "iron in their souls." Both Marshall and McNair understood this and pondered what to do with the many officers who were clearly unsuitable for the commands they held. While it was personally more painful to relieve Regular Army friends and acquaintances who did not measure up, the relief of National Guard senior officers posed political and public-relations problems that could damage popular support for the mobilization. Before the great maneuvers, they had already fired some commanders and expected to get rid of others. Between the Louisiana and Carolinas maneuvers, matters came to a head.

On October 7 McNair sent Marshall a list with comments on the corps and division commanders. Seven of the original corps commanders had already been relieved, but they were all regulars. Six of the original eighteen National Guard division commanders had also lost their commands, and McNair thought that another nine should probably go. A week later, he expanded his critique: "The National Guard is built on an unsound foundation, in that its officers have had little or no training as such. The Guard now is or soon will be occupying space and facilities which could be used to better advantage for new units, organized soundly, and led adequately." Because of this situation, McNair recommended that the Guard be demobilized.[42]

Marshall was aware of the political explosion that would result if he endorsed such a drastic solution. Besides, he was more sympathetic to the Guard and had been somewhat cautious in getting rid of senior Guard officers. He came to realize, however, that his desire to give them ample opportunity to succeed had delayed the preparation of their units. Demobilizing the Guard was out of the question, but age, incompetence, and lack of military training cost all but two of the senior Guard generals their commands.[43]

Although a higher percentage of regular field-grade officers were relieved than their Guard equivalents and a good many regular generals lost their commands as well, there remained a general impression that the Guard officers had been unfairly treated. Secretary of War Henry L. Stimson talked about this with Marshall and McNair when he urged that at least one Guard colonel be placed on a promotion list in late

October. They saw his point and came up with two names, but they also stood up for their policy in regard to senior commanders. As a rule, the Guard officers simply did not have the training that Leavenworth and the War College experience had given their regular counterparts, and the war of movement that Marshall anticipated demanded such a background.[44]

Given the criteria that Marshall and McNair established, the officers they considered to replace those they relieved were regulars. As early as July, McNair sent five names to Marshall as possible division commanders; among them was William H. Simpson. He had headed the Military Intelligence faculty at the Army War College but was in command of a regiment in the Second Division when he received his first star. He served as assistant commander of that division for a few months before he commanded a large replacement training center. In October 1941 Simpson, who became a major general in September, took over the 35th, the National Guard unit involved in the "Yoohoo" incident. Even though they had participated in the Louisiana maneuvers, Simpson thought they still needed training down to the basic level.[45]

During the GHQ maneuvers, parachute troops made their debut while the field artillery experimented with light observation planes. Only one company of parachutists took part in the Louisiana maneuvers; the entire 502d Parachute Battalion participated in the Carolina exercises, but these were essentially token appearances. Eleven spotter planes piloted by civilians with artillery officers as observers flew more than 3,000 missions beginning in the summer and through the fall maneuvers. The evolution of these new elements of warfare had just recently begun.[46]

Soon after he took office, the chief of field artillery, Robert M. Danford, began arguing for the field artillery's control of air observation in order to direct fire more effectively. In January 1939 he made a formal proposal to the chief of the Air Corps, but Hap Arnold rejected it. Although Arnold had little interest in giving such support to the ground forces, he did not want to give up control of any air function. He and other airpower advocates were concerned with strategic bombardment, not with the problems of directing artillery fire. Besides, he did not believe that light aircraft had much chance of survival on the modern battlefield. Danford was not deterred. Again and again in maneuvers, he saw that the existing system did not work. When he made another effort in late 1940, the General Staff disapproved on the organizational point that the Air Corps should control air elements.[47]

After the Louisiana maneuvers of 1940, an unusually qualified battery commander who was disgruntled by the poor air support decided to state the case. Not once during four months of field problems had an air observer actually adjusted the fire of his battalion. During his twenty years of service, Captain William W. Ford had had some experience as an aerial observer, but, more to the point, he was a qualified pilot. In an article published in the *Field Artillery Journal* in April 1941, Ford made a strong case for light, unarmored aircraft, which would not need hard landing fields, to remain close to the firing batteries. If they were part of a firing battalion, the pilots and observers could keep up with the gun positions and targets instead of trying to locate both when called to the scene. As a pilot, he also made a strong case as to the viability of light aircraft. Danford was pleased to have such a well-articulated argument at hand. Yet, after the apparent success of the "Grasshopper Squadron" in the GHQ maneuvers, Danford was still unable to make progress in changing the opinion of the General Staff. Finally, he took the unusual step of going directly to the secretary of war. Henry L. Stimson had been a field artillery regimental commander in World War I. Stimson was interested and referred him to the assistant secretary, John J. McCloy, who approved. Arnold grudgingly consented to let the field artillery test its concept with its own planes. General Marshall approved on December 3, and ten days later Danford called Ford to Washington to work out the plans for the project.[48]

During World War I, Billy Mitchell had toyed with the idea of inserting troops by air behind enemy lines, but it was some ten years later that a couple of Air Corps lieutenants and a sergeant made some practical experiments at Brooks Field, just outside San Antonio. Claire L. Chennault, Benjamin W. Chidlaw, and Sergeant Erwin H. Nichols dropped a six-man machine-gun team, but the Army continued to show no interest. Nor was there much interest stirred when, in 1931, the commanding general of the Panama Canal Department moved a field artillery battalion ninety miles by air across the isthmus or when, the next year, Captain George C. Kenney air transported and landed a small infantry detachment behind the opponents' front line during a maneuver.

The Russians and Germans, however, had pursued the possibilities of airborne troops during the 1930s. In May 1940, in the early stages of their campaign against Belgium and France, the Germans demonstrated the value of parachute and glider troops when they used them to capture a formidable Belgian border fort, Eben Emael.

A year before that dramatic incident, the War Department had begun to consider the possibility of parachuting a small force, to be quickly reinforced by other troops flown in and landed, behind enemy lines. On May 1, 1939, Major General Robert M. Beck, assistant chief of staff for operations and training, ordered the chief of infantry to study this concept. When the chief of infantry asked for transport planes, Beck forwarded the request to the chief of the Air Corps. The Air Corps involvement became the sticking point. The Air Corps Board at Maxwell Field had made a study of efforts to develop airborne troops in Europe and had been unimpressed. However, the commandant of the Air Corps Tactical School disagreed and wanted their branch, not the infantry, to organize such a group. Hap Arnold then concluded that the Air Corps Board and the Infantry Board should do a joint study but that nothing should be done unless the chief of staff ordered further consideration.

A few months later, in early January 1940, General Marshall apparently pushed the issue. The Infantry Board at Fort Benning came up with a plan by the end of February, and in mid-March the chief of infantry recommended the organization of a test platoon. Throughout these months, a courtly major in the chief of infantry's office, William C. Lee, was a key supporter of the concept. On June 25 the adjutant general ordered the formation of a test platoon with all personnel to come from the 29th Infantry, the school troops at Fort Benning.[49]

Bill Ryder and Bill Yarborough, who had returned from the Philippines in the spring, were in that regiment awaiting assignment to the next class in the Infantry School. Ryder, who had done some flying as an observer in the Philippines, was particularly impressed with the possibilities of airborne warfare and had written several memos to the Infantry Board on the organization, equipment, and training of a parachute unit. He reminded the regimental commander of his research and great interest in this when he sent in his formal application on June 29. Bill Yarborough also volunteered, but neither he nor Ryder thought that they had much chance of being selected, since both were married and had children. They did make a pact, however, that if one were selected, he would try to get the other assigned as soon as possible.

Since there was little basis on which to choose between the lieutenants who volunteered, the Infantry Board decided to test their knowledge of airborne warfare. As it happened, the officer who made up the test relied in part on Ryder's memos. Not surprisingly, Bill made the highest grade. On July 1 he was elated when he got a phone call: "Ryder, come right on over, you've been selected and our first job is to write a TO&E (Table of Organization and Equipment) for the platoon." On the same day, regimental Special Order No. 127 announced the names of the six sergeants and 42 privates first class and privates who would make up the platoon.[50]

They moved into tents near Lawson Field on the Benning reservation and promptly began a rigorous eight-week training program. While there were physical conditioning and instruction in tactics and demolitions, the focus was on parachute packing, preparation for jumping (which included a week in Hightstown, New Jersey, where they made controlled jumps off the 250-foot towers similar to the ones used for entertainment at the New York World's Fair), and, finally the actual jumps—five in all. For instruction in parachute packing and maintenance as well as the jumping, they depended on Warrant Officer Harry "Tug" Wilson and four riggers who came down from Chanute Field. As riggers, they were experienced parachutists.

After a couple of weeks, Ryder went to the Infantry Board and requested that another officer be assigned in case he was injured. True to his promise, he requested Yarborough, but the 29th's colonel, who had just ordered Bill to Camp Jackson, refused to release him. Ryder then asked for and got Second Lieutenant James A. Bassett, who joined the platoon and completed the training.

By mid-August the time had come to jump. The night before, Bill received word that because of a defect in the stitching, the parachutes had been recalled for checking. Since it would take at least a couple of days to check and, if necessary, repair the chutes, Ryder decided to give his men a two-day pass rather than keep them waiting on the post. On the morning of the initial jump, August 16, he went up first. As the B-18 flew at 1,500 feet over the cleared field adjacent to Lawson Field, Bill had three major concerns. Most of all, he wanted to make a good

Bill Ryder (extreme right) and his platoon board the plane for another jump, Lawson Field, Georgia, October 19, 1940. Their instructor, Harry Wilson (in uniform), stands at the door. Courtesy of William T. Ryder.

impression on his men. Then he worried about fouling his chute and, finally, about not landing properly. All went well, and he never forgot the absolute "silence" and the feeling that "you really don't want to come down." And the landing was "very easy."

He went back up to stand by the door and watch the reactions of his men as Tug Wilson, the jump master on the other side of the door, yelled "Go!" and slapped them on the rump. The most taxing moment of the day came when the first man, who had won the post by lottery and had turned down a hundred-dollar offer to yield it, refused to jump. Visions of five or six or more also refusing, which would possibly result in a "hell of a stigma," worried Bill. But William N. "Red" King stepped up and promptly jumped, as did every one else in the platoon. It was well that they did, as the chief of infantry had already recommended forming a battalion of parachute troops.[51]

With training and qualifying jumps done, Bassett took some of the men to Chanute for training in rigging while Ryder set about creating a parachute school. On October 1 the battalion was activated with Major William M. Miley, athletic officer at Fort Benning, as its commander. Meantime both Bill Ryder and Bill Yarborough had received their promotions to captain. Then Yarborough succeeded in getting back to Benning and completed his jump training in January and took command of a company in the 501st Parachute Battalion. Already plans for more battalions and a Provisional Parachute Group with Bill Lee as the commander were under way.

In those formative days, Yarborough's inventiveness served the new arm well. He designed the "jump wings" insignia, boots, and a coverall for jumping and took out a patent with Tug Wilson for a multipurpose parachute-delivery container. He also wrote articles about the parachutists who were becoming famous. *Life* magazine featured a paratrooper on the cover of the May 12, 1941, issue and had several pages of photos. Hollywood paid tribute as RKO Pictures sent a film crew to Benning to get action shots for *Parachute Battalion,* with Bill standing in for Robert Preston in two jumps.[52]

At West Point, Jim Gavin, who was teaching tactics, studied the action at Eben Emael as well as the works of the British military writer J. F. C. Fuller and the tactics of Stonewall Jackson at Second Manassas, and grasped the common threads of mobility and deep penetration. Such tactics were apparently the future of war, and he wanted to be a part of it. While he studied history and current events and taught cadets, he also corresponded with Ryder and Yarborough about developments at Benning. Mindful of the necessity for good physical condition, he secretly jogged on trails through the woods of the Military Academy reservation. In those days, jogging was so rare that "people would think you were crazy" if they saw you running.

In the spring of 1941 he applied for assignment to the parachute troops and was chagrined when the superintendent did not endorse the request because he wanted to keep him as a teacher. To make the turndown more galling, the superintendent added: "he is not peculiarly fitted for this type of duty." Disappointed but not shaken in his resolve, Jim went to the War Department to see if a friend could get him a suitable replacement in the Tactics Department while Ryder urged Bill

Lee to work for Gavin's transfer. Their efforts paid off, and Jim was able to complete his parachute qualification by the end of the summer. Assigned as a company commander in one of the newly formed battalions, Gavin did not stay long, since he was promoted to major. Both Ryder and Yarborough used their influence with Lee to have Jim assigned as the S-3 (organization and training officer) of the Provisional Parachute Group. On the basis of their acquaintance with him in the Philippines, they were convinced that he was the best man to develop training and tactical doctrine. During his first months as S-3, Gavin wrote *Tactics and Technique of Air-Borne Troops,* which was later published as *Field Manual 31-30.* To fight in the war of rapid movement that he envisioned, parachute troops had to be self-reliant and flexible. Organization, equipment, training, and tactics should all be focused to those ends. In late November the 502d Parachute Battalion jumped en masse at Fort Bragg, North Carolina. As chief umpire of the exercise, Jim oversaw the troops practicing offensive and defensive actions. This was the largest such jump to date, but within a few months airborne regiments emerged and, before too long, divisions. Airborne was definitely on its way.[53]

✤

The rapid expansion during the mobilization and the changes in organization, armament, and equipment that accompanied it were stressful for many of the old enlisted regulars. Although there were promotions for many and commissions for a few, many mourned the disappearance of their world of the garrison Army. Some were unable to keep up with the great changes while others recognized the opportunity. After almost a quarter of a century at West Point, William L. Banks left the Cavalry Detachment to be a sergeant in a newly organized field artillery unit at Fort Sill, Oklahoma. Within a few months he became a first sergeant. Norbert L. Craine, who had been first sergeant of a company in the 29th Infantry for fifteen years at Fort Benning, went to Camp Blanding, Florida, as a sergeant major in November 1940 and was later given a reserve commission as a captain. Al Zawadski became a first sergeant in the Third Armored Division and eventually went to Officers Candidate School and earned a commission in the summer of 1942.[54]

When Staff Sergeant Victor Vogel saw a War Department letter in 1940 offering regular enlisted men the opportunity to apply for commissions, he applied. After a few weeks without hearing anything, he went to San Francisco to check at an administrative headquarters. Elated to hear that he would soon receive a commission as a first lieutenant, he started back to the bus station. En route a man stopped him and asked where he should sign up. Vogel did not know what he was talking about. Taken aback, the civilian answered: "The draft." The sergeant had never heard of it. After buying a newspaper that headlined the Selective Service registration, Vogel realized what "a secluded world" the Army was.[55]

Even before the avalanche of draftees and National Guardsmen hit the Army in the fall of 1940, there had been great changes. The change in organization from four to three regiments in the infantry divisions, and the accompanying reorganization on down the line to squad level, affected all soldiers, who had to learn the appropriate new drill. At the same time there was a spate of new weapons. Field artillerymen had to begin working with 105mm howitzers instead of the World War–vintage French 75s. Infantrymen who were used to the Springfield '03 rifle, the Browning automatic rifle (BAR), the water-cooled heavy .30-caliber machine gun, and the Stokes mortar kept the machine gun but replaced the Springfield with the M-1 Garand, the Stokes with the new 60mm mortar, and received an improved version of the BAR as well as a new air-cooled light .30-caliber machine gun and the M-1 carbine.[56]

There was grousing among the men who bore the brunt of these changes. The Garand was not as well balanced as the Springfield and did not seem to have its pinpoint accuracy. Besides, who knew what a recruit might do with a rifle that had semiautomatic capability. The M-1's saving grace was that, after firing, its recoil did not pound the shoulder as severely as the Springfield. The new squad drill looked awkward to those used to the old, and there was concern that promoting the squad leader from corporal to sergeant might go to his head. The most impressive change was in the daily routine of soldiering. No longer were there free afternoons or an emphasis on intramural athletics. The focus was squarely on strenuous training.[57]

Mixing draftees with cadres of old soldiers was a hectic experience for both. By mid-1941, draftees made up from a quarter to half of the men in regular divisions, which made more of an impact than the Guardsmen who were called into active service in their separate units. Tension and friction were inevitable as these civilians moved into the barracks and became a part of the squads and sections of the combat units. In the fall of 1941, the War Department created a Research Branch in the Morale Division to determine the extent of this disruption. They made their first major survey on December 8, 1941, the day after Pearl Harbor, when a team questioned members of an infantry division.[58]

What they found was not surprising. There was a clash of cultures between the military and the civilian worlds that the regulars and the draftees represented. Those who had volunteered had served longer and, in many cases, considered the Army their career. The draftees were basically concerned with getting back to civilian life. Aside from homesickness and the lack of privacy in the squad bays and open toilets in the barracks, there were the hierarchical authoritarian structure, the discipline, the regimentation, the deeply rooted traditional way of doing even the most minute task, the demand for "spit and polish," and, of course, close-order drill. There was a lot they did not like about the Army.[59]

As far as many draftees were concerned, the regulars in their units only made their lives worse. Usually their immediate superiors, who supervised and instructed them, were recently promoted regulars. These men generally were not as well educated as the draftees. To make the situation more difficult in the new units, the cadres often did not consist of the best of the regulars. A new field artillery battalion commander reported that the nineteen NCOs he received were drunks. An infantry company commander was unhappy with his first sergeant, who had a third-grade education and who had spent most of his twenty years of service tending the furnaces in officers' quarters. Later the War Department put a stop to the older units using cadres to get rid of less desirable soldiers. In the first survey made by the Research Branch, 32 percent of the draftees were high school graduates and another 16 percent had completed college, with the comparable regulars' education levels respectively 20 and 3 percent. The researchers found that the sergeants had the least education of any of the enlisted men; a third had not gone beyond grade school. One of the draftees complained: "It doesn't do any good to be bossed by men inferior in every way except length of service." Another pointed out: "There is no more reason for making a fifteen year Pfc a staff sergeant than there is in making a ditch digger a construction engineer."[60]

In turn, the regulars deplored the loss of the stability that had under-girded the Army before the mobilization. They thought the draftees were treated better than they had been when they were recruits, and there was a lessening of the discipline and a corresponding decline in the authority of noncoms. They believed that this was a blow to general morale and the professionalism and esprit that they had known before the influx of the civilians. One old soldier groused that the selectees "gripe too much," while another believed that many were "too smart for their own good."[61]

Some of the regulars did not share this dark view of the newcomers. George Waple, who had dropped out of high school to enlist in 1938 in the Third Cavalry, was promoted to corporal just before a group of one-year volunteers joined his troop. At nineteen he was in charge of the training of the twelve new recruits. He thought they were "a great bunch of men." Gene E. Harris, who had been in the 11th Infantry two years before the draft, thought this infusion "upgraded" the Army. "We had college men as riflemen. We could solve problems that weren't written in manuals. We were moving into situations that require think-ing on our own. The spit & polish, the parade ground drill was another world. We were moving into combat."[62]

As the nation prepared for war, it was obvious that blacks would be involved. To be sure, a Texas senator called up memories of the Browns-ville and Houston riots in an effort to bar an antidiscrimination clause in the Selective Service bill, but Congress easily overruled him. The gov-ernment, its military services, and most whites nevertheless supported segregation and assumed that this would not change. Many blacks, how-ever, hoped that the emergency would open up an opportunity to im-prove their situation.

As early as 1937, Army mobilization regulations specified that blacks be represented in the same proportion as their percentage of the total population and that they serve in combat as well as service branches except for the Air Corps. There was a qualification—"Unless conditions require modification in the interests of national defense"—and the 1940 detailed plan had only 5.8 percent blacks in organizations—considerably less than the 10 percent population ratio. Black leaders pressed for appropriate representation in all branches of the Army as well as for desegregation. The presidential election of 1940, in the midst of the mobilization, worked to blacks' advantage when they presented their case to President Franklin D. Roosevelt, who was running for an unprecedented third term. A few weeks before the election, Roosevelt agreed to their recommendations except the crucial one of desegregation. His decision was helped by the announcement of the appointment of William H. Hastie, dean of Howard University Law School, who had been the first black federal judge, as adviser to the secretary of war and the nomination of Benjamin O. Davis for promotion to brigadier general.

There had been a black civilian adviser to the secretary during World War I, but there had never been a black general in the Army. The black press was enthusiastic. Davis was very surprised. He was then serving as the instructor and colonel of the black National Guard regiment in New York City. Since mandatory retirement was only a few months away, he assumed that this was his last assignment. He had never voted and evidently had no inkling that politics might bring about his promotion. The response of friends must have pleased him. The new general, who had served his entire career as one of fewer than ten blacks in the regular officer corps, had achieved his position despite overwhelming odds, but to him the reason was clear: "I did my duty. That is what I set out to do—to show that I could make my way if I knew my job."[63]

In January 1941 Davis took command of a brigade of the Second Cavalry Division at Fort Riley. The Ninth and Tenth Cavalry regiments, which were being brought up to strength, made up his command. Except for his son, who served as his aide, and some chaplains and medical officers, all the officers under his command were white. Off duty, there was no socializing aside from formal calls. Since Davis was slated to retire in June, his command time was limited. However, when he did retire, he was immediately called back to active duty to serve as an inspector general and adviser on racial relations and issues.[64]

Many blacks were eager to enlist in the Army, as it offered more economic security, better opportunity for advancement, and more general respect than virtually all available civilian jobs. In the summer of

1940, when the War Department organized additional regular black units—a field artillery regiment, two coast artillery regiments, and several quartermaster and chemical companies—blacks flocked to recruiting stations. With the advent of Selective Service that fall, the Army created another four regiments and assorted other black units to accommodate the draftees. The change in the number of blacks in the Army was impressive. In the summer of 1939, 3,640 blacks were on duty. By the end of November 1941, the total had increased almost twenty-seven times, to 97,725. Yet the ratio to white soldiers did not fulfill the Army's, and the president's, commitment. The black increase in the percentage of the total Army was from 2 percent in 1939 to just under 6 percent two years later. And, whatever advantages the Army offered over civilian life, it remained segregated.[65]

George Marshall spoke for the Army, the president, and the majority of the whites of that period when he reminisced about the segregation issue: "there was no hope of settling that at that time . . . we had enough on our hands to get a fighting Army." He realized that this was an outrageous denial of equal rights, but he could not see the military moving beyond its civilian masters in this regard. As it was, maintaining segregation led to difficulties in proper assignments for the great influx of volunteers and draftees, in providing cadres for their training as well as separate housing and locating camps. He did come to believe that his decision to send northern blacks into southern camps was "one of the most important mistakes I made in the mobilization." The blacks bore the burden of that mistake as well as of segregation. For the Army, keeping blacks in segregated units and separate housing, however, was a bureaucratic problem. Locating camps for large numbers of blacks was a political problem; many communities objected to having black units stationed in their vicinity. Yet it was the black volunteer or draftee who was assigned to a segregated unit who wound up not being sent to a camp because there was not enough segregated housing, or who went to another post because of its isolation—such as Fort Huachuca in the Arizona desert.[66]

To complicate matters even more, white stereotypes of all blacks as uneducated southern farm laborers were wide of the mark in the early 1940s. In contrast to the blacks in the Army during World War I, those who entered the service in the later period were better educated, and a significantly larger number lived in the north. In World War I, 86 percent of northern black soldiers and 97 percent of those from the South had only a grade-school education or less. A generation later the Army found that 37 percent of the northern blacks and 67 percent of the southerners were in this low-education category. And, as compared to 20 percent of the black soldiers from the North at the earlier time, 32 percent claimed northern residence in 1941.[67]

Blacks who wound up in southern camps were subjected to Jim Crow rules of segregated seating on trains and buses and facilities and to white law officers and civilians, who might take offense at any breach of local laws and customs. Anger was endemic, and violence could explode at any time. At Fort Benning, Georgia, a black private was lynched in the spring of 1941 on the reservation, and the crime remained unsolved. At Fayetteville, near Fort Bragg in North Carolina, during that summer there were several incidents involving white military policemen and black soldiers. The explosion came when MPs boarded a bus and attempted to quiet down an unruly group of drunken black soldiers by beating them with their clubs. One of the blacks grabbed a policeman's pistol and opened fire. One black and one white were killed and several others wounded in the melee. General Davis led the resulting investigation. Although he understood the significance of racism in the situation, he blamed poor leadership by local commanders.[68]

Training of the black units suffered because of a shortage of qualified cadres. There were too few regulars, and most of them had spent much of their time looking after horses and performing service chores. None had the background to serve as cadre for artillery or engineer units. Although the Army did send white NCOs to cadre the new coast artillery regiments, it still called on the Ninth and Tenth Cavalry and the 24th and 25th Infantry for cadres for other new units. This policy affected the training of these old units once they were brought up to wartime strength and began their own combat training. Then, cadres were taken from the newly organized units to go to more recently created organizations.

William Banks's experience reflects the turbulence of those days. After twenty-four years at West Point, he was selected to go to the field artillery regiment organized at Fort Sill in August 1940. He went as a supply sergeant while others from his detachment at West Point became first sergeants. Within a few months he also made first sergeant. In 1942, selected again for a cadre, he left this unit to report to Fort Huachuca, where he had served as a trooper some thirty years earlier. From there he went to Camp Atterbury as a battalion sergeant major for another field artillery regiment. Age caught up with him. The strenuous training was too much. "I thought I was in good physical condition but the muscles in both my legs would freeze on me." In the spring of 1943, at fifty, he retired as a master sergeant with thirty years of service.[69]

While Sergeant Banks was in the last phase of his military career, Vernon Baker began his in the summer of 1941. Unlike Banks, who had grown up in a segregated southern community, Baker was from Cheyenne, Wyoming. He spent a couple of years at Father Flanagan's Boys' Town in Nebraska and later graduated from high school in Iowa. He shined shoes and worked as a porter on the Union Pacific Railroad, so he knew and understood the limits that racism imposed. At his sister's urging, he considered enlisting in the Army because it offered not only a good, steady job but also, he thought, respect. Initially turned away because there were no vacancies, he succeeded on his next attempt in June 1941.

After a few days at Fort Leavenworth, he was sent to Camp Wolters, Texas, for basic training. It amazed and irritated him to have to move to a segregated rail car in Kansas, but an incident after his arrival in Texas infuriated him. He boarded a bus and promptly sat down behind the driver. The man turned and shouted: "Hey, Nigger. Get up and get to the back of the bus where you belong!" Baker leaped up and clenched his fist. An old black man restrained him. "You planning to die your first day in Texas?" The man calmed him down and then explained the customs of segregation. Baker learned to live with these humiliations, but his anger seethed.[70]

Meanwhile blacks in the military realized some progress during the mobilization period. The Army had opened up branches such as the Air Corps, which had heretofore been closed, and had promised appropriate representation throughout the Army. The Tuskegee pilot training program, the appointment of Dean Hastie, and the promotion of General Davis were causes for pride. But segregation remained, and several of the president's promises were unfulfilled. Increasingly, Hastie's constant hammering on the issue of segregation caused the civilian and military leaders in the War Department to dismiss his views as impractical.

Meantime, they accepted and worked with Davis, who worked within the system. Later the *Pittsburgh Courier,* a popular black newspaper, demanded victory over enemies abroad and victory over racism at home—"Double V"—but the time had not yet come for such a drastic reform.[71]

✦

In late November 1939 Thelma Fadner Watson wrote a long, newsy letter to her parents. She enjoyed life at Schofield Barracks and was looking forward to returning to the States the next summer, but she was not sure what she would return to. "We hear so much about upheavals in the Army at home." Some officers were unable to take their families with them to new assignments, while others were unable to get quarters on post. Mobilization was making life uncertain not only for those in uniform but also for their families. As Eleanor Mathews Sliney, whose husband was an instructor in the Field Artillery School at Fort Sill, noted, "the short, sharp tempo of preparedness" interrupted the peaceful routine they had known for so many years. Virginia Weisel Johnson liked Fort Warren, Wyoming, but the 20th Infantry was gone much of the time. "The few brief moments I saw Johnny, I felt I should shake his hand and introduce myself."[72]

Benny Bolté and her family had become comfortable in Washington. Charlie's assignments as a student and instructor at the Army War College, followed by a brief tour in the office of the chief of the Air Corps, kept them there for four years. The mobilization caught up with the newly promoted lieutenant colonel when he was ordered to Jacksonville, Florida, as the operations and training officer in the Fourth Corps in the fall of 1940. There were no government quarters, so they had to search for a home. David was in the tenth grade in Hill School in Pottstown, Pennsylvania, hence could be with them only during vacations; but the younger children, Phil and Damara, remained. Benny was athletic, and she knew the children would also enjoy the ocean, so they settled in Atlantic Beach in a house just fifty yards from the ocean. She and the children swam every day. Since they had only one car, Charlie usually commuted by bus twenty-three miles to his office. In May 1941 the War Department sent him on a special observer's mission to London. In the following months, when neither he nor Benny knew when he would return or where he would go if he did return, she opted to stay in Atlantic Beach with the children. She had spent her life in the Army, hence had no family home. As David recalled, "It was a civilian world and we were not civilians."[73]

The last years of the 1930s were a time of major life changes for Mauree Pickering Mahin. Two of her daughters married, and her father died. She liked the two years she spent at Fort Snelling, while Frank enjoyed being back with a regiment again. In 1937 they moved to Indianapolis, where for three years he was senior instructor with the National Guard. In September 1940 Mahin, now a colonel, went to Fort Bragg to take command of the 60th Infantry, which, like the rest of the Ninth Division, was just organizing. His brigade commander was Forrest Harding, who was highly impressed with him. Since quarters were not available on post, Mauree found a house at Pinehurst, fifty miles away. Frank was working night and day with his regiment, so he came home only a couple of times a week. In May 1941 the Mahins learned that they could get quarters on the post in the middle of the summer, so they gave up the house. Before they were able to move, their third daughter, Elizabeth, announced that she was getting married. Although they had no home, the Mahins decided to have the wedding at Bragg. They stayed with friends who rallied together with the commanding general and other friends to furnish all that they needed for the occasion. As Mauree remembered, "Nothing was ours except the Bride!"[74]

The Watsons were also in the Ninth Division at Fort Bragg, where Bob commanded a company in the 39th Infantry. It was a hectic time. As the tempo of training increased, Bob, who had only three regular NCOs to help train a company of draftees, could not get home very often. After almost a year with little social life and no servant to help with the housework, Thelma was depressed. The basic problem, however, was "always the nagging fear that he will be sent to some damned outpost where I can't go, or—war. I think, & so does Bob, that next spring may see an American Expeditionary Force setting sail for somewhere."[75]

On Corregidor in the summer of 1940, Grace Weaver wrote her parents: "Every day we get bigger and bigger rumors over here. Most of them not true." She and her family were scheduled to go home in a few months. In December General Marshall decided to make a basic shift in War Department policy about the defense of the Philippines.

Doubling the number of Philippine Scouts, building up the strength of the 31st Infantry, and shipping antiaircraft guns as well as constructing additional airfields were hardly enough to make the islands appear invincible to the Japanese. But they did indicate a recognition of the threat. Just before the Weavers' transport was due to sail in February, the increased defense effort changed their plans. The doctor would have to stay. "Every thing is in a turmoil over here," she wrote on February 17, 1941. "No one seems to know anything other than that gradually the women and children are being evacuated."[76]

The evacuation orders were a complete surprise to Nancy Taylor, the seventeen-year-old daughter of an officer stationed at Philippine Department headquarters. "I was having the time of my life when orders came . . . I was devastated." Although Navy dependents had begun to leave in November, the first group of Army wives and children did not leave until February. Nancy and her mother boarded the transport *Republic* in May. The band on the Manila pier played "Harbor Lights" as all said tearful goodbyes. Nancy stared at the pier until it disappeared in the distance as the ship headed out to sea.[77]

✶

From 1898 to 1941, two momentous developments—the emergence of the United States as a world power and a revolution in warfare—radically changed the Army. After more than a century as a frontier constabulary, the Army defeated the Spanish in Cuba and the Philippines, then battled nationalists and other foes in the latter, and established garrisons there as well as in Hawaii and later in Panama. In 1917 President Woodrow Wilson deemed it necessary to intervene in order to defeat the Germans in the World War. Within eighteen months, a massive mobilization raised and transported two million American soldiers to France to tip the balance on the Western Front. From the continental perspective of policing the frontier and maintaining a tiny coastal defense force, the Army planners had to expand their vision to consider the possibilities of fighting wars across not only the Pacific but also the Atlantic.

Technology precipitated the revolution in warfare. Tanks and trucks replaced horses and wagons, while the airplane came into its own, resulting in the organizations of Armored Force and Air Force. A poignant example of the relative brevity of that more-than-four-decade span occurred in the War Department in the spring of 1943. Major General Guy V. Henry, who had graduated from West Point in 1898, fought in the Philippines, and devoted his life to horses through his service as chief of cavalry, had come out of retirement to head the Inter-Allied Personnel Board. It fell to him to interview Bill Dunn, who sought a pilot's rating and a captaincy in the Air Force after becoming the first ace in the Eagle Squadron of the RAF. He had also been an infantryman in both the American and Canadian armies. Henry liked Dunn's cocky attitude and saw that he got his American wings as well as captain's bars. In parting, he paid him his highest compliment: "In the old days you'd have made a good cavalryman."[78]

While machine guns and high-trajectory field artillery guns predated the Spanish-American War, they continued to improve and forced planners to come up with new tactics for the combat arms. Field telephones and radios facilitated control and made possible the development of the rapid concentration of massed artillery fire. The use of poison gas in World War I led to the organization of a chemical corps to prepare to use and defend against that terrible weapon.

Fortunately, on the verge of these great changes, the Army had as secretary of war a man who grasped the necessity for change and created institutions required to deal with this new world. By stating the Army's purpose—"the real object of having an Army is to provide for war"—and adding that "the regular establishment in the United States will probably never be by itself the whole machine with which any war will be fought," Elihu Root fixed the course for the twentieth century. During his five years in the War Department he worked with Congress to standardize the state militias and to establish a chief of staff and General Staff to coordinate the Army's activities. He created the Army War College, which he envisioned as the keystone of an educational system for officers. After graduates demonstrated their value during the World War, the school system became increasingly important in the next two decades, when there was time for study and academic work, since, for the first time in the nation's history, there was real peace. Captains learned how to handle divisions on paper, and majors became familiar with theoretical corps and field armies as well as national strategic thought in classrooms. As Omar Bradley pointed out, "Those of us who wanted to get ahead studied at home a lot."[79]

The soldiers' work changed as many had to deal with the new technological developments. Some became airplane mechanics, others operated the new communication systems, while many learned how to drive trucks and tanks. Cavalrymen had to give up their horses, while infantrymen mastered the new machine guns and mortars. A few even began jumping out of airplanes. For all that, there was a sameness about soldiering: discipline, regimentation, drills, and barracks life.

There was also a sameness about garrison life that wives and children experienced in their "world within the world," as a *Fortune* magazine writer described it. Unlike their civilian cousins, they moved frequently—on occasion to exotic locales—and, as they came to realize during the Depression, they had basic security that was lacking outside. For the officers and their wives, there was a social whirl that few middle-class civilians could have afforded.[80]

Most civilians had little knowledge of and less interest in the regulars. This was a reflection of the traditional antimilitary sentiment that dated back to the animosity toward the British occupying troops in the decade before the War of Independence. In war, of course, there was enthusiasm for the soldiery; after all, most of those who fought were civilians temporarily in uniform. This mood quickly evaporated with demobilization. As Secretary of War John W. Weeks pointed out in 1921, "The American people are traditionally opposed to the existence of a large standing army."[81]

Despite the great changes in the early twentieth century in their country's position on the world scene and in the tools of warfare, Americans' traditional antimilitary view remained essentially the same. *Fortune* magazine made the point more succinctly in 1935: "nobody loves the Army. In peace it all but rots." The fact that the War Department's relative share of federal expenditures in the 1920s and 1930s was smaller than in the 1880s, as it plunged to about half (7.2 percent) of the earlier figure in 1936, shows that Congress responded to the national will to put as little money as possible in the Army. In the same period, however, the percentage of the labor force in the military tripled from 1890 to 1939 (.06 percent). This still was a force so small that many civilians, like their ancestors, probably never saw a regular.[82]

This situation changed drastically in the mobilization of 1939–1941. For the first time in the nation's history, there was a large peacetime mobilization and conscription. Although political debate continued throughout this period as to whether there was a real emergency and as to the necessity of military preparation, the Army increased from what had been essentially a third-rate-power strength to just under nine-fold—almost 1,650,000 officers and men. In July 1941 George Marshall looked back on the expansion and hailed the regulars' contribution as "the invaluable leaven . . . without which developments to date would have been impossible." To him, it was clear that "what has happened is history."[83]

While the regulars prepared for war, their families coped with the demands of the crisis. Amidst the tumult of the great changes, few had the time or the inclination to look back as they anticipated the uncertain future. Years later, Virginia Weisel Johnson came to understand the significance of the occasion when she and her husband left Fort Warren, Wyoming, just as the bugles sounded retreat. As was the custom, they stood at attention. "Although we didn't realize it . . . we had seen the last of the 'old' Army."[84]

On December 7, 1941, the war came.

Postscript

O N A COLD Saturday afternoon in April 1940, Sandy Nininger sat
in his room at West Point and wrote a letter to his parents. A
tall, quiet, sensitive man, Alexander R. Nininger Jr. impressed his fellow
cadets with his interest in art, books, music, and the theater. On this
afternoon, however, the war in Europe engrossed him. After the recent
German invasion of Norway, he wrote his family that "heated argument, wild conjecture, and excited rumors" were circulating throughout
the cadet corps. He pondered the meaning of the war to him and his
fellows. "My generation . . . is faced with a future of burden, despair,
and disillusionment, a future that we feel holds bottomless pits, that
may cease abruptly for any one of us at any time."

When he graduated fourteen months later, war was much closer to
the United States. Sandy chose infantry as his branch and volunteered
for the Philippines. After a brief course at the Infantry School at Fort
Benning, he sailed for Manila and joined the 57th Infantry, a Scout
regiment. On January 12, 1942, in the bitter fighting on Bataan, he volunteered to take out some snipers. Killed in the ensuing fight, he was
the first soldier to be awarded the Medal of Honor in World War II.[1]

The war that had seemed such an exciting prospect to Jimmy Collins
and his three companions when they toured Europe in the summer of
1939 did prove to be exciting, but it also held its share of tragedy. Jimmy
led a field artillery battalion in the fighting in Europe, while George
Zethren commanded a bomber squadron, and Charles Bowman was
killed in a bombing raid over Germany. Harry Kinnard wound up besieged in Bastogne during the Battle of the Bulge. As operations officer
of the 101st Airborne Division, he suggested to the division commander,
Tony McAuliffe, that he use his impulsive response "Nuts" as his formal
reply to the German request for surrender.[2]

And so the regulars scattered throughout the great Army that fought
in World War II. The irrepressible Buck Lanham, whom a difficult

colonel initiated into the Army, commanded the 22d Infantry, which fought one of the most terrible battles of the war, in the Huertgen Forest. He won the admiration of the novelist and war correspondent Ernest Hemingway. Some forty-six years after he attempted to go to war with his father's company in 1898, Brigadier General Gardiner Helmick led the Fifth Corps artillery from Normandy into the heart of Germany. Benjamin O. Davis earned the respect of those with whom he came into contact as he used his position as an inspector general to improve race relations within the Army. It must have been a great pleasure to decorate his son, Colonel Ben Davis, who won laurels as commander of the first black fighter squadron and group. Meantime Noel Parrish, as a colonel, remained in command of the Tuskegee training program throughout the war [3]

Although the pace of the prewar mobilization had shaken the Army out of its peacetime routine, it picked up dramatically after Pearl Harbor. By the spring of 1945 more than 8 million men were in the mightiest force in the nation's history. This expansion by a factor of more than forty since the fall of 1939 illustrates the enormity of the complex tasks involved in organizing and bringing this force to bear on the Japanese and the Germans. In March 1945, with American troops across the Rhine, Prime Minister Winston Churchill congratulated George Marshall and hailed him as "the true organizer of victory."[4]

Shortly after the war, when Churchill visited the Pentagon and talked with the chiefs of services, he expressed amazement at the speed with which the United States had expanded its small peacetime force into a "mighty army." It was "an achievement which the soldiers of every other country will always study with admiration and with envy." Even more stunning, however, was the emergence of the large numbers of commanders and staffs "capable of handling enormous masses." He confessed that this was a "mystery as yet unexplained."[5]

The generals present at that meeting could have told him. Virtually all the senior commanders and key staff officers had spent their adult lives in the Regular Army. Many of them had known each other at one or more stages of their careers. Over the years of working together, they measured each other's character, dedication, and ability. The round of assignments with increasing responsibilities helped shape them. But, most of all, the schools gave them the vision of what should be done in war when they would be called upon to plan for vast operations and lead huge organizations. Even before the war began, George Marshall had seen enough of the conduct of the graduates in handling great responsibilities during the mobilization to assert that the school system "had declared a huge dividend."[6]

From December 1941 to September 1945, war dominated the media, and generals made headlines. Men unknown outside garrison limits throughout much of their lives appeared on the cover of *Life* magazine: MacArthur, Eisenhower, Spaatz, Eaker, Simpson, Truscott among them. George Patton, who had graced the cover in full color during the mobilization period, appeared again during the war. He, Eisenhower, and MacArthur became as well known as the president and Hollywood stars.[7]

After years of slow promotion, when it appeared that a colonelcy was likely to be the end of a successful career, stars fell in abundance. Marshall, who remained chief of staff throughout the war, became a five-star general of the Army along with MacArthur, the supreme commander of the Southwest Pacific, Eisenhower, the supreme commander of Allied Forces in Europe, and Hap Arnold, who stayed at the helm of the Air Force until the war ended.

Devers and Bradley commanded Army groups in the campaigns in northern Europe while Mark Clark led the Fifth Army and later an Army Group in Italy; all earned four stars. As did Vinegar Joe Stilwell, the commander of the China, Burma, and India theater, who eventually led the Tenth Army on Okinawa. His successor in China was Al Wedemeyer, who wore three stars and established more congenial relations than Vinegar Joe with the Chinese.

Among the other field army commanders were Patton and Simpson. The former led a corps in North Africa, the Seventh Army in Sicily, and the Third Army in its spectacular dash across France. He won the fame he craved and became a full general. In the last weeks of the war, Simpson's Ninth spearheaded the American advance toward Berlin. He was a lieutenant general, as was Lucian Truscott, who proved to be as successful as a division, corps, and Fifth Army commander, as he had been on the polo fields during the interwar period.

Matt Ridgway led the 82d Airborne Division in Sicily and in Normandy before he became an airborne corps commander with three stars.

Lightning Joe Collins earned his nickname for the dash with which he handled the Seventh Corps in combat in Europe. He and Wade Haislip were among the lieutenant generals who commanded corps, as was Troy Middleton. Both he and Ralph Huebner had enlisted as privates in 1910, and both commanded corps, but Middleton wore three stars while Huebner had only two.

Except for two National Guardsmen, all the divisions that saw combat had regulars in command. Charlie Bolté led the 34th Division in the last nine months of the Italian campaign while Tom Finley commanded the 89th in Patton's Third Army. Twenty years after enlisting as a private, Jim Gavin succeeded Ridgway as commander of the 82d Airborne Division. At thirty-seven he was one of the youngest major generals, and under his command the 82d Airborne added to its laurels as one of the most celebrated divisions in the Army.

Ira Eaker's first impulse when he heard about Pearl Harbor was to call Hap Arnold. Tooey Spaatz answered the phone.[8] The two were together in England at the beginning of the American bombardment campaign. Eaker, who became a lieutenant general, commanded the Eighth Air Force while Tooey with four stars headed the Strategic Air Force. As major generals and commanders, respectively, of the IX and XIX Tactical Air Commands, Pete Quesada and O. P. Weyland deviated from the Air Force emphasis on strategic bombardment. Quesada commanded the air cover at D-Day and pioneered close air-support techniques in Normandy. He continued to support the First Army after the breakout from the beachhead while Weyland helped clear the way for Patton's Third Army. Colonel Jake Smart, the fighter pilot who enjoyed his Panama tour so much, was a key staff officer in the Pentagon and then commanded a bomber group and wound up as a prisoner of war.

As he predicted to Mark Clark, Lesley McNair never got combat command, but he was wounded while observing the fighting in North Africa and ultimately killed by American bombs in Normandy. Mauree Mahin's husband, Frank Mahin, got a second star and division command in the spring of 1942 but lost his life in an air crash that summer. The war continued for Mauree, who had two sons-in-law in uniform and a son who graduated from West Point in time to fight in Europe.

One of the most charming men in the Army as well as a leading interwar intellectual, Forrest Harding led the 32d Division in the Buna campaign in New Guinea but was not given the support he considered necessary to overcome the Japanese. MacArthur relieved him, but he retained his two stars. Carlos Brewer, who deserved much of the credit for developing the Time on Target technique that gave American artillery the ability to concentrate and mass fire rapidly, had an Armored Division in training but lost his two stars because his division did not meet the appropriate status for overseas service. Later he got to Europe as a field artillery group commander.

As the Seventh Army's engineer, Gar Davidson wore a star and demonstrated as much competence in that capacity as he had shown as coach of the Army football team during the 1930s. Doc Martin was wounded as a battalion commander in North Africa but returned to combat as a colonel in command of the Seventh Armored Division's artillery in the fighting at St. Vith during the Battle of the Bulge. Bill Yarborough participated in the first combat jump in North Africa and fought in Italy while Bill Ryder headed the Jump School at Benning. Both became colonels and regimental commanders.

When the Japanese attacked Hawaii, James Jones, who was at Schofield Barracks, pondered the meaning of this attack. "I remember thinking . . . that none of our lives would ever be the same." He was later wounded in the fighting on Guadalcanal. After the war, he wrote *From Here to Eternity* and other novels that made him one of the nation's leading authors. Many noncoms such as Al Zawadski, Mike Varhol, Francis Walski, Norbert Craine, and Lawrence Curtis became officers. Charles Willeford stayed in the ranks. As a tank commander in Patton's Army he was wounded and decorated for valor. After the war he continued in the Army but transferred to the Air Force before he retired. Then he launched a successful career as a novelist in the suspense and mystery genre.[9]

After the war, many of the regulars stayed in the Army while others served their nation in a variety of ways. After Marshall retired, Eisenhower succeeded him as chief of staff. Later he retired to become president of Columbia University before returning to uniform as the NATO commander and became president of the United States in 1953. George Marshall came out of retirement to serve as secretary of state and secretary of defense in the post-1945 era. His plan for the rehabilitation of war-torn Europe earned him the Nobel Peace Prize. Bradley,

Collins, and Ridgway were chiefs of staff, and Charlie Bolté served as vice chief of staff, while Tooey Spaatz became the first chief of staff of the independent Air Force in 1947. Troy Middleton, who had retired before the war to be a dean at Louisiana State University, retired again and went back to LSU, where he became president a few years later.

William L. Banks went back to West Point after he retired and was a civilian employee at the Military Academy until he retired again. In the adjacent community of Highland Falls, he was active in the Episcopal church and in civic affairs. George S. Schuyler, who had enlisted not long after Banks, had become an officer during World War I but left the Army and became a journalist. Active at first as a leftist and years later as a conservative, he was one of the most famous columnists in the black press.[10]

Jim Twitty transferred to the Army Air Force and stayed until retirement after the war, then launched a career as an artist. He taught at the Corcoran School of Art in Washington, D.C., for a decade and had paintings in major galleries and museums throughout the nation. Noel Parrish, who retired as a brigadier general, followed a different path in retirement. He earned a doctorate in American history at Rice University and taught at Trinity University in San Antonio and the Air War College.

Benny and Charlie Bolté retired to Alexandria, Virginia, in the mid-1950s. They kept up with many of their Old Army friends while their sons, both of whom graduated from West Point, were wounded in the Korean War and later saw combat in Vietnam, where Phil was wounded again. Benny was active in local historical and church work and continued to ride horseback for years. They lived to see both sons retire from the Army.

In the spring of 1986 Benny took the review of the Corps of Cadets at West Point on the centennial anniversary of her father's graduation. Two years later the secretary of the Army awarded her the Outstanding Civilian Service Medal as a tribute to her life's work as an "exemplary Army wife and mother . . . a role model and a standard for others to emulate." As the years passed, age brought heavier burdens. In February 1989 Charlie died at ninety-three. Benny, whose eyesight and hearing were failing, was also having trouble with back pain and began to spend much of her time in bed. David, who lived nearby, visited daily; Damara and Phil came as often as they could.

When David said to her one day that he hated to see her in such condition, she responded: "I don't know why you should when I don't mind." She was then ninety-seven and despite her physical difficulties was still mentally alert. She could no longer read or even watch television, but she told Phil: "I can lie here and reflect on all the experiences that I have had and I am not bored at all." And those experiences were many: the long voyages across the Pacific, the varied conditions of life in Leyte, China, and Alaska as well as various Stateside posts, and the stint in the mansion in Heidelberg when Charlie commanded the American troops in Europe. A few days after her ninety-eighth birthday, she died on January 8, 1998, probably the last Army wife who had lived through the radical transformation of the Army in the twentieth century.[11]

ESSAY ON SOURCES AND ACKNOWLEDGMENTS

R ATHER than provide a list of books that are already cited in the notes, I shall mention only a few published sources, focusing instead on the manuscripts, questionnaires, and interviews that I collected from participants. I also want to acknowledge the many people who have helped me in my research.

The basic source for the Regular Army's activities is the *War Department Annual Reports*. Although they are not as complete after World War I, as reports of subordinate commanders were no longer included, they remain a rich source of information. Reports by the secretary of war, the commanding general (initially), and later the chief of staff summarized major issues and policy decisions, while the adjutant general and the surgeon general provided personnel and health information. All *WDAR* citations in the notes are from the government serial set.

Another useful source, though only occasionally cited, is the *Official Army Registers*, an annual government publication containing brief career data about all regular officers. For West Pointers, a more complete source that includes assignments and their dates supplied by the graduates every decade up to 1950 is the *Biographical Register of the Officers and Graduates of the U.S. Military Academy at West Point since Its Establishment in 1802*, edited initially by George Cullum. *Who Was Who in American History: The Military* (Chicago, 1975) contains names of wives and children as well as biographical information about generals. Charles J. Sullivan, *Army Posts and Towns: The Baedeker of the Army* (Burlington, Vt., 1926), provides invaluable descriptions of the posts of that period.

I researched in several institutions but concentrated on three: the National Archives, Washington, D.C.; the U.S. Army Military History Institute (MHI), Carlisle, Pennsylvania; and the Special Collections and Archives Division of the United States Military Academy Library at West Point, New York. Throughout the more than three decades I have worked on this project, Timothy K. Nenninger has been a stalwart in finding records for me at the National Archives. At MHI and West Point, I searched for unpublished memoirs and relevant personal papers. There was also a wealth of material at MHI in the Senior Officer

Oral History Program, consisting of transcripts of interviews of retired generals by Army War College students. Richard Sommers and David Keough helped me at MHI, as did Marie Pappas Capps and Alan Aimone at the United States Military Academy (USMA). Larry I. Bland at the George C. Marshall Library (Lexington, Virginia), Duane J. Reed at the U.S. Air Force Academy Library (Colorado Springs), George Hicks of the Airmen Memorial Museum (Suitland, Maryland), and Jack Rosen at the National Jewish Welfare Board Archives (New York City) were also most helpful.

At the University of Wisconsin–Madison, I had excellent research assistants for one or two years at a time in Jerry M. Cooper, Russell Gilmore, Richard Kehrberg, and Edgar F. Raines. Others who helped in my research include William M. Belote, Thomas Buckley, Jeffrey J. Clarke, Elliott V. Converse III, Lorenzo M. Crowell, Joseph T. Glatthaar, Stacy Gran, Mark R. Grandstaff, Scott Harrison, Elliott Johnson, Brian M. Linn, Jay Luvaas, Janice McKenney, Richard B. Meixsel, Allan R. Millett, Rod Paschall, Robert D. Ramsey III, John F. Votaw, Richard Werking, and Russell F. Weigley.

During a visit to MHI in 1980, I was impressed by a typescript memoir, "The Monkeys Have No Tails in Zamboanga," by Charles F. Ivins. Witty as well as informative, this manuscript did not cover his entire career. Since his address was attached, I sent him a slate of questions. A week later I was shocked to read a newspaper story about the deaths of Colonel and Mrs. Ivins. She was an invalid, and he suffered from terminal cancer, so they made a suicide pact. When I picked up my mail that morning, I found a brief note, written the day before the day he died—"I am in a nursing home and am toting 82 years around with me. Things are difficult."—attached to three pages of answers to my questions. This episode dramatically illustrates the need to contact in a timely manner participants who can contribute to research.

I assumed from the onset of my research that I would depend a great deal on the memories of participants. Secondary and published primary sources would be the foundation, but I hoped to glean from interviews, questionnaires, and letters information that would enable me better to understand and describe the experiences of the people who lived this part of history. From earlier research, I had some interviews that proved to be helpful. In the mid-1950s I questioned Mansfield Robinson about his service in the 24th Infantry from 1889 to 1913. In my research on previous books about Peyton C. March and the American effort in World War I, I talked with Douglas MacArthur and several others whose interviews were relevant to this book. As Forrest C. Pogue's research assistant, I interviewed several people, including Benjamin D. Foulois. Most of the interviews specifically for this book were conducted in the 1970s. In addition to formal question-and-answer sessions, most of which are on tape, I took notes on conversations with a few of these people. Altogether I have interviews with more than seventy-five people. Charles DeVallon Bolles, Douglas E. Clanin, Paul J. Jacobsmeyer, James Harvey Short, Charles E. Twining, and C. Michael Williams interviewed seven people for me. Over the years I interviewed several people more than once, but Charles L. and Adelaide Poore Bolté contributed the most interviews and conversations. In the notes I have provided a date only for each of the multiple interviews and for Mrs. Bolté's two questionnaires. Esther Anken, Amy Arntsen, and Larry Bland transcribed most of these interviews.

When I considered using questionnaires, Don Rickey Jr., who had used them in his research on the Indian-fighting Army *(Forty Miles a Day on Beans and Hay)* and had prepared those used in the MHI's Spanish-American War veteran survey, advised me as to form. I gathered more than 320 from wives, children, and enlisted men. Most of these answered in the 1970s. Some of these soldiers later became officers. Responses varied from cursory comments to extensive remarks. William L. Banks, whom I also interviewed, made the most extensive comments, while Lawrence B. Curtis, Eugene G. Hogan, and James W. Twitty wrote brief memoirs. Others sent photos and other material. Mark R. Grandstaff and Brian M. Linn lent me questionnaires that they had collected in their research. Brian also let me use notes on his interview with Richard W. Ripple. Earl F. Stover gave me photocopies of chaplains' records and also sent notes on interviews with Edward Warfield (by Lee A. Thigpen Jr.) and Dorsie W. Willis (by Lewis K. Combs).

Noel F. Parrish talked with me, answered my questionnaire, and then lent me his scrapbook and gave me relevant chapters of his memoir. Elizabeth Sorley Lyon let me copy Lewis S. Sorley, "Some Recollections"; and Douglas V. Johnson Jr. gave me a copy of Douglas V. Johnson, "Keep 'em Rollin'." Garrison H. Davidson gave me copies of his and his wife's memoirs; Richard H. Groves sent copies of his grand-father's letters and his mother's memoir. I interviewed James S. Watson about his childhood in the 1930s and 1940s, and he let me copy his mother's letters. Edwin Todd Wheatley lent me his parents' scrapbook for copying. David G. Brenzel filled out a questionnaire and let me copy a brief memoir and the letters he wrote from Corregidor. William E. Carraway corresponded and lent me for copying extensive material from his years in the 15th Infantry in China. Aln D. Warnock gave me a copy of his unpublished memoir; John G. Westover sent me the section of his memoir about his Citizens' Military Training Camp experience and other pre–World War II military experiences. John F. Votaw and Charles P. Summerall III allowed me to research in the memoir of Charles P. Summerall. After a joint interview with the airborne pioneers William T. Ryder and William P. Yarbrough, the former let me copy photos and orders, while the latter and his wife, Norma Tuttle Yarbrough, lent me their scrapbook for copying. Eventually the tapes, transcripts, and research notes will go to the George C. Marshall Library in Lexington, Virginia.

In appreciation for their contributions, I list all of those who gave me interviews, answered my questionnaires, or corresponded with me on this subject. Jacob E. Smart responded most completely, with a sixty-one-page typed letter. When someone else did the interview, the interviewer's last name is in parentheses following that of the interviewee. Those who answered questionnaires are listed separately as enlisted men, wives, and children. Some answered in two categories. A few sent photos, menus of holiday dinners, and copies of official documents. Most of those whom I contacted (sixty-five) enlisted in the 1930s, but forty-five began their service in the years 1919–1929, with seventeen enlisting before World War I (one as early as 1900) and eight during the war. Three did not date their enlistments. Many of these men who were noncommissioned officers before World War II became officers. Others, including one full general and two lieutenant generals, served only a year or so before either entering West Point or receiving a commission from the ranks. Among the wives who responded, several were married to enlisted men, and some of the children who answered my questionnaire had enlisted fathers.

INTERVIEWS

Henry S. Aurand, William L. Banks, Gilmer M. Bell, Percy P. Bishop, Adelaide Poore Bolté, Charles L. Bolté, David E. Bolté, Philip L. Bolté, Omar N. Bradley, W. Fritz Breidster (Williams), Arthur R. Brooks, Beverly F. Browne, Clovis E. Byers, Mark W. Clark, James L. Collins, J. Lawton Collins, Norbert L. Craine, Benjamin O. Davis, Benjamin O. Davis Jr., Ruth McCombs DeMattia, Jacob L. Devers, William R. Dunn, Ira C. Eaker, Paul C. Febiger, Bonner F. Fellers, Thomas D. Finley, Berenice Fiske, Benjamin D. Foulois, Stephen O. Fuqua (Jacobsmeyer), David St. P. Gaillard (Bolles), Geoffrey Galwey, James M. Gavin, Sidney C. Graves, Wade H. Haislip, Thomas T. Handy, Charles D. Herron, John L. Hines Jr., George W. Hinman, Clarence R. Huebner, Charles S. Johnson, Robert P. Johnson, Charles T. Lanham, John W. Leonard, Douglas MacArthur, Orville W. Martin, Anthony C. McAuliffe, Charles E. McCombs, Elnora Davis McLendon, Theodore R. Milton, John W. Norwood, Louis M. Nuttman (Short), Robin Olds, Noel F. Parrish, Lillian Auring Perry, Edward P. Quesada, Matthew B. Ridgway, Charles D. Roberts, Mansfield Robinson, Walter J. Rouse, William T. Ryder, Charles A. Sanders (Clanin), Frank B. Scahill (Twining), Martha McCombs Schneider, Ada Baker Shelton, William H. Simpson, Carl Spaatz, Ruth Harrison Spaatz, Isaac Spalding, George L. Stackhouse, Arthur J. Stanley, Jane Bigelow Stevenson, Imogene Hoyle Taulbee, Virginia Fiske Timberman, Lewis Turtle, James W. Twitty, Kenneth F. Vars (Twining), James S. Watson, George W. Weber, Albert C. Wedemeyer, Norma Tuttle Yarbrough, William P. Yarbrough, Louis S. Yassel, Alphonso S. Zawadski.

CORRESPONDENCE

Michael Buckley Jr., Bradford G. Chynoweth, Albert P. Clark, Bruce C. Clarke, Garrison H. Davidson, Paul S. Davison, Harold H. Elarth, William P. Ennis Jr., Thomas D. Finley, James M. Gavin, Andrew J. Goodpaster, John W. Hammond, Haywood S. Hansell Jr., John E. Harris, Charles F. Ivins, Tom Jones, Noe C. Killian, William N. Leonard, Mauree Pickering Mahin, Orville W. Martin, Frederick P.

Munson, John E. Olson, Bruce Palmer Jr., Russell P. Reeder, Holland L. Robb, Jacob E. Smart, Edwin V. Sutherland, Walter Warlimont, Alexander M. Weyand, Otto P. Weyland, Roscoe B. Woodruff, Charles W. Yuill.

QUESTIONNAIRES

ENLISTED MEN

Sydney P. Andrews, Narcisco Arce, Numa P. Avendano, Silas C. Azbell, William L. Banks, Carlton J. Barnes, Tommie J. Baugh, Otto E. Bauman, Frank I. Beard, Lewis Beaulieu, Gilmer M. Bell, Robert L. Bergeron, William A. Bowling, Wilfrid A. Bowman, Frank Bozoski, Jack Bradley Jr., James H. Brady, David G. Brenzel, Gussie A. Buckner, James J. Bynum, Ralph L. Cadwallader, Leonard Cattivera, Jess W. Cloud, Reisig Conrad, Theodore J. Conway, Norbert L. Craine, Lawrence B. Curtis, Ralph O. Cypher, Louis M. DiCarlo, Marshall C. Dickinson, Walter Dillon, Theodore L. Dobol, Francis T. Dockery, Frank L. Doyle, John W. Dulin III, William R. Dunn, Rudy F. Etley, Isadore Ferguson, Eugene E. Forbes, Alberto Garcia, James M. Gavin, Mese E. Geissner, Athol W. George, Ramón Gómez-Cintrón, Felix L. Goodwin, Leland R. Goodwin, Frank E. Hagan, Samuel M. Halliburton, Raymond L. Hammond, John J. Hannon, Walter Hansen, Gene E. Harris, Edward J. Hayes, Patrick J. Hayes, Mike Henley, James C. Hicks, George C. Hodgen, Eugene G. Hogan, John J. Hoodock, David L. Hopkins, Charles A. Horton, Chester E. Horton, Rufus W. House, William A. Howell, John M. Jackson, Robert P. Johnson, Johnny W. Jones, James B. Joslin, John L. Key, John N. Lillie, Roland O. Linker, Woodrow Littrell, Dave Livesay, Jerome Lowrey, George E. Maker, James C. Maples, William H. March, S. Morgan Martin, Anthony Mayeski, Joseph J. Mayor, Eugene H. McDermit, Troy H. Middleton, Curtes Mitchell, George R. Moe, Arch R. Morris, Victor Murdock, William R. Nabors, Frank E. Orcutt, Frank Palasky, George S. Pappas, Noel F. Parrish, Alfonson C. Passero, Heman W. Peirce, Andrew Pemper, William Peterson, Andrew W. Piehl, Hubert P. Poe, Lucious President, Sam T. Prophet, John Randall, Basil Rauch, Alva L. Reams, Reginald M. Rice, Ramōn Rivera, Walter J. Rouse, Walter N. Ruffin, Leo P. Sanders, Frank B. Scahill, Eugene E. Schneider, Robert L. Scott,

James H. Short, William A. Shrenk, Richard M. Sibley, Frank Skorniak, Walter W. Smith, Charles L. Southern, George L. Stackhouse, George W. Stocks, Roy F. Sulzberger, Estel A. Thompson, M. J. Thompson, William C. Tiller, James W. Twitty, James E. Vance, Michael C. Varhol, Hoberr C. Wade, Francis, J. Walski, Edward Warfield, Howard F. Wehrle III, Robert W. Wendt, Marvin J. White, August L. Williams, Lester G. Williams, Slone Williams, Dorsie W. Willis, Louis H. Wilson, March Worsham, Joseph M. Wozniak.

WIVES

Helen Townsley Allen, Margaret C. Almond, Dorothy Potter Benedict, Ruby Mundell Berry, Adelaide Poore Bolté, Louise Adams Browne, Eleanor Fletcher Buckley, Edith Morgan Cabell, Elizabeth Fleming Carter, Sarah Shanks Chamberlin, Adelaide Chain Cottrell, Miriam Blount Craig, Marjorie Hinds Cruse, Elizabeth Rumbough Donaldson, Hester Nolan Donovan, Frances Dwyer Ennis, Dorothy Anderson Goodpaster, Grace Wilson Groves, Velma G. Hennessy, Evelyn Hruby, Florence Ricketts Jackson, Harriet Howze Jones, Katherine Selfridge Kellond, Marion Anderson Lillie, Gladys E. Linker, Katherine Swift McKinney, Margaret Brown Mueller, Frances Z. Norman, Margaret Casteel Pickering, Burtram O. Pierce, Phyllis Corbusier Pierson, Eleanor Bishop Powell, Carol Palmer Power, Ellen Erwin Rehkopf, Marian Sanford Robb, Caroline Johanna Rouse, Mary Reed Royce, Susie Coley Smythe, Virginia Fiske Timberman, Maida Davis Turtle, Tere Rios Versace, Elizabeth Embick Wedemeyer, Anne Rumbough West, Rachel Forbush Wood, Alice Gray Woodruff, Mildred Parker Yount, Gay Reaves Yuill.

CHILDREN

Helen Townsley Allen, Jancie Robb Anderson, Jo Jones Bates, Margie Hoskins Bloxom, Adelaide Poore Bolté, Philip L. Bolté, Devol Brett, Robert W. Brockway, George S. Brown, Louise Adams Browne, Stephen W. Burres, Margaret Forsythe Camp, Thomas J. Camp Jr., Jacqueline Thompson Campbell, Elizabeth Fleming Carter, Sarah Shanks Chamberlin, Bradford G. Chynoweth, Howard W. Clark, Rose

Loughborough Clark, Alice Hines Cleland, Jess W. Cloud, Francis J. Clune Jr., James L. Collins, Theodore J. Conway, Winifred Stilwell Cox, Virginia Ridgway Crawford, Marjorie Hinds Cruse, Phyllis Batson Davis, Michael S. Davison, William R. Desobry, Elizabeth Rumbough Donaldson, Hester Nolan Donaldson, Mara Coffey Donaldson, Thomas Q. Donaldson IV, Ernest F. Easterbrook, Frances Dwyer Ennis, William P. Ennis Jr., Robert J. Farnsworth, Thomas D. Finley, Sarah Scott Foulk, William F. Freehoff Jr., Fielding L. Greaves, Michael J. L. Greene, Marjorie Harwood Greer, Grace Wilson Groves, Margaret Brown Guest, Laurence Halstead Jr., Haywood S. Hansell Jr., Anne G. Hawkins, Thomas R. Hay, Elizabeth P. Hoisington, Willard A. Holbrook Jr., Frank L. Hoskins Jr., Hamilton H. Howze, Mary Henry Howze, Robert L. Howze Jr., Margaret Uncles Huffman, Robert P. Johnson, Harriet Howze Jones, Dorothy Bevans Kramer, John C. H. Lee Jr., Julian B. Lindsey, Elizabeth Sorley Lyon, William H. Marsh, Ethel Mason Matheson, Paul J. Matte Jr., Robert G. Matte, Katherine Winans Maxwell, Charles E. McCombs, Fitzhugh McMaster, Margaret Bradley Mellboom, Alice Beukema Miller, Margaret Brown Mueller, Frederick P. Munson, Robin Olds, Harriette Marshall Olson, John E. Olson, David E. Ott, Joyce Helmick Ott, Nina Garfinkel Page, Bruce Palmer Jr., Williston B. Palmer, George S. Patton III, Cornelia Getty Peale, Roland E. Peixotto, Margaret Casteel Pickering, Phyllis Corbusier Pierson, James H. Polk, Carol Palmer Powell, Eleanor Bishop Powell, Russell P. Reeder, Robert C. Richardson III, Harry N. Rising Jr., Eleanor R. Robb, Haywood B. Roberts, Haywood B. Roberts Jr., Charles C. Ross, Lelia Brady Ryan, Adrian St. John, Karl L. Scherer, Edward C. Smith, Charles L. Spettel, George L. Stackhouse, Jane Bigelow Stevenson, Roy F. Sulzberger, Patrick H. Tansey, Dorothy Tebbetts, Virginia Fiske Timberman, Ruth Patton Totten, Harry W. Urrutia, Robert L. Walsh, Frances Murray Walsh, Anna Rumbough West, William W. West III, Patricia Henry Williams, Alexander S. Wotherspoon, Dorothy Devine Wurster, Mildred Parker Yount, Charles W. Yuill Jr.

NOTES

ABBREVIATIONS

AG	Adjutant General
ANJ	*Army and Navy Journal*
CG	Commanding General
CS	Chief of Staff of the Army
Cullum Register	George W. Cullum, *Biographical Register of the Officers and Graduates of the U.S. Military Academy at West Point, N.Y., since Its Establishment in* 1802, vol. V, ed. Charles Braden (Saginaw, Mich., 1910, suppl. 1900–1910); vols. VIA and VIB, ed. Wirt Robinson (Saginaw, Mich., 1910–1920)
QMG	Quartermaster General
IG	Inspector General
JAG	Judge Advocate General
LC	Library of Congress, Washington, D.C.
MHI	U.S. Army Military History Institute, Carlisle Barracks, Pa.
NA	National Archives, Washington, D.C.
OAR	Official Army Register
QMG	Quartermaster General
RG	Record Group
SG	Surgeon General
SW	Secretary of War
USAFA	United States Air Force Academy
USMA	United States Military Academy
WCD	War College Division
WDAR	*War Department Annual Report*
WHS	Wisconsin Historical Society, Madison

PROLOGUE

1. Edward M. Coffman, *The Old Army: A Portrait of the American Army in Peacetime, 1784–1898* (New York, 1986), 3.

1. THE ARMY BEGINS A NEW ERA

Epigraph: Lewis S. Sorley to author, October 4, 1957.

1. In the fall of 1897 the largest garrison was Fort Leavenworth, Kansas (848), while eight posts had less than 100. On April 1, 1898, there were 2,143 officers and 26,040 enlisted men, but 2,264 had enlisted in February and March; *WDAR* (1897), CG, 102–109; (1898), SW, 144, AG, 276.

2. Graham A. Cosmas, *An Army for Empire: The United States Army in the Spanish-American War* (Columbia, Mo., 1971), 85; Gilbert C. Fite and Jim E. Reese, *An Economic History of the United States* (Boston, 1973), 267, 269, 275, 279, 285; James L. Abrahamson, *America Arms for a New Century: The Making of a Great Military Power* (New York, 1981), chap. 2; George B. Duncan, "Reasons for Increasing the Regular Army," *North American Review* 166 (April 1898), 455–456.

3. Duncan, "Reasons for Increasing the Army," 451–452, 457; Cosmas, *Army for Empire*, 89–97, 101–110 (quotations on 96); William A. Ganoe, *The History of the United States Army* (New York, 1924), 373; Edward M. Coffman, *The Old Army: A Portrait of the American Army in Peacetime, 1784–1898* (New York, 1986), 272.

4. Russell A. Alger, *The Spanish-American War* (New York, 1901), 7; Theodore Roosevelt, quoted in *Annual Report of the American Historical Association for the Year 1912* (Washington, D.C., 1914), 194; Cosmas, *Army for Empire*, 98, 101–109, 134.

5. Bertha Barnitz Byrne Peelle, "Autobiography," 37, USMA; Cosmas, *Army for Empire*, 100; Eli A. Helmick, "From Reveille to Retreat," 61, MHI.

6. Guy V. Henry Jr., "A Brief Narrative of the Life of Guy V. Henry Jr.," 1, 3–4, 7 (quotation), 19–20, MHI; John Bigelow Jr., *Reminiscences of the Santiago Campaign* (New York, 1899), 1, 9; Jane Bigelow Stevenson, interview.

7. Helmick, "From Reveille to Retreat," 62.

8. Martha Summerhayes, *Vanished Arizona: Recollections of the Army Life of a New England Woman* (1911; reprint, Lincoln, Neb., 1979), ix, 287–288; Coffman, *Old Army*, 230; Alger, *Spanish-American War*, 6; John P. Dyer, *From Shiloh to San Juan: The Life of "Fightin' Joe" Wheeler* (Baton Rouge, 1961), 221.

9. William Paulding, "A Few Words on My Army Life, 1874–1913," MHI, 74; Robert S. Offley, "Autobiography," 19, MHI. Bivens quoted in Herschel V. Cashin, *Under Fire with the 10th Cavalry* (1899; reprint, New York, 1970), 61. Willard B.

Gatewood, *Black Americans and the White Man's Burden, 1898–1903* (Urbana, 1975), 44–51.

10. Mauree Pickering Mahin, *Life in the American Army from the Frontier to Distaff Hall* (Washington, D.C., 1967), 43.

11. Beaumont B. Buck, *Memories of Peace and War* (San Antonio, 1935), 55, 57; Charles Gerhardt, "Summary of Military Career," 20, MHI; Grace Bunce Paulding, Memoir, 23–24 (quotations on 23), 150; MHI; W. S. Nye, *Carbine and Lance: The Story of Old Fort Sill* (Norman, 1943), 298–299.

12. George Kennan, *Campaigning in Cuba* (New York, 1899), 4; *WDAR* (1897), CG, 97; (1898), AG, 276; (1899), SG, 389.

13. George B. Duncan, "Reminiscences: 1882–1905," 76, copy in author's collection; Henry C. Corbin, "Autobiography," 48, 123 (quotation), Corbin Papers, LC; Cosmas, *Army for Empire*, 123, 130.

14. Cosmas, *Army for Empire*, 193 (staff officer quotation); Duncan, "Reminiscences," 76; Helmick, "From Reveille to Retreat," 65; Mahin, *Life in American Army*, 43.

15. Lewis S. Sorley, "Some Recollections," 53, 55 (first quotation), in possession of Elizabeth Sorley Lyon; William Paulding, "A Few Words on Army Life," 80 (second and third quotations); Alger, *Spanish-American War*, 288–289; David F. Trask, *The War with Spain* (New York, 1981), 190.

16. Sorley, "Some Recollections," 57; Trask, *War with Spain*, 317.

17. Cosmas, *Army for Empire*, 70, 75, 88, 188–189; T. Bentley Mott, *Twenty Years as Military Attaché* (New York, 1937), 57. Alger lists units in both expeditions; hence one can estimate the regular-volunteer ratio (*Spanish-American War*, 310–311, 329). See also Benjamin D. Foulois with C. V. Glines, *From the Wright Brothers to the Astronauts: The Memoirs of Major General Benjamin D. Foulois* (New York, 1968), 7, 9–12.

18. Cosmas, *Army for Empire*, chap. 8; Trask, *War with Spain*, 324–335; Sorley, "Some Recollections," 58; Bigelow, *Reminiscences of Santiago Campaign*, 128, 150–151; Mary C. Gillett, *The Army Medical Department, 1865–1917* (Washington, D.C., 1995), 130–131. The 24th's commander's report is in the unpaginated William G. Miller, *The Twenty-fourth Infantry: Past and Present* (Fort Collins, 1972, paperback reprint); Mansfield Robinson, interview, September 8, 1954; and author's interview with him published in Hopkinsville *Daily Kentucky New Era*, July 5, 1951; William T. Anderson to George A. Myers, October 18, 1898, George A. Myers Papers, Ohio Historical Society, Columbus; Jack D. Foner, *Blacks and the Military in American History* (New York, 1974), 80–82.

19. Matthew F. Steele to Stella Folsom Steele, August 28, 1898, Matthew F. Steele Papers, MHI; Offley, "Autobiography," 33; Alger, *Spanish-American War*, 437;

William Paulding, "A Few Words on Army Life," 84–95; Grace Paulding, Memoir, 26–31 (quotation on 28).

20. The combined total of combat deaths in Puerto Rico and the Philippines was twenty; *WDAR* (1898), 273. For deaths from disease in Cuba, see ibid., 274. For typhoid fever, see *WDAR* (1899), 618–626; Henry, "Brief Narrative," 20; Alger, *Spanish-American War,* 411–418; Cosmas, *Army for Empire,* 264–277.

21. Henry, "Brief Narrative," 21. A complete list of the black NCOs who became officers is in Cashin, *Under Fire,* 359–361. Marvin A. Kriedberg and Merton G. Henry, *History of Military Mobilization in the United States Army,* 1775–1945 (Washington, D.C., 1955), 162–163; Trask, *War with Spain,* 325–326; Benjamin O. Davis, "The Family Tree and Early Life," unpaginated memoir lent by Elnora Davis McLendon; Benjamin O. Davis, interview with Marvin E. Fletcher and author; Marvin E. Fletcher, *America's First Black General: Benjamin O. Davis, Sr., 1880– 1970* (Lawrence, Kans., 1989), 4–18.

22. Graham A. Cosmas, "Military Reform after the Spanish-American War: The Army Reorganization Fight of 1898–1899," *Military Affairs* 35, no. 1 (1971), 12–18. For requirements for officers in the volunteers and a list of regular officers who went into the volunteers, see *WDAR* (1899), AG, 16–21.

23. Henry, "Brief Narrative," 22–24 (quotation on 22); *WDAR* (1899), AG, 21.

24. *WDAR* (1899), AG, 4. The foldout after page 10 shows variations in strength in both regulars and volunteers from May 1898 to June 1899. Cosmas, *Army for Empire,* 175–176, 296, 299; Bigelow, *Reminiscences of Santiago Campaign,* 166.

25. *WDAR* (1899), AG, 30, 40 (quotation), IG, 112; Coffman, *Old Army,* 141, 330.

26. Lewis S. Yassel, interview.

27. Foulois, *From Wright Brothers to Astronauts,* 14–15.

28. Davis, "Family Tree and Early Life"; Fletcher, *America's First Black General,* 18–20.

29. Davis, "Family Tree and Early Life"; Fletcher, *America's First Black General,* 20–22; Davis, interview.

30. George Van Horn Moseley, "One Soldier's Journey," I: 45–67, Moseley Papers, LC, quotations on 49, 50, and 61. Thomas McGregor Appointment, Commission, and Promotion File, 5173 ACP 1878, RG 94, NA.

31. After the arrival of the reinforcements, the situation calmed down. Other Indians were taken into custody, and all the troops except for one company left by October 23; *WDAR* (1899), 23–25. The regiment had three men killed and fifteen wounded in Cuba; *The Third Infantry or "The Old Guard of the Army"* (n.p., n.d.), 38–40, pamphlet, MHI.

32. Stephen R. Remsberg, "United States Administration of Alaska: The Army Phase, 1867–1877; A Study in Federal Governance of an Overseas Possession" (Ph.D. diss., University of Wisconsin, 1976), chaps. 2, 10, and appendix. One of the first

officers to go into Alaska in 1897 was Wilds P. Richardson, who later commanded the North Russian expedition in 1919; *WDAR* (1898), CG, 180–181. The correspondence about Spaulding, who later became a distinguished historian of the Army, is in *WDAR* (1899), CG, 110–114.

33. This garrison was about a third of the 499 officers and men stationed in Alaska; *WDAR* (1899), AG, 6; Charles A. Booth, Diary, June–December 1899, USMA Library.

34. *WDAR* (1899), CG, 28–74; Jerry M. Cooper, *The Army and Civil Disorder: Federal Military Intervention in Labor Disputes, 1877–1900* (Westport, Conn., 1980), chap. 7; Coffman, *Old Army*, 246–254. See Harvey Meyerson, *Nature's Army: When Soldiers Fought for Yosemite* (Lawrence, Kans., 2001), for a detailed study of the Army's involvement in protecting this national park.

35. Mansfield Robinson, interview, August 6, 1956; *WDAR* (1899), 22; Willard B. Gatewood Jr., *"Smoked Yankees" and the Struggle for Empire: Letters from Negro Soldiers, 1898–1902* (Urbana, 1971), 240.

36. *WDAR* (1899), 6, 15–16. For a list of the locations and dates of moves of all regular Army units, see *Circular Showing the Distribution of Troops of the Line of the United States Army: January 1,, 1866 to June 30, 1909,* War Department, AG, 1909.

37. Yassel interview; Foulois, *From Wright Brothers to Astronauts,* 16–17.

38. Helmick, "From Reveille to Retreat," 87–89, 102.

39. Duncan, "Reminiscences," 130–134; Cosmas, *Army for Empire,* 299; *WDAR* (1899), AG, 33–34; Thomas D. Finley, "The Finleys and the Army," 67, copy in author's collection; Lewis E. Gleeck Jr., *Over Seventy-five Years of Philippine-American History: The Army and Navy Club of Manila* (Manila, 1976), 3; Elihu Root Orders, October 27, 1899, no. 60, file 403, RG 407, NA; Matthew F. Steele to wife, September 20, 1899, MHI.

40. Duncan, "Reasons for Increasing the Army," 452; idem, "Reminiscences," 130–136 (second and third quotations on 135 and 136).

41. Peelle, "Autobiography," 38; Adelaide Poore Bolté, telephone interview, January 28, 1990.

42. Grace Paulding, Memoir, 9, 32–34 (quotation on 33); Henry, "Brief Narrative," 24; Mahin, *Life in American Army,* 46.

43. Larry I. Bland and Sharon R. Ritenour, eds., *The Papers of George Catlett Marshall,* 4 vols. (Baltimore, 1981), I: 8; Larry I. Bland, ed., *George C. Marshall Interviews and Reminiscences for Forrest C. Pogue* (Lexington, Va., 1991), 48–49, 100; Forrest C. Pogue, *George C. Marshall: Education of a General* (New York, 1963), 48.

44. Cosmas, *Army for Empire,* 308.

45. *WDAR* (1899), AG, 34–35, Chief Signal Officer, 753; Henry, "Brief Narrative," 24.

46. Lewis S. Sorley, letter, October 4, 1957.

2. THE COLONIAL ARMY

Epigraph: John H. Parker, "Memories of the Service," 52, USMA.

1. The *Rocky Mountain News* cartoon appears in Thomas A. Bailey, *A Diplomatic History of the American People* (New York, 1950), 519. Charles Francis Adams is quoted in Robert L. Beisner, *Twelve against Empire* (New York, 1968), 113.

2. The strength figures are from the secretary of war's reports (SW) in *War Department Annual Reports: 1899–1916.* For comparisons with the foreign armies, see *WDAR* (1900), SW, 239; (1914), SW, 10.

3. I. B. Holley Jr., *General John M. Palmer, Citizen Soldiers, and the Army of a Democracy* (Westport, Conn., 1982), 104; *WDAR* (1902), 291; Charles H. Franklin, "History of the Philippine Scouts, 1899–1934," Army Historical Division study, 1935, 8–9, RG 407, NA; Aaron L. Friedberg, *The Weary Titan: Britain and the Experience of Relative Decline, 1895–1905* (Princeton, 1988), 220.

4. Graham A. Cosmas, "Securing the Fruits of Victory: The U.S. Army Occupies Cuba, 1898–1899," *Military Affairs* 38 (October 1974), 86, 90. For details of the occupation, see David F. Healy, *The United States in Cuba, 1898–1902* (Madison, 1963); *WDAR* (1900), SW, 4; (1901), SG, 714–717; Mary C. Gillett, *The Army Medical Department, 1865–1917* (Washington, D.C., 1996), 239–249.

5. *WDAR* (1909), Commander of the Army of Cuban Pacification, 241; (1903), SW, 2; (1904), Military Secretary, 249. See also Allan R. Millett, *The Politics of Intervention: The Military Occupation of Cuba, 1906–1909* (Columbus, 1968); *WDAR* (1908), Commander of the Army of Cuban Pacification, 416.

6. *WDAR* (1899), SW, 17; (1900), AG, 13, and Lieutenant General, Commanding, 293; (1904), Military Secretary, 249; (1908), SW, 5. Details of organization and pay are in *WDAR* (1901), AG, 117. See also Charles J. Crane, *The Experiences of a Colonel of* Infantry (New York, 1923), 430; Ramón Gómez-Cintrón, questionnaire, 1973.

7. Goethals received a direct promotion to major general and the thanks of Congress for his work. See his entry in Wirt Robinson, ed., *Biographical Register of Officers and Graduates of the U.S. Military Academy at West Point, N.Y., since Its establishment in 1802,* vol. VI-A (Saginaw, 1920). *WDAR* (1911), SW, 8; (1912), SW, 16, and AG, 433; (1914), SW, 7; (1915), CS, 141; Gillett, *Army Medical Department,* 263–278; Marie D. Gorgas and Burton J. Hendrick, *William Crawford Gorgas: His Life and Work* (Garden City, N.Y, 1924), 254. Robert L. Eichelberger, "Memoir," E 21, III E 37-3, copy lent by Jay Luvaas.

8. *WDAR* (1914), SW, 7; (1916), SW, 7–10, 31; John S. D. Eisenhower, *Intervention! The United States and the Mexican Revolution, 1913–1917* (New York, 1993).

9. *WDAR* (1916), SG, 558 (first quotation); Lowell Thomas, *Woodfill of the Regulars: A True Story of Adventure from the Arctic to the Argonne* (Garden City, N.Y., 1929),

152 (second quotation); see also 113–115, 149, 203. Adelaide Poore Bolté, interview, April 3, 1986 (third quotation); *WDAR* (1900), SW, 4–5; (1903), CG, Department of Columbia, 45; (1906), AG, 611; (1907), AG, 244; (1908), AG, 417. In 1972 the Alaskan Command prepared *The Army in Alaska*, Pamphlet 360-5, 48, 50, 53. Alfred F. Hurley, *Billy Mitchell: Crusader for Air Power* (Bloomington, 1975), 10; Wilds P. Richardson, "The Army in Alaska," *Infantry Journal* 22 (May 1923), 515.

10. *WDAR* (1900), SW, 12–13, 19, and AG, 12–13; (1901), SG, 692–693; Allan R. Millett, *Semper Fidelis: The History of the United States Marine Corps*, rev. ed. (New York, 1980), 163. Richard H. Groves, ed., "The Papers of Chaplain Leslie Richard Groves," 597, 604–699 (quotation on 642), copy in author's collection; Earl F. Stover, *Up from Handymen: The United States Army Chaplaincy, 1865–1920* (Washington, D.C., 1977), 134–135.

11. *WDAR* (1906), Military Secretary, 567; (1912), SW, 7, and AG, 433; Patrick J. Hayes, telephone interview, May 11, 1974 (first quotation); Walter J. Rouse, letter, November 2, 1972 (second quotation), and interview, Holley, *General John M. Palmer*, 220–227 (second quotation on 221); Adelaide Poore Bolté, interview, August 4, 1971; Mildred Parker Yount, letter (last quotation); Edward M. Coffman, "The American 15th Infantry Regiment in China, 1912–1938: A Vignette in Social History," *Journal of Military History* 58 (January 1994), 57–74; Dennis L. Noble, *The Eagle and the Dragon: The United States Military in China, 1901–1937* (Westport, Conn., 1990).

12. Warren Dean, Journal, October 12, 1900, USMA Library; Groves, "Papers of Leslie Richard Groves," 677; James L. Abrahamson, *America Arms for A New Century: The Making of a Great Military Power* (New York, 1981), 93; Richard D. Challener, *Admirals, Generals, and American Foreign Policy, 1898–1914* (Princeton, 1973), 181–182, 233 ff. (TR quotation on 182); James H. Belote and William M. Belote, *Corregidor* (New York, 1967), 27–30. William Belote gave me the notes and drafts of relevant chapters. Brian M. Linn, *Guardians of Empire: The U.S. Army and the Pacific, 1902–1940* (Chapel Hill, 1997), chap. 4.

13. Matthew F. Steele to Martha Folsom Steele, October 1, 1899, Steele Papers, MHI. *WDARs* for 1900–1908 show that the garrison exceeded 250 in only two years. Anne Goodwin Winslow, *Fort DeRussy Days: Letters of a Malihini Army Wife (1908–1911)* (Honolulu, 1988), v, vii, xii, 79 (second quotation), 98 (third quotation), 114–115. Walter S. Schuyler Journal, January 15—May 25, 1909, copy lent by Allan R. Millett; Walter J. Rouse, questionnaire and interview; Carl Spaatz, interview (quotations); *WDAR* (1910), CG, Department of California, 133–134; (1911), SG, 480–481; (1912), SG, 709; (1915), CS, 141, and SW, 121 (last quotation). For locations and descriptions of the Hawaiian posts, see Charles J. Sullivan, *Army Posts and Towns: The Baedeker of the Army* (Burlington, Vt., 1926), 22–30.

14. *WDAR* (1903), SW, 2; (1914), SW, 7; (1915), CS, 141; Glenn A. May, *Social Engineering in the Philippines: The Aims, Execution, and Impact of American Colonial*

Policy (Westport, Conn., 1980), xiv, xix, 7, 19, 123, 125, 179–181; John M. Gates, *Schoolbooks and Krags: The United States Army in the Philippines, 1898–1902* (Westport, Conn., 1973), chap. 2. Linn, *Guardians of Empire,* chap. 2.

15. Franklin, "Philippine Scouts," 1–12. See also James R. Woolard, "The Philippine Scouts: The Development of America's Colonial Army" (Ph.D. diss., Ohio State University, 1975); Edward M. Coffman, "Batson of the Philippine Scouts," *Parameters* 7, no. 3 (1977), 68–72; idem, "The Philippine Scouts, 1899–1942: A Historical Vignette," in the International Commission of Military History, *ACTA* 3, TEHERAN 6–16 VII 1976 (Bucharest, 1978), 68–79.

16. Heath Twitchell, *Allen: The Biography of an American Officer, 1859–1930* (New Brunswick, N.J., 1974), chap. 6. Woolard, "Philippine Scouts," 66–67, 152–158, 242–244, 257–258.

17. Richard B. Meixsel, "United States Army Policy in the Philippine Islands, 1902–1922" (Master's thesis, University of Georgia, 1988), 21–23, 57; Franklin, "Philippine Scouts," 16; *U.S. Statutes at Large,* vol. 31, 753; *Official Army Register:* 1902, 506–507; Douglas Porch, *The French Foreign Legion: A Complete History of the Legendary Fighting Force* (New York, 1991), 188; John Masters, *Bugles and a Tiger: A Volume of Autobiography* (New York, 1956), 86.

18. James Parker, *The Old Army: Memories 1872–1918* (Philadelphia, 1929), 222; Pearl M. Shaffer, "Reminiscences of an Army Career," 67, MHI; *WDAR* (1903), CG, Department of Texas, 97, and CG, Philippines Division, 136–137; (1912), CS, 255–256; (1913), CS, 164; Meixsel, "Army Policy in Philippine Islands," 5, 10–12, 18–20, 46, 74–75, 80, 83–84, 106.

19. Linn, *Guardians of Empire,* chap. 2; José M. Quisumbing, *The American Occupation of Cebu: Warwick Barracks, 1899–1917* (n.p., 1983), chap. 5.

20. *WDAR* (1901), SW, 31–32; (1902), AG, 291. The definitive history of the conflict is Brian M. Linn, *The Philippine War, 1899–1902* (Lawrence, Kans., 2000), 125.

21. William Weigel, "Foreword from Division Commander," *Infantry Journal* 30 (April 1927), 339; Edward M. Coffman, *The Hilt of the Sword: The Career of Peyton C. March* (Madison, 1966), 22; Mansfield Robinson, interview, August 6, 1956 (quotation); Benjamin D. Foulois, Diary, November 14–15, 1899, Foulois Papers, LC; George B. Duncan, "Memoir," 168 (quotation), University of Kentucky Library; Michael J. Lenihan, "I Remember, I Remember," 30, MHI.

22. Benjamin D. Foulois to his mother, February 7, 8, 16, and October 3, 16, 1900, Foulois Papers, LC. The quotations are from his letters of March 12, 1900, and April 10, 1901.

23. See picture of mounted detachment in Foulois Photo Album, USAFA Library. Parker, "Memories of the Service," 74–75; Charles D. Herron, interview, November 7, 1964.

24. Samuel P. Lyon to wife, February 27, March 6 and 17, 1900, MHI (quotations

from first two letters); Brian M. Linn, *The U.S. Army and Counterinsurgency in the Philippine War, 1899–1902* (Chapel Hill, 1989), 57, 85, 166–167; Glenn A. May, *Battle for Batangas: A Philippine Province at War* (New Haven, 1991), 160, 181, 192–194, 290.

25. Duncan, "Memoir," 193; William Eggenberger to his mother, May 4, 1900, MHI; Warren Dean, Journal, February 4, 1901, MHI; Linn, *U.S. Army and Counterinsurgency*, 145; May, *Battle for Batangas*, 181, 192–194, 200, 240, 257–259. See also David L. Fritz, "The Philippine Question: American Civil/Military Policy in the Philippines, 1898–1905" (Ph.D. diss., University of Texas, 1977), chap. 8; and Richard E. Welch Jr., "American Atrocities in the Philippines: The Indictment and the Response," *Pacific Historical Review* 43 (1974), 233–253.

26. Warren Dean, Journal, March 16, 1901; Duncan, "Memoir," 171–184; Linn, *U.S. Army and Counterinsurgency*, 42–44; Gates, *Schoolbooks and Krags*, 228–229; Glenn A. May, "Why the United States Won the Philippine-American War, 1899–1902," *Pacific Historical Review* 52 (1983), 353–377.

27. William Eggenberger to Mother and All, September 29, 1900, MHI; Samuel P. Lyon to wife, March 17 and 28, 1900, MHI; Benjamin D. Foulois to his mother, December 30, 1900, Foulois Papers.

28. The report of the court-martial, General Orders, no. 80, Headquarters of the Army, July 16, 1902, no. 444399, RG 153, NA, quotes Smith. Parker, "Memories of the Service," 87–88. Mary Reaume to Drum, letter no. 21 (1902), Drum Papers, MHI; Gates, *Schoolbooks and Krags*, 172–173; William T. Sexton, *Soldiers in the Sun: An Adventure in Imperialism* (Harrisburg, Pa., 1939), 256.

29. Benjamin D. Foulois with C. V. Glines, *From the Wright Brothers to the Astronauts: The Memoirs of Major General Benjamin D. Foulois* (New York, 1968), 27 (quotation); John W. Norwood, *Fifty Thousand Miles with Uncle Sam's Army* (Waynesville, N.C., 1912) 39 (quotation), 47; Allan R. Millett, *The General: Robert L. Bullard and Officership in the United States Army, 1881–1925* (Westport, Conn., 1975), 165–168; Donald Smythe, *Guerrilla Warrior: The Early Life of John J. Pershing* (New York, 1973), 96, 161–162; Hugh L. Scott, *Some Memories of a Soldier* (New York, 1928), 283, 287; Wayne W. Thompson, "Governors of the Moro Province: Wood, Bliss, and Pershing in the Southern Philippines, 1903–1913" (Ph.D. diss., University of California–San Diego, 1975), 1–2.

30. Benjamin D. Foulois to mother, March 25, 1902 (first quotation), August 16, October 22 and November 8, 1903 (second quotation), June 12, 1904, February 7, 1905 (other quotations), Foulois Papers; Wood quoted in Thompson, "Governors of the Moro Province," 59; Foulois, *From Wright Brothers to Astronauts*, 27–31, 36–41; Millett, *The General*, 168.

31. Cornelius C. Smith Jr., *Don't Settle for Second: Life and Times of Cornelius C. Smith* (San Rafael, Calif., 1977), 88; Scott, *Some Memories*, part IV; Percy P. Bishop, interview.

32. Millett, *The General*, 137–138. On General Order no. 100, see Linn, *U.S. Army and Counterinsurgency*, 23–24, 49–50; and Gates, *Schoolbooks and Krags*, 206–207.

33. Mansfield Robinson, interview, August 6, 1956; Batchelor's report to the Adjutant General, 1st Division, 8th Army Corps, December 28, 1899, in William G. Muller, *The Twenty-fourth Infantry: Past and Present* (reprint, Fort Collins, n.d.), app. 4 (unpaginated).

34. Groves to wife, February 2, 1901; Groves, "Papers of Leslie Richard Groves," 810 (first quotation); Lewis S. Sorley, "Some Recollections," 62 (second quotation), in possession of Elizabeth Sorley Lyon; Richard Johnson, "My Life in the U.S. Army, 1899–1922," 102 (last quotation), MHI. Willard B. Gatewood Jr., *"Smoked Yankees" and the Struggle for Empire: Letters from Negro Soldiers, 1898–1902* (Urbana, 1971), 247, 252–254, 257–258, 268, 271, 277, 284, 289, 295, 300, 308; idem, *Black Americans and the White Man's Burden: 1898–1902* (Urbana, 1975), ix–x, 190, 276, 278–285, 288–290. The unit strengths are on foldouts following page 30 in *WDAR* (1900), AG. See also *ANJ*, October 4, 1902, 106; and May 23, 1903, 952.

35. Gatewood, *Black Americans*, 302–307 (quotation on 303); Johnson, "My Life in U.S. Army," 46–47, 49, 130–140 (quotation on 136).

36. The four chaplains were Allen Allensworth, William T. Anderson, George W. Prioleau, and Theophilus G. Steward; Stover, *Up from Handymen*, 53, 90–92; *WDAR* (1899), AG, 16–17; Gatewood, *Black Americans*, 207, 274.

37. Lynch retired a major in 1911; John Hope Franklin, ed., *Reminiscences of an Active Life: The Autobiography of John Roy Lynch* (Chicago, 1970). In the Benjamin O. Davis Papers at MHI, there is a brief typescript note about Green by Mack C. Nance, who was a member of the escort party; Marvin E. Fletcher, *America's First Black General: Benjamin O. Davis, Sr., 1880–1970* (Lawrence, Kans., 1989), 23.

38. Fletcher, *America's First Black General*, 25–30; Fletcher's and my interview with General Davis (quotation); Benjamin O. Davis, "The Family Tree and Early Life," unpaginated memoir, copy in author's collection.

39. *WDAR* (1899), IG, 82; (1901), SW, 31.

40. The figures are from *WDAR* (1902), SW, 30. The adjutant general had slightly different figures: 1,740 newly commissioned out of 2,749 combat officers, with the same number of West Pointers and almost the same number (615) of ex-volunteers, and 477 civil-life appointees and 376 from the regular ranks. He also pointed out that 216 commissioned from the volunteers were appointed first lieutenants; *WDAR* (1902), AG, 288–289. Benjamin D. Foulois to mother, May 10, 1901, Foulois Papers; Linn, *Guardians of Empire*, chap. 1.

41. Geoffrey D. Galwey, "Once upon a Horse," 60 (first quotation), author's collection; Lyon to wife, July 6, September 14, 1900, January 15, 1901 (second quotation), Samuel P. Lyon Papers, MHI; Duncan, "Memoir," 164–165, 220 (third quotation);

George Van Horn Moseley, "One Soldier's Journey," I: 69, George Van Horn Moseley Papers, LC; Smythe, *Guerrilla Warrior*, 94.

42. Benjamin D. Foulois to mother, July 13, August 25, September 19, 1901 (quotation), Foulois Papers; Foulois, *From Wright Brothers to Astronauts*, 25–26.

43. Larry I. Bland, ed., *George C. Marshall Interviews and Reminiscences for Forrest C. Pogue* (Lexington, Va., 1991), 125–134, 140–142 (quotation on 125); Larry I. Bland and Sharon R. Ritenour, eds., *The Papers of George Catlett Marshall*, 4 vols. (Baltimore, 1981), I: 24–26; Forrest C. Pogue, *George C. Marshall: Education of a General, 1880–1939* (New York, 1963), 70–79; Russell F. Weigley, *History of the United States Army* (New York, 1967), 317–318.

44. Seventy-nine percent of the field-grade officers, including all the regimental commanders of the volunteers, were regulars. Altogether 227 regular officers and men served as officers in the volunteers, and 983 wartime volunteers held commissions; *WDAR* (1899), AG, 17–21; Millett, *The General*, 155; Crane, *Experiences of a Colonel*, 323; Parker, *The Old Army*, 370.

45. Roosevelt quoted in Hermann Hagedorn, *Leonard Wood: A Biography*, 2 vols. (New York, 1931), I: 240.

46. Roy K. Flint, "The United States Army on the Pacific Frontier, 1899–1939," in *The American Military in the Far East*, ed. Joe C. Dixon (USAFA, 1980), 146–147; Foulois, *From Wright Brothers to Astronauts*, 41; Bland, *Marshall Interviews*, 140.

47. *WDAR* (1905), CG, Department of Mindanao, 311; Moseley, "One Soldier's Journey," I: 70 (first quotation); Bland, *Marshall Interviews*, 133–134, 139–140, 142 (second quotation); Edward M. Coffman, "The AEF Leaders' Education for War," in *The Great War, 1914–1918: Essays on the Military, Political, and Social History of the First World War*, ed. R. J. Q. Adams (College Station, 1990), 151–156.

3. LIFE AND TRAINING IN THE PHILIPPINES

Epigraph: Grace Bunce Paulding, "Memoir," 64, MHI.

1. Adelaide Poore Bolté, interview, August 4, 1971; Mauree Pickering Mahin, *Life in the American Army from the Frontier Days to Army Distaff Hall* (Washington, D.C., 1967), 56; *WDAR* (1910), AG, 155.

2. Rita Wherry Hines, "Old Army Days," 1–2, copy in author's collection; Uncle Dudley (John W. Norwood), *Fifty Thousand Miles with Uncle Sam's Army* (Waynesville, N.C., 1912), 65; Mahin, *Life in American Army*, 52–55; Benjamin O. Davis, "The Family Tree and Early Life," unpaginated memoir lent by Elnora Davis McLendon; Benjamin D. Foulois to mother, July 22, 1899, Foulois Papers, LC.

3. Norwood, *Fifty Thousand Miles*, 66; Eli A. Helmick, "From Reveille to Retreat: An Autobiography," 119, MHI; *Circular Showing the Distribution of Troops of the*

Line of the United States Army: January 1, 1866–June 30, 1909 (Washington, D.C., 1909), 56; *WDAR* (1901), IG, 204–209.

4. *WDAR* (1902), SW, 300; (1905), SW, 41; (1909), QMG, 28–29; Graham A. Cosmas, *An Army for Empire: The United States Army in the Spanish-American War* (Columbia, Mo., 1971), 218–219, 299.

5. Hines, "Old Army Days," 3–4; Norwood, *Fifty Thousand Miles*, 7, 66–67; Matthew F. Steele to wife, September 20, 1899, MHI; *WDAR* (1907), CG, Northern Division, Report, 83.

6. Helmick, "From Reveille to Retreat," 120; Clarence Lininger, *The Best War at the Time* (New York, 1964), 89; Norwood, *Fifty Thousand Miles,* 6; William J. Lanyon to his parents, March 3, 1899, in "Local War Letters from the Philippines, 1899–1900," *The Columbian* (Journal of the Columbia County, Pa., Historical Society) 3 (April 1974), 16; *WDAR* (1901), AG, 205–209; Richard Johnson, "My Life in the U.S. Army, 1899—1922," 12–14, MHI.

7. M. F. Steele to wife, September 28, 29, 30, and October 12 and 13, 1899, MHI; Samuel P. Lyon to wife, July 5 and 6, 1899, MHI; William Eggenberger to mother, February 21, 1899, MHI; E. Hoffman Price, "Trooper of the 15th Horse," 48–61, USMA; Norwood, *Fifty Thousand Miles,* 5; Richard H. Groves, ed., "The Papers of Chaplain Leslie Richard Groves," 265, copy in author's collection; William L. Adams, *Exploits and Adventures of a Soldier Ashore and Afloat* (Philadelphia, 1911), 288–290.

8. Steele to wife, September 23–30, October 1, 4, 12, 13, 17, 20, 21, 1899, MHI; William Paulding, "A Few Words on My Army Life, 1874–1913," 109–110, MHI; Hines, "Old Army Days," 4–5; George B. Rodney, *As a Cavalryman Remembers* (Caldwell, Idaho, 1944), 25, 29–31; Mahin, *Life in American Army,* 82; Grace Wilson Groves, "Recollections," 63, copy provided by Richard H. Groves.

9. Hines, "Old Army Days," 5; Grace Groves, "Recollections," 55; Grace Paulding, "Memoir," 98–99; Karl L. Scherer, questionnaire.

10. Adelaide Poore Bolté, interview, April 3, 1986; Hines, "Old Army Days," 4–5; William Farrington, ed., *Cowboy Pete: The Autobiography of Major General Charles H. Corlett* (Santa Fe, 1974), 33–34.

11. Mahin, *Life in American Army,* 78–82; Benjamin D. Foulois to mother, August 3, 1902, Foulois Papers.

12. Adelaide Poore Bolté, interview, April 3, 1986; Charles D. Rhodes, "Diary of the China Relief Expedition," July 1–August 11, 1900, USMA.

13. Mahin, *Life in American Army,* 52, 59; Johnson Hagood, "Down the Big Road," 150, MHI; Florence Price Batson, Diary, May 13, 1901, copy provided by Phyllis Batson Davis.

14. Walter L. Finley to wife, December 18, 1900 (quotations), January 19 and March 7, 1901; typescript excerpts provided by Thomas D. Finley.

15. R. H. Groves, "Papers of Leslie Richard Groves," 509, 901; Stella Steele to husband, June 8, 1902, MHI.

16. R. H. Groves, "Papers of Leslie Richard Groves," 303, 867; Steele to wife, October 22 (quotation) and 24, 1899; Mahin, *Life in American Army*, 59–65 (quotation on 65); William Eggenberger to mother, March 25, 1899, MHI; William B. Gatewood Jr., *Black Americans and the White Man's Burden, 1898–1903* (Urbana, 1975), 281–282, 285.

17. John M. Gates, *Schoolbooks and Krags: The United States Army in the Philippines, 1898–1902* (Westport, Conn., 1973), chap. 2; Virginia F. Mulrooney, "No Victor, No Vanquished: United States Military Government in the Philippine Islands, 1898–1901" (Ph.D. diss., University of California at Los Angeles, 1975), 53–58, 82–88. The population figure, 244,732 in 1901, comes from *The American Almanac, Year-Book, Cyclopaedia, and Atlas* (New York, 1903), 120.

18. Alexander S. Wotherspoon to author, April 18, 1973; Mahin, *Life in American Army*, 64; Hines, "Old Army Days," 9; W. Paulding, "A Few Words on Army Life," 73–74.

19. William W. Harts, "His Story," 23–24, author's collection; Vernon G. Olsmith, *Recollections of an Old Soldier* (San Antonio, 1963), 6; R. H. Groves, "Papers of Leslie Richard Groves," 316; James B. Erwin, Diary, September 13, 1906, copy provided by Mrs. Robert M. Wilson.

20. R. H. Groves, "Papers of Leslie Richard Groves," 309, 395, 409, 410 (quotation), 533. Estimate of Army women in Manila is in Matthew F. Steele to wife, December 5, 1899, MHI.

21. Warren Dean, Diary, December 11, 1900, USMA; Mahin, *Life in American Army*, 67; Hines, "Old Army Days," 11–12; R. H. Groves, "Papers of Leslie Richard Groves," 764.

22. Edith Moses, *Unofficial Letters of an Official's Wife* (New York, 1908), 20. Her husband was Bernard Moses.

23. Stella Steele to Matthew Steele, January 18 (quotation) and October 11, 1901, MHI; R. H. Groves, "Papers of Leslie Richard Groves," 496, 499, 547; Hines, "Old Army Days," 10.

24. Richard B. Meixsel, "United States Army Policy in the Philippine Islands, 1902–1922" (Master's thesis, University of Georgia, 1988), 33–37; Hugh S. Johnson, *The Blue Eagle from Egg to Earth* (Garden City, N.Y., 1935), 42; "Camp John Hay, Baguio," *Infantry Journal* 30 (April 1927), 353–354; Margaret MacMillan, *Women of the Raj* (New York, 1988), 173, 193–198; *WDAR* (1907), 23; Mahin, *Life in American Army*, 127 (first quotation); Hagood, "Down the Big Road," 151–152; Guy V. Henry Jr., "A Brief Narrative of the Life of Guy V. Henry Jr.," 53, MHI; Frank S. Clark, *The Chronicle of Aunt Lena* (Charlotte, N.C., 1960), 56 (last quotation).

25. Hagood, "Down the Big Road," 155–157 (quotation on 156); Clark, *Chronicle of Aunt Lena,* 56; Henry, "Brief Narrative," 53.

26. R. Johnson, "My Life in U.S. Army," 20; R. H. Groves, "Papers of Leslie Richard Groves," 829; Alice Blackwood Baldwin, *Memoirs of the Late Frank D. Baldwin, Major General U.S.A.* (Los Angeles, 1929), 38–40; Helmick, "From Reveille to Retreat," 126–127; MacMillan, *Women of the Raj,* 7, 12, 42; Veronica Bamfield, *On the Strength: The Story of the British Army Wife* (London, 1974), 136.

27. R. Johnson, "My Life in U.S. Army," 21–22 (quotation on 22); Marvin E. Fletcher, *The Black Soldier and Officer in the United States Army: 1891–1917* (Columbia, Mo., 1974), 109–111; Meixsel, "Army Policy in Philippine Islands," 13–14.

28. Moses, *Unofficial Letters,* 344; Lewis S. Sorley, "Some Recollections," 64, lent for copying by Elizabeth Sorley Lyon; Hugh L. Scott, *Some Memories of a Soldier* (New York, 1928), 285, 315.

29. R. H. Groves, "Papers of Leslie Richard Groves," 542; James Parker, *The Old Army: Memories, 1872–1918* (Philadelphia, 1929), 224–225, 236–240, 355 (quotation), 361–367; Steele, Rotary Club Talk, June 18, 1941, MHI; Scott, *Some Memories,* 320.

30. Moses, *Unofficial Letters,* 349–350; John H. Parker, "Memories of the Service," 75 (quotation), USMA; Charles J. Crane, *The Experiences of a Colonel of Infantry* (New York, 1923), 466, 471–475; William G. Haan, "Grafton Case," February 11, 1907, Haan Papers, WHS; R. Johnson, "My Life in U.S. Army," 20, 119–120; 164–165 (quotation).

31. William Lassiter, "Memoir," USMA, III: 3–4.

32. Mahin, *Life in American Army,* 84–96, 112 (quotation on 92).

33. Ibid., 96–104. Pershing referred to the cool, bracing climate in his annual report; *WDAR* (1911), CG, Department of Mindanao, 233.

34. Charles D. Herron, interview; Sidney M. Martin, questionnaire, October 29, 1976; Sorley, "Some Recollections," 77–78; Norwood, *Fifty Thousand Miles,* 69.

35. Lowell Thomas, *Woodfill of the Regulars: A True Story of Adventure from the Arctic to the Argonne* (Garden City, N.Y., 1929), 26, 31–33; Rodney, *As a Cavalryman Remembers,* 131–132.

36. Boone to Mr. and Mrs. Lesker Adamson, January 31, 1902, Indiana Historical Society, Indianapolis.

37. Helmick, "From Reveille to Retreat," 130; Alexander S. Wotherspoon to author, April 18, 1973.

38. Earl F. Stover, *Up from Handymen: The United States Army Chaplaincy, 1865–1920* (Washington, D.C., 1977), 110, 123; Gates, *Schoolbooks and Krags,* 86–87, 136–139, 199, 217, 271, 277; Helmick, "From Reveille to Retreat," 127–128.

39. Parker, "Memories of the Service," 76–80 (quotations on 76 and 79); Helmick,

"From Reveille to Retreat," 127; Thomas, *Woodfill of the Regulars,* 56; Glenn A. May, "Why the United States Won the Philippine-American War, 1899–1902," *Pacific Historical Review* 52 (1983), 361. See also idem, *Social Engineering in the Philippines: The Aims, Execution, and Impact of American Colonial Policy, 1900–1913* (Westport, Conn., 1980), 77–79, 85, 87, 94–95, 123, 125; Louis S. Yassel, interview, 1972.

40. Benjamin D. Foulois to mother, November 4, 18 (quotations), 24, December 23, 1900, April 18, 1901, Foulois Papers; Benjamin D. Foulois with C. V. Glines, *From the Wright Brothers to the Astronauts: The Memoirs of Major General Benjamin D. Foulois* (New York, 1968), 23; *ANJ,* June 13, 190.

41. Edith Morgan Cabell to "Too" (1971), copy in author's collection; questionnaires from Frederick P. Munson and Bradford G. Chynoweth; and Paul C. Febiger, interview.

42. Thomas D. Finley, questionnaire; Sidney C. Graves, interview; Jack W. Heard, *The Pictorial Military Life History of Jack Whitehead Heard* (San Antonio, 1969), 14–17 (last quotation on 15); Adelaide Poore Bolté, questionnaire and interview (August 4, 1971); Mahin, *Life in American Army,* 105–106; Grace Paulding, "Memoir," 105; Alexander S. Wotherspoon to author, April 18, 1973.

43. Hincs, "Old Army Days," 14; Carolyn Richards Whipple, *Victory at Eighty* (New York, 1975), 47.

44. Cornelius C. Smith Jr., *Don't Settle for Second: Life and Times of Cornelius C. Smith* (San Rafael, Calif., 1977), 53; *WDAR* (1908), CG, Department of Mindanao, 269; Mahin, *Life in American Army,* 103–110; Grace Paulding, "Memoir," 101–105 (quotation on 105).

45. Hines, "Old Army Days," 14–25 (quotations on 24 and 25); Norwood, *Fifty Thousand Miles,* 68–73; John W. Norwood, interview; Philip Reade, Diary, August 15, 1904, University of Wisconsin–Stout Area Research Center.

46. *WDAR* (1902), SG, 589 (first quotation), 590; R. Johnson, "My Life in U.S. Army," 37(second quotation), 43; Thomas, *Woodfill of the Regulars,* 29, 36; Benjamin D. Foulois to mother, July 8 and December 10, 1901, February 2, 1902, Foulois Papers; Hines, "Old Army Days," 20.

47. *WDAR* (1904), CG, Department of Mindanao, 281; (1907), CG, Department of of Mindanao, 306; (1911), CG, Department of Mindanao, 240.

48. *WDAR* (1908), CG, Philippines Division, 238; R. Johnson, "My Life in U.S. Army," 150–153.

49. Thomas, *Woodfill of the Regulars,* 45–46, 58–59; Louis S. Yassel, interview, December 1, 1972.

50. R. Johnson, "My Life in U.S. Army," 59–60, 65, 69–70.

51. Philip Reade, Diary, July 11, 13, 18, 19, 31, and August 10, 1906, University of

Wisconsin–Stout Area Research Center; Thomas, *Woodfill of the Regulars*, 41, 57–58; *WDAR* (1909), SG, 157–158.

52. Mary C. Gillett, *The Army Medical Department, 1865–1917* (Washington, D.C., 1995), 354–355. For a chart that gives the statistics for venereal disease and alcoholism from 1873 through 1912 see *WDAR* (1913), SG, 457. Also see ibid., 468; (1915), SG, 436; (1916), SG, 470, 529.

53. *WDAR* (1903), CG, Philippines Division, 210; John Whiteclay Chambers II, *The Tyranny of Change: America in the Progressive Era, 1890–1920* (New York, 1992) 163; R. Johnson, "My Life in U.S. Army," 150, 153.

54. Statistics in the annual reports are for the previous year; thus *WDAR* (1916) gives figures for the calendar year 1915. Edward M. Coffman, *The Old Army: A Portrait of the American Army in Peacetime, 1784–1898* (New York, 1986), 388; *WDAR* (1902), SG, 622; (1905), SG, 140, 145; (1909), SG, 123–124, 162; (1912), SG, 682, 692; (1916), SG, 533, 575.

55. *WDAR* (1905), SW, 8; (1910), SW, 17; (1911), SG, 407, 486–487 (second quotation on 487); (1912), SW, 11 (first quotation), SG, 662, 715; (1913), SG, 430; (1917), SG, 527; Coffman, *Old Army*, 389; Gillett, *Army Medical Department*, 349.

56. *WDAR* (1912), SW, 12 (first quotation); (1913), SW, 11; (1914), SG, 336 (second quotation); (1916), SG, 469.

57. Price, "Trooper of the 15th Horse," 16, 67–68, 84–85, 99. Army legal records indicate that the rate of homosexuality was low. Since sodomy was a court-martial offense under Article of War no. 62, the Judge Advocate General's Department reported that from 1899 through 1917 (the year covered was from July 1 of the previous year through June 30 of the year of the report), there was a total of 372 cases, of which 308 were in the period 1911–1917. See the judge advocate general's reports in the *WDARs* for 1899–1917.

58. Price, "Trooper of the 15th Horse," 16, 122–124; R. Johnson, "My Life in U.S. Army," 59–60, 142–143.

59. Helmick, "From Reveille to Retreat," 125–126; Hines, "Old Army Days," 19; Gillett, *Army Medical Department*, 294–299, 302–304.

60. WDAR (1908), SW, 22; Steele, Rotary Club Talk, June 18, 1941; Philip Reade, Diary, July 19, 1904 (first quotation), University of Wisconsin–Stout Area Research Center; William Eggenberger to family, July 7, 1899 (second quotation), MHI. See also his letters of May 18, November 11, 1900, and July 14, 1901.

61. The admission rate was just under 823 per 1,000 in 1912. In the 1890s the Army had the best average over a decade, with 1,429 per 1,000; *WDAR* (1913), SW, 10–11, SG, 411, and the chart showing admissions from 1819 to 1912 on 415; (1914), SW, 1. Also see the study of Army health from 1820 to 1917 in *WDAR* (1918), SG, 337 ff. Statistics showing averages each decade for admissions are on 343. Gillett, *Army Medical Department*, 191–193, 348–349.

62. Gillett details these efforts in *Army Medical Department,* chaps. 9–11.

63. Harts, "His Story," 28–29; *WDAR* (1902), CG, Philippines Division, 195–197; (1903), CG, Philippines Division, 165; (1905), CG, Department of Luzon, 274; (1907), SW, 23.

64. *WDAR* (1910), CG, Philippines Division, 183–184; (1916), SG, 565; Meixsel, "Army Policy in Philippine Islands," 59–63, 88; James H. Belote and William M. Belote, *Corregidor* (New York, 1967), 17–19.

65. Meixsel, "Army Policy in Philippine Islands," 26–27, 108–109; Henry, "Brief Narrative," 53.

66. R. Johnson, "My Life in U.S. Army," 183, 190; *WDAR* (1907), SG, 113; (1917), SG, 342, 500.

67. Caroline S. Shunk, *An Army Woman in the Philippines* (Kansas City, Mo., 1914), 64–66, 85–87, 90, 97 (first quotation), 101–102 (last quotation).

68. Shunk, *Army Woman in Philippines,* 78; Bertha Barnitz Byrne Peele, "Autobiography," USMA, 41; Grace Groves, "Recollections," 56–57, 61, 95 (quotation on 56).

69. Grace Groves, "Recollections," 58; Forrest C. Pogue, *George C. Marshall: Education of a General, 1880–1939* (New York, 1963), 126.

70. Ola Bell, Diary, December 24, 1909, USMA; Shunk, *Army Woman in Philippines,* 178.

71. Frederick G. Knabenshue to Stephen C. Mills, February 1, 1910, Mills Collection, MHI; William Lassiter, "Notes and Diaries," IX: 68, USMA; Shunk, *Army Woman in Philippines,* 94, 100.

72. Lassiter, "Notes and Diaries," IX: 67–68; Shunk, *Army Woman in Philippines,* 39–42.

73. Shunk, *Army Woman in Philippines,* 80–81, 98; Lassiter, "Notes and Diaries," IX: 69; Pogue, *George C. Marshall,* 126; Larry I. Bland, ed., *George C. Marshall Interviews and Reminiscences for Forrest C. Pogue* (Lexington, Va., 1991), 171; Katharine C. Kingman, Diary, August 20–September 14, 1906, USMA; Heard, *Pictorial Military Life,* 42–43.

74. Ola Bell, Diary, November 17, 19, 20 (quotation), 21, 28, 1910, USMA; Henry, "Brief Narrative," 52; Lahm to father, December 14, 1911, July 17, 1912 (quotation), August 16, 1913, Frank P. Lahm Collection, Historical Research Center, Maxwell Air Force Base, Ala.; W. Cameron Forbes, "Polo in the Philippine Islands," *The Rasp,* 1913 (Mounted Service School yearbook), 237–240; Stephen C. Reynolds, "The Manila Polo Club," ibid., 241–245; *Howtizer,* 1904 (West Point yearbook), 176. See also *WDAR* (1910), CG, Department of the Missouri, 83; *ANJ,* September 25, 1909, 93.

75. *WDAR* (1907), CG, Philippines Division, 221; (1908), SW, 87, CG, Philippines Division, 202; (1909), AG, 239–240.

76. *WDAR* (1908), SW, 11–12, CS, 353; (1909), CS, 192–194; Lawrence F. Abbott, ed., *The Letters of Archie Butt: Personal Aide to President Roosevelt* (Garden City, N.Y., 1924), 167–169; Edgar F. Raines Jr., "Major General J. Franklin Bell and Military Reform: The Chief of Staff Years, 1906–1910" (Ph.D. diss., University of Wisconsin, 1976), 490; Matthew M. Oyos, "Theodore Roosevelt: Commander in Chief" (Ph.D. diss., Ohio State University, 1993), 136–139.

77. *WDAR* (1914), JAG, 228; Coffman, *Old Army,* 282; Adams, *Exploits and Adventures,* 280–281; William T. Anderson to AG, Philippines Division, December 22, 1908 (copy provided by Earl Stover); Price, "Trooper of the 15th Horse," 66, 67 (quotation), 71, 91–93, 101–102; *WDAR* (1910), CG, Department of Mindanao, 251.

78. Ola Bell, Diary, December 3, 5, 14, 1909, and January 1, 1910, USMA; Henry, "Brief Narrative," 52; Shunk, *Army Woman in Philippines,* 67, 79, 92–93; Hugh Johnson, *The Blue Eagle,* 39 (quotation).

79. Hugh Johnson, *The Blue Eagle,* 43 (quotations); Gillett, *Army Medical Department,* 355.

80. R. Johnson, "My Life in U.S. Army," 185–187.

81. Meixsel, "Army Policy in Philippine Islands," 86; Price, "Trooper of the 15th Horse," 74–79; *WDAR* (1905), CG, Department of Mindanao, 319–311; (1907), CG, Philippines Division, 240–241, CG, Department of Mindanao, 307.

82. War Department General Oorder no. 44, March 1, 1906; Raines, "J. Franklin Bell and Military Reform," 485; *WDAR* (1904), CG, Department of Luzon, 225; (1908), CG, Philippines Division, 206; Frank E. Vandiver, *Black Jack: The Life and Times of John J. Pershing* (College Station, 1977), I: 408–411, 417–421, 438; Ralph W. Kingman, Diary, March 18, April 19, May 1 and 3, June 12–14, 17–21, August 8–10, 1907, USMA.

83. Ola Bell, Diary, July 26 and 28, 1910, USMA; Meixsel, "Army Policy in Philippine Islands," 53–56, 79, 93.

84. Marvin E. Fletcher, *America's First Black General: Benjamin O. Davis Sr., 1880–1970* (Lawrence, Kans., 1989), chap. 3; Bernard C. Nalty, *Strength for the Fight: A History of Black Americans in the Military* (New York, 1986), 110–111; *ANJ,* July 25, 1914.

85. Benjamin O. Davis to Sarah Overton, March 1, 1918 (first quotation), 23 (second quotation), June 3 (third and fourth quotations), August 5, 17, September 10 and 20, 1918, Davis Collection, MHI.

86. Ralph W. Kingman, Diary, June 12, 1907, UMSA; Lassiter, "Memoir," III: 8, 9; Edgar F. Raines Jr., "The War Department General Staff and the Japanese War Crises, 1906–1909," copy in author's collection; Belote and Belote, *Corregidor,* 27–30; Joan M. Jensen, *Army Surveillance in America, 1775–1980* (New Haven, 1991), 105–108.

87. Hagood, "Down the Big Road," chap. 20; Brian M. Linn, *Guardians of Empire:*

The U.S. Army and the Pacific, 1902–1940 (Chapel Hill, N.C., 1997), 107; Mansfield Robinson, interviews, September 8, 1954, and August 6, 1956; War Department Special Order no. 219, September 19, 1913.

88. Larry I. Bland and Sharon R. Ritenour, eds., *The Papers of George Catlett Marshall*, 4 vols. (Baltimore, 1981), I: 83 (quotation); Pogue, *George C. Marshall*, 120–124; Charles D. McKenna, "The Forgotten Reform: Field Maneuvers in the Development of the United States Army, 1902–1920" (Ph.D. diss., Duke University, 1981), 159–160.

89. Henry H. Arnold, *Global Mission* (New York, 1949), 44; Bland and Ritenour, *Papers of Marshall*, I: 79; Pogue, *George C. Marshall*, 124.

90. Pogue, *George C. Marshall*, 125–128 (quotation on 125); Bland and Ritenour, *Papers of Marshall*, 85–92.

91. *WDAR* (1915), SW, 120–121; Shunk, *Army Woman in Philippines*, 84; Grace Groves, "Recollections," 58.

4. ENLISTED MEN IN THE NEW ARMY

Epigraph: Gilmer M. Bell, questionnaire.

1. Alfred Reynolds, *The Life of an Enlisted Man in the United States Army* (Washington, D.C., 1904), 7; Leonard Wood to Russell B. Harrison, June 10, 1911, no. 6942; and Newton D. Baker to Edward D. Duffield, January 7, 1916, no. 1230, both in Chief of Staff File, 1907–1916, RG 165, NA.

2. *WDAR* (1902), AG, 330, and IG, 406; (1916), AG, 265; (1912), AG, 467; (1916), CS, 165.

3. *WDAR* (1904), CS, 225–226, and AG, 256; (1905), AG, 402; (1910), SW, 14; (1914), AG, 170, and SG, 439. The quotation is from *WDAR* (1901), AG, 41.

4. The Army statistics are from AG annual reports. The Navy statistics are from Frederick S. Harrod, *Manning the New Navy: The Development of a Modern Naval Enlisted Force, 1899–1940* (Westport, Conn., 1978), 52, 176–177.

5. Although the adjutant general gave the percentage of foreign-born every year, the surgeon general tabulated them annually by nationality as well as by the medical causes for rejection in the *WDAR*s for 1900–1916. The Navy's figures are from a table (Harrod, *Manning the New Navy*, 181) of naturalized citizens and noncitizens as part of the total force.

6. *WDAR* (1905), SW, 5–6.

7. William L. Banks, interviews, May 10, 1973, and February 9, 1980; questionnaire; copies of Banks's Notes for Byron Price, copies provided by Byron Price; *WDAR* (1912), AG, 460, 463; Marvin E. Fletcher, *The Black Soldier and Officer in the United*

States Army, 1891–1917 (Columbia, Mo., 1974), 28–29, 71–72; Harrod, *Manning the New Navy*, 57–58; *WDAR* (1910), AG, 176 (quotation).

8. George S. Schuyler, *Black and Conservative: The Autobiography of George S. Schuyler* (New Rochelle, N.Y., 1966), 2, 23, 28–30 (quotations on 28 and 30); questionnaires based on interviews by chaplains with Mike Henley, Dorsie W. Willis (Lewis K. Combs), and Edward Warfield (Lee A. Thigpen Jr.), copies provided by Earl T. Stover.

9. Lowell Thomas, *Woodfill of the Regulars: A True Story of Adventure from the Arctic to the Argonne* (Garden City, N.Y., 1929), 11–12, 19, 22–23; Martin Blumenson and James L. Stokesbury, *Masters of the Art of Command* (Boston, 1975), 43; Patrick J. Hayes, George E. Maker, Sidney M. Martin, Walter J. Rouse, questionnaires; and Sidney M. Martin to author, October 29, 1976.

10. Questionnaires from Clarence R. Huebner and Troy H. Middleton; Frank J. Price, *Troy H. Middleton: A Biography* (Baton Rouge, 1974), 14, 23–25, 33–34, 38.

11. Edwin F. Glenn, "The Recruit Depot, Columbus Barracks, Ohio," *Journal of the United States Infantry Association* 2, no. 2 (October 1, 1905), 6; *WDAR* (1905), Military Secretary, 403; Edward M. Coffman, *The Old Army: A Portrait of the American Army in Peacetime, 1784–1898* (New York, 1986), 336–340. Fort Slocum was known as Davids Island in the nineteenth century.

12. *WDAR* (1905), Military Secretary, 404; (1906), SW, 14; (1908), AG, 411; (1909), AG, 259, 265.

13. *WDAR* (1906), Military Secretary, 592; (1907), AG, 232–233 (second quotation on 233); (1909), AG, 259 (first quotation); (1910), JAG, 242.

14. William L. Banks, interviews, May 10, 1973, and May 2, 1978; also Banks Notes for Byron Price; R. R. Jackson to William H. Taft, April 27, 1912; George A. Dodd endorsement, July 18, 1912 (quotation); AG to Secretary of War, August 13, 1912, no. 1932951 (quotation); Charles T. Smart to AG, May 6, 1915; George A. Dodd endorsement, May 11, 1915, no. 2285100, all in AG Document File, 1890–1917, RG 94, NA.

15. C. C. Lyon, *Experience of a Recruit in the United States Army* (Washington, D.C., 1916), 3; Newton D. Baker to Lyon, June 21, 1916, no. 2476114, AG Document File, 1890–1917, RG 94, NA; Glenn, "Recruit Depot, Columbus Barracks," 30; *WDAR* (1910), SG, 369; (1916), SG, 682.

16. The quotations are from Lyon, *Experience of a Recruit*, 3 and 7; and Glenn, "Recruit Depot, Columbus Barracks," 17. Also see ibid., 8 and 15.

17. Schuyler, *Black and Conservative*, 34; Glenn, "Recruit Depot, Columbus Barracks," 9 and 15.

18. Lyon, *Experience of a Recruit*, 5, 7, 9–10; Glenn, "Recruit Depot, Columbus Barracks," 8–10, 14–15, 32; *WDAR* (1911), AG, 227, and CG, Department of Mindanao, 240 (quotations); (1912), AG, 462.

19. Schuyler, *Black and Conservative,* 36–39, 48, 76–83 (quotations on 39, 38, 76, 77, 80, 83); Walter J. Rouse, interview (quotations).

20. *WDAR* (1902), CG, Department of the Missouri, 56; Patrick J. Hayes, telephone interview; Arthur J. Stanley, interview; William L. Banks, interview, May 10, 1973; Banks to author, June 28, 1973; Banks Notes for Price.

21. *WDAR* (1901), CG, Army, 147; (1904), IG, 288; (1906), CG, Pacific Division, 169–170; Reynolds, *Life of Enlisted Man,* 13–14, 17; Richard Johnson, "My Life in the U.S. Army, 1899–1922," 71, MHI; Schuyler, *Black and Conservative,* 45.

22. Reynolds, *Life of Enlisted Man,* 18–19; *WDAR* (1902), SW, 21; (1903), IG, 448–449; (1905), IG, 448.

23. *WDAR* (1901), CG, Army, 15–16, and IG, 142; (1902), CG, Department of the Missouri, 55.

24. *WDAR* (1911), CG, Department of California, 193; (1911), IG, 271 (quotation); *Sixth Regiment of Field (Horse) Artillery, USA, Fort Riley, Kansas: Illustrated Review* (Denver, 1910), 65.

25. War Department, General Order no. 44, March 1, 1906; *WDAR* (1906), SW, 46–47, and CG, Department of the Gulf, 46–49; Edgar F. Raines Jr., "Major General J. Franklin Bell and Military Reform: The Chief of Staff Years, 1906–1910" (Ph.D. diss., University of Wisconsin–Madison, 1976), 485–486; Johnson, "My Life in U.S. Army," 50, 52–53, 77–78.

26. *WDAR* (1907), CS, 176; Banks Notes for Price; *Sixth Regiment of Field Artillery,* 66–68.

27. Coffman, *Old Army,* 278–280, 355; William A. Ganoe, *The History of the United States Army* (New York, 1924), 419; *WDAR* (1903), SW, 25–26; (1907), SW, 94; (1908), CG, Department of the East, 31; Schuyler, *Black and Conservative,* 57; *WDAR* (1911), IG, 270 (quotation); *ANJ,* October 26, 1912.

28. *WDAR* (1901), CG, Department of the Missouri, 254; (1902), IG, 399, and CG, 3 (quotation); (1903), AG, 429; (1905), SW, 39; Walter J. Rouse, interview.

29. *WDAR* (1903), CG, Department of the Missouri, 81; (1908), CG, Department of the Gulf, 64–65; William L. Banks, interview, May 10, 1973 (first quotation); Banks Notes for Price; Johnson, "My Life in U.S. Army," 75–76 (second quotation on 75); Schuyler, *Black and Conservative,* 57 (third quotation); Robert L. Bullard, "What Is the Matter with Army Athletics?" (last quotation), Bullard Papers, LC; *WDAR* (1905), SW, 39.

30. Charles D. McKenna, "The Forgotten Reform: Field Maneuvers in the Development of the United States Army, 1902–1920" (Ph.D. diss., Duke University, 1981), 59–60, 99, 102, 109, 129, 158, 161; Johnson, "My Life in U.S. Army," 75–77.

31. William L. Banks, interview, May 10, 1973; Banks Notes for Price.

32. "Notes for Chief Signal Officer in re Policies" (quotation), Foulois Papers, LC.

Enlisted ranks and pay are in *WDAR* (1907), SW, 67; Rebecca Robins Raines, *Getting the Message Through: A Branch History of the U.S. Army Signal Corps* (Washington, D.C., 1996), 119–122.

33. R. Raines, *Getting the Message Through*, 127; Edward Ward, interview by Royal Frey and others, December 1, 1959; Vernon L. Burge, "Early History of Army Aviation," copy in author's collection; George E. Hicks, "The First Enlisted Airman," *Sergeants,* June 1989, 10–12, and July 1989, 10–13; Charles D. Chandler and Frank P. Lahm, *How Our Army Grew Wings* (reprint, New York, 1979), 77–80, 118, 122, 244–245.

34. William Loeb to William H. Taft, May 22, 1907; J. Franklin Bell to William P. Duvall, May 25, 1907, no. 4560-1; Shelton report, July 31, 1907; *WDAR* (1907), SW, 66–113 (quotation on 79), and CG, Northern Division, 78; Harrod, *Manning the New Navy,* 198. Desertion statistics from 1830 through 1914 are in *WDAR* (1914), JAG, 276 (foldout); Gilbert C. Fite and Jim E. Reese, *An Economic History of the United States* (Boston, 1973), 271; *Military Laws of the United States,* 2 vols. (Washington, D.C., 1921), II: 1125.

35. *WDAR* (1907), SW, 67, 72–76, 80, 85, 90, and CG, Northern Division, 75; (1905), JAG, 481; (1904), SW, 7; questionnaires from William L. Banks and Gilmer M. Bell; *The Statistical History of the United States from Colonial Times to the Present* (Stamford, Conn., 1965), 73.

36. *WDAR* (1902), SW, 22; (1907), SW, 75, 96; Reynolds, *Life of Enlisted Man,* 9, 16–17.

37. Reynolds, *Life of Enlisted Man,* 15–16; *WDAR* (1901), AG, 105–111; (1902), IG, 401, 429; (1907), SW, 96, and CG, Northern Division, 77 (quotation); William L. Banks, interview, May 10, 1973.

38. Reynolds, *Life of Enlisted Man,* 12–13; *WDAR* (1900), Acting Commissary General, 500; (1908), CG, Department of the East, 35; W. W. Wotherspoon to Robert Shaw Oliver, June 16 and November 15, 1909, WDGS Report no. 4154, CS Correspondence, RG 165, NA.

39. *WDAR* (1905), SW, 36–37, and CS, 377–379, and CG, Department of the East, 18–19; (1906), CG, Department of the Missouri, 104, 106.

40. Shelton report, July 31, 1907; Schuyler, *Black and Conservative,* 55; *WDAR* (1905), CS, 382; Leslie R. Groves to AG, January 29, 1909, no. 1485804; J. Franklin Bell to the Secretary of War, November 30, 1909, no. 1436700-J, both in AG Document File, RG 94, NA.

41. Ernest F. Easterbrook, *The Soldier and the Cross: A Biography of My Father, Edmund Pepperell Easterbrook* (Carmel, Calif., 1985), 36, chap. 6; Earl F. Stover, *Up from Handymen: The United States Army Chaplaincy, 1865–1920* (Washington, D.C., 1977), 164–165, 168–169.

42. Stover, *Up from Handymen,* 160; *WDAR* (1899), SW, 41–42 (quotation). AG

questions and results of the poll are in ibid., 93–94. For two responses, see ibid., 103 (second quotation) and 213 (last quotation). The statistics are on 275–279.

43. Stover, *Up from Handymen*, 160–161; War Department, General Order no. 5, February 2, 1901 (*WDAR* [1901], AG, app., 73–77), put the congressional ban into effect; ibid., CG, 148; (1903), CS, 142, and CG, Department of Texas, 112 (first quotation); (1904), IG, 292; (1905), CS, 379; (1907), SW, 100; (1916), SG, 470 (second quotation); "Effects of Abolishing the Canteen," *Infantry Journal* 4 (November 1907), 423–433. See long-term graphs on desertion (*WDAR* [1914], JAG, app.) and alcoholism (*WDAR* [1913], SG, 452); Mary C. Gillett, *The Army Medical Department, 1865–1917* (Washington, D.C., 1995), 354.

44. A soldier stood a slightly better chance of acquittal in the intermediate court, which averaged an 87 percent conviction rate from 1912 through 1916; Harrod, *Manning the New Navy*, 199; Reynolds, *Life of Enlisted Man*, 21–23 (quotations on 22 and 23); Articles of War 75, 809, and 83, in *Regulations for the Army of the United States*, 1904; David A. Lockmiller, *Enoch H. Crowder: Soldier, Lawyer, Statesman* (Columbia, Mo., 1955), 134; *WDAR* (1911), JAG, 284; (1916), JAG, 318; (1917), JAG, 223.

45. *WDAR* (1910), AG, 174, and JAG, 241; (1912), JAG, 490–491.

46. Questionnaires from Gilmer M. Bell, Walter Hansen, George E. Maker, and Sidney M. Martin; Patrick J. Hayes, telephone interview, May 11, 1974. Nor did old soldiers steal. Major General Tom R. Stoughton (retired), deputy governor of the Soldiers Home, commented in an interview in 1972 that no theft had been reported there in four years.

47. Gilmer M. Bell, questionnaire (first quotation); Patrick J. Hayes, telephone interview (second quotation); Mike Henley, questionnaire; Schuyler, *Black and Conservative*, 68. See JAG reports in *WDAR*s for those years.

48. In 1912 the judge advocate general began listing the strength and number of summary court trials at every post in an effort to exert pressure on this issue. See *WDAR* (1912), JAG, 492–493; (1906), JAG, 665–666; (1910), JAG, 240–241; (1916), JAG, 318.

49. Coffman, *Old Army*, 378–379; Lockmiller, *Enoch H. Crowder*, 136–137, 149; *WDAR* (1907), SW, 24–25.

50. E. H. Crowder to AG, May 20, 1914, Court-Martial no. 84967, JAG, RG 153, NA; War Department, General Order no. 48, June 25, 1914; Benjamin M. Koehler File, no. 58077, AG General Correspondence File, 1890–1917, RG 94, NA; *WDAR* (1915), JAG, 254.

51. Coffman, *Old Army*, 202, 204, 224–225; Reynolds, *Life of Enlisted Man*, 25; *WDAR* (1907), SW, 70–71, 102. "Does the present system of promoting men from the ranks benefit the Army?" unsigned paper attached to J. F. Bell Memo, March

27, 1907, no. 1897-3; and T. W. Jones Memorandum Report, April 27, 1907, no. 1897-4, both in War Department General Staff Records, RG 165, NA.

52. Vernon G. Olsmith, *Recollections of an Old Soldier* (San Antonio, 1963), 3–7, 112–117. In 1909 there were 4,209 officers, 546 from the Army, 1,838 from civil life (including those who came in from the volunteers during the Philippine War), and 1825 West Pointers; *WDAR* (1909), SW, 10–11. For annual increments, see AG reports. Harrod, *Manning the New Navy*, 106.

53. *ANJ*, June 10, 1911, 1240; Leroy Eltinge File, AG no. 39626, RG 94, NA; Lewis Landes, "Jews in the United States Army and Navy," in *The American Jewish Year Book 5677: September 28, 1916 to September 16, 1917* (New York, 1916), 76–79. Also see correspondence in no. 123115, AG Central File, RG 94, NA; Stover, *Up from Handymen*, 176 and app. 4; John Higham, *Strangers in the Land: Patterns in Nativism, 1860–1925* (New York, 1969), 160–161.

54. Simon Wolf to William H. Taft, May 3, 1911, quoting Garrard's comment; Summary of Results of Preliminary Examination of Private Frank Bloom, January 16, 1911; Taft to Secretary of War, May 8, 1911 (second quotation); Dickinson to Taft, May 9, 1911 (third quotation); Taft to Dickinson, May 11, 1911, all in AG no. 1702681, RG 94, NA; *ANJ*, June 10, 1911, 1240.

55. Bloom's examination results, efficiency reports, and other relevant correspondence, including Henry L. Stimson to AG, March 4, 1913 (quotation), are in AG no. 1702681, RG 94, NA. Bloom and Garrard entries in *Official Army Register* for 1922.

56. In addition to those in the four regiments, a few blacks including Richard Johnson were in the Hospital Corps and the Signal Corps; Fletcher, *Black Soldier and Officer*, 66–67, 71, 79, 116 (Young quotation), 153–159. G. W. Read to Commanding Officer, Columbus Barracks, November 27, 1916, no. 2496329, filed with no. 2476114, AG Document File, 1890–1917, RG 94, NA; *WDAR* (1910), AG, 176 (second quotation); Garna L. Christian, *Black Soldiers in Jim Crow Texas, 1899–1917* (College Station, 1995), 49 (last quotation).

57. Taft to Culbertson, June 4, 1906, in *WDAR* (1906), SW, 26; Christian, *Black Soldiers in Jim Crow Texas*, 70.

58. Steward to Adjutant, 25th Infantry, June 30, 1906. Copies of this letter as well as others that Hoyt forwarded are filed with his letter to the Military Secretary, July 1, 1906, AG Miscellaneous File, no. 73, RG 94, NA.

59. *WDAR* (1906), SW, 26–35 (second quotation on 33 and third on 31), and app. B, 255–364 (first quotation on 256). In addition to Fletcher (*Black Soldier and Officer*, chaps. 9 and 9) and Christian (*Black Soldiers in Jim Crow Texas*, chap. 4), I relied on John D. Weaver, *The Brownsville Raid* (College Station, 1992). The Penrose quotation is from 160. Willis' comment is in *New York Times*, December 31, 1972. The last two quotations are from *ANJ*, November 24, 1906, 343, and April 18, 1908,

877; photocopies of clippings from New York and Massachusetts newspapers, author's collection.

60. On the Athens incident, see Weaver, *Brownsville Raid,* 91; and Marvin Fletcher, "War on the Streets of Athens," unpublished paper. For Walla Walla, see Coffman, *Old Army,* 379–381; *ANJ,* November 17, 1906; and Charles E. Hay to Major Porter, December 26, 1906, no. 20.754, JAG Office File, 1894–1912, RG 153, NA.

61. *WDAR* (1910), AG, 175. For Army desertion rates from 1830 to 1914, *WDAR* (1914), AG, 276; Schuyler, *Black and Conservative,* 65–68; *ANJ* on communities' protests, January 2, 1909, 480, and September 25, 1909, 88; *ANJ* on the Honolulu riot, January 29, 1916, 697; and February 5, 1916, 725.

62. Shelton added: "So also are married officers"; *WDAR* (1907), SW, 97; *ANJ,* December 14, 1907, 375.

63. William T. Anderson's Monthly Report of August 1, 1904, copy from Earl F. Stover; Frank N. Schubert, *Buffalo Soldiers, Braves, and the Brass: The Story of Fort Robinson, Nebraska* (Shippensburg, Pa., 1993), 67–68.

64. *WDAR* (1899), SG, 385–386; (1900), IG, 134; (1905), CG, Department of the Gulf, 49.

65. Roy F. Sulzberger, telephone interview; *WDAR* (1904), SG, 167.

66. George L. Stackhouse, questionnaire (quotation); Stackhouse, interview.

67. *WDAR* (1904), CG, Department of Texas, 133; (1910), CG, Department of Texas, 104.

68. *WDAR* (1907), Board of Visitors, USMA, 181–186; (1908), Superintendent, USMA, 17; Robert P. Johnson, questionnaire; Johnson, interview (quotation); also his essays in USMA.

69. Charles E. McCombs, questionnaire; McCombs, telephone interview, March 16, 1975; joint interview with McCombs and his sisters, Ruth DeMattia and Martha Schneider, May 23, 1975; Lillian Auring Perry, interview. For pay, see *Official Army Register, 1913,* 622.

70. *WDAR* (1907), SW, 99–102, 113 (quotation on 99); Louis S. Yassel, interview; Martha McCombs Schneider, interview; Charles E. McCombs, questionnaire.

71. Mrs. E. J. Erazmus to William H. Taft, November 10, 1912, filed with John Biddle to Editor, *American Magazine,* December 19, 1912, WCD no. 6292, RG 165, NA; Robert K. Evans to AG, December 28, 1912, T. H. Barry, Endorsement, January 3, 1913, WCD no. 7519–1, RG 165, NA.

72. M. M. Macomb to Chief of Staff, September 18, 1914; George B. Duncan to Chief of Staff, July 23, 1914, both WCD no. 7519-32, RG 165, NA. The post with the highest enrollment in the Department of Texas in 1910 was Fort Sam Houston, with twenty. Two other posts only had three each; *WDAR* (1910), CG, Department of Texas, 104. See also *WDAR* (1906), CG, Pacific Division, 169–170.

73. Douglas MacArthur to Chief of Staff, November 14, 1913, filed with supporting letter by Brigadier General M. M. Macomb, November 15, 1913, WCD no. 7519–21, RG 165, NA. Also filed under this number is Leonard Wood to Chief, War College Division, December 9, 1913, in which he commented that the secretary of war wanted such courses offered.

74. Harrod, *Manning the New Navy*, 92–94. The strength figures do not include the 5,000-plus members of Philippine Scout units; *WDAR* (1916), AG, 236–238, and SW, 37 (quotation), and CS, 162.

75. William L. Banks, interview, May 10, 1973; Thomas, *Woodfill of the Regulars*, 206–218 (quotation on 217).

5. THE MANAGERIAL REVOLUTION

Epigraph: William H. Simpson, interview, August 17, 1971.

1. *WDAR* (1899), SW, 56–70 (quotations on 58 and 69).

2. Walter Millis, *Arms and Men: A Study in American Military History* (New York, 1956), 173–181; James E. Hewes Jr., *From Root to McNamara: Army Organization And Administration, 1900–1963* (Washington, D.C., 1975), 8 (quotation).

3. *WDAR* (1909), SW, 7, and AG, 232.

4. Jacob L. Devers, interview; Carlo D'Este, *Patton: A Genius for War* (New York, 1995), chaps. 1 and 3; William H. Simpson, interview, August 17, 1971 (quotation).

5. D'Este, *Patton*, 62–63, 66; Jacob L. Devers, interview; William H. Simpson, interview, August 17, 1971.

6. *Howitzer* (1909), 208–209; Jacob L. Devers, interview; William H. Simpson, interview, August 19, 1971.

7. William H. Simpson, interview, August 17, 1971; *Howitzer* (1908), 14 (second quotation); William H. Simpson, interview, August 20, 1971 (third quotation); William H. Simpson to author, December 30, 1978; Sidney Forman, *West Point: A History of the United States Military Academy* (New York, 1950), 158–161.

8. Jacob L. Devers, interview; *Howitzer* (1909), 64.

9. Martin Blumenson, ed., *The Patton Papers: 1885–1940* (Boston, 1972), 119 (first quotation), 121, 124 (third quotation), 125, 137, 146, 153; William H. Simpson, interview, August 20, 1971 (second quotation); *Howitzer* (1909), 76, 247–253.

10. Stephen F. Ambrose, *Duty, Honor, Country: A History of West Point* (Baltimore, 1966), 244–245; *Howitzer* (1909), 231; Blumenson, *Patton Papers*, 173 (quotation).

11. Hugh L. Scott, *Some Memories of a Soldier* (New York, 1928), 420; Blumenson, *Patton Papers*, 169; *Howitzer* (1909), 14, 16.

12. Blumenson, *Patton Papers,* 153, 156; Jacob L. Devers, interview; *Howitzer* (1909), 101; Cullum Register, vol. VIB.

13. William A. Ganoe, *The History of the United States Army* (New York, 1924), 432; *WDAR* (1906), CS, 554; Gilbert C. Fite and Jim E. Reese, *An Economic History of the United States,* 3d ed. (Boston, 1973), 271.

14. *New York Times,* June 12, 1909; *WDAR* (1908), SW, 87; (1909), SW, 7, 10–11, 12, 14, and AG, 239; Edward M. Coffman, *The Old Army: A Portrait of the American Army in Peacetime, 1784–1898* (New York, 1986), 49.

15. Henry S. Aurand to author, September 1, 1978; *WDAR* (1908), SW, 29; (1909), SW, 8; Emanuel R. Lewis, *Seacoast Fortifications of the United States: An Introductory History* (Annapolis, 1979), 77–93.

16. Boyd L. Dastrup, *King of Battle: A Branch History of the U.S. Army's Field Artillery* (Fort Monroe, Va., 1992), chap. 6.

17. Beverly. F. Browne to author, February 26, 1959 (quotation); Dastrup, *King of Battle,* 152–153, 158–159; Oliver L. Spaulding, *The United States Army in War and Peace* (New York, 1937), 405–406.

18. Robert M. Danford, "Edmund L. Gruber," *Assembly,* 1 (April 1942), 11; *WDAR* (1909), SW, 8.

19. Jacob L. Devers, interview.

20. Blumenson, *Patton Papers,* 185, 193, and 195 (quotation).

21. Ibid., 231; D'Este, *Patton,* chap. 10.

22. Blumenson, *Patton Papers,* 260–263, 267, 282; Robert Wooster, *Nelson A. Miles and the Twilight of the Frontier Army* (Lincoln, Neb., 1993), 208, 247; *WDAR* (1915), CS, 163, and QMG, 365–368; (1916), SW, 22.

23. Blumenson, *Patton Papers,* 264, 265, 267 (quotation); D'Este, *Patton,* 139, 146, 152.

24. Courses are described in detail in the *Rasp*s for 1912 and 1913. See the latter, 256, 258, and 259, for Patton's races.

25. Guy V. Henry Jr., "A Brief Narrative of the Life of Guy V. Henry, Jr.," MHI, 34–50 (first quotation on 37); Guy V. Henry Jr. to the Secretary, Mounted Service School, October 16, 1911 (third quotation); Henry T. Allen to the Chief of Staff, October 27, 1911; Walter C. Short to "Teddy" (Charles D. Rhodes), May 5, 1911; Short to Rhodes, telegram, June 5, 1911 (second quotation), all in General Staff Miscellaneous Correspondence: 1907–1916, RG 165, NA.

26. Henry, "Brief Narrative," 36 (last quotation) and 43 (first quotation); *WDAR* (1913), CS, 156, 158 (second quotation). Joseph T. Glatthaar provided me with a copy of Wood to L. L. Lomax, January 23, 1911, Lomax Papers, Virginia Historical Society, Richmond.

27. Wade H. Haislip, interview (first quotation); William H. Simpson, interview, August 17, 1971 (other quotations).

28. D'Este, *Patton,* 153. The data on foreign service come from the Cullum Registers, vols. V and VIB.

29. William H. Simpson, interview, August 17, 1971, and notes from a second interview that night; McGee entry in Cullum Register, vol. VIB; H. H. Elarth to author, March 17, 1975.

30. Robert L. Eichelberger, "Memoirs," E 16–17 (third quotation), and III E 35 (first two quotations), MHI; D. Clayton James, *The Years of MacArthur: 1880–1941* (Boston, 1970), 106 (last quotation); Forrest C. Pogue, *George C. Marshall: Education of a General, 1880–1939* (New York, 1963), 113–114; *WDAR* (1911), SW, 12–13, and AG, 239–242; Charles D. Chandler and Frank P. Lahm, *How Our Army Grew Wings* (New York, 1979), 184–185.

31. Eichelberger, "Memoirs," III E 36–40, E 18–23.

32. After World War I, there were 250 machine guns in an infantry regiment; Edgar F. Raines Jr., "Major General J. Franklin Bell and Military Reform: The Chief of Staff Years, 1906–1910" (Ph.D. diss., University of Wisconsin, 1976), 434; William H. Simpson, interview, August 17, 1971; David A. Armstrong, *Bullets and Bureaucrats: The Machine Gun and the United States Army, 1861–1916* (Westport, Conn., 1982), 128; *WDAR* (1908), SW, 42 (quotation).

33. Raines, "Bell and Military Reform," 408–433 (quotation on 422); John H. Parker, "Memories of the Service," 94–103, USMA; Armstrong, *Bullets and Bureaucrats,* 46–47, 96–119, 131, 141, 150, 155–156, 163.

34. *Infantry Drill Regulations: 1911,* 2d ed. (Washington, D.C., 1917), 127; Parker, "Memories of the Service," 95; Blumenson, *Patton Papers,* 212; Armstrong, *Bullets and Bureaucrats,* 139, 141, 144, 152–154, 171, 181, 184, 189, 195; Raines, "Bell and Military Reform," 433–434; Ernest N. Harmon, "Personal Memoirs of Major General E. N. Harmon, U.S.A. Retired," 9, MHI; Charles D. Herron, interview.

35. Chandler and Lahm, *How Army Grew Wings,* 189, 191; Eichelberger, "Memoirs," III E 35 and E 17–18; Larry I. Bland and Sharon R. Ritenour, eds., *The Papers of George Catlett Marshall,* 4 vols. (Baltimore, 1981), I: 54; Benjamin D. Foulois with C. V. Glines, *From the Wright Brothers to the Astronauts: The Memoirs of Major General Benjamin D. Foulois* (New York, 1968), 92–94.

36. Chandler and Lahm, *How Army Grew Wings,* 80, 295–298 (quotation on 295); *WDAR* (1908), SW, 44.

37. Foulois, *From Wright Brothers to Astronauts,* 42–46.

38. Benjamin D. Foulois to Captain Cowan, January 12, 194, Foulois Papers, LC; Foulois, *From Wright Brothers to Astronauts,* 54–57; Chandler and Lahm, *How Army Grew Wings,* 152–154 and chap. 11; Frank P. Lahm to his father, October 2, 1908,

Lahm Papers, U.S. Air Force Historical Research Center, Maxwell Air Force Base, Ala.; Johnson Hagood, "Down the Big Road," 107, MHI.

39. Foulois, *From Wright Brothers to Astronauts*, 60, 62; Frank P. Lahm to father, August 1, 1909, Lahm Papers (quotation).

40. Foulois, *From Wright Brothers to Astronauts*, 1, 63–65 (quotation on 64); Fred Howard, *Wilbur and Orville: A Biography of the Wright Brothers* (New York, 1987), 305–306; Frank P. Lahm to father, August 1, 1909, Lahm Papers.

41. Frank P. Lahm to father, September 5, 1909, Lahm Papers; Foulois, *From Wright Brothers to Astronauts*, 66–67; Chandler and Lahm, *How Army Grew Wings*, 162–165.

42. Chandler and Lahm, *How Army Grew Wings*, 166–167; Foulois, *From Wright Brothers to Astronauts*, 3–5 (first quotation on 4), 73–76 (second quotation on 75); Benjamin D. Foulois, interview (last quotation); Logbook for Airplane no. 1, February 3, 1910–July 22, 1911; monthly report to Chief Signal Officer, April 1, 1910, both in Foulois Papers.

43. Benjamin D. Foulois to Chief Signal Officer, September 1, 1910, Foulois Papers; Foulois, *From Wright Brothers to Astronauts*, 75–77; *WDAR* (1910), SW, 30; Chandler and Lahm, *How Army Grew Wings*, chap. 12.

44. *ANJ*, October 29, 1910; *WDAR* (1912), Chief Signal Officer, 965–967; Chandler and Lahm, *How Army Grew Wings*, 320.

45. H. H. Arnold, *Global Mission* (New York, 1949), 15 and chap. 2; Cullum Register, 1920; Frank P. Lahm to father, October 13, 1913, Lahm Papers; *WDAR* (1915), Chief Signal Officer, 740–748; Chandler and Lahm, *How Army Grew Wings*, chap. 15 and 269.

46. Foulois, *From Wright Brothers to Astronauts*, 84; Chandler and Lahm, *How Army Grew Wings*, 88, 222–225, 247–248; E. B. Potter and Chester W. Nimitz, eds., *Seapower: A Naval History* (Englewood Cliffs, N.J., 1960), 391.

47. Chandler and Lahm, *How Army Grew Wings*, 316–319, 269; Otto L. Nelson, *National Security and the General Staff: A Study in Organization and Administration* (Washington, D.C., 1946), 48, 175–176.

48. Ruth Harrison Spaatz, interview (quotation); Foulois, *From Wright Brothers to Astronauts*, 112 and chap. 8; Alfred F. Hurley, *Billy Mitchell: Crusader for Air Power* (Bloomington, Ind., 1975), 20–21.

49. *ANJ*, January 3, 1903, October 8 and 29, 1904, August 26, 1905, April 24, 1915 (quotation).

50. D'Este, *Patton*, 55–58, 102–105, 117–121, 130, 137, 146 (quotation); David M. Katzman, *Seven Days a Week: Women and Domestic Service in Industrializing America* (New York, 1978), 57; Harold Katz, "The Decline of Competition in the Automobile Industry, 1920–1940" (Ph.D. diss., Columbia University, 1970), 41.

51. Carolyn Richards Whipple, *Victory at Eighty* (New York, 1975), 15, 38–65.

52. Louise Adams Browne, questionnaire and interview.

53. Eli A. Helmick, "From Reveille to Retreat," 181 (quotation), MHI.

54. D'Este, *Patton,* 120–122, 150–151; Whipple, *Victory at Eighty,* 61. The quotations are from questionnaires from Thomas D. Finley, Marjorie Hinds Cruse, and Adelaide Poore Bolté (October 1972); and Bradford G. Chynoweth, *Bellamy Park* (Hicksville, N.Y., 1975), 42.

55. Questionnaires from Edith Morgan Cabell, Sarah Shanks Chamberlain, Bradford G. Chynoweth, Alice Hines Cleland, Marjorie Hinds Cruse, Elizabeth Rumbough Donaldson, Thomas D. Finley, Haywood S. Hansell Jr., Harriet Howze Jones, Katherine Winans Maxwell, Phyllis Corbusier Pierson, and Russell P. Reeder Jr.; interviews with Adelaide Poore Bolté (August 4, 1971), Mark W. Clark, Thomas D. Finley (November 27, 1982), Berenice Fiske, John L. Hines Jr., and Matthew B. Ridgway; Mauree Pickering Mahin, *Life in the American Army from the Frontier to Distaff Hall* (Washington, D.C., 1967), 83; Bernard A. Byrne, "Modern History of Bernard Albert Byrne," USMA.

56. Interviews with Mark W. Clark and Matthew B. Ridgway; Russell P. Reeder, *Born at Reveille: Memoirs of a Son of West Point* (New York, 1966), 44.

57. Matthew B. Ridgway, interview; Thomas R. Hay, questionnaire; Adelaide Poore Bolté, questionnaire (October 1972) and interview (August 4, 1971); Jenny Bigelow, Diary, October 14, 1902, February 2 and 6, March 9, 1903, John Bigelow Papers, USMA.

58. Questionnaires of Ernest F. Easterbrook, Thomas D. Finley, Thomas R. Hay, Harriet Howze Jones, and Russell P. Reeder Jr.; interviews of Adelaide Poore Bolté (November 9, 1984), Mark W. Clark, Thomas D. Finley (November 27, 1982), Matthew B. Ridgway, and Virginia Fiske Timberman; Grace Wilson Groves, "Recollections," 40–41, 48, author's collection.

59. Hester Nolan Donovan, questionnaire; interviews with Mark W. Clark, Thomas D. Finley (November 27, 1982), and Matthew B. Ridgway; Groves, "Recollections," 95.

60. Interviews with Adelaide Poore Bolté (August 4, 1971) (quotation), Mark W. Clark, Sidney C. Graves, Paul C. Febiger, Thomas D. Finley (November 27, 1982), and Imogene Hoyle Taulbee. Questionnaires from Adelaide Poore Bolté (October 1972), Sarah Shanks Chamberlain, Bradford G. Chynoweth, Marjorie Hinds Cruse, and Karl L. Schrer; Reeder, *Born at Reveille,* 5–6, 52, 58.

61. Jane P. Bigelow, Diary, John Bigelow Papers, USMA; Jane Bigelow Stevenson, interview (quotation), questionnaire, letter to author, February 8, 1976, and undated MS., author's collection.

62. Adelaide Poore Bolté, interview, November 9, 1984, and telephone interview, January 28, 1990; Mahin, *Life in American Army,* 122, 133–149 (quotations on 133).

63. Helmick, "From Reveille to Retreat," 171, 197; interviews with Mark W. Clark, Thomas D. Finley (November 27, 1982), and Matthew B. Ridgway; Chynoweth, *Bellamy Park,* 51.

64. Coffman, *Old Army,* 277 (first quotation); *WDAR* (1901), SW, 20–25 (second quotation on 21, third on 23); (1902), SW, 187–193; (1900), IG, 149; Ira L. Reeves, *Military Education in the United States* (Burlington, Vt., 1914), chap. 12; Timothy K. Nenninger, "The Army Enters the Twentieth Century," in Kenneth J. Hagan and William R. Roberts, eds., *Against All Enemies: Interpretations of American Military History from Colonial Times to the Present* (Westport, Conn., 1986), 227–231.

65. Coffman, *Old Army,* 274–276; *WDAR* (1904), CG, Department of the Visayas, 245 (quotation).

66. Timothy K. Nenninger, *The Leavenworth Schools and the Old Army: Education, Professionalism, and the Officer Corps of the United States Army, 1881–1918* (Westport, Conn., 1978), 59–65; Ewing E. Booth, *My Observations and Experiences in the United States Army* (Los Angeles, 1944), 84–88.

67. Matthew F. Steele to wife, September 8, 1903, Steele Papers, MHI; Nenninger, *Leavenworth,* 68–70; Edgar F. Raines, "Major General J. Franklin Bell, U.S.A.: The Education of a Soldier, 1856–1899," *Register of the Kentucky Historical Society,* 83 (autumn 1985), 315–346.

68. Nenninger, *Leavenworth,* chap. 5. Also see Reeves, *Military Education,* 210–212.

69. Nenninger, "Army Enters Twentieth Century," 73, 86–94; Helmick, "From Reveille to Retreat," 170; Larry I. Bland, ed., *George C. Marshall Interviews and Reminiscences for Forrest C. Pogue* (Lexington, Va., 1991), 152; Fay W. Brabson, Diary, October 5, 1906, MHI.

70. Nenninger, *Leavenworth,* 94–98; Carol Reardon, *Soldiers and Scholars: The U.S. Army and the Uses of Military History, 1865–1920* (Lawrence, Kans., 1990), 69–75 and chap. 7; Thomas E. Griess to author, September 20, 1996.

71. Matthew F. Steele to wife, September 3 and 4, 1903, October 6, 1906, July 18, 1908, Steele Papers; Helmick, "From Reveille to Retreat," 169; Bland, *Marshall Interviews,* 157, 160 (quotation).

72. Paul B. Malone, "The Army School of the Line," *Infantry Journal,* 6 (January 1910), 512–532; Fay W. Brabson, Diary, November 2 and 5, 1906, January 7, 15, and March 24, 1907; Helmick, "From Reveille to Retreat," 171.

73. *WDAR* (1907), Commandant, Infantry and Cavalry School, Staff College, and Signal School, 235–236; Booth, *Observations and Experiences,* 92; *Commandants, Staff, Faculty, and Graduates of the General Service Schools, Fort Leavenworth, Kansas, 1881–1926* (Fort Leavenworth, 1926), 30–31; Charles D. Herron, "The Four Generals" (first two quotations), unpaginated, copy in author's collection ; Fay W. Brabson, Diary, June 29, 1907 (third quotation); Bland, *Marshall Interviews,* 157 (fourth quotation).

74. Fay W. Brabson, Diary, August 17, September 6, October 18, November 25 and 28, December 25, 1906, January 12 and 27, February 16 and 17, April 8, 11, and 30, May 24, June 29, 1907.

75. Pogue, *George C. Marshall*, 100–102; Booth, *Observations and Experiences*, 93–94; Nenninger, *Leavenworth*, 85–87, 97–101; Reardon, *Soldiers and Scholars*, 56–57; 67–76; Matthew F. Steele to wife, July 2, 3, 4, 6, 8, 10, 14, and 16, 1908, Steele Papers; Marshal's Gettysburg Lecture, George C. Marshall Library; Charles D. Herron, interview (first quotation); Bland, *Marshall Interviews*, 153–154, 160 (second quotation).

76. (Army War College) *Directory: Present and Former Staff and Faculty Graduates and Students by Class Etc.: 1905–1987* (Carlisle Barracks, Pa., 1987), 72–74; George P. Ahern, "A Chronicle of the Army War College, 1899–1919," MHI; Henry P. Ball, *Of Responsible Command: A History of the U.S. Army War College* (Carlisle Barracks, Pa., 1994), 96–97, 106, 115, 128, 137.

77. Helmick, "From Reveille to Retreat," 173–179; Ball, *Of Responsible Command*, 117–118; Nenninger, *Leavenworth*, 122–124.

78. Ahern, "Army War College," 199, 228, 258; Allan R. Millett, *The General: Robert L. Bullard and Officership in the United States Army, 1881–1925* (Westport, Conn., 1975), 222–232; Hunter Liggett, *AEF: Ten Years Ago in France* (New York, 1927), 292–295; Nenninger, *Leavenworth*, 123.

79. Henry L. Stimson and McGeorge Bundy, *On Active Service in Peace and War* (New York, 1947), 39; George Van Horn Moseley, "One Soldier's Journey," I: 92, Moseley Papers, LC.

80. Nenninger, *Leavenworth*, 78, 117–118; Moseley, "One Soldier's Journey," 79; WDAR: 1905, CG, Department of Texas, 145 (first quotation); Wilson B. Burtt, "Tactical Instruction of Officers," *Infantry Journal*, 10 (September 1913), 180 (second quotation); Coffman, *Old Army*, 285 (last quotation).

81. There were 251 Staff College and 236 War College graduates in the classes of 1905 through 1916. Of the 202 general staff officers appointed from 1904 through 1916, 112 had no postgraduate military education. Nenninger, *Leavenworth*, 158, 159; (Army War College) *Directory* (1987), 72–74; WDAR (1916), IG, 300–301; Helmick, "From Reveille to Retreat," 176; I. B. Holley Jr., *General John M. Palmer, Citizen Soldiers, and the Army of a Democracy* (Westport, Conn., 1982), 242.

82. Helmick, "From Reveille to Retreat," 188–192; William Lassiter, "Memoir," II: 32–34, III: 63–66, USMA (quotations on II: 33 and III: 64, 66).

83. Charles P. Summerall, "The Way of Duty, Honor, Country," 72–73, 79 (quotation on 73), First Division Museum—Cantigny.

84. WDAR (1902), SW, 296; Lawrence F. Abbott, ed., *The Letters of Archie Butt, Personal Aide to President Roosevelt* (Garden City, N.Y., 1924), 41; Hewes, *From Root to McNamara*, 10; Raines, "Bell and Military Reform," 86, 191–195.

85. Hewes, *From Root to McNamara,* 13; Nelson, *National Security and General Staff,* 102–106; Moseley, "One Soldier's Journey," 113; Johnson Hagood, *The Services of Supply: A Memoir of the Great War* (Boston, 1927), 15–21.

86. WDAR (1905), CG, Department of Texas, 152; Fleet file 18900, Record Cards to Correspondence, 1903–1912, Department of Texas, RG 393, NA.

87. Nelson, *National Security and General Staff,* 151–166 (quotation on 162); Stimson and Bundy, *On Active Service,* 33–36.

88. WDAR (1902), SW, 293 (quotation); (1911), SG, 439–440; Stimson and Bundy, *On Active Service,* 37–38; Scott, *Some Memories,* 545–547; Nelson, *National Security and General Staff,* 167, 170–171, 174–176, 182.

89. WDAR (1912), SW, 18–19; Stimson and Bundy, *On Active Service,* 38–39; Holley, *General John M. Palmer,* 191, 201 (quotation), 203–211; John M. Palmer, *Washington, Lincoln, Wilson: Three War Statesmen* (Garden City, N.Y., 1930), 313–315; Moseley, "One Soldier's Journey," 106–107; Lassiter, "Memoir," 6–8 (second and third quotations).

90. Coffman, *Old Army,* 274–278, 281–284; WDAR (1899), SW, 58; Reardon, *Soldiers and Scholars,* 21–22; Nenninger, *Leavenworth,* 121, 127–128; Allan R. Millett, *Military Professionalism and Officership in America* (Columbus, Ohio, 1977), 17–18.

91. Russell F. Weigley, *History of the United States Army* (New York, 1967), 320–323; Nenninger, *Leavenworth,* 113–114; Pogue, *George C. Marshall,* 100, 102–105, 115–117; Bland, *Marshall Interviews,* 159, 170–171; WDAR (1910), AG, 201; Charles D. McKenna, "The Forgotten Reform: Field Maneuvers in the Development of the United States Army, 1902–1920" (Ph.D. diss., Duke University, 1981), 225–231.

92. Bland, *Marshall Interviews,* 159; John M. Gates, *Schoolbooks and Krags: The United States Army in the Philippines,* 1898–1902 (Westport, Conn., 1973), 67–70; Russell F. Weigley, "The Elihu Root Reforms and the Progressive Era," in *Command and Commanders in Modern Warfare,* ed. William Geffen (Colorado Springs, 1969), 11–30; Andrew J. Bacevich Jr., "Family Matters: American Civilian and Military Elites in the Progressive Era," *Armed Forces and Society,* 8 (spring 1982), 405–418.

93. James L. Abrahamson, *America Arms for a New Century: The Making of a Great Military Power* (New York, 1981), 148–149; Holley, *General John M. Palmer,* 135–138; Pogue, *George C. Marshall,* 381, n. 17; Douglas MacArthur, *Reminiscences* (New York, 1964), 44 (quotation); Merch B. Stewart, "Soldiering—What Is There in It?" *Harper's Weekly,* December 11, 1909, 16–17; idem, "The Shame of the Uniform," *Harper's Weekly,* May 24, 1913, 12–13.

94. Frank E. Vandiver, *Black Jack: The Life and Times of John J. Pershing,* 2 vols. (College Station, 1977), I: chap. 13; Pogue, *George C. Marshall,* 110–111; Holley, *General John M. Palmer,* 214–217; Moseley, "One Soldier's Journey," 109–113; Lewis S. Sorley, "Some Recollections," 91–98 (quotation on 95), copy in author's collection; Lassiter, "Memoir," vol. VIII; John T. Greenwood, "The U.S. Army Military

Observers with the Japanese Army during the Russo-Japanese War (1904–1905)," *Army History*, 36 (winter 1996), 1–14.

95. Weigley, *History of Army*, chap. 15.

96. *WDAR* (1909), CS, 215; (1910), SW, 22–23, and AG, 204–205; (1911), AG, 238; Raines, "Bell and Military Reform," 167.

97. *WDAR* (1914), CS, 136–137; (1915), CS, 152; (1906), SW, 25; (1908), SW, 25; and CG, Department of the Colorado, 151 (quotation), 152; Scott, *Some Memories*, 533–541.

98. *WDAR* (1906), SW, 18–25; (1910), AG, 205–207; (1913), SW, 18–19; Gaines M. Foster, *The Demands of Humanity: Army Medical Disaster Relief* (Washington, D.C., 1983), chap. 4.

99. Hermann Hagedorn, *Leonard Wood: A Biography*, 2 vols. (New York, 1931), II: 131 (quotation), 159–160, 193; *WDAR* (1913), SW, 19–21; (1914), CS, 81–83; (1916), AG, 275–276; Pogue, *George C. Marshall*, 136–138; John Garry Clifford, *The Citizen Soldiers: The Plattsburg Training Camp Movement, 1913–1920* (Lexington, Ky., 1972), 71, 79, and chaps. 4 and 6.

100. Lassiter, "Memoir," IX: 39; *WDAR* (1911), AG, 238–242; (1912), SW, 13; (1913), SW, 9–10; (1914), CS, 135–136; (1915), CS, 152; John S. D. Eisenhower, *Intervention: The United States and the Mexican Revolution, 1913–1917* (New York, 1993), 218–223.

101. Mahin, *Life in American Army*, 160; D'Este, *Patton*, 160–161.

102. *WDAR* (1916), SW, 7; Scott, *Some Memories*, 519–521; Moseley, "One Soldier's Journey," 133–136; George Van Horn Moseley to author, October 3, 1958.

103. William H. Simpson, interviews, August 19 and 17, 1971; Donald Smythe, *Guerrilla Warrior: The Early Life of John J. Pershing* (Indianapolis, 1973), 222, 227, 229, 264.

104. Foulois, *From Wright Brothers to Astronauts*, chap. 8 (quotation on 136).

105. Roger G. Miller, "Wings and Wheels: The 1st Aero Squadron, Truck Transport, and the Punitive Expedition of 1916," *Airpower History* 42 (winter 1995), 20–22; *WDAR* (1915), QMG, 365–367.

106. *WDAR* (1916), SW, 7–10, 31; (1917), SW, 9; Miller, "Wings and Wheels," 24.

107. D'Este, *Patton*, 162–163, 169, 172–177 (quotation on 163).

108. *WDAR* (1916), SW, 11–13; John K. Mahon, *History of the Militia and the National Guard* (New York, 1983), 148–151; Allan R. Millett and Peter Maslowski, *For the Common Defense: A Military History of the United States of America* (New York, 1984), 324–325.

109. Moseley, "One Soldier's Journey," 136–137; Dwight D. Eisenhower, *At Ease: Stories I Tell to Friends* (Garden City, N.Y., 1967), 119 (quotations).

110. *WDAR* (1917), SW, 9–10, and SG, 350.

111. Hugh A. Drum to wife, August 4, 1914, Drum Papers, MHI; Joseph T. Dickman, *The Great Crusade: A Narrative of the Great War* (New York, 1927), 2–6 (quotation on 3); Nenninger, *Leavenworth*, 127.

112. Dickman, *The Great Crusade*, 1–2, 6–7; Millett, *The General*, 291–294; Liggett, *AEF*, 1–2; Leonard P. Ayres, *The War with Germany: A Statistical Summary* (Washington, D.C., 1919), 21; William H. Simpson, interview, August 17, 1971 (quotation).

6. THE WAR TO END ALL WARS

Epigraph: Hunter Liggett, *AEF: Ten Years Ago in France* (New York, 1928), 249.

1. Frederick Palmer, *Bliss, Peacemaker: The Life and Letters of Tasker H. Bliss* (New York, 1934), 106–107.

2. N. K. Averill to Chief, Army War College, December 21, 1912, WCD no. 7267-16, RG 165, NA; *WDAR* (1914), SW, 10.

3. Edward M. Coffman, *The War to End All Wars: The American Military Experience in World War I* (Lexington, Ky., 1998), 8, 24, 42–43; James G. Harbord, *The American Army in France: 1917–1919* (Boston, 1936), 18.

4. Otto L. Nelson, *National Security and the General Staff: A Study in Organization and Administration* (Washington, D.C., 1946), 180–184, 217, 225; Coffman, *War to End All Wars*, 8–9.

5. John M. Palmer, *Washington, Lincoln, Wilson: Three Wartime Statesmen* (Garden City, N.Y., 1930), 322; Harbord, *American Army*, 103–104; Michael E. Bigelow, "Brigadier General Fox Conner and the American Expeditionary Forces" (Master's thesis, Temple University, 1984), 42–46.

6. John H. Parker, "Memories of the Service," 154, USMA; Coffman, *War to End All Wars*, 24–29, 43–46.

7. Leonard P. Ayres, *The War with Germany: A Statistical Summary* (Washington, D.C., 1919), 16, 21–22, 26, 28–30; Peyton C. March, *The Nation at War* (Garden City, N.Y., 1932), 47–48.

8. Lucian K. Truscott Jr., *Twilight of the U.S. Cavalry: Life in the Old Army, 1917–1942* (Lawrence, Kans., 1989), 4 (first two quotations); Charles L. Bolté, interviews, November 9, 1964 (third quotation), and August 4, 1971.

9. Truscott, *Twilight of Cavalry*, 1, 4–11 (quotation on 8).

10. Orville W. Martin, interview; Guy V. Henry Jr., "A Brief Narrative of the Life of Guy V. Henry, Jr.," 55, 57, MHI; *Howitzer* (1921), 205 (this is the yearbook of the later-designated class of 1919); Stephen E. Ambrose, *Duty, Honor, Country: A History of West Point* (Baltimore, 1966), 255–256.

11. Lowell Thomas, *Woodfill of the Regulars: A True Story of Adventure from the Arctic to the Argonne* (Garden City, N.Y., 1929), 217–221 (quotation on 219); Martin

Blumenson and James L. Stokesbury, *Masters of the Art of Command* (Boston, 1975), 44; Arthur L. Koch, "A Story about a Soldier," 96–103, MHI.

12. George S. Schuyler, *Black and Conservative: The Autobiography of . . .* (New Rochelle, N.Y., 1966), 86–93; Bernard C. Nalty, *Strength for the Fight: A History of Black Americans in the Military* (New York, 1986), 110–111.

13. Donald Smythe, *Pershing: General of the Armies* (Bloomington, Ind., 1986), 83; Frederick Palmer, *Newton D. Baker: America at War*, 2 vols. (New York, 1931), II: 228.

14. James G. Harbord, *Leaves from a War Diary* (New York, 1925), 201; Liggett, *AEF*, 259; F. Palmer, *Newton D. Baker*, II: 229.

15. William J. Snow, *Signposts of Experience: World War Memoirs* (Washington, D.C., 1941), 11, 171–177; *American Decorations* (Washington, D.C., 1927), 730.

16. George C. Marshall, *Memoirs of My Service in the World War: 1917–1918* (Boston, 1976), 1–2, 7–8, 14 (first quotation); George B. Duncan, "Reminiscences of the World War," 19, Special Collection, University of Kentucky Library; Sidney C. Graves, interview, July 20, 1963; Robert L. Bullard, Diary, January 2, 1918 (second quotation), Bullard Papers, LC.

17. Benjamin D. Foulois with C. V. Glines, *From the Wright Brothers to the Astronauts: The Memoirs of Major General Benjamin D. Foulois* (New York, 1968), 124–125, 140–141, 143, 147, 156–157, 159, 180–183; William Mitchell, *Memoirs of World War I: From Start to Finish of Our Greatest War* (New York, 1960), 11, 15, 134–135, 165–166 (quotation on 166); Alfred F. Hurley, *Billy Mitchell: Crusader for Air Power* (Bloomington, Ind., 1975), 2, 21; Coffman, *War to End All Wars*, 189–191, 195–198.

18. Carlo D'Este, *Patton: A Genius for War* (New York, 1995), 190, 191, 204 (first quotation), 205 (second quotation), 210–211, 225.

19. Douglas MacArthur, interview; Edward M. Coffman, *The Hilt of the Sword: The Career of Peyton C. March* (Madison, Wis., 1966), 288, n. 37.

20. Sidney C. Graves, interview, July 20, 1963 (first quotation); Larry I. Bland, ed., *George C. Marshall Interviews and Reminiscences for Forrest C. Pogue* (Lexington, Va., 1991), 197 (other quotations).

21. Clarence R. Huebner, interview, July 17, 1963; *American Decorations*, 353 and 720.

22. Marshall, *Memoirs*, 139; *American Decorations*, 741; Coffman, *War to End All Wars*, 303–304.

23. J. M. Palmer, *Washington, Lincoln, Wilson*, 340; Hugh A. Drum to Mary Reaume Drum, November 11, 1918, Drum Papers, MHI; Douglas MacArthur, interview; Edward M. Coffman, "The AEF Leaders' Education for War," in *The Great War, 1914–1918*, ed. R. J. Q. Adams (College Station, 1990), 155–156.

24. D'Este, *Patton,* 254–265, 272 (last quotation), 275–276; *American Decorations,* 492, 752 (first quotation).

25. Charles L. Bolté, interview, November 9, 1964; William H. Simpson, interview, August 17, 1971. His citation is in *American Decorations* (767), as are Parker's (489, 751), Middleton's (743), and Woodfill's (120). Frank J. Price, *Troy H. Middleton: A Biography* (Baton Rouge, 1974), 66, 67–69; Blumenson and Stokesbury, *Masters of Art of Command,* 42, 46–47.

26. Matthew B. Ridgway, *Soldier: The Memoirs of Matthew B. Ridgway* (New York, 1956), 32 (first quotation); Omar N. Bradley and Clay Blair, *A General's Life: An Autobiography* (New York, 1983), chap. 5; J. Lawton Collins, *Lightning Joe: An Autobiography* (Baton Rouge, 1979), 7–24; Dwight D. Eisenhower, *At Ease: Stories I Tell to Friends* (Garden City, N.Y., 1967), chap. 10; Jacob L. Devers, interview (last quotations).

27. Lewis S. Sorley, "Some Recollections," 101–109, USMA; Eli A. Helmick, "From Reveille to Retreat," 234 (quotation), 239, 246–248, MHI.

28. D'Este, *Patton,* 122, 192, 194, 195 (quotation); Ruth Ellen Patton Totten, questionnaire.

29. Adelaide Poore Bolté, interviews, August 4, 1971 (quotation), and November 9, 1984. David Bolté gave me answers from his mother about this period on September 7, 1997.

30. Mauree Pickering Mahin, *Life in the American Army from the Frontier Days to Army Distaff Hall* (Washington, D.C., 1967), 147, 159–161, 163, 169, 171–173, 176–189 (quotation on 184).

31. Garna L. Christian, *Black Soldiers in Jim Crow Texas: 1899–1917* (College Station, 1995), 146–168; Nalty, *Strength for the Fight,* 101–106; Arthur E. Barbeau and Florette Henri, *The Unknown Soldiers: Black American Troops in World War I* (Philadelphia, 1974), 28–32.

32. Barbeau and Henri, *The Unknown Soldiers,* 70–71, 75–77, 79, and chaps. 7 and 8; Florette Henri, *Black Migration: Movement North, 1900–1920* (Garden City, N.Y., 1975), 293–294, Coffman, *War to End All Wars,* 231–233, 314–319.

33. Barbeau and Henri, *Unknown Soldiers,* 23, 181–184; Henri, *Black Migration,* 318–321.

34. Benjamin O. Davis to Sarah Overton, March 1, June 29, July 10 and 16, 1919 (quotations from last two letters), MHI.

35. Edward M. Coffman, "The Intervention in Russia, 1918–1920," *Military Review* 68 (September 1988), 60–71.

36. Robert L. Eichelberger, "Memoirs," E 81–109, III 52, IV 13–14, MHI.

37. *WDAR* (1920), CS, 240; Alfred E. Cornebise, *The Amaroc News: The Daily Newspaper of the American Forces in Germany, 1919–1923* (Carbondale, 1981), xiv–xviii,

201, 212; Forrest C. Pogue, *George C. Marshall: Education of a General,* 1880–1939 (New York, 1963), 191–192.

38. J. Lawton Collins, interview (first two quotations); Collins, *Lightning Joe,* 25, 34; Robert L. Bullard, *Fighting Generals* (Ann Arbor, 1944), 93 (last quotation).

39. *WDAR* (1920), SG, 612 (quotation); (1921), SG, 71, 191; Cornebise, *Amaroc News,* 183–185; Steven N. Collins, "Disguised Hostility: The U.S. Occupation of the Rhineland after the First World War and the German Response," paper in author's collection.

40. *WDAR* (1921), SG, 190; Heath Twitchell, *Allen: The Biography of an Army Officer, 1859–1930* (New Brunswick, N.J., 1974), 216 (quotation); Collins, *Lightning Joe,* 36; Ernest F. Easterbrook, *The Soldier and the Cross: A Biography Of My Father, Edmund P. Easterbrook* (Carmel, Calif., 1985), 65.

41. Elizabeth Lewis Wheatley to her family, October 11, 1921 (quotation), printed in *Horton* (Kans.) *Headlight Commercial,* December 15, 1921, clipping in Wheatley Scrapbook; copies of scrapbook and 1921 diary in author's collection.

42. Collins, *Lightning Joe,* 36–41; Ernest F. Easterbrook, questionnaire; and Henry E. Thomson to author, August 8, 1986.

43. Wheatley Scrapbook (quotation); Twitchell, *Allen,* 250.

44. *Report of the Chief of Staff:* 1919, 240; Clarence C. Clendenen, *Blood on the Border: The United States Army and the Mexican Irregulars* (New York, 1969), 344–350.

45. Arthur J. Stanley, interview (first quotation); Clendenen, *Blood on the Border,* 352–355 (last quotation on 355).

46. Arthur R. Brooks, interview; Clendenen, *Blood on the Border,* 355–356.

47. *WDAR* (1919), SW, 26–27; (1920), AG, 263–264; Russell C. Langdon to W. G. Haan, August 24, 1919, Haan Papers, WHS; Bradley and Blair, *A General's Life,* 47.

48. *WDAR* (1919), SW, 31, and AG, 518–520; (1920), SW, 15–17 (first quotation on 17), and AG, 280–281, 303–304; W. G. Haan to Julius Kahn, February 1, 1921 (last quotation), Haan Papers.

49. Frank L. Winn to W. G. Haan, July 29, 1919 (quotation), Haan Papers. Also see William M. Weigel to Haan, July 2, 1919; Edwin B. Winans to Haan, November 17, 1919, ibid.; Coffman, *Hilt of the Sword,* 164–165; Thomas, *Woodfill of the Regulars,* 315–320; Blumenson and Stokesbury, *Masters of Art of Command,* 51; Schuyler, *Black and Conservative,* 93.

50. Interviews with Arthur Raymond Brooks, J. Lawton Collins, George W. Hinman, and William H. Simpson (August 17, 1971); Eisenhower, *At Ease,* 155; *WDAR* (1920), AG, 267–268; Edward M. Coffman and Peter F. Herrly, "The American Regular Army Officer Corps between the World Wars: A Collective

Biography," *Armed Forces and Society*, 4 (fall 1977), 56. The resignation figures are in the *Official Army Registers* for 1920, 1921, and 1922.

51. Manuel M. Eskind to the Commandant, November 25, 1918, no. AG 351.24, RG 407, NA (quotation); interviews with Orville W. Martin and Alfred C. Wedemeyer; Ambrose, *Duty, Honor, Country*, 262.

52. Douglas MacArthur, interview (quotation); Douglas MacArthur, *Reminiscences* (New York, 1964), 77–83; Ambrose, *Duty, Honor, Country*, chap. 13; D. Clayton James, *The Years of MacArthur, 1880–1941* (Boston, 1970), chap. 10.

53. Jacob L. Devers, interview.

54. Bradley and Blair, *A General's Life*, 51 (first quotation); Maxwell D. Taylor, *Swords and Plowshares* (New York, 1972), 28; Earl H. Blaik, *The Red Blaik Story* (New Rochelle, N.Y., 1960), 39; Douglas MacArthur, interview (second quotation).

55. *WDAR* (1920), SW, 5; Coffman, *Hilt of the Sword*, 162, 199, 198, 188.

56. J. M. Palmer, *Washington, Lincoln, Wilson*, 365 (first quotation); W. G. Haan to Irving A. Fish, September 22, 1919; Edwin B. Winans to Haan, November 17, 1919 (second quotation), both WHS; Coffman, *Hilt of the Sword*, 199–202.

57. Coffman, *Hilt of the Sword*, chaps. 14 and 15.

58. Maurer Maurer, *Aviation in the U.S. Army, 1919–1939* (Washington, D.C., 1987), 3, 19–29, 41–43; John F. Shiner, *Foulois and the U.S. Army Air Corps, 1931–1935* (Washington, D.C., 1983), 12, 15–16; Foulois, *From Wright Brothers to Astronauts*, 186–188; *Army Reorganization Hearings*, House Committee on Military Affairs, 66th Cong., 1st sess., 899–924, 924–973 (first quotation on 932); Benjamin D. Foulois, interview (second quotation).

59. Eisenhower, *At Ease*, 157–179 (quotations on 169, 173); D'Este, *Patton*, 286, 289–302; Timothy K. Nenninger, "The Development of American Armor, 1917–1940" (Master's thesis, University of Wisconsin–Madison, 1968), 55–64.

60. *WDAR* (1920), SW, 9–14, and AG, 252; (1921), SW, 9, 11; Russell F. Weigley, *History of the United States Army* (New York, 1967), 399–400; William A. Ganoe, *The History of the United States Army* (New York, 1924), 483–484; John M. Lindley, *"A Soldier Is Also a Citizen": The Controversy over Military Justice, 1917–1920* (New York, 1990), 173–175.

61. Ganoe, *History of Army*, 485.

62. Liggett, *AEF*, 249; Clovis E. Byers, interview.

7. THE ARMY IN LIMBO

Epigraph: J. Lawton Collins, interview.

1. *WDAR* (1922), SW, 13; *The National Defense Program—Unification and Strategy*, House Committee on Armed Services Hearing, 81st Cong., October 1949, 604;

Charles L. Bolté, interview, October 8, 1973; Clovis E. Byers, interview; William W. Ford, *Wagon Soldiers* (North Adams, Mass., 1980), 102; James M. Gavin, interview; Douglas V. Johnson, "Keep 'em Rollin'," memoir, 235, copy in author's collection.

2. WDAR (1931), SW, 40, and SG, 23–24; (1932), SW, 58; (1935), SW, 4; (1938), SW, 29; Larry I. Bland and Sharon R. Ritenour, eds., *The Papers of George Catlett Marshall*, 4 vols. (Baltimore, 1981), I: 420; interviews of Charles T. Lanham and Thomas T. Handy.

3. WDAR (1932), SW, 55 (quotation); (1926), SW, 44; Bland and Ritenour, *Papers of Marshall*, 236–240; Donald M. Kington, *Forgotten Summers: The Story of the Citizens Military Training Camps* (San Francisco, 1995), 10–11, 66–67, 138, 140; John K. Mahon, *History of the Militia and the National Guard* (New York, 1983), 180; *The Army Almanac* (Washington, D.C., 1950), 324.

4. Edward M. Coffman and Peter F. Herrly, "The American Regular Army Officer Corps between the World Wars," *Armed Forces and Society*, 4 (November 1977), 60, 63, 65, 72; WDAR (1935), SW, 47–48 (quotation on 47).

5. Bernard C. Nalty, *Strength for the Fight: A History of Black Americans in the Military* (New York, 1986), 136.

6. Marvin Fletcher, *America's First Black General: Benjamin O. Davis, Sr., 1880–1970* (Lawrence, Kans., 1989), 67, 79, and chap. 4; Elnora Davis McLendon, interview (first quotation); Benjamin O. Davis Jr., *Benjamin O. Davis, Jr., American: An Autobiography* (Washington, D.C., 1991), 10 (last quotation).

7. Benjamin O. Davis Jr., "Introduction," in Fletcher, *America's First Black General*, x.

8. Davis was the fourth black graduate of West Point. In 1949 Wesley A. Brown became the first black graduate of Annapolis; Jesse J. Johnson, *Black Armed Forces Officers, 1736–1971* (Hampton, Va., 1971), 160, 162; *Howitzer* (1936), 112 (first quotation); Benjamin O. Davis Jr., interview (second quotation); William P. Ennis Jr., "Senior Officer Oral History Program," 49, MHI.

9. Shea Schwartz to Harry L. Gluckman, October 15, 1936 (quotation), and Israel Weinstein to Gluckman, October 31, 1936, both in Folder: Nazi Propaganda in the Army, box 2, National Jewish Welfare Board Archives, New York. There were thirteen rabbis holding reserve commissions as chaplains in 1924; Army and Navy Committee Minutes, November 17, 1924, box 1, ibid.; Rabbi Charles Sydney to Harry L. Glucksman, January 29, 1923, Folder: Charles Sydney, box 3, ibid.; Rabbi B. A. Tintner to Report to Jewish Welfare Board, February, 1938, Folder: West Point 1938, box 189, ibid.

10. J. Lawton Collins, *Lightning Joe: An Autobiography* (Baton Rouge, 1979), 314; Elwood R. Quesada, interview, April 28, 1988; Thomas A. Hughes, *Over Lord: General Pete Quesada and the Triumph of Tactical Air Power in World War II* (New York, 1995), 62–63.

11. "Who's in the Army Now?" and "Why an Army?" *Fortune*, 12 (September 1935). All quotations are from the first article, 39, 40, 132, 135.

12. *WDAR* (1932), SW, 64–67; (1930), SW, 141–142; (1935), SW, 5 (quotation), 46; (1938), SW, 36; Coffman and Herrly, "American Regular Army Officer Corps," 55–56; "Who's in the Army Now?" 39.

13. *WDAR* (1935), SW, 46; Edward M. Coffman, *The Old Army: A Portrait of the American Army in Peacetime, 1784–1898* (New York, 1986), 49; Coffman and Herrly, "American Regular Army Officer Corps," 67.

14. Albert C. Wedemeyer, interview (first quotation); Anthony C. McAuliffe, interview (second and fourth quotations); Bland and Ritenour, *Papers of Marshall*, I: 380 (third quotation); Henry S. Aurand, "A Statistical Study of the Class of 1915, United States Military Academy," 13–15, copy in author's collection; *The Halfway Book: Class of Nineteen Twenty-three* (West Point, 1938), 88; W. Fritz Breidster, interview with C. M. Williams, February 19, 1981 (last quotation); *Assembly*, 42 (September 1983), 135–136.

15. *WDAR* (1935), SW, 5.

16. Eleanor Mathews Sliney, *Forward Ho!* (New York, 1960), 133 (first quotation); interviews with James M. Gavin, Charles T. Lanham, and John W. Leonard; "Who's in the Army Now?" 39. Army pay levels were printed in the annual *Official Army Registers*. *WDAR* (1932), SW, 70–72; (1933), SW, 41; (1934), SW, 64–65; (1935), SW, 6. For the CPI, see Stanley Lebergott, *Manpower in Economic Growth: The American Record since 1800* (New York, 1964), 524; Statistics Branch Special Report no. 229 on the Financial Status of Officers, Records of the War Department General and Special Staffs, RG 165, NA; questionnaires from Floyd E. Dunn (second quotation) and Columbus B. Lenow in officer questionnaires, AG 240 (10–4–33), Bulky File 8-2, RG 407, NA; questionnaires from Maida Turtle and Tere Rios Versace.

17. *WDAR* (1933), SW, 3–11 (quotation on 10); (1934), SW, 9; D. Clayton James, *The Years of MacArthur: 1880–1941* (Boston, 1970), 418.

18. Bland and Ritenour, *Papers of Marshall*, I: 659; Forrest C. Pogue, *George C. Marshall: Education of a General, 1880–1939* (New York, 1963), 274–280, 308–311.

19. Charles S. Johnson, interview; *WDAR* (1933), SW, 6–8, 41; Bland and Ritenour, *Papers of Marshall*, I: 665.

20. Charles T. Lanham, interview.

21. *WDAR* (1934), SW, 197; (1935), SW, 13, 127; (1936), SW, 95; (1939), SW, 90; (1940), SW, 66; James, *Years of MacArthur*, 423.

22. George W. Weber, interview (first quotation); *WDAR* (1935), SW, 3; John L. Hines Jr., interview, April 12, 1984 (second quotation); Melvin Zais, "Senior Officers Oral History Program," interview by William L. Golden and Richard C. Rice, 12–17 (last quotation on 13), MHI.

23. W. D. Connor, 2d Endorsement, December 29, 1934 (quotation), to Herman Beaukema, Academic Board, December 17, 1934, copy in author's collection.

24. Johnson Hagood, "Down the Big Road," chap. 42, MHI; Chief of Staff to the Secretary of War, February 18, 1936 (quotation), in press release, Francis B. Mallon Papers, MHI.

25. Charles L. Bolté, interview, August 4, 1971; Adelaide P. Bolté, questionnaire, September 1973; interviews with J. Lawton Collins, Benjamin O. Davis Jr., Elnora Davis McLendon, Jacob L. Devers, Clarence R. Huebner, C. T. Lanham, Anthony C. McAuliffe, M. B. Ridgway, and Albert C. Wedemeyer; Pogue, *George C. Marshall*, 280; Virginia Weisel Johnson, *Lady in Arms* (Boston, 1967), 17.

26. Interviews with Clovis E. Byers, Mark W. Clark, Bonner Fellers, John L. Hines Jr. (April 12, 1984), and John W. Leonard.

27. Coffman, *Old Army*, 82, 87–88; William H. Simpson, interview, August 17, 1971; Dwight D. Eisenhower, *At Ease: Stories I Tell My Friends* (New York, 1967), 216. In the 1930s Major General George Van Horn Moseley made extreme right-wing anti-Semitic statements; James, *Years of MacArthur: 1880–1941*, 384, 399, 411.

28. Lucian K. Truscott Jr., *The Twilight of the U.S. Cavalry: Life in the Old Army, 1917–1942* (Lawrence, Kans., 1989), 68–70 (quotations on 70).

29. "Who's in the Army Now," 40.

30. V. W. Johnson, *Lady in Arms*, 6–14; questionnaires from Dorothy Potter Benedict, Marian Sanford Robb, and Rachel Forbush Wood.

31. Maurine Clark, *Captain's Bride, General's Lady: The Memoirs of Mrs. Mark W. Clark* (New York, 1956), 5, 9, 12, 15, 18, 22, 23 (quotations on 22 and 23).

32. Thelma Fadner Watson to mother, June 8, 12, 13 (first quotation), 15, and October 3, 1930 (second quotation), lent by James S. Watson; James S. Watson, interview.

33. Questionnaires from Margaret Hinds Cruse, Eleanor Bishop Powell, and Adelaide Poore Bolté, August 1973; Grace Wilson Groves, "Recollections," 79, 82, 107–109, 114–117, 123, author's collection.

34. Adelaide Poore Bolté, interviews, August 4, 1971, November 9, 1984, and April 3, 1986; Damara Bolté, letter to author, June 3, 1998.

35. Adelaide Poore Bolté, questionnaire and memoir, October 1972 (quotation), and interview, April 11, 1984; Margaret Brown Mueller, questionnaire.

36. Katharine Hollister Smith, "My Life," 20, MHI; Susie Coley Smythe, questionnaire; Carlo D'Este, *Patton: A Genius for War* (New York, 1995), 286, 333, 343.

37. Groves, "Recollections," 123, 129, 149, 157; Thelma Watson to mother, August 31, 1936; James S. Watson, interview.

38. Thelma Fadner Watson to Grace Fadner Bastian, November 26, 1933, September 30, 1936 (first quotation), February 5 (second quotation) and December 14, 1940; James S. Watson, interview.

39. Questionnaires from Grace Wilson Groves and Tere Rios Versace; James S. Watson, interview; V. W. Johnson, *Lady in Arms,* 9. According to the Cavalry School's 1943 Regulations, sec. VI, p. 14, orderlies' pay ranged from eight dollars a month if assigned from 8:00 A.M. to 4:30 P.M. at a single house or to one officer to twelve dollars if assigned fulltime. The Regulations specify that as many as five officers could employ one orderly, to whom each would then pay two dollars.

40. Questionnaires from Adelaide Poore Bolté, October 1972 and August 1973.

41. Questionnaires from Margaret Casteel Pickering and Eleanor Bishop Powell; Vernon G. Olsmith, *Recollections of an Old Soldier* (San Antonio, 1963), 137, 153; Rachel Forbush Wood, questionnaire (last quotation) and letter to author, March 5, 1976.

42. Louise Adams Browne, questionnaire; Thelma Fadner Watson to Grace Fadner Bastian, February 13, 1938; D'Este, *Patton,* 381; Smith, "My Life," 54–55 (quotation on 55); Groves, "Recollections," 155. Susie Coley Smythe sent one of these programs with her questionnaire. Also see questionnaires from Marjorie Hinds Cruse, Harriet Howze Jones, Margaret Brown Mueller, Phyllis Corbusier Pierson, and Rachel Forbush Wood; Leslie Anders, *Gentle Knight: The Life and Times of Major General Edwin Forrest Harding* (Kent, Ohio, 1985), 127–128.

43. Adelaide Bolté, questionnaire, August 1973; David L. Bolté, telephone interview, June 17, 1998; Tere Rios Versace, questionnaire; Sliney, *Forward Ho!* 137–138; Pogue, *George C. Marshall,* 261.

44. John L. Hines Jr., interviews, April 12, 1984, and April 14, 1985; Louis S. Yassel, interview (first quotation); D'Este, *Patton,* 308 367–368 (second quotation on 367); Guy V. Henry Jr., "A Brief Narrative of the Life of Guy V. Henry, Jr.," 63, MHI; Truscott, *Twilight of Cavalry,* 112–116.

45. D'Este, *Patton,* 336, 359 (quotation), 744, 879.

46. Eleanor Bishop Powell, questionnaire; Albert C. Wedemeyer, interview; Smith, "My Life," 41, 47–48; Truscott, *Twilight of Cavalry,* 117; Clark, *Captain's Bride,* 54.

47. Clark, *Captain's Bride,* 33; Sliney, *Forward Ho!* 142; D'Este, *Patton,* 289; Groves, "Recollections," 128; Margaret Almond, questionnaire.

48. Questionnaires from Edward C. Smith (first quotation), Jo Jones Bates, William F. Freehof, Frank L. Hoskins Jr., William N. Leonard, Leila Brady Ryan; John A. Heintges, "Senior Officers Oral History," interview by Jack A. Pellicci, 8–9, 18 (last quotation), MHI.

49. Clark, *Captain's Bride,* 63–64; Adelaide Poore Bolté, interview, April 11, 1984.

50. Questionnaires of Jo Jones Bates, William N. Leonard, Janice Robb Anderson, Margie Hoskins Bloxom, Margaret Forsythe Camp, Thomas Q. Donaldson IV, Margaret Uncles Huffman, Frederick P. Munson, Harry N. Rising Jr., Eleanor Robb, Dorothy Devine Wurster, and Charles W. Yuill Jr.

51. Questionnaires from William N. Leonard, Harry N. Rising Jr., Devol Brett,

Jacqueline Thompson Campbell, Howard W. Clark, Elizabeth P. Hoisington, Robin Olds, Hariette Marshall Olson, Joyce Helmick Ott, Ruth Ellen Patton Totten.

52. Questionnaires of Mary Henry Howze (first quotation), Alice Beukema Miller (second quotation), Bruce Palmer Jr. (last quotation), James L. Collins Jr., George S. Patton III, Adrian St. John, and Patricia Henry Williams; Theodore R. Milton, interview.

53. Questionnaires from Bruce Palmer (first quotation), Alice Beukema Miller (second quotation), and Dorothy Devine Wurster.

54. Questionnaires from Jacqueline Thompson Campbell (first quotation), James H. Polk (third quotation), and Theodore J. Conway (fourth quotation); Theodore R. Milton, interview (second quotation).

55. Charles T. Lanham, interview.

56. Interviews with Clovis E. Byers, Frank B. Scahill, and Albert C. Wedemeyer; Russell P. Reeder, *Born at Reveille: Memoirs of a Son of West Point* (New York, 1966), 132, 138–140; Eisenhower, *At Ease*, 196–197.

57. Interviews with Mark Clark and Thomas D. Finley (January 29, 1983).

58. James M. Gavin, interview.

59. E. F. Harding, "Piddling," in *The Infantry Journal Reader*, ed. Joseph I. Greene (Garden City, N.Y., 1943), 218; Charles T. Lanham, interview.

60. James H. Bruns, "The Dead Hand," in Greene, *Infantry Journal Reader*, 64–65.

61. The Superior Board report and Pershing's endorsement are in Entry no. 23, Reports of AEF Boards, RG 120, NA. William O. Odom, "The Rise and Fall of United States Army Doctrine: 1918–1939" (Ph.D. diss., Ohio State University, 1995), 37–41; Michael E. Bigelow, "A Live Issue: Major General Fox Conner and the Development of the Triangular Infantry Division, 1920–1938," paper in author's collection.

62. Clarence R. Huebner, interview, August 5, 1971 (first quotation); Odom, "Rise and Fall of Army Doctrine," 56–97 (quotation on 70); John K. Mahon and Romana Danysh, *Infantry, Part I: Regular Army* (Washington, D.C., 1972), 48–58.

63. Bland and Ritenour, *Papers of Marshall*, I: 412; Pogue, *George C. Marshall*, chap. 15; Charles T. Lanham, interview.

64. Interviews with Charles T. Lanham and J. Lawton Collins; Collins, *Lightning Joe*, 44–55; Barbara Tuchman, *Stilwell and the American Experience in China, 1911–45* (New York, 1971), 117, 123–125; Anders, *Gentle Knight*, 119–136; Pogue, *George C. Marshall*, 257–258.

65. Bradley defined these rudiments as giving a free hand to a subordinate, helping if he hesitated, and relieving him if he failed; Omar N. Bradley, *A Soldier's Story* (New York, 1951), 20 (first quotation); Collins, *Lightning Joe*, 51; Tuchman, *Stilwell,*

130; Odom, "Rise and Fall of Army Doctrine," 193; Charles L. Bolté, interviews, May 26, 1964, and April 14, 1985; Pogue, *George C. Marshall,* 269 (second quotation).

66. Odom, "Rise and Fall of Army Doctrine," 104–105; Collins, *Lightning Joe,* 46–47; Carlos Brewer to Commandant, Field Artillery School, February 5, 1944, Folder "FDC Development at Fort Sill," Army Center of Military History, Washington, D.C.; Thomas T. Handy, interview (quotations).

67. As quoted in John M. Devine to W. W. Carr, April 10, 1944, Army Center of Military History. In addition to Brewer, Sidney F. Dunn (February 21, 1944) and R. G. Barkalow (February 4, 1944) to Commandant, Field Artillery School, FDC Development Folder, ibid., are comprehensive reminiscences of this period.

68. H. L. C. Jones (February 23, 1944) and George V. Keyser (February 11, 1944) to Commandant, Field Artillery School, FDC Development Folder, ibid., are particularly good on the latter part of these developments, in which Hones played a crucial role. See also Leslie J. McNair (February 7, 1944) to Commandant, Field Artillery School, ibid. The best account is Riley Sunderland, "Massed Fire and the FDC," *Army,* May 1956, 56–59.

69. *WDAR* (1935), SW, 52; Anthony C. McAuliffe, interview (first quotation); Orville W. Martin to author, January 22, 1980 (second quotation); Orville W. Martin, interviews, December 27, 1979 (third quotation), and March 9, 1985; Ford, *Wagon Soldiers,* 84; Boyd L. Dastrup, *King of Battle: A Branch History of the U.S. Army's Field Artillery* (Fort Monroe, Va., 1992), chap. 7, 208.

70. John K. Herr, "Reminiscences," chap. 2, 16, Holbrook Family Collection, USMA; James H. Polk, "Senior Officer Oral History," by Roland D. Tausch, 30, MHI.

71. Geoffrey Galwey, "Once upon a Horse," 112–113 (quotation on 112), copies of excerpts in author's collection; Norman Spencer, "Tommy Tompkins," *Cavalry Journal,* 18 (December 1994), 8–10.

72. Theodore R. Milton, interview; Lucian K. Truscott III, preface to Truscott, *Twilight of Cavalry,* xv (quotation); Ernest N. Harmon, *Combat Commander: Autobiography of a Soldier* (Englewood Cliffs, N.J., 1970), 54.

73. *WDAR* (1933), SW, 20; George S. Patton and C. C. Benson, "Mechanization and Cavalry: Can Fighting Machines Replace the Mounted Soldier?" *Army Ordnance,* 10 (March–April 1930), 336–338; Martin Blumenson, ed., *The Patton Papers, 1885–1940,* 2 vols. (Boston, 1972), I: 741, 840, 843–844, 868; D'Este, *Patton,* 346, 349. For background on mechanization, see Timothy K. Nenninger, "The Development of American Armor, 1917–1940" (Master's thesis, University of Wisconsin–Madison, 1968); Robert W. Grow, "The Ten Lean Years: From the Mechanized Force (1930) to the Armored Force (1940)," copy in author's collection; and Vincent J. Tedesco, "'Greasy Automatons' and 'The Horsey Set': The U.S. Cavalry and Mechanization, 1928–1940" (Master's thesis, Pennsylvania State University, 1995).

74. Timothy K. Nenninger, "Organizational Milestones in the Development of American Armor, 1920–40," in *Camp Colt to Desert Storm: The History of the U.S. Armored Forces,* ed. George J. Hofmann and Donn A. Starry (Lexington, Ky., 1999), 39–41.

75. Grow, "Ten Lean Years," 5; Charles G. Mettler, obituary of Chaffee, *Assembly,* 1 (April 1942), 13–15; Nenninger, "Development of American Armor," 131, 140, 148.

76. Henry, "Brief Narrative," 64–70 (quotation on 65); Grow, "Ten Lean Years," 7–8, 13, 23.

77. Nenninger, "Development of American Armor," 106, 109. A picture of the Combat Car, T-5, designed in 1933, with its specifications is in Grow, "Ten Lean Years," 53.

78. Grow, "Ten Lean Years," 16, 31–35 (quotation on 33).

79. Ibid., 60, 69, 71; *The Rasp: 1926* (Cavalry School annual published at Fort Riley), 57; Nenninger, "Organizational Milestones," 18; idem, "Development of American Armor," 172.

80. Herr, "Reminiscences," 17 (first quotation), and his Army War College Lecture, September 19, 1938, Holbrook Family Collection, USMA; Mary Lee Stubbs and Stanley R. Connor, *Armor-Cavalry, Part I: Regular Army and Reserve* (Washington, D.C., 1969), 53; Grow, "Ten Lean Years," 78; L. W. Cramer, "Portee Cavalry: An Experiment with Commercial Trucks," *Cavalry Journal,* 15 (March 1991), 4–6; Truscott, *Twilight of Cavalry,* 103 (second quotation); Lewis Sorley, *Thunderbolt from the Battle of the Bulge to Vietnam and Beyond: General Creighton Abrams and the Army of His Times* (New York, 1992), 30 (last quotation).

81. Polk, "Oral History," 28; Jack W. Heard, *The Pictorial Military Life History of Jack Whitehead Heard* (San Antonio, 1969), 121; John L. Hines Jr., interview, April 12, 1984.

82. *Official Army Register* (1925), 835; John F. Whiteley, *Early Army Aviation: The Emerging Air Force* (Manhattan, Kans., 1974), 96. The uniform regulation change for the rest of the Army came on December 31, 1926. Randy Steffen, *The Horse Soldier, 1776–1943,* vol. IV: *World War I, the Peacetime Army, World War II, 1917–1943* (Norman, 1979), 51; H. H. Arnold and Ira C. Eaker, *This Flying Game* (New York, 1936), chap. 5.

83. James M. Gavin, interview, June 15, 1978; Jacob E. Smart to author, August 11, 1989.

84. Paul W. Tibbets, *Flight of the Enola Gay* (Reynoldsburg, Ohio, 1989), 42 (first quotation). The plane was a Consolidated PT-3. Jacob E. Smart to author, August 11, 1989 (second quotation); Edmund C. Lynch, *Views of an Early Bird: Life in the Army Air Corps* (Austin, 1990), 31–32.

85. Arnold and Eaker, *This Flying Game,* chap. 6; Maurer Maurer, *Aviation in the United States Army, 1919–1939* (Washington, D.C., 1987), 54; *West Point of the Air,*

pamphlet in Noel F. Parrish Scrapbook, copy in author's collection; Noel F. Parrish, interview (first quotation); idem, "Memoir," Randolph chapter, 9 (second quotation), copy in author's collection.

86. Noel F. Parrish, interview (quotation); Parrish, "Memoir," Fort Crockett chapter, 1–3, 6–7, 10–12.

87. Parrish interview (quotation). Also see his memoir chapters on Chanute and Wright-Patterson.

88. Parrish, "Memoir," Wright-Patterson chapter, 39, and Barksdale chapter, 15, 18 (quotation), 20; Elwood R. Quesada, interview, April 8, 1983.

89. Parrish interview (quotation). Benjamin D. Foulois with C. V. Glines, *From the Wright Brothers to the Astronauts: The Memoirs of Major General Benjamin D. Foulois* (New York, 1968), 220–221.

90. Alfred F. Hurley, *Billy Mitchell: Crusader for Air Power* (Bloomington, Ind., 1975), 108; James P. Tate, *The Army and Its Air Corps: Army Policy toward Aviation, 1919–1941* (Maxwell Air Force Base, Ala., 1998), 59; Foulois, *From Wright Brothers to Astronauts*, 260.

91. H. H. Arnold, *Global Mission* (New York, 1949), 118 (first quotation) and 120 (last quotation); Hurley, *Mitchell*, 104 (other quotations), also 105–108; Tate, *Air Corps*, 42–43.

92. Hurley, *Mitchell*, 111; Tate, *Air Corps*, 48.

93. Edward M. Coffman, *The Hilt of the Sword: The Career of Peyton C. March* (Madison, Wis., 1966), 224; John F. Shiner, *Foulois and the U.S. Army Air Corps: 1931–1935* (Washington, D.C., 1983), 258; Tate, *Air Corps*, 89; Secretary of War Harry H. Woodring, Statement, May 28, 1940, Cater Files, 1938–42, Center of Military History.

94. Foulois, *From Wright Brothers to Astronauts*, 206; Tate, *Air Corps*, 40–41, 47, 102–105; Shiner, *Foulois and Air Corps*, 25–31; Robert K. Griffith Jr., *Men Wanted for the U.S. Army: America's Experience with an All-Volunteer Army between the World Wars* (Westport, Conn., 1982), 77.

95. Tate, *Air Corps*, 143–147, 150–151; Shiner, *Foulois and Air Corps*, 193–198.

96. IG to Chief of Air Service, February 13, 1926; H. H. Arnold, Statement, February 17, 1926, both in William Mitchell Papers, Special Collections, USAFA; Dewitt S. Copp, *A Few Great Captains: The Men and Events That Shaped the Development of U.S. Air Power* (Garden City, N.Y., 1980), 48–51.

97. Elwood R. Quesada, Lecture at USAFA, April 7, 1983 (first quotation), author's collection. Quesada also characterized Spaatz in this lecture. Thomas M. Coffey, *Hap* (New York, 1982), 96–97, 104, 125, 155; David R. Mets, *Master of Airpower: General Carl A. Spaatz* (Novato, Calif., 1988), 36, 40, 62–63, 81, 89 (second quotation); James Parton, *"Air Force Spoken Here": General Ira Eaker and the Command of the Air* (Bethesda, Md., 1986), 115–116.

98. Parton, *"Air Force Spoken Here,"* 32, 44, 46, 70 (quotation), 87, 89, 96, 114–115; Ira C. Eaker, interview; Quesada, Lecture at USAFA, April 7, 1983.

99. From 1936 to 1940, 65 percent of the total graduates finished at ACTS, according to the best brief account of the school; Peter R. Faber, "Interwar U.S. Army Aviation and the Air Corps Tactical School: Incubators of American Airpower," in *The Paths of Heaven: The Evolution of Airpower Theory,* ed. Philip S. Meilinger (Maxwell Air Force Base, Ala., 1997), 211–212, 214; Martha Byrd, *Kenneth N. Walker: America's Untempered Crusader* (Maxwell Air Force Base, Ala., 1997), 23; Mets, *Master of Airpower,* 56–59; Parton, *"Air Force Spoken Here,"* 97–99.

100. Hugh Knerr, "The Vital Era: 1887–1950," memoir, 103 (first quotation) 108, USAFA; Hughes, *Over Lord,* 53 (second quotation), 54 (third quotation). See Faber's discussion of this concept, "Interwar U.S. Army Aviation," 216–221.

101. Claire Chennault fought a rearguard action for fighters. See his *Way of a Fighter: The Memoirs of Claire Lee Chennault* (New York, 1949), 23, 28; Maurer, *Aviation in Army,* 354–355; Byrd, *Walker,* 37.

102. An ACTS course certificate dated June 4, 1935, showed that students were required to ride eighty-six hours during the school year; Lawrence S. Kuter Papers, USAFA. Elwood R. Quesada, interview, April 28, 1988 (first two quotations); O. P. Weyland to author, October 27, 1978 (last quotation).

103. Foulois, *From Wright Brothers to Astronauts,* 274, 279; also see 278–280; Shiner, *Foulois and Air Corps,* 91, 257, 263, 265.

104. Omar N. Bradley, interview; Timothy K. Nenninger, *The Leavenworth Schools and the Old Army: Education, Professionalism, and the Officer Corps of the United States Army, 1882–1918* (Westport, Conn., 1978), 129–130, 157; idem, "Leavenworth and Its Critics: The U.S. Army Command and General Staff School, 1920–1940," *Journal of Military History,* 56 (April 1994), 201.

105. Invictus, "The Legion of the Lost," in Greene, *Infantry Journal Reader,* 156, 158; Mark W. Clark, interview (first quotation); Collins, *Lightning Joe,* 43; Timothy K. Nenninger, "Creating Officers: The Leavenworth Experience, 1920–1940," *Military Review,* 69 (November 1989), 60; William H. Simpson, interview, August 17, 1971 (second and third quotations).

106. Nenninger, "Leavenworth," 202–203; Daniel D. Holt and James W. Leyerzapf, eds., *Eisenhower: The Prewar Diaries and Selected Papers, 1905–1941* (Baltimore, 1998), 47, 50; Truscott, *Twilight of Cavalry,* 142–146; G. L. Byroade, List of Individual Research Papers from the Second Year Course, September 8, 1930, Archives, Combined Arms Research Library, U.S. Army Command and General Staff College.

107. Charles L. Bolté, interview, April 14, 1985; Thomas D. Finley, interview, February 5, 1983; Nenninger, "Creating Officers," 61–62.

108. Eisenhower, *At Ease,* 48 (first quotation), 58; Truscott, *Twilight of Cavalry,* 147 (second quotation).

109. Nenninger, "Leavenworth and Its Critics," 221–224; Ennis C. Whitehead to "Hege," November 12, 1937 (first quotation), Air University, Maxwell Field, Ala.; Elwood R. Quesada, interview, April 8, 1983 (second quotation); Arnold, *Global Mission*, 128 (third quotation); DeWitt S. Copp, *A Few Great Captains: The Men and Events That Shaped the Development of U.S. Air Power* (Garden City, N.Y., 1980), 313–314; St. Clair Street, "What Principles Should Govern the Strategical Employment of the Air Force, with Particular Consideration to the Most Suitable Objectives?" March 23, 1934, Combined Arms Research Library, U.S. Army Command and General Staff College.

110. Charles L. Bolté, interview, April 14, 1985 (first two quotations); Anders, *Gentle Knight*, 184.

111. Larry I. Bland, ed., *George C. Marshall Interviews and Reminiscences for Forrest C. Pogue* (Lexington, Va., 1991), 306, 605 (quotation); Bland and Ritenour, *Papers of Marshall*, I: 702–703, 707–708.

112. Bland and Ritenour, *Papers of Marshall*, I: 625; Terence J. Gough, "Soldiers, Businessmen and U.S. Industrial Mobilisation Planning between the World Wars," *War and Society*, 9 (May 1991), 70–71; Henry P. Ball, *Of Responsible Command: A History of the U.S. Army War College* (Carlisle Barracks, Pa., 1994), 198; Bland and Ritenour, *Papers of Marshall*, I: 625; Coffey, *Hap*, 117; Holt and Leyerzapf, *Eisenhower*, 178.

113. Holt and Leyerzapf, *Eisenhower*, 179; Gough, "Soldiers, Businessmen and Mobilisation Planning," 71.

114. Collins, *Lightning Joe*, 86–88 (quotation on 87); Gough, "Soldiers, Businessmen and Mobilisation Planning," 70, 72.

115. Eisenhower, *At Ease*, 204 (first quotation); Ball, *Of Responsible Command*, 154, 185, 204–206, 212, 214; Collins, *Lightning Joe*, 90 (second quotation); *Directory: Present and Former Staff and Faculty, Graduates and Students* (Carlisle Barracks, Pa., 1987), 74–91.

116. Ball, *Of Responsible Command*, 193–194, 218, 248; Collins, *Lightning Joe*, 91–92; Olsmith, *Recollections*, 148; Bradford G. Chynoweth, *Bellamy Park* (Hicksville, N.Y., 1975), 134; Charles L. Bolté, interview, October 21, 1986. His projects are filed under nos. 3-1937-3 and 6, Army War College File, MHI.

117. Blumenson, *Patton Papers*, I: 889–892; Chynoweth, *Bellamy Park*, 133–134.

118. Chynoweth, *Bellamy Park*, 133; Ball, *Of Responsible Command*, 229.

119. Henry G. Gole, *The Road to Rainbow: Army Planning for Global War, 1934–1940* (Annapolis, 2002); Ball, *Of Responsible Command*, 199–200, 225–227, 240, 246; Collins, *Lightning Joe*, 93–94; Charles L. Bolté, interview, October 21, 1986.

120. Charles L. Bolté, interview, October 21, 1986; Collins, *Lightning Joe*, 91 (first quotation); William H. Simpson, interview, August 17, 1971 (second quotation).

121. The adjutant general reported these statistics: *WDAR* (1931), 212; (1934), 190; (1935), 40; (1938), 80.

122. Alfred C. Wedemeyer, *Wedemeyer Reports!* (New York, 1958), 49–62 (first two quotations on 50); Wedemeyer, interview (last quotation); Keith E. Eiler, "The Man Who Planned the Victory: An Interview with Gen. Albert C. Wedemeyer," *American Heritage,* 34 (October–November 1983), 39.

123. Walter Warlimont to author, June 1, 1966.

124. Anthony C. McAuliffe, interview; Noel F. Parrish, "New Responsibilities of Air Force Officers," *Air University Review,* 23 (March–April 1972), 15–16; Omar Bradley and Clay Blair, *A General's Life* (Norwalk, Conn., 1995), 53; Reeder, *Born at Reveille,* 144–148; M. B. Ridgway, interview; Coffey, *Hap,* 133–134; "Van Fleet and Football," folder 14, box 5, Van Fleet Papers, George C. Marshall Library, Lexington, Va.; Geoffrey Galwey, interview 2, September 21, 1974; Charles T. Lanham, interview (last quotation).

125. John W. Thomason Jr., "The Case for the Soldier: A Commentary on Critics," *Scribner's Magazine,* April 1935, 211; Wade H. Haislip, interview.

126. J. Lawton Collins, interview.

8. SOLDIERING IN THE 1920S AND 1930S

Epigraph: The United States Army as a Career (Washington, D.C., 1929, 3.

1. In 1924 there was a change from the dark bronze to the brighter brass, and sabers were abolished in the cavalry in 1934; Randy Steffen, *The Horse Soldiers, 1776–1943: The United States Cavalryman: His Uniforms, Arms, Accoutrements, and Equipment, vol. IV: World War I, the Peacetime Army, World War II, 1917–1943* (Norman, 1979), 29, 37, 126; William J. Smith, *Army Brat: A Memoir* (New York, 1980), 49; George S. Pappas, Memoir, 3, 30, author's collection.

2. Lucian K. Truscott Jr., *The Twilight of the U.S. Cavalry: Life in the Old Army, 1917–1942* (Lawrence, Kans., 1989), 35.

3. *WDAR* (1921), SW, 22; questionnaires from John W. Dulin III, Basil G. Rauch, and Louis H. Wilson.

4. *WDAR* (1919), TAG, 518–519; (1920), CS, 156, 170–172, and TAG, 279–280.

5. *WDAR* (1919), SW, 30–31; (1920), SW, 17 (quotations), CS, 194–195, and SG, 643; Robert K. Griffith, *Men Wanted for the U.S. Army: America's Experience with an All-Volunteer Army between the World Wars* (Westport, Conn., 1982), 33–34. The poster is labeled Recruiting Series no. 3 (author's collection).

6. *WDAR* (1920), SG, 641, 644 (quotation), 646 (second quotation), 647, 649; and (1921), SG, 179 (last quotation).

7. Edward M. Coffman, *The Hilt of the Sword: The Career of Peyton C. March*

(Madison, Wis., 1966), 221; *WDAR* (1922), SG, 20; (1923), SG, 12; Griffith, *Men Wanted*, 86, 91.

8. Griffith, *Men Wanted*, 94, 149–152, 162, 183, 206. The strength figures do not include Philippine Scouts; *WDAR* (1932), SG, 237; (1935), CS, 43; (1936), SG, 89; (1940), SW, 58; Russell F. Weigley, *History of the United States Army* (New York, 1967), 416–417.

9. Griffith, *Men Wanted*, 32; questionnaires from William L. Banks, Tommie J. Baugh, Felix L. Goodwin, and Robert P. Johnson; *WDAR* (1925), SG, 19; (1935), SG, 5, 6; Bernard C. Nalty, *Strength for the Fight: A History of Black Americans in the Military* (New York, 1986), 85.

10. Benjamin O. Davis Jr., *Benjamin O. Davis, Jr., American: An Autobiography* (Washington, D.C., 1991), 58 (quotation); William L. Banks, interview (May 10, 1973) and questionnaire; William G. Muller, *The Twenty-fourth Infantry Past and Present* (Fort Collins, Colo., 1972), unpaginated, but under 1921 and 1922 in the chronicle; *Historical and Pictorial Review: Tenth Cavalry of the United States Army, Camp Funston—Fort Riley, Kansas, 1941* (n.p., n.d.), 32.

11. William L. Banks, interview, May 3, 1978, and notes; M. T. Dean, ed., "Twenty-third Anniversary Day Program, U.S. Military Academy Detachment of Cavalry, West Point, N.Y.: Saturday, March 22, 1930."

12. William L. Banks, interviews, May 10, 1973 (quotations), January 11 and May 3, 1978, and questionnaire; Robert P. Johnson, questionnaire (quotation); *News of the Highlands* (Highland Falls, N.Y.), June 27, 1974.

13. Mike Henley, questionnaire.

14. Tommie J. Baugh, questionnaire; copies of Stephen O. Fuqua letter of commendation, September 24, 1929; Edward P. Earle, Announcement of Band Concert, September 24, 1929; Promotion warrants of February 5, 1930, and July 24, 1936; and certificates of completion of various courses; and photo of captured 29th Infantrymen; copies in author's collection; Davis, *Benjamin O. Davis*, 58.

15. Questionnaires from William L. Banks, Tommie J. Baugh (quotations), Mike Henley, Lucious Prescott, Slone Williams, and March Worsham.

16. There is a photograph of some thirty troopers mounted for a fox hunt at Leavenworth on Easter Sunday 1934, in *Historical and Pictorial Review: Tenth Cavalry*, 33.

17. "Status Sheets Showing Districts Covered by Representatives of Army and Navy Service Department with Analyses of Their Activities and Expenditures as of January 1, 1927," Folder: Army and Navy, 1917, box 1, National Jewish Welfare Board Archives, New York; Alphonso S. Zawadski, interview (quotations).

18. James M. Gavin to author, October 29, 1975 (quotation). He recalled that Roth had reached the rank of lieutenant colonel during World War II. See also James M. Gavin, *War and Peace in the Space Age* (New York, 1958), 38.

19. Coffman, *Hilt of the Sword*, 3 (last quotation), 16 (second quotation), 30 (first

quotation). The statistics are in the adjutant general's report in *WDAR*s for 1922 through 1941.

20. Questionnaires from Heman W. Peirce (first quotation), John J. Hoodock (second quotation), and John Randell; Griffith, *Men Wanted,* 44.

21. Questionnaires from Otto E. Bauman, Leland R. Goodwin (first quotation), Gene E. Harris (second quotation), and Michael C. Varhol (third quotation); Gaylord J. Parrish to Noel F. Parrish, July 22, 1930 (last quotation), Noel F. Parrish Collection, LC; Noel F. Parrish, interview, October 11, 1974.

22. Parrish interview (quotations); Noel F. Parrish, "Memoir," Prologue, copy in author's collection.

23. James M. Gavin, interview, June 15, 1978 (quotation); Gavin, *War and Peace,* chap. 2.

24. Sketch in Parrish Scrapbook, copy in author's collection; James W. Twitty, "Memoir," 5 (first quotation), author's collection; Rufus W. House, questionnaire (second quotation).

25. Interviews with Theodore R. Milton and Noel F. Parrish.

26. Twitty, "Memoir," 6; Parrish interview; Rufus W. House, questionnaire.

27. Francis L. Walski, "Memoir," 5–6, author's collection; Eugene E. Forbes, questionnaire.

28. Griffith, *Men Wanted,* 96–97; questionnaires from Louis M. DiCarlo, Francis T. Dockery, William A. Howell, Francis L. Walski, and Hobert B. Wade.

29. Charles Willeford, *Something about a Soldier* (New York, 1986), 66–70 (quotations on 70).

30. *WDAR* (1922), TAG, 200.

31. Twitty, "Memoir," 2–4 (quotation on 3); James W. Twitty to author, November 10, 1990.

32. Alphonso S. Zawadski, interview; Michael C. Varhol, questionnaire.

33. Eugene C. Hogan, Memoir, unpaginated typescript, author's collection (quotations); John J. Hannon, questionnaire.

34. Edward R. Halvorson, questionnaire, lent by Mark R. Grandstaff; Mark R. Grandstaff, *Foundation of the Force: Air Force Enlisted Personnel Policy, 1907–1956* (Washington, D.C., 1997), 39.

35. Pappas, Memoir, 18; Willeford, *Something about a Soldier,* 10 (first quotation), 20, 187–206 (last quotation on 202); Parrish, "Memoir," Prologue, 17 (second quotation).

36. Victor Vogel, *Soldiers of the Old Army* (College Station, 1990), chap. 4; Twitty, "Memoir," 24.

37. Twitty, "Memoir," 15–16.

38. Alphonso S. Zawadski, interview; Michael C. Varhol, questionnaire.

39. Pappas, Memoir, 30; Hogan, Memoir, 3–5.

40. Grandstaff, *Foundation of the Force,* 25–30; questionnaires from Steven B. Davis and Edward R. Halvorson, lent by Mark R. Grandstaff.

41. Bernard S. Kolp, interview by Donald Weckhorst, lent by Mark R. Grandstaff.

42. George S. Pappas, "The Army's Pre-WWII Prep Schools," *Assembly* 56 (July–August 1998), 48–50; William P. Yarborough, interview; Robert L. Scott Jr. to author, April 2, 1977; Scott, *The Day I Owned the Sky* (New York, 1988), 6–8: James H. Short, questionnaire (last quotation).

43. James M. Gavin, interview; Gavin, *War and Peace,* 30–33; T. Michael Booth and Duncan Spencer, *Paratrooper: The Life of Gen. James M. Gavin* (New York, 1994), 38–40.

44. James W. Twitty, interview and "Memoir," 17, 28.

45. For desertions from 1830 to 1914, see *WDAR* (1914), JAG, app. D, facing 276. For 1907–1926 statistics, see *WDAR* (1926), TAG, 165. For 1921–1940, see *WDAR* (1940), TAG, 47; Griffith, *Men Wanted,* 43–48.

46. TAG printed rates of desertion in all branches along with the general Army rate throughout this period in *WDAR*s. Willeford, *Something about a Soldier,* 225; questionnaires from Tommie J. Baugh (quotation) and Norbert L. Craine.

47. Alphonso S. Zawadski, interview.

48. Griffith, *Men Wanted,* 100, 201; Raymond L. Hammond to author and questionnaire; Rauch earned a doctorate and became a history professor at Barnard College; Basil G. Rauch, questionnaire.

49. Questionnaires from Theodore J. Conway and William R. Dunn; Twitty, "Memoir," 3; Willeford, *Something about a Soldier,* 61.

50. The top enlisted grade received $45 before the war, $51 during the war, $74 in 1920 and 1921, and $124 in 1922; Griffith, *Men Wanted,* 34, 67–68, 91, 153–154, 158, 237–238 (pay chart on 237); Edward M. Coffman, *The Old Army: A Portrait of the American Army in Peacetime, 1784–1898* (New York, 1986), 346; *WDAR* (1937), SW, 4; Willeford, *Something about a Soldier,* 99 (quotation), 160–162.

51. Vogel, *Soldiers of Old Army,* 81–82; Twitty, "Memoir," 13.

52. Questionnaires from William R. Dunn, Rufus W. House, and Michael C. Varhol; Twitty, "Memoir," 13.

53. For pay comparison, see Alphonso S. Zawadski, interview; questionnaires from Robert L. Bergeron, Francis T. Dockery, John J. Hannon, Eugene C. Hogan, Willie R. Nabors, Arthur W. Piehl, Eugene C. Schneider, Robert E. Wendt, August L. Williams, and Joseph M. Wozniak. For those who sent money home, see Alphonso S. Zawadski, interview; questionnaires from Tommie J. Baugh, James A. Bynum,

Felix L. Goodwin, Eugene C. Hogan, Alphonso C. Passero, William C. Tiller, and Michael C. Varhol; and Gavin, *War and Peace*, 31.

54. Alphonso S. Zawadski, interview; Michael C. Varhol, questionnaire; Smith, *Army Brat*, 33–36; Willeford, *Something about a Soldier*, 82–83, 106.

55. Smith, *Army Brat*, 72–81 (first two quotations on 75); Alphonso S. Zawadski, interview; questionnaires from James C. Hicks, George C. Hogden, William A. Howell, Noel F. Parrish (last quotation), Michael C. Varhol.

56. JAG statistics are in *WDAR* (1926), 186; (1927), 202; (1928), 236; (1929), 248; (1930), 363; (1931), 220; (1932), 244). For medical statistics on alcoholism, see *WDAR* (1930), SG, 136; (1937), 60; (1938), 55–56; (1941), 54. Drug addiction statistics are usually next to those of alcoholism; *WDAR* (1932), SG, 87.

57. Questionnaires from William R. Dunn, Raymond L. Hammond, George R. Moe, Sam T. Prophet, William A. Shrenk, Charles L. Southern, and Michael C. Varhol; Smith, *Army Brat*, 153.

58. Brian M. Linn, *Guardians of Empire: The U.S. Army and the Pacific, 1902–1940* (Chapel Hill, 1997), 131–132; questionnaires from Jack Bradley, Norbert L. Craine, and Estel A. Thompson; O. P. Weyland to author.

59. Noel F. Parrish, interview, questionnaire, and "Memoir," 22; Alphonso S. Zawadski, interview; questionnaires from Theodore R. Milton (quotation), William A. Shrenk, and Michael C. Varhol.

60. *WDAR* (1925), SG, 111–112.

61. *WDAR* (1920), SG, 678–679 (quotations on 679); (1923), SG, 66; (1925), SG, 121. Some veterans who aired their resentment about the severe punishment were Leonard Cattivera, Marshall C. Dickinson, Raymond L. Hammond, George E. Harris, Jerome Lowery, and Charles L. Southern (see questionnaires).

62. Howard F. Wehrle, questionnaire (quotations); Willeford, *Something about a Soldier*, 153, 168–169.

63. The chart is in *WDAR* (1940), SG, 42. See also *WDAR* (1924), SG, 11; (1934), 37; (1936), 32; (1940), 39; (1941), 41.

64. *WDAR* (1929), SG, 2; (1930), 2; (1932), 20–23; (1936), 6, 9, 57; (1941), 4.

65. *WDAR* (1928), SG, 4, 163; (1932), 100, 101; (1933), 70; (1936), 55; (1939), 74; (1940), 67, 68.

66. Questionnaires from Jack Bradley, Jess Cloud, Walter Dillon, William R. Dunn, Alberto Garcia, Jerome Lowrey, Noel F. Parrish, and Estel A. Thompson.

67. Questionnaires from Robert L. Bergeron, M. J. Thompson, Lester G. Williams, and Joseph M. Wozniak.

68. Smith, *Army Brat*, 53.

69. Griffith, *Men Wanted*, 202–204.

70. Parrish, "Memoir," Prologue, 19; Theodore R. Milton, interview; Smith, *Army Brat*, 44, 47, 55–56, 59.

71. Questionnaires from Evelyn Hruby, Caroline Rouse (first quotation), Ruby Mundell Barry, and Florence Ricketts Jackson (second quotation); Smith, *Army Brat*, 9 (last quotation).

72. Questionnaires from Ruth Mundell Barry and her three daughters—Barbara Jane Barry Apple (first quotation), Mary Ellen Barry Carns, Kathryn Rose Barry Mulcahy—Robert W. Brockway (last quotation), Jess W. Cloud, John N. Lillie, and Margaret Bradley Mellboom; Smith, *Army Brat*, 12, 81, 170.

73. Twitty, "Memoir," 7 (first two quotations); William R. Dunn, questionnaire (last quotation); Smith, *Army Brat*, 61–62.

9. THE ARMY IN PACIFIC OUTPOSTS, 1919–1940

Epigraph: Larry I. Bland and Sharon R. Ritenour, eds., *The Papers of George Catlett Marshall*, 4 vols. (Baltimore, 1981), I: 274.

1. Eli A. Helmick, "From Reveille to Retreat: An Autobiography," 281–284 (quotations on 283), MHI; Joseph W. A. Whitehorne, *The Inspector General of the United States Army, 1903–1939* (Washington, D.C., 1998), 345–348; Charles H. Franklin, "History of the Philippine Scouts, 1899–1934," 19–27, Historical Section, Army War College, RG 407, NA.

2. Charles Willeford, *Something about a Soldier* (New York, 1986), 37 (quotation); the average percentage is based on figures from SW reports in *WDAR*s for those years, as in (1934), SW, 191. For Hawaii and Philippine garrisons from 1902 through 1941, see Brian M. Linn, *Guardians of Empire: The U.S. Army and the Pacific, 1902–1940* (Chapel Hill, 1997), 253–254.

3. *WDAR* (1925), SW, 12. Statistics are in the *WDAR*s as noted above.

4. Forrest C. Pogue, *George C. Marshall: Education of a General, 1880–1939* (New York, 1963), 227; Adelaide Poore Bolté, questionnaire supplement; Rachel Forbush to Mother, March 6, 1921, copy in author's collection.

5. Edward M. Coffman, "The American 15th Infantry Regiment in China, 1912–1938: A Vignette in Social History," *Journal of Military History* 58 (January 1994), 59, 69 (quotations); Bland and Ritenour, *Papers of Marshall*, I: 299 (last quotation); Dennis L. Noble, *The Eagle and the Dragon: The United States Military in China, 1901–1937* (Westport, Conn., 1990), 32–33; Charles L. Bolté, Senior Officer Oral History by Arthur J. Zoebelein, MHI, 42.

6. Pogue, *George C. Marshall*, 228, 232–234; Bland and Ritenour, *Papers of Marshall*, I: 264, 266, 270 (quotation), 271.

7. Pogue, *George C. Marshall*, 238–240; Bland and Ritenour, *Papers of Marshall*, I:

283 (quotation), 284; Matthew B. Ridgway, *Soldier: The Memoirs of Matthew B. Ridgway* (New York, 1956), 35–36.

8. W. D. Connor to AG, January 22, 1926, AG File, no. 350.05, RG 94, NA. He forwarded his letter to Ambassador J. V. A. MacMurray on January 13, 1926 (quotations); J. C. Castner to AG, July 30, 1928, AG File, no. 319.12, RG 94, NA.

9. Eli A. Helmick to the Chief of Staff, October 22, 1925, and J. C. Castner to IG, June 3, 1927, in no. 333.1, IG Reports, RG 159, NA; W. D. Connor to AG, December 4, 1925, and J. C. Castner to AG, December 27, 1926, AG File, no. 333.3, RG 94, NA; Alfred C. Wedemeyer, interview; and Charles L. Bolté, oral history, 35.

10. The regiment's weekly magazine, *The Sentinel*, at MHI, indicates the great emphasis on sports; Alfred C. Wedemeyer, interview; William E. Carraway, "Life in China with 15th Infantry—1933–36," copy in author's collection.

11. Charles L. Bolté, interview, October 12, 1975. William E. Carraway, who was a captain in the 15th at the time, permitted me to copy several of the lectures given in this school. These include topics taken from newspaper accounts—such as "Japan's Secret War Plan Revealed" and "Nippon Influence in North China Is Virtual Control"—as well as historical background; Robert L. Smalser, ed., *History of the 31st U.S. Infantry and 1988–1989 Yearbook* (Fort Sill, Okla., 1989), chap. 4; Allan R. Millett, *Semper Fidelis: The History of the United States Marine Corps* (New York, 1991), 225.

12. Stephen O. Fuqua Jr., interview by Paul J. Jacobsmeyer, July 11, 1989 (first two quotations), and telephone interview, January 13, 1990 (last quotation); *The Sentinel*, February 12, 1938, MHI.

13. Adelaide Poore Bolté, interview, August 4, 1971 (first two quotations), and questionnaire supplement (last two quotations). See also "Conditions of Service in China," *Infantry Journal* 29 (August 1926), 171.

14. Bland and Ritenour, *Papers of Marshall*, I: 281, 295 (quotation); Pogue, *George C. Marshall*, 236–237; Leslie Anders, *Gentle Knight: The Life and Times of Major General Edwin Forrest Harding* (Kent, Ohio, 1985), 81; Adelaide Poore Bolté, questionnaire, October 1972.

15. Rachel Forbush to Mother, May 8, 1921; Forbush to Dad, July 18, 1921; Forbush to Parents, December 7, 1921.

16. "Conditions of Service in China," 174; Lilian Stewart Burt to mother, September 3, 1932, Burt Papers, MHI; *The Sentinel*, October 16, 1925, 8; Ken Webber, "Mongolian Meander," copy in author's collection; Charles L. Bolté, oral history, 43–44; Carraway, "Life in China."

17. During the Korean War, Phil Bolté remembered enough Chinese to be able to identify the first Chinese soldier his unit captured in the fall of 1950; Philip L. Bolté, telephone interview; Lilian Stewart Burt to mother, December 1, 1933, MHI; Adelaide Poore Bolté, interview, August 4, 1971; David L. Bolté, telephone interview;

Francis J. Clune, questionnaire supplement; Winifred Stilwell Cox, questionnaire; Norma Tuttle Yarborough, interview; Douglas V. Johnson, "Keep 'em Rollin'," 173, copy in author's collection.

18. Frank Bozoski, questionnaire; Charles G. Finney, *The Old China Hands* (New York, 1963), 13. This autobiographical novel gets across the flavor of that service.

19. "Conditions of Service in China," 168–169; *The Sentinel*, February 12, 1938, 2; Anders, *Gentle Knight*, 80, 106.

20. John G. Westover, *A Papago Traveler: The Memories of James McCarthy* (Tucson, 1985), 91; Christmas 1935 menu, copy in author's collection.

21. Jack Bradley Jr., questionnaire; Margaret Bradley Mellblom, "Mama and the Soiled Doves" (a short story about her parents in China) and questionnaire; Charles L. Bolté, oral history, 45; and William E. Carraway to author, November 9, 1972.

22. Bland and Ritenour, *Papers of Marshall*, I: 273 (quotation); Charles L. Bolté, oral history, 41; Frank Bozoski, questionnaire.

23. Rachel Forbush to Mother, May 8, 1921, copy in author's collection.

24. Finney, *Old China Hands*, 14; *WDAR* (1939), SG, 55.

25. *WDAR* (1921), SG, 71. See the annual reports throughout the 1920s and 1930s for statistics; *WDAR* (1931), SG, 119; Pogue, *George C. Marshall*, 240.

26. Statistics are from SG annual reports. In particular, see *WDAR* (1934), SG, 35; (1939), SG, 40; William E. Carraway, "A Case of Military Justice in China," October 26, 1972, copy in author's collection; Francis J. Clune (son), questionnaire supplement; Noble, *Eagle and Dragon*, 128–129.

27. Linn, *Guardians of Empire*, 62, 68; Johnson, Keep 'em Rollin'," 120–122; interviews with William T. Ryder (first quotation) and William P. Yarborough (the other quotations), *Howitzer* (1936), 193, 221.

28. William P. Yarborough, interview; and Charles F. Ivins, "The Monkeys Have No Tails in Zamboanga," 36, MHI.

29. Franklin, "Philippine Scouts," 21–22, 29, 33, 40.

30. Francis A. Ruggles to Assistant Chief of Staff, War Plans Division, March 19, 1925, WPD no. 1799-7, Philippine File, RG 185, NA.

31. John E. Olson, *Anywhere—Anytime: The History of the Fifty-seventh Infantry, PS* (n.p., 1991), 8; James M. Gavin to author, October 29, 1975; Johnson, "Keep 'em Rollin'," 133–134; Norma Tuttle Yarborough, interview.

32. A combined invitation and program to the 57th Infantry Barrio Fiesta, May 8–9, 1937, is in the Edwin T. Wheatley Scrapbook, copy in author's collection.

33. Ivins, "Monkeys Have No Tails," 1, 47 (both quotations), 137–138.

34. Ibid., 32, 51–53, 94, 97–100; Olson, *Anywhere—Anytime*, 11.

35. Johnson, "Keep 'em Rollin'," 148–149, 152–153.

36. James M. Gavin, *War and Peace in the Space Age* (New York, 1958), 37–38 (first two quotations); T. Michael Booth and Duncan Spencer, *Paratrooper: The Life of Gen. James M. Gavin* (New York, 1994), 62, 63 (last quotation); Edwin V. Sutherland to author, July 21, 1990.

37. Richard Johnson, "My Life in the U.S. Army, 1899–1922," 185, 200, 207–211, 218, 224–226 (quotation on 225), MHI; Richard B. Meixsel, "Camp Stotsenburg and the Army Experience in the Philippines: A Brief History," *Bulletin American Historical Collection* (American Association of the Philippines) 22 (July–September 1994), 21, 23.

38. Willeford, *Something about a Soldier*, 13, 39–43, 46–48, 71–74, 77–78 (quotations on 39, 77, and 40).

39. Ibid., 35–36, 40, 50–51.

40. Ibid., 61–63, 83–84, 141; *WDAR* (1928), SG, 111; (1939), SG, 258.

41. James H. Belote and William M. Belote, *Corregidor* (New York, 1980), chaps. 1 and 2. Bill Belote gave me their notes and drafts of the pre–World War II section. Linn, *Guardians of Empire*, 91–92, 227–228; Ewing E. Booth, *My Observations and Experiences in the United States Army* (n.p., n.d.), 298.

42. David G. Brenzel, questionnaire (first and last quotations), "Confessions of a POW," letter to Mother, Don, and Pat, December 27, 1940 (last quotation), and letter to Mother and kids, May 18, 1941, copies in author's collection; Herbert F. Markland and Shawn A. Welch, "A Coast Artilleryman's Experience at Fort Mills," *Coast Defense Study Group Journal*, February 1995, 4–15.

43. Questionnaires from Phyllis Corbusier Pierson (first quotation), Eleanor Fletcher Buckley (second quotation), Elizabeth Dade Embick Wedemeyer, and Margaret Forsythe Camp; Ada Baker Shelton, interview; Charles H. Bogart, ed., "Letters from Corregidor—and the Aftermath," *Periodical* (Journal of the Council of America's Military Past) 18 (October 1991), 36 (last quotation).

44. Virginia Weisel Johnson, *Lady in Arms* (Boston, 1967), 30–31; Bogart, "Letters from Corregidor," 36; Eleanor Fletcher Buckley, questionnaire.

45. Buckley questionnaire.

46. Bogart, "Letters from Corregidor," 36 (quotation), 37 (photo).

47. Ibid., 36, 38. Harriette Marshall Olson, questionnaire.

48. Questionnaires from Mary Henry Howze, Nina Garfinkel Page (first quotation), and Patricia Henry Williams (second quotation).

49. Questionnaires from Paul J. Matte and Robert G. Matte.

50. Ivins, "Monkeys Have No Tails," 9.

51. Maurer Maurer, *Aviation in the U.S. Army: 1919–1939* (Washington, D.C., 1987), 50, 76, 96; Linn, *Guardians of Empire*, chap. 9.

52. Jacob E. Smart, "Recollections," 1–9 (quotations on 3), copy in author's collection.

53. Ibid., 10–12 (quotations on 10, 11), 14.

54. Ibid., 13.

55. Ibid., 14–15 (last quotation on 14), 36–37 (other quotations on 36).

56. Ibid., 18 (last quotation), 36–39 (first quotation on 36, others on 39).

57. Holland L. Robb to author, February 4, 1973; questionnaires from Marian Sanford Robb, Eleanor Robb, and Janice Robb Anderson.

58. Questionnaires from Fielding L. Greaves, Adrian St. John, and Howard W. Clark.

59. Lawrence E. Curtis to author, October 4, 1972 (first two quotations); Robert L. Bergeron, questionnaire (last quotation).

60. Gavin, *War and Peace,* 31 (first quotation); questionnaires from James C. Hicks, Andrew Pemper (second quotation), M. J. Thompson (fourth quotation); Lawrence E. Curtis to author, October 4, 1972 (third and last quotations). VD statistics are in the SG's annual reports in *WDAR* (1932), 70; (1936), 32. Drug use was not considered a problem. The surgeon general reported in 1935 that there were only forty-six discharged as drug addicts in the years 1932–1934. Of the eighteen officers and men discharged in 1934, eight were in Panama; *WDAR* (1935), SG, 48.

61. Lucian K. Truscott, *The Twilight of the U.S. Cavalry: Life in the Old Army, 1917–1942* (Lawrence, Kans., 1989), 26; Eleanor Mathews Sliney, *Forward Ho!* (New York, 1960), 150–151.

62. Truscott, *Twilight of Cavalry,* 27–28.

63. *Official Program: Schofield Barracks Horse Show, June* 8 & 9, 1934, 4.

64. William Wallace Ford, *Wagon Soldier* (North Adams, Mass., 1980), 80–83 (quotation on 80).

65. Charles P. Summerall, "The Way of Duty, Honor, Country," 140–143 (quotation on 140), First Division Museum Library at Cantigny, Wheaton, Ill.; Linn, *Guardians of Empire,* 153, 195–199.

66. Linn, *Guardians of Empire,* 42; Summerall, "Duty, Honor, Country," 142; Orville W. Martin, interviews, December 27, 1979 (quotation), and March 9, 1985; Anthony C. McAuliffe, interview.

67. The head of the board was Major Henry H. Arnold, who commanded the Army Air Force during World War II; Martin Blumenson, ed., *The Patton Papers: 1885–1940* (Boston, 1972), 784, 787–788, 811–816, 819; and Carlo D'Este, *Patton: A Genius for War* (New York, 1995), 338.

68. D'Este, *Patton,* 357–362; Blumenson, *Patton Papers,* 907–916 (quotations on 916).

69. Band photo in *The Bark of the Twenty-seventh Infantry, Schofield Barracks, Oahu, Hawaii: Organization Day, May* 2nd, 1939, 21; Anders, *Gentle Knight,* 175–181 (quotations on 176, 179); Linn, *Guardians of Empire,* 254.

70. Verone Gruenther Davidson, "From Here to Maternity," 56, copy in author's collection; Maida Davis Turtle Questionnaire.

71. *Official Program: The Hawaiian Division Annual Horse and Transportation Show:, Schofield Barracks, June* 10 & 11, 1932, 10; *Official Program: Schofield Barracks Horse Show, June* 8 & 9, 1934, 11, 41; Louise Adams Browne Questionnaire. Truscott, *Twilight of Cavalry,* 45; D'Este, *Patton,* 336, 358, 360–36; Ford, *Wagon Soldier,* 81.

72. Ruth Ellen Patton Totten Questionnaire; Vernon G. Olsmith, *Recollections of an Old Soldier* (San Antonio, 1963), 215, 222; Sliney, *Forward Ho!* 153, 164; *Official Program:* 1932, 10–11, 13, 46–51; Truscott, *Twilight of Cavalry,* 31, 34; Grace Wilson Groves, "Recollections," 127, author's collection; Anthony C. McAuliffe, interview; Anders, *Gentle Knight,* 192.

73. Anders, *Gentle Knight,* 177–178 (quotation on 178); Truscott, *Twilight of Cavalry,* 31; Orville W. Martin, interview, December 27, 1979; V. Davidson, "From Here to Maternity," 59; Harriet Howze Jones, questionnaire.

74. Questionnaires from Louise Adams Browne, Harriet Howze Jones, and Frank L. Hoskins Jr.; Ford, *Wagon Soldier,* 87; Garrison H. Davidson, "Grandpa Gar," 63–64A, copy in author's collection.

75. D'Este, *Patton,* 336–337; Ruth Ellen Patton Totten, questionnaire; Olsmith, *Recollections,* 212–214.

76. Questionnaires from Margie Hoskins Bloxom, Frank L. Hoskins Jr., Charles C. Ross (second quotation), and Patrick H. Tansey Jr. (first quotation).

77. Robert W. Brockway to author, August 18, 1978, and questionnaire.

78. Thelma Fadner Watson to her parents, April 28, 1938, copy in author's collection.

79. Frank B. Scahill, interview by Charles E. Twining; Richard W. Ripple, interview by Brian Linn, and Robert W. Kenney to Brian Linn, February 4 and 16, 1994, Brian M. Linn Collection, College Station, Tex.

80. Questionnaires from Frank Bozoski and Eugene G. Hogan.

81. Questionnaires from Frank Bozoski, George C. Hodgen, and John J. Hoodock.

82. Emil E. Matula, "Company D, 35th Infantry," 17, Linn Collection.

83. Frank B. Scahill, interview (first two quotations); Linn, *Guardians of Empire,* 116 (last quotation); SG reports in *WDAR*.s

84. *The Bark* (1939); *Official Program,* 1932, 13; G. H. Davidson, "Grandpa Gar," 65.

85. Summerall, "Duty, Honor, Country," 144; Frank B. Scahill, interview; Linn,

Guardians of Empire, 116–117; Frank Bozoski, questionnaire; Eugene G. Hogan, "Memoir," 10, author's collection.

86. Hogan, "Memoir," 3, 5; questionnaires from Eugene G. Hogan, Francis T. Dockery, and John J. Hannon; Frank B. Scahill, interview.

87. Eugene G. Hogan, questionnaire; Linn, *Guardians of Empire,* 117; Anders, *Gentle Knight,* 193.

88. Eugene G. Hogan, questionnaire; Robert W. Keeney to Brian M. Linn, February 16, 1994; Dick White to C. L. Sharrow Jr., February 26, 1937, Linn Collection.

89. Questionnaires from William A. Bowling and John J. Hannon; Hogan, "Memoir," 2, 10; Summerall, "Duty, Honor, Country," 143–144.

90. *WDAR* (1937), SG, 46, 60; questionnaires from Frank Bozoski, John J. Hannon, and Eugene G. Hogan; Robert W. Keeney to Brian Linn, February 4, 1994, Linn Collection; Linn, *Guardians of Empire,* 124, 126, 128, 130–133.

91. Hogan, "Memoir," 4; questionnaires from Francis T. Dockery, Athol W. George, James C. Hicks, John L. Key Jr., Dave Livesay, and George L. Stackhouse.

92. Richard W. Ripple, interview with Brian Linn, Linn Collection; Linn, *Guardians of Empire,* 125–126, 135–136.

93. Truscott, *Twilight of Cavalry,* 43–44 (quotations on 44); Richard W. Ripple, interview, and Robert W. Keeney to Brian M. Linn, February 16, 1994, Linn Collection.

94. Frank MacShane, *Into Eternity: The Life of James Jones, American Writer* (Boston, 1985), 27, 30, 105–107, 133.

95. Hogan, "Memoir," 11.

10. MOBILIZING FOR WAR

Epigraph: WDAR (1941), CS, 56.

1. James L. Collins Jr., interview; Harry W. O. Kinnard to Collins, November 6, 1981, author's collection.

2. Forrest C. Pogue, *George C. Marshall: Ordeal and Hope, 1939–1942* (New York, 1966), 15, 457 n. 19; idem, *George C. Marshall: Education of a General, 1880–1939* (New York, 1963), 2, 297, 301, 312, 314, 319, 327, 330, 342 407 n. 1.

3. *WDAR* (1923), SW, 24; (1940), AG, 26; Pogue, *George C. Marshall: Ordeal,* 10–11, 61, 63; Larry I. Bland, Sharon R. Ritenour, and Clarence E. Wunderlin, eds., *The Papers of George Catlett Marshall,* vol. II (Baltimore, 1986), 355–356; *The Army Almanac* (Washington, D.C., 1950), 310, 625–626, 693 310, 693; *Logistics in World War II: Final Report of the Army Service Forces* (Washington, D.C., 1993), 10.

4. Bland, Ritenour, and Wunderlin, *Marshall Papers,* 345 (quotation), 357; Pogue,

George C. Marshall: Ordeal, 16, 19, 22, 33, 39–44, 46–47, 49, 82, 87, 91–99, 139–141, 158–160.

5. Omar N. Bradley, *A Soldier's Story* (New York, 1951), 20; idem, preface to Pogue, *George C. Marshall: Ordeal,* ix; see also 7, 8, 11–15. J. Lawton Collins, *Lightning Joe: An Autobiography.* (Baton Rouge, 1979), 95–97; Maxwell D. Taylor, *Swords and Plowshares* (New York, 1972), 38–40.

6. Mark A. Stoler, *Allies and Adversaries: The Joint Chiefs of Staff, the Grand alliance, and U.S. Strategy in World War II* (Chapel Hill, 2000), 17; Louis Morton, "Germany First: The Basic Concept of Allied Strategy in World War II," in *Command Decisions,* ed. Kent R. Greenfield (Washington, D.C., 1960), 12, 13, 15.

7. Morton, "Germany First," 21–46.

8. Albert C. Wedemeyer, *Wedemeyer Reports!* (New York, 1958), 62; Keith E. Eiler, "The Man Who Planned the Victory: An Interview with Gen. Albert C. Wedemeyer," *American Heritage* 34 (October–November 1983), 39; Charles E. Kirkpatrick, *An Unknown Future and Doubtful Present: Writing the Victory Plan of 1941* (Washington, D.C., 1990), 35, 48–50, 55–56, 124; Taylor, *Swords and Plowshares,* 40.

9. Eiler, "Man Who Planned," 40 (first quotation); Kirkpatrick, *Unknown Future,* 56, 57 (second quotation); Wedemeyer, *Wedemeyer Reports!* 67 (last quotation).

10. The estimate was 8,795,658, while 8,157,386 were in the Army in March 1945. The Army peaked at ninety divisions during World War II; Kirkpatrick, *Unknown Future,* 100–101, 113, 115, 123; Eiler, "Man Who Planned," 40 (quotations).

11. Haywood S. Hansell Jr., *The Air Plan That Defeated Hitler* (Atlanta, 1972), 65–67, 69–71, 78–80, 85, 94 (quotation), 96; Martha Byrd, *Kenneth N. Walker: Airpower's Untempered Crusader* (Maxwell Air Force Base, Ala., 1997), 67–68, 70, 74.

12. Bland, Ritenour, and Wunderlin, *Marshall Papers,* 345; Pogue, *George C. Marshall: Ordeal,* 82–83; Larry I. Bland, ed., *George C. Marshall Interviews and Reminiscences for Forrest C. Pogue* (Lexington, Va., 1991), 189, 305–306; Russell F. Weigley, *History of the United States Army* (New York, 1967), 461.

13. Mark W. Clark, *Calculated Risk* (New York, 1950), 9–15 (first and fourth quotations on 13); Clark, interview (other quotations); Pogue, *George C. Marshall: Education,* 316; idem, *George C. Marshall: Ordeal,* 83; Bland, *Marshall Interviews,* 305–306.

14. Leslie Anders, *Gentle Knight: The Life and Times of Major General Edwin Forrest Harding* (Kent, Ohio, 1985), 186 (first quotation); Bland, Ritenour, and Wunderlin, *Marshall Papers,* 191 (second quotation); Dwight D. Eisenhower, *At Ease: Stories I Tell to Friends* (Garden City, N.Y., 1967), 240, 244 (last quotation).

15. Bland, *Marshall Interviews,* 310–312 (quotation on 311); DeWitt S. Copp, *A Few Great Captains: The Men and Events That Shaped the Development of U.S. Air Power* (Garden City, N.Y., 1980), 121–122, 434–436.

16. Pogue, *George C. Marshall: Education,* 320–323 (quotation on 323); Copp, *A Few*

Great Captains, 453, 455–456; David R. Mets, *Master of Airpower: General Carl A. Spaatz* (Novato, Calif., 1988), 108.

17. Copp, *A Few Great Captains*, 447; Henry H. Arnold, *Global Mission* (New York, 1949), 180, 181; Dik A. Daso, *Hap Arnold and the Evolution of American Airpower* (Washington, D.C., 2000), 160–161; Mets, *Master of Airpower*, 104; James Parton, *"Air Force Spoken Here": General Ira C. Eaker and the Command of the Air* (Bethesda, Md., 1986), 114.

18. Bland, *Marshall Interviews*, 312.

19. Elwood R. Quesada, Lecture at USAFA, April 7, 1983; Wesley F. Craven and James L. Cate, *The Army Air Forces in World War II*, vol. I: *Plans and Early Operations, January 1939 to August 1942* (Chicago, 1948), 104, 115; Arnold, *Global Mission*, 205, 206, 241, 247; Pogue, *George C. Marshall: Ordeal*, 49, 86.

20. Arnold, *Global Mission*, 215–239 (quotation on 235); Craven and Cate, *Army Air Forces*, I: 127–128, 130, 134–135; 318; Mets, *Master of Airpower*, 109–112; Thomas A. Hughes, *Over Lord: General Pete Quesada and the Triumph of Tactical Air Power in World War II* (New York, 1995), 70–74.

21. Arnold, *Global Mission*, 219; Parton, *"Air Force Spoken Here,"* 120; Jacob Smart to author, August 11, 1989; James H. Howard, *Roar of the Tiger* (New York, 1991), 57; Craven and Cate, *Army Air Forces*, I: 487–489.

22. Craven and Cate, *Army Air Forces*, I: 110–111.

23. Noel F. Parrish, interview; Jacob Smart to author, August 11, 1989.

24. Parrish interview (quotation); Noel F. Parrish, "Memoir," Randolph chapter, II, 37, and Glenview chapter, 22, 28–29, 34, copy in author's collection.

25. Parrish, "Memoir," Glenview chapter, 55–60 (quotation on 56); Bernard C. Nalty, *Strength for the Fight: A History of Black Americans in the Military* (New York, 1986), 143–144; Benjamin O. Davis Jr., *Benjamin O. Davis, Jr., American: An Autobiography* (Washington, D.C., 1991), 69–70.

26. Davis, *Benjamin O. Davis, Jr.*, 76 (first quotation); see also 44–45, 63–70, 77, 83–86, 89; Noel F. Parrish, interview; Nalty, *Strength for the Fight*, 146–147; Charles W. Dryden, *A-Train: Memoirs of a Tuskegee Airman* (Tuscaloosa, 1997), 95 (last quotation).

27. Lucian K. Truscott Jr., *Twilight of the U.S. Cavalry: Life in the Old Army, 1917–1942* (Lawrence, Kans., 1989), 186–187. See also idem, *Command Missions: A Personal Story* (New York, 1954), 16.

28. Truscott, *Command Missions*, 15. The quotations are from Truscott, *Twilight of Cavalry*, 159 and 160.

29. Timothy K. Nenninger, "Organizational Milestones in the Development of American Armor, 1920–1940," in *Camp Colt to Desert Storm: The History of U.S. Armored Forces*, ed. George F. Hofmann and Donn A. Starry (Lexington, Ky., 1999),

57–60; Vincent J. Tedesco III, "'Greasy Automatons' and 'The Horsey Set': The U. S. Cavalry and Mechanization, 1928–1940" (Master's thesis, Pennsylvania State University, 1995), 92, 94, 102–104; Robert W. Grow, "The Ten Lean Years: From the Mechanized Force (1930) to the Armored Force (1940)," 88, copy in author's collection; Christopher R. Gabel, *The U.S. Army GHQ Maneuvers of 1941* (Washington, D.C., 1992), 22–24.

30. Martin Blumenson, ed., *The Patton Papers: 1885–1940* (Boston, 1972), 947, 949, 951–956 (first quotation on 956). See also idem, *The Patton Papers: 1940–1945* (Boston, 1974), 10, 12; Carlo D'Este, *Patton: A Genius for War* (New York, 1995), 379–385 (second quotation on 385); Nenninger, "Organizational Milestones," 60; Bland, Ritenour, and Wunderlin, *Marshall Papers,* 601.

31. D'Este, *Patton,* 380 (first quotation); Blumenson, *Patton Papers: 1940–1945,* 31, 38–39, 45 (last quotation on 39).

32. Richard Steinbach, Memoir, 95–98 (quotations on 97 and 98), MHI.

33. Blumenson, *Patton Papers: 1940–1945,* 14–15, 23.

34. Ibid. 40–41 (second quotation on 41); Jacob L. Devers, interview (first and last quotations); Gabel, *GHQ Maneuvers,* 53; D'Este, *Patton,* 403–404; John Cranston, "Patton Museum Exhibit Depicts Long and Hard Road to Racial Integration," *Patton Museum Bulletin* 6 (May 2000), 4–5.

35. Blumenson, *Patton Papers: 1940–1945,* 43; D'Este, *Patton,* chap. 27; Kirkpatrick, *Unknown Future,* 107–108; Gabel, *GHQ Maneuvers,* 52, 80–82, 84, 87–90, 110–111, 121–122, 124–125, 146, 162, 175–178; Gabel, "World War II Armor Operations in Europe," in Hofmann and Starry, *Camp Colt to Desert Storm,* 144–147; Gabel, *Seek, Strike, and Destroy: U.S. Tank Destroyer Doctrine in World War II,* Leavenworth Papers no. 12 (Fort Leavenworth, Kans., 1985), 14–18.

36. Gabel, *GHQ Maneuvers,* 5, 9–11, 50, 59, 127, 192 (first quotation), 194, Bland, Ritenour, and Wunderlin, *Marshall Papers,* 97 and 98 (other quotations); Collins, *Lightning Joe,* 102–103.

37. Clark, *Calculated Risk,* 15–16 (quotation on 15). Also see Mark W. Clark, interview; Gabel, *GHQ Maneuvers,* 49, 50, 64; Pogue, *George C. Marshall: Ordeal,* 100–101.

38. Steinbach, Memoir, 102–103 (quotation on 102); Collins, *Lightning Joe,* 113; Gabel, *GHQ Maneuvers,* 69.

39. Collins, *Lightning Joe,* 114.

40. Gabel, *GHQ Maneuvers,* 148, 188.

41. Daniel D. Holt and James W. Leyerzapf, eds., *Eisenhower: The Prewar Diaries and Selected Papers, 1905–1941* (Baltimore, 1998), 530 (first quotation), 532, 537, 538, 541 (last quotation); Eisenhower, *At Ease,* 242–243.

42. Holt and Leyerzapf, *Eisenhower,* 545 (first quotation); Lesley J. McNair to

Marshall, October 7, 1941, Marshall Papers, George C. Marshall Library, Lexington, Va.; McNair to Marshall, October 14, 1941, AG no. 353.8 (10-14-41), AG Classified Document File, 1940–1942, RG 407, NA (quotation). The report by Hilton H. Railey is with this letter.

43. McNair applied those three criteria in his comments in his letter to Marshall, October 7, 1941. Bland, *Marshall Interviews,* 578; Pogue, *George C. Marshall: Ordeal,* 99–101; Gable, *GHQ Maneuvers,* 117.

44. Bland, Ritenour, and Wunderlin, *Marshall Papers,* 655–657. Stimson's diary notes on this occasion are quoted in a footnote on 656–657. Pogue, *George C. Marshall: Ordeal,* 99; Bruce Jacobs, "Senior Leadership: The Myths of Yesteryear," in *National Guard,* July 1982, 262–263.

45. McNair to Marshall, July 10, 1941, Marshall Papers; William H. Simpson, interview, August 20, 1971.

46. Gabel, *GHQ Maneuvers,* 107, 126, 181–182, 190–191.

47. Edgar F. Raines Jr., *Eyes of Artillery: The Origins of Modern U.S. Army Aviation in World War II* (Washington, D.C., 2000), 29–38.

48. Ibid., 40–41, 50–51, 59–63; William W. Ford, *Wagon Soldier* (North Adams, Mass., 1980), 106–107, 113, 117–119.

49. Claire L. Chennault, *Way of a Fighter* (New York, 1949), 16–17; Clay Blair, *Ridgway's Paratroopers: The American Airborne in World War II* (Garden City, N.Y., 1985), 30; R. M. Beck Jr. to Chief of Infantry, May 1, 1939; L. R. Fredendall to Assistant Chief of Staff, G-3, May 6, 1939; Walter Weaver to H. H. Arnold, September 7, 1940, with enclosure of the Air Corps Board report of September 6, 1940; H. H. Arnold to AG, October 19, 1939, all in AG 580 (51-39 Sec. 1), AG Central Decimal File, 1926–1939, RG 407, NA. For the chronology of documents pertaining to the airborne from January 2 to November 19, 1940, see Paul J. Mueller to Executive Officer, Office Chief of Infantry, November 19, 1940, copy in author's collection.

50. William T. Ryder, interview; Ryder to CO, 29th Infantry, June 29, 1940, and 29th Infantry SO no. 127, July 1, 1940, copies in author's collection.

51. Ryder interview (quotations). Extra pay for hazardous duty was discussed in E. W. Fales to AG, March 19, 1940, AG no. 580 (5-1 Sec. 1), AG Central Decimal File, 1926–39, RG 407, NA; John T. Ellis Jr., "The Airborne Command and Center," 3–5, Study no. 25, Historical Section, Army Ground Forces, RG 337, NA; Samuel T. Williams to the Chief of the Test Section of the Infantry Board, July 1, 1940, copy in author's collection.

52. William P. Yarborough, interview; Patent no. 2314914 (March 30, 1943), Yarborough articles in *The Pointer* 19 (October 10, 1941), 8–11, and *Recruiting News,* March 1942; Yarborough to father, April 22, 1941, comment on photo of Yarborough jumping, Yarborough Scrapbook, copies in author's collection.

53. James M. Gavin, interview (first quotation); James M. Gavin, *War and Peace in the Space Age* (New York, 1958), 40–46 (last quotation on 45); T. Michael Booth and Duncan Spencer, *Paratrooper: The Life of Gen. James M. Gavin* (New York, 1994), 73–77.

54. Interviews with William L. Banks (May 10, 1973), Norbert L. Craine, and Alphonse Zawadski.

55. Victor Vogel, *Soldiers of the Old Army* (College Station, 1990), 110–111 (quotations on 111).

56. *WDAR* (1941), CS, 60, 69; John K. Mahon and Romana Danysh, *Infantry*, Part 1: *Regular Army* (Washington, D.C., 1972), 58.

57. Vogel, *Soldiers of Old Army*, 105–108.

58. The standard basic training for the draftees took thirteen weeks; *WDAR* (1941), CS, 53, 57; Samuel A. Stouffer et al., *The American Soldier: Adjustment during Army Life*, 4 vols. (Princeton, 1949), I: 9–10, 12, 61.

59. Stouffer et al., *American Soldier*, I: 55, 57, 61, 66, 71, 78.

60. William P. Ennis Jr., Senior Officers Oral History, 61; and John A. Heintges, Senior Officers Oral History, 81, 83, MHI. The Research Branch found that 30 percent of the regulars had some high school, while 47 percent had only a grade-school education. The draftees had respectively 31 percent with some high school and 21 percent grade school. Both groups had more education than draftees in World War I. World War I draftees included 5 percent college graduates, 4 percent high school graduates, 12 percent some high school, 79 percent grade school. These figures are from Stouffer et al., *American Soldier*, I: 59–63, 68 (quotations).

61. Stouffer et al., *American Soldier*, I: 68 (quotations); questionnaires from Frank E. Orcutt, Arthur W. Piehl, Heman W. Pierce, Sam T. Prophet, M. J. Thompson, William C. Tiller, and James E. Vance.

62. George H. Waple III, *Country Boy Gone Soldiering* (n.p., 1998), 55, 73–74 (first quotation on 73); questionnaires from Gene E. Harris (last quotation), Walter Dillon, and Walter N. Ruffin.

63. Ulysses G. Lee, *The Employment of Negro Troops*, United States Army in World War II: Special Series (Washington, D.C., 2000), 38, 40–43, 48–50, 52, 68, 72–76, 79 (first quotation on 40); Nalty, *Strength for the Fight*, 135–140; Marvin Fletcher, *America's First Black General: Benjamin O. Davis, Sr., 1880–1970* (Lawrence, Kans., 1989), 80, 84–85; Elnora Davis McLendon, interview with Marvin Fletcher and author, March 21, 1972; Benjamin O. Davis, interview with Fletcher and author (last quotation).

64. In the Tenth Cavalry, for example, there were only one chaplain and one medical officer; *Historical and Pictorial Review: Tenth Cavalry of the United States Army— Camp Funston—Fort Riley, Kansas* (n.p., n.d.), 47, 81; Fletcher, *America's First Black General*, 86, 88–90.

65. Lee, *Employment of Negro Troops*, 69–71, 77–78.

66. Bland, *Marshall Interviews*, 459 (quotations); Lee, *Employment of Negro Troops*, 93–94, 96–102, 107.

67. The Army's Research Branch did not conduct a detailed survey of blacks until March 1943; hence these statistics are from that period; Stouffer et al., *American Soldier*, I: 488–491.

68. A majority of southern blacks preferred to be stationed close to home; ibid., 550, 554,557, 562; Nalty, *Strength for the Fight*, 164–165; Fletcher, *America's First Black General*, 93.

69. William Banks, interview, May 10, 1973; the quotation is from notes of a conversation that day rather than the taped interview. Lee, *Employment of Negro Troops*, 107–109.

70. Vernon Baker with Ken Olsen, *Lasting Valor* (Columbia, Mo., 1997), 26, 73, 85–87, 90, 101–103, 116, 138–139, 285 (quotations on 85 and 86). As a lieutenant in Italy, he earned the Medal of Honor.

71. Stouffer et al., *American Soldier*, 516; Lee, *Employment of Negro Troops*, 145–147; Fletcher, *America's First Black General*, 94.

72. Thelma Watson to parents, 29, 1939, James S. Watson Collection, Madison, Wis.; Eleanor Mathews Sliney, *Forward Ho!* (New York, 1960), 203; Virginia Weisel Johnson, *Lady in Arms* (Boston, 1967), 47–51 (quotation on 48).

73. The quotation is from David L. Bolté in a joint interview with Adelaide Bolté, September 30, 1993; Adelaide Bolté, interview, August 4, 1971.

74. Mauree Pickering Mahin, *Life in the American Army from the Frontier Days to Distaff Hall* (Washington, D.C., 1967), 210–217 (quotation on 214); Anders, *Gentle Knight*, 200.

75. Thelma Watson to parents, August 7, 1940; to Grace, December 14, 1940; September 14 (quotation) and November 11, 1941, James S. Watson Collection; James S. Watson, interview.

76. Charles H. Bogart, "Letters from Corregidor—and the Aftermath," *Periodical* (Journal of the Council of America's Military Past) 18 (October 1991), 37, 40; Pogue, *George C. Marshall: Ordeal*, 179.

77. Nancy Taylor Evans, "An American Teen in Pre-war Manila," *Assembly* 52 (November 1993), 23–24 (quotation on 23).

78. William R. Dunn, *Fighter Pilot: The First American Ace in World War II* (Lexington, Ky., 1982), 111–113 (quotation on 113).

79. *WDAR* (1899), SW, 58 (first two quotations); Omar N. Bradley, interview (last quotation).

80. "Who's in the Army?" *Fortune*, September 1935, 136.

81. *WDAR* (1921), SW, 22. See also Edward M. Coffman, "The American Army in Peacetime," *Military Review* 72 (March 1992), 49–59.

82. "Who's in the Army?" 136 (quotation); *The Statistical History of the United States from Colonial Times to the Present* (Stamford, Conn., n.d.), 718; Peter Karsten, *Soldiers and Society: The Effects of Military Service and War on American Life* (Westport, Conn., 1978), 11.

83. *WDAR* (1941), CS, 56.

84. Johnson, *Lady in Arms,* 50.

POSTSCRIPT

1. A. R. Nininger to parents, April 13, 1940, Nininger Papers, USMA (quotations); James H. Short to author, August 17, 1989; *Howitzer* (class of 1941), 251; Bill Yenne, *"Black 41": The West Point Class of 1941 and the American Triumph in World War II* (New York, 1991), 80–81, 91–91.

2. James L. Collins Jr., interview; Chalres B. MacDonald, *A Time for Trumpets: The Untold History of the Battle of the Bulge* (New York, 1985), 512.

3. Bickford Sylvester, "Hemingway's Unpublished Remarks on War and Warriors," in *War and Society in North America,* ed. J. L. Granatstein and R. D. Cuff (Toronto, 1971), 136–137; Charles G. Helmick Service Record, Special Collections and Archives, Nimitz Library, U.S. Naval Academy, Annapolis. Richard Werking and Gary A. LaValley provided this document.

4. Forrest C. Pogue, *George C. Marshall: Organizer of Victory,* 1943–1945 (New York, 1973), xi.

5. Winston S. Churchill, *The Hinge of Fate* (Boston, 1950), 387.

6. *WDAR* (1941), CS, 56.

7. For a large sampling of covers, see *Life Goes to War: A Picture History of World War* II (New York, 1978).

8. James Parton, *"Air Force Spoken Here": General Ira C. Eaker and the Command of the Air* (Bethesda, Md., 1986), 126.

9. Frank MacShane, *Into Eternity: The Life of James Jones, American Writer* (Boston, 1985), 40; George Hendrick, ed. *To Reach Eternity: The Letters of James Jones* (New York, 1989), xxiii; Don Herron, *Willeford* (Tucson, 1997), 81, 88; Charles Willeford, *Something about a Soldier* (New York, 1986), dustjacket biographical sketch.

10. For Banks's later years, see *News of the Highlands* (Highland Falls, N.Y.), June 27, 1974.

11. Adelaide Poore Bolté, Outstanding Civilian Service Medal citation (quotation), copy provided by David Bolté; Philip Bolté to author, October 27 and December 16, 1997, and e-mail to author, February 28, 2002. Obituaries are in the *New York Times,* February 13, 1989, and the *Washington Post,* January 10, 1998.

INDEX